Secret Histories

Secret Histories

READING TWENTIETH-CENTURY
AMERICAN LITERATURE

DAVID WYATT

The Johns Hopkins University Press
Baltimore

© 2010 The Johns Hopkins University Press
All rights reserved. Published 2010
Printed in the United States of America on acid-free paper
2 4 6 8 9 7 5 3 1

The Johns Hopkins University Press
2715 North Charles Street
Baltimore, Maryland 21218-4363
www.press.jhu.edu

Library of Congress Cataloging-in-Publication Data
Wyatt, David, 1948–
Secret histories : reading twentieth-century American literature / David Wyatt.
p. cm.
Includes bibliographical references and index.
ISBN-13: 978-0-8018-9711-5 (hardcover : alk. paper)
ISBN-10: 0-8018-9711-4 (hardcover : alk. paper)
ISBN-13: 978-0-8018-9712-2 (pbk. : alk. paper)
ISBN-10: 0-8018-9712-2 (pbk. : alk. paper)
1. American fiction—History and criticism.   2. History in literature.   3. United
States—In literature.   4. Literature and history—United States—History.   I. Title.
PS374.H5W93 2010
810.9´35873—dc22   2009052701

A catalog record for this book is available from the British Library.

*Special discounts are available for bulk purchases of this book. For more information,
please contact Special Sales at 410-516-6936 or specialsales@press.jhu.edu.*

The Johns Hopkins University Press uses environmentally friendly book materials,
including recycled text paper that is composed of at least 30 percent post-consumer
waste, whenever possible. All of our book papers are acid-free, and our jackets and
covers are printed on paper with recycled content.

John Auchard

Jones DeRitter

Charles Feigenoff

Alan Filreis

John Meredith Hill

Robert Kolker

David McWhirter

Jon Megibow

Howard Norman

Barney O'Meara

Miles Parker

Stanley Plumly

Jahan Ramazani

Robert Schultz

David Van Leer

Tim Coffin (1948–94)

We must disenthrall ourselves, and then we shall save our country.

—*Abraham Lincoln, Message to Congress, December 1, 1862*

CONTENTS

In the 1950s, reading William Faulkner, Toni Morrison began to detect "a special kind of courage," the courage demonstrated by any writer who sets out to tell the secret history of his country. This was a courage she herself would demonstrate when it came to her great rewriting of *Absalom, Absalom!* (1936) in *Beloved* (1987). The Faulkner-Morrison relation is one of the more dramatic examples of American literature as the result of what Faulkner termed "a happy marriage of speaking and hearing," where the speaker is the precursor who calls forth in the later listener-reader-writer an answering act of creation. "My reasons, I think, for being interested and deeply moved by his subjects," Morrison says, "had something to do with my desire to find out something about this country and that artistic articulation of its past that was not available in history, which is what art and fiction can do but sometimes history refuses to do."

When Morrison claims that fiction can do something that history sometimes refuses to do, she speaks directly to the exigence behind my project, to my deep belief that American literature is the secret history of the United States. I mean by this nothing fancy or obscure, but simply that in reading American literature we are given the chance to recognize and refeel the emotional, cultural, and political burdens of a specific and collective past. Our novels, poems, plays, and short stories provide a medium for imagining how it felt—then—to be alive in our country, and to see how that experience plays out—now—in the present in which we happen to be reading.

This book grows out of the changing experience of teaching, over more than thirty years, a course entitled "Twentieth-Century American Literature." These were the years in which the opening of the canon was the major intellectual event, and I have attempted to capture some of the richness of this ever-expanding universe by offering commentary on fifty-four twentieth-century American authors. The length of the list has been determined, in part, by the physics of bookmaking; this is a big book, and at some point one needs to stop. Indeed, at one point I determined that it was necessary to remove chapters about American poetry and drama, and to center this project on fictional and nonfictional prose. Even given this genre limitation, I regret the exclusion of many who still deserve to be read. I take some comfort, however, in the thought that any selection from such an embarrassment of riches is bound to be partial in the end.

In writing the story of a secret history, I have tried to honor the meaning to be found in sequence; to this end, the chapters succeed each other in a rough chronology. Within each chapter the author remains the focal principle. Some authors get as little as a page, some many more. Although the quantity of attention paid to a particular author does argue for a sense of relative importance, each choice also reflects my sense that here is a writer who uncovers something crucial in our national story. I group writers by way of obvious affinity, although Chester Himes, for instance, appears in a chapter on the Depression when he might just as well fit into the pages on the Second World War. Conceived less as a reference work than as an internally coherent narrative, my book is structured so that a reader who chooses to dip in, say, to sample the few pages on Toshio Mori can do so, I hope, and leave it satisfied.

Each chapter—except those on Hemingway, Faulkner, Morrison, and Roth, authors for whom, surely, relations stop nowhere—consists of a set or series of clustered authors, and some of the clusters involve juxtapositions that may seem unlikely. The juxtapositions—or any of the moments in which I find myself *reminded* of a kindred text—are meant to dramatize how one reader's memory of his reading works. When T. S. Eliot says "I associate" about his mental leaps in *The Waste Land* (1922), he provides a model for this activity. Although in no way duplicating Eliot's achievement, my book, like his great poem, invites a reader to follow out the associative pathways grooved by years of reading in another human mind. By this method I mean to invoke the process by which, over a lifetime of encounter, certain prose works in the American procession begin to speak—and listen—to each other. The possible exchanges are of course infinite, and I have explored here only a few of them, leaving much of that work to my reader, who will, quite naturally, "associate" as well.

My book dramatizes one reader's experience of "listening" to twentieth-century American literature. While this experience is necessarily subjective, as is the encounter with any art form, I also mean to argue that what is heard is actually there, a reality external to any one mind. I am making truth claims, that is, about a structure of interrelationships among literary texts, claims about patterns of family resemblance and their continual refigurings in the procession of American literature. Of course, settling on the texts that ought to be seen as making up this procession is a matter of ongoing debate, as the community of writers creates more books and as the community of readers and critics continues to decide which ones to hand on to the next generation.

In putting this book together, I have attempted to create a structure open enough to accommodate a wide variety of texts, while also trying to follow out a number of through-stories. I explore the unresolved tension in the lives of women between the search for work and the search for love, as well as the reclamation of the body as a site over which a woman can assert responsibility and control. The book wrestles with the tentacles of "corporation land," as Norman Mailer calls it, an octopus that destroys the future of the nation as it augments in strength. It studies war and the ways in which war depreciates all our terms while also opening up the possibility of strange clemencies and empathies, even for and with the enemy. It unpacks the meaning or our "innocence," to use Faulkner's word—the willful striving not to know what we know and to believe ourselves, as Americans, unburdened by ideology.

Each of these stories claims its place in the ongoing rewriting of America, but the most powerful and moving through-story I recover here is one of union imagined as interracial family romance—a romance sometimes played out in families of origin, other times in families created out of consensual affiliation. One of the deepest subjects of the book, then, could be called love.

"Love" is always a historically embedded experience, one bound up with and to a certain extent created by the history of the novel. I owe much to old masters like Leslie Fiedler, who long ago put "Love and Death in the American Novel" on the critical map. But what do I mean—now—in the first decade of the twenty first century, as I look back and talk about love in the literature of the twentieth? It is a question to which I can give only a partial answer here, since "love," in American literature, remains a word and an experience whose meaning and force undergo continual refiguration.

To attempt a definition, nevertheless: Love is a word for the effort involved in a reader's attempt to achieve empathetic union with a text, an experience that also figures forth the ways in which "love" in the real world might be achievable, especially among those unrelated by birth or national origin. I borrow this sense of the word from chapter 8 of *Absalom, Absalom!*, where Shreve McCannon says, "And now . . . we're going to talk about love." He says this as part of a conversation with Quentin Compson. The two young men, one from Canada and one from Mississippi, have met as freshmen at Harvard. Shreve is quickly drawn into Quentin's obsessive retellings of the story of the Thomas Sutpen family, stories that have been in turn imposed on Quentin in the summer before his arrival in Cambridge. As the novel draws to a close, Quentin and Shreve home in on the central mystery of the Sutpen family story, the question of why a stranger named Charles Bon, a man who befriends Henry Sutpen at the University of Mississippi and who then courts and wins the hand of Henry's sister Judith, is, in 1865, shot down by Henry at the gates to the Sutpen mansion where Judith waits in her wedding gown.

Shreve proposes to talk about love in preparation for the culminating scene in the novel, the one in which the two Harvard freshmen alive in 1910 succeed in becoming "compounded" with the two young Confederate soldiers alive in 1865, all in an attempt to understand why Henry Sutpen shot Charles Bon. In order to so compound—to join with their nineteenth-century counterparts in an act of empathetic imagination—Shreve and Quentin have already agreed to "overpass," to abandon any competitiveness or ego-driven relationship to the story they are both so urgently trying to recover:

> "And now," Shreve said, "we're going to talk about love." But he didn't need to say that either, any more than he needed to specify which he he meant by he, since neither of them had been thinking about anything else; all that had gone before just so much that had to be overpassed and none else present to overpass it but them, as someone always has to rake the leaves up before you can have the bonfire. That was why it did not matter to either of them which one did the talking, since it was not the talking alone which did it, performed and accomplished the overpassing, but some happy marriage of speaking and hearing wherein each before the demand, the requirement, forgave condoned and forgot the faulting of the other—faultings both in the creating of this shade whom they discussed (rather, existed in) and in the hearing and sifting and discarding the false and conserving what seemed true, or fit the preconceived—in order to overpass to love, where there might be paradox and inconsistency but nothing fault nor false.

It is a lot to ask of the reader, "to overpass to love." But Faulkner and the other authors read in this secret history of the United States continue to ask it of us. *Absalom, Absalom!* models this activity as well as any novel I know, one that involves a surrender of self in the collaborative work of reading the past. When Quentin and Shreve arrive at their third and final surmise about Henry's motives, a surmise that Charles is asked to articulate—"*So it's the miscegenation, not the incest, which you cant bear*"—they come upon one of the deepest secrets in American life, the fact that slavery was based on a sexual commingling so profound that any notion of racial difference was consumed by it and, even more, that a "spot of Negro blood" can have become for this culture an obsession that trumps the universal taboo against incest.

This, of course, is an insight Faulkner's reader must generate, and one arrives at it by way of entering into the felt logic and timing of the offered surmise. One is asked to recognize the final and climactic confrontation between Thomas Sutpen and Henry and between Henry and Charles as taking place in an italicized passage imagined jointly by Quentin and Shreve, an event that has as its only warrant the gathering knowledge of where this collective act of storytelling—"the two of them creating between them, out of the rag-tag and bob-ends of old tales and talking, people who perhaps had never existed at all anywhere"—has led them. This version has authority precisely because it admits "paradox and inconsistency," because it is partial, and because it calls on the reader to become the cocreator rather than the mere inheritor of the American past.

When Shreve uses the word "love," he is talking specifically about Charles's love for his half-sister Judith, a doomed and fatal attraction. After Shreve's sentence about love, Faulkner breaks off from quoted dialogue and returns the narrative to the third person. He moves away from the question of love between a man and a woman, that is, and toward a description of the kind of love that Quentin and Shreve—and, by extension, the reader—are experiencing. "Love" is the word Faulkner chooses because it is the best word we have for the fusion of mindfulness and self-forgetting that goes into the writing or the reading of a page. Love forgives and condones and forgets the inevitable faults involved in the making of anything in order to complete the act of creation with an equally generative act of listening. And Morrison, among Faulkner's heirs, most powerfully understands this.

⚜   ⚜

Literature has always understood the congruence between matters intimate, social, and political. If the marriage story is the staple of the novel, the family romance has long been a figure for the intrigues and conflicts of American nation-building. Lincoln calls this "the work we are in," a work concerned with how the parts of a thing might fit into the whole. If my book has one word to say, then, it would be *Union*, the word Lincoln came round to as the point of the Civil War. The word for Lincoln named a complex metaphor, one that best figured the relation of the individual states to the American nation. All metaphor deals, in some sense, with union, since all metaphor attempts to find, as Wordsworth maintains, similitude in dissimilitude. The Civil War itself became a painful ordeal of such finding, a search for a new set of metaphors around which a nation conceived in liberty could be reconceived, and Lincoln's speeches are the site in which the process most vividly plays itself out.

In his "House Divided" speech, Lincoln also calls on his listeners to attend to his carefully marshaled "string of historical facts," facts that have been obscured by his opponents but can be shown to be, by way of Lincoln's careful exposition, a series of acts leading the nation inexorably toward civil war. The facts—from the Missouri Compromise of 1820 to the Dred Scott Case of 1857—all give "evidences of design." It is Lincoln's purpose to uncover the secret history behind this design, one that cloaks itself under the phrase "*sacred right of self government*," while all the time promoting the extension of "slavery." And in so doing, he seeks to expose the fissure that divides a house.

As an experiment in nation-building, the United States remains a powerfully metaphoric exercise, one that originates out of the words of the founders and that returns continually to questions about what Toni Morrison calls "the join." Not only was the United States the greatest poem, in the eyes of Lincoln's contemporary Walt Whitman, but its very survival depended on the willingness of its citizens to be gathered together by way of a metaphor, the original call to "a more perfect union." Metaphors are, finally, what we fight for, and American literature provides our essential store of them. Of course, how to achieve more perfect unions, between citizen and nation, black and white, self and soul, along with all that stands in the way of doing so, is the heart of the story.

And so, amid the various through-stories that I have named—the American stories of women, "combination," war, and innocence—the overarching narrative is one of family romance and nation-building. My book explores the struggle between union and disunion as it plays itself out in American literature in the wake of the Civil War, with a starting point that circles around *The Souls of Black Folk* (1903), a text that prophesies that the problem of the twentieth century will be the problem of the color line. It also takes inspiration from Lincoln's metaphor of the nation as a family that lives in one house, however divided. While I often gather writers of color into chapters of their own, in order to explore their intrafamilial resemblances, I also mix things up, and the entire volume conceives of the literature of the century as an ongoing family conversation that culminates in a black writer's answer to a white one—in Morrison's refigurings of Faulkner.

In *Shadow and Act* (1964), Ralph Ellison provides a metaphor for understanding the struggle of the writer's imagination against its influences as a figure for the American mind dealing with the ghost of slavery. "While one can do nothing about choosing one's relatives," Ellison writes, "one can, as artist, choose one's 'ancestors.'" The major trope in his book is freedom, or choosing, a capacity that apparently includes the ability to regulate one's anxiety of influence. Lost in the shuffle between Ellison's named black and white fathers is the name of William Faulkner. Ellison does allow that "as for the Negro minority, he has been more willing perhaps than any other artist to start with the stereotype, accept it as true, and then seek out the human truth which it hides." But in a book so committed to the values of international modernism, it is not high praise when Ellison calls Faulkner "the greatest artist the South has produced." Faulkner enters Ellison's critical narrative largely through tantalizing asides, as in the remark, made on the occasion of receiving the National Book Award, that "except for the work of William Faulkner something vital had gone out of American prose after Mark Twain." Faulkner's name does not appear in the lists of writers Ellison cites as perhaps more important to him than his living folk tradition, lists including names like "Eliot, Pound, Gertrude Stein and Hemingway." Yet, near the end, Ellison discloses that "Faulkner has given us a metaphor," the metaphor of his book's title, *Shadow and Act*.

Ellison then describes a scene from *Intruder in the Dust* (1948) in which Chick Mallison falls through the ice and "into the depth of a reality which constantly reveals itself as the reverse of what it had appeared before his plunge. Here the ice—white, brittle, and eggshell thin—symbolizes Chick's inherited views of the world, especially his Southern conception of Negroes." Chick suddenly finds himself thrust into the position of the shadow. The shadow is the Negro, and the Negro shadows the white act. In the beginning was not the shadow, but the act, Ellison concludes, yet priority here does not confer freedom or power. It confers indebtedness and entanglement, since the act only exists and has meaning in tension with the shadow. Ellison's book ends by arguing that the repressed will return, where the repressed can be understood as the Negro, the unconscious, the father or mother-in-art—as whatever is kept down.

Ellison here acknowledges and appropriates a late novel by Faulkner. He thereby creates a literary genealogy in which he becomes one of Faulkner's heirs. The borrowings and refigurings in his essay are interracial, an active crossing and an inspiring across the color line. It is a movement, however conflicted, toward affiliation. The novel from which Ellison borrows the trope of shadow and act, *Intruder in the Dust*, also acts out a fantasy of affiliation, one in which a white boy, a black boy, and an old white woman come together in order to help a black man, Lucas Beauchamp, get out of jail. In doing so, they in turn refigure Huck and Tom and Jim and the much more ironic and yet sadly illuminating attempt, one made at the end of *Adventures of Huckleberry Finn* (1884), "to set a free nigger free." Through Ellison, Twain and Faulkner are brought together in "a join," as Morrison might call it, an ingathering of relation that echoes the reformation of human bonds, beyond blood ties, attempted in the novels themselves.

Not every story read in the following pages involves family, or a reconfiguration of it. Sometimes the most that can be imagined are tactical regroupings, if only of the self with a more adaptive sense of self. Sometimes "the join" cannot be achieved. Edward Said, from whom I borrow the term "affiliation," knows how powerfully filiation—the seemingly natural bonds of family and blood—can work to inhibit the choosing of whom to learn from, and whom to love, and so also work to keep so many characters in American literature, and in American life, less than free.

Nevertheless, the essential story told in these pages will be the ongoing struggle to connect across difference within relations of enlivened freedom. Any achieved connection between characters depends, of course, on the ongoing connection between a story and its reader, and we will often find that the reader's experience *of* these texts replicates the kinds of joining occurring *within* them. The culminating example of this work occurs in Morrison's *Beloved*.

"Tell me," Beloved likes to say to her sister Denver, "Tell me how Sethe made you in the boat." Beloved asks to be told a story, and the story is one that she, like Quentin Compson, has heard before. A burden is placed on the storyteller; it would now seem to be Denver's task to do something for or to Beloved. But *Beloved* is a novel in which the speaker of a story repeatedly discovers her profound dependency on the hearer of it. When Denver begins to tell her sister the story of how she was made, Morrison writes that "Denver was seeing it now and feeling it—through Beloved." The "it" Denver sees and feels is the story she has been urged to tell. And she can now feel the story she already knows because she is being held by the attention of a passionate listener. The experience begins to build on itself: "And the more fine points she made, the more detail she provided, the more Beloved liked it. So she anticipated the questions by giving blood to the scraps her mother and grandmother had told her—and a heartbeat. The monologue became, in fact, a duet as they lay down together, Denver nursing Beloved's interest like a lover whose pleasure was to overfeed the loved." The two sisters here live out an intimate exchange and a momentary union that enlivens both speaker and hearer, an exchange not only of sisterly love but that partakes as well, by way of Morrison's figurative language, of both maternal and sexual love. Yet the ultimate form of connection and creation here—one also being literally enacted—is between the two "sides" of a storytelling act. Denver speaks, Beloved listens, and the two of them do the best they can "to create what really happened, how it really was." In refiguring the overpassing scene between Quentin and Shreve, Morrison also offers up a new and bracing allegory of the experience of reading itself. Just as Denver is a figure for Morrison, for the willing and responsive author, so Beloved is Morrison's figure for the ideal and even hungry reader, the reader both of her novel and of the tradition it renews. It is to such a listener, as well, that I offer my book.

This book is dedicated to the men who helped me make it.

First, to Bob Schultz, who read every word and who gently urged me to confront the many occasions on which I had not quite said what I meant to say. In the give-and-take between my versions and his discreet and eloquent revisions, we lived out the experience of call-and-response that is the subject of this book.

My friend and office mate Howard Norman offered me the hospitality of his home on Wednesday nights, as well as a constant supply of books and talk about them. He is the great reader of my acquaintance, a man always seeking to convert intelligence into a useful melancholy.

I see John Auchard on Tuesdays, when I sit with him in the kitchen of his Sixteenth Street apartment over the dinner he has cooked us. Conversation with John stops nowhere, and so gave me a sense of the complex scale I have aimed for in this book, one in which a child perhaps can wade and an elephant can swim.

Every Wednesday during the school year, Stanley Plumly and I have lunch and talk about poetry. Watching the full flowering of Stanley's career over the past few years, as a poet and as a critic, has reinforced my sense that American literature is alive and well.

Reading Robert Kolker's prose is like drinking clear water. The talks with him at the College Inn, or on my back porch in Charlottesville, have led me to strive for an answerable clarity.

I didn't see enough of Jody DeRitter, Charlie Feigenoff, and Jay Hill, and when I did see them, it was usually at the beach. They remain passionate readers of work beyond their fields, especially inspiring when smoking cigars in a hot tub.

Jahan Ramazani has a hot tub of his own, and the two of us sometimes get together for a long soak on a winter night. There I am reminded that the man I met when he was eighteen has become the most knowledgeable and devoted scholar of poetry that I know.

David Van Leer and Miles Parker visit us every year at our cottage on Cape Cod.

I remember the day that David gave me his list of the books that ought to make it into this book, one that carried all the authority of his deep learning, and I remember too how Miles Parker leavened our sometimes gossipy conversation with his wisdom and wit.

Al Filreis has spent the last decade raising his two children and pursuing his busy career, and I have not seen enough of him. But his presence nevertheless makes itself felt in the following pages, especially as this student-become-teacher convinced me early on that literature is always telling a story about history.

Jon Megibow loves the big, difficult, encyclopedic novels, and I am grateful to him for sitting me down one day and patiently explaining just what was up with *Gravity's Rainbow*. I am grateful too for the chance to enjoy this good cook's many gracious dinners.

David McWhirter passed through town at a key moment in my researches, convincing me to give Eudora Welty a second look. I am in his debt as well for alerting me to the novels of Ellen Douglas.

Since my freshman year in college, Barney O'Meara has been the constant friend. Barney and Mary's farm, in Rappahannock County, is where Ann and I were married, and it is the place I come to for rest and recovery, for harvesting a little wood, and for the comfort of Barney's accepting presence.

It was with Tim Coffin, in my junior year in high school, that I first discovered and enjoyed intimate conversation. He died far too young, at the peak of life, but his spirit lives on, I hope, in the fact of these pages, and in the continuing sense that being serious is also having fun.

●   ●

At the University of Maryland, I have been fortunate to be a member of a sane, open-hearted department, one that continues to find ways to bring out the best in its teacher-scholars. My students are to be thanked for teaching me more, I am sure, than I teach them. A GRB award from the university in support of this project helped me to bring it to a conclusion.

Chapters 4 and 11 have appeared as articles in *The Hopkins Review*. Permission to reprint them is gratefully acknowledged, as is the longtime support of John Irwin, who published my work over thirty years ago in *The Georgia Review* and who helped me place my sixth book, as he did my first one, with the Johns Hopkins University Press.

In the summer of 2008, my sister Meleesa Wyatt sat down with my original manuscript—then at 640 pages—and read and proofread it with great care. She caught many errors and also responded with the enthusiastic intelligence that makes her presence such a delight.

For over twenty years, *The Southern Review* was a willing publisher of the essays

I sent it. I would like to thank its editors for permission to reprint portions of "Norris and the Vertical," "Ann Beattie," and "Faulkner's Hundred." Thanks as well to *The South Atlantic Quarterly* for permission to reprint portions of "Shepard's Split."

Finally, to my wife Ann, who is such a pleasure to come home to every Thursday night, and who rolled over in bed one morning and said "I've got your title," as she had.

Secret Histories

CHAPTER ONE

The Body and the Corporation

NORRIS ◆ CHAMBERS

*T*he phrase "secret history" is <u>Michael Herr's</u> and comes from a passage in *Dispatches* (1977). Herr is writing about the problem of determining when the war in Vietnam began:

> You couldn't find two people who agreed about when it began, how could you say when it began going off? Mission intellectuals like 1954 as the reference date; if you saw as far back as War II and the Japanese occupation you were practically a historical visionary. "Realists" said that it began for us in 1961, and the common run of Mission flack insisted on 1965, post-Tonkin Resolution, as though all the killing that had gone before wasn't really war. Anyway, you couldn't use standard methods to date the doom; might as well say that Vietnam was where the Trail of Tears was headed all along, the turnaround point where it would touch and come back to form a containing perimeter; might just as well lay it on the proto-Gringos who found the New England woods too raw and empty for their peace and filled them up with their own imported devils. Maybe it was already over for us in Indochina when Alden Pyle's body washed up under the bridge at Dakao, his lungs all full of mud; maybe it caved in with Dien Bien Phu. But the first happened in a novel, and while the second happened on the ground it happened to the French, and Washington gave it no more substance than if Graham Greene had made it up too. Straight history, auto-revised history, history without handles, for all the books and articles and white papers, all the talk and the miles of film, something wasn't answered, it wasn't even asked. We were backgrounded, deep, but when the background started sliding forward not a single life was saved by the information. The thing had transmitted too much energy, it heated up too hot, hiding low under the fact-figure crossfire there was a secret history, and not a lot of people felt like running in there to bring it out.

This passage not only provides the present book with its title but makes four important points about <u>the ways in which literary art works</u>. First, the range and audacity of Herr's field of allusion argue that a writer can and continually does create the context within which he is to be understood. Second, the echoes set up between these allusions—they enforce the recognition that Vietnam and the Trail

of Tears involve wars against what Bruce Springsteen, in "Born in the U.S.A."
(1984), calls with some irony the "yellow man" and his North American descendants—argue for overdetermined and previously overlooked connections in the
vast array that is the American past. Third, the breathlessness of the syntax and
sheer scale of Herr's sentences show a mind thinking and betray an ambition to
find a form adequate to contain its associations and to allow their consequences
to be felt. Fourth, the willingness to admit into evidence something that "happened in a novel" alongside what may have happened in fact summons art to the
task of making secret history, a task that the passage not only identifies but chooses
to enact.

Herr makes a crucial distinction here between two kinds of history. By "straight
history" he means to evoke official, euphemistic, committee-generated language.
Straight history does not include the first-rate scholarship of a James M. McPherson's *Battle Cry of Freedom* (1988) or a Richard Rhodes's *The Making of the Atomic
Bomb* (1986), works of imagination as moving and artful as any strong novel. By
"straight history," Herr refers to something like the stories taught in the public
schools or invoked at a political convention. Frances Fitzgerald has shown the ways
in which high school textbook history reinforces rather than questions the nation's
myths of itself and thereby fails in the task of providing a critical-minded citizenry.
What Elizabeth Bishop (1911–79) writes in "Crusoe in England" (1971) about the
love of the two men on the island applies also to the Texas School Board–approved
version of the nation's story: "None of the books has ever got it right."

Straight history and secret history are both versions of a third thing, what we
call the "real." The distinction between two modes of narrating the past is in no
way meant to argue that the past did not happen in a particular way. That way may
be forgotten, or unrecorded, or occluded. It is in any case not directly recoverable.
The "real" is, instead, always mediated, always subject to the work of interpretation, if only by way of the words we use to acknowledge how lost it may actually
be. As my student Ted Kaouk argues: "The problem with 'straight history' is not
that it isn't up to *telling* all there is to tell. Nothing is. Poetry itself can only evoke
the impossibility of telling it all. No, what straight history refuses to do is admit
the limitations of representation. It is not that 'something wasn't answered' about
what happened in Vietnam but rather 'it wasn't even asked,' where 'it' might be
understood as the question that itself refuses the entire notion of a complete and
satisfactory answer."

Herr's book gives the phrase "secret history" a precise and original meaning. By
"secret history," he does not mean to invoke a story that has been intentionally hidden. Secret history is, simply, the counter-record generated by art. It is not so much
the story *behind* the story as the story *alongside* the story, one ever available to the

determined reader who finds it hidden, if at all, in plain sight. It is secret only in the sense that many may fail to recognize it as history, and that, when they do, they must work to acquire it. And it remains so often secret because so many of us consent to attend, instead, to one or another of the self-congratulatory or self-pitying and memory-suppressing narratives that dominate our public life.

❀   ❀

Hemingway's *In Our Time* captures the dilemma of the secret historian in a story called "Soldier's Home," in which Harold Krebs returns from the trenches of World War I. "By the time Krebs returned to his home town in Oklahoma the greeting of heroes was over." At first, Krebs doesn't want to talk about the war. "Later he felt the need to talk about it but no one wanted to hear it. His town had heard too many atrocity stories to be thrilled by actualities."

Straight history is found in the atrocity stories that comfort, in their melodramatic distortion; secret history is found in the actualities that threaten, in their deflation of the heroic. Krebs finds that "to be listened to at all he had to lie," and so he stops talking about the war. Hemingway's aesthetic of silence—"You'll lose it if you talk about it," Jake Barnes maintains in *The Sun Also Rises* (1926)—issues, in part, from the sense of there being no audience prepared to listen to the kind of stories he has to tell.

Krebs's solution is to retreat from the world of "girls" and to begin reading about the war. "It was a history and he was reading about all the engagements he had been in. It was the most interesting reading he had ever done . . . Now he was really learning about the war." Writing—art—doesn't simply capture experience after the fact; it creates the capacity to recognize and to feel it, perhaps for the first time. If Krebs is lucky, he's reading something like *A Farewell to Arms*.

Hemingway, like Krebs, went to the war. When he came back, he couldn't talk about it. One solution was to write his history of it, in the 1929 novel. Like Krebs, Hemingway knew that a single man's experience carried no particular authority. He discovered that the way forward lay in *study*. So he began, like Krebs, to read about the war. He did extensive research, as Michael Reynolds has shown, and he reconstructed the retreat from Caporetto—an action of which he had no first-hand knowledge—with exactitude. He understood that people needed not more atrocity stories but an account that combined the highest standards of scholarship with all the imaginative reach he could muster. He needed to tell the story in such a way as to explain why Frederic Henry, like Nick Adams and Harold Krebs, chose to make "*a separate peace*"; he needed to understand why the war had led, as Henry James (1843–1916) said of it, not to honor or to glory but to "a depreciation of all our terms."

❀   ❀

On an April morning in 1901, the world became aware for the first time that eleven men, including an agent of the Pacific and Southwestern Railroad and a United States Marshall, engaged in a gunfight with eleven ranchers near the town of Guadalajara in the San Joaquin Valley of California. The gunfight was the culmination of a dispute growing out of the settlement of Tulare County. The ranchers, who moved into the area in the 1870s, had built irrigation ditches in the hot, flat, dry valley and transformed it into wheat country. Two years without rain had brought the prospect of a big crop and "a chance to pay off our mortgages and get clear of debt and make a strike." Then the railroad decided to raise grain-hauling rates to a new level: "All—the—traffic—will—bear."

At the same time that it is raising its rates, the P. and S. W. decides to grade its lands for sale, at twenty dollars an acre. When the railroad initially invited the settlers onto its land—land it had been granted by the federal government in alternating sections twenty miles in depth all along its line—it also agreed to sell to the settlers in preference to any other applicants and at a price based on the value of the land without improvements. The circular advertising this offer also stated that the lands in question would thereafter be "*offered at various figures from $2.50 upward per acre.*" Now, eight years after Annixter, the owner of the Quein Sabe Ranch, "came in on it and improved it," as he says to a railroad agent, the P. and S. W. proposes to sell it to him at eight times the price he expected to pay.

In response to this double squeeze, the ranchers form a league to nominate—or to buy—new railroad commissioners who will move to keep hauling rates down. When the scheme fails and the ranchers fall deeper into debt, the railroad moves its people in and begins to evict the ranchers from their homes. It is on the day of the first eviction that the shoot-out occurs.

The climactic scene arrives as something heard:

> Instantly the revolvers and rifles seemed to go off of themselves. Both sides, deputies and Leaguers, opened fire simultaneously. At first, it was nothing but a confused roar of explosions; then the roar lapsed to an irregular, quick succession of reports, shot leaping after shot; then a moment's silence, and, last of all, regular as clock-ticks, three shots at exact intervals. Then stillness.

It unfolds as something seen:

> Delaney, shot through the stomach, slid down from his horse, and, on his hands and knees, crawled from the road into the standing wheat. Christian fell backward from the saddle toward the buggy, and hung suspended in that position, his head and shoulders on the wheel, one stiff leg still across his saddle. Hooven, in attempting to rise from his kneeling position, received a rifle ball squarely in

the throat, and rolled forward upon his face. Old Broderson, crying out, "Oh, they've shot me, boys," staggered sideways, his head bent, his hands rigid at his sides, and fell into the ditch. Osterman, blood running from his mouth and nose, turned about and walked back. Presley helped him across the irrigating ditch and Osterman laid himself down, his head on his folded arms. Harran Derrick dropped where he stood, turning over on his face, and lay motionless, groaning terribly, a pool of blood forming under his stomach. The old man Dabney, silent as ever, received his death, speechless. He fell to his knees, got up again, fell once more, and died without a word. Annixter, instantly killed, fell his length to the ground, and lay without movement, just as he had fallen, one arm across his face.

Of course, all this happens in a novel, in Frank Norris's (1870–1902) *The Octopus* (1901). Given its insistent emphasis on the vertical—a recurring trope is of a human figure standing against a vast, horizontal landscape—Norris could have shown no greater respect for his characters than in this careful notation of the way each body falls. This is very hard to take, however well we have been prepared. There are, for me, few more moving scenes in American fiction, and much of its power is due to the skill with which Norris has included me as a *bystander*. I have been preparing to "stand in . . . in *one* fight" with these characters, as Annixter puts it, but when the fight comes, the fact of its suddenness is belied by the deliberate slowness with which I am asked to take it in. Having been ready, I had thought the readiness all. The gap between my stunned sense of dispossession and the author's calm disposition of the plot suggests, instead, that not the readiness, but the ripeness, is all.

The fact of the deed is established first through the ear. Sound must penetrate in order to be heard; by opening ourselves to these roars and reports we are compelled to acknowledge the event as literally internalized. The vulnerability of the ear then gives way to the distancing power of the eye. The trouble here is that we have not seen the fight and get only its carefully visualized aftermath. Whatever those sounds meant, the eye sees that it has opened too late. We are left looking on—standing by—without being able to help. What good then does it do to be ready? Norris's climax reminds us, in its structure and in its effect, of the ways in which we read or watch a tragedy—that the greatest power its audience ever has is the power to care and to wish, and that it is the powerlessness of these feelings to affect events, once they have been aroused, that makes them arouse in turn a sense of pity and fear.

In the spring of 1899, twenty-nine-year-old Frank Norris, Chicago-born and San Francisco–raised, spent eight weeks on the San Anita Rancho, near Hollister,

California. He had just published *McTeague* (1899) and went to the rancho in order to gather impressions for a new novel, one he intended to base on an event that had occurred in Tulare County some twenty years earlier.

Norris went to Hollister the way John Ford (1895–1973) went to Monument Valley, in search of a site that would provide his story with an answerable if enlarged historical scale. The area around Hollister resembled only a little the place in the San Joaquin Valley where the previous incident had taken place. Norris may have bagged wheat on the threshing platform of the San Anita; he certainly set out to conflate its landscapes with those of the great valley. Hollister lay in the rolling earthquake country between spurs of the Coast Range; Tulare was an arid country with distant horizons. If Tulare lacked the romance of antiquity, Norris could supply it by importing a copy of the mission a few miles west of Hollister, San Juan Bautista. The Morse Seed ranch nearby, an agricultural impossibility in the San Joaquin, became the magical seat of one of his heroines. And the coast live oak migrated over the mountains to shed in Tulare its welcome shade.

Norris based the action of *The Octopus* on events that took place in 1880 at a place called Mussel Slough. During the 1870s, settlers in the San Joaquin did take up land along the right-of-way owned by the Southern Pacific Railroad with the pledge that they could one day buy the land at $2.50 upward an acre. The railroad was built, the ranchers improved the land, and then, when the Southern Pacific acquired clear title, it offered the land for sale at prices between $17 and $40 an acre. After losing ejectment suits, members of the Grand Settlers' League confronted a U.S. Marshall and would-be purchasers of their land near the town of Hanford in the Mussel Slough district of Tulare County. Firing broke out, and after the dust settled, one railroad agent and three settlers lay dead. Three settlers died thereafter, five were sentenced to prison, and others were hunted down and killed by the railroad's hired guns. After losing one more court battle, most of the settlers moved away, and those who stayed accepted the railroad's terms.

There are a number of "Notable Memorials to Mussel Slough," as one omnibus essay has it, including a novel by Josiah Royce (1855–1916), friend of William James (1842–1910) and fellow member of the Harvard philosophy department, called *The Feud of Oakfield Creek* (1887). Among the documentary sources that survive is a letter written to the Visalia *Delta* by Mary E. Chambers, a sister of one of the men killed by railroad guns. "I would like to state a little of my own experience since coming on these lands," she writes; she and her husband had moved to Tulare County in January of 1870.

"I shall never forget my first impression of the country. I was so discouraged with the looks of it, that I did not want to look out of the wagon. Nothing but cattle and horses, sheep and hogs, till it looked like one vast corral, with no more appearance of vegetation than a well-swept floor." Mary and her husband have never farmed before; the stockmen look upon them as intruders; they must buy everything at Stockton, at a "very high price." They travel eight days to purchase their first supply of seed; wild cattle plunder their crop. Mary plants a garden five miles from her home, and she gets up at four in the morning and walks the distance in order to weed it.

"Nothing could be done without ditches," so the Chamberses join with other settlers to build their first irrigation project. "These very men who are termed by this company as squatters . . . were the men who built this ditch, and who have made a success of it; but who can say at what cost! I have known men, when they were working on those ditches, to grind corn in their coffe-mills to make their bread, and take their frying-pan with them and depend on catching fish for their meals. Just let this great corporation think of that a moment!" Mary and her husband continue their struggle, planting "five successive crops without ever raising anything." Then the railroad land grader arrives, and "Up went our land from $2.50 to $22 per acre. And why? Because we had a house, barn, orchard, alfalfa pasture, flower garden, ditches, and a well cultivated farm." When it becomes clear that the settlers cannot afford to purchase the land they have improved, the railroad comes in "like thieves in the night" to dispossess them. "Coming in after most of the farmers' bedtime, and on the day of our picnic, when they supposed that every one would be at the picnic, and they could murder the few who would offer resistance."

Like *The Octopus*, Mary Chambers's letter is a document from the past. It survives in the archive, in the files of a newspaper office, and in a book published by the Settlers Committee in 1880. Norris's novel is the version of the Mussel Slough affair that has passed into the economy of reading; indeed, it is the only means by which all but a few scholars are likely to retain any awareness of what happened over 120 years ago on a May morning in Tulare County. Neither text has pride of place when it comes to the facts; each constructs a version of what happened, and each aims to promote a certain effect. Had the letter by the determined settler somehow entered the canon and gained a place in the classroom, it, too, could be credited with creating a usable past. That it did not says more about the vagaries of publishing, text distribution, and the politics of canon formation than it does about the letter's verbal power.

But we must work with what we can recover, put across, and keep in view. When it comes to Mussel Slough, as well as the wider issues it calls up, *The Octopus* is what we have. And the intensity of the artistic performance makes it more than a mere record, or "memorial." Beyond all the lawyers' briefs and newspaper articles and scholarly analyses, the novel offers us a secret history commensurate with the unresolved and still urgent political and emotional burdens of the event.

If *The Octopus* looks backward twenty years, it is even more, as is any intelligent historical novel, a secret history of its own moment. In the words of Theodore Roosevelt, who ascended to the presidency in the year *The Octopus* was published, the true and worthy subject for any fighting man is "that combination between business and politics which I was in after years so often to oppose." Writing here in his *Autobiography* (1913), Roosevelt refers to an insight experienced in 1882, when Norris would have been only twelve. But the novelist, even more rapidly than the politician, came to the knowledge that the issue of the age was concentration of power.

The turn-of-the-century trusts represented "combination," Louis Brandeis was to write—"concentration intensive and comprehensive." In the years in which Norris grew to maturity, the incorporation of America accelerated with locomotive force. The twenty-six industrial mergers that occurred between the end of the Civil War and 1890 multiplied sixfold in the next seven years. Records for the incorporation of capital were set and then broken in 1898 and 1899. The process culminated in the 1901 creation by J. P. Morgan of U. S. Steel, which placed 60 percent of the nation's steel production under the control of one corporation. The word "corporate" comes from *corporare*, to make into a body, and *The Octopus* dramatizes the consequences of an actual human body going up against the interests of a corporate one.

The experience of ranching in Tulare County, as Mary Chambers lived it, was lived as a chronology, a brute and unpredictable sequence. In our daily lives, we live as she did, in existential time. The future remains unknown and comes as it comes.

But, in our reading and our remembering lives, we enjoy a different relationship to time. The past need not be experienced as an unfolding path but presents itself to us, rather, as an echoing field. We know that some events preceded or followed others, that causes can perhaps even be adduced, and yet we also know that much of the meaning of the past—or what we call "history"—can be found in the answerable patterns we make out of it. The empowering value of the past has nothing to do with its being "over" and everything to do with the freedom of imaginative movement afforded by it and in it. Toni Morrison alludes to this entitlement when she writes that "history is more infinite than the future." And the most compelling and lasting versions of that history—the ones destined to outlast the straight histories and to replace them as the effective contents of our memories—are those provided by literature.

Why by our literature? Because to the "what happened" artful writing adds the "how it felt." "*How it felt to me*," Joan Didion writes in *Slouching towards Bethlehem*; this is what her work attempts to recover and commemorate. In so framing the task, she speaks not only to a writer's responses but to a reader's. As Eudora Welty wrote in 1965, "great fiction shows us not how to conduct our behavior but how to feel."

How do such works enable us to feel? Care is the key: as Sheldon Sacks argues in *Fiction and the Shape of Belief* (1967), a novel is a represented action with characters about whose fates we are made to care. A novel is a "history," as *Tom Jones* subtitles itself, one that uses all the means available to art to arouse, complicate, and release emotion. In *Hunger of Memory*, Richard Rodriguez writes eloquently about making this discovery:

> Another summer I determined to read all the novels of Dickens. Reading his fat novels, I loved the feeling I got—after the first hundred pages—of being at home in a fictional world where I knew the names of the characters and cared about what was going to happen to them. And it bothered me that I was forced away at the conclusion, when the fiction closed tight, like a fortune-teller's fist—the futures of all the major characters neatly resolved. I never knew how to take such feelings seriously, however. Nor did I suspect that these experiences could be part of a novel's meaning.

Rodriguez reminds us that the recognition scenes for which we so often read—those passages where the text gathers itself into a moment of maximum emotion—demand, as Gloucester says in *King Lear*, that we "see it feelingly." The kind of care induced by reading is a complex fate, however, since with response comes responsibility.

So what do I feel—what perhaps does any reader feel—when taking in the shoot-out scene? I feel shock, then loss, then anger, then awe. I feel the complicated responsibilities of a bystander described in my first pass at unpacking the scene. These feelings are overdetermined by all the means used by Norris to prepare me for the moment of crisis. They are provoked and guided by form. "It is forms," Jean-Luc Godard maintains, "that tell us finally what lies at the bottom of things." In the pages that follow, I will focus on literary form—on narrative structure, metaphor, repetition, point of view, ellipsis, allusion—in order to uncover the distinct ways in which literature works upon us.

Norris believed that a novel gathered momentum toward a "pivotal event"—in the case of *The Octopus*, toward the shoot-out. He wrote to a friend that the thing was meant to accelerate "all of a sudden to a great big crushing END, something that will slam you right between your eyes and knock you off your feet." In keeping with Norris's formal commitment to a pivotal event, *The Octopus* orders response through its repeated foreshadowings of an inevitable fall. In a half sentence from part 2, Norris advances a formula that sums up the novel's three key incidents and hearkens toward a fourth and climactic one: "that abrupt swoop of terror and impending death dropping down from out of the darkness, cutting abruptly athwart the gayety of the moment, come and gone with the swiftness of a thunderclap." What does this describe but the invasion of the Other, the early collision of the locomotive with the sheep, and Delaney's abruption into the barn dance? And what does it anticipate but the felling of the men on the Lower Road? These three acts of foreshadowing are characterized by their abruptness. Loss comes suddenly in this world; what dawns gradually, through this pattern of repetition, is that loss will come.

Foreshadowing thus operates throughout *The Octopus* to draw us into an action about which we care. The genius of Shakespeare, Coleridge argues, lies in his ability to produce "expectation in preference to surprise." The genius of Norris lies, as he writes in "The Mechanics of Fiction" (1901), in "preparation of effect." By extending to us the opportunity to recognize pattern and so to anticipate events, Norris confers on us, in the manner of the great tragic dramatists, a sense of implication in and responsibility for the promised end. Our foreknowledge is purchased, of course, by a lack of power; the characters are dignified by suffering a surprise we are asked to experience as an expectation fulfilled.

In a novel so overpoweringly visual, Norris chooses to fulfill his design by way of an act of listening. The shoot-out arrives, as I have said, as something heard. "At first, it was nothing but a confused roar of explosions." Norris signals the imminent importance of sound by twice using the word "audible" in the pages leading up to the guns going off. Norris even provides a stand-in for the overhearing reader in the figure of Presley, the unengaged spectator who arrives at the irrigation ditch with the ranchers but who does not stay with them. "Presley withdrew," Norris writes, "to watch what was going on."

But watching alone will not serve here. Hearing is required, or, more properly, listening. I choose the word *listening* because listening entails the active will to hear and the faith that the sound so engaged will have both meaning and force. It is what we go through with the ranchers here—especially our willingness to listen as well as to "watch"—that distinguishes us from Presley and makes us cocreators and sufferers of Norris's climactic scene.

Our experience of the shoot-out acts as a paradigm of the recognition scenes that will preoccupy me in the pages that follow and that comprise the heart of my secret history. Recognition Scene, Scene of Instruction, Pedagogical Moment— whatever label we apply to such occasions, they involve an exchange of knowledge, or a decision not to exchange it. The knowledge is often passed on in the form of a story, or, as in *The Octopus*, by way of a dramatic confrontation or tableau. These scenes enact an allegory of the author's relationship with and responsibility toward the reader. They concern themselves as much with how knowledge gets transferred as with what can be known. In staging such scenes, the artistic burden cannot be separated from the moral one: they become a test of both timing and tact. Although not every pedagogical moment involves an experience of overhearing, or represented listening, each operates in my narrative as a figure for attentiveness, for the sort of open but suspicious mind that can divine the secret history any text worth reading hides in plain sight.

CHAPTER TWO

Double Consciousness

JOHNSON ✦ CHESNUTT ✦ DU BOIS ✦ WASHINGTON

A boy discovers, by being told not to stand up with the "white scholars" in his class, that he is "colored." "Mother, mother," he cries when he gets home, "tell me, am I a nigger?" "I am not white," she answers, "but you . . . the best blood of the South is in you." The boy goes on to take up piano. On the way to enroll in college in Atlanta, he is diverted by a craps game and ends up becoming a cigar maker in Jacksonville. Moving north, he becomes a professional gambler as well as "the best ragtime player in New York." A millionaire who likes his playing takes him to Europe as a servant-companion. After a pleasant sojourn, the narrator decides to return to the United States to pursue music, especially study of "the old slave songs." At Macon, Georgia, he strikes out "into the interior." One night he hears the galloping of horses and mutterings about "some terrible crime." "A crowd of men, all white," gathers at the railroad station. A "poor wretch" is chained to a railroad tie and burned alive. On the return journey north, the narrator feels "unbearable shame" and realizes the emotion "that was driving me out of the Negro race." He resolves to make money, in real estate. "Then I met her." She is "dazzlingly white." A courtship begins; he finally tells her "I love you," and that "there is something more." She flees. Meeting him again months later, she confesses her love. "We were married the following spring . . . First there came to us a little girl, with hair and eyes dark like mine . . . Two years later there came a boy, who has my temperament, but is fair like his mother." The wife dies giving birth to the son. "I shall never marry again." The narrator concludes that "I am an ordinary successful white man who has made a little money." But he ends, in his last sentence, with the thought that "I have sold my birthright for a mess of pottage."

What an American story! Wandering, vagrancy, upward mobility, courtship, denial, marriage, parenthood, success—and all that crossed by race, a factor that determines everything and nothing. What allows the unnamed narrator to escape its strictures is his appearance, one by which even he—the big recognition scene occurs when racial identity is publicly disclosed and imposed—is taken in. And, of course, if race can be this easily dissembled, then what, exactly, is it?

Never used here is the word "black"—the term simply does not apply. At moments of extreme racial awareness, the narrative retreats from specificity behind questions ("Am I a nigger?"), euphemism ("best blood"), or abstract nouns ("something more"). While being black is an overwhelming cultural fact for most Negroes, trapping them in a cycle of abuse sanctioned by lynching, the narrator lives out his race as a performance, an identity function that exists insofar as he is willing to acknowledge it.

The great fantasy of James Weldon Johnson's (1871–1938) *Autobiography of an Ex-Colored Man* is that race is an experience to which one can consent. The "ivory whiteness" of his skin allows the narrator to move at will across the color line, and yet the crises of his story involve an experience of unchosen or anguished identification with his blackness. These are moments of shame: the "sword thrust" in the classroom; the lynching in Georgia; the rejected proposal, when his wife-to-be begins to weep. To step out of blackness, on the other hand, proves relatively painless, its greatest price being the guilt expressed in Johnson's last sentence.

And of course the book itself, like its narrator, engages in an act of passing: it is a novel masquerading as an autobiography. In its step-by-step documentary tone (a life, unlike a story, cannot have happened otherwise), the *Autobiography* purchases a kind of necessity for a character who enjoys a fantastic freedom. The *Autobiography* was first published anonymously, in 1912. An editor's note in the Dover Thrift Edition tells us that "it fooled many readers with its authentic tone." But it did not become "widely successful" until reissued in 1927 under its author's name. Then it became clear that this "autobiography" had nothing to say about vast stretches of its author's life, such as his founding of the first black daily paper in America, his work for the NAACP in the South and the West, or his successful lobbying in 1921–22 for the passage of the Dyer-Lynching Bill.

Johnson's book did not achieve standing until its truth came to be seen as constructed. Once people knew that this was not an "authentic" story but one Johnson had made up, then they wanted to read it. Like the narrator of the novel itself, readers did not want to remain trapped on the level of the literal. The history of the book's reception thus allowed readers to reenact its central dynamic, the continual rediscovery that assumptions we make about types (of literary genres, of races of people) determine the generosity of our response.

❖   ❖

Why is it so liberating to think of the self as a performance rather than an essence? And why does the performing self have so much to do with the experience of race? One answer circles around the word "passing." Only in the United States, where the conventions regarding race are so complex and so arbitrary, did the color line become a zone of radical self-making. The endless sets of laws that tried and failed to encode racial identity, the disproportionality of the "one drop" rule, the unique availability of black women to the sexual appetites of white men—all this and more subjected the racialized body to a carnival of interpretation. Whereas a civil war was fought to maintain the fiction of the black-white binary, American literature had long since moved on, fascinated by the price both individuals and the culture remained willing to pay to defend the purity of a whiteness that never had and never could exist in practice.

In 1896, *Plessy v. Ferguson* established as lawful "separate but equal" facilities for the nation's white and black citizens. The Dred Scott case had gone so far as to argue that Negroes are "beings 'of an inferior order.' " Charles Chesnutt (1858–1932) quotes this language from the 1857 Supreme Court decision in his 1900 novel, *The House Behind the Cedars*. The brevity of Chesnutt's publishing career suggests that the nation was not yet ready for the claim his complex fictions made upon it; his first two books, each a short-story collection, appeared in 1899, and he was to publish only two more novels after *The House Behind the Cedars*: *The Marrow of Tradition* in 1901 and *The Colonel's Dream* in 1905.

Chesnutt's first novel does much more than did either *Plessy v. Ferguson* or *Dred Scott v. Sandford* to complicate the enforceability of laws regarding color. Separate but equal might prove workable, in a clumsy sort of way, where racial differences could be distinguished. But in a hierarchy based on physical appearance, and one even more undergirded by the ineluctable metaphor of "blood," how was separate but equal to be maintained when blackness or whiteness could not be discerned by the eye?

John Warwick practices law in South Carolina. Following a decade-long absence from his North Carolina home—the house behind the cedars—he retrieves his beautiful sister Rena and brings her to the town of Clarence. There she is courted by George Tryon, the man she agrees to marry. On a chance visit back to Patesville, where Rena has returned to care for her sick mother, Tryon discovers that Rena is "a negro." He renounces her; she decides to teach school. Pursued by a new suitor, as well as the repentant George, Rena flees into a swamp. Having resolved to "give up the world for love," George arrives at the house behind the cedars only to find that Rena is dead.

Plot summary reduces *The House Behind the Cedars* to another tragic mulatto story. But Chesnutt's art draws its reader instead into an excruciating reenactment of the undecidability of race. He does this by deploying the technique of "*deliberately withheld meaning*" that Conrad Aiken (1889–1973) found so central in Faulkner. What Chesnutt's story withholds is genetic evidence, the kind of information found on birth certificates. Like Johnson's *Autobiography*, Chesnutt's novel chooses to indulge in an act of passing, to offer itself as a marriage plot rather than a story of renounced or unacknowledged origins.

In his second paragraph, Chesnutt delivers a portrait of John Warwick. He is "tall, dark, with straight, black, lustrous hair, and very clean-cut, high-bred features." The description is unexceptional; like any other nineteenth-century novel, *The House Behind the Cedars* attempts to fix character by way of appearance. Since the word "black" is preceded by the word "straight," to describe John's hair, only a suspicious reader would infer anything racial from the offered adjectives. Yet John's mind and eye prove highly attentive to the fact of the color line. On arriving in his hometown, he sees the Patesville bell tower and thinks of how it "had clamorously warned all negroes, slave or free," of the curfew. As he continues his walk, John sees a "colored policeman" and thinks—the story begins "a few years after the Civil War"—of the marks left by the conflict.

After dropping in on Judge Straight's office, John finds himself walking behind a "strikingly handsome" young woman with an "ivory" neck. She is kind to an old black woman; she pulls a "negro child" out of a mudhole. We watch him, watching her. We suspect—and we suspect this not only because of the text's highly charged racial awareness but because we know that Chesnutt was African-American and maybe because we have read in the introduction that in a letter to his editor Chesnutt had written that "the subject of the book" is "a colored girl who passed for white"—that both characters are black.

Chesnutt layers the opening chapter with a second level of speculation, one having to do not with race but with relationship. Who is this woman to this man? He senses "something familiar" about her. Then he sees her enter the house behind a row of dwarf cedars and murmurs to himself, "It must be Rena." The reader is left to wonder—is she a lover, a friend, a sister? Chesnutt then makes Warwick himself the object of the gaze. As John throws a backward glance at the house, he "scarcely" notices two men across the street, looking at him. "I jes' wonder who dat man is," the younger man observes. If the question has been race—what a man is—it shifts to identity, to a matter of who he is.

John gazes at the town, and at Rena; Frank gazes at John; the reader watches them all. What can be known by looking at people turns out to be very little, and yet on the vagaries of physical appearance the convention called "race" is based. (In his essay "The Courts and the Negro" [undated typescript], Chesnutt would be careful to quote the language of Plessy on the point that race is "a distinction which is founded in the color of the two races.") Chesnutt withholds information concerning his characters' genetic and relational status so as to set us adrift in a sea of surmises. By refusing to identify his characters for us, he implicates readers in the preemptive and reductive guessing game race is here revealed to be.

John performs his elected identity so well that he even takes his mother in. On his second day in Patesville, he visits the house behind the cedars with a message for Molly Walden, who greets John at the front door. He tells her that the message is from her "son" and then sits down in her parlor. Molly scans his face with a puzzled look. Then an "electric spark" of sympathy flashes between them. "John, my John!" Molly cries, "It *is* John."

Chesnutt stages this scene without commentary. It is up to us to be shocked at the alienating power of John's performance; it is up to us to give this failed recognition scene its parabolic force. For what is race in America but a vast and failed recognition scene, one in which the power of a visually based and yet visually unstable set of conventions blinds us to our common humanity and reaches so far down into the roots of being that it can render mothers unable to recognize their sons?

And yet John's homecoming is a triumph, of sorts. His mother's response confirms that John has mastered his act, an impersonation that powerfully enhances his personal freedom. What is lost to family ties is gained in social mobility. And here lies the difficulty in assessing the literature of passing: do we celebrate the John Warwicks and the Coleman Silks (in an anticipation of Philip Roth's title, *The Human Stain*, John refers to his mixed blood as "that stain"), as free artists of themselves—as heroes of performativity—or do we read them as tragically dispossessed, race traitors cut off from their origins who have sold their birthright, as Johnson's narrator says at the end of his narrative, "for a mess of pottage"?

The novel of passing belongs to the American fictions of family romance—the recurring syndrome in fairy tales in which the parents of origin are replaced "by others of better birth"—of which *The Great Gatsby* (1925) is a central instance. Like Gatsby, John sets out to become "a new man." He leaves home, renames himself (Walden becomes Warwick), marries a rich girl, gets a profession, and buries his past. As in *Gatsby*, his identity is revealed in stages. Nick tells Gatsby's background story three times before he gets to the shocking fact delivered in chapter 8—a fact Nick has known from the beginning of his narration, which is all delivered after the action of the story has ended—that Gatsby "took" Daisy years ago, an act of original sexual possession rendering absurd the idealizing and adolescent repossession he attempts in the novel's present. The final version of John's story, told in chapter 17, is also the most reductive. Not until after George renounces Rena, over halfway into the novel, does Chesnutt tell us "about the past life," about the fact that John and Rena's mother is "a bright mulatto" impregnated and set up in the house behind the cedars by a white man.

To pretend to be what one is not: the American passing story goes back as least as far as Olaudah Equiano (1745–97), surfaces in novels as distinguished as *Clotel* (1853) and *Passing* (1929), and persists on into Chang-rae Lee's *A Gesture Life* (1999) and Philip Roth's *The Human Stain* (2000). Of course, under the regime of racial and ethnic difference, a character understood to be ethnically Korean or racially black is often judged, as Werner Sollers writes, to be an "impostor" rather than a "self-made man." While I read passing as a welcome challenge to identity politics, it is finally much different to pass as a Jay Gatsby than as a Doc Hata or a Coleman Silk. Coleman's act of passing knowingly protests against the strictures of race. Gatsby's embrace of a lightness of being acts as an unwitting critique of the promise that every American is entitled to the pursuit of happiness. The ground gained and the price paid by way of each act of passing could not be more different.

The force of John Warwick's story depends, as does Gatsby's, on its author's decision to begin near the end of it. To come upon a character without an origin story or a detailed genealogy is to be deprived of the ability to categorize. Instead, the reader must scramble to piece together a profile and, in so doing, can come to realize that identity depends on how stories are told. Taking men—or fictional characters—as we find them changes our sense of what it is about people that counts. Chesnutt's Warwick and Fitzgerald's Gatsby present the self not as a pedigree, but a conjecture. And the release of the "past life" in tantalizing stages—Molly refers early on to "the old story," and in chapter 7 Chesnutt alludes to "the family secret"—allows, in both cases, the reader to participate in the wishful fantasy of a painless rise, to begin with achieved status rather than with the repudiations involved in achieving it.

Of course, the novel turns out to be less John's than Rena's story. He maintains his performance of whiteness, while she is destroyed by the discovery of her blackness. If John is the Gatsby figure, Rena is more like Faulkner's Charles Bon, undone by her position "along the border-line." In another odd recognition scene, George and Rena encounter each other, by accident, in Patesville, and they do so in a way that allows him to divine that she is black. Yet in this moment Rena *looks* like she has always looked. George's perception of race in the scene is based on knowledge extrinsic to the moment of looking. It is based on something he has *heard* and, thus, can be taken as the seminal instance, in the American literature of the twentieth century, of race as a rumor, as the product of a vast whispering campaign in which the classifying of bodies is gossiped into being.

While visiting Doctor Green in Patesville, George is told that "a young cullud 'oman" is in the drugstore nearby and that she is worth a look. The young woman is Rena. But when George then peers through the window, he sees not Rena but what has been said about her. He sees that "a negro girl had been foisted upon him for a white woman." Yet Rena's color has not changed; when George first looks through the drugstore window, and he sees only her back, she looks "like a lily on its stem." Here is the moment of reciprocal recognition:

> When Rena's eyes fell upon the young man in the buggy, she saw a face as pale as
> death, with starting eyes, in which love, which once had reigned there, had now

given place to astonishment and horror. She stood a moment as if turned to stone. One appealing glance she gave,—a look that might have softened adamant. When she saw that it brought no answering sign of love or sorrow or regret, the color faded from her cheek, the light from her eye, and she fell fainting to the ground.

The two characters are here joined together in an exchange that argues for likeness rather than difference. The woman turns to "stone;" the man is likened to "adamant." Their eyes fall on each other; in each case, a "glance" registers a feeling. And each loses "color," drained of the very physical marker that maps out the racial divide.

In this climactic scene, in which a look almost kills, George *sees* nothing new. As the system of signs by which race is signified breaks down, or is proven unreliable, words—Rena has been designated a "cullud 'oman"—rush in to sustain the fiction of racial difference. Here as elsewhere in the novel, race is revealed as the product of stories people tell themselves—or have told—about their origins. Chesnutt's America, like Jean Toomer's, proves a nation of "*hearsay descents.*" The most powerful instance of such a case is given to us by Faulkner: the fact that in *Light in August* (1932) Joe Christmas is merely said to be black in no way discourages him from internalizing the designation and from acting out his self-destructive response to it. By delaying the telling of the Walden family history until a few chapters after Rena faints away, Chesnutt allows the reader, along with George, to gather the hints and rumors about Rena's "identity" and to make of them, in contrast to or in concert with George, what he or she will.

As if to alert us to the task facing us in chapter 15, Chesnutt interposes into the middle of the preceding chapter a direct address to the reader:

If there be a dainty reader of this tale who scorns a lie, and who writes the story of his life upon his sleeve for all the world to read, let him uncurl his scornful lip and come down from the pedestal of superior morality, to which assured position and wide opportunity have lifted him, and put himself in the place of Rena and her brother, upon whom God had lavished his best gifts, and from whom society would have withheld all that made these gifts valuable. To undertake what they tried to do required great courage. Had they possessed the sneaking, cringing, treacherous character traditionally ascribed to people of mixed blood—the character which the blessed institutions of a free slave-holding republic had been well adapted to foster among them; had they been selfish enough to sacrifice to their ambition the mother who gave them birth, society would have been placated or humbugged, and the voyage of their life might have been one of unbroken smoothness.

Chesnutt takes a firm stand here. Passing is not judged to be, as Johnson's narrator appears to judge it, a betrayal of the race. It is an act of courage.

The efficacy of such claims for Chesnutt, and for his characters, may be difficult for a contemporary reader to appreciate. Over a century later, people in love move much more easily across the color line, seeking a happiness they are more likely to find. Miscegenation has ceased to be, in most quarters, a scandal, or even a term of use. Racial intermixing is no longer perceived, except by crackpots, as much of a threat to anything. If the courage to pass is something of a dead issue, what remains of Chesnutt's novel that we can make use of in the present?

What made passing such a scandal was that it gave evidence of prior sexual congress between the races, a joining together that, since it surely had occurred at a white man's pleasure and on his terms, also provided a powerful and embodied argument against the practicability of the taboo against it, let alone the many state laws prohibiting miscegenation. Most Americans no longer worry about this taboo. But the social fact of race—of discrimination based on color—remains a deeply intransigent issue, and it is John's performance of whiteness, rather than Rena's destruction by the racializing gaze, that has the most liberating consequences for how we live now.

John plays the Coleman Silk figure to the end; he never drops the mask of whiteness. In school he fights off every imputation of blackness: "to himself he never admitted the charge." "You are aware, of course, that you are a negro?" Judge Straight asks the young John, in the chapter that revisits the Walden family history. " 'I am white,' replied the lad." For John, race becomes a matter of refusing the attribution of the sign. Grasping early on that race is a complex and deeply self-contradictory system of signification, and recognizing that "no external sign" marks him off from the white boys on the street, John claims the "privilege" of "choosing" his race. Of course, this choice comes at a price. When he invites Rena to pass, along with him, he welcomes her to "the populous loneliness of his adopted country." At the end, Rena returns to her native roots. The last lines of the novel are spoken by a black man, who has been asked to identify the dead woman in the house behind the cedars. "A young cullud 'oman, suh, Mis' Molly Walden's daughter Rena." Rena dies as her mother's daughter, while John lives on as no man's son.

But the freedom he gains at such cost is a salutary one. If John's story can be taken as plausible, then the notion of race as determining, essential, or even ascertainable simply breaks down. At the extreme edges of the color line, whiteness or blackness turns out to be a performance that highly skilled actors can choose to take on. And once this possibility is allowed, the whole logic of race collapses, since a color line that cannot be policed, given the infinite gradations of the players along it, is really no line at all.

✦   ✦

"To get to a place where you could love anything you chose—not to need permission for desire—well now, *that* was freedom." Paul D thinks this to himself in
the climactic chapter of *Beloved*. Isn't this the implied object not only of the long
march of American literature—one thinks of the terrible sublimations of Nathaniel
Hawthorne's Hester Prynne—but of any imaginative work whatsoever? And isn't it
a heart-stopping irony to discover that one of the most satisfying and believable
love stories imagined by our literature takes place between two ex-slaves named
Sethe and Paul D? They are good people—they deserve and are worthy of each
other—and their story had a kind of happy ending. Of course, the "veil" of race
stands in their way, as it does between George and Rena; both of Morrison's characters are openly black, and Sethe, especially, must learn to love her blackness. *Beloved* is a triumph in many ways, a culminating work in the tradition, and no more
so than when it imagines the human project as one in which every individual can
enjoy "the freedom to love."

Not simply the freedom to own land, or travel, or vote, or sit in the front of the
bus, but the freedom to love—whether such freedom exists becomes the true test
of a nation's promises fulfilled. Only once all the other freedoms are in place can
this ultimately satisfying freedom—it is what we live for—be enjoyed. In this account of the still-unfinished movement from slavery to freedom, the key event in
the liberation of both black and white Americans would not be the Civil Rights Act
of 1964 but a Supreme Court decision of 1967, *Loving v. Virginia*, in which miscegenation laws were once and for all deemed unconstitutional. Virginia had passed
the first of these laws in 1662, declaring sexual intercourse between whites and
blacks twice as evil as fornication between two whites.

"The freedom to love" is a phrase Morrison borrows from W. E. B. Du Bois
(1868–1963). He uses it at the end of chapter 1 of *The Souls of Black Folk* (1903),
where the phrase expresses his understanding that the story of race in America is
all about men and women and how they get together. Du Bois knows that such
stories are most powerfully handled in the novel form, in books like *The House Behind the Cedars*, *Absalom, Absalom!*, and *Beloved*. The history of the novel could be
said, in fact, to constitute the secret history of the origin and course of love. The
structure of linked essays making up *The Souls of Black Folk* does not lend itself to
the telling of a love story. Instead, it accomplishes an analysis as essential for the
beginning of the century as is Richard Rodriguez's at the end. Here is the key paragraph from *Brown* (2002):

> When I began this book, I knew some readers would take "race" for a tragic
> noun, a synonym for conflict and isolation. Race is not such a terrible word for

me. Maybe because I am skeptical by nature. Maybe because my nature is already mixed. The word race encourages me to remember the influence of eroticism on history. For that is what race memorializes. Within any discussion of race, there lurks the possibility of romance.

What Rodriguez imagines as a romantic commingling Du Bois experiences a century earlier as a tragic family feud. The "two figures" who typify for him the conflict that gave rise to the Civil War are a white man and a black woman:

> The one, a gray-haired gentleman, whose fathers had quit themselves like men, whose sons lay in nameless graves; who bowed to the evil of slavery because its abolition threatened untold ill to all; who stood at last, in the evening of life, a blighted, ruined form, with hate in his eyes;—and the other, a form hovering dark and mother-like, her awful face black with the mists of centuries, had aforetime quailed at that white master's command, had bent in love over the cradles of his sons and daughters, and closed in death the sunken eyes of his wife,—aye, too, at his behest had laid herself low to his lust, and borne a tawny man-child to the world, only to see her dark boy's limbs scattered to the winds by midnight marauders riding after "damned Niggers."

Du Bois here presents the American couple as the owner and his slave.

For Du Bois, however, that blacks and whites have from the nation's founding shared an erotic history in no way equates with "the freedom to love." Their racially mixed children embody instead a legacy of sexual coercion. The Civil War brings with it an end to this "intimacy"—it is a quaint word—between the races. Two centuries of white-on-black rape give way to the period of lynching, in which the loss of control over black male bodies gets projected back onto those bodies as an imagined desire for white women for which the black male is then preemptively punished. It was seeing the charred knuckles of a lynched Negro prominently displayed in a white store owner's window on Atlanta's Mitchell Street that shocked Du Bois out of his stance as a "detached scientist" and set him, in 1899, on the course of a fighter for African-American rights.

The one lynching story Du Bois elects to tell in *The Souls of Black Folk* is about John Jones. After an education in the big city, John returns to the town of Altamaha to teach in the Negro school. There he runs afoul of his double, the white John who has also gone away to school and whose father closes the Negro school after an idle word from his son about John Jones being "dangerous." That afternoon the black John sees his "dark sister struggling in the arms of a tall and fair-haired man"—the white John—and brains him with a tree limb. Then he waits for the posse and its "coiling twisted rope." This time the black man did it; this time he is guilty. Not of raping the white woman, but of acting on "the pent-up hatred" over the repetition of the age-old crime.

Through all of this history, Du Bois writes, the marks of mixture survive:

> The red stain of bastardy, which two centuries of systematic legal defilement of Negro women had stamped upon his race, meant not only the loss of ancient African chastity, but also the hereditary weight of a mass of corruption from white adulterers, threatening almost the obliteration of the Negro home.

This is the tragic irony of race in the United States, that the two peoples so radically distinguished by law and custom were all the while enjoying the most intimate possible union.

"Union" proves the key problem for Du Bois, union among races, regions, halves of the self. He captures the problem with a single "and": "to be both a Negro and an American." The famous passage about double consciousness elaborates the dilemma:

> The Negro is a sort of seventh son, born with a veil, and gifted with second-sight in this American world,—a world which yields him no true self-consciousness, but only lets him see himself through the revelation of the other world. It is a peculiar sensation, this double-consciousness, this sense of always looking at one's self through the eyes of others, of measuring one's soul by the tape of a world that looks on in amused contempt and pity. One ever feels his twoness,—an American, a Negro; two souls, two thoughts, two unreconciled strivings; two warring ideals in one dark body, whose dogged strength alone keeps it from being torn asunder.

Du Bois here defines the Negro problem as "one" thing being split into "two." It is a problem of division. The greater problem—the more challenging issue for the century—would be to imagine ways in which two could become as one. It is a problem of integration. D. H. Lawrence grasped the figurative issue early on when he argued, in *Women in Love* (1921), against "meeting and mingling." The solution to division and separateness is not simply to merge everything together; the metaphor of the "melting pot" is not only wishful, but crude. Lawrence instead imagines love as "a star balanced with another star." He complains repeatedly in *Studies in Classic American Literature* (1923) of the national obsession with "MERGING," the wishing away of difference in an indiscriminate fusion. What he calls for is a "recognition of souls." You can only have a recognition of souls when you acknowledge the distance between them, the intrinsic otherness of one human from another. And this leads to the further insight, shared by all authors who grasp the race problem, that the faculty required to bridge the divide is not identification but empathy, not a feeling for but a feeling with. Knowing this, Chesnutt asks his reader to "put himself in the place of Rena and her brother." In direct contrast to identification, the empathy here requested celebrates the fact that the object of its attention does not need to be "like" the self in order to solicit its interest and concern.

Du Bois understands the problem of the color line as a crisis of figuration. To speak of race is to speak figuratively, and this is why, in the paragraph following the one in which George "sees" Rena as black, Chesnutt inserts the phrase "figuratively speaking." Du Bois is groping his way forward here, testing out the efficacy of each chosen word. What the twentieth century needed, he sensed, was a word or an image adequate to a complex demand: a bringing together of two (or more) "strivings" without erasure of the differences between them. In the three monologues that conclude part 2 of *Beloved*, Toni Morrison imagines such an accomplishment, by way of the word "join." The entire force of Gore Vidal's (b. 1925) *Lincoln* (1984) comes to rest on the word "Union," a complex metaphor originating in the Constitution that the sixteenth president decides to put forward as the thing worth fighting for. Moreover, "union" is a word that has proven itself useful and true both then and now because, unlike the word "confederacy," it covers the case in which a number of states are united in a way that holds them together while respecting their individual borders.

When Du Bois goes on to claim, in the paragraph following the passage on the veil, that the American Negro longs to "merge" his "double self into a better and truer self," he relies on a verb that Lawrence deplores. "In this merging," Du Bois continues, "he wishes neither of the older selves to be lost." The paradoxical force of this sentence makes it a more successful putting of the case. The sentence balances a will toward merging against a wish to maintain the integrity of older selves. Such a paradox—it may well be the American dilemma—can best be apprehended through what Hart Crane (1899–1932) called the "logic of metaphor," an act of figuration that invites the mind to acknowledge the pleasure of finding similitude in dissimilitude. If race is a massive fabrication, a verbal construction that over three centuries became an increasingly unwieldy conceit, then it can only be unbuilt through a self-aware refiguration of that jungle of signs into a new and more compelling set of metaphors.

Du Bois figures a condition of doubleness and division through the metaphor of the veil. The metaphor carries with it apocalyptic overtones: at the moment of Christ's death the veil of the temple is rent and the bodies of the saints rise from their graves. Hence, the veil can figure forth an eventual *un*veiling; it is a kind of self-consuming artifact. And this unveiling has in fact already occurred, since the veil carries with it, Du Bois reminds us, the compensating gift of "second-sight." Second sight doesn't merely see; it sees through. The Negro sees through "this

American world"; by virtue of his racial positioning he is gifted with a unique ability to look into the hidden workings of the culture. Du Bois implies as much in
"The Forethought," where he announces that "herein lie buried many things which
if read with patience may show the strange meaning of being black here at the
dawning of the Twentieth Century." He goes on to promise that the "you"—the
white reader—can also uncover "truth hidden." "This meaning is not without interest to you, Gentle Reader; for the problem of the Twentieth Century is the problem of the color line."

There is a price to be paid, however, for being a seer: the Negro cannot see himself "except through the eyes of others." By imaging the experience of being black
as a matter of the gaze, Du Bois reduces the problem of race in America to a question of point of view. Could we but see each other differently, or escape the determining perspective of the hegemonic gaze, then, the logic of the metaphor argues,
what we call race would disappear. And could the Negro no longer see himself
through the eyes of others, he would gain the final freedom, the freedom to love
the self.

Of course, the "divine event" for the Negro was not the rending of the veil but
emancipation. This "was the key to a promised land." But emancipation has not
actually occurred: "the freedman has not yet found in freedom his promised land."
Like *Huckleberry Finn*, *The Souls of Black Folk* sets out to explain why it is yet necessary to indulge in what appears to be a redundant project, why a Jim who has already been freed by his owner must be imprisoned in the smokehouse and then
subjugated to Tom Sawyer's elaborate attempts, as Huck puts it, "to set a free nigger
free." Like Twain, who finished his novel in the 1880s, Du Bois departs from the
ironic awareness that the Civil War has succeeded only in delivering the black man
up to another and more subtle form of enslavement. Du Bois goes on to catalogue
all the terrors of the Ku Klux Klan, the strictures of the Jim Crow laws, the humiliations of the segregated railroad car. In but one instance does he imagine a post–
Civil War African-American life "not yet darkened" by the veil. And he does so by
paying the price of losing his only son.

Burghardt Du Bois died of diphtheria in 1899 at the age of two. His father tells
his story in chapter 11, "Of the Passing of the First-Born." The reference to Exodus
and the final plague visited upon Egypt places the loss within a biblical context, as
if it answered to some part of God's design. And, as the story unfolds, the father
searches out a reading of his son's death that can redeem it as providential. He arrives, finally, where Sethe arrives, in *Beloved*: "I took and put my babies where
they'd be safe."

Safe from what? From "sorrow." From the shame and self-hatred and sheer
dirtying of the self that double-consciousness engenders. "Well sped, my boy, be-

fore the world had dubbed your ambition insolence, had held your ideals unattainable, and taught you to cringe and bow. Better far this nameless void that stops my life than a sea of sorrow for you." Du Bois here offers up his boy, Abraham-like, as a sacrifice to the sufferings of the race. This is the price that must be paid, and is daily paid, by the souls of black folk in America, a civic death difficult to prefer to death itself.

Du Bois's son dies before he knows about race. "He knew no color-line, poor dear—and the Veil, though it shadowed him, had not yet darkened half his sun." His sacrifice is also a delivery and an escape. When Sethe finally gets to the moment of sharing with Paul D why she killed Beloved—a moment never fully articulated—the prose with which Toni Morrison surrounds her suddenly again remembers Du Bois. On her final flight from schoolteacher, Sethe, we are told, "collected every bit of life she had made, all the parts of her that were precious and fine and beautiful, and carried, pushed, dragged them through the veil."

Morrison inherits from Du Bois the awareness that to be black and a parent in the United States means to bring children into a world all too willing to hurt them. Rather than have them suffer such "bitter meanness," Du Bois and Morrison imagine the ultimate way out. That they would be forced to embrace this solution places a maximum burden on the imagination of the "Reader," to whom Du Bois again commends his book, in "The Afterthought." There he asks that *my book not fall still-born into the world-wilderness.*" Only the reader can give birth to the force and meaning of its central parable. The reader gives birth to the story by acknowledging that for a black mother or a father in America—during slavery or after it—it can be felt better to see a beloved child die than to have him live "Within the Veil."

* *

"Criticism of writers by readers . . . is the soul of democracy," Du Bois argues in his chapter on Booker T. Washington (1856–1915). The word "criticism" tolls like a bell throughout *The Souls of Black Folk*, and precisely because a critical spirit is what Washington's vision appears to lack. Eager to pacify a North "weary of the race problem," Washington's embrace of "a gospel of Work and Money" represents, for Du Bois, a complete submission to the American ideology. "So thoroughly did he learn the speech and thought of triumphant commercialism" that he has come to operate entirely within the dominant discourse. He has learned the master's language, and his profit on it is that he has learned to compromise.

Against Du Bois's "critical" approach, Washington deploys one we might call "strategic." Houston Baker characterizes these antithetical responses as "the deformation of mastery" and the "mastery of form." Du Bois wants to pull apart, to analyze, to reveal contradictions; Washington wants to overcome resistance (a "critical" member of an audience requires "thawing out"), to achieve "sympathy," to assuage. He subverts from within, he does not attack from without. If Du Bois's "singing book" comes bearing an urgent message about love, Washington's autobiography quietly insinuates an equally vital lesson about work.

In its last paragraph, *Up from Slavery* (1901) pictures its hero doing what he does best, giving a speech before the city council and the state legislature in Richmond. "I delivered my message," Washington writes. While Washington's book is thoroughly message-driven, it understands that for "effective medicine" to achieve a cure, it must be "administered," as are the messages in his speeches, "in the form of a story." And this is the advantage Washington enjoys over Johnson, Chesnutt, and Du Bois: his having lived such a life that it can be turned into the form of a story, one that embodies the American "up."

Up from Slavery—the most strategic move made by the book is in the choice of the first word in the title. For Du Bois, born into freedom and the relative comfort of Great Barrington, Massachusetts, experience comes as a fall. As it does with Johnson's narrator, "the revelation" of race first bursts upon Du Bois during a day at school. The boys and girls in the classroom are exchanging greeting cards. "The exchange was merry, till one girl, a tall newcomer, refused my card—refused it peremptorily, with a glance. Then it dawned upon me with a certain suddenness that I was different from the others . . ." The moment generates the metaphor of the veil, as the sentence continues: "or, like, mayhap, in heart and life and longing, but shut out from their world by a vast veil." *The Souls of Black Folk* proceeds from this moment of fall, one that opens out onto an experience of continuing loss and failed promises.

For Washington, born into slavery, there is nothing to do but rise. "I was born a slave on a plantation in Franklin County, Virginia." This opening sentence purchases for its author the immense authority of the slave narratives, the rich variety of which would have been largely unknown to the reading public in 1901. Along with *Narrative of the Life of Frederick Douglass* (1845), Washington's story assumed its place as one of the first widely read slave narratives, although this is not where the interest falls. The memories of his first five or six years under slavery—Washington can only guess at the year of his birth—are not richly elaborated. Instead, he emphasizes what he does not know in order to remind us that he, like all slaves, was systematically deprived of personal and collective memory. "I am not quite sure," he writes in his first paragraph. "I suspect," he continues, "As nearly as I have been able to learn," "I do not know." Booker's not knowing culminates on his first day of school, when, as the teacher calls the roll, he realizes that he does not know his last name and so "calmly told him 'Booker Washington,' as if I had been called by that name all my life." This moment of self-naming sets the tone of improvisation and self-making that gives the book its resolutely adaptive spirit.

Knowing so little, then, the newly named Washington's project comes to be to live forward so as to acquire a story that can be claimed, remembered, told. His five-hundred-mile journey from West Virginia to the Tidewater, the days spent sleeping under a Richmond sidewalk, the arrival at Hampton with fifty cents in his pocket, and the task first assigned him there, sweeping the floors—all this testifies not only to the narrator's persistence and good luck but to the sheer distance across which he has the potential to rise. Lifting becomes a central metaphor, not just an implication of the famous refrain from his 1893 Atlanta Exposition Address—"Cast down your bucket where you are"—but for the striving self. "In order to lift them up," Washington writes, about his arrival at Tuskegee. He is speaking here about his people. The eminence that he will achieve becomes his key argument for the possibility of African-American social mobility.

So he begins. When he opens his school of thirty students, he is the only teacher. He secures a loan to buy an abandoned plantation. He resolves to make the students build their own school, to "use their hands." Starting with nothing more, as he later claims, than "a few quilts and pumpkins and chickens," he will, in the course of thirty years, lift Tuskegee up into a college of 2300 acres, forty buildings, and 1100 students. It is a story of creation ex nihilo, a truly God-like act of building out, and it is also one that in its necessary reliance on brick making and food preparation and even proper toothbrushing makes an eloquent case for the centrality of work in the human enterprise.

Washington's narrative may have a message, then (that "we must do something besides teach them mere books"), but its story best exemplifies its moral. It is a story of successful uplift. Washington did it. And he enacts the moment of understanding this on the day he receives an invitation from Harvard to receive an honorary degree. Sitting on his Tuskegee verandah, the letter from Cambridge in his hand, he is most moved not by the "recognition" by Harvard but by his own story:

> My whole former life—my life as a slave on the plantation, my work in the coal-mine, the times when I was without food and clothing, when I made my bed under a sidewalk, my struggles for an education, the trying days I had had at Tuskegee, days when I did not know where to turn for a dollar to continue the work there, the ostracism and sometimes oppression of my race,—all this passed before me and nearly overcame me.

Washington here apprehends that he has less a "message" to deliver than something "administered . . . in the form of a story." If the most disturbing word in his book is the often-repeated epithet "humble," to describe the station of his people, it too serves a rhetorical strategy, since the more it is repeated, the more the ascent of the story's central character gets accented. His truly has been, as he argues in his big speech, the story of a "great leap." *Overcame*, Washington writes, about the moment of savoring on his front porch: we shall overcome by living overcoming lives.

The shape of Washington's story thus authorizes his central metaphor, of the hand. The metaphor cuts two ways. As he explicates it in the Atlanta Address, it is a figure for the separate but equal status of the races. "In all things that are purely social we can be as separate as the fingers, yet one as the hand in all things essential to mutual progress." Here the logic of the metaphor fails him, perhaps from too fine a reading of its component parts. The hand-finger dichotomy simply makes no sense. Fingers do not do any real work in any significantly separate way. And to "separate" fingers from the hand, as if the component parts really could be uncoupled, is to mistake a superfluity of signifiers for a distinction that does not obtain in fact. The fingers *are* the hand, and no amount of poetic license will render them otherwise. Because he misreads his own metaphor—because he does not acknowledge how profoundly integrated black and white bodies have, in America, always been—he can thus arrive at the disabling conclusion that "agitation of questions of social equality is the extremest folly." As if black and white in the United States were or ever could be separated—and this from a man who allows in the third paragraph of his narrative that his father may have been "a white man."

Earlier in his speech, however, when Washington speaks of "the productions of our hands," he deploys the metaphor of the hand in a way that does real and important cultural work. One of Washington's signal contributions, beyond enacting the romance of uplift, was to enhance America's sense of the "beauty and dignity" of labor. The number of canonical texts that deal with how most of us spend our days—working—is scandalously few. Washington's story and his message and his central metaphor converge on the awareness that in the new century, as the gods disappeared over the horizon and left us alone to build therefore our own world, what there was left to do was "to love work for its own sake."

When the students arrive at Tuskegee, they arrive believing in a crippling and false distinction. "They had not fully outgrown the idea that it was hardly the proper thing for them to use their hands, since they had come there, as one of them expressed it, 'to be educated, and not to work.'" There is as much dignity, Washington teaches them, "in tilling a field as in writing a poem." It turns out that the hand is not a figure to be contrasted to the fingers but to the mind. And the hand is to be contrasted to the mind in order to be fully integrated with it; tilling and writing are complementary activities. The word "verse" comes from the word "vertere," to turn, as the hand turns the plow at the furrow's end. The joint cultivation of hand and mind, Washington argues, produces the complete human person; a full life is one in which body is not bruised to pleasure soul, nor soul bruised to pleasure body. That this insight about the value of embodied knowledge would issue from an ex-slave—a man who had every reason to dissociate himself from the body as an expression of the self—stands as the deepest and least appreciated irony of Washington's knowing and canny performance.

CHAPTER THREE

Pioneering Women

AUSTIN ❧ EATON ❧ STEIN ❧ ELIOT ❧ WILLIAMS ❧ CATHER

*D*id American women writing in the twentieth century succeed in writing beyond the ending, in Rachel DuPlessis's phrase, the ending in which a woman's hopes are curtailed or altogether defeated? In 1899, Kate Chopin's (1850–1904) heroine walks into the Gulf of Mexico. Six years later, in *The House of Mirth*, Lily Bart dies her lonely death. Gertrude Steins's Anna, Melanctha, Lena—they all suddenly wither and pass. Even Thelma and Louise, eight decades later, steer toward oblivion, although the viewer is left with the solace of last seeing them suspended in midair.

Some imagined women do escape the closed ending: one thinks of Thea Kronberg in *The Song of the Lark* (1915), singing "The Ring of the Nibelung," or Janie on her porch, at the end of *Their Eyes Were Watching God* (1937), retelling her hard-won story. Yet the literature of the century contains fewer such cases than the changes on the ground might seem to warrant. In 1920, the Nineteenth Amendment brought the right to vote; in 1964, the Civil Rights Act included a provision called Title VII, which forbade discrimination in employment based on sex; in 1965 and 1973, *Griswold v. Connecticut* and *Roe v. Wade* allowed for a woman's control over the process of reproduction. It is possible to argue that the biggest change in the social world during the last one hundred years, bigger, even, than the movement we call "Civil Rights," was the opening up of possibility in the lives of American women. That our literature proceeds from a less than wholehearted conviction of achieved satisfaction argues for something deeply and persistently unrequited in those lives.

Mary Austin (1868–1934) presents a dramatic case of an American writer—too often a woman—who slips from fame to obscurity within a few years of her death. During her highly productive career, Austin published seven novels, plays, collections of folklore, studies in mysticism, and a brilliant autobiography. Her two best books were the short-story collections *The Land of Little Rain* (1903) and *Lost Borders* (1909). Austin lived a highly public life: she beachcombed with Jack London and George Sterling at Carmel; toured England with Herbert Hoover; huddled with H. G. Wells over his marital difficulties; and received a rose from Conrad, on her departure from England. The first woman to convert the arid landscapes of California and New Mexico into a literary subject, Austin would have been, in

1920, on anyone's list of the major living American writers. But by 1940 she was being dropped from the anthologies, and it would be almost forty years before her work would again find a place in the college classroom. Part of the reason for the eclipse has to do with Austin's interest in stories that, at midcentury, Americans had lost the capacity to hear.

The great subject of Austin's career is her search for a story that has "a woman in it." She must look for such a story in out-of-the-way places, mostly in the high deserts of the American Southwest. Subject and setting enjoy an intimate connection in Austin's work: both are marginal, underfunded, unstoried. And each refuses, in its own way, to come forth. Like the Woman at the Eighteen-Mile and the Walking Woman, "the earth is no wanton to give up all her best to every comer, but keeps a sweet, separate intimacy for each." There is something untellable in a woman's story, Austin's practice suggests, or at least a something that only two women, in a moment "of fullest understanding," can share.

In the climactic scenes in her two strongest short stories, both published in *Lost Borders*, Austin finally tracks down and compels a woman to "give up" her story. The reluctance with which these stories are given up stands in inverse proportion to the culture's desperate need for them. And Austin makes it plain that only some-one like herself, a ferocious female listener, can compel these stories forth.

The title character in "The Woman at the Eighteen-Mile," when Austin finally finds her, makes her auditor promise not to repeat her words. Mary has tracked the story as she would a lost love: "All this time the story glimmered like a summer is-land in a mist, through every man's talk about it, grew and allured, caressing the soul. It had warmth and amplitude, like a thing palpable to be stroked." *A thing palpable to be stroked*—there is a suggestion here that a woman's relationship to her story can be as intimate as any she shares with a lover or a child. It is, in any event, a thing to be closely held.

These are women who have lost everything but their stories, and the sharing of them can compromise a trust. Austin wants the Woman's story, but she wants as much to preserve solidarity with her, and so she must not force the moment of disclosure:

> If it were not the biggest story of the desert ever written, I had no wish to write it. And there was the Woman. The story was all she had, absolutely all of heart-stretching, of enlargement and sustenance. What she thought about it was that that last elusive moment when she touched the forecast shadow of his destiny was to bind her to save his credit for his children's sake.

"*His* credit"—the irony of many of these acts of withholding is that they protect the integrity of an experience with a man.

Austin keeps a kind of faith with the Woman at the Eighteen Mile by structuring her story in such a way that the Woman's testimony will not convict her man. Austin begins by telling us of her long-standing desire "to write a story of Death Valley that should be its final word." She then meets a teamster who gives her a fragment of the story about Lang's murder, the most famous incident in the region. His is a pure act of *habeas corpus*: he cites the fact of the murdered body and nothing more. Left with only "the middle of an idea, without any definiteness, as to where it began or ended," Austin tracks the story for seven years. She gradually shores up a host of fragments:

> There was a mine in it, a murder and a mystery, great sacrifice, Shoshones, dark and incredibly discreet, and the magnetic will of a man making manifest through all these; there were lonely water-holes, deserted camps where coyotes hunted in the streets, fatigues and dreams and voices in the night. And at last it appeared there was a woman in it.

Austin knows the Woman and remembers her as "one of the very few people I had known able to keep a soul alive and glowing in the wilderness, and I was to find that she kept it so against the heart of my story. Mine!" Austin finally tracks the Woman to her lair, and there, halfway through a story of only eight pages, she begins to tell her story.

"For her the heart of the story was the man, Whitmark." This is the man linked by common gossip to the murder, and Austin can feel the pieces begin to fall into place: "I sat within the shallow shadow of the eaves experiencing the full-throated satisfaction of old prospectors over the feel of pay dirt . . . It was as good as that. And I was never to have it!" As Austin listens to the story, "the one thing the Woman made plain to me in the telling was the guilt of Whitmark." But because she still loves Whitmark, and still considers herself "honored" to have been "witness to the intimation of his destiny," the Woman has made Austin promise that if she tells her everything she will "not use it." So Austin is reduced to giving us her reaction to the strike, not the gold itself, with the reader left to infer what she will from the omissions. The focus shifts from Whitmark's guilt to his love, to the one moment the Woman feels able and privileged to tell. "The crux of the story to her was one little, so little, moment, that owing to Whitmark's having been taken with pneumonia within a week afterward, was rendered fixed beyond change or tarnish of time."

For two years, Whitmark and the Woman, each married to others, have experienced the happiness of working side by side in a great venture in the mines. "He had never known what it meant to have a woman concerned in his work, running neck and neck with it, divining his need, supplementing it not with the merely

feminine trick of making him more complacent with himself, but with vital reme-
dies and aids." They have been careful, however, not to touch; throughout everything, the Woman remains solicitous both of Whitmark's "name" and of the feelings of his surviving "wife and his children." Now the time has come for his return
home. As they ride together toward the point of departure, each seems caught up
in a mixture of triumph and gloom. The moment comes to say good-bye. It is
Whitmark's prophetic statement on leave-taking that the Woman feels compelled
to report: "'I have *missed* you so.' Just that, not good-bye, and not *shall* miss you,
but 'I *have* missed you *so.*'" The power of this farewell for Austin's imagination
would be difficult to exaggerate. She has been searching for the biggest story of the
desert. By the time she gets it, she has promised not to tell it. Of course, she manages to tell it after all. The sheer juxtaposition of the teamster's report with the
Woman's story links Whitmark to Lang's murder. Beyond that, the Woman expresses by way of Whitmark her profound awareness of the way we *do* miss each
other, of the taking for granted that turns the days and years into a history of un-
tended love, or, even worse, of the ways in which we waste away the present by anticipating its departure. There is no more powerful summary in Austin of her
steady foreknowledge of the inevitability of erotic loss.

And it is these moments that ought to be valued, too, as the true "pay dirt" in
fiction. Along with reading for the promised scene of violence, can we not also
learn to read for the awful daring of a moment's surrender to feeling? What the
woman has to say is not only hard and true and heartbreaking—even the best of us
do, sometimes, miss each other—but formally elegant. The italics shift. When she
repeats Whitmark's good-bye, the emphasis moves from "*missed*" to "*have*" and
"*so,*" as if she senses that it will not do merely to repeat what he has said. She revises
the rhythm and therefore the meaning of the sentence, giving it, in its second iteration, an even more personal and desperate force.

Whitmark's "I have missed you so" acknowledges the fact that while he and the
Woman have worked together, they have not felt free to love each other. Because of
the strictures against love across the marriage line, they have been condemned to
miss each other, even while working together. For them, there has not been—and
there will not be, in part because of Whitmark's sudden death—a chance to integrate love and work.

The last story in *Lost Borders* reconfigures "the Woman at the Eighteen-Mile"
into the lineaments of gratified desire. "The Walking Woman" also unfolds through
the activities of seeking, meeting, and talking. Austin's "wish for a personal encounter" with the Walking Woman sends her out, again, after a figure of hearsay.
Bits of local lore drift back: she had been seen at the Maverick at the time of the Big
Snow, at Tres Piños when they brought home the body of Morena, and at Tunawi

at the time of the cloudburst. "She came and went, oftenest in a kind of muse of travel which the untrammeled space begets, or at rare intervals flooding wondrously with talk." It is talk Austin is after, and as the story unfolds, the Walking Woman's own account gradually begins to crowd out the rumors. A figure built up out of "the contradiction of reports about her" finally stops to talk to Mary in her own voice, and what she tells her is, for all its losses, a far happier story.

Of all the stories surrounding the Walking Woman, there is one worth her telling, the story about the "three things which if you had known you could cut out all the rest." In a sandstorm on the south slope of Tehachapi she had come upon the camp of the shepherd Filon Geraud. They run together with the wind:

> The flock traveled down the wind, the sand bit our faces; we called, and after a time heard the words broken and beaten small by the wind . . . Such was the force of the wind that when we came together we held one another and talked a little between pantings . . . we slept by turns; at least Filon slept . . . I lay on the ground when my turn was and beat with the storm. I was no more tired than the earth was . . . we kept the flock together.

After the wind drops and they cook their first meal, Filon comes over to her side of the fire:

> I stayed with Filon until the fall . . . All that summer in the Sierras, until it was time to turn south on the trail. It was a good time, and longer than he could be expected to have loved one like me. And besides, I was no longer able to keep the trail. My baby was born in October.

Filon moves on, with the flock, and the baby does not stay for long: "And whenever the wind blows in the night . . . I wake and wonder if he is well covered." With all else lost, the Walking Woman is able to keep the trail.

It was while living this story, then, that the Walking Woman got the three things she and Austin agree one cannot live without. They agree in their one moment of reported dialogue, in which Austin is allowed to speak the story's climactic words:

> "To work together, to love together," said the Walking Woman, withdrawing
>   her hand again; "there you have two of the things, the other you know."
> "The mouth at the breast," said I.
> "The lips and the hands," said the Walking Woman.
> "The little, pushing hands and the small cry."

In "The Basket Maker," the central story in Austin's 1903 collection *The Land of Little Rain*, Austin uses the story of the Shoshone woman Seyavi in order to develop a more chastening model of female development. Seyavi knows the five stages that are a woman's lot: girlhood ("she danced and dressed her hair"), marriage, motherhood, artistry (she "made baskets for the satisfaction of desire"), and cronedom. But she knows them *in sequence*. Where a man can expect to have a career, a wife, and a child all at once, a woman—and Seyavi provides Austin's most compelling model of a completed life cycle—is allowed to experience each of "the things" only in turn. "Love and work," Freud is said to have answered, when asked what life is all about. "Love *or* work," Austin answers, when she ventures, through Seyavi's story, a woman's response to the same question.

What a woman wants, Austin argues, is pretty much what a man wants. And she wants these things, also, to overlap in time. The "three things . . . were good any way you got them," the two women agree, but "best if . . . they were related to and grew each one out of the others." The objects of the Walking Woman's desires are entirely conventional; it is the way she gets them—all at once—that makes her story so awe-inspiring, just as the extremity of the surmise requires Austin to imagine this happiness as so briefly held. The fantasy of getting and having all three things at once, as a woman, is a fiction too extreme for the imagination to long entertain.

The uncanny power of these two women to anticipate or remember each other's experience raises their encounter up almost beyond the reach of words. The preemptive intimacy between listener and teller gives the story its radical force; it is as if Mary and the Walking Woman already possess a knowledge of the very things that have never before been and that here finally do get expressed. "The Walking Woman" is a touching story, one in which the solidarity of women in their fate is expressed through their ability to give and accept the comfort of a hand. At the point where the Walking Woman speaks of her love for Filon, she places her hand on Mary's arm. A remembering Mary then says, "I do not know why at this point the Walking Woman touched me." She wonders whether "in some flash of forward vision, encompassing the unimpassioned years, the stir, the movement of tenderness were for *me*." As in "The Woman at the Eighteen-Mile," the final communication assumes that the future, for both Mary and her informant, will be unimpassioned. The tender acknowledgement of this is the final gift of the story. Sharing that realization compensates, as much as anything can, for the "things" that have been and will be lost.

"To work and to love and to bear children," Austin writes at the end of "The Walking Woman." "*That* sounds easy enough. But the way we live establishes so many things of much more importance." A century later, "the way we live" had come down to one big variable: who does the housework. What we have discovered, after ten decades of slow liberation for women, is that gender roles arise from and are rationalized by the division of labor. To the extent that women do work once reserved for men, and that men also begin to cross over, the whole apparatus called gender begins to disappear. But as women entered the workplace and still attempted to be wives and mothers—to lay claim to Austin's three things—they discovered a key element of the old arrangements holding fairly constant: Men were not willing to do "house" work. Nora Grey, a respondent to the 1955 Kelly Longitudinal Study, summed up the problem this way: "Much of our trouble has centered around my husband's unwillingness to do work around the house."

It may sound like a small thing, but insofar as men expected and women could not help but attempt the delivery of a comfortable and well-organized place in which to live, the burdens on "liberated" women, as the century wore on, began to approach the intolerable. Marilynne Robinson (b. 1943) was therefore prophetic in her choice of title for her 1981 novel, *Housekeeping*. It is the task of keeping house from which the women in her story walk away. As they do so, they quietly argue that the division of labor in the home is the true last frontier, an ongoing negotiation that, if resolved, will yield much happier lives even as it dissolves the last vestiges of what it once meant to be a "man" or a "woman."

Austin invites us to listen to "the secret talk of women." The phrase is from "Mrs. Spring Fragrance," the title story in the collection published in 1912 by Edith Maud Eaton, "the first Asian American fictionist." Eaton—her pen name was Sui Sin Far—was born in England in 1865 to a Chinese mother and an English father. The family migrated to North America in 1872. Eaton began publishing short stories in the late 1890s, in magazines like *Overland*, *Century*, and *Good Housekeeping*. She never married, and she died in 1914, in Montreal.

By "secret talk," Eaton does not mean to invoke a freestanding nonpatriarchal language available to women alone. (The fantasy of a "nonpatriarchal" language uniquely available to women not only receives no support from the serious study of linguistics but only succeeds in essentializing and ghettoizing those who are believed to have access to it. Caliban is the most eloquent voice in *The Tempest* precisely because he has learned to use the "master's language" better than the master can.) The talk between these two women stays secret because it is deemed inconsequential or beyond notice; it is verbal exchange not yet crossing over into recognized speech.

As the story opens, Mrs. Spring Fragrance, who lives in Seattle with her merchant husband, talks with her young neighbor Laura about frustrated love. Sitting nearby, Mr. Spring Fragrance "could not help receiving the words which were borne to him through the open window." He gets up and moves out of range, "not wishing to hear more of the secret talk of women." The gesture argues that such talk remains secret for lack of a responsive audience; men, and even many women, are not yet ready to deem it worthy of publication. As in Austin, Eaton acknowledges this reluctance by alluding to conversation she will not represent: "For a long time Mrs. Spring Fragrance talked. For a long time Laura listened. When the girl rose to go, there was a bright light in her eyes." In the project of the story, Mrs. Spring Fragrance will travel to San Francisco to unarrange Laura's arranged marriage and thereby set her free to have the man she wants. Her ability to manipulate social conventions stands in stark contrast to her unwillingness to talk directly about them.

Reticence will remain a dominant feature in twentieth-century writing by women, a stance toward self-uncovering that culminates in the poetry of Elizabeth Bishop. "Friday was nice," she writes, in her poetry's supreme moment of erotic encounter: "Friday was nice, and we were friends." This line of writers exploits the authority of the *tacit*. Their writing often deals with things meant to be intuited rather than directly expressed. The reticence issues less from some anxiety over the difficulty of representation itself, as in the furious iterations of Faulkner, than from the sense that a woman's experience must be protected from unsympathetic or un-hearing "ears." Verbal exchange between the sexes tends to go one way, at least according to Mr. Spring Fragrance: "This is America," he says to himself, "where a man may speak to a woman, and a woman listen." As if in response to this impasse, Willa Cather falls back on the word "incommunicable" in the last sentence of *My Ántonia* (1918). When it comes to love, Austin has made the prior, counterintuitive, and oddly plausible claim that "a man's story like that is always so much more satisfactory because he tells you all the story there is, what happened to him, and how he felt about it, supposing his feelings are any part of the facts in the case; but with a woman it is not so. She never knows much about her feelings, unless they are pertinent to the story, and then she leaves them out."

Surely such reticence is overdetermined: by an instinct for self-protective secrecy; by the power advantage of conserving one's special knowledge; by the rueful awareness that to put words on feelings is to risk the distorting of them. A style devoted to the "thing left out" is a time honored strategy for generating an uncanny mood or a sense of the sublime, a strategy most famously exploited by Hemingway. All of these instincts, motives, and strategies are available to and can be located in writing by men as well as by women. What Austin and Eaton also suggest is that feelings become the thing left out—in stories by women—because the tradition has not offered them adequate narratives or capable auditors.

In its marvelous ending, Eaton's story redresses this lack. Her mission having been accomplished, Mrs. Spring Fragrance returns to her home in Seattle. Her husband has missed her so much that he has stopped eating and sleeping. She is lighthearted at the reunion, but "something" rises in his throat that prevents him "from replying" with happiness at her return. He pleads business and prepares to leave the house. Laura rushes in to thank Mrs. Spring Fragrance; he pauses on the doorstep. Forgetting her husband for a moment, his wife begins to tell "all about" her trip. Mr. Spring Fragrance reenters the house and hangs up his hat. "I have been listening to you and Laura," he says. She mentions his business, and he replies that "It is not important to me now . . . I would prefer to hear again about Ah Oi and Man You and Laura and Kai Tzu." In the space of ten pages, a husband has been converted from a dismissive overhearer to an eager listener. And what he chooses to listen in on is an American love story, one in which the desires of the young are allowed to overcome.

Thus, the story is all about the fulfillment of wishes: that love will triumph over convention, that men will consent to listen to women. Cutting against all this is the political standing of the Chinese-American citizen. The impasse not here resolved concerns Mr. Spring Fragrance's brother. At the end of the story he is still being held in a detention pen in California. In the wake of the Exclusion Act of 1882, all "laborers" of Chinese origin were excluded from entry into the United States. While this effectively ended Chinese immigration, Chinese who could pass as "merchants" or U.S. citizens by birth or derivation were still allowed to enter the country. In 1912, those seeking entry were held on Angel Island, in San Francisco Bay, and subjected to prolonged detention and interview. Over the decades, the walls of these barracks filled up with poems, protests against having dreams of a new country end with confinement in "a wooden building."

This is the situation in which Mr. Spring Fragrance's brother finds himself. We never hear about what happens to him.

In a profoundly American solution, private happiness is accomplished within the ongoing and glossed-over pain of an unresolved political conflict. Eaton even indulges in some black humor when she has a white neighbor admit that for "real Americans" detention pens are "against our principles." To this Mr. Spring Fragrance replies, "I offer the real Americans my consolations that they should be compelled to do that which is against their principles." Eaton is only able to imagine a partial adjustment in the province of the "real." Sexual politics prove subject to adjustment outside the public arena—they become a matter of domestic maneuvering—but racial politics remain unredressed.

❧   ❧

Gertrude Stein (1874–1946) proposed a radical kind of audition: "listening to repeating." In *The Autobiography of Alice B. Toklas* (1933), her most accessible work, she does not connect this activity with gender. There she is one among the boys, a "genius" along with Picasso and Whitehead. Alice sits with the wives. But, in *Three*

Lives (1909), Stein had already made it plain that when it comes to being listened to, men and women have considerably different experiences. Jeff Campbell goes at Melanctha Herbert with words. She talks back, tries to deflect him by "wandering," by refusing a foolish self-consistency. He thinks his job is to analyze and correct her, and she is drawn into his game. At the same time she replies in a way that does not do to him what he does to her—which is to *define* her: "Sometimes you seem like one kind of a girl to me, and sometimes you are like a girl that is all different to me, and the two kinds of girls is certainly very different to each other, and I can't see any way they seem to have much to do, to be together in you." Melanctha resists Jeff's reductions by persisting in being a "sometimes" self, by believing, like Emily Dickinson, in the right to "internal difference, / Where the Meanings are." In the end, she and Jeff separate, she wanders a bit more, and then she suddenly dies.

"Slowly every one in continuous repeating," Stein writes in *The Making of Americans* (1925), "to their minutest variation, comes to be clearer to some one." She describes her biggest book as a "history of learning to listen to repeating," and she links this activity with love. In any prolonged relationship what comes to be loved is what the partner repeats. "Sometimes it takes many years of knowing some one before the repeating in that one comes to be a clear history of such a one." Stein also saw that attention has its downward curve. One day will come not only the discovery that in our repeating we become clearer to each other but the disillusionment of "finding that no one can really ever be agreeing with you completely in any thing." Friends are made and then people who have been fighting beside you "each one of them splits off." This is the plot of *The Autobiography*. Friends like Matisse and Hemingway are made and lost, re-made and re-lost. To accept this lack of complete agreement is the beginning of old age. People who can't accept it keep "always looking."

The "bottom" question asked by *The Autobiography* is a simple one: is anyone listening to me? The book traces a double fable in which Stein's pioneering appreciation of Cezanne, Picasso, and Matisse is not matched by a corresponding enthusiasm, in the wider world, for her work. The happiest moments come when a piece of writing is accepted for publication. When her sister-in-law is "deeply moved" by *Three Lives*, Stein is immensely pleased. "In those days she never asked any one what they thought of her work, but were they interested enough to read it. Now she says if they can bring themselves to read it they will be interested."

Stein makes the case by way of her story that the key romance in our lives is the romance of reception. Is there an audience—a listener adequate to the force of what we have to say? Stein's work repeatedly acts out the scene of a powerful speaker confronted with an inadequate listener. And much of this frustration has to do with Stein's chosen mode of expression, the notorious "difficulty" of her work.

For the pleasure of the text, its easy identifications and suspense-relieving recognitions, she substitutes a more strenuous and alienating discipline, what we might call *the joy of reading*.

Stein wrote out of the conviction that word choice was above all a matter of placement. The challenge for any real writer lay along the syntagmatic axis. "Vocabulary in respect to prose," she maintained in "Poetry and Grammar" (1935), "is less important than the parts of speech, and the internal balance and the movement within a given space." Words are chosen less as meaningful referents than for their cadence and their syntactical force. Her allegory of grammar—she fought it like the War in Heaven—elevated the verb over the noun (nouns are "completely not interesting"), the adverb over the adjective. The comma she deemed "servile." If such claims seem a little abstract, or even silly, it is useful to remember Borges: "there is nothing more human . . . than grammar."

Stein's argufying made key features of language dramatically clear. However, in her preference for placement over reference, and for argument over story, Stein can forego much of the realm of affect. Except for what she calls a few "poignant incidents" in *Three Lives*, her more programmatic work refrains from asking us to feel. "Nor should emotion itself be the cause of poetry or prose," she writes, and she worked hard to purge from her writing the ordinary sorts of pleasures, especially the narrative building-up to a climactic moment in which character stands isolated by a deed.

Just as words, for Stein, find their function by way of their internal balance and movement within a given space, so identity is social, relational. *The Autobiography* deals with life among friends and enemies; there is little interior life. Opinions are rendered, but motives are not plumbed. It is a journey to the exterior. When Bishop ends a poem by writing, "we are driving to the interior," she makes a little joke about where she will not take us. There will be no direct assault on consciousness, no thought torment, no dark night of the soul. The self, insofar as it has an inside, is to be evoked by the outside, by how it appears, where it stands, what it sees. Depth is expressed by surface. Hemingway, Stein's pupil, would refer to this technique as giving the reader "the sequence of motion and fact which made the emotion."

Stein tells us that after *Three Lives* was published she changed her style. "Hitherto she had been interested only in the insides of people, their character and what went on inside them, it was during that summer that she first felt a desire to express the rhythm of the visible world." Always "tormented by the problem of the external and the internal," she proposes to turn her focus from the second to the first. Surely this must strike us as an odd claim. Has not Stein from the get-go approached the inner life as a kind of superstition, the province of depth psychologists who want to translate fascinating behavior into mere unconscious motive? How is one to square this career claim with Stein's lifelong gift for physical description, as when she notices a "wild quality" in Alice Derain "that perhaps had to do with her brutal thumbs and was curiously in accord with her madonna face." In *The Autobiography*, writing like this is meant to differentiate between real, living people. But, in *Three Lives*, Stein has already turned the practice on its head. There her physical descriptions of imagined human bodies become so generic as to be self-consuming. "Melanctha Herbert was a graceful, pale yellow, intelligent, attractive negress." Stein begins here in order to move past such a way of describing. *Three Lives* argues that people—women, immigrant Americans, African-Americans—cannot be gotten at in words such as these, by way of adjectives and the huge part they have played in the novelistic abbreviation of character, by way of the furniture of a life, from the outside.

Three Lives empties out the language of seeing people as types, and it does so by repeating it. The word "blue" provides a key here and is aligned along a differential continuum that includes the adjectives "Rose," "black," "yellow," " white," and, finally, "blue." It is important that these adjectives are also words of color.

"Rose" is, of course, a proper noun—the first name of a character, Melanctha's friend Rose Johnson—as well as the first word of "Melanctha." "Black" occurs next, in the second paragraph, as part of a cascade of eight adjectives hurled in one sentence at Melanctha and Rose. "Yellow" is Stein's choice to gesture at Melanctha's skin color. "White" refers to something that cannot be seen, her "blood." And then comes "blue." "Sometimes the thought of how all her world was made, filled the complex, desiring Melanctha with despair. She wondered, often, how she could go on living when she was so blue." Stein repeats the word "blue" four more times on this page, before she is done with it.

Rose, black, yellow, white, blue: five color words. One functions as a person's name and the name of a flower. The second describes a category of American whose skin in no way can or ever does conform to the intensity of zero brilliance entailed by the word "black." Another word that presumes to describe skin color, "yellow" in fact actually refers to no visible aspect of Melanctha's skin but to the felt sense of lighter and darker shades occurring along a continuum. "White" refers to an assumed inheritance that shines out from Melanctha's skin, but again, as with "black," corresponds to no actual skin color available to a human body. It refers to the uncanny fact that a good proportion of those Americans referred to as "black" have actually "been half made," as Stein writes, "with real white blood." And "blue," the five-times-repeated *blue*, what is this but a color word that utterly confounds the realms of inside and outside, assigning as it does to Melanctha—on top of already being black, yellow, and white—a blueness having nothing to do with how she looks and everything to do with a permanent female depression that proves the adaptive and eloquent response to a world in which color words, or any words that collude in keeping the social world "regular," operate with such careless force?

All five words are metaphors. None of them function as mere or accurate descriptors. It is naïve, Stein insinuates, to think that they describe anything, or that fundamental social and political distinctions can be maintained by them. And yet, of course, such distinctions are created and maintained by such words. Stein reveals here that skin, like words, is differential. Bodies—skin colors—have meaning and are given relative value in light of the internal balance and movement within a given space.

And yet the social space in which Stein's women find themselves has no internal balance. "She did not belong to any society that could stop them," Stein writes about the Good Anna. "Them" here refers to men—specifically to men who abuse animals—and "society" refers to the world as men control it. Anna's voice, normally a "pleasant one," becomes "high and piercing" when she calls out to the teamsters and to the other wicked men. For Anna, like her author, life is a romance of reception, one in which her cry goes unheard.

Jeff does not beat Melanctha, but he browbeats her. The struggle between the two characters betrays a conflict within Stein herself, a conflict between being a talker and a listener:

> There was a time when I was questioning, always asking, when I was talking, wondering, there was a time when I was feeling, thinking and all the time then I did not know repeating, I did not see or hear or feel repeating. There was a long time then when there was nothing in me using the bottom loving repeating being that now leads me to knowing. Then I was attacking, questioning, wondering, thinking, always at the bottom was loving repeating being, that was not then there to my conscious being. Sometime there will be written a long history of such a beginning.
>
> Always then there was a recognition of the thing always repeating, the being in each one, and always then thinking, feeling, talking, living, was not of this real being. Slowly I came to hear repeating. More and more then I came to listen, now always and always I listen and always now each one comes to be a whole one in me.

Does Stein claim her right to belong to the society of talkers—of men—or should she sit with the wives, with the listeners? In *The Autobiography*, Stein rejects any special interest in "the cause of women." She claims, instead, a proscribed space, the space of *theory*.

Stein proceeds from the assumption that literature always already knows everything theory knows. While Ferdinand de Saussure, off in Geneva, is delivering the lectures that would later be gathered into *Course in General Linguistics* (1906–11), she is having fun with the word "blue." "Melanctha," and indeed all of Stein's work, can be read as a deeply informed and highly encoded theorization of the status of the "sign." Yes, the sign (the word "blue") is composed of a signifier (the "sound image" *blu*) and a signified (the "concept" of a color we agree to call "blue"). Yes, when the word "blue" is uttered the transaction occurs wholly within, one could argue, a linguistic space: what is "referred to" by the utterance of the word is a distributed continuum of concepts (our words for the various colors) rather than a perceptual field in the world. Yes, to ponder this dynamic is to conclude that language is differential rather than referential, that to speak and to listen is to find oneself at play among an order of words where words have meaning in relation to where they are positioned along an axis composed of . . . other words.

One can figure this out by reading Stein or by reading de Saussure. Then the question is what to do with this knowledge. Stein does not encourage us to conclude, given our subjection to the dance of signification, that language is arbitrary (in perhaps his most influential formulation, de Saussure maintains that "*the linguistic sign is arbitrary*") or that saying something meaningful is impossible. She does not make the despairing move that misreaders of Derrida typically make. She encourages us to keep playing; she encourages us, like Eliot, to "construct something / Upon which to rejoice." De Saussure, hardly a systematic theorist, would in some of his statements seem to agree. *Langue* may exist as a self-contained whole, but "execution is always individual," he argues, "and the individual is always its master." The call is not to *aporia* or to mind-spin or to a nihilism about the efficacy of words: the call is to more making. The Stein / de Saussure insight ought to liberate rather than demoralize us; it ought to give us permission, as Emerson did seventy years earlier, to recognize that we live in a vale of collective language-making and that the task, as always, is to "build therefore your own world."

Stein does not conceive of language, then, as a prison-house by which we are constrained. It is more like Conrad's destructive element in which we must immerse ourselves. Then the deep, deep sea will keep us up. Like water, like air, language precedes us and makes life possible. Its priority—the fact that its rules and vocabularies are bequeathed to us—need no more create an anxiety of influence than literature itself, those beautiful words and thoughts that return upon us, when we are feeling our oats, with a certain alienated majesty. All this is there, Stein's practice argues, for the taking and the remaking. She was so far ahead of her century that her work was often read as mere provocation, but it is long since time to acknowledge that her radical critique of words carelessly assigning identity and essence, her profound awareness of the talking/listening dynamic as it is inflected by gender, and her warning that such repeatings imperil the human (rather than the male or female, black or white) pursuit of happiness made her the first and perhaps the twentieth century's most compelling theorist of anti-foundational thinking and of the right to a *jouissance* that it would take the French thirty more years to name.

✦   ✦

While Willa Cather (1873–1947) can be linked to Stein by a shared sexual preference, her highly decorous novels present none of Stein's argumentative and even rebarbative surface. Cather stays home, while Stein emigrates, and Cather embraces the American West Stein was born into but in which she could find "no there there." With William Carlos Williams, Cather believed that "the classic is the local fully realized, words marked by a place." She spent the middle forty years of her adult life in New York, but it was her exposure to the country's prairies and small towns that granted Cather the material she could not resist. Born in Virginia's Shenandoah Valley, she was taken to Webster County, Nebraska, at the age of nine. Early on in *My Ántonia*, she confers on Jim Burden the pleasure and the shock of this felt sense of arrival. He lies down in the pumpkin patch, under the singing wind, and feels entirely happy. "I was something that lay under the sun and felt it, like the pumpkins, and I did not want to be anything more . . . that is happiness; to be dissolved into something complete and great." In passages like these, Cather links back to Austin's deep-rooted sensibility, and one is perhaps not surprised to learn that the two writers were friends and that parts of *Death Comes for the Archbishop* (1927) may have been written in Austin's Santa Fe adobe.

The classic or the local; to leave or to stay. Did inspiration arise from European or American "ground?" From both surely, any strong writer would have answered, and yet during the 1920s even the most generous imaginations could square off over how openly "American" American writing ought to be. T. S. Eliot gave one answer, William Carlos Williams another. The question came down to whether some universalizing term like "tradition" would be allowed to trump the more modest claims of a word like "region." In what ways could a part of the whole—in this case, a geographically bounded stretch of American ground—come to stand in for the entire "union" itself?

Eliot (1889–1965) borrows the content for his poems and essays largely from high, European culture, fighting his fight on Old World ground. Williams (1883–1963) would argue that our "rudeness" as Americans "rests all upon the unstudied character of our beginnings" and that the beginnings essential for our understanding occur on American ground. Red Eric, Columbus, Cortez, De Soto, Cotton Mather, Père Sebastian Rasles, Daniel Boone, Edgar Allan Poe, Abraham Lincoln—these are the touchstones in his tradition. Whereas Eliot, born in St. Louis into a family of ministers and businessmen, offers us Ezekiel, Virgil, Dante, the Upanishads, Chaucer, Thomas Kyd, John Donne, Arnaut Daniel, Baudelaire, and the Tarot. The mind that speaks *The Waste Land* is a citizen of everywhere and nowhere; it is hard to imagine a neighborhood in which it would vote. "The historical sense compels a man to write not merely with his own generation in his bones," Eliot maintains in "Tradition and the Individual Talent" (1919), "but with a feeling that the whole of the literature of Europe from Homer and within it the whole of the literature of his own country has a simultaneous existence and composes a simultaneous order." It is odd that we do not more readily remember it, that phrase in the great sentence about the whole of the literature of Europe, where Eliot alludes as well to "the whole of the literature of his own country." The only guidance provided by the essay as to what that country might be comes by way of the adjectives "European" and "English." And of course in due time Eliot would become not only an Anglican but a British citizen.

Eliot was born in St. Louis; Williams, in Rutherford, New Jersey. Each man attended an Ivy League school. Then Eliot left the country. Williams stayed home, building up a practice as a general practitioner and in the course of his doctoring career delivering thousands of babies. He devoted his life not only to helping the people of his home area but to finding the beauty in the weeds and the broken glass lying along the roads to the contagious hospitals where he worked.

In the American Grain was published three years after *The Waste Land* and launches a powerful counterresponse to it. With Eliot, Williams is devoted to "books"; the debate, rather, is over which ones to read. But even Williams, a partisan of all things homemade, harbors doubts about their adequacy. Williams finds himself in Paris, chatting with Valery Larbaud about the New World. "We have no books, I said." Larbaud answers:

> There you are wrong. Two or three are enough, to have shown a beginning. Have you not yourself proven that there is meat—
>
> Yes (so he had read what I intended!), the early records—to try to find—something, a freshness; if it exist.

Here, after glibly dismissing the writing of his country, Williams happily stands corrected and quickly proceeds to revise his point. He demonstrates the very ability to respond (to an argument, to a place) that is his subject. The paragraph is worth quoting at length:

> I said, It is an extraordinary phenomenon that Americans have lost the sense, being made up as we are, that what we are has its origin in what *the nation* in the past has been; that there is a source in AMERICA for everything we think or do;

that morals affect the food and food the bone, and that, in fine, we have no conception at all of what is meant by moral, since we recognize no ground our own—and that this rudeness rests all upon the unstudied character of our beginnings.

Throughout his dialogue with Larbaud, Williams is looking for a metaphor. He tries out the words "origin" and "source," then settles on "ground." As in Eliot's "Tradition and the Individual Talent"—and on this point the two passionately agree—the "we" can only think and be (have "conception") by way of studying all that "has been."

Williams continues:

We have no defense, lacking intelligent investigation of the changes worked upon the early comers here, to the New World, the books, the records, no defense save brute isolation, prohibitions, walls, ships, fortresses—and all the asininities of ignorant fear that forbids us to protect a doubtful freedom by employing it. That unless everything that is, proclaim a ground on which it stand, it has no worth; and that what has been morally, aesthetically worth while in America has rested on peculiar and discoverable ground. But they think they get it out of the air or the rivers, or from the Grand Banks or wherever it may be, instead of by word of mouth or from records contained for us in books—and that, aesthetically, morally we are deformed unless we read.

As the poet listens to himself worry the question of Americans and their capacity for study, he settles on a place where he can stand and comes to rest, in the last word of the paragraph, on the activity that will allow us to work it. We are grounded in and by books, and kept grounded by reading.

"Ground" is Williams's big pun. No American writer is more committed to the actual American earth and to the renovating effects of a passionate love for it. Again and again, Williams urges penetration of the ground. In his sexual myth of the conquest, "one is forced on the conception of the New World as a woman." The challenge becomes how to handle her. Will one make "walls," like the Puritan, or "touch," like the Spaniard. It is all a rather messy construction, with oversimplified binaries and too much enthusiasm for a continental deflowering that equates with the act of rape, and Annette Kolodny has provided the necessary critique of it. But the ecstasy is what matters, the emphasis on giving (the English gave "parsimoniously" while the Spanish "gave magnificently") rather than resistance. Instead of the man-boy in front of *The Waste Land*'s Hyacinth Girl, whose limbs freeze and whose eyes fail, Williams offers us De Soto, a "sperm" committed to the middle of the Mississippi's great stream.

"It is *this* to be moral," Williams argues, when he finally gets to the story of Père Sebastian Rasles:

> To be *positive*, to be peculiar, to be sure, generous, brave—TO MARRY, to *touch*— to *give* because one HAS, not because one has nothing. And to give to him who HAS, who will join, who will make, who will fertilize, who will be like you yourself: to create, to hybridize, to crosspollenize, not to sterilize, to draw back, to fear, to dry up, to rot. It is the sun.

"Ground" is a pun, then, and the claims about a moral relationship to it are also poetic claims. We are sustained by two kinds of relation: by our actual embrace of the local conditions, and by our own writing and reading about them. To be grounded is to consent to exist in both dimensions.

❧   ❧

Cather never made any apologies for the limitations of her American West, and she persisted in believing that even its most far-flung frontiers had the capacity to absorb and redefine Europe. *Death Comes for the Archbishop* is a romance of transplantation and a fierce defense of the ways in which the Old World can become the New. Her novel accomplishes a reconciliation of inheritances that Eliot and Williams never quite accomplished. Gone here is any anxiety of influence; when Cather invokes a successive overlayering of traditions, the elements of the present echoing the past do not inscribe some pattern of decline. Thus, the "thick Indian blankets" in Father Latour's Santa Fé adobe hang "on the walls like tapestries." A site of relaxed fusion, his study contains a wooden chest "beautifully carved" by "native carpenters," a "walnut 'secretary' of the American make," and "silver candlesticks" from France. Cather faces West, as well as East, for her sense of a deep and usable past, and the outcome of her novel has everything to do with the landscape in which she sets her story.

Throughout her career Cather remained so alive to the beauty of the American Southwest as never to doubt that it could be the site of a cultural refounding. *The Song of the Lark* and *The Professor's House* (1925) also turn on the promise of the Southwest, and each novel figures the region as a site of refuge and rebirth. When Cather transports Thea Kronberg to Panther Canyon and Tom Outland to Blue Mesa, she takes them to a place where they can fulfill or connect with "fragments of their desire." But these obviously female spaces offer sex without the sex. While the work there is companionable, it is not, finally, ecstatic. Big decisions get made— I will go to Germany; I will become a singer, Thea promises herself; I will excavate but not betray the secrets of Blue Mesa, Tom intends—but an available partner is never joined with or found. The heroine or hero remains lonely, fulfilled in work, by way of this restoring place, but not in love. Formally, these "holidays" in the

Southwest may appear as interruptions of the narrative, long short stories set apart in books or parts of their own. But they are more than tonic digressions. In *The Professor's House*, for example, Tom's Book Two repeats many of the images and motifs from the Professor's Book One, arguing for a deeper continuity between Chicago and the Southwest than may be immediately apparent.

"The difficulty was that the country in which he found himself was so featureless—" Cather writes about Father Latour's arrival in New Mexico. The comedy of the story hangs on that dash, since the sentence completes itself as the novel will, by admitting the opposite of the case: "featureless—or rather, that it was crowded with features, all exactly alike." Latour's challenge is to learn to read this place, one that by the day of his death will have become crowded with association and life. His Southwest proves a site of "constantly refined tradition," just like Father Vaillant's onion soup. While Cather is careful to embed her argument in such homely images—here, surely, in the humble contents of a meal, is where cultural identity survives—she also makes a larger, even a "figural," claim. This desert calls up the Holy Land, as in the juniper that the lost priest shortly encounters, whose two lateral, flat-lying branches "could not present more faithfully the form of the Cross."

In the logic of Eric Auerbach's concept of "figura," figures and events from the Old Testament anticipate figures and events in the New. It is a model of influence in which what comes second is not a belated copy but a promised fulfillment. One might even argue that Auerbach reads the Western literary tradition as a happy unfolding—a progress, if you will, toward a greater and deeper apprehension of "reality." In light of Father Latour's ongoing discoveries of the humble, moving, and eloquent adaptations of Catholic practice in the desert environment, the most salient being the brown Madonna, the Virgin of Guadaloupe, it is similarly possible to claim that Cather's Southwest does not merely rhyme with the Old World; it may actually improve upon it.

Cather does not indulge in a naïve primitivism that prizes the aboriginal Indian presence over the importations of the European latecomers. Rather, she views the Southwest as a site in which to respond to Stanley Kunitz's (1905–2006) invitation to "Live in the layers, / not on the litter." To live at the end of a history of conquest is to inherit a sense of neither triumph nor decline but of interpenetration. Annette Kolodny has powerfully redefined the meaning of the word "frontier," not as a moving line of settlement in which civilization replaces savagery, but as a "liminal landscape of changing meanings on which distinct human cultures first encounter one another's 'otherness' and appropriate, accommodate, or domesticate it through language."

This is where we all live now, Cather implies, in a landscape of invaded and contested sites where any claim to purity or priority has become happily lost. Accordingly, at Laguna, Father Latour finds himself unable to make out whether the church painting has been done by Spanish missionaries or Indian converts. The Southwest is not a uniquely layered site—many inner cities would do as well—but simply the particular frontier that provides the most complementary setting for Cather's exemplary love story.

By way of the bell in the pueblo of Santa Fé, Cather makes her most subtle case for an unfraught crossing among cultures. When Father Latour hears it, he is carried back to Rome and then further, to Jerusalem. At breakfast, Father Vaillant tells him that its inscription is in Spanish, and that it was brought from Mexico City in an oxcart. A good deal of silver in the bell accounts for its beautiful tone. "And the silver of the Spaniards was really Moorish, was it not?" Father Latour asks. Father Vaillant accuses him of trying to make the bell an "infidel," but Latour persists in his friendly "belittling":

> Belittling? I should say the reverse. I am glad to think there is Moorish silver in your bell. When we first came here, the one good workman we found in Santa Fé was a silversmith. The Spaniards handed on their skill to the Mexicans, and the Mexicans have taught the Navajos to work silver; but it all came from the Moors.

Thus, it turns out, as the conversation will go on to reveal, the Angelus by which Latour feels so charmed that morning "is really an adaptation of a Moslem custom." In passages like this, Cather advances a vision of tradition and the individual talent that is prophetically multicultural. Two years after *In the American Grain*, she has activated Williams's definition of the moral, which is "to hybridize."

Not every cultural practice can achieve its graceful refiguration, Cather allows: Latour finds the "old warlike Church" of Acoma grim and gray, a depressingly outsized building for the task at hand. Carrying huge timbers forty miles from the San Mateo Mountains to the top of the mesa was a grandiose exercise in portage, nothing more. What has any of this architecture to do, the priest wonders, with "types of life so old, so hardened, so shut within their shells, that the sacrifice on Calvary could hardly reach back so far." And the most thriving import of all, of course, were the Old World's "contagious diseases," the measles and scarlatina and whooping cough that have reduced to less than one hundred adults the pueblo of the Pecos.

Cather's decision to end her novel with the expulsion of the Navajos from their ancestral land emphasizes, perhaps, that, when it comes to the meeting of European and Native American cultures, the refusals have been more numerous than the borrowings. She anticipates this recognition in Latour's musings on his guide Jacinto, in whom he senses "a long tradition, a story of experience, which no language could translate to him." Saved from the storm by taking refuge in a kiva, the priest feels a "repugnance" for this "hospitable shelter." During the last weeks of the bishop's life, he remarks that he has lived to see the righting of two great wrongs. "I have seen the end of black slavery, and I have seen the Navajos restored to their own country." Yes, the Navajos were driven to the Bosque Redondo, three hundred miles from their own country, and yes, when the farming country proved no home for nomadic shepherds, the government "admitted its mistake" and restored them to their land near the Four Corners. They are returned to a reservation, a piece of land with wholly geometrical borders. That it was to prove of all Indian reservations to be the most prosperous and photogenic lends to Latour's hopeful conclusions about the Navajos ("God will preserve" the Indian) a sense of the exception that proves the rule.

"She exists wherever a human being has learned to live without joy." The sentence appears in Ellen Glasgow's (1873–1945) preface to *Barren Ground* (1925). The claim is made about her heroine, Dorinda. The phrase is repeated at the end of Cather's *The Professor's House*, when St. Peter concludes that he will have to learn to live "without joy." Edith Wharton (1862–1937) makes a similar claim for Newland Archer, at the end of *The Age of Innocence* (1920): "Something he knew he had missed: the flower of life." By *joy*, each writer means the same thing—a passionate, sexual, bodily love. Glasgow and, to a lesser extent, Cather present this life without joy as an achievement, as something almost devoutly to be wished for. Whether writing about male or female characters, each author writes, when deploying this phrase, out of her experience of being a woman. The logic and power of the implicit claim—that it is better, or at least stoically necessary, to so live "without"—flow from a firsthand experience of the "extra tasks" that Freud maintained were intrinsic to the project of being a woman in culture as he knew it.

When Freud writes in his essay "Femininity" (1933) that "a man's love and a woman's are a phase apart," he points to the asymmetry at the heart of heterosexual love. The extra task the woman must perform is to give up her mother. "A boy's mother," Freud argues, "is the first object of his love, and she remains so during the formation of his Oedipus complex, and, in essence, all through his life." An adult male heterosexual love still allows for the love of a woman. The female body of the mother is replaced by the female body of the wife. Every finding is a re-finding.

A girl's mother is also the first object of *her* first love. But an adult female heterosexual love requires that she replace her first love with a man. Every finding, for her, is a reminder of losing. The female body of the mother is replaced by the male body of the husband. One way for a woman to avoid this extra task is to fall in love with a woman.

But, of course, Cather lived in a culture where same-sex desire was proscribed. How could such a finely tuned soul have felt anything but denied its "joy" in a country that would have to wait seventy-six more years before its Supreme Court would finally strike down, in *Lawrence v. Texas* (2003), the last of the nation's sodomy laws? "The petitioners are entitled to respect for their private lives," that decision would read. "The State cannot demean their existence or control their destiny by making their private conduct a crime."

Cather respects the privacy of her characters for many reasons, and one of them may have been a deeply historical sense that the sharing of certain intimacies, at least in print, is premature. As Tom Outland says, about his discoveries in the Southwest: "We were reluctant to expose these silent and beautiful places to vulgar curiosity." Godfrey St. Peter later uses the same word: "my friendship with Outland is the one thing I will not have translated into the vulgar tongue." In both cases the "we" here alludes to a male-male intimacy that the vulgar cannot comprehend. The word may remind us of Williams's term "rudeness," and of the need to embrace this fact about ourselves as the first step toward translating our experience into a more responsive and liberating language.

Father Latour and Father Vaillant remain composed to the end, and the priest who has been ordered to depart for Colorado will allow himself only one tear, dropped from an averted gaze, at the thought of parting. Cather represents through them a powerful same-sex love but one that is not yet free to speak its name. Their parting allows for no recognition scene, no declaration of feeling. The reader is allowed sufficient evidence of it, nevertheless. On his deathbed, in the last paragraph in which his consciousness is recorded, Latour thinks of Vaillant. "He was standing in a tip-tilted green field among his native mountains, and he was trying to give consolation to a young man who was being torn in two before his eyes by the desire to go and the necessity to stay." Latour here remembers the person he most surely loves and remembers their moment of leaving France. What binds the two men together, beyond their country of origin and shared faith and years together in the desert, is their habit of renunciation. They have defined life as a constant leave-taking, as letting things go. "It was the discipline of his life to break ties," Cather writes about Father Vaillant, "to say farewell and move on into the unknown." The two men are connected, that is, by a commitment to separation and to separateness, a habit the vast distances of the Southwest continually reward and reinforce.

The big scene between the two men occurs late in the novel, when Vaillant is leaving for Colorado. Latour tells Vaillant that he must take both of the mules, Contento and Angelica. "They have a great affection for each other; why separate them?" Father Latour can ask the question on behalf of one pair but not on behalf of another. But whether the mules separate or remain together, they continue to share in the priests' fate. Both pairs are cut off, by nature or by choice, from generation. Latour is very firm about "celibacy" and sees it as a question "thrashed out many centuries ago." The one priest who breaks his vows of celibacy is pushed off a mesa. But if one is denied—by choice—both sexual love and child raising, how is one then to fill a life? "A life need not be cold, or devoid of grace in the worldly sense," Latour thinks to himself, the day Vaillant rides away, "if it were filled by Her who was all the graces." So Latour gives the standard theological answer. It is the novel's most hollow moment of consolation. We trust the narrative much more when it dwells on Latour's "feeling of personal loneliness" than when it moves so quickly to relieve it. And we trust it because we know that if love as most human beings know and want it is to be denied him, then his loneliness is his reward and his portion, as it is the portion of every one of us when we separate ourselves from the body and its hungers and experience ourselves alone. "What is lonely is a spirit," A. C. Bradley writes, and Father Latour's embraced and unapologetic loneliness is the surest warrant of the reality of his spiritual life.

Whatever joy she permitted herself in her private life, Cather chooses here, as does Elizabeth Bishop in "Crusoe in England," to image her ideal human love as the love between two men. Bishop's poem, discreet as it is, allows for the additional possibility of a sexual love, although she consigns it mostly to the white space between the printed lines of the poem, and to a sexy but easily overlooked pun: "Just when I thought I couldn't stand it / another minute longer, Friday came." Cather's novel refuses to suggest even this much—to gesture toward such an *arrival*. Insofar as *Death Comes for the Archbishop* is a love story, then, it does not choose to express what its author and its characters may have wanted, or not even known that they had wanted, but what their culture was willing to permit. Whatever kinds of inter-penetration New Spain and the country that conquered it were to allow, the free-dom of two women to love openly lay beyond any ending Cather could consign to the page.

CHAPTER FOUR

Performing Maleness

HEMINGWAY

Whenever I teach a course in twentieth-century American literature, a task I perform at least once a year, I begin with Hemingway (1899–1961). Not with *The Sun Also Rises* (1926), but with *In Our Time*, and with its second story, "Indian Camp." Why not begin with "On the Quai at Smyrna," the first story in the book? In reading a career so obsessed with beginnings—with the excitement and peril of setting out, and with the difficulty of moving forward with hope—why finesse the whole issue by not starting where Hemingway himself appears to ask us to start?

In Our Time is itself a repeated act of beginning, a book Hemingway reconfigured twice. The first version was published in Paris as *in our time* in January 1924 and consisted solely of the language games of the italicized vignettes. A year later Hemingway brought out *In Our Time*. The 1925 version interposes fourteen short stories among the vignettes, a sequence that begins with "Indian Camp." ("Indian Camp" was the first of the nine stories Hemingway wrote in a burst of creativity during the winter and spring of 1924.) In 1930, Hemingway brought out a third version of *In Our Time*, now beginning with "On the Quai at Smyrna." A first version of the story had been written in 1926, and a revised version—the one we now have—was added by Hemingway at the request of Maxwell Perkins, his editor at Scribners. The copyright page of contemporary editions reads: " 'On the Quai at Smyrna' was first published as the introduction to the 1930 edition of IN OUR TIME."

Despite the pride of place given to "On the Quai at Smyrna" in the final published version, forty years of reading Hemingway have convinced me that "Indian Camp" is the true beginning of Nick Adams's story and of Hemingway's career. "*No end and no beginning,*" the voice speaking in chapter 2 says in evident horror at the retreat from Adrianople. In positing ends and beginnings, stories impose a punctuation that experience itself does not provide. Given the contours of his life and the temper of his imagination, Hemingway had an easier time inventing ends than in imagining beginnings. As a consequence, in his first book he provides the definitive moment of setting out and also proceeds to obscure it. The initiation Nick Adams undergoes in "Indian Camp" is the key recognition scene in Hemingway's work and one of the most significant in the American literature of his century, a pedagogical moment so foundational and so terrifying that Hemingway eventually chose to protect the reader from its uncanny power by appearing to locate his beginning somewhere else.

The major obstacle to understanding *In Our Time* arises from the history of its publication as driven by the desire to start with a false start. This claim is bolstered by the fact that, in the original submission to publisher Horace Liveright in 1925, Hemingway positioned "Up in Michigan" as the first story in the sequence and "Indian Camp" as the second. After Liveright objected to the sexuality in "Up in Michigan," Hemingway agreed to replace it with "The Battler" and moved "Indian Camp" to the head of the book. By deciding, finally, not to begin with Nick, Hemingway distracts attention from the psychological and toward the technical, away from Nick's romance of education and growth and toward the experiment with voice that links "On the Quai at Smyrna" more powerfully to the vignettes than to the short stories. Our attention will nevertheless be directed toward Nick Adams as the core figure, and we will come to follow his story as the most compelling dimension of the book.

Nick's story culminates in "Big-Two-Hearted River," in which he returns to the landscape of "Indian Camp" in order to restart his story on his own terms. Between the beginning and the return, Nick sees his father humiliated, ends an affair, drinks and talks with a friend, confronts incest and homosexuality, is wounded in war, and then passes through a series of veiled avatars—a numb veteran, a friend of a jailed revolutionary, a partner in three failed marriages—before reentering the text as the anxious husband in "Cross-Country Snow" who plucks his mind out while skiing in lieu of confronting the "hell" of his wife's pregnancy. After all this, in the careful smoothing of the ground and pitching of the tent at the end of part 1 of "Big Two-Hearted River," Nick creates the "good place" he can enter and emerge from, reborn. In direct contrast to the body of the woman in "Indian Camp," whose screams, Dr. Adams says, are "not important," the tent embodies the natal space as clean and empty and as the complete construction of the male. So Nick makes his own mother, and he finds her uncanny still: "Already there was something mysterious and homelike."

We misread Hemingway when we reduce him to the champion of a "code" or the rhetoric of "not talking"; nowhere in his early work does he *recommend* to us the behavior of his central characters. He takes upon himself instead a much more difficult task: portraying the cost of the performance of being male. Nick's career as a man culminates in the vignette interposed between parts 1 and 2 of "Big Two-Hearted River," an event that appears to belong to the sequence of interchapters but which surely originates from Nick's unexcavated psyche.

The vignette in chapter 15 deals with the hanging of Sam Cardinella, a scene in which a male character loses control of his sphincter muscle while being urged to "*Be a man, my son.*" The vignette thus acts out issues of emotional courage, shame, and loss of control central to Nick's story. The return to his trout streams has been going well enough—Nick is managing to have things in the woods pretty much his own way—so why does Hemingway obtrude this awkward and ugly episode into the middle of the regression-in-the-service-of-the-ego that is Nick's fishing trip?

The question brings us back to the intercalary structure of *In Our Time*. The decision to interpolate short stories within the already existing vignettes foregrounds ellipsis as the dominant formal feature of the text. *In Our Time* is everywhere characterized by "The Thing Left Out," as Julian Smith calls it. "Big Two-Hearted River" is "about coming back from the war," Hemingway was to write in *A Moveable Feast*, "but there was no mention of the war in it." Instead, we must infer Nick's degree of shell shock from his obsessively tidy mental and physical habits. The most important and suggestive omissions, however, are the transitions between the original and the interpolated material. Do the spaces between the stories and the vignettes connect or separate? Because life here emerges as a series of gaps punctuated by crises, reading *In Our Time* trains us to infer, to search for patterns of continuity underlying seemingly disjointed episodes. The eventual continuity to be discovered reveals a life history obsessively unified: the "development" of a character who feels present even when absent, as in the suite of three marriage stories in which Nick never appears but where the characters clearly stand in for and act out the possibilities of love both in Nick's adulthood and in "our time."

At the end of part 1 of "Big Two-Hearted River," Nick executes a mosquito, curls up under his blanket, and goes to sleep. The Sam Cardinella vignette follows. Then we turn the page, to part 2 of the story. "In the morning the sun was up and the tent was starting to get hot." So we read the Sam Cardinella passage during the interval in the narration when Nick could be dreaming. In this brilliant act of sequencing (in the back-and-forth with his editor about the 1930 edition of *In Our Time*, Hemingway refused to rearrange the sequence of stories or vignettes: "Max *please believe me* that the chapters are where they belong") Hemingway reveals the vignettes as nightmares haunting the minds of the main characters. They are the dream work through which Nick rehearses all he has not yet come to resolve. Presented with these two kinds of material, with the manifest content of the stories and the latent content of the vignettes, the reader is asked to piece together a reading of Nick's life in the same way an analyst constructs a sense of his patient. Hemingway thus confers on his reader a role of immense difficulty and dignity. He issues a call for a profound act of listening that testifies to his trust in our power to confront "things" from which Nick himself will often turn away, as Nick's failed education becomes an occasion for the reader's painful and potentially educative effort of understanding.

Given all this, on the first day of my course, I begin where Hemingway really begins, with the opening sentences of "Indian Camp":

> At the lake shore there was another rowboat drawn up. The two Indians stood waiting.
>
> Nick and his father got in the stern of the boat and the Indians shoved it off and one of them got in to row. Uncle George sat in the stern of the camp rowboat. The young Indians shoved the camp boat off and got in to row Uncle George.
>
> The two boats started off in the dark. Nick heard the oarlocks of the other boat quite a way ahead of them in the mist. The Indians rowed with quick choppy strokes. Nick lay back with his father's arm around him. It was cold on the water. The Indian who was rowing them was working very hard, but the other boat moved further ahead in the mist all the time.
>
> "Where are we going, Dad?" Nick asked.

By the time Nick asks his question, it has become the reader's, too. The darkness that shuts off sight here does more than disorient; it presents departure as risky. Origins are murky, just as ends will prove too certainly known. The one thing we will see clearly in "Indian Camp" is death, when we are invited to gaze, lingeringly, at the cut throat of the self-slaughtered husband. The one thing Nick cannot look at is birth: "Nick did not watch. His curiosity had been gone for a long time." Our not being able to see where we start contrasts sharply with Nick's being asked to see how all of us will, finally, stop.

Yet for all its obscurity about specific contours, this opening makes us confront the fact of priority. We enter a world already filled with objects. "Another" has gone before us. Repetition of definite articles, as in "the two Indians," suggests that this is a world with which we are already familiar. The casualness of the narrator contrasts with the ignorance of both character and reader and encourages us to pretend that we are, in fact, at home here. The contrast between our stark ignorance of where we are and a tone implying our prior knowledge renders the scene, like Nick's tent, at once "mysterious and homelike."

Hemingway approaches the terror of the sublime through the sensation of the uncanny. In his essay "The 'Uncanny,'" Freud begins with the etymology of the word. "The German word 'unheimlich' is obviously the opposite of *heimlich* . . . meaning 'familiar.'" Freud then produces a prolonged dictionary entry on the word *heimlich* that results in the surprising conclusion that "among its different shades of meaning the word *heimlich* exhibits one which is identical with its opposite, *unheimlich*. What is *heimlich* thus comes to be *unheimlich*." The word for "homelike" in German "is a word the meaning of which develops towards an ambivalence, until it finally coincides with its opposite, *unheimlich*." And out of this ambivalence—Freud is at pains to point out that it is not a contradiction—he develops his theory that "the 'uncanny' is that class of the terrifying which leads back to something long known to us, once very familiar." To something, perhaps, like and yet unlike Nick's tent, which is where his journey begins and ends.

This complementarity of meanings does not argue that what is "familiar" *becomes* "mysterious," but that it is always already so, that the human condition is to be not at home at home. At the end of part 2 of "Big Two-Hearted River," Nick confronts the swamp. "He did not feel like going on into the swamp." The swamp is not "clean and compact" like the male trout Nick cleans while gazing at it. As if in answer to Nick's fantasy of the clean, well-lighted tent, the swamp insists on the inescapability of the mother's uncanny body. "This *unheimlich* place," Freud argues, "however, is the entrance to the former *heim* [home] of all human beings, to the place where everyone dwelt once upon a time and in the beginning." Nick has suffered a premature exposure to the dark and uncertain place out of which life emerges and of which living and loving must therefore be a part. Sex and birth cross the hard fact of personal limitation with the harder facts that we are not the original possessors of our first source, and that our first source must be lost. Nick's story details the refinement of his defenses against the untimely onset of this unbearable knowledge.

"Indian Camp" is therefore not only a key recognition scene but a failed one. It serves up one of the most moving examples in our literature of how knowledge *should not* be put across. Dr. Adams jokes with Nick about being an "interne," but his son's likely age—he can be no older than twelve or thirteen—sets up the scene as a cruelly botched attempt at sex education. How such knowledge gets transferred between the generations remains, in the United States, a continuing scandal, and the father here only aggravates the son's anxiety by refusing to acknowledge the son's desperate attempts to ward off the experience. Nick copes with the bloody birth by "looking away" or by focusing on the synecdoche of "his father's hands." The prose assists him in these maneuvers by falling back on words like "it," "things," and "something," abstract nouns standing in for concrete but unspeakable terms like "the cutting open" and "placenta." We see here the birth not only of Nick's fear of birth and beginnings but of the Hemingway style, one mustered on behalf of a lost son who is being asked to take in more than he can bear.

Given the fact that Hemingway shows Nick to be tender and handles him with such tenderness, it is difficult for me to understand how any reader could continue to read this story or any other by Hemingway as a celebration of machismo.

Hemingway begins and proceeds from a vision of life as an uncontrollable mystery on a bestial floor, one that generates in his characters the conviction that the readiness is all. While we may wish to object to the narrowness of the vision, we are required, in all fairness, to credit Hemingway with the possession of at least as much sympathy for and understanding of his characters as any one of his faithful readers. The problem, of course, is that the Hemingway myth continues to usurp an open reading of the work. Tobias Wolff (b. 1945) is eloquent on this point: "the man who lived in these stories was not the steely warrior-genius whose image had so fogged my first impressions. He was in most respects an unremarkable, even banal man who got things wrong and suffered from nervousness and fear, fear even of the workings of his own mind, and who sometimes didn't know how to behave . . . I judged him, but I also understood that he'd allowed me to, and this was chastening. Knowing that readers like me would see him in Nick, he had given us a vision of spiritual muddle and exhaustion almost embarrassing in its intimacy. The truth of these stories didn't come as a set of theories. You felt it on the back of your neck."

The unready Nick scrambles to compensate for his untimely exposure to human ends and beginnings by turning a fear into a disbelief: "In the early morning on the lake sitting in the stern of the boat with his father rowing, he felt quite sure that he would never die." The story ends with this sentence. This is not a celebration of a glib overcoming of fear but a bow to the courageous management of terror. If Dr. Adams is the bad teacher, insensitive and ill-prepared, Hemingway is the good one, the man who shares with us an honest if solemn vision of the way he feels things are and who also provides us with a set of strategies for dealing with them. These strategies, again, are not recommended but held up for scrutiny and as a generous reminder that a personal style is indistinguishable from the mechanisms of defense that protect each of us from things we, like Nick, cannot "stand."

❖   ❖

Nick's Indian Camp is not only the scene of a personal initiation but a crucial site of American memory, the primal and largely forgotten ur-place out of which the United States was violently born. Hemingway's response to this uncovering is not to deal with it but to leave; his characters spend most of their time recovering the pleasures of the civilized Europe that became so thoroughly transformed when it took up the errand of colonizing North American ground. The uncanniness haunting Hemingway's work may arise as much from this repressed and collective memory as it does from a family romance unique to a specific home.

Hemingway founded his style on a theory of controlled omission articulated in *A Moveable Feast*. He is describing here an effect created by withholding key information from the story "Out of Season":

The real end . . . was omitted on my new theory that you could omit anything if you knew that you omitted and the omitted part would strengthen the story and make people feel something more than they understood.

Under the pressure of this theory, Hemingway's early style becomes a crafty calling attention to what goes without saying. Roland Barthes defines ideology as what *"goes without saying,"* and Hemingway's deployment of the "omitted" could be described as *the style of ideology itself,* an ongoing instruction in the ways in which what is not said continually haunts and informs what is. As with the psyche, so with the culture of "our time": each structure has its secrets, the entire unspoken realm of interests served that sends up the taken-for-granted. Hemingway's style evokes the absent presence and workings of a secret history in both self and world, a history to which we have access only through the very words that refuse to "say" it. His development as a writer involves the bringing to light of this secret history, an act of working-through that makes his career a model for the work I am attempting in this book. This process culminates in *For Whom the Bell Tolls* (1940).

In chapter 19 of the novel, Robert and Pilar engage in a prolonged debate about divination. "Do you believe in the possibility of a man seeing ahead what is to happen to him?" Robert is asked. Since rehearsing for the end has long been the preoccupation of the Hemingway hero, the reader might expect Robert to give a positive answer. But Robert responds that such forebodings are only "evil visions," projections of what one fears, and therefore need not be accepted: "Seeing bad signs, one, with fear, imagines an end for himself and one thinks that imagining comes by divination . . . I believe there is nothing more to it than that." Pilar counters by asserting that she can "divine events from the hand" and even smell death in advance. Robert, in a playful mood, encourages her to instruct him in the ways of the odor of mortality. The scene of instruction culminates in an astonishing passage:

> "Then," Pilar went on, "it is important that the day be in autumn with rain, or at least some fog, or early winter even and now thou shouldst continue to walk through the city and down the Calle de Salud smelling what thou wilt smell where they are sweeping out the *casas de putas* and emptying the slop jars into the drains and, with this odor of love's labor lost mixed sweetly with soapy water and cigarette butts only faintly reaching thy nostrils, thou shouldst go on to the Jardín Botánico where at night those girls who can no longer work in the houses do their work against the iron gates of the park and the iron picketed fences and upon the sidewalks. It is there in the shadow of the trees against the iron railings that they will perform all that a man wishes; from the simplest requests at a remuneration of ten centimos up to a peseta for the great act that we are born to and there, on a dead flower bed that has not yet been plucked out and replanted,

and so serves to soften the earth that is so much softer than the sidewalk, thou wilt find an abandoned gunny sack with the odor of the wet earth, the dead flowers, and the doings of that night. In this sack will be contained the essence of it all, both the dead earth and the dead stalks of the flowers and their rotted blooms and the smell that is both the death and birth of man."

If this is overdone it is also bravely done, a complete violation of the Hemingway style along with an admission that the content of our fantasy lives is often an overheated mishmash, which, once brought to light, ought to have no power to haunt us. Of course, there is also a logic to these imaginings, one that reiterates the career-long conflation of birth and death. Life begins and ends in a "dead . . . bed"; the site of love houses the oracle of death. But solemn readings have little place here, since what ought to be celebrated is Hemingway's willingness to throw all the materials of his main obsessions into a "sack." Pilar's fantasy is unique in his work for its explicitness, its self-consciousness, and its patent absurdity. If this is a lurid triumph of the uncanny, it is also a triumph *over* it, one so unblinking and so thorough that it clears the way for Robert to love Maria.

As this remarkable passage reveals, the act of leaving things out operates for Hemingway as a conscious principle rather than as an unconscious mechanism of mind; the author cannot both mimic repression and fall victim to it. "Feel . . . more," Hemingway writes. The iceberg principle, as it is sometimes called (in the 1932 *Death in the Afternoon* Hemingway maintains that "the dignity of movement of an iceberg is due to only one eighth of it being above water"), is founded on a generosity not always acknowledged by Hemingway's critics. I call Hemingway's calculated elision "generous" because it is attempted in the service of feeling, a prompting in the reader of a collaborative surmise that generates what could be called the Hemingway sublime. The sublime results from encounter with a text encouraging the reader to believe, as Longinus maintains, that he has produced what he has heard. The books that we think of as the purest examples of the Hemingway style, *In Our Time* and *The Sun Also Rises*, do generate this effect. Yet, when Hemingway came to write his biggest, best, and most ambitious book, *For Whom the Bell Tolls*, he decided to put things back in. And he took particular care to remember the American Indian.

This work began even earlier, in the 1927 story "Now I Lay Me." The story deals with an American wounded in Italy during the Great War; it would seem to position itself about as far from America as one could get. The unnamed narrator passes the time thinking of the trout streams back home and saying prayers for all the people he has ever known. The "earliest thing" he can remember is the attic in his grandfather's house. In that attic is a family treasure, "jars of snakes and other specimens that my father had collected as a boy." The family moves to a new house and the specimens are moved to a basement. Then, one day the boy and his father come home to find a fire burning in the front yard.

> "I've been cleaning out the basement, dear," my mother said from the porch. She was standing there smiling, to meet him. My father looked at the fire and kicked at something. Then he leaned over and picked something out of the ashes. "Get a rake, Nick" he said to me. I went to the basement and brought a rake and my father raked very carefully in the ashes. He raked out stone axes and stone skinning knives and tools for making arrow-heads and pieces of pottery and many arrow-heads. They had all been blackened and chipped by the fire.

In this moment of maximum grief, the father hands the son his shotgun and sends him into the house. The gun is heavy and bangs against the son's legs.

What is this but an image of an American man publicly unmanned by a wife who casually discards the carefully gathered remains of a pre-"American" past? *That* he collects such things arouses her furious housekeeping, an act of cleansing that is also an uncensored expression of contempt for the activity of remembering. When we see the boy handed the shotgun, a weight he can barely manage, there is little hope he will prove any more capable of preserving a cultural legacy or of resisting those forces that would just as soon incinerate it.

Yet Robert Jordan does remember. On the night before the attack on the bridge, he returns in his mind, voluntarily, to his family history. It's a story implicated with Indian fighting. Robert's grandfather fought in the Civil War, and then he fought the Indians on the plains. "Do you remember," Robert says to himself,

> the cabinet in your father's office with the arrowheads spread out on a shelf, and the eagle feathers of the war bonnets that hung on the wall, their plumes slanting, the smoked buckskin smell of the leggings and the shirts and the feel of the beaded moccasins? Do you remember the great stave of the buffalo bow that leaned in a corner of the cabinet and the two quivers of hunting and war arrows, and how the bundle of shafts felt when your hand closed around them?

By putting these questions to Robert in the second person, Hemingway allows Robert's reverie to take on the quality of a dutiful and disciplined rehearsal, an act of the mind performed for the sake of the health of the mind. He also equates honest remembering with the willingness to hold in mind the fate of the American Indian.

As the reverie begins to build, a Hemingway character comes about as close to free association as one will ever get. Robert's memory moves on to the grandfather's saber and to his Smith & Wesson. There is a memory of a conversation during which Robert is allowed to hold the gun, and of the grandfather's refusal to speak of the Civil War: "I do not care to speak about it, Robert."

"Then after your father had shot himself with this pistol"—so begins the following paragraph. Robert remembers being given the suicide weapon and remembers riding with it and a friend up to the Bear Tooth plateau, where he drops it in a deep lake. When Chubb says "I know why you did that with the old gun, Bob," Robert answers him as his grandfather had earlier answered: "Well, then we don't have to talk about it."

Grandfather and grandson both choose not to talk about the past even while they cherish relics that embody it. As a novelist writing about defeat and as a man who saw himself caught up in "retreats" and "holding attacks," Hemingway perhaps here quietly identifies with the dignified remnants of the vanquished foe. Few territorial conquests have been as total as that suffered by the Native Americans living in the area that became the United States, and the silent tokens of these vanished Americans bequeath the victors a complex reservoir of pride and shame.

Furthermore, these relics also speak of a price that has been paid by the middle generation, by the "one that misused the gun." Robert wonders whether the fear his grandfather "had to go through and dominate and just get rid of finally in four years of that and then in the Indian fighting . . . had made a *cobarde* out of the other one the way second generation bullfighters almost always are." The Indians were good at turning those who had to fight them into men: the emphasis here is on the heroics—not the squalor—of the conquest. And the self-slaughtered father becomes Hemingway's crucial instance of the fact that what makes one man can break another. The distinctions drawn here between the generations, however, are not entirely convincing: Robert will later contemplate, in extreme pain, doing what his father did; and Hemingway himself, so hard on the man who takes his own life, did request and receive the Smith & Wesson his father "misused," a misuse that was to repeat itself thirty years later.

Yet the father does have something to teach the son, something bound up with Indians. It is an awkward knowledge. Embarrassment is the most powerful emotion Robert feels when he brings back his father. In imagining a meeting with his grandfather, Robert realizes that "both he and his grandfather would be acutely embarrassed by the presence of his father." Embarrassment is surely what the boy in "Now I Lay Me" feels as he watches his father rake through the fire. And embarrassment is a little of what an older Nick Adams feels, in "Ten Indians" (published in 1927) and "Fathers and Sons" (published in 1933), stories in which Hemingway approaches an understanding of the place of Indians in his psychic economy.

It is no accident that an Indian woman lies at the center of Nick's fall. If this is the moment in which the identity of Hemingway's "self-character" is formed, in all its troubled and—for Hemingway—moving complexity, then the construction of that identity, her presence would argue, depends on the felt, if not the acknowledged, presence of the gendered and racial other. She is the ultimate example of the thing left out, so physically present, so culturally and emotionally "unimportant." "Her screams are not important," Nick's father tells him. The inescapable uncanniness at the heart of things has everything to do with Nick's apprehension of this mysterious and homelike figure, just as the defenses that compose the self are born out of his struggle to differentiate himself from the alterity she bodies forth. And she will go with him. She goes with him precisely insofar as he attempts to repress the felt urgency of all she makes him recognize and feel. That Indians are so often reduced to relics in Hemingway's accounts of them argues for his awareness of the ways in which the mind is haunted by and even hangs on to the uncanny psychic material it also attempts to put aside. In the scene at Indian Camp, then, Hemingway becomes an archaeologist of the American unconscious, if we define that structured space as the preserve of a normative white male who maintains his pride of place in the larger culture by being "not-like" the female and the racial others whose existence in fact provides him with an identity.

In *Our America* (1995), Walter Benn Michaels argues that any struggle against the Indian in Hemingway masks a deep identification with him, a dynamic in which the expectant father in "Indian Camp" becomes the central figure. Michaels reads the father's suicide as "more a consequence of his inability to tolerate his wife's actually producing a baby than of his inability to tolerate her suffering" and then links this inability with the uneasiness about marriage and procreation so prevalent in Hemingway's work. For Michaels, Jake Barnes's impotence and Frederic Henry's feeling "trapped" by Catherine's pregnancy register cultural rather than psychological anxieties. "The refusal of procreation is the mark of racial purity," he maintains, where this purity is something that the Native American is taken to represent and that his white opponent can somehow hope to emulate or even appropriate. Michaels proceeds to read Hemingway's early career as a response to a perceived threat to "native" American identity aroused by the waves of immigration that crested against the exclusionary Immigration Act of 1924.

Hemingway's stories about Indians typically involve a father, a son, and an uncanny secret about human beginnings or endings. And the secret connecting birth and death is the secret of sex. Sex initiates the catastrophe of "Indian Camp," and the expectant father punishes himself for "the crime of death and birth," as Yeats would have it, with the ax wound that will put him in the top bunk where he will hear the birth screams that provoke him to cut his own throat. He is reduced to expressing himself through silence and self-annihilating violence; there is no cultural space left in which he can "be a man." Nick's own father rather unsuccessfully attempts to translate the meaning of the scene to his inquiring son. In this inaugurating story, fathers are represented as implicated in a process they can neither control nor comprehend. They can no more pass on an enabling knowledge than they can protect the son from a premature exposure to the facts of life.

But Hemingway was a developing soul, and on no subject was he more willing to overpass to love than on the question of the weak or uninstructive father. He makes a first attempt at this in "Ten Indians," where the father elects to convey to Nick the awkward knowledge that he has seen Nick's Indian girl "threshing around" with another boy. Nick cries in response and thinks to himself, "My heart's broken." "Fathers and Sons" refigures this story, in a finer tone.

"Fathers and Sons" creates an intimacy across three generations unique in Hemingway's fiction. The memory of Indians is not merely the occasion for this intimacy, but the essential experience out of which the main character has developed any capacity for it. When the story begins, Nick Adams is now thirty-eight years old, driving through the familiar landscape of Northern Michigan. As he drives, he starts thinking about his father.

Nick thinks that his father had been as sound on fishing as he was "unsound on sex." He forgives the father this lapse, choosing to believe that when it comes to sex "each man learns all there is for him to know about it without advice." The adequacy of Nick's sex education would seem to be a matter that has been raised and then put to rest.

But the story goes on to restage two scenes of instruction in which Dr. Adams demonstrates his unsoundness on the "whole matter," episodes in which he conveys his thoughts about buggery and mashing. Nick's mind then drifts back. His "own education in those earlier matters had been acquired in the hemlock woods behind the Indian camp." Nick remembers Trudy, the Indian girl who offers him actual physical experience rather than "direct sexual knowledge." Nick's thoughts turn to his father again, to Nick's adolescent rage with him, and to the fact that his sister is the only person in his family he can stand the smell of. Then a voice interrupts him.

"What was it like, Papa, when you were a little boy and used to hunt with the Indians?" It is the voice of Nick's son, riding in the front seat next to him. He is a boy ten or eleven years old, a boy of about the same age as the Nick who crosses the lake in the dark with his father in "Indian Camp." Yet the initiation about to take place will be far different for this son than it was for Nick.

It is the first mention of the boy in the story, and it comes near the end. For all the reader knows, Nick has been driving alone. Nick's son asks about the Indians and what they were like to be with. "It's hard to say," Nick answers. Then, in the very next sentence, Nick remembers and does not give voice to what being with Trudy was like. "Could you say she did first what no one has ever done better and mention plump brown legs, flat belly, hard little breasts, well holding arms, quick searching tongue, the flat eyes, the good taste of mouth, then uncomfortably, tightly, sweetly, moistly, lovely, tightly, achingly, fully, finally, unendingly, never-endingly, never-to-endingly, suddenly ended, the great bird flown like an owl in the twilight, only in daylight in the woods and hemlock needles stuck against your belly."

Nick, by way of Hemingway's prose, shares this memory with the reader; he does not impart it to his son. And so the entire machinery of omission—albeit here in the service of a notion of sex education perhaps more humane than Nick's father's—gets reproduced. Nick's experience of sex is private, sweet, and unbearable; he will be of little use to his son in spelling things out. And perhaps he cannot and even should not try to do so. Failing in this—or succeeding, since the words a reader brings to bear here have everything to do with a private conviction about a personal matter—Nick will convey much more: that the inner life is the deepest life but that "You'll lose it," as Jake Barnes says, "if you talk about it." The getting at it without talking about it is, of course, both the triumph and the limitation of the Hemingway style. Here that style works in the service of an awareness that each of us harbors a secret sexual history that is the token of our having most intensely lived, a history that does and probably should remain incommunicable. In conferring upon the reader a knowledge withheld from a character, Hemingway also anticipates the many scenes of instruction to come—in Welty, Baldwin, Morrison, and others—where not talking serves a supremely pedagogical purpose.

Hemingway's stories about Indians are those in which he courts the possibility of talking about "things," *things* being the favorite abstract noun that unnames the very referent it pretends to invoke. Remarkably full of messy emotions and embarrassing incidents, these stories challenge any easy characterization of the Hemingway style *as a style*, especially one dedicated to surface above depth. "Fathers and Sons" does, after all, share with the reader an explicitly sexual memory not shared with Nick's son, as if to remind us that literature is perhaps the best place for such secrets to come to light. Certain kinds of knowledge can only come from strangers. Thus, in the scene in the car, where an older Nick Adams finds a way to pass on a part of his knowledge to an inquiring son, Hemingway gives Nick the opportunity not only not "to do that business that my father did"—to him, at Indian Camp—but to share with his reader a memory of an achieved pleasure taken in the body that testifies to Nick's having grown into the man we had hoped he might become. And that man turns out to be Robert Jordan.

＊   ＊

In describing Hemingway's project as "narrow," I mean to acknowledge that his concern with the experience of maleness and a critical assessment of its costs and pleasures is an obsessive one that does not allow for the introduction of ulterior points of view. This not-trying to enter into the minds of the female or racial other makes for a monologic style. The central figure in "Indian Camp" is both a woman and a Native American, and Hemingway clearly refrains from attempting to represent her subject-position. No more does Faulkner attempt to speak *through* Dilsey. Is this a failure of imagination, or a prudent admission of its limits? A writer's limitations and strengths are intimately related, and we miss Hemingway's essential achievement if we ask it to have been other than it was. The consistency of the Hemingway voice has, however, encouraged some readers to mistake it as an argument on behalf of a "code." Thus, Hemingway not only is reduced to a maker of recipes for behavior but is dismissed as betraying his vision when he attempts to modulate his style.

For Whom the Bell Tolls is the book in which Hemingway puts aside the Hemingway style. Instead of leaving things out, this novel puts things in. It is a long book about a short time. The ratio between its 471 pages and the three days covered allows for close attention to moments and feelings that have previously gone unattended. Rather than killing time (in *A Farewell to Arms*, Frederic Henry admits that except for loving Catherine "the rest of the time I was glad to kill"), this novel fills it. "I am an old man who will live until I die," Anselmo declares in the opening pages, and this acceptance of both the years given and the inevitable end of them signals a new and mortal patience. Instead of omitting the awkward and the terrifying, this novel articulates them. The love scenes with Maria are silly and embarrassing, as love so often is. Here you'll lose it if you *don't* talk about it, including the supreme embarrassment of having been raped. Robert's reply to her story is to tell Maria—she is speaking here to Pilar about what he has said—that "nothing is done to oneself that one does not accept and that if I loved some one it would take it all away." Hemingway breaks through here, against the entire history of his defenses, to the freedom implicit in a love based on a mutual acknowledgment of what has been "done."

In the same way, the potentially crippling force of Robert's past is not denied return but is openly assimilated into a more inclusive imaginative scheme. He understands his father and forgives him, but he will not emulate him. Robert Jordan refuses to take his life at his own hand. The overriding obsession that has dominated Hemingway's fiction—trying to control the end—is absorbed into a multiplicity of truths. The beauty of the "high plateau," Robert Jordan thinks, as he lies behind the machine gun, is just "as true as Pilar's old women drinking the blood down at the slaughterhouse. There's no *one* thing that's true. It's all true."

The ending of the novel chooses to celebrate the power of "making believe" over fantasies that the traumas of our personal histories make us believe. The power of the imagination over a sense of fate culminates in Robert's good-bye to Maria. When he says, "I go with thee," he gives his entire life up to a saving fiction. "Go, go," Robert keeps saying, "stand up and go and we both go." This is not merely a comforting way of speaking; metaphor here *is* truth. For Maria to "go" is also to have their love stay, survive. Eve experiences this recognition about her love for Adam, at the end of *Paradise Lost*: "with thee to go / Is to stay." For Maria to go and survive and live is the only way to keep the chain of loving and remembering alive. As Zora Neale Hurston claims on the last page of *Their Eyes Were Watching God*, about Janie's love for Tea Cake, "he could never be dead until she herself had finished feeling and thinking." Robert will always "go" with Maria in her heart, which is the only way, Hemingway has come to understand and accept, that any of us—in life or in death—ever really do go with anyone.

CHAPTER FIVE

Colored Me

TOOMER ❧ HURSTON

*I*f what we call "race" in the United States entails an ongoing crisis of figuration, perhaps it is best to begin with a poem by Jean Toomer (1894–1967), entitled "Portrait in Georgia":

> Hair—braided chestnut,
>   coiled like a lyncher's rope,
> Eyes—fagots,
> Lips—old scars, or the first red blisters,
> Breath—the last sweet scent of cane,
> And her slim body, white as the ash
>   of black flesh after flame.

Something is looked at here; we are being offered a portrait. Hair—Eyes—Lips—Breath: the nouns that open four of the first five lines give us parts of a body. But the immense compression of the performance, the swiftness of the comparisons, and the decision to cast it as a sentence fragment all work to defeat the intelligence almost successfully and to argue that only poetry—and poetry asking us to work this hard to unpack it—can capture and contain the human situation Toomer here attempts to convey.

Parts of a body, followed by dashes. The dashes here work like equal signs. Hair (it is "braided chestnut" hair) is "coiled like a lyncher's rope." Eyes=fagots. Lips are "old scars." Breath is "the last sweet scent of cane." The fifth comparison, of "her slim body" to the color of ash, receives no dash. Five comparisons, with one "like" and one "as." Two similes, three metaphors.

Where do these comparisons come from? They can only arise from an eye and a mind looking at and thinking about "her slim body." The body is female, a "her." It has braided chestnut hair, so it is probably—almost certainly—white. But who is the gazer? And from what sort of history and standpoint does that gazer's excruciatingly bittersweet motive for metaphor arise?

"Portrait in Georgia" is the last poem in the first section of *Cane* (1923), the section exploring the fate of women in the South. It is positioned directly before "Blood-Burning Moon," Toomer's lynching story. By the time we get to the poem, then, we know that women are on Toomer's mind, and we have learned a lot about how they are seen. Toomer concurs with Laura Mulvey's claim that woman is "*to-be-looked-at-ness*." Stories like "Becky" ("No one ever saw her") and "Carma" ("she feels my gaze") continually advert to the drama of the male gaze. In "Fern," Toomer even posits a female character able to resist and redirect it. When a glance rests on Fern's face, it "thereafter wavered in the direction of her eyes." "Wherever they looked, you'd follow them and then waver back." Fern's resistance to being possessed sexually or visually is embodied in "the nail in the porch post just where her head came which for some reason or other she never took the trouble to pull out." An adaptive version of Prufrock's pin, which fixes him like a bug to a wall, and a forecasting of the nail on which Kabnis will hang the robe of his old self on the last page of *Cane*, Fern's nail is the unassailable token of an identity she conserves and will not surrender to the depredations of the gaze.

Of course, the dynamic in "Fern" stands in ironic relation to the dynamic in "Portrait in Georgia," since the short story envisions a black woman being looked at by a black man. "What white men thought of Fern I can arrive at," the narrator admits, "only by analogy." The brilliance of the poem flows from Toomer's decision to require its reader to examine the *object* of the gaze and then to reason back to the identity of the gazer. This process allows us to act out the complex associations and terrifying consequences attendant on the unidentified gazer's point of view.

"Portrait in Georgia" can in fact be read as a poem about the responsibilities and dangers of reading, where the central text offered up by the culture to the reading eye is the white female body. The body here is read from the top down: from hair, to eyes, to lips. The reading culminates in a fusion of the four synecdoches into a whole, a "body." And this body is reminiscent, a sight that generates a simile. It is "white as the ash / of black flesh after flame." The poem ends in fire. It ends with fire and a lyncher's rope, with the ever-available and all-too-frequent consequence of the very act of reading the poem asks us to perform. And the only point of view routinely punished, in Georgia, for so reading a white woman's body, with such care and desire, was a black man's.

His gazing has a result; he can be lynched for it. And the gazer knows he very well might be. This is why he moves so rapidly through his associations. Yes, the chestnut hair is beautiful, but also killing; the appraisal of it can hang you. Yes, the lights of the eyes give off a kind of fire, but also one that consumes the gazer, like the fagots gathered around the lynch victim's feet. Lips are scars because they invoke an opening in the skin, the opening raised by a whip on one's back. Or, in a second comparison, lips are like the first red blisters raised on a body as it is being burned. The breath is sweet like cane, but sugar cane only becomes sweet when rendered by fire, a sweetness purchased by the labor of black bodies. And the last association, of her body to the whiteness of ash—this association raises the poem not only to the level of the great poems in the tradition but to prophecy itself. Lynching is the consequence of the black male gaze openly directed against a white female body. (We remember that Emmet Till was lynched for whistling at a white woman.) And yet the final consequence of that act of hysterical cultural revenge is to produce "white" ash. All bodies, white and black alike, become alike—*become the same color*—when they are burned. In this terrifying and transcendent image, Toomer reminds us that the races and all their distinctions will, inevitably, return to the same dust from which all bodies also initially arise. This education in the logic of metaphor equals anything provided by the conceits of John Donne's "A Valediction Forbidding Mourning."

And yet—and yet—this was a gaze that simply didn't exist! There is virtually no record of black-on-white rape in the American South before the latter decades of the twentieth century. Toomer gives us here the *fantasy* of a gaze. It is a fantasy projected onto black men, one arising out of white pride, guilt, and sexual anxiety. This imaginary black gaze is used by white men as a way of fantasizing about raping white women, the more magnolia-scented the better. It thus allows them to regain some measure, if only indirectly, of the sexual power and patriarchal authority lost with defeat in the Civil War. In *Dutchman* (1964), Amiri Baraka (b. 1934) literalizes the fantasy of a rapacious black male gaze and shows it being teased into being. A white woman on a New York subway accuses a black man of "staring" at her. He tries to stay cool; she keeps after him. She tells him that you like to "run your mind over people's flesh." When he finally responds by cutting loose with a tirade filled with sexual and racial rage, she stabs him.

Once he has been assigned this desiring or rapacious gaze, the black man is then preemptively punished for a crime he is assumed to continually commit. This is the burden of Faulkner's "Dry September" (1931), a story beginning with the word "rumor" and then proceeding to show how the rumor plays itself out on the white body of Miss Minnie Cooper and the black body of Will Mayes. "Through the bloody September twilight, aftermath of sixty-two rainless days, it had gone like a fire in dry grass—the rumor, the story, whatever it was." The last sentence of the story is given no period because this is a story that goes on. "Happen?" McClendon answers, to the question "Did it really happen?" He goes on. "What the hell difference does it make? Are we going to let the black sons get away with it until one really does it?" The rumor is always in the air; it is indigenous, a spontaneous combustion, part of the weather. "Whatever it was."

"In a world ordered by sexual imbalance," Laura Mulvey argues, "pleasure in looking has been split between active/male and passive/female. The determining male gaze projects its phantasy onto the female figure, which is styled accordingly."

Toomer's poem unpacks the ways in which, in the United States, a racial imbalance complicates a world always already ordered by sexual imbalance. The four key and interdependent figures in this dynamic find themselves caught up in a circuit of desire by which they are "styled accordingly." In *Soul on Ice* (1968), Eldridge Cleaver (1935–98) assigns the players in this national allegory their hard-earned names: the Omnipotent Administrator (the white man); the Supermasculine Menial (the black man); the Ultrafeminine (the white woman); the Amazon (the black woman). Cleaver's story is of a man who chooses to act out the projected fantasy; his book begins with the release of physical anger in rape. He quickly opts instead for the fulfillment of imaginative strength through style.

What has alienated Cleaver, he comes to realize, is gender as well as race, the split between the male and female that generates the pathos of existence in a gendered body. Sex is the "Primeval Mitosis," the division of divisions. We all suffer from it, Cleaver argues. And the quest for fusion becomes at once a shared universal—Cleaver is relentlessly heterosexual—and the "dynamic of history."

But the white male, Cleaver reasons, has refused to participate in the pathos of gender, which involves the continual acceptance of limitation, by distracting attention toward race. In America the white male fear of racial mixing, Cleaver comes to believe, is a way of finessing the issue of sexual adequacy, because at the bottom of his resistance to miscegenation is less the fear that the white woman's purity will be defiled than that his own merely human adequacy will stand revealed. You cannot assign the realm of physical work away from your own privileged body without also calling into question the potency of that body. "Race fears," Cleaver argues, "are weapons in the struggle between the Omnipotent Administrator and the Supermasculine Menial for control of sexual sovereignty." The prevailing system of sexual access, even into Cleaver's day, expresses the anxiety of the patriarch before the menial: "I will have sexual freedom . . . I will have access to the white woman and I will have access to the black woman. The black woman will have access to you—but she will also have access to me. I forbid you access to the white woman. The white woman will have access to me, the Omnipotent Administrator, but I deny her access to you, the Supermasculine Menial." Rape is Cleaver's rebellion against this logic; lynching has provided the traditional enforcement of it. Cleaver comes to see that for the black man to take on the project of rape is to act out a fantasy rooted in white alienation and anxiety. This discovery allows him at the end of *Soul on Ice* to recover and express his respect and desire for his black "sisters," who have been crowded out, in his inner life, by the irrepressible image of the white woman, by what he goes on to call "the Ogre." Cleaver writes rather than rapes his way free and reveals along the way that in his country a racial politics is also always a sexual politics.

As Cleaver argues, the goal of the racial allegory policed by lynching was to prevent racial mixing between white women and black men. Yet the entire system allowed for and even assured an ongoing mixing in the other direction. And here we come to the vexing role of the Ultrafeminine in the circuit of desire. Toomer's portrait represents a body so desirable that it kills the onlooker. Yet it seems churlish to blame the to-be-looked-at for causing the black man's death. Ex-slave Harriet Jacobs would answer that she is no more innocent than is any other symbolic figure granted a status as "pure," since the purity of one such figure depends on the defilement of another. In *Incidents in the Life of a Slave Girl* (1861), Jacobs provides a telling anecdote about the active complicity of the slave owner's wife in maintaining the order that consigns her to the pedestal. The complicity of the Ultrafeminine culminates in an astonishing scene in the chapter called "The Jealous Mistress." Mrs. Flint, tormented by her husband's open seduction of Linda, as Jacobs calls herself, begins visiting Linda's room at night. "She whispered in my ear, as though it was her husband who was speaking to me, and listened to hear what I would answer." By consenting to impersonate the very man who would betray her, and by directing her anger at the victim rather than the author of the crime, the white woman achieves a total identification with the oppressor and so styles herself as an enforcer of what Jacobs calls the "patriarchal institution," although she is also psychically torn apart in the process.

"Portrait in Georgia" encodes an entire interracial history in seven lines of verse. It is a victory won through form, where the grammar of the sentence, absent as it is of either an active subject or an enabling verb, suspends before our gaze the components of a process that repeats itself, without any apparent human agency. The final and resolving simile posits a collapse of the distinction between black and white on which slavery was based, and does so by appealing to a verifiable physical fact. Toomer appeals to the color of ash. If the poem reveals racial difference as constructed not out of facts but out of metaphors serving the interests of class and sexual politics, it also demonstrates that the way out of such an impasse is to think like a poet, to invite us to unpack race as a set of complex figures or tropes. Race is a thing we have made and can therefore unmake.

The deepest issues in *Cane* have to do with fusion and separation; Toomer, who called himself a "reconciler," strives through his writing for "a spiritual fusion analogous to the fact of racial intermingling." As the poem models a strategy for the reconciling of difference (about Paul, Toomer writes, "Suddenly he knew that people saw, not attractiveness in his dark skin, but difference"), it joins the 1920s debate about the nature and mission of poetry.

The debate turned upon the question of how far to reach for similitude. "Tis a very old strife," Emerson writes in *English Traits* (1856), "between those who elect to see identity, and those who elect to see discrepancies." Toomer pushed hard for identity; he possessed that "instinct of seeking resemblances" that, in a wonderful premonition of one twentieth-century solution, Emerson calls "an affirmative action." Samuel Johnson had complained that in metaphysical poetry "the most heterogeneous ideas are yoked by violence together," but Eliot prizes such violent yoking, and in the year in which *Cane* was being written he published his famous defense of Donne and his wide-ranging conceits. In Eliot's allegory, the Metaphysicals experience no divorce between thought and feeling and are most integrated when their metaphors are at their most audacious. A conceit for the oneness of two souls in love, for instance, Donne's image of the "twin compasses" finds likeness in difference even while it honors the inescapable tension between two human beings. Each lover is imaged as one leg of the compass, and the two touch only at the apex or when the roaming arm returns home to the fixed foot. With Wordsworth, then, Donne commits to finding "similitude in dissimilitude," a process Eliot describes as "forming new wholes."

In his own day, Eliot argues, this capacity has been lost. Human beings no longer feel their thought and suffer instead from a "dissociation of sensibility." No phrase better sums up the condition of the male characters who inhabit the second section of *Cane*. "John's body is separate," Toomer writes, "from the thoughts that pack his mind." John, the narrators of "Avey" and "Box Seat," and especially Paul, in "Bona and Paul," are men in search of a metaphor—a reconciling conceit—but they are not quite up to the task. "The poet," Eliot maintains, "must become more and more comprehensive, more allusive, more indirect, in order to force, to dislocate if necessary, language into his meaning." Seeking evidence of Toomer's cherished fantasy of "an unmixed human race," these characters bear a heavy burden. Each strives to bridge a gap between the self and a woman. But the way they set about the task only widens the gap.

The key phrase comes from Kabnis: "I talk." "Kabnis" begins with an address to a "sweetheart," but there is no one there. In "Avey," the male self is reduced to narrative, to explanation. "I traced my development . . . I described . . . I pointed out." He talks, and, meanwhile, Avey falls asleep. It's all a little too reminiscent of *The Waste Land* and the blinded frozen lover before Eliot's Hyacinth Girl. These are speakers marooned in analysis paralysis. Commitment to monologue signals their dissociation from everything but an obsessive inner life.

Even Paul, the most ambitious and appealing of the bunch, finds himself driven back upon his own thoughts. He wants to sleep with Bona and to convince her of the possibility of a new order of color, but his most intense move toward her takes place in an interior monologue turning on the word "know." "I'd like to know you whom I look at. Know not love." Paul misses the pun in the word "know," since at this point he's thinking only about a kind of mental possession rather than knowing "in the Biblical sense." Worse, he says all this not to Bona, but to himself. And she is somehow expected to read his mind. When he resurfaces from the monologue, he says to her,

> "And you know it too, don't you Bona?"
> "What, Paul?"
> "The truth of what I was thinking."

Trying to resolve differences by way of monologue, in Toomer as in Eliot, only results in being more cut off.

"Bona and Paul" takes as its project the reconciling of inner and outer difference: between thought and feeling, man and woman, black and white. It is one of the most ambitious short fictions ever written about the longing to escape double consciousness. The story begins with a frenzy of similitudes, as Bona searches for similes adequate to her sense of Paul. "He is a candle . . . He is a harvest moon. He is an autumn leaf. He is a nigger." Bona's search for a nonrestrictive language here collapses into what "all the dorm girls say," and it will fall to Paul to work through the crisis of figuration.

As Paul and Bona dance, they also "clot." "Art and Helen clot. Soon, Bona and Paul." They come, physically, together. But as they dance, they talk. Bona accuses Paul of a "failure to make love." Paul replies, "Mental concepts rule you." Here they seem to act out Yeats's mordant observation that sexual love is founded on spiritual hate. Mentally at war, they are physically close. "The dance takes blood from their minds and packs it, tingling, in the torsos of their swaying bodies. Passionate blood leaps back into their eyes. They are a dizzy blood clot on a gyrating floor." Dance here brings the mind down into the body. But in deploying the word "blood" and in repeating the word "clot," Toomer takes a considerable risk. Yes, the metaphor of clotting argues for a mingling of Bona's white with Paul's black blood. But to achieve that mingling on the level of "blood" is to give new life to the very dead metaphor that has shored up for centuries a false scientism about racial difference. Fortunately, as Toomer proceeds through this paragraph and the remaining few that conclude the story, he moves away from the essentializing metaphor of blood and toward the obvious concoctions of color.

"Bona and Paul" ends with an apotheosis of color, and purple is the central one. This is Paul speaking to the "uniformed black man," as he and Bona leave the Crimson Gardens:

> I came back to tell you. To shake your hand, and tell you that you are wrong. That something beautiful is going to happen. That the Gardens are purple like a bed

of roses would be at dusk. That I came into the Gardens, into life in the Gardens with one whom I did not know. That I danced with her, and did not know her. That I felt passion, contempt and passion for her whom I did not know. That I thought of her. That my thoughts were matches thrown into a dark window. And all the while the Gardens were purple like a bed of roses would be at dusk. I came back to tell you, brother, that white faces are petals of roses. That dark faces are petals of dusk. That I am going out and gather petals. That I am going out and know her whom I brought here with me to these Gardens which are purple like a bed of roses would be at dusk.

Paul then shakes the black man's hand and looks up to see that Bona is gone. Poised between the same options Gatsby faces at the end of Fitzgerald's chapter 6, Paul chooses his "unutterable vision" over Bona's "perishable breath."

Why purple? Because it is the blend of Paul's own "rosy-black" skin and the "pink"-white faces that haunt him throughout the story, because it is the noble color through which Paul and Toomer can fantasize about the merging of all colors and the differences based on them in a new "American race." Again, the metaphor must have its logic: purple is the color that the mixtures of these two skin colors would, literally, produce. This is the "something beautiful" that is going to happen. It will be a world in which black men, like the doorman, can stop dressing up in livery. As in Stein, color here exists along a spectrum, a play of infinite gradations in which difference is lost in the differential.

Paul's wish is hedged about with ironies. A man and a woman again leave a garden to found a new human "race," but Adam somehow looses track of his Eve. We are left with two men alone, and the vision can only be imparted through monologue. Paul remains stuck on the verb "to know." On the facing page, we see two arcs mirroring each other, the symmetrical but broken and unconnected halves of a potential circle. The house is still divided, and when we turn the page, we find Kabnis in his "whitewashed" cabin, where the "cracks between the boards are black." These cracks are the lips the night winds use for whispering. Toomer here provides an image of the "white" house that is America infiltrated by the black voices it has banished to its periphery. Seeing Kabnis in this space reminds us once again that *Cane* provides an inventory of ways to live out one's blackness, and that leaving blackness behind is not one of them.

Like the fantasy of color that ends "Bona and Paul," the form of *Cane* is a triumphant mixture, one that blends genres as readily as it imagines a mixture of peoples. As in the walls of Kabnis's cabin, this structure asserts the permeability of all containers. Form as interpolation—I am speaking here not only of the intermixture of poetry and prose but of the visual cues the shifting arcs provide—was a principle governing not only *The Souls of Black Folk* but the *Cantos* (1915–69), *Spring and All* (1925), and *U.S.A.* (1938). Toomer here lays claim to being a master of the intercalary form, and, as in *In Our Time*, he asserts a more than playful connection between the individual parts. The poems in *Cane*, like Hemingway's vignettes, provide the "lore" that conditions the minds of the main characters. They whisper, like the voices outside Kabnis's room, a collective fate.

In breaking ground for Hemingway's experiment with intercalary form, *Cane* reminds us, as Eric Sundquist has so convincingly shown in *To Wake the Nations* (1993), that American literature and African-American literature form an indivisible tradition. Moreover, the experience of influence does not simply flow in one direction, from white to black. Kabnis's whitewashed room provides, in fact, a powerful figure for that tradition, where the "dominant" white space is continually haunted by and therefore compelled to internalize the sounds and souls of black folk.

What makes *Cane* especially moving is its refusal to deliver wholeheartedly on its central fantasy of blending. Toomer chooses instead to poise the symbolic resolutions, at the end of "Bona and Paul" and at the end of "Kabnis," where the hero completes his Orphic ascent while Carrie's "gaze" follows him up the stairs, against a sense of narrative irresolution. Kabnis and Paul have their vision, but in each case they leave the woman behind. Arguing for social change by way of the logic of metaphor is one thing—a possible thing. But imagining a new human story, an imitation of an action that requires nerve and risk-taking and marching in the street, is much harder to do.

❖   ❖

The double consciousness afflicting Toomer's male characters is in many ways indistinguishable from the spiritual and psychological crisis Eliot lays out in "The Metaphysical Poets" (1922). What makes the work of the Harlem Renaissance so crucial to its time are the ways in which its key texts continually make connections about a black predicament that is also a human one. For "double consciousness" as Du Bois conceives it acts not only as a curse but as a *resource*. It provides those condemned to it a kind of "second sight" highly adapted for dealing with modernity. This second sight feels, if not knows, that life is full of loss and self-alienation. Insofar as Emerson has used the phrase "double consciousness" as early as 1843, in "The Transcendentalist," perhaps the condition can be thought of as not only a modern burden but an American one.

Alain Locke's (1885–1954) great anthology, *The New Negro* (1925), is an illustrated text that mixes poetry, short fiction, drama, and criticism. In its argument, as in its structure, it mirrors the vision laid down by *Cane*. While some contributors to the anthology do appeal to black "characteristics" and to a kind of innate folk wisdom or "emotional endowment," the more compelling voices argue that the black artist, like any other cultural worker, finds herself alone with America, stranded in a place denying her any spontaneous or organic link to the past. Locke himself maintains that "there is little evidence of any direct connection of the American Negro with his ancestral arts" and that a black sensibility confronts various forms of African art with as "misunderstanding an attitude as the average European Westerner." When Arthur Schomberg (1874–1938) argues that "history must restore what slavery took away," he issues a call to make stories that do not yet exist, or that must be brought into the public arena through the slow diligence of the years. Precisely because African-Americans have been systematically deprived of cultural memory and of most of the means by which it is recorded, they are also empowered to live out the consequences of being modern with a potentially enabling self-awareness. Whereas Eliot finds himself almost crushed by the burden of the past, the individual African-American talent confronts the tradition as not to be forgotten, or evaded, but consciously and with great difficulty to be *reconstructed*. In fact, the African-American imagination might best be conceived of, at any interval of its unfolding, as a modern one, if by "modernity" we mean that sense of existing at a historical juncture where the continuity with the past has been broken and where the artist finds herself stranded in the "now" ("modo"=now), and where only a skeptical and self-conscious effort can construct a usable past. What else is jazz but a wild embrace of a radical impurity, a celebration of the "fusion," to use Locke's word for what the spirituals accomplish, of highly eclectic musical precedents in the continual call to improvise a form?

Of course, the facts on the ground always condition artistic energies, even of a renaissance, and the years in which Toomer and Hurston came to maturity were bleak ones for African-Americans. The 1890s and first decades of the twentieth century saw a worsening situation for America's black citizens. The old Southern conservatives had left a small space for "the Talented Tenth," but rising radicals such as James K. Vardaman wanted to give them nothing. As the Snopes replaced the Sartorises, black Americans entered "the Nadir," as one of Du Bois's disciples called it. In 1890 the "Mississippi Plan" required black voters to pay a two-dollar poll tax, take a literacy test, and recite from memory and interpret clauses in a new state constitution. *Plessy v. Ferguson* formalized separate but unequal education in 1896. As the century turned, lynchings were on the rise, with ninety-one reported in 1901 alone. In 1906 black soldiers of the Twenty-fifth Infantry regiment allegedly shot up a Texas town in what came to be known as the Brownsville Raid. After the fall elections, Roosevelt signed orders discharging 167 out of 170 soldiers from the regiment without honor. A race riot broke out in Atlanta that fall, with a mob of ten thousand whites beating every black person it could find on the city streets. By 1910, the franchise had been effectively denied to Southern blacks; Virginia reapportioned voting districts five times in seventeen years in order to nullify black ballots. The Ku Klux Klan was reborn at Stone Mountain in 1915, a year before being glamorized in D. W. Griffith's *The Birth of a Nation*. It all culminated in the "Red Summer" of 1919, when the murder of a black civilian by a white sailor in Charleston, South Carolina, sparked urban riots that spread to Longview, Texas, and then to Washington, D.C., Chicago, Knoxville, and Omaha. In that same year the Senate once again failed to pass an antilynching bill. This casual and reflexive racism was formalized in the Immigration Act of 1924, which reached far beyond African-Americans to entirely exclude the Japanese, to cut immigration from Southern and Eastern Europe, and to reduce Jewish immigration to a trickle.

Against all this, what sort of renaissance could be imaginable? Against all this, Zora Neale Hurston (1903–60) steps aside. Not that she was herself immune to the "humiliating" effect of Jim Crow laws, as when in 1932 she was hustled into a laundry closet at a Brooklyn internist's office and then hurried out the back door. But her upbringing in the independent and all-black town of Eatonville, Florida, and her fortune in being sponsored by Alain Locke at Howard and by Franz Boas at Columbia distanced her somewhat from a felt sense of depredation. Deciding to focus on "racial health" rather than on black life as a "tragedy of color," Hurston became a scholar-storyteller of the adaptive energies of African-American life.

Hurston's scholarly career can be read as a dramatic enactment of the workings of the uncertainty principle. She took as her subject a study of the "folk." In order to study them, she had to "stand off," to become trained, and therefore alienated, as an academic anthropologist. About the Brer Rabbit cycle, she was to write, "it was fitting me like a tight chemise. I couldn't see it for wearing it. It was only when I was off in college, away from my native surroundings, that I could see myself like somebody else and stand off and look at my garment." As in *The Education of Richard Rodriguez*, Hurston had to leave home and even risk losing it in order to become a "scholarship girl."

In 1925 Hurston arrived in New York with "a lot of hope" and fifty cents in her pocket. She had come to enroll at Barnard after winning a prize for her short story "Spunk." Her first job for Boas was to stand on a Harlem street corner and to measure the skull sizes of passersby with a pair of huge calipers. Boas then sent her South on the first of many expeditions to recover and record African-American folklore, "the art people create," as she called it, "before they find out there is such a thing as art." Her study of hoodoo involved an initiation in which she lay nude for sixty-nine hours, face down on a couch, without food or water, with her navel touching a snake skin. This is the work that was to produce her ingathering of seventy folktales in the 1935 *Mules and Men*.

But the romance of the participant-observer led Hurston to conclude that too much distance from her subject would not serve it, however much the observer might also get in the way. "It did not do," she said in 1935, "to be too detached as I stepped aside to study them. I had to go back, dress as they did, talk as they did, live their life, so that I could get into my stories the world I knew as a child." Soon after writing these lines, Hurston abandoned folklore as an academic subject, traveled to Haiti, and in seven straight weeks produced *Their Eyes Were Watching God* (1937).

Hurston's novel commemorates her love affair with a man of West Indian descent she had met in New York in 1931. "I tried to embalm all the tenderness of my passion for him in *Their Eyes Were Watching God*," she wrote. It certainly is a high romance, "the most convincing . . . novel of Blacklove," June Jordan (1936–2002) argues, "that we have." It is impossible to imagine Sethe and Paul D without it; Hurston here invents the flawed man who comes and goes but who somehow assists the heroine in the discovery that she is her own "best thing." Hurston goes so far as to have Janie say that the man "makes" the woman. "But you come 'long," Jamie says to Tea Cake after the hurricane, "and made somethin' outa me." Of course, he will also turn and bite her, as if to repay, in a terrifying parody of what Eve does to Adam during the gift of the fall.

Janie begins and ends her narrative as single, back where she started, on a porch of her own. Her experience of her three husbands comes to us as a parenthesis within this larger fact; these ventures at marriage have generated her "story." Chapters 2 through 20 unspool out of the last two words in chapter 1: "Janie talked." Janie's progress through what she calls the "love game" is important; it allows her to discover pleasure in her body (Tea Cake affirms that her "comfortable" is "mine too") and to rebalance the division of labor, to work "long side" her man picking beans in the Everglades. But the love game above all allows Janie to develop a power that frees her even of the need for love. Through it, she finds her own voice.

"They all leaned over to listen while she talked." This sentence describes the behavior of the all-white male jury and of the eight or ten white women in the court room who lean forward to listen to Janie tell what happened with Tea Cake. The sentence takes in the reader as well. Framed by the two front porch scenes in which Janie rehearses her life story for Phoeby, the novel is structured as a prolonged scene of instruction not only in how to love but in how to listen. Like Beloved's avid listening to Denver, "Phoeby's hungry listening helped Janie to tell her story."

In both Hurston and Morrison, the listener calls forth the story. Hurston so sets up her novel as to urge its auditor to lean like that jury, or like the reader in Wallace Stevens's (1879–1955) "The House Was Quiet and the World Was Calm," who "leaned above the page / Wanted to lean, wanted much most to be / The scholar to whom his book is true." This is why Hurston chooses not to render Janie's testimony at the trial in Janie's voice. Instead, she delivers it in the third person: "She had to go way back to let them know how she and Tea Cake had been with one another." The scene is not about Janie's voice; by now, we know that she's found one. Instead, the scene dramatizes empathetic listening. What Janie most fears in this moment is not death but "misunderstanding." And she succeeds in putting her story across. It has been a big day for her:

> The sun was almost down and Janie had seen the sun rise on her troubled love and then she had shot Tea Cake and had been in jail and had been tried for her life and now she was free. Nothing to do with the little was left of the day but to visit the kind white friends who had realized her feelings and thank them.

By way of the power of Janie's voice, this all-white audience has been made able to "realize" her feelings and so can vote to find her not guilty. It is like a gift, a gratuitous moment of interracial understanding that stands to the side of the main story, which occurs in a virtually all-black world, a scene inviting generations of non-black readers to recognize themselves as potential realizers, too, of Janie's story.

As Janie arrives home, she moves through a world of talk: "A mood come alive. Words walking without masters." The paragraph following these sentences runs together ten unassigned and hostile questions directed at Janie by what Elizabeth Bishop will later call "the family voice." Here the social self is constituted out of gossip, a machine that appears to run of itself by putting its "mouf on things." Janie comes back the way Morrison's Sula does after her ten years away, in a storm of shit. The gossipers slowly begin to acquire names: Pearl Stone, Mrs. Sumpkins, Lulu Moss, Phoeby Watson. Their curiosity is represented as prurient rather than eliciting; sitting in a kind of perpetual "Judgment," "They wants to be there and hear it *all*." Janie's crime, in their eyes, is not killing Tea Cake but choosing not to "stop and say a few words with us." Phoeby defends her from this charge and then gets up to take Janie some supper.

The audiences have been set up: the group mind that covets deference rather than real knowledge, and the sole friend, "eager to feel and do through Janie." The core problem is "envy," a problem Sula also faces. In Hurston's world, as in Morrison's, envy is the symptom of an unlived and therefore unstoried life.

Janie begins by making a few distinctions. She accepts Phoeby's word "understandin'" as central to their task and says that "tellin'" has no use unless "understandin'" accompanies it. So the call to listen feelingly is made. Janie also admits that because Phoeby is a long-time kissin'-friend, she counts on her "for a good thought. And Ah'm talking to you from dat standpoint." Fulfilled narrative depends on the good will of the listener, a disposition depending in turn on the acceptance of the limited "standpoint," a unique and stylized subject position, as the only place from which narrative can originate.

Much of the charm of Janie's story arises from its refusal to dwell on the standard developmental crises. Hurston takes care of the discovery of sexual desire in fewer than seven pages. Janie kisses Johnny Taylor over the gatepost, Nanny yells at her, and "that was the end of her childhood." To the question of racial identity, Hurston gives even less space.

As a girl in West Florida, Janie plays mostly with white children and "didn't know Ah wuzn't white till Ah was round six years old." She finds out about her color by way of a class photograph in which everybody gets pointed out "except a real dark little girl" that she cannot "recognize" as herself. "Dat's you," she is told. "Aw, aw! Ah'm colored!" she replies. "Den dey all laughed real hard. But before Ah seen de picture Ah thought Ah was just like de rest."

That's it. That's the scene. Hurston immediately cuts away to a recounting of the inevitable separation, as the years go by, of black from white playmates, giving Jamie's response to her discovery of color no more thought. Compared to the "chasm of misgiving and fear" opening out into Johnson's narration when he "gazes in his looking-glass," or to the "shadow" that sweeps across Du Bois when the revelation of his race first bursts upon him, Hurston handles Janie's realization with extreme coolness. By minimizing the amount of attention afforded this conventional moment of trauma, Hurston quietly suggests that taking it so hard only reifies racial categories. And the laughter with which Hurston surrounds Janie's reenactment of the mirror phase may also argue that a formulation like Lacan's is perhaps more melodramatic than accurate, taking too seriously the inevitable alienation and fragmentation of self, a form of self-pity based on a nostalgia for wholeness and control that may be a luxury of the male.

It is men who in Janie's story insist on speaking with a "big voice" and who refuse to admit and adjust to the fact that their will to "tell" entirely depends on someone else's—usually a woman's—consenting to "listen." Hurston knows there is nothing so revealing of a person as the way she talks. She also knows that an entire gender has been allowed and even encouraged to treat the scene of conversation as a form of argufying in which egos vie for dominance rather than for "understandin.'"

The men in Joe Starks's store behave as if a conversation is something one can *win*. They like "big arguments." But they mistake size and pseudo-seriousness for real exchange. "It must have been the way Joe spoke out without giving her a chance to say anything one way or another that took the bloom off of things." "You need tellin'," Joe says, and so Janie gradually learns "to hush." She has already joined the word "tellin'" with the word "understandin'" in order to invoke the kind of exchange productive of a good story. But Joe reduces the meaning of the verb "tell" to a simple command, as in "You sho loves to tell me whut to do." Joe never grasps the fact that the only kind of telling worth attempting is the kind willing to shift into listening. "Too busy listening tuh yo' own big voice," as Janie says of him, Joe is finally killed by Janie's back talk. "When you pull down yo' britches, you look lak de change uh life." In the face of this blast, all his meanings and vanity bleed away like a flood. The shock of the moment has less to do with the taunt—it's a good joke, not a great one—than with the sudden revelation of the force of Janie's anger and the fragility of Joe's pride.

When Janie interrupts the conversation about the mule, an animal Joe has bought so that he can set it free, Hambo says that she "put jus' de right words tuh our thoughts." But Joe, jealous of Janie's verbal entry into the male realm of words, bites down hard on his cigar and doesn't say a thing. And of course the mule's story is also Janie's: both have been forced to work without rest, and both (Janie senses that this is an allegory about emancipation) depend on a "Lincoln"-like figure to gain their rest. "You have tuh have power tuh free things," Janie concludes.

Janie answers the "big" male voice not only by grasping the point of its meandering conversation but by meeting its abstractions with the economy and force of concrete images. When Sam and Walter indulge in their Socratic dialogue about "nature" versus "caution," they become so caught up in digressions and one-upmanship that they have to ask themselves, "Well what *is* mah point?" Janie continually brings experience back to the particular. She has learned "to live," as she says, "by comparisons," as in "love is lak de sea. It's uh movin' thing." Her story proves worth listening to because she has taught her mind to work like a poet's. Of course, most of these images belong to Hurston and her third-person narrative voice. But they are assigned to Janie, summoned on her behalf, in a novel where the distinction between narrator and character proves generously indistinct.

The most famous of these images may be of Janie's pear tree:

> She was stretched on her back beneath the pear tree soaking in the alto chant of the visiting bees, the gold of the sun and the panting breath of the breeze when the inaudible voice of it all came to her. She saw a dust-bearing bee sink into the sanctum of a bloom; the thousand sister-calyxes arch to meet the love embrace and the ecstatic shiver of the tree from root to tiniest branch creaming in every blossom and frothing with delight. So this was a marriage! She had been summoned to behold a revelation. Then Janie felt a pain remorseless sweet that left her limp and languid.

If this is a marriage, it will take Janie three tries before she achieves such a state. And she will finally be left alone. Hurston unapologetically embraces Janie's search for sexual and emotional reciprocity, however short-lived. She does not denigrate man-woman love simply because it does not last. There is a gallantry to Hurston's imagination, a refusal to be cast down before the foreknowledge of inevitable erotic loss. Like the Walking Woman and the Woman at the Eighteen-Mile, Janie values her experiences precisely because there are so few of them. And, like those characters as well, what is left Janie, finally, of "heart-stretching, of enlargement and sustenance," as Mary Austin writes, is her story.

The image of the tree does more than connect the reader with the intensity of Janie's experience. It connects *Their Eyes Were Watching God* with the American literary tradition as it has played its variations on a foundational Western myth. A woman and a tree: what does this identification not call up but the Daphne story, the enduring legend about emotional aliveness and the defenses that protect it, even at the price of its own extinction? Henry Louis Gates points out that Hurston's Janie inverts the case of Walker's Celie, who decides to "make myself wood" rather than to submit any further to Mr._____'s humiliations. But the "ebony chain of discourse," as Gates styles it, also reaches back to Chesnutt, whose Po' Sandy says, out of a desire to hide and deaden himself like Celie, "I wisht I wuz a tree," or across the color line to Austin, to whom, in *Experiences Facing Death* (1931), "God happened to Mary under the walnut tree," and where she feels "herself in the bee and the bee in the flower and the flower in God." In Louise Glück's (b. 1943) "Mythic Fragment," the female child refuses the gift of sex offered by Apollo—which typically comes as a rape—and cries out to her father to save her, to trap her "in a tree forever." And of course there is Morrison's Sethe, with her "tree" on her back, the numb pattern of scars raised by a whipping she can still remember and yet which her dead skin can no longer feel.

In this great image of the tree, Janie refuses to "step aside." She identifies; she fuses. She feels an "ecstatic shiver." Hurston gives ecstasy its conventional meaning here, of sexual transport. It is a moment of "creaming" and "frothing." That's good; that's the marriage Janie will, on her third try, go on to find. In the novel's second big ecstatic moment, where Janie stands beside her husband in the storm, Hurston deepens our understanding of the word and reveals that ecstasy is the true cure for double consciousness, the unfallen version of it.

Ecstasy means, literally, "to stand beside." Ecstasy and double consciousness each involve a self standing beside itself. But with ecstasy as Hurston will finally represent it, the awareness takes the form of "true self-consciousness," to use Du Bois's phrase, rather than a painful and unreconciled striving. Thoreau, in his chapter on "Solitude," discovers ecstasy in a certain way of thinking rather than in the joining of two bodies:

> With thinking we may be beside ourselves in a sane sense. By a conscious effort
> of the mind we can stand aloof from actions and their consequences and all

things, good and bad, go by us like a torrent. We are not wholly involved in Nature . . . I only know myself as a human entity; the scene, so to speak, of thoughts and affections; and am sensible of a certain doubleness by which I can stand as remote from myself as from another. However intense my experience, I am conscious of the presence and criticism of a part of me, which, as it were, is not a part of me, but a spectator, sharing no experience, but taking note of it, and that is no more I than it is you.

While this may sound like a state of alienation or division, it is rather, as Stanley Cavell argues in *The Senses of Walden* (1972), one of "absolute awareness of self without embarrassment," the condition into which Janie is delivered when she finds that her story is done. Only a "spectator" who views the self as a "scene" is able to translate its "thoughts and affections" into a story. Cavell is careful to distinguish this way of being beside ourselves from ordinary self-consciousness:

> What *we* know as self-consciousness is only our opinion of ourselves, and like any other opinion it comes from outside; it is hearsay, our contribution to public opinion. We must become disobedient to it, resist it, no longer listen to it. We do that by keeping our senses still, listening another way, for something indescribably and unmistakably pleasant to all our senses. We are to reinterpret our sense of doubleness as a relation between ourselves in the aspect of the indweller, unconsciously building, and in the aspect of the spectator, impartially observing. Unity between these aspects is viewed not as a mutual absorption, but as a perpetual nextness, an act of neighboring or befriending.

What could be a better description of the state Janie achieves, as she pulls in the horizon around herself like a great fish net and calls in her soul to come and see?

In *Beloved*, Sixo calls the Thirty-Mile Woman "a friend of my mind." With Morrison, Hurston chooses to represent the self-befriending described by Thoreau as something that can be earned by going through the ecstasies of love. Love as Janie comes to have it is about being beside someone in a sane sense. The hurricane brings out a moment of verbal reckoning between Tea Cake and Janie, where they once again choose not to "stand aside," but *beside*:

> "Ah reckon you wish now you had of stayed in yo' big house 'way from such as dis, don't yuh?"
> "Naw."
> "Naw?"
> "Yeah, naw. People don't die till dey time come nohow, don't keer where you at. Ah'm wid mah husband in uh storm, dat's all."

Wid mah husband in uh storm. What does this not describe but Janie's and Tea Cake's joint and unending struggle against the corrosions of "double consciousness," their earning of a self-acceptance, through the love of the other, beyond anxiety or embarrassment? "Ah never *knowed* you wuz so satisfied wid me lak dat," Tea Cake responds, to Janie, as he drops to his knees and puts his head in her lap. Then the wind comes back with triple fury and blows out the light.

Of course, Janie will also be asked to stand beside Tea Cake in an *insane* sense: there is no overlooking the terrible violence he attempts to inflict on her at the end, a product of his rabies, surely, but also a violence that echoes backward through the two-way physical abuse that also punctuates Janie's relationship with him. Michael Awkward has taken the lead in emphasizing Tea Cake's "flaws," down to and including his wish to maintain a traditional division of labor in which Janie will wear whatever his money can buy. This is not a marriage of unmitigated ecstasy—but then, no one's is. Hurston's willingness to admit such flaws is a way of admitting that Janie's third marriage, in its best moments, is an image of possibility, a projection of one black woman's desire that such things might be so. It is in light of such hopes that I read the climactic scene in the novel as the final act in a romance, with the understanding that romance deals less with actualities than with the shape and strength of human desire.

And so the wind comes back with triple fury and blows out the light. Hurston then proceeds to deliver her title: "They seemed to be staring at the dark, but their eyes were watching God."

I have often pondered the meaning of this wonderful title and have been content to savor it as one of the resonant and irreducible enigmas, like a line from Bob Dylan. In the margin of my copy of the novel I find that I have written, "To watch God is to *have life*." Well, that sounds pretty good. Another thing to say, perhaps, is that the watching is directed outward, at God, at the third thing. This scene knows nothing of a gaze that looks at the self through the eyes of others. This gaze doesn't look at the self at all. After all the violence-inflected gazing that so determines black lives in Hurston, as well as in Toomer, what is delivered here is a gaze-filled, if temporary, rehabilitation of the visual. Janie and Tea Cake have been brought to an apprehension of "beauty," to use Thoreau again, which "has gradually grown from within outward, out of the necessities and character of the indweller, who is the only builder—out of some unconscious truthfulness, and no bleness, without ever a thought for the appearance." By consenting to work "long side" and to respond and listen to each other, they have uncovered, if only momentarily, the voice that is great within them, here blown back upon them as a storm of love.

CHAPTER SIX

The Rumor of Race

FAULKNER

*I*n making a comparison between Faulkner (1897–1962) and Hemingway, Robert Penn Warren (1905–89) also raises the issue, in any writer's work, of the career:

> I just mean that every man has only one story. He doesn't know what his story is, so he keeps on fiddling with the possibilities of that story. Every writer, no matter how trivial, and every writer, no matter how great, has only one tale; and the great writers have more versions of it. Shakespeare has more versions of it than Milton does . . . And Faulkner has more than Hemingway. But you have to assume the central story.

Whether or not one accepts Warren's rankings, the notion of a central story, repeatedly fiddled with, comports pretty well with my experience of reading Faulkner and Hemingway, an experience that turns upon the question of memory.

Faulkner is a patron of remembering; Hemingway, of forgetting. This is one reason why Faulkner's style includes so much and Hemingway's so little. Hemingway's approach to experience was to chase after it but not to carry it around. His prized moment is one filled with sensory pleasure and emptied of painful memory. Faulkner, who lived a much quieter life, allowed himself to be invaded by the burden of a familial, regional, and national past. His prized moment is one in which a character or narrator gathers the many versions of the past together and becomes compounded with them. The story that haunted them both, and produced such contrary reactions, was the history of their country.

Hemingway wrote about America as an expatriate or an outsider, even when he wrote about life up in Michigan. He became the first modern chronicler of the American imperium, of the extension of our power into the world of nations. In the wounds suffered by his characters he *anticipates* the cost of this expansion of the national will. Frederic Henry above Plava becomes Billy Pilgrim fifty years later, another innocent abroad wounded in a foreign war. Even the early stories set in the United States are suffused with a sense of elegy, of the already-lost and the impossibility of return. Nick's experience at Big Two-Hearted River proceeds from the assumption that the hero has lost the "good place" and will never again feel at home at home. The response to this loss is an elliptical style, one devoted to the technique of the thing left out and to a syntax that reproduces through rhythm a speaker's or character's central defense mechanisms, as well as to a general refusal to speak directly about the big feelings of the heart.

Faulkner places himself within a regional American myth and takes responsibility for its simultaneous construction and deconstruction. His work *recollects* the cost to Americans of a prior and unfinished war at home. Quentin Compson is Henry Sutpen fifty years earlier, wounded in a civil war. Faulkner deploys a recurring cast of characters, situates them in a specific landscape, and asks them to relive key moments in an epic of region building. The point of the reenactment is to demonstrate that the facts on the ground are irrecoverable and that the task of the artist or the Southern citizen is to provide an answerable version of the past while acknowledging its essential indeterminacy.

Hemingway usually knew what he was leaving out and devoted himself to making the reader sense, through indirect means, this knowledge. Faulkner's omissions work in an opposite fashion, as admissions of an honest and courageous ignorance. Why did Henry shoot Charles Bon? Faulkner truly doesn't know, and the possible answers are various enough and contradictory enough to generate vertigo rather than a filling in of the blanks. Hemingway writes an existential novel, one dedicated to the pleasures and anxieties of being and to a continual preparation for death. Faulkner writes an epistemological novel, one obsessed by the work of knowing and haunted by events that precede a storyteller's birth.

In a letter written in 1957, John Steinbeck maintained that "a novelist, perhaps unconsciously, identifies himself with one chief or central character in his novel. Into this character he puts not only what he thinks he is but what he hopes to be. We can call this spokesman the self-character." Both storyteller and story-taker, Quentin Compson acts as Faulkner's "self-character." Quentin appears in two of the greatest novels, *The Sound and the Fury* (1929) and *Absalom, Absalom!* (1936). Quentin was also the original narrator of the short story that grew into "The Bear" and then into *Go Down, Moses* (1942), where he was replaced by Isaac McCaslin. Each of these novels deals with the burden of being a son. And what these sons do is listen.

Quentin listens to his father, and to Rosa; Ike listens to the hunters and their "best of all talking"; Chick Mallison listens to Lucas Beauchamp and to Gavin Stevens. A relentless voice pours forth into an inevitable ear: narration typically preempts conversation. The test of a good listener is his ability to retell with a difference. Ike celebrates his majority by wresting the narrative of his life away from the third person: "then he was twenty-one. He could say it, himself." Development comes to be measured by the growing authority and autonomy of voice; a character has grown up when he has learned to resist being entrapped by the "rhetoric of re-tellings" into a mere repetition of the past.

Faulkner's first Yoknapatawpha novel, *Flags in the Dust*, opens with one old man shouting a memory at another. Old Falls tells the story of the gallant Colonel John Sartoris, Civil War hero, to his son Bayard. The opening phrase "As usual" makes it plain, in the *Sartoris* version of the novel, that this is a scene of habitual retelling. (*Flags* was first published as *Sartoris* in 1929 and appeared in its original and uncut version only in 1973.) In *Flags*, Bayard's irritated response to a question by Old Falls—"Do I have to tell you that every time you tell me this damn story?"—makes the same point. Bayard's frustration is that he has exchanged his father's life of deeds for one of received words. This rueful awareness becomes conscious in "An Odor of Verbena," a story Faulkner completed a year after publishing *Absalom*, in a scene where Bayard, here given a second chance by Faulkner and reimagined as a young man of twenty-four, kisses his stepmother Druscilla and as he does so thinks to himself, "those who can, do, those who cannot and suffer enough because they cant, write about it." Bayard will, consequently, go on to "do" something remarkable, to ride into town and walk across the square and up the stairs to face his father's killer unarmed, an act that avenges his father's murder and unmans the killer without resorting to the kind of "doing" that merely renews the cycle of revenge.

Only by coming to imagine a resolution in which symbolic action is able to stand in for literal doing was Faulkner able to write his way out of the anxiety driving the first half of his career, the fear that he is a Quentin figure who merely receives stories he cannot help repeating and the best of which—as in Henry Sutpen's case—he cannot hope to emulate. "*I have heard too much, I have been told too much; I have had to listen to too much.*" Quentin says this to himself, in chapter 6 of *Absalom*. This is the true Faulknerian cry of the heart, the protest of the younger and receiving generation against being asked, once more, to shoulder the unbearable burden of the past.

And yet only through narration can narration be conquered. When it comes to listening to stories, the Quentin in *Absalom* begins as a draftee and ends as a volunteer: not in the Civil War—the Great Missed Event—but in the ongoing guerilla struggle of family life, the outcome of which is determined by the control of information and how it gets dispensed. By evolving from reluctant listener to active teller, Quentin refigures the one-way transaction of the Faulknerian scene of instruction into an open-ended give-and-take. The irony of Quentin's achievement, accomplished with Shreve's help in the winter of 1910, is that he cannot profit from it; he will take his own life in the following spring. Quentin kills himself for many reasons, but one of them is the implicit comparison between himself and Henry

Sutpen that develops out of his retelling of the Sutpen family story. Quentin's loss proves, however, the reader's gain, as the generosity, imaginative reach, and sheer courage Quentin displays, in probing deeper into a story that will make him feel even worse about his own, provide a model of how to become a capable auditor and therefore an empowered legatee of our national past.

In *The Sound and the Fury* Mr. Compson makes a distinction between the meaning of the word "was" and the meaning of the word "again." "Again. Sadder than was. Again. Saddest of all. Again." Not that things have happened and are over but that they are repeated—this is the source of human sadness. Faulkner loves the prefix "re-," the one that signals the "again." "*Maybe nothing ever happens once and is finished*," Quentin thinks to himself, in chapter 7 of *Absalom*. He is not happy in the thought. For what he discovers in the retellings of the novel is his status as a belated and failed copy of Henry Sutpen, the son and brother who, also caught up in an incestuous triangle with his sister, succeeds in punishing the "brother seducer," as John T. Irwin calls him, and thereby becomes the "brother avenger" Quentin cannot succeed in being for his beloved sister Candace.

Action in *Absalom* happens as a response to an insult, where the deepest and most abiding insult is being "born too late." At the core of the book is the insult suffered by Sutpen, at fourteen, when he approaches the big house and is turned away at the front door by the black face and told to go around to the back. Sutpen conceives his design as a response to this moment. Faulkner gives us the reaction before the cause; we are introduced to Sutpen and his design in the novel's second paragraph but do not come upon the insult until we are well into chapter 7. Faulkner repeats this strategy of "*deliberately withheld meaning*," as Conrad Aiken calls it, with the other insults in the book. In the opening scene we are made aware that Rosa is in a rage of "impotent yet indomitable frustration" over something Sutpen did long ago, but we are not given any mention of his "*bald outrageous words*" until page 139, and then, ten pages later, the notion that Sutpen and Rosa might breed "like a couple of dogs" comes as a paraphrase by way of Shreve. We learn on page 199 that Sutpen's first wife Eulalia did not prove "incremental to the design" and so he therefore "put her aside." But we do not learn about her "Spanish" blood until page 208, and even then the claim retains only the authority of surmise, one meant to stand in for the assumption that Eulalia is in fact part "negro." This strategy of putting a reaction before a cause requires a reader to remain in a state of unknowing. "But why?" Quentin asks, five pages in. As we read on, the "But why?" moments only multiply.

Because the black man at the front door insults Sutpen, Sutpen will insult Eulalia Bon, and Ellen Coldfield will be insulted by the citizens of Jefferson on her wedding day, and Charles will be turned away by Sutpen, and Sutpen will insult

Rosa, and because Rosa then heads for town Sutpen will insult Wash Jones, and because Wash Jones feels insulted he will cut down Sutpen with a scythe. So the closed feedback loop of insults snaps shut. The ultimate insult is framed as a question by Rosa very early on, and it is also the biggest question the novel will address: "*why God let us lose the War.*"

Faulkner's great gift to his country was to uncover the effect of slavery on the white heart and mind. He came to understand the Civil War as Lincoln did, in the Second Inaugural Address: "If we shall suppose that American Slavery is one of those offences which, in the providence of God, must needs come, but which, having continued through His appointed time, He now wills to remove, and that He gives to both North and South, this terrible war, as the woe due to those by whom the offence came, shall we discern therein any departure from those divine attributes which the believers in a Living God always ascribe to him?" Lincoln here argues that the war is something God "gives" the nation, and that it has been given to both North and South. It is an earned consequence; it is "the woe due" to us.

But Lincoln doesn't so much argue as suggest, or suspend. The entire set of claims is embedded in an "If . . . then" construction, and in a sentence ending with an overwhelming question, perhaps the most desperate rhetorical question generated by the war. The sentence asks us to "suppose," to surmise that slavery is an offence somehow within the providence of God to bestow, something he allows to "come." But what the Lord giveth, he has now willed to take away. Unless we can make sense of this war, which leaves neither side free from pain and complicity and an uneasy truce, we may be required to conclude that God is in a state of "departure" from himself and that the seat of providence is now vacant.

Faulkner was the author who had the gumption to take up Lincoln's question—not in order to justify the ways of God to man, but in order to free his countrymen from unusable pasts. Only through the form and experience of a novel in which questions are raised but not readily answered would it be possible, he knew, to penetrate the tangle of psychosexual, political, and economic anxieties and interests that "American Slavery" and its legacy had become. Earlier in the Second Inaugural Address, Lincoln had described slavery as a "peculiar and powerful interest" and had maintained that "all knew that this interest was, somehow, the cause of the war." The words "all knew" argue that there is a knowledge of the war we all possess, while the word "somehow" admits the causality to be so complex that this knowledge may never achieve full realization. The nation had to wait seventy-one years—from 1865 to 1936, the year in which *Absalom* was published—for Lincoln's sentence to receive an adequate explication. How slavery was "somehow" the cause of the war, and how the peculiar and powerful conventions that comprise race in

America continued to play themselves out, through and beyond his lifetime, was the most urgent question Faulkner ever took up.

Faulkner saw his beloved South as a region that had failed to recover from an insult. It had failed to recover because it had reacted to the insult as Sutpen did to his insult—by repeating it. The Jim Crow laws were perhaps the most obvious evidence of this. The emotional and intellectual work Faulkner did in writing the novels that led up to *Absalom* allowed him to see that the war could not be refought. It could only be understood and, in some sense, forgiven. And this, in turn, became a work of acknowledgment—not of the woe done *to* oneself, by others, an endless and finally useless question, but of the woe done *by* oneself, a woe inflicted by the self-regarding emotion of guilt and the other-regarding emotion of rage.

The great drama in Faulkner's career is his replacement of a myth of repetition with a myth of forgiveness. Each myth deals with the way stories end. Revenge requires that endings get repeated, that there is no end to them. Forgiveness allows that endings can be revised. Through figures like Bayard Sartoris in "An Odor of Verbena," Faulkner tried to model on the level of the individual's story a way in which the South, and the North, might move from repetition to forgiveness. This process was not a matter of repaying a debt; there can be no literal reparation for a harm this deep, and reparation is in any case a sort of watered-down revenge. It was to be a matter of acknowledgment, or "overpassing," to use the word supplied in chapter 8 of *Absalom, Absalom!* That acknowledgment depended, in turn, on a full understanding of how slavery was "somehow" the cause of the war, and of how both sides had profited from and therefore allowed the offence to play itself out.

The way we come to this knowledge has as much value as the knowledge itself. Faulkner's decision to deliberately withhold (the phrase "deliberately withheld" actually appears in a speech by Sutpen in chapter 7) continually reminds the reader that meaning is a function of the sequence in which knowledge is delivered. Encouraged to supply answers to the novel's many "But why?" moments, the reader learns to speculate on the basis of partial knowledge and to accept that certainty is not available. As if to signal this distinction, Faulkner enjambs the words "certainty" and "knowledge" in a sentence about Judith in chapter 4, where the relevant part of the sentence compares her kind of waiting for news to the way other Southern women wait: "none to ask her about brother and sweetheart while they talked among themselves of sons and brothers and husbands with tears and grief perhaps but at least with certainty, knowledge." The comma positions the second noun as appositive to the first. It's an ironic marker, since the novel works against any casual parallel between the two words.

The biggest "But why?" of the novel has to do with the act that destroys Sutpen's design. Why does Henry shoot Charles? This is above all what a reader wants to *know.* A series of lesser questions, some posed as early as the first page, lead up to the asking of this big one. Since, as Robert Frost (1874–1963) says, "the best way out is always through," we might as well begin where Faulkner asks us to begin, in order to remind ourselves of how we come to ask the big questions.

The opening sentence is a long one:

> From a little after two oclock until almost sundown of the long still hot weary dead September afternoon they sat in what Miss Coldfield still called the office because her father had called it that—a dim hot airless room with the blinds all closed and fastened for forty-three summers because when she was a girl some- one had believed that light and moving air carried heat and that dark was always cooler, and which (as the sun shone fuller and fuller on that side of the house) became latticed with yellow slashes full of dust motes which Quentin thought of as being flecks of the dead old dried paint itself blown inward from the scaling blinds as wind might have blown them.

Hemingway wanted to write "one true sentence." He defined this sort of sentence as "declarative." The sentence was to be, above all, short: the average sentence length in "Big Two-Hearted River" is twelve words. The simplicity of the sentence is meant to belie the complexity of the forces it seeks to express and contain. What is omitted from the sentence is often the better part of its meaning.

Hemingway's sentence stops short; Faulkner's sentence runs on. There are vir- tually no personal memories in Hemingway's early novels, whereas Faulkner's style is ruminative, meant to mimic the sense that in thinking back on the past relations stop nowhere and that putting a period to a thought is premature.

Absalom's opening sentence starts with time. In *The Sound and the Fury* Mr. Compson had already told Quentin that "time is your misfortune," and Quentin "kills time" tearing the hands from a watch. Quentin and Henry and Charles and Sutpen are all linked in their desire to take revenge against this misfortune. Yet as precise as the opening sentence is about numbers—"two oclock" and "forty-three summers"—we are given no information about when this story's calendar starts.

"Because her father had called it that": like the neighbor in Frost's "Mending Wall," Rosa is a narrator who "will not go behind" her "father's saying." She remains stuck in what an authority calls something. To her own cost she keeps her room "airless" because of what "someone had believed" about heat and cool. Rosa lives inside an ideology, a set of beliefs that govern her without being questioned or even known. This is her "innocence," a trait she shares with Sutpen. Rosa comes closest to losing her innocence in the scene with Clytie on the stairs, in chapter 5, where the woman with the "*coffee-colored face*" reaches out to stop her from going up- stairs "to find" Charles Bon's murdered body. Touch—the ineradicable truth of bodies—threatens to topple Rosa's "*furious immobility*" and to break through the "*eggshell shibboleth of caste and color too.*" The likening of an ideological shibboleth to the fragility of an "eggshell" is a clear echo of *Hamlet*, where the prince marvels that armies stoked by nationalism will fight over "a little patch of ground / That hath in it no profit but the name"—that men will fight and die for a fantasy, or "even for an eggshell." Faulkner, like Shakespeare, distinguishes between characters who break through this eggshell and those who don't, and the token of liberation is to modulate one's voice and to revise one's story.

But the eggshell reference is also an echo forward toward Ralph Ellison (1914–94), who adopts the metaphor in the passage from *Shadow and Act* quoted in the "To the Reader" section at the beginning of my book. When Chick Mallison falls into the ice-coated creek on Lucas Beauchamp's farm, he finds himself, according to Ellison and in language that cannot be found in *Intruder in the Dust*, looking upward through ice that is "white, brittle and eggshell-thin." The eggshell metaphor here is Ellison's invention, his riff on Faulkner. The logic of the metaphor argues that Chick is being invited, as if from below, to look through and suddenly to discover the flimsiness and the thinness of the white, Southern ideology. Its shibboleths—its assumed, repeatable, unquestioned "truths"—are of no more strength and substance than an eggshell. And yet an eggshell is also, of course, very tough and resistant to breakage; it is hard to crush an egg by squeezing one's hand around it. No, the way to break through an eggshell is to pierce it, or to cut it, as Clytie's touch threatens to pierce through Rosa's stubbornly held mental and physical virginity. "*There is something in the touch of flesh with flesh,*" Faulkner writes, "*which abrogates, cuts sharp and straight across the devious intricate channels of decorous ordering.*" To "abrogate" means to repeal a law. Clytie herself stands for the abrogation of the nation's antimiscegenation laws; she is the daughter of a white man and a black slave, hence the repeated emphasis on the telltale signifier of blended color, Clytie's "*coffee-colored face.*" Yet even Clytie is subsumed by the shibboleths about color. When Rosa refers to Clytie as an "*instrument,*" she gets at the irony of her behavior in the scene, which is to act on behalf of Sutpen's design and to protect its secrets. Yet her touch also allows Rosa, momentarily at least, to see through the design and the shibboleths on which it is founded. What touch here threatens to do is what, in America, it has always done, which is to produce coffee-colored bodies like Clytie's, to reveal the power of human will and desire to repeal all laws enacted to contain them, especially along the color line.

The novel opens with a closed room. *Absalom* deals with how the spaces people build become traps from which they cannot escape: Sutpen will be crushed by his design and the house that embodies it. The action of the story often takes place in liminal spaces: doorways, stables, attics, Wash Jones's rotting porch, the mansion's front gate. History happens in the margins, Faulkner will reveal, away from the official and triumphal spaces, often out of sight. Containers are made in order to be shattered, even as the room in which Quentin here finds himself slowly deliquesces under the pressure—the blinds are closed and fastened—of an imaginary wind.

Striking above all about this opening sentence is its sheer size. Faulkner's syntax expresses a will to comprehend, to interconnect, to include. The piling up of adjectives in unpunctuated series argues for modification as a potentially infinite process. Faulkner's frequent reliance on the parenthesis operates as a rhythmic device, certainly, one that asks us to hold—or that permits us to catch—our breath. But the parenthesis also acts as a moral force, a syntactic reminder that qualifications are often called for, that categories bleed into each other, and that more can and almost always should be said.

In the paragraph that his sentence begins we also learn that this will be a novel of "telling" and "listening," that Miss Coldfield has brought Quentin to this airless room in order to make him the auditor of her story. We trip quickly over the novel's first "re-" word, recapitulation. So this is a story that has been told before. Then Sutpen bursts into view: "Out of quiet thunderclap he would abrupt (man-horse-demon) upon a scene peaceful and decorous as a schoolprize water color." The hero is delivered in the form of a tableau. Then Faulkner sets the "immobile" crew in motion, and they are seen to "overrun suddenly the one hundred square miles." This is the first of those moments of "furious immobility" that capture the will to achieve an identity free from and beyond the only medium—time—through which any identity can ever be worked out.

While beginnings deserve special scrutiny, to proceed at the pace I have set here would be to write a book about *Absalom* longer than the novel itself. Two more features of chapter 1 do, however, require glossing. The first has to do with narrative suspense. Faulkner apparently has little interest in it, since he gives away his climax only four pages in, during the meandering sentence in which Quentin questions why Rosa has chosen him as her scribe and that also casually mentions the fact that her nephew "shot the fiance to death before the gates to the house." So Henry will shoot Charles. The "What happened?" interests Faulkner far less than the "But why?" behind it; the word "why" can be found six times on pages 8 and 9 alone. By so readily summarizing the plot to come, Faulkner begins to direct attention away from action and toward the motives sending it up.

Finally, we come to the wrestling scene with which the chapter ends. Ellen runs down to the stable to find "her husband and the father of her children standing there naked and panting and bloody to the waist and the negro just fallen evidently, lying at his feet and bloody too." Henry clings to her and vomits, while Judith and Clytie look on from the loft.

Sutpen's revenge is based on getting back at a black face, and an entire social order, that turned him away from a front door. But here, over twenty years after the insult, Sutpen reveals himself as sublimely careless about maintaining the distinctions central to his design. Race and class differences collapse completely in the wrestling scene, however much Sutpen remains the one standing. In an uncanny recapitulation of his fathering of Charles Bon, Sutpen again produces a black body covered in blood. It's a little like "Indian Camp," where looking upon a confusion of realms and roles also sickens a son.

This is the novel's first great scene of touch. There aren't many of them, only three more really: the two between Rosa and Clytie at the bottom of the stairs, and the scene where Wash Jones says "*I'm going to tech you, Kernel.*" "*But let flesh touch with flesh,*" Rosa allows, "*and watch the fall of all the eggshell shibboleth of caste and color too.*" Above all, Charles wants the "physical touch" of his father's "flesh." Flesh "*abrogates,*" and the anger or desire that moves one body toward another undercuts all social orders and designs, even to the point of producing children, like Charles, who not only embody the contradictions of those social orders and designs but will bring them crashing down. Henry vomits because he has a vested interest in the hierarchy his father here so casually disregards, while Judith and Clytie look on wide-eyed because in some way they already know that as women in the South, of whatever color, they can never be, in the phrase Sutpen applies to Eulalia, "adjunctive or incremental" to the lust for patrimony that drives the "design."

Sutpen here betrays a remarkable naïveté about the decorum any successful outcome of his project would require. As Mr. Compson will go on to say, "His trouble was innocence." "Innocence" is Faulkner's greatest one-word gift to us, a word on which he confers a desperately important meaning. Repeated seventeen times in chapter 7, the word tolls like a bell through Quentin's account, acquiring with each sounding out of its syllables an increasingly sinister force.

"His trouble was innocence," Quentin says of Sutpen, in reference to his response to the insult at the front door. "Innocence" may seem an odd choice. Why not simply say "ignorance"? Because ignorance is simply a state of not knowing, while innocence, as Faulkner will go on to show and as Chang-rae Lee so eloquently puts it in *A Gesture Life*, is "wanting not to know what I know." Innocence is a smug or a proud or at best a willful not-knowing, a turning away from the possibilities and the work of knowing always being offered the self in preference for a self-protective state of bad faith. The implied opposite of "innocence," as Faulkner and Lee deploy the term, is not "guilt" but "knowledge." Innocence is not the legal status of being "not guilty," but rather the moral and epistemological condition of actively not wanting to know what we know.

How do I know this? By reasoning out the implications of the wrestling scene, surely, or the touching scene with Rosa and Clytie, but above all by considering Sutpen's reaction to the insult at the front door. Faced with the turning away at the door, Sutpen has two options: he can react as he does, in shame and anger, or he can analyze what has happened, try to understand it. His not doing this—his responding with "innocence" rather than with curiosity or empathy—is offered up by Faulkner as one of the reasons why God let the South lose the Civil War.

The Civil War was fightable because the planter class that owned the big houses and the slaves to support them was able to mobilize the energies of poorer white men with little vested interest in the class of life that slave labor made possible. As early as Bacon's Rebellion, large landowners had recognized that their survival depended on driving a wedge between the white and the black labor pools in the South. In 1676, Nathaniel Bacon led a militia of poor whites and blacks against the Indian tribes along the Virginia frontier. When the Governor of Virginia accused Bacon of treason—largely out of fear of Bacon's armed and "Rabble Crew"—Bacon marched his force on Jamestown and burned it to the ground. The rebellion was eventually put down, but not before raising the specter of "English and Negroes in Armes." The General Assembly decided to conquer by dividing. Once the rebellion ended, the white rebels were pardoned, but the black rebels, freemen or indentured servants, were not. Virginia quickly began to pass laws that worked against any solidarity between black and white, including a measure in 1691 that prohibited the "abominable mixture and spurious issue" of black-white unions. The child of a white mother and a black man would be consigned to servitude for thirty years. A century later, when the Revolution came, every white man who fought for Virginia was promised in return a "sound Negro" slave.

Racism and the comfort it offered to otherwise underfunded white egos was used, then, from the 1670s on, as a distraction from the oppressive realities of the class system, one that trapped most white men in a feudal economy in which little mobility was possible. (Even during the decade in which Faulkner wrote his novel, it was clear that the order of the New South disenfranchised poor whites as well as blacks, since during the Depression voter turnout in states like Virginia and Mississippi hovered at 20%.) It is no accident that as Sutpen and his family migrate out of the Appalachians and down into the Tidewater, the word "nigger" begins to infiltrate Quentin's narrative. For the first time in his life, Sutpen finds himself in a world with other than white bodies. At first, Sutpen seems to be getting it: "He had learned the difference not only between white men and black ones, but he was learning that there was a difference between white men and white men." The first kind of learning has to do with race; the second, with class. Sutpen's innocence consists in his allowing race to trump class in his personal story just as it has and will continue to do so in the history of his region.

"How it was the nigger told him," Quentin puts it, "even before he had had time to say what he came for, never to come to that front door again but to go around to the back." There it is, the insult. So what does Sutpen do? He decides not to analyze, but to repeat. He concludes that "to combat them you have got to have what they have that made them do what he did. You got to have land and niggers and a fine house to combat them with." In this way, the reproduction of class occurs. By reacting in this way to the insult that is class, our great novels show us, from *Sister Carrie* (1900) to *The Bonfire of the Vanities* (1987), that Americans continue to sell their souls.

Sutpen decides to deal with the insult not by breaking the chain of insult that is culture or by revising the conditions that make insults possible but by putting himself in a position to be able to inflict one. And so he will get his repetition. The "nigger" will again appear—and this time as a body that Sutpen has fathered—at a front door. He, too, will be turned away. And the repetition of the insult will destroy the design.

This is the logic of Sutpen's story, a story not unlike Gatsby's. Both Gatsby and Sutpen refuse to believe in the irrevocability of experience. Both believe, as Gatsby says, that you can "repeat the past." This involves returning "to a certain starting place" and beginning again as if the interval between then and now had never occurred. For Gatsby, the starting place is Daisy; for Sutpen, it's the mansion door. Faulkner shows that by persisting in his innocence, Sutpen brings about an endless chain of insults that results in the utter destruction of the very "interests," to use Lincoln's word, he sets out to preserve. This is what American innocence does, and is kept in place in order to do, because "innocence" is, after all, Faulkner's word for ideology, where the essential assumption of the American ideology is that we do not have one. We are . . . innocent.

Sutpen's alternative was to leave that front door and to begin to think and to make connections and to see that he and the black face at the front door were in a similar place. That the poor whites tumbling out of the mountain valleys were oppressed in ingenious if not in equal ways, and that the spurious and innocent sense of superiority a racialist discourse conferred on those poor whites was a sop thrown to them by the powers-that-be in order to reconcile them to that place. That the closer enemy was not the abolitionists up North but the men who controlled money and power and discourse in the South, and that the real War of Rebellion ought to have been fought against them, if a war was what was wanted. And that these two faces, on either side of that front door, could not and did not join forces to create a new social order in which no man's labor could be owned by another man and in which every man's labor was fairly compensated is one of the reasons, Faulkner understands, why God let the South lose the war.

When it comes to answering such urgent historical questions, Faulkner knows that only patience and rereading are of any use ("you re-read, tedious and intent," Mr. Compson says, about his effort to grasp the Sutpen story), and that this is a collective work that never ends. Yet he also shares with Sutpen a rage for summary in a moment of "furious immobility." Early on in *Absalom*, Faulkner acknowledges the teller's and the tale's desire to be fulfilled in a single instant:

> It (the talking, the telling) seemed (to him, to Quentin) to partake of that logic-and reason-flouting quality of a dream which the sleeper knows must have oc-curred, stillborn and complete, in a second, yet the very quality upon which it must depend to move the dreamer (verisimilitude) to credulity—horror or plea-sure or amazement—depends as completely upon a formal recognition of and acceptance of elapsed and yet-elapsing time as music or a printed tale.

Faulkner asks his reader to make way between two imperatives: the desire for expla-nation or the "complete," and the acceptance that we can only be moved to feel and therefore to understand by having to proceed through an open-ended and "yet-elapsing" temporal sequence, even a sequence as deferring and complex as the se-quence of *Absalom, Absalom!* Literature knows that we can only be moved in time, however much we may wish to be delivered from it. And we are moved in and by time because as time passes and we pass through it, it passes utterly, forever, once and for all. We cannot repeat the past, not in the way Gatsby thinks we can. We can only reimagine it. And we do so not in order to change the past—it cannot be changed—but to alter our attitudes toward it, so as to gain a more abundant life.

So why does Henry shoot Charles Bon? In answer to this question, the novel offers three conjectures. As always in Faulkner, the order and the timing of the conjectures supply the better part of their meaning.

The first is that Charles is already married, and therefore marriage to Henry's sister Judith would be bigamy. This conjecture surfaces early on, at the beginning of chapter 4, where Mr. Compson asserts that "Henry loved Bon" and repudiated his birthright for a "man who was at least an intending bigamist." Mr. Compson speculates that Henry was told about Bon's marriage to the octoroon during the Christmas of 1860. Bigamy would seem to more than explain the case. But given that Henry waits until 1865 to shoot Charles, it apparently doesn't do the trick. So Mr. Compson provides an explanation for the delay: Henry places Charles on "probation" in hopes that he will dissolve his existing marriage and only shoots him, as Mr. Compson continues to believe, when he fails to do so.

The second motive surfaces three-quarters of the way into the novel, at the be-ginning of chapter 8. Here Sutpen tells Henry "they cannot marry because he is your brother." This speculation comes to us by way of Shreve and is meant to refigure the exchange between Sutpen and Henry during the Christmas of 1860. Shreve and Quentin, who assume the burden of narration in chapter 5, have come to doubt the persuasiveness of Mr. Compson's bigamy theory, in part because of Henry's five-year delay, and so replace it with a much more powerful inducement to action, with the threat of incest.

Faulkner wants to show, however, given the psychosexual and sociopolitical order in which Henry has been raised, that not even incest will suffice to motivate the killing of a figure about whom so many ambivalences swirl. Shreve and Quentin soon see that the incest theory does not hold up; it doesn't hold up, first of all, because Henry rejects it as a "lie," and then, when he discovers it not to be a lie, he is still willing to say "I don't believe it." Henry loves Bon, feels for him in all the complex ways in which a younger sibling is drawn to an older, a country boy to a city man, and a brother of the bride to a prospective brother-in-law who, if he has to imagine the man who has "seen and touched parts" of the sister's body "he will never see and touch," is somehow able to say to Bon, "I want that man to be you." Long before any narrator even contemplates that Henry and Bon might be brothers, Mr. Compson speculates that, for Henry, the most effective protection of Judith's "virginity" would be to allow Bon to marry Judith and so to achieve, his identification with Bon being that profound, "the pure and perfect incest: the brother realising that the sister's virginity must be destroyed in order to have existed at all, taking that virginity in the person of the brother-in-law, the man whom he would be if he could become." On this theory, Bon's marrying Judith allows Henry to keep them both; long before Bon's literal kinship with Henry and Judith is suspected, the narrative has contemplated a drive toward fusion in Henry in comparison with which the mere fact of literal incest will prove a trifle.

And it does prove to be, because after being told that Charles is his older brother, Henry still does not act. He does not act in part because the Civil War interrupts his conversation with Charles and in part because now, since they are both soldiers, "maybe the war," Henry thinks, "would settle it."

Thus, Shreve and Quentin find themselves compelled to conjecture a third and final motive. It is because Henry takes no action and refuses Charles's offer to let him shoot him in the back, and because he keeps asking Charles "Don't you know yet what you are going to do?" and because he still does nothing as the Federal picket lines grow more numerous and encircling around the dwindling Confederate army—Henry even suffers Charles to carry him back, when he is wounded, from Pittsburg Landing—that Quentin and Shreve feel compelled to make this move. And so, near the end of chapter 8, some twenty pages from the novel's closing scene, they come up with their answer: Sutpen summons Henry to his tent in Carolina and tells Henry that Bon's *"mother was part negro."*

And that's it. That's what it takes. After hearing this, Henry will ride side by side with Bon right up to the gate of Sutpen's Hundred and then shoot him dead. *Miscegenation trumps incest.* This is what Faulkner has come to tell us.

Miscegenation and incest are old and pervasive themes in American literature; there is nothing new in locating them at the heart of our secret histories. But Faulkner does something entirely new with these themes, while also revealing that a reader's experience of the form of his complex and difficult novel is the key to understanding its urgent meanings.

There is, of course, something terribly counterintuitive and downright wrong about the order in which these three conjectures enter the narrative, not to speak of the relative importance Henry assigns to each. Any one of the conjectures could prove sufficient grounds for what Henry finally chooses to do. But surely the only sensible sequencing of motives, in ascending order of force, would be as follows: Bigamy—Miscegenation—Incest. Or even: Miscegenation—Bigamy—Incest. But to produce miscegenation as the trump card, the motive overriding a resistance in Henry that cannot be overridden even by the fear of transgressing the deepest and most universal human taboo—well, this is another of Faulkner's gifts to us, his exposure of the utter absurdity and fratricidal logic of a social order that allows a mere rumor (we are never certain that Charles is, in fact, black, and race is always and everywhere, as Faulkner and Chesnutt and all the rest have come to show us, itself a complicated whispering campaign) to determine who we will be allowed to love, an order even willing to countenance incest before it will permit a "*nigger,*" as Charles says, "*to sleep with your sister.*"

This is all more than enough to ask for, worth the price of admission. But of course it's the *way* Faulkner ushers us into and through these recognitions that gives them their overpassing force. To separate out the content of Faulkner's vision from its impelling form may be a requirement of literary criticism, but it is not a separation that need occur in the reader's experience. A significant portion of that experience consists in simply waiting for the three motives to be produced and in recognizing the absurdity of that sequence. This we have already done. Another part—perhaps the better part—of the experience Faulkner's novel offers us has to do with cocreation. By way of Quentin and Shreve, Faulkner invites us not simply to recognize Henry's motives, but to provide them.

By the time we get to chapter 8, we have learned to speculate. We have learned that the talking of the four narrators, so full of guesses and gaps in knowledge, assumes a reader willing to entertain surmise and to remain in uncertainties, without any irritable reaching after fact and reason. Of course, we also long for facts and reasons; no one is capable of remaining forever in negative capability. But we come to learn that facts don't explain much, that knowledge is always provisional, and that explanations only beget more if not better explanations. In chapter 8 we are called to a further task, which is to recognize our own complicity in the making of the offered outcome. Faulkner accomplishes this recognition through the metaphor of compounding.

The great scene of compounding begins on page 289, as Quentin and Shreve together contemplate their final imagining of what happened between Henry and Charles. Donald Kartiganer judges this scene "the great imaginative leap of the novel," one set up by Faulkner in two earlier passages. In the first, Quentin and Shreve achieve a moment in which their voices become indistinguishable: "It might have been either of them and was in a sense both: both thinking as one, the voice which happened to be speaking the thought only the thinking become audible." Here Faulkner talks about a moment of cocreation, but he does not enact it. Then, a little more than twenty pages later, he gives us this:

> Shreve ceased. That is, for all the two of them, Shreve and Quentin, knew he had stopped, since for all the two of them knew he had never begun, since it did not matter (and possibly neither of them conscious of the distinction) which one had been doing the talking. So that now it was not two but four of them riding the two horses through the dark over the frozen December ruts on that Christmas eve: four of them and then just two—Charles-Shreve and Quentin-Henry, the two of them both believing that Henry was thinking *He* (meaning his father) *has destroyed us all.*

In this passage, Faulkner makes a second and more effective try at the compounding he seeks. Quentin and Shreve once again lose a consciousness of a distinction between their voices. The speaker-listener hierarchy happily breaks down. Moreover, they join with their subjects, with the characters of whom they speak. Faulkner argues here that "four" become "two," and that's good. But the two hyphens that connect "Charles-Shreve" and "Quentin-Henry"—visually at least—also divide them. And the pairing off is too neat, too symmetrical, with outsiders grouped against insiders. While this passage moves much closer to the moment Faulkner will produce, it still registers as more about compounding than of it.

Faulkner identifies his final compounding passage as another try by repeating the verb "ceased." Here is the moment:

> He ceased again. It was just as well, since he had no listener. Perhaps he was aware of it. Then suddenly he had no talker either, though possibly he was not aware of this. Because now neither of them was there. They were both in Carolina and the time was forty-six years ago, and it was not even four now but compounded still further, since now both of them were Henry Sutpen and both of

them were Bon, compounded each of both yet either neither, smelling the very smoke which had blown and faded away forty-six years ago from the *bivouac fires burning in a pine grove, the gaunt and ragged men sitting or lying about them . . .*

As the passage moves from plain text to italics, it moves from the moment of compounding in 1910 into the surmise being constructed about what happened in 1865. The italics signal a shift away from the present or the factual and into the past and the imagined. The italicized passage will continue for six pages. In it, Henry is summoned to Sutpen's tent, is told that Bon's mother is part Negro, and then returns to the fire and to Charles, who says to Henry, "*So it's the miscegenation, not the incest, which you cant bear.*" Charles says this to Henry before Henry says anything of substance to him; he knows this truth without needing to hear it articulated and takes upon himself the burden of voicing it, even at his own cost.

In this scene, both "listener" and "talker" cease to exist as the power relation involved in any scene of rendition and audition gives way to a space and a time in which empathetic imagining is possible. Quentin and Shreve have earned this condition, one that allows them to experience "the join," as Toni Morrison calls it. They "both" become Henry and "both" become Bon. This compounding is the result of an empathy so great that it can go on to produce, in the italicized pages that follow, an answer to the "But why?" of the novel that not only resolves the reader's uncertainties but provides a message of supreme national importance.

I use the word empathy because Faulkner here dramatizes his conviction that the purpose of writing and reading is to achieve a *feeling with*. The opposite of identification (the undergraduate sentiment "I can relate to that"), empathy acknowledges that feeling "with" always occurs across a gap of otherness and can occur only because such a gap exists. Quentin and Shreve can imagine the beautiful and terrifying scene they produce because they have worked so hard to understand Henry and Charles—especially Charles. I would urge my reader to reread chapter 8 and will promise you that what you will be struck by is the extreme tenderness and solicitude mustered in it for Charles. "Think of his heart then," Shreve says to Quentin, as he urges him to feel what the spurned son must have felt as he entered Sutpen's house for the first time and waited, in a waiting that would prove endless, for the slightest sign of acknowledgment from his father's hand.

The compounding achieved has little to do with Quentin and Shreve being "like" Henry and Charles, although in many ways they surely are alike. It is a matter of recognizing that in the creation of any story there is a responsibility to imagine with generosity and courage, emotions that here carry us far beyond the bigamy-incest surmises and toward a conjecture that is extreme but that also feels emotionally and politically right. Quentin and Shreve keep talking and listening until they find a way to come upon the central fact—a fact here revealed in all its absurd and paltry and yet uncanny force—that let the South lose the war. Henry will finally shoot Charles because he is black. Step by step, the narrators create a story in which an American "innocence" founded on a cruel and casual racism is revealed not only as unknowing but as murderous and, finally, suicidal.

The reader here is the fifth rider. Implicit in the compounding of narrator with character is the compounding of reader with text. The logic of the metaphor is all about moving from passive reception to active participation. And what the reader is invited to do is to feel the feelings and to arrive at the insights I have already outlined.

This activity is what Faulkner means by "overpassing to love." Truth in fiction, as in life, is something we collectively make, and this compounding of voices and imaginations deserves—along with what happens in the happy bedroom—to be called an act of love. What Quentin and Shreve and the empathetic reader come up with may not be true, and that's the point. Instead, in Rosa's phrase, they create "*a might-have-been which is more true than truth*." Wallace Stevens would call it a fiction. A fiction is something made that we consent to believe in, a story that helps us to make sense of the world and that is answerable to the depth of our need and to the capacity of our feelings. Those who consent to believe in a fiction "stick to the nicer knowledge of / Belief, that what it believes in is not true." In the kind of fiction Faulkner writes, answers to questions like "Why does Henry shoot Charles?" remain dependent on the ever-expanding state of the reader's knowledge. Reading becomes an experience of constructing an answer, not arriving at one. The answer is tangled up in stories tangled in history, and the form most answerable to those tangles is that of the novel itself. The "truth," as Sethe calls it, may be "simple," but the approach to it is necessarily slant.

In chapter 8 of *Absalom, Absalom!* Charles Bon does not receive the "acknowledgment" he seeks. For him, it is a failed scene of recognition. He is even asked to speak the self-annihilating words: "*So it's the miscegenation, not the incest, which you cant bear.*" Quentin and Shreve imagine these words in Charles's mouth because the machinery of race depends on having its victims spell out their own doom, internalize the oppressor. Charles imparts this knowledge at great cost to himself and to the considerable benefit of the reader. For that reader, this is a fulfilled recognition scene, the most dramatic example offered in twentieth-century American literature of the power of a cocreated fiction to provide a usable past.

If God let the South lose the war, Faulkner's entire canon argues, He surely did not allow the North to "win" it. "*Maybe nothing happens once and is finished,*" Quentin agonizes, and of nothing is this truer than the war itself. The Civil War could only have been won and therefore considered over if the people it set out to free were in fact set free. "All knew," after all, that slavery was "somehow" the cause of the war. Lincoln holds this truth, like the founding truths, to be self-evident. And if it is, also self-evident is the failure of the war to free anyone. This is the burden of *Huckleberry Finn* and, in its turn, of Faulkner's last strong novel, *Intruder in the Dust*. These novels reveal the fatal flaw in the "design" of emancipation: if you have the power to set someone free, then that person remains still in your power. This is why Twain chooses to end his novel with the much-misunderstood episode in which Tom proposes, to Huck's amazement, to imprison Jim in the smokehouse (he has already been manumitted by his owner) and then to proceed "to set a free nigger free." The terrible fact about freedom is that it cannot be given. It must be *taken*—but that is a story for a later chapter.

CHAPTER SEVEN

The Depression

DREISER ❧ FITZGERALD ❧ YEZIERSKA ❧ DI DONATO ❧ HIMES
❧ FARRELL ❧ STEINBECK

*N*o, I don't like work," Marlowe says, near the end of chapter 1 of *Heart of Darkness* (1902). "I had rather laze about and think of all the fine things that can be done. I don't like work—no man does—but I like what is in the work,—the chance to find yourself. Your own reality—for yourself, not for others—what no other man can ever know." What a fine thought this is, that work is the activity through which we find ourselves. From Upton Sinclair's (1878–1968) *The Jungle* (1906) through Tillie Olsen's (1910–70) "I Stand Here Ironing" (1956) to Philip Roth's *American Pastoral* (1997), American literature has taken on the job of finding itself in work. Yet, given that it is through work that most Americans do, in fact, define themselves—our opening question is "What do you do?"—the productions of our days have never quite evolved into a salient fictional subject. As William Dean Howells wrote in 1911, "The American public does not like to read about the life of toil. What we like to read about is the life of noblemen and millionaires . . . If our writers were to begin telling us on any extended scale how mill hands or miners or farmers or iron-puddlers really live, we should soon let them know that we do not care to meet with such vulgar and commonplace people." Only in the decade of the 1930s, when for so many Americans the possibility of work was lost, did how we make a living begin to assume pride of place. Even then, a set of complex resistances—or perhaps they were awarenesses—limited that "work" of representation and led to surprising results.

Near the end of *An American Tragedy* (1925), as Clyde Griffiths awaits execution, he retraces "his unhappy life." He thinks of his few, brief, intense moments, and of losing it all, "the beauty of the days—of the sun and rain—of work, love, energy, desire." So life consists of work, love, energy, desire. It's a pretty good list. What's interesting about the list is the way in which the first word—work—gets subsumed, in Theodore Dreiser's (1871–1945) account, by the last three. "Dreiser is widely regarded as the strongest of the novelists," David Denby writes, "who have written about America as a business civilization." Yet the way people make a living—the eight or the ten or the sixteen hours a day that labor and management put into making a business run—receives little attention from Dreiser or the other novelists who write about this civilization. The open and stunning secret of these novels is that in them, as Michael Denning argues in *The Cultural Front* (1997), "work itself resists representation."

Yet work is something American literature does manage to talk about, insofar as work becomes a subject and an experience, as the century unfolds, increasingly bound up with any talk about love. As early as 1909, Mary Austin had given us the story of the Walking Woman and the "three things" that make for a full life: work, love, and a child. Austin's story clearly longs for an integration and a balance among these three things. As the Walking Woman argues, "there were three things which if you had known you could cut out all the rest, and they were good any way you got them, but best if, as in her case, they were related to and grew each one out of the other." And Mary, the narrator of the story, seems to agree: "To work and to love and to bear children. *That* sounds easy enough." Yet in the very moment of asserting the possible easiness of achieving the three good things, Mary admits to how we somehow choose otherwise. "But the way we live establishes so many things of much more importance." Austin represents this conflict as especially acute in the lives of women and links it to built-in imbalances in the accepted division of labor. But, as the writers examined in this chapter come to see, the tension between the things we say we want and "the way" we actually live also proves a deeply American problem, one that can leave men, as well as women, either unable to find work or, when they find it, unable to experience it as related to and growing out of the other good things.

* *

Clyde Griffiths hates the evangelical religion that sends his family members out into the streets and knows that he needs to find work in order to break with them. He also feels "himself above the type of labor which was purely manual." After a brief stint as a bellboy, he will flee Kansas City and end up at his uncle's collar factory in New York, doing just what he doesn't want to do. He is placed in the shrinking room. Dreiser devotes two pages to "the manufacturing end of the game," where, in a dank basement, amidst an enormous clatter and rattle, thousands of collars are submerged in steaming water and then hung out to dry on hot steam pipes. Dismayed when he chances upon his nephew sleeveless and sweaty and hard at work in the shrinking department, Clyde's uncle promotes him to the stamping room, where Clyde moves to a desk and presides over the labors of a dozen young women and where he meets Roberta Alden, the woman he will impregnate and for whose murder he will be found legally guilty.

In a novel of almost nine hundred pages, Dreiser devotes about ten to the experience of the working day—and this from a writer who seems inclined to agree with Uncle Griffiths that "the one really important constructive work of the world" is "material manufacture." Yet somehow the world of material and its transformation receives little play here. Clyde's first impression of the shrinking room culminates in vagueness and generalization; it is a site of "various processes." It's not simply that Dreiser's interests lie, finally, elsewhere, with love, and energy, and desire. It's that even the workplace itself finds work ineluctable, a little unreal. Alan Dugan's (1923–2003) "On a Seven-Day Diary" (1963) recurs to the word "and" in order to suggest that when it comes to work, the whole is lesser than the parts:

Oh I got up and went to work
and worked and came back home
and ate and talked and went to sleep.
Then I got up and went to work
and worked and came back home
from work and ate and slept.
Then I got up and went to work
and worked and came back home
and ate and watched a show and slept.
Then I got up and went to work
and worked and came back home
and ate steak and went to sleep.
Then I got up and went to work
and worked and came back home
and ate and fucked and went to sleep.
Then it was Saturday, Saturday, Saturday!
Love must be the reason for the week!
We went shopping! I saw clouds!
The children explained everything!
I could talk about the main thing!
What did I drink on Saturday night
that lost the first, best half of Sunday?
The last half wasn't worth this "word."
Then I got up and went to work
and worked and came back home
from work and ate and went to sleep,
refreshed but tired by the week-end.

Dugan manages to get Austin's three things into the poem, but none seem related to, or grow out of, the others. The poem's structure reveals that there is no "main thing" in the speaker's life except the recurring "then" of getting up and going to work.

In *An American Tragedy*, the very routines of work allow for a continuous escape from it, as Clyde senses near the end of a summer's work day:

> And over all the factory, especially around two, three and four in the afternoon, when the endless repetition of the work seemed to pall on all, a practical indifference not remote from languor and in some instances sensuality, seemed to creep over the place. There were so many women and girls of so many different types and moods. And here they were so remote from men or idle pleasure in any form, all alone with just him, really. Again the air within the place was nearly always heavy and physically relaxing, and through the many open windows that reached from floor to ceiling could be seen the Mohawk swirling and rippling, its banks carpeted with green grass and in places shaded by trees. Always it seemed to hint of pleasures which might be found by idling along its shores. And since these workers were employed so mechanically as to leave their minds free to roam from one thought of pleasure to another, they were for the most part thinking of themselves always and what they would do, assuming that they were not here chained to this routine.

While this is a profound evocation of the inherently alienating quality of repetitive manual labor, it is much more than that. Dreiser reveals work as that from which we are absent, a way of passing the time that is also a way of killing it, unless, of course, a work can be found to command the attention of the imagination as well as the busyness of the hands.

It turns out that there is very little about business in this novel about America as a business civilization. Dreiser is not simply making a point about where we, as human beings—and he, as a writer—would rather be. He is questioning whether production has much at all to do with identity in a culture of consumer capitalism. Why is it that fantasy and "the call . . . of sex" so pervade the workplace? Not only because Clyde is a man in a room full of women. The workplace itself has been subsumed by the endless play of desire, where the desire of young bodies for each other becomes an expression of the culturally encoded message that a worker's and a citizen's function is to want things. Work escapes representation, in part, because our real work is not production but consumption, because in our world making cannot hope to compete with shopping.

Clyde spends much of Book One of *An American Tragedy* trying to buy Hortense what she wants, a fur coat. It's a matter of exchange; if he buys it, "she might even be willing to yield herself to him." The largest human shopping project has to do with this search for a partner, with the ideology of romantic love. Clyde will fix upon his ultimate love object, the rich and beautiful Sondra Finchley, precisely as Jay Gatsby does. "It excited him too," Nick says about Gatsby, "that many men had already loved Daisy—it increased her value in his eyes." This is how advertising works. Desire in a consumer culture—especially "love"—moves toward mimetic desire, an imitation of the way "many men" have "already loved." So Sondra is sold to Clyde, given all the cultural messages he so willingly accepts, as an attractive and already-desired package. "Her voice is full of money," Gatsby says about Daisy, thus making clear the connection between love and the ultimate commodity.

Clyde lives in a continual state of want. When Clyde first looks at Sondra, she arouses in him a "stinging sense of what it was to want and not to have." "Want" must be kept unsatisfied if the consumer is to do his job, which is to keep the market churning. "Love" is the word the market gives to the constant advertising and exchange of desirable bodies. And this then, Dreiser reveals, is the true human work, the activity that rationalizes all the other ad-induced desires and that commands, rightly, Dreiser's attention.

Of course, the only thing worse than wanting and not having is getting what you want. " 'Happiness' is, after all, a consumption ethic," Joan Didion writes, and the problem with fulfilled consumption is that with fulfillment, happiness ends. Therein lies the genius of the founding fathers, who guaranteed only a right to the "pursuit of happiness." Compare also the last sentence of *Sister Carrie* (1900), in which the heroine's restless rocking represents her always-deferred arrival at her goal: "In your rocking chair, by your window, shall you dream such happiness as you may never feel." Possession brings diminishment, as Richard Poirier says about the story narrated by Nick Carraway. Once Gatsby gets Daisy, "his count of enchanted objects had diminished by one." And so the goal, for writers about desire, is to keep their characters in *pursuit* of happiness by not allowing them to get what they want.

An American Tragedy can seem at first glance a holdover achievement, a voice from twenty years before. Since the publication of *Sister Carrie* in 1900, Dreiser had been at war with censors, publishers, and a public resistant to the dark news he felt compelled to bring. The result was a breakdown in 1902, a gap of eleven years between *Sister Carrie* and *Jennie Gerhardt*, and another gap of ten years between *The Genius* (1915) and his masterpiece of 1925. If *An American Tragedy* appears a throwback, it also belongs very much to its cultural moment. Published in the same year as F. Scott Fitzgerald's (1896–1940) *The Great Gatsby*, it shares with that novel a similar vision of the logic of desire. In the great kiss scene at the end of chapter 6, Fitzgerald, by way of Nick, is careful to protect Gatsby from any too-easy realization of his wish. Considerable energy in the scene goes into hesitation, into holding off:

> He knew that when he kissed this girl, and forever wed his unutterable visions to her perishable breath, his mind would never romp again like the mind of God. So he waited, listening for a moment longer to the tuning fork that had been struck upon a star. Then he kissed her. At his lips' touch she blossomed for him like a flower and the incarnation was complete.

Gatsby here experiences his incarnation, his fall into flesh. In kissing Daisy he chooses against "the pap of life" at the top of the "ladder" that mounts to a secret place above the trees and chooses in favor of the real, perishable woman who stands at the bottom of the ladder. The phrase "So he waited" captures his reluctance to make this choice. It is a fall, out of ideation and into experience. And this is rarely a good thing in Fitzgerald, since it brings an end to longing, requires an acceptance of limitation, and calls upon the self to want what it has.

This is the fantasy at the heart of the American Dream, here embodied as the desire for a woman: that the choosing self can at once get what it wants and also remain true to a "Platonic conception" of itself in which possibilities are kept forever open. Gatsby keeps choosing or "taking" Daisy ("eventually he took Daisy one still October night") and then pretending as if he has never chosen or taken her. Gatsby believes he can "repeat the past," and what this means, for him, is that he can pretend it never happened. He can also conveniently forget his sexual experience with Daisy because he is not in love with her but rather with "some idea of himself," as Nick imagines, "that had gone into loving Daisy." He is in love, that is, with the shape and strength of his own desire.

Through the metaphor of the ladder, Nick images Gatsby's choice as one between going up and going down. At the top of the ladder is the pap of life and the "milk of wonder"; at the bottom, the living, dying Daisy. (Another way to think about his metaphor of climbing up versus falling down is to recall the General Motors ladder of consumption, inaugurated in the 1920s, where the car buyer begins his purchasing career at the bottom, with Chevrolet, and ascends, over the years and as his purchasing power increases, to the tip-top—through Pontiac, Buick, Oldsmobile, and, finally, to a Cadillac. It is a fast and expensive car, driven by Daisy, that will run down the working-class Myrtle.) It looks to be a choice between transcendence and personality. At the end of the novel, in its last sentence, Fitzgerald reconfigures the choice as horizontal, not vertical: he flips the ladder onto its side. "So we beat on, boats against the current, borne back ceaselessly into the past." If we think of Gatsby's ladder as tipping toward the left, and lying on its side, then the image of the rower against the current suggests that the choice is not a spatial but a temporal one, a choice not of up or down but of back or forward. By replacing the image of the ladder-climber with the image of the rower, Fitzgerald reminds us that Gatsby's enemy has always been time.

The rower tries to fare forward, into the future and away from "the past." But in order to row, he must face backward, and, despite his best efforts, the strength of the current works against him and bears him "ceaselessly" back. By superimposing the logic of the one metaphor on the logic of the other, Fitzgerald makes a complex argument about the real object of the American Dream, about the fact that despite the rower's apparent efforts he is actually being carried back toward what he really wants.

In the kiss scene, Gatsby wants to climb up, although he finally chooses to descend. By refiguring his ambitions as temporal rather than spatial, Fitzgerald reveals that hidden within that desire for "transcendence" is something deeply regressive, a refusal to go and grow forward in mortal time. In the paragraph that precedes the novel's last sentence, Nick speculates that Gatsby, chasing a dream out ahead of him, "did not know that it was already behind him." The image of the rower reinforces the point. Gatsby has called his dream "hope," has embodied it in Daisy, and has gone in search of it. But it has always already been behind him, since it has always been a regressive dream. What we call "hope" in America, Fitzgerald is arguing, is really nostalgia, the longing for a primary wholeness and oneness and purity that never existed and that we confuse with something that never can or could be out ahead of us. So what such male characters are really in love with and chasing after is their own "innocence" rather than any embodied, limited, mortal thing, especially a thing as compromised by sexuality and otherness as a woman's body.

"Clyde had a soul that was not destined to grow up." If Gatsby hesitates, Clyde wavers. Clyde can be defined by his betweenness, a sense of being poised—or caught—between options. It's not that choice is beyond him but rather too often upon him. As Roberta says to Clyde, about her pregnancy, "You can get someone to get me out of this or you can marry me." Clyde sees himself as a victim of that "or," tormented by the fact that choices exist. To this conception of himself he remains true almost to the bitter end; it even becomes part of his legal defense. As opposed to Fitzgerald, who hands his hero's story over to an empathetic Nick, Dreiser maintains third-person control. Rather than soliciting sympathy for his protagonist, he reveals him to be in thrall to a "cowering sense of what society would think and do."

⁕   ⁕

The alternative to Clyde's adaptability is Sara Smolinsky's resistance. Also published in 1925, Anzia Yezierska's (ca. 1885–1970) *Bread Givers* begins with one woman working at home—"I had just begun to peel the potatoes for dinner"—and another wearily returning from her failed search for work in the world. Meanwhile, "Father" has his own room for study and prayers, gets the "fat from the soup and the top from the milk," and is "so busy working for Heaven" that it is left to the women in the family to provide for life "here, on earth."

Yezierska correlates the problem of work with "the problem of Father." Reb Smolinsky spends his time reading the Torah rather than making money, which he relies on his girl children to do. Religion as practiced here is organized for the convenience of the father: he attends temple and lodge meetings, while his daughters iron, fabricate boxes, or hawk herring in the street. Yet the very dynamic that depends on her labors discounts the value of the female. "The prayers of his daughters didn't count because God didn't listen to women. Heaven and the next world were only for men." Yezierska is unsparing in her portrayal of the smugness and selfishness and above all the hypocrisy of the patriarchal structure; the copious praise Reb Smolinsky dishes out is only for himself. When his wife dies, he promptly replaces her with the widow upstairs. While continually disclaiming interest in the comforts of this world, or denigrating the importance of producing something of value in it, he ensures that the women around him will spend their energies looking after his material needs. He is a taker, not a bread giver.

Unlike Clyde, Sara sees through the social contract and resolves to achieve a "silent aloofness" within it. Yezierska images her choice as one made between two doors. There is the one she walks out of, the door to her father's house: "I stepped into the next room, seized my hat and coat, and walked out." She then seeks a room of her own: "This door was life. It was air. The bottom-starting point of becoming a person." What Sara will do in that room is study.

Like Sara, Anzia Yezierska left home young, at the age of seventeen. Born in Russian Poland in the early 1880s, she emigrated to the United States with her family in the 1890s. Night school, a little college, and two marriages followed. She would eventually give the child of her second marriage to its father and embark on a writing career. Her first short story was published in 1915; collections of short stories and four novels followed. Goldwyn studios made two movies based on her work, but the prints and the negatives have not survived. In 1950, after an eighteen-year writing silence, Yezierska published a fictionalized autobiography, *Red Ribbon on a White Horse*. She died in Claremont, California, in 1970. As Sally Ann Drucker points out, Yezierska "was the only immigrant Jewish woman from Eastern Europe of her generation who wrote any body of fiction in English."

Sara solves the problem of father by stealing his power. She takes on the man's plot, the story of mastery through knowledge. On the night she gives up her love of Max Goldstein, she turns back to her books and recommits to her desire "to learn, to know, to master by the sheer force of her will." At school she tells the teacher "I want the knowledge that is the living life." Since Sara is the narrator of her own story, one in which she continually declares the reasons for her choices and perceives the contradictions in the system she resists, by the time she makes this statement it is clear to the reader that this is a knowledge she already possesses, which is a knowledge of how power reproduces itself in the present, in her Lower East Side.

It is perhaps therefore not surprising that, at the moment when Sara re-chooses work over love, she openly identifies with her father. "I had lived the old, old story which he had drilled into our childhood ears . . . I had it from Father, this in-grained something in me that would not let me take the mess of pottage." Reb then shows up and curses Sara for renouncing Max. She realizes, once again, that she is alone. "I had to give up the dreams of any understanding from Father as I had to give up the longing for love from Max Goldstein. Those two experiences made me clear to myself. Knowledge was what I wanted more than anything else in the world. I had made my choice. And now I had to pay the price."

The brilliance of Sara's solution to the problem of Father is to fashion a believable outcome that takes place in this world and largely on its terms. Sara will finally acquire the knowledge she seeks, find work as a teacher, and gain the love of a good man. If it sounds like a fairy tale—this is one of the rare American novels in which a heroine is allowed to put the "and" back into "Arbeiten und Lieben"—her happy ending comes off as hard-earned and plausible because Sara refuses the fantasy of revolutionary change, which is another way, Yezierska implies, of "working for heaven." She grasps that only by way of the Father can the problem of Father be defeated, and so, like any other Caliban figure, she steals the master's language and learns to deploy it with surpassing force. "It's from him," Hugo Seelig reminds her, "that you got the iron for the fight you had to make to be what you are now."

By appropriating the Jewish tradition of sublimation of self into study, Sara gains the understanding of how to best the father at his own game without reproducing his bitterness and self-regard. Her upbringing in a tradition of the Book endows her with a belief in and a capacity for what William Blake calls "Mental Fight," the most effective weapon against the "tyranny" of the father and the discourse that rationalizes it. Sara wins through to a mobility of the spirit in a world that remains, fundamentally, patriarchal, but one in which she has nevertheless also taught herself how to clear a space (no image has been more important for the liberation of women in the twentieth century than that *room*) where she can become what her father has never been for her, an adult who provides not only bread but loving care.

✦   ✦

Clyde Griffiths possesses none of Sara's will to study. Yet, despite Clyde's submission to the received, Dreiser creates a fictional world in which he is held responsible for the shape of his story. Clyde's freedom can be measured by his ability to project a future. He begins doing this with a vengeance after reading a newspaper account about drowning. "If only such an accident could occur to him and Roberta," he thinks. He even refines the tense of the fantasy: "*could it but occur.*" From this point on, until the drowning scene that ends Book Two, Clyde remains in the grip of such considerations. "It would have to be toward evening, of course . . . But, damn it, he would not listen to such thoughts." But listen he does, and so becomes acquainted with his unforeseen capacities.

In a sequence of experimental scenes, Dreiser reveals Clyde as hard at work on his fantasy. As Clyde waits for and then meets Roberta at the station platform, Dreiser interposes a series of parentheses in which the anxious lover's mind adverts to irrelevant or strangely salient details. A moment of self-rebuke—"The blackness of this plot of his!"—is followed by this: "(*Those nine black and white cows on that green hill side.*)" We might call this the verbal precipitate of the psychic experience of guilt. Dreiser stages Clyde's choice as a debate between two voices, the voice of "Clyde" versus the voice of "the darkest and weakest side." That voice addresses Clyde as "you," and Clyde responds. Whatever Dreiser may have believed about determinism and free will, he here offers a powerful experience of a self in debate. "But you must choose—choose! And then act." It's like watching Faust and Mephistopheles; by splitting Clyde into these two voices, Dreiser also elicits the sense of agency that drama and its characters in conflict typically create.

Given this orgy of premeditation, it is simply not credible for Clyde to suggest, in his interview with lawyer Belknap, that "nor had he intentionally killed her at the last," or to argue that "it had been an accident." Clyde deploys a rhetoric of the accidental, but the novel does not quite believe him. We have read the story Clyde here retells his lawyer, and so we know that by way of his "plans and deeds" Clyde has played an active part. Clyde misconstrues the nature of responsibility in appealing to the notion of having been, at the moment of Roberta's drowning, in a "trance." However confused he felt at that moment—and Dreiser shows him, as Denby argues, in "an anguished state in which shame tries, but fails, to overtake desire"—he is, by way of all he has done and not done, still responsible. Responsible, I say, not guilty: in the legal question of guilt, which turns out to be a product of a game called the law, neither Dreiser nor his reader can have much interest.

Taking responsibility for what has happened is the only cure for Clyde's deeply divided and wavering self, and for a vagrancy of soul he can only heal by accepting the gravity and irrevocability of what that self has wrought. To acknowledge this,

Dreiser implies, is worth more than any exoneration before the court; it is to find, finally, work fit for man. As Blake also maintains, every man performs a Last Judgment upon himself continuously, and, despite the ambiguity of our motives and the vagaries of our moods, the ultimate vanity lies in not accepting one's part in the thing done.

Dreiser's novel therefore turns out to be, in my reading, not a naturalist tract but a work of supreme moral seriousness, where the word *moral* is understood to imply not a list of rights and wrongs but rather the truthfulness of the self before the self. Of course, Dreiser remains interested in all that stands in the way of this and that makes taking responsibility so difficult an accomplishment. Clyde has a bad case of Sutpen's "innocence." Governed by his cowering sense of what society would think and do, he operates out of a supreme outer-directedness that never questions the values and standards that arouse and finally punish his longing. Moreover, Dreiser reveals society as structured to so arouse and so punish. Dreiser's response to this awareness is not to reduce Clyde to a determined victim of an infernal system, but to reveal his "innocence" as what makes him guilty. He is guilty of the very thing, according to Cynthia Ozick (b. 1928), that so infuriates the imagination of William Gaddis and propels his fierce denunciations: he is guilty of "false belief."

For how can one talk about determinism in the face of this relentlessly interior book, one in which the prose is devoted to the flow of mood as it responds to what other people think? "Because their moods were so brisk and passionate," Dreiser writes about his young strivers, "they were often prone to fix on the nearest object." Clyde lives in an entirely socially constructed world—it's made-up and artificial—one driven by rules and class uncertainties and longings to like and to be liked. Clyde responds to these pressures, surely, as he feels caught in various binds. But these have to do with an unquestioned and unquestioning culture, a world people have made and that is then experienced, as is the shrinking room, as a machine that runs itself. Dreiser writes about characters whose desires are placed outside themselves and who enjoy no vantage point from which to imagine a realm of resistance. "Of the opinion of society in general and what other people might say, Roberta stood in extreme terror." If "what people might say" does drive behavior, this is hardly a determinism. Given that a Hester Prynne, so circled round, has the courage and the wit to say, in *The Scarlet Letter*, "What we did had a consecration of its own," why cannot these characters venture half as much? Never do they imagine differently, outside "society's" box.

Dreiser's story allows his reader a freedom, however, that his characters do not claim. The power of the novel's three-part structure arises from the contrast between the first two books and the third. The structure anticipates that of Norman

Mailer's *The Executioner's Song* (1979). The first movement of Mailer's equally vast book presents the story of Gary Gilmore and his crime. The second movement delivers the mediation of the story—by the media (including Mailer) and by the law.

Book Two ends with Roberta's drowning. Book Three is devoted to Clyde's arrest and trial. It provides two retellings of Clyde's story: one by the prosecution, and one by the defense. Neither is as satisfying or convincing as the account Dreiser provides in Books One and Two. Both retellings are argumentative reductions meant to serve a process called the "law." Dreiser makes the case that when it comes to judging a life, the conventions of a novel are much more persuasive than those of a trial.

Dreiser's retellings have a purpose far different, then, than Faulkner's. They work differently because Clyde's motives and his strategy for dealing with them have not been withheld from us. Since the novel's third-person free indirect discourse has given us such full access to Clyde's "plans and deeds," any introduction of ambiguity by Clyde or his lawyers comes off as rationalizing. We know what we know; we have gone through the story with Clyde, in linear fashion, step by step. The contrast between the lawyer's backstory, invented to exculpate Clyde, and the story we have read makes the simple point that any number of narratives can be invented to fit a set of facts. But the weight and detail of those first two books, when placed against the lawyer's inventions, have prepared us to be suspicious of any use of story that treats story as an excuse.

One fact never changes: Roberta's drowning, however it occurred, is the outcome Clyde wanted. Only by reasoning back from the outcomes in which he is involved can Clyde—or anyone else, Dreiser suggests—know what his "motives" are. The novel thus calls for a reckoning. It is a structure designed for revealing responsibility and for testing self-respect. "People with self-respect," Joan Didion argues, "have the courage of their mistakes. They know the price of things." Didion's formula hearkens back to Yezierska's, when she describes Sara's resolve: "I had made my choice. And now I had to pay the price." Clyde must also pay the price for his false belief, where the price is not execution but self-recognition. And this is what Clyde will come round to in the days before he dies. "It was a lie," says the narrative voice that has so intimately shared his journey, "that he had experienced a change of heart."

As if to signal that this recognition is Clyde's work and his challenge, Dreiser offers him an earlier and a failed self-recognition scene. "Clyde . . . was called upon to witness a scene identified with Roberta, which, as some might think, only an ironic and even malicious fate could have intended or permitted to come to pass." The "some" who might think this include Clyde, who experiences the scene as an utter humiliation. But the real irony is that the scene affords Clyde an opportunity for the recognition of pattern and therefore the call to analysis he will sadly avoid.

While motoring north to the lakes with Sondra and her friends, the driver of the car becomes lost and asks Clyde to seek directions at a nearby farmhouse. At the front door, Clyde discovers it to be the Alden farm. The path is unkempt, the roof decayed and sagging, the chimney broken. At the door he is met by a man in an old, threadbare coat and baggy, worn jeans. It is Roberta's father. The man comes out into the yard and points Clyde along the way. In approaching and then leaving the Alden house, Clyde runs through a complex series of emotions. While he is "astonished" to realize that this is Roberta's home and hesitates about going forward, he feels "an identification of this lorn, dilapidated realm with Roberta and hence himself." While this identification causes him to wish to turn around and run, it nevertheless occurs.

Having experienced the identification, Clyde proceeds to dismiss it. As he approaches the house, he becomes "dejected" and experiences "the most troubled and miserable of thoughts." Nearing the door, however, he has begun to dissociate himself from the scene: "How far he had traveled away from just such a beginning as this!" And, by the time he hurries away from Mr. Alden, he has redefined his initial identification as voluntary, even arbitrary: "Oh, why had he ever been so foolish and weak as to identify himself with her in this intimate way?"

Of course, Clyde and Roberta are irrevocably identified. They come from the same class, and however far they travel, this will always remain, as the prose goes on to say, "the world from which he sprang." All Clyde feels in the evoked presence of this world is chagrin. His identification is unwilling and, finally, put from him. He cannot forgive himself his origins, cannot say, as Nick does about his Middle West near the end of *Gatsby*, "I am part of that." The man at the front door is Clyde, is his past. But no more than is Sutpen is Clyde willing to trade his "innocence" for empathy and analysis, for the work of knowing and self-knowing that could free him from the snobbism and the will to rise that bring him so fully to grief.

+   +

We remember the 1930s as the decade of labor, as a depression in which Americans were thrown out of work. By 1933, 25 percent of the work force was jobless. Throughout the decade the unemployment rate never fell below 14 percent. David M. Kennedy calculates that the Depression years witnessed the "loss of some 104 million person-years of labor" and some $360 billion in economic output, had 1929 job levels held. On the day Pearl Harbor was bombed, the nation still had three million unemployed, and the average factory was up and running only forty hours a week. Despite the best efforts of the New Deal, only the economic buildup required by the war finally pulled the nation out of the Depression.

The process of economic recovery, backed by an activist federal government, led to a high-water mark for union status and power. The Wagner Act of 1935, "the most radical piece of legislation in twentieth-century American history," guaranteed unions the right to organize and to collective bargaining. The giant sit-down strike at General Motors in 1937 led to a final recognition of the UAW-CIO as the "sole voice" of GM employees. That strike had attacked the metaphor at the heart of GM's promise to car buyers, its ladder of automobile models. The strike worked because it focused on choking off production at Fisher Body Plant Number One in Flint, the plant where bodies for GM's 1937 versions of Pontiacs, Buicks, Oldsmobiles, and Cadillacs were produced.

By 1945 there were fifteen million unionists. Midcentury workers saw a doubling of real wages, a trend that peaked in the late 1960s. From this period on—the decline can perhaps be marked from the day in the spring of 1970 when "hardhats" attacked an antiwar demonstration in New York—wages and union membership began to stagnate. By 2000 American workers were putting in more hours per year than in any other industrial country and a CEO was earning up to 400 times more than a wage earner in the same firm. Wal-Mart and Manpower, Inc., had become the nation's two largest employers. And union membership hovered at sixteen million, only one million more than it had been sixty years before. Thirty percent of American workers had been unionized in 1945; by the end of the century, the figure had dropped to 13.5 percent.

In his magisterial *Freedom from Fear* (1999), David M. Kennedy argues that "perhaps the New Deal's greatest achievement was its accommodation of the maturing immigrant communities that had milled uneasily on the margins of American society for a generation and more before the 1930s." Clyde Griffiths hails from an older America, Protestant stock now gone to seed and forced to make a living peddling religion in the streets. Pietro Di Donato (1911–92) and James T. Farrell (1904–79) write, by contrast, out of the heart of "maturing" immigrant communities and about characters searching, like Clyde, for "constructive work." A decade later, Chester Himes will chronicle the attempt of African-Americans to find a place on the assembly line. And Steinbeck, in *In Dubious Battle* (1936) and *The Grapes of Wrath* (1939), explores an agricultural crisis as it reduces a proud and native-born yeomanry to the status of the Mexican migrant workers who even today stoop and reach in California's fields and orchards. These novels focus on young men named Paul, and Studs, and Bob, and Tom. None will find satisfactory work.

＊   ＊

Pietro Di Donato was born in West Hoboken, New Jersey, to parents who had emigrated from Abruzzo. His bricklayer father was killed on Good Friday in 1923 when a building collapsed and buried him in concrete. In order to support his seven siblings, Pietro took up the trowel. Wandering into a library during a strike in the building trades, he discovered French and Russian novels. The result was "Christ in Concrete," a short story that appeared in *Esquire* in 1937 and was quickly expanded into a novel. In 1939, *Christ in Concrete* edged out *The Grapes of Wrath* as a selection of the Book-of-the-Month Club.

Di Donato's novel plunges us into its world of work with a suddenness that anticipates Geremio's fall: "March whistled stinging snow against the brick walls and up the gaunt girders. Geremio, the foreman, swung his arms about, and gaffed the men on." The men are Italian immigrant stonemasons, now bricklayers. The work is hard, exposed, unpunctuated: "fifteen chisel point intoned stone thin steel whirred and wailed through wood liquid stone flowed with dull rasp through iron veins and hoist screamed through space." Geremio warns his supervisor that they are "pushing the job." Then the underpinning collapses, and "the bottom of their world" gives way. Geremio shoots down through the empty wooden forms of a foundation wall, "his blue swollen face pressed against the form and his arms outstretched." A concrete hopper overturns and begins "sealing up the mute figure."

So Geremio becomes Christ in concrete; he is entombed standing with his arms outstretched. All this happens on Good Friday, as it had to Pietro's father. The point made is that work, for these immigrant men, is a crucifixion; the laborer's body is there to be mutilated. Luigi's pick slips and causes a boulder to fall, and he is immobilized. "The stone has fixed my legs, and now," he says to his sister, "I shall be your stone." The material worked becomes the man.

No American novel better makes the case that men are subdued to the element they work in. Paul's fate is to inherit his "father's trowel." "He reached the trowel down into the mortar. Slice down toward him, edgewise twist in quick short circle and scoop up away from him. The trowel came up half-covered with mortar—but how heavy! He dropped it back into the tub and worked the trowel back and forth in the mortar just as he had seen the brick layers do." And so Paul's story becomes, like his father's, about the rhythm of labor: the pride in it, the relief from it, the exhaustion of it. It's a work of the hands that can destroy the hands; the Swedish carpenter loses four fingers when the wheel at the top of the hoist sheers them down to his palm.

Di Donato's story ends in 1929, with another crash, the stock market collapse that sends men out "in futile search of wall." His godfather, soon to fall to his death as well, prophecies that "all shall be shut to the hands that labor." As the possibility of working evaporates, Annunziata, Paul's mother, retreats into her Catholic belief in an otherworldly salvation. By their labors these men have perhaps raised structures, as Hart Crane has it, that "*lend a myth to God*," but Paul has no truck with such thinking. For him, the experience of labor and its costs lead inexorably to the loss of belief: "Here where we are is our only life," he cries out to his failing mother, just before he crushes her crucifix in his hands. Annunziata sickens and dies, while clinging to her faith. The full force of the novel comes to rest, like a collapsing structure, on the deaths of the two figures—God, and the Italian-American mother —that comfort and rationalize and therefore stand in the way of these men freeing their souls from the "sentence to stone."

Christ in Concrete ends in a struggle between a mother's traditional faith and a son's emerging class consciousness. *An American Tragedy* opens and closes with scenes of evangelical religion practiced on the street, the paltry world from which Clyde Griffiths sprang and which simply chugs along, oblivious to his fate. Faith is something Clyde's parents try to sell, but their son senses early on that there is little demand for it. "The work his parents did was not satisfactory to others," Clyde observes. James T. Farrell's *Studs Lonigan* trilogy also troubles the question of whether in a world of labor—or its lack, unemployment—the religion housed in churches can be anything more than the opiate of the people. Denied the work that would give his life as *animal laborans* its hard-earned meaning, Studs withdraws into a baroque and underfunded inner life. "A mood of opposition": the phrase is applied by Farrell, to Studs, in chapter 6 of *Young Lonigan*, but the exact phrase also surfaces early on in *An American Tragedy*. Like Clyde, and like Bob Jones, in Chester Himes's *If He Hollers Let Him Go*, Studs proves a creature of mood. It is mood—the inner weather that blows through the self—that becomes for each of these characters a destination and a destiny. Self-generated and seemingly independent of the will, mood proves a sort of possession, a demonic force that stands in for all the vanishing authorities. Moods are what these characters have instead of choate feelings: to put it another way, a mood is a feeling that has not been disciplined into shape by a coherent religious vision or by a practical education.

If we judge this movement—to mood from developed religion or practical education—to have been a decline, Norman Mailer foresees a further decline. By the late 1960s, Mailer feels obliged in *The Armies of the Night* to defend "mood" against the encroachments of a technology that threatens to sanitize it. Mood for Mailer is the token of the natural man and the survival of the ungovernable and vital animal self. "For years he had been writing about the nature of totalitarianism, its need to render populations apathetic, its instrument—the destruction of mood. Mood was forever being sliced, cut, stamped, ground, excised, or obliterated; mood was a scent which rose from the acts and calms of nature, and totalitarianism was a deodorant to nature." As Mailer admits to Robert Lowell, after hearing his speech at the Department of Justice, mood brings with it the gift of surprise:

> "I was affected by what you said. It took me out of one mood and put me in another."
> "What sort of mood, Norman?"
> "Well, maybe I was able to stop brooding over myself."

Mood saves the self from the "brooding" self; like the speaker in Frost's "Dust of Snow," the sufferer of moods has one belief—that they will change. So the crow that shakes down on him a dust of snow

> Has given my heart
> A change of mood
> And saved some part
> Of a day I had rued.

But the problem with mood—the downside of the upside—is that, as Emerson declares in "Circles," "our moods do not believe in each other." Mood may fill the psychic space vacated by a vanishing and soul-structuring faith, but mood also refuses to stay still. Mood thus becomes the token of a radical instability, the outer-directedness of a self largely subject to market forces. Dreiser repeatedly describes Clyde as a creature of a "vacillating, indefinite, uncertain mood," and it is a mood shift—Clyde's "change of heart"—that he offers up as his best defense against the charge of murdering Roberta.

❖   ❖

"I felt . . . I felt . . . I felt," Bob Jones repeats, as he narrates the mood swings dominating Chester Himes's (1909–84) deeply interior novel about a black man trying to hang on to work in the shipyards of Los Angeles. In chapter 12 of *If He Hollers Let Him Go*, Bob awakes from a violent dream and begins policing his feelings. "I started drawing in my emotions, tying them, whittling them off, nailing them down." The strategy fails, as Bob cycles through feeling "fragile," then "a dead absolute quiet," then a "hard, grinding nonchalance," and then, finally, to feeling "better." For all his efforts, Bob's inner life spirals out of his control.

In moving through the external world, Bob lives a continually interrupted life as well: the alarm lifts him out of his dream-ridden sleep; the red light catches him at the corner of Manchester; a racial insult breaks up his winning crap game; a typed note ruins his dinner with Alice. But a more primal "pressure" here is an internal one, the ongoing and unresolvable argument Bob conducts within himself about race. "Race was a handicap, sure, I'd reasoned. But hell, I didn't have to marry it." Yet some compulsion makes him keep entering that space. In the climax of the story, Bob notices a closed door. Madge, the blonde who will accuse him of rape—a version of Cleaver's "Ogre"—is behind it. "I noticed a closed door, put my hand on the knob, and pushed inside to see what it might hold."

The closed room is an image of Bob's highly pressurized psyche, from which only a change of mood can deliver him. "The irritation ironed quickly out of me and I got that bubbly, wonderful feeling again." Bob is *homo interruptus*, hooked on the promise of the next "I felt." Himes mobilizes these moods in order to dramatize Bob's struggle to maintain an inner space—the "room of being," as William James (1842–1910) calls it in *Pragmatism* (1907)—free from "white folks sitting on my brain." Bob's moodiness, we might argue, is largely an index of his cultural position as a black man.

But Bob is also a hurried and tenderized male whose hysteria results, as well, from the shape and tempo of his work. "All of a sudden I began rushing to get to work on time." The anger-producing drive to work generates a sense of speedup that replicates the rhythm of ship assembly.

In 1926, there were only 33,000 African-Americans living in Los Angeles. Himes moved to the city in 1942. Between 1942 and 1945, 340,000 blacks emigrated to California. Those who found work in the industries of war found it mostly in shipbuilding, since aircraft construction remained highly segregated. Himes held twenty-two jobs during the war, only two of them involving skilled work. The first was at the Kaiser Shipyard No. 1 in Richmond, across the bay from San Francisco; the second, as a shipwright's helper in San Pedro. In 1945 he published his findings about the racial and economic landscape in Los Angeles in his story about Bob Jones, Madge, and the Atlas Shipyards.

Himes became a writer in prison, while serving a term for armed robbery. After his arrest, he had been handcuffed, hung upside down, and pistol-whipped until he confessed. Paroled in 1936, he went to work for the Ohio Writer's Project. Four years later he landed in Los Angeles with a list of contacts from Langston Hughes (1902–67) and the intention of doing some screenwriting. He soon saw that there was no place for him in Hollywood. In *The Quality of Hurt* (1972), Himes was later to write that "Los Angeles hurt me as much as any city I have ever known—much more than any city I remember from the South."

The reason Bob Jones got his shipyard job was because President Roosevelt signed Executive Order 8802, and the reason he signed it was because A. Philip Randolph, head of the Brotherhood of Sleeping Car Porters, had threatened a march on Washington of a hundred thousand Negroes if he didn't. Randolph met with Roosevelt in June of 1941 to address the employment policies of defense-related industries as well as segregation in the military. The Office of Production Management was refusing to enforce antidiscrimination language in existing defense contracts, and the head of North American Aviation had gone so far as to announce that his firm "would not employ Negroes." In the face of such policies, as well as the pressure from Randolph, Roosevelt issued an order forbidding "discrimination in the employment of workers in defense industries or government because of race, creed, color or national origin." The order marked the first move by the federal government on behalf of black citizens since Reconstruction.

Himes the novelist does attend to the physical processes of work:

> The air was so thick with welding fumes, acid smell, body odour, and cigarette smoke; even the stream from the blower couldn't get it out. I had fifteen in my gang, twelve men and three women, and they were all working in the tiny, cramped quarters. Two fire pots were going, heating soldering irons. Somebody was drilling. Two or three guys were hand-riveting. A chipper was working on the deck above. It was stifling hot, and the din was terrific.

Bob likes his job and is good at it. But he is continually drawn away from the work by the need to mediate the human relations of the job site. Looking for a tacker to help another all-Negro gang, Bob has to waste time jockeying for "advantage" with the white leaderman who doles out the assignments. He is offered Madge, who responds that "I ain't gonna work with no nigger." Bob calls her a "cracker bitch." For his trouble, Bob is demoted to the level of a mechanic. He turns for relief to a crap game, gets in a fight with a white man, asks for a sick pass, and goes home.

So much for Bob's day at work. Work turns out to be about the sexual and racial politics of the workplace. Like Bob's inner life, it consists of a series of interruptions. Bob's inability to compose an integrated psyche is mirrored in the refusal of the material and social world to offer him the simple chance to do his job. As Bob leaves the shipyard, he is moved by "the size of it, the immensity of the production." The work has turned him into a patriot; he has gone from wanting the Japanese to win the war to feeling "included in it all. I had never felt included before. It was a wonderful feeling."

Like every other feeling in the novel, this one does not last. Harassed by the lynching plot out of a job he does happily and well, Bob ends up being forcibly drafted. The two Mexican youths sent off with him at the end look at Bob and say, "Looks like this man has had a war." They are moved to say this because they have detected Bob's socially conferred vocation, the one-man self-defense industry in which he has always been employed, full-time. Bob's tragedy is that his culture will not permit him a working life steady enough to allow him to become acquainted with work's routine alienations.

✦   ✦

Near the middle of the second novel in the *Studs Lonigan* trilogy, *The Young Manhood of Studs Lonigan* (1934), Studs attends Mass. This extended scene comprises the trilogy's climax—and its nadir. Studs finds himself in a pew "with a girl beside him." The fantasies unfold: of religious rapture, worldly triumph, sexual possession. Studs's feelings shuttle between "elation" and "sorrow": as high in emotion as he rises, by the end of the Mass he will sink as "low."

The scene reveals Studs as a man of "too many feelings." Studs doesn't move through these feelings; they move through him. "Perhaps he had scorned a vocation, and that was the reason why he was always feeling that there was something in life that he could never seem to get." His moodiness and lack of inner stability become a measure of what is missing for Studs. Mood is what Studs has instead of work, or love—or even God.

Written between 1929 and 1935, the *Studs Lonigan* trilogy follows Studs from his graduation from St. Patrick's grammar school in 1916 to his death in 1933. It is a story of ruin. By the end of the second novel, the stock market crash is imminent and jobs in Chicago have begun drying up. Near the end of the third novel, Studs's father correlates the "break in the stock market" with the morning of New Year's Day of that same year, when Studs was found drunk and unconscious in the street. "Both of these days had brought upon him troubles that now linked up in one whole series that was breaking him." Farrell published *Young Lonigan*, the first novel in the trilogy, in 1932. He could not have known what was coming. And yet so much that was to arrive for his country during the Depression can be "linked up," as it will be in the trilogy that unfolds, by the ever-present imminence of Studs's inevitable fall.

Studs will fall, in part, because of his refusal to acquire a language adequate to the density of his inner life and the complexity of his social station. There is a terrifying gap between the knowingness of Farrell's prose and what it is given Studs to know. Farrell dramatizes the gap on the first page of the novel. We see Studs in the bathroom at St. Patrick's, facing the mirror, "with a sweet caporal pasted in his mug.'" Farrell here surrenders the idiolect of his opening sentence to the sensibility of his hero; in such a phrase, Studs might describe himself. But the performance of masculinity is too self-conscious and clichéd to maintain control, and Farrell swiftly reasserts himself in the astonishing three-page-long paragraph that follows. "St. Patrick's meant a number of things to Studs. It meant . . ." And so we are off, off into a series of eight sentences all beginning with the promising phrase "It meant," a cascade of memories and associations of such thick description as to exceed any verbal performance of which Studs himself might be capable, an incapacity Farrell signals when he winds up the "It meant's" by dropping back into a register that belongs to Studs: "St. Patrick's meant a lot of things. St. Patrick's meant . . . Lucy."

This astonishing paragraph contains an even more astonishing sentence, the ninth one beginning with "It meant":

It meant Bertha trying to pound lessons down your throat, when you weren't interested in them; church history and all about the Jews and Moses, and Joseph, and Daniel in the lion's den, and Solomon who was wiser than any man that had ever lived, except Christ, and maybe the Popes, who had the Holy Ghost to back up what they said; arithmetic, and square and cube roots, and percentage that Studs had never been able to get straight in his bean; catechism lessons . . . the ten commandments of God, the six commandments of the church, the seven capital sins, and the seven cardinal virtues and that lesson about the sixth commandment, which didn't tell a guy anything at all about it and only had words that he'd found in the dictionary like adultery which made him all the more curious; grammar with all its dry rules, and its sentences that had to be diagrammed and were never diagrammed right; spelling, and words like apothecary that Studs still couldn't spell; Palmer method writing, that was supposed to make you less tired and made you more tired, and the exercises of shaking your arm before each lesson, and the round and round ⬤⬤⬤⬤⬤ and straight and straight ⫶⫶⫶⫶⫶ , and the copy book, all smeared with ink, that he had gone through, doing exercise after exercise on neat sheets of Palmer paper so that he could get a Palmer method certificate that his old man kicked about paying for because he thought it was graft; history lessons from the dull red history book, but they wouldn't have been so bad if America had had more wars and if a guy could talk and think about the battles without having to memorize their dates, and the dates of when presidents were elected, and when Fulton invented the steamboat, and Eli Whitney invented the cotton gin or whatever in hell he did invent.

This sentence does two things at once. On the one hand, it shows how Studs's mind skips over the surface of things, reducing incoming information to an undifferentiated and breathlessly overwhelming flow. In words like "bean," "dry," "guy," and "hell," Farrell allows the vocabulary of the sentence to collapse into Studs's habitual vagueness and resentment. Education reduces itself to a mere list, a barrage of data that makes Studs feel bad.

The shape of the sentence also models a way of managing meaning differently, differently than the ways in which Studs's highly distractible mind will manage it. The clauses tumble through kinds of knowing and categories of cultural literacy, from church history, to arithmetic, to the catechism, to grammar, to spelling, to penmanship, to the wars and presidents and inventions of American history itself. A mind could hold all this together, the linking semicolons imply. Richard Rodriguez testifies that education "allowed me to shape into desire what would have remained indefinite, meaningless longing." And Farrell here shapes a sentence for our education.

The sentence reveals that Studs's education contains within it a set of cultural assumptions and messages, a sort of propaganda for the soul: that piety is the first thing; that truths can be reduced to numbers and lists, and must be hidden behind euphemisms, like "adultery"; that the mastery of language consists in the formalism of grammar and spelling; that gentility (the Palmer method) can stand in for personal style; that history is and can only be found interesting because of the violence that underwrites it.

Under the "straight history" being force-fed to Studs there lies a "secret history" awaiting discovery. Studs does not convert his impatience with and contempt for what and how he is being taught into such a discovery, although doing so remains an ever-available possibility with even the narrowest of educations, as Richard Wright's *Black Boy* will show. But Studs is no more "interested" in decoding the secret history embedded in his Catholic school curriculum than he is in learning its content. He prefers to live on the level of the inchoate. As he admits to himself, later on, while sitting with Lucy in the oak tree, "he couldn't even say a damn thing about how it all made him want to feel."

Farrell takes up Dreiser's burden, to supply the "heart's speech" and "to speak for people who cannot speak for themselves." Farrell was to describe himself as a man who had escaped Studs's fate: "An American writer of plebian origin . . . is brought up on banalities, commonplaces, formal religious fanaticism, spiritual emptiness, an authoritative educational system (it is less so now than it was in my day), Horatio Algerism and so on . . . He doesn't begin with a consciousness of the complications which are the source material of writers in a more sophisticated culture, and he doesn't absorb forms and traditions. His subject matter is his own world around him, and from that he gradually expands." The knowingness and sheer stylistic bravery of the novel's opening salvo of sentences testify to Farrell's hard-won and unillusioned education, one acquired on the streets of Chicago and in three years at its great university.

Farrell wrote that "the story of Studs Lonigan was conceived as the story of the education of a normal American boy in this period." To the extent that *Studs Lonigan* is a *Bildungsroman*, it dramatizes a failed education. His social institutions fail to nourish Studs, and his health will be insulted by Prohibition and its bootleg gin. Farrell attributes Studs's decline to "spiritual poverty." Irish immigrants, as William A. Gleason has shown, were in the nineteenth century often excluded from the "leisure ethic" and its call for a life of self-improvement as opposed to deadening toil, "welcome as useful hands but considerably suspect as whole bodies." Nearly a century later, according to Farrell, the Irish have advanced—materially:

Their lives were dedicated to work, to advancing themselves, to saving and thrift, to raising their families. They rose socially and economically. Ultimately many of them owned buildings and conducted their own small business enterprises. They became politicians, straw bosses, salesmen, boss craftsmen, and the like. And they became tired. Their spiritual resources were meager.

Studs will never find satisfactory utterance or satisfying work, and he will eventually come to feel displaced by the Bob Joneses of the world. His father makes the familiar case: "America was a fine country. And all these foreigners came here to take jobs away from Americans who have a right to them . . . They're exciting the niggers down in the Black Belt, telling them they're as good as white men and they can have white women." So Farrell depicts the emergence of the angry white male. The irony in Lonigan's position is that the Irish in America *became* white; "Anglo-Saxon," the nineteenth-century label for whiteness, did not originally take the Irish in. In 1852 a sermon could be delivered in Boston on "The Dangerous Classes," "negroes, Indians, Mexicans, Irish, and the like." As the Irish began to promote their own whiteness, some began to oppose suffrage for blacks. The 1863 New York draft riots marked an Irish uprising against the rich who could buy their way out of the fight and against the black laborers and servants on behalf of whom the war was being fought. The Irish were in fact forced to compete with free blacks for the menial jobs beyond which they were rarely allowed to rise. In 1830, a majority of servants in New York City were black; by 1850, a majority of them were Irish. Irish women went on to become a dominant proportion of the nation's working women; by 1900, 54 percent of Irish women in America were classified as servants or waitresses. Most of these women, like Stein's Good Anna, remained unmarried. (Farrell himself was the son of a domestic servant.) Meanwhile, Irish men began to dominate municipal politics and to become the salesmen and craftsmen Farrell describes. "I never thought," says Studs's father, "that once they started coming, they'd come so fast." Sadly, this sentence applies not to the successful integration of the Irish into America but to the reason for the Lonigans' eventual flight from the inner city. Modestly secure and content with the building up of their Chicago neighborhood, the Lonigans finally move out, as Studs says, only when "there is scarcely a white man left."

Studs may complain about being squeezed out of a job, but we never see him hard at work. There is some talk about him helping out with his father's painting and decorating business. What we see Studs doing is gambling, strolling, partying, or, like Clyde, chasing girls. He will, at the end, plan to marry and settle down, only to die of a heart attack. This is the organ that has been overworked—overworked by Studs's relentlessly moody flight to the interior. Studs passes the time at the looking glass. "He felt a little goofy, remembering how . . . he'd looked at himself in the mirror, and assured himself that he was a man." Studs lives trapped in his self-regarding gaze, an anxious brooding over his maleness and his Irish Catholic goodness. Farrell's discovery is that latent in the successful immigrant assault on a place in the American sun is an extreme self-consciousness about social standing. This becomes the real work of Studs's days, the assessment of his relative position. "He wondered if the people in the car noticed him, asking themselves who he was and what he was, and wondering if he might be more than they were." Plagued by the ever-present possibility of comparison, Studs equates "passing the time" with looking at people strolling in the streets and "asking himself how many of them were better off than he was." In gaining his entitled, second-generation immigrant status, Studs has lost any sense that identity is his to shape from within, a thing that can be made, built, worked for.

＊　　＊

Clyde and Gatsby and Bob and Studs remain trapped in their moods, and they do so, in part, because they fail to enter into a working dialogue with the women they pretend to desire. As "love" objects, Sondra, Daisy, Madge, and Lucy remain projected rather than real, the ultimate and obsessive prize of a failed education. The education fails because these male characters refuse the possibility of study, the work of seeing through the culture that Sara so powerfully models. Oppressed in various ways, Sara has feelings about this oppression and acts on them. She gains agency insofar as she takes responsibility for the shape of her inner life. And then she is able to find satisfying work.

Each of these authors reveals the inseparability of the problem of work from the problem of love. The underemployed male will not find a satisfactory vocation so long as he remains in thrall to an imaginary partner who really stands in for some idea of himself that has gone into loving her. Strangely enough, it was John Steinbeck (1902–68), in writing about the collapse of the family farm in the 1930s, who came to an understanding of this fundamental impasse and who was able to frame a response to it in *The Grapes of Wrath*.

A serious downturn in the farm economy was almost ten years old at the time of the stock market crash. But a crisis in farming was more perennial than decade-specific, and it had to do with the open secret of American agriculture: overproduction. The United States simply had too many farmers growing too much food. Farmers habitually responded to depressed prices for their goods by increasing supply, which only further depressed prices. In 1930, farmers still comprised 30 percent of the workforce, but personal incomes in rural America had been losing ground for decades to those in urban areas; as far back as 1890, city dwellers could claim three times the wealth of people living in the country. The Depression only exacerbated these trends; in 1934, the average farm household took in only $167 a year. The New Deal responded with a system of price supports and payouts to farmers that persist to this day, a propping-up of a key economic sector that was to make it a "ward of the state," while the structural problems involved in agriculture went unredressed.

In 1936 Steinbeck published a deeply political novel about making a living off of the land. While he maintained that "I have used a small strike in an orchard valley as the symbol of man's bitter warfare with himself" and that he was "not interested in strike as a means of raising men's wages," *In Dubious Battle* reads, in fact, as a powerful evocation of the union ideal. Through a careful manipulation of his structures of imagery, Steinbeck unfolds a story about Jim Nolan's emergence from "great shadows" into "unshaded light." His embrace of the labor movement marks his liberation from false consciousness, from a sort of Plato's cave of selfishness. Jim even reads *The Republic*, and his story becomes a fictional democratization of that very hierarchical book. For Steinbeck, only when laborers organize into a political movement—take on a public voice and initiate public action—do they have a chance of becoming citizens, men.

The real work of the novel is not apple picking but building a union. What matters is not the crop harvested or the object produced but the solidarity felt. "Something . . . grows out of a fight like this," Jim argues. "Suddenly you feel the great forces at work that create troubles like this strike of ours. And the sight of these forces does something to you, picks you up and makes you act. I guess that's where authority comes from." Jim's access of authority is also Steinbeck's; this is the novel in which he learns to write, a triumph of rhythm as well as figuration in which a "slow sullen movement," as Steinbeck describes it, builds an overpowering suspense that culminates in Jim's apotheosis and death.

The Grapes of Wrath also dwells on the ingathering of force. When Casy talks as a preacher about everyone being part of a "great big soul," he is talking, on a political level, about what we call a union. Casy will move away from a spiritual and toward a secular sense of the coming together he seeks. "Been tryin' to start a union," he tells Tom, on the night he is killed. Tom incorporates both notions of solidarity into his speech of departure to Ma:

> I'll be all aroun' in the dark. I'll be ever'where—wherever you look. Wherever they's a fight so hungry people can eat, I'll be there. Wherever they's a cop beatin' up a guy, I'll be there. If Casy knowed, why, I'll be in the way guys yell when they're mad an'—I'll be in the way kids laugh when they're hungry an' they know supper's ready. An' when our folks eat the stuff they raise an' live in the houses they build—why, I'll be there.

If Tom here invokes the Emersonian Oversoul and the perpetual American flight to the interior, he is also talking, in a very practical sense, about the redistribution of American incomes and land. His speech is one of our literature's most powerful evocations of the unending work of building a more perfect "Union," a work the novel conceives of as dependent on the various working people's "unions" also built along the way.

Once Casy drops out of the novel, however, Steinbeck appears to lose sight of a practical solution to the Joads' economic condition. His beautiful ending in the marooned barn, where Rose of Sharon offers her breast to the old and dying man, offers a symbolic rather than a narrative resolution to the story. As J. P. Hunter has shown, the moment invokes the survivors in the ark, the taking of communion, the nativity itself. Steinbeck deftly echoes these forms of sharing and even blessedness, but the Joads remain, nevertheless, without food or work. Despite his theories of the "group-mind" and his interest in the phalanx, Steinbeck remained something of a romantic individualist. "The most precious thing in the world is yourself," he wrote in 1950, "your individual, lonely self." It is a view difficult to square with the movement "from 'I' to 'we'" Steinbeck himself seems to accept as the fundamental impulse of his "union" novel.

The Grapes of Wrath begins with wind and ends with rain. Steinbeck focuses on processes largely beyond individual control: banking, agribusiness, the weather. For all his anger at bigness, he is not terribly interested in an analysis of the economic forces that displace the Joads. Steinbeck works instead to particularize the members of the ever-expanding Joad family and to look beyond radical economic and political solutions to their plight.

Steinbeck's real contribution is to understand that the "union" we seek cannot be accomplished without dismantling the nuclear family and the division of labor that underwrites it. Ma Joad becomes, in this reading, the central figure in the novel. The change in her behavior and the evolution of her vision make a prophetic case for the ways in which work will and should, in the nation's future, be re-divided.

Ma begins as a defender of traditional gender roles and of the patriarchal family. When Casy asks the Joads to take him along, on the trip to California, Ma defers to her male child. "Ma looked to Tom to speak, because he was a man, but Tom did not speak." In anticipation of her later assertiveness, Ma then seizes the opening given. "She let him have the chance that was his right, and then she said, 'Why, we'd be proud to have you.'" Still, when Casy attempts to help salt the pork, she tells him, "It's women's work." "It's all work," the preacher replies. "They's too much of it to split it up to men's or women's work." Casy anticipates Ma's change of heart, one to which only dispossession and hardship can bring her.

Everything shifts when Ma picks up the jack handle. Pa has agreed to send the others ahead in the truck while Tom and Casy stay behind to fix the Wilson's car, and Ma, in protest, picks up the jack handle in order to keep "the family unbroke." Her "revolt" is made on behalf of the institution in which she waits for the man to speak. "The whole group" watches the revolt, watches to see an anger in Pa that does "not rise." They see that "Ma had won." Her victory temporarily holds the family together, while its very success begins to break the family apart in a profound and permanent way.

Ma's career reveals that what we call "gender" is based on a traditional division of labor that, when it collapses, exposes the roles assigned to men and to women as the artificial things that they really are. Steinbeck means to show that what we call a "man" or a "woman" has everything to do with the work each figure is allowed and expected to do. Pa has this recognition at the Weedpatch camp, after Ma takes away from him the decision about staying when she says "We'll go in the mornin'." "Seems like times is changed," he said sarcastically. "Time was when a man said what we'd do. Seems like women is tellin' now. Seems like it's pretty near time to get out a stick."

Ma responds tartly to the threat of violence that underwrites a husband's power: "Times when they's food an' a place to set, then maybe you can use your stick an' keep your skin whole. But you ain't a-doin' your job, either a-thinkin' or a-workin'. If you was, why, you could use your stick, an' women folks' sniffle their nose an' creep-mouse aroun'. But you jes' get you a stick now an' you ain't lickin' no woman you're a-fightin', 'cause I got a stick all laid out too." Doing his "job" is what makes a man a man; once he fails to provide the food that the woman is then expected to cook, a job Ma in all of her newfound power never fails to perform, the woman picks up a stick too. The authority comes from accomplishing the provision. In the face of his loss of a provider's role, Pa retreats to nostalgia, to the memory of work undone on his lost farm. "Spen' all my time a thinkin' of home . . . thinkin' how the willow's los' its leaves now. Sometimes figgerin' to mend that hole in the south fence. Funny! Woman takin' over the fambly. Woman sayin' we'll do this here, an' we'll go there. An' I don' even care."

When Pa gives up—"Seems like our life's over an done"—Ma answers him with an argument based on an emotional rather than a physical division of labor. "It ain't Pa. An' that's one more thing a woman knows. I noticed that. Man, he lives in jerks—baby born an' a man dies, an' that's a jerk—gets a farm an' loses his farm, an' that's a jerk. Woman, it's all one flow, like a stream, little eddies, little waterfalls, but the river, it goes right on. Woman looks at it like that." Even if "woman" wins out here as the more adaptive gender, one gifted with a felt unity of experience, the very distinctions drawn reinscribe a troubling notion of difference. For Ma to make such a case is to regress, since any argument for essential differences between the sexes tends toward a privileging of one set of differences over another. Binaries are unstable and like to become hierarchies.

This is why the great scene in *The Grapes of Wrath*, my favorite in all of Steinbeck's work, brings Ma and Pa together in a way that positions them beyond arguments about roles or notions of difference. It takes place in chapter 22, at the nice government camp, on the day Tom finally finds work. In it, Ma and Pa think and speak in ways that achieve the novel's most complex experience of "union."

Pa sees sadness in Ma's face and asks her, "Why have you got to mope?" In the long paragraph that follows, she answers him:

> She gazed at him, and she closed her eyes slowly. "Funny, ain't it. All the time we was a-movin an' shovin', I never thought none. An' now these here folks been nice to me, been awful nice; an' what's the first thing I do? I go right back over the sad things—that night Grampa died an' we buried him. I was all full up of the road, and bumpin' and movin', an' it wasn't so bad. But now I come out here, an' it's worse now. An' Granma—an' Noah walkin' away like that! Walkin' away jus' down the river. Them things was part of all, an' now they come a-flockin' back. Granma's a pauper, an' buried a pauper. That's sharp now. That's awful sharp. An' Noah walkin' away down the river. He don' know what's there. He jus' don' know. An' we don' know. We ain't never gonna know if he's alive or dead. Never gonna know. An' Connie sneakin' away. I didn' give 'em brain room before, but now they're a-flockin' back. An' I oughta be glad 'cause we're in a nice place." Pa watched her mouth while she talked. Her eyes were closed. "I can remember how them mountains was, sharp as ol' teeth beside the river where Noah walked. I can remember how the stubble was on the groun' where Granpa lies. I can remember the choppin' block back home with a feather caught on it, all crisscrossed with cuts, an' black with chicken blood."

In this deeply poetic catalogue, Ma gives the reader a plot summary of the novel, an inventory of loss. The past comes back in concrete images, mountains sharp as old teeth and a white chicken feather black with blood. The mountains work as a selected memory because they looked sharp, like the loss of Granpa and Noah. The association is not adventitious but accurate, necessary. The paradox that cessation of movement brings with it not peace but pain—time to go "back over the sad things"—also receives its just acknowledgment. Ma's closed eyes signal this as an internal reverie, a production of her elegiac imagination.

The content of Ma's speech is moving enough, testimony to her having cultivated a mind and a language worthy of the weight and complexity and integrity of her experience. But she also has a listener. "Pa watched her mouth while she talked."

Steinbeck is adept at tracing the development of the "lonely mind," in Tom, in Casy, in Ma. But what lifts this passage up to greatness is its status as a dialogue, an interval of human exchange in which two "I's" become part of a fully realized "we."

The passage continues:

> Pa's voice took on her tone. "I seen the ducks today," he said. "Wedgin' south— high up. Seems like they're awful dinky. An' I seen the blackbirds a-settin' on the wires, an' the doves was on the fences." Ma opened her eyes and looked at him. He went on, "I seen a little whirlwin', like a man a-spinnin' acrost' a fiel'. An' the ducks drivin' on down, wedgin' on down to the southward."
>
> Ma smiled. "Remember?" she said. "Remember what we'd always say at home? 'Winter's a-comin' early,' we said, when the ducks flew. Always said that, an' winter come when it was ready to come. But we always said, 'She's a-comin' early.' I wonder what we meant."
>
> "I seen the blackbirds on the wires," said Pa. "Settin' so close together. An' the doves. Nothin' set so still as a dove—on the fence wires—maybe two, side by side. An this little whirlwin'—big as a man, an' dancin' off acrost' a fiel'. Always did like the little fellas, big as a man."
>
> "Wisht I wouldn't think how it is home," said Ma. "It ain't our home no more. Wisht I'd forget it. An' Noah."
>
> "He wasn't ever right—I mean—well, it was my fault."
>
> "I tol' you never to say that. Wouldn' a lived at all, maybe."
>
> "But I should a knowed more."

I cannot think of a more striking example in our literature of two people becoming one. Not by having sex, or swearing allegiance, or agreeing to think alike. The union accomplished here is wholly unself-conscious and fully dramatized. It bespeaks a marriage in which a man and a woman have taught each other to feel by listening carefully to how each partner speaks.

Buried within Ma's reverie is the metaphor of thoughts as a flock of birds: "I didn' give 'em brain room before, but now they're a-flockin' back." By repeating the word "a-flockin' "—Ma has already used it once—Ma's speech draws attention to the implicit comparison of thoughts to birds, and it does so in a way that a refrain might function in a poem. Perhaps the force of this simple repetition enables Pa to pick up on the metaphor.

When Pa begins to respond, he does not say anything so banal as "I know what you mean." He answers her in kind: "I seen the ducks today." By adverting to his seeing of the ducks and the blackbirds and the doves, Pa extends Ma's trope. His speech plays with the sense that things are coming "a-flockin' back" in painful and unpredictable ways, and he also pacifies the terror implicit in the image—Ma can't control her thoughts—by literalizing it. All he is talking about, for all he consciously knows, are flocks of birds. But through long practice and respectful attention, he has learned how to hear and to respond. Ma and Pa are here "compounded" as surely as are Quentin and Shreve. And, as in Faulkner, the greatest tribute their author can pay to this accomplished marriage of true minds is to represent it as a commingling of voices: "Pa's voice took on her tone."

Ma and Pa's great exchange makes a strong case for the difference between a feeling and a mood. Feelings, we might say, are moods taken seriously, inner promptings for which responsibility is taken. Moods befall the self; feelings belong to the self. Ma and Pa each have feelings here, and they find an idiosyncratic and yet interdependent language in which to express them. They have learned how to experience their feelings by listening. Marriage proves, in their case, a form of supreme education, a continual refinement and curtailment of the self in which each partner is called upon to imagine and to adjust to the other. We learn to have feelings, Steinbeck argues here, through the unending work of acknowledging the feelings a partner is having.

This heartbreaking scene models a union that moves beyond what is "his" or "hers." Through a kind of dialogue poem—the same dynamic can be found at work in Frost's "The Death of the Hired Man" and in "West-Running Brook"—Steinbeck presents the intimate activities of speaking and listening and changing one's speech accordingly as the model for divisions healed. Casy ventures that "we was holy when we was one thing." The holiness he seeks has to do with how we live and work together: "But when they're all workin' together, not one fella for another fella, but one fella kind of harnessed to the whole shebang—that's right, that's holy." Steinbeck's gift to us is to image a process where separate wills and voices come together in a union without giving up their unique tones and standpoints, as well as to remind us that while this struggle must eventually extend to the workplace, the work of re-forming how we work begins at home.

CHAPTER EIGHT

The Second World War

MORI ❖ VONNEGUT ❖ PYNCHON ❖ SILKO ❖ HERSEY

*T*he winning of a war can be a defeat for the imagination. In the sixty years since the two unconditional surrenders, narratives of "The Greatest Generation" have crowded out accounts of the pain and alienation and bad behavior that are inevitably the experience of war. Triumph can become a tiresome subject, however, and sensing this, turn-of-the-century movies such as *Saving Private Ryan* (1998) and HBO's *Band of Brothers* (2001) substitute decency for heroism as the quality being celebrated. While these toned-down approaches, shot in muted browns and grays, mark an advance on mere self-congratulation, they have probably not displaced the image of the good and glamorous war long ago laid down by the garish camera filters of *South Pacific* (1958).

For anyone looking back at the history of the twentieth century, the war is in the way. It marks a breach in time that separates the "before" from the "after." In *The Gathering Storm* (1948), Winston Churchill describes the First and Second World Wars as a "Thirty Years War." This was a European and an East Asian civil war won by two outside powers, the United States and the Soviet Union. The conflict then gave way to the cold war, "won" by the United States in 1989. The price for winning was stalemate in Korea and defeat in Vietnam. After a decade as the world's unchallenged superpower and the moving force in Panama, the Gulf War, Bosnia, and Somalia, the United States was shocked into an anxious state of readiness on September 11, 2001, when the reality of an aggression already twenty years underway announced itself. Even so swift a summary argues for the truth of William Styron's (1925–2006) prophecy, one made in *The Long March* (1952), that his country has gone "astray . . . in the never-endingness of war."

Given the immensity of the thing, it remains puzzling that more good American writing did not come out of World War II. If it was not quite the "Unwritten War," as Daniel Aaron calls the Civil War, the response did appear delayed. It took twenty years before the best of the big books started coming: *Catch-22* (1961), *Slaughterhouse-Five* (1969), *Gravity's Rainbow* (1973). Kurt Vonnegut opens his novel by addressing the matter of the delay:

> I would hate to tell you what this lousy little book cost me in money and anxiety
> and time. When I got home from the Second World War twenty-three years ago,

I thought it would be easy for me to write about the destruction of Dresden, since all I would have to do would be to report what I had seen. And I thought, too, that it would be a masterpiece or at least make me a lot of money, since the subject was so big.

But not many words about Dresden came from my mind then—not enough of them to make a book, anyway.

Perhaps Heller and Vonnegut and Pynchon had to wait for Vietnam to ramp up before being liberated into the vision of endless repetition of error that offered them a structural understanding of and a narrative handle on the experience of the war.

In *Wartime* (1989), his book about "the psychological and emotional culture of Americans and Britons during the Second World War," Paul Fussell maintains that "the real war is unlikely to be found in novels." Fussell supplies at least two reasons for this. First, the war was a series of blunders that no one wanted to acknowledge; and second, its essential feature—combat—is the soldier's work, and, like other kinds of work, it escapes representation. In his edition of *The Norton Book of Modern War* (1991), Fussell quotes historian Robert J. Spiller on this point:

> Because the soldier's history of war does not readily submit to the orderly requirements of history, and because, when uncovered, it often challenges the orderly traditions by which military history has shaped our understanding of warfare, the soldier's war has been the great secret of military history. And within this special, secret history of war, the darkest corner of all has had to do with war's essential, defining feature—combat, what it is like to have lived through it, and to have lived with one's own combat history for the rest of one's life.

Fussell's subsequent selections reveal that the soldier's letters and diaries provide the most "illuminating testimony" about the war.

But Fussell moves beyond Spiller in arguing that the Second World War had about it a unique absurdity, one that generates in him a felt sense of outrage and that places the experience beyond the reach of words. "It was a savage, insensate affair, barely conceivable to the well-conducted imagination (the main reason there's so little good writing about it) and hardly approachable without some currently unfashionable theory of human mass insanity and inbuilt, inherited corruption." Fussell never takes up the question of the worthwhileness of the war and the assumption most Americans still make about its having to be fought. His angry and somewhat reductive account deprecates the value of historical analysis (the war is about some universal like "inherited corruption") and so leads him to conclude that "something close to silence was the byproduct of experience in the Second War."

Of course, among the first responders to the war we can find "good writing" in novels by Chester Himes, Norman Mailer, and James Jones (1921–77). In *If He Hollers Let Him Go*, Himes supplies a pioneering account of the toll taken on the black male psyche by "the war of machines" at home. *The Naked and the Dead* (1948) offers up the platoon or "melting pot" novel that became the template for so many war films. Jones waits until 1951 to publish *From Here to Eternity*. By taking a running start at the war in a long book ending with Pearl Harbor, Jones suggests that the real "soldier's war" is less combat itself—nine out of ten American soldiers provided support for those actually firing guns—and more the sheer bureaucracy and boredom and strangely comforting regimentation of army life.

I would follow Peter Biskind in viewing the movie Western as one of the more profound responses to the war. From *Fort Apache* (1948) to *The Searchers* (1957), John Ford's Westerns take up, while displacing the story backward in time, the problem of decommissioning and reabsorbing into civilian life a huge army of men. In *Fort Apache*, Henry Fonda's Colonel Thursday cannot forgive the army his demotion in rank following the Civil War or his transfer to an outpost in the West, and so he continually disrupts the rituals of the fort and spurns the social order in which a future for his daughter might be possible. In *The Searchers*, John Wayne's Ethan Edwards is a Confederate soldier still on the loose in 1868 and a man proud of not having shown up for the surrender. In the movie's opening scene his slow return, on horseback, with the woman he loves standing in the doorway—a woman married to his brother—makes everybody in the frame and in the theater strain to look, and he remains unassimilated at the end, a man again seen through a doorway, doomed to stay outdoors and to turn away from the enfolding shadows of family life.

The movie set in the 1940s that comes closest to capturing the unbridgeable distance between those who fought and those who stayed home is William Wyler's (1902–81) *The Best Years of Our Lives* (1946). It does so especially in the heartbreaking awkwardness of the breakfast reunion scene between husband Frederic March and wife Myrna Loy. March has returned from the war the night before and has fallen asleep, alone, in the marriage bed. In the morning, Loy brings him his breakfast. The scene plays out as if these two, long married, have forgotten how to touch, how to love. They circle each other warily and politely—Loy is a paragon of empathy and patience—until March finally overcomes his diffidence, grabs her, and gives her a big kiss.

Coming back. Coming home. The awkwardness and the felt unreality of reentry are some of the war's richest subjects. How do we bring the knowledge gained from war back into a world of peace? As Vonnegut was to show, and as the following passage by another writer demonstrates, the attempt to make the transit between the war and the postwar can leave the protagonist feeling "unstuck in time." The writer here is returning to a home in Los Angeles and is anxious about the coming reception:

> In our isolated world we had overprepared for shows of abuse. If anything, what greeted us now was indifference. Indeed, if the movements of this city were an indication, the very existence of Manzanar and all it had stood for might be in doubt. The land we drove away from three and a half years earlier had not altered a bit. Here we were, like fleeing refugees, trekking in from some ruined zone of war. And yet, on our six-hour drive south, we seemed to have passed through a time machine, as if, in March of 1942 one had lifted his foot to take a step, had set it down in October of 1945, and was expected just to keep on walking, with all the intervening time erased.

The author of this passage is Jeanne Wakatsuki Houston (b. 1934). She writes here about having gone off to her war, one that leaves her feeling like an exile in the culture of her choice. It was not a war in which a majority of American combatants fought. One clue given here to the identity of her special battlefield is the word "Manzanar."

In Errol Morris's (b. 1948) *The Fog of War* (2003), former Secretary of Defense Robert McNamara, one of the primary architects of America's war in Vietnam, offers a list of things to do in order to win war. First on his list is "Empathize with your enemy." If there is anything to be learned from war, it is presumably how to "win" one, a task that McNamara sees as dependent on imagining the other. McNamara's point is a tactical rather than a moral one. He makes it by way of a comparison between the governmental response to the Cuban Missile Crisis and the response to the war in Vietnam. People in the Pentagon and State Department knew Russian Premier Nikita Khrushchev well, were able to imagine his possible reactions during the showdown over missiles in Cuba, and were therefore able to calibrate a response to his bluff that worked. If we had understood the Vietnamese as fully as we did the Russians, McNamara argues, we might have been able to fashion a more desirable outcome to America's longest war. As a long-term strategy, empathizing with the enemy, a task to which literature habitually calls us, could have an even more salutary effect than ensuring victory. By anticipating the perspective of and therefore the just and proper treatment of our enemies, such empathy might act as a preventative measure against even the need for "preventative" war.

As the century unfolds, war actually begins to diffuse national identity even as it attempts to shore it up. This development transforms the work American fiction has to do. As an extended war leads to a globalization of American power, Americans not only find themselves exported to new and strange places but find new groups of people imported in. War's inevitable diasporas and alliances complicate the narrative, as other national histories come to "join" the story of the American nation. In the effort to defeat the enemy other, often marked as a racial other, the American "house" becomes not so much subdivided as hybridized. In Chang-rae Lee's *A Gesture Life* (1999), for instance, as Doc Hata emigrates to New Jersey, he not only becomes an American but brings with him his experience as a soldier in the Japanese Army and his suppressed identity as an ethnic Korean. His struggle to integrate these three selves mirrors the difficulty faced by the larger culture in acknowledging and assimilating such new arrivals.

In the pages that follow, I will focus on the experience of the "postwar" and the challenge of reentry in the lives of Americans who were defined as or came to be identified with the enemy. These are people who were exiled by the war or never included in its triumphant progress. The story begins with the Japanese-American writer Toshio Mori (1910–80), who was relocated to a domestic concentration camp. It then moves through the novels of Kurt Vonnegut (1922–2007) and Thomas Pynchon (b. 1933), writers who imagine their characters lost in a "Zone" where war aims and even personal and national identities begin to break down. Leslie Marmon Silko's (b. 1948) *Ceremony* maps out the psychic and geographic terrain still available to a returning Native American soldier after his home place has been invaded by the technology of the bomb and his dreams have revealed to him the cultural and even biological continuities with the enemy he had been sent to fight. I conclude with John Hersey (1914–93) and his attempt in *Hiroshima* to go through the experience of being under the atomic "flash."

　　　　　　　*　　　*

From the standpoint of the Japanese, Pearl Harbor was anything but a surprise attack. For them, what happened in 1941 was the end of something. "For forty years," Kevin Starr argues, "California had been at war with the Japanese, foreign and domestic, although this war had never made the history books." Starr is dating the start of this war from the "Keep California White" campaigns that began before the turn of the century and that were increasingly focused on the Japanese. Starr's chapter, "Shelling Santa Barbara," in *Embattled Dreams* (2002), volume 6 of his *Americans and the California Dream* series, reminds us that the Second World War compelled Americans out of their characteristic isolationism and into intimate contact with the peoples of an enemy nation. The isolationism proved a trait so stubborn that Philip Roth can find himself still brooding on it in his 2004 *The Plot Against America*, a novel that fantasizes Roosevelt's defeat by Lindberg in 1940, and a book that could have in turn been inspired by Philip L. Dick's (1928–82) *The Man in the High Castle* (1962), a brilliant conjuring of an "alternate present" in which Dick imagines an America divided up after a victory by Germany and Japan. "Germany" and

"Japan," like "Korea," "Vietnam," and "Afghanistan," are simply names for the stories of peoples that would become, ineluctably, part of the American story.

The story of modern Japan is inseparably linked with that of the United States. In 1853, Matthew Perry had forced the "opening" to Japan that prompted the Meiji restoration. Japan's new rulers replaced the three-hundred-year-old Tokugawa shogunate with a highly efficient bureaucracy and a crash program of modernization. Emigration from Japan at last became legal. The result was migration to Hawaii and then to California, with the first Japanese immigrants arriving on the mainland in 1869. By the First World War, these *issei* dominated the growing of many of California's fruits, flowers, and vegetables, and this despite the fact that immigrating Japanese were prohibited from becoming U.S. citizens.

In 1913 an Alien Land Law prevented "Asians" from owning land in California. Since the Chinese had long been reduced in numbers and morale by the Exclusion Act of 1882, the new law was clearly aimed at the Japanese. Japanese farmers nevertheless persisted in their highly productive activities—in these years George Shima became known as the "potato king" of California—by leasing agricultural plots from white landlords. The 1924 Immigration Act, in which the nation followed the lead provided by California, singled out the Japanese as "aliens ineligible for citizenship" and effectively shut off immigration to the United States from Asia.

The high tide of governmental action against the Japanese came in February 1942, when Franklin Roosevelt signed Executive Order 9066. Indulging in the characteristic euphemism and lumping together with which Japanese-Americans had been addressed, the order created "military areas" from which "any or all persons may be excluded." Although Japanese-Americans were not explicitly named in the order, it was aimed at them, and this despite the fact that in 1941 they comprised a mere 0.1 percent of the country's total population. And so the roundups began—or continued, as some *issei* had been detained as early as December 7. Nearly 120,000 *issei* and *nisei* were removed from their homes and held in temporary quarters, including stables at the Santa Anita race track. Eventually 171 special trains would ship them to ten concentration camps scattered throughout the West. Meanwhile, by the summer of 1942, the United States had won the Battle of Midway and had alleviated any threat of a Japanese invasion of the mainland. Although rumor was rampant and a submarine or two did surface and fire a desultory shot off the coasts of Oregon and California, Monica Sone (b. 1919) reminds us, in *Nisei Daughter* (1953), that during this period "there had not been a single case of sabotage committed by Japanese living in Hawaii or on the mainland." Some thirty-three thousand Japanese-American men would eventually serve in the U.S. armed forces, including the members of the 442nd Regimental Combat Team, which became the army's most decorated unit.

Toshio Mori was the first Japanese-American writer to record the effects of re-location and life in the camps. Born into the greenhouse culture of the East Bay, Mori began writing short stories about that life in the 1930s. The collection *Yoko-hama, California* was scheduled for publication in 1941. Instead, Mori was shipped to Topaz, Utah, where he became the camp historian. By the time Mori's book was finally published, in 1949, he had added two stories to the collection, both written in the camps.

The gap between the proposed and the actual publication date of *Yokohama, California* mirrors the breach in time caused by the war in the Japanese-American experience. The challenge Mori faced as a writer and a citizen was to reconcile the "before" with the "after" and to defend the possibility of a life in the present. How was a writer to imagine reentry into a culture that had suspended his freedoms and confiscated the property of his community without giving way to feelings of hope-lessness or revenge?

One of the two stories written during the war is called "Slant-Eyed Americans." In it, Mori argues that the war *creates* racial difference, a new and reductive identity category. The epithet "slant-eyed" never surfaces in the text of the story. It appears only once, in the title, hovering over the world of the story as an emerging and in-escapable label that now applies even to the younger brother in the family, an American soldier on a furlough home. The sudden intrusion of the epithet into the family had, in fact, a long history, one that generated its consequences. As Kevin Starr argues, it was just such language and treatment that had since the early years of the century "succeeded in provoking a number of highly placed people in the Japanese government to view war with the United States as the only adequate re-sponse to the racial insults that were being offered."

The second story Mori wrote at Topaz is called "Tomorrow is Coming, Chil-dren." It is the strongest and the most political story in the volume. By positioning it in the leadoff spot, Mori not only gives it pride of place but frames and thereby overshadows the following stories, all written before the war, with a felt awareness of what is coming.

If Mori's book had been published in 1941, it would have opened with the story "The Woman Who Makes Swell Doughnuts." In the story, a man enters a space of uncanny hospitality, magically available food, and unhesitating female nurturance. But it is only a space he passes through. He gets the best of both worlds; he gets to eat his breakfast and to leave it too. Little talking occurs; the man can "taste the si-lence." The woman's little house is a "depot," a world that gives without taking. "But outside," the narrator knows, "outside of her little world there is dissonance, huge-ness of another kind, and the travel to do."

It is this "outside" that haunts the characters in Mori's prewar stories and that prefigures the loss to come. "Outside" proves less an alien space than an uncontrollable future. This is why the book ends with another story about a woman cooking called "Tomorrow and Today," a story also set in the years before the war. We are free to read it under the shadow of "tomorrow" and an awareness of history, or immersed in "today's" immediate pleasures. Yet, in the final words of the book, a sense of foreclosure triumphs: "it is her day that is present and the day that is tomorrow which is her day and which will not be."

Mori also signals that time is our misfortune in the lovely way he says farewell to the woman who makes swell doughnuts. "She is still alive, not dead in our hours, still at the old address on Seventh Street, and stopping the narrative here about her, about her most unique doughnuts, and about her personality, is the best piece of thinking I have ever done. By having her alive, by the prospect of seeing her many more times, I have many things to think and look for in the future." But "most stories would end with her death," he concedes.

Mori's book unfolds as a war of tenses, a struggle between being present and nostalgia. The war *produces* nostalgia and suffuses even the most powerfully remembered pleasure with a sense of unreality. The opening story, one of the two added to the collection after the war, begins with a voice that says, "Long ago children, I lived in a country called Japan." This story was first published in 1943 in the camp magazine *Trek*, in English and in Japanese translation. Whatever it meant in 1943 has been superseded by its function as an introduction to the published collection. The unstoppable events of history—Pearl Harbor, the battles in the Pacific, the relocation, Hiroshima, the Japanese surrender, the release from the camps— give the phrase "long ago" the power to conjure an endless recession of possibility. "Japan," in such a sentence, becomes as distant as the moon.

"Tomorrow is Coming, Children" attempts to counter this felt loss with a brave cheer. The grandmother-narrator is recalling her departure from Japan to California where her husband awaits; she presents the journey as a thing she is determined and willing to do. Mori has her tell her story in such a way that her departure becomes a figure for the difficult response to the past the postwar Japanese will be called on to make. "Turn back?" she says, remembering her doubts as the steamer crossed the Pacific. "A steamer never turns back for an individual. Not for death or birth or storm. No more does life." As she begins her story, she sounds nostalgic, but at every opportunity where she might turn back or express regret at leaving the country of her birth, she renounces or moves quickly through that emotion.

Her story, it turns out, is being told from the middle of the conflict. On the last page of his story, Mori deftly establishes her specific location: "If there were no war we would not be in a relocation center." The grandmother will not indulge in bitterness but seizes the war as an "opportunity" to choose again, to reenact the commitment to America she and virtually all the *issei* have long since made. In order to bring her fellow immigrants to this recognition, she shifts into the third person. "War has given your grandmother an opportunity to find where her heart lay. To her surprise her choice had been made long ago, and no war will sway her a bit." Not "*my* surprise" but "*her* surprise": with this simple substitution, Mori renders her choice generic, representative.

"Come back," her sister and brother in Japan have written the grandmother. "But I did not return," she says. It is difficult to imagine a writer giving a character a more painful and courageous sentence. *But I did not return*. Even in the wake of the camps, and in the sure expectation of opprobrium from those who would have her renounce the country that imprisoned her, the grandmother chooses that country. Hers is a story about re-choosing, about the second will more wise that confirms the initial commitment, even in the face of abuse and betrayal. Mori's strategy of delay—his withholding from the reader the knowledge that the grandmother is speaking from one of the relocation camps—gives us the nostalgia first. It sounds like nostalgia for Japan. But the longing here expressed, the longing so decorously controlled, is not for the lost country of origin but for the lost country of adoption, an America she hopes to reenter and that she will not abandon even if it has abandoned her.

＊　　＊

The aerial bombing of civilian populations during World War II marked a radical break with the standing rules of engagement. Bombing is about taking effect at a distance. Meant to position the attacker at a spatial remove from the target, bombing carries with it a whiff of unreality, of a magic trick performed from the air. "It was all impersonal," Paul Tibbets, pilot of the *Enola Gay*, was to say about the Hiroshima run. The very possibility of such things being uttered made the actual experience of bombing a challenge for the postwar imagination. In *Slaughterhouse-Five*, Kurt Vonnegut found a way to collapse the distance between the sky and the earth by positioning his hero under his own country's bombs.

More people are said to have died in the firebombing of Dresden than in the atomic bombing of Hiroshima. Vonnegut quotes a figure of 135,000; the *Oxford Companion to World War II*, 50,000; David M. Kennedy, in *Freedom from Fear*, 35,000. There is a pathos in the divergence between such sums, a sad testimony to their inability to convey the loss they attempt to express. The power of numbers to justify rage and grief is an abiding illusion. Those who lived through September 11 may recall a grudging acceptance as the initial casualty figures did not rise, but fell.

Two days after the end of the Second World War in Europe, Billy Pilgrim finds himself riding in a coffin-shaped wagon back toward the slaughterhouse to look for souvenirs. The wagon is pulled by two horses. Billy feels happy in the wagon, so good that he will later designate his sun-drenched wagon ride as his "happiest moment." He is now located in what Pynchon calls "the Zone," that liminal terrain of "moonlike ruins" located somewhere between war and peace where anything can happen. So Billy meets the "horse pitiers," a German couple who see something Billy has missed. "They were noticing what the Americans had not noticed—that the horses' mouths were bleeding, gashed by the bits, that the horses' hooves were broken, so that every step meant agony, that the horses were insane with thirst." The horse-pitiers croon to the horses and make Billy get out of the wagon and look at them. "When Billy saw the condition of his means of transportation, he burst into tears. He hadn't cried about anything else in the war."

We cry for things pointed out to us, things noticed and stylized by art. How does Vonnegut get us to do this? By leaving the pity out and by making it thereby an emotion we must supply. Vonnegut's shell-shocked narrative, with its fantasy of a planet where all moments can be experienced as copresent and therefore removed from the endless chronicle of loss, expresses the numbness from which Billy continually struggles to awake. There is nothing worse than becoming "unstuck in time." It may look like a solution, to float so free of the irreversible. But it is only in the sequence we call history that commitments can be made and emotions felt. They are felt precisely because everything invested in will, inevitably, be lost.

Vonnegut sets up the fantasy of Tralfamadore as a self-consuming one. Its residents can "look at any moment that interests them." Time is there arrayed like space. They "can look at all the different moments just the way we can look at a stretch of the Rocky Mountains." It is perhaps a bombardier's view, another version of the American fantasy of being able to live "in the present," as Emerson writes in "Self-Reliance," "above time."

The downside of the upside is that because of the reach of their vision, the Tralfamadorians also "know how the Universe ends." (They will blow it up.) They look on this knowledge dispassionately: "The moment is *structured* that way." The power to transcend time, it turns out, renders moot the point and value of any action. Tralfamadore is structured as a seductive denial of the human condition, which the Talfamadorians accurately describe as a condition in which "one moment follows another one, like beads on a string." Once an earthly "moment is gone it is gone forever."

Whatever we mean by freedom, Hannah Arendt reminds us, depends on the fact of our "natality," our contingent birth into the world in a specific moment in time, our subsequent existential uncertainty, and the necessity for action despite our not knowing what the future will bring. Billy is cursed, not blessed, by the loss of this condition. Arriving in Dresden as a prisoner of war, "Billy, with his memories of the future, knew that the city would be smashed to smithereens and then burned—in about thirty more days. He knew, too, that most of the people watching him would soon be dead. So it goes." So it goes, he thinks. "So it goes" becomes the mantra of Billy's God-like eye and his burned-out heart, a reflexive defense against the foreknowledge being continually brought home to him about the war, a protection purchased by the inability to act or to feel.

In his life after the war, "Billy cried very little." The epigraph to the novel invokes the Christ child of the Christmas carol, another character with a God's-eye view: "*No crying he makes.*" The not-crying has to do with the extent of the perspective. The most human thing about us—the thing that makes pity and empathy and love at all possible—is our not knowing how things will turn out, and our acting and caring anyway.

The literature of war calls on us to recognize and to feel pain, our enemy's and our own. As Wilfred Owen wrote, about his experiences in the trenches of Flanders, "The Poetry is in the pity." "Pity the men who had to *do* it," Rumfoord says to Billy, about the British and American flyers who bombed Dresden. "I do," Billy replies. To extend pity to one's own side, even in victory, is to acknowledge that the suffering inflicted on those under the bombs is accompanied by the guilt and sorrow felt by those who drop them.

When the bombing in *Slaughterhouse-Five* comes, it comes, like the shoot-out in *The Octopus*, as something heard and not seen. "*Listen,*" Vonnegut begins, as he ends his first chapter, the one about how hard it has been to write his book:

> Listen:
> Billy Pilgrim has come unstuck in time.

The call to the reader is to *listen*. As the novel approaches its climax, the word "listening" begins to crop up. "God is listening," Kilgore Trout tells Billy's sister, at Billy's eighteenth wedding anniversary party. This is a strange and welcome riff on the more familiar "God is watching you." What prompts Billy to associate backward to the day of the bombing is the effect of hearing a barbershop quartet, whose singing at the party generates in him "powerful psychosomatic responses." He lay down and "remembered it shimmeringly—as follows":

> He was down in the meat locker on the night that Dresden was destroyed. There were sounds like giant foot-steps above. Those were sticks of high-explosive bombs. The giants walked and walked. The meat locker was a very safe shelter. All that happened down there was an occasional shower of calcimine. The Americans and four of their guards and a few dressed carcasses were down there, and nobody else. The rest of the guards had, before the raid began, gone to the

comforts of their homes in Dresden. They were all being killed with their families.

Why not allow us to see the bombing? The destruction of Dresden was, after all, a visual spectacle, one visited upon a "skyline" unique in Europe, a skyline "intricate and voluptuous and enchanted and absurd." Part of the pain resides in the seemingly gratuitous ruination of a city of such gratuitous beauty. But to render the firebombing in a visually explicit way would be to court the pornographic, Vonnegut implies, to conjure an image as damaging to one's sensibility as the "dirty picture" Roland Weary caries with him, "of the woman attempting sexual intercourse with a Shetland pony." Billy has no choice but to look at the photograph, over and over: Weary "had made Billy Pilgrim admire that picture several times."

In taking in the firebombing of Dresden, the aesthetic challenge faced by the writer and the emotional challenge faced by the reader is "to imagine what was happening to the people on the ground." By situating us *under* the ground, with Billy Pilgrim in the meat locker of the slaughterhouse, Vonnegut requires the reader to do just this. We are not allowed, like the residents of Tralfamadore, to "look at any moment that interests us." We are asked to take in the bombing of Dresden as unique, incomparable, unseeable. What we are not allowed to believe is that it is unimaginable. When Billy revisits his memory of the bombing and finally reproduces the moment for the reader, he does not do so by coming unstuck in time. It is not a heartless grazing among interesting moments. Instead, he thinks hard. "Billy thought hard about the effect the quartet had had on him, and then found an association with an experience he had had long ago. He did not travel in time to the experience. He remembered it shimmeringly—as follows." *Thought— found—remembered*, Vonnegut writes. These are verbs of agency. They describe a man in charge of what he is doing. Billy chooses to open himself to this memory in the way the reader chooses to open Vonnegut's book. We may come to look, but we stay to listen.

✦   ✦

The core action of *Gravity's Rainbow* takes place during the eight months from December 18, 1944, to September 14, 1945. It takes a long time to get to September. The difficulty in reading the novel is not Joycean, not a matter of having to follow the private logic of a stream of often hermetic thoughts and words. Joyce's subject is, finally, consciousness. Pynchon's subject is plot and character—the temptation to make it and to care about it.

Pynchon asks his reader to negotiate extreme and unannotated shifts in point of view. While every section of the novel is narrated by an all-seeing third-person voice, that voice continually alters its perspective and attempts to occupy the many standpoints of a huge cast of characters. For each section of the novel, Pynchon provides a focal character. Thus, sections 1 and 2 of the novel belong to Pirate Prentice, section 3 to Teddy Bloat, section 4 to Tyrone Slothrop, and so on. We typically come into awareness of the focal character in each section at some point well along in our reading of it. Pynchon's obsessive use of the ellipsis forwards this process, cutting like a dissolve in film, acting as a device for shifting between thoughts and situations without expository transitions. The knowledge of where we are and who we are with thus usually arrives too late to prevent us from getting lost. And this is how Pynchon wants it, a reader set all-too-terribly free to make his way through a Zone where the search for narrative pattern ("assertion-through-structure") and the identification of and with people in the story become an endless work.

"Keep cool, but care," Pynchon advises, in *V* (1963). As we read on into *Gravity's Rainbow*, the nature of our experience instructs us to distribute attention evenly across the focalization shifts. As we do this, we learn to keep cool—to cease to care in the usual ways—about the two traditional pleasures of the text, character and plot.

The pleasure provided by character is the pleasure of identification. It is a pleasure a little like what is offered by war, the pleasure of taking sides. But *Gravity's Rainbow* offers us so many characters and creates so many surprising intersections between them, not to speak of those who simply fade from view, that side-taking comes to feel premature. Slothrop, the ostensible hero of the story, continually pops up and disappears, finally diffusing, near the end, into the free play of the Zone.

The last sentence in which Slothrop functions as the subject of an active verb can be found on page 694, and it begins as follows: "Slothrop sits on a curbstone watching it." He is watching a scrap of newspaper with the headline

MB DRO

ROSHI

By the last mention of Slothrop, fifty more pages on, he has become the subject of a discussion of his function in the text. "There is also the story about Tyrone Slothrop, who was sent into the Zone to be present at his own assembly—perhaps, heavily paranoid voices have whispered, *his time's assembly*—and there ought to be a punch line to it, but there isn't. The plan went wrong. He is being broken down instead, and scattered." Slothrop's story yields "no clear happiness or redeeming cataclysm." Some say he was just a "rallying point," others a "pretext." So it goes.

The upside of a novel without a hierarchy of characters lies in the reader's possible discovery of his solidarity with people on all sides and therefore of "the connectedness of the world." Herein lies the promise of the Zone: "maybe for a little while all the fences are down, one road as good as another, the whole space of the Zone cleared, depolarized, and somewhere inside the waste of it a single set of co-ordinates from which to proceed without elect, without preterite, without even a nationality to fuck it up . . ." Pynchon asks us to care equally about all of his charac-ters, petty or big-hearted, good or bad. We all belong to the "preterite," Pynchon implies, because we are all equal before the fact of our inevitable death. Anyone who is going to die—which is everyone—deserves our compassion. The elect attempt to make themselves exceptions to this rule. They buy into the illusions—religion, sex-ual perversion, corporate raiding, bureaucratic efficiency, rocket-building—that will somehow set them apart, render them special, and therefore protect them from the knowledge most worth having, which is that they are dying.

The pleasure of plot is the pleasure of expectation fulfilled, of a story whose end is consonant with its beginning and where the middle creates the requisite diver-sion and suspense. Pynchon chooses to blow his climaxes. At the moment when Enzian the Herero Schwartzkommando and Tchitcherine the Soviet intelligence officer finally meet, Pynchon has them miss each other. This is the promised face-off: we have been told that "they will meet face to face," and they have been looking for each other hard. In the event, Pynchon so structures the moment as to "blind" Tchitcherine and to have him climb up the road from the streambed in search of food and cigarettes:

> Enzian on his motorcycle stops for a moment, mba-kayere, to talk to the scarred, unshaven white. They're in the middle of the bridge. They talk broken German. Tchitcherine manages to hustle half a pack of American cigarettes and three raw potatoes. The two men nod, not quite formally, not quite smiling, Enzian puts his bike in gear and returns to his journey. Tchitcherine lights a cigarette, watch-ing them down the road, shivering in the dusk. Then he goes back to his young girl beside the stream. They will have to locate some firewood before all the light is gone.
>
> This is magic. Sure—but not necessarily fantasy. Certainly not the first time a man has passed his brother by, at the edge of the evening, often forever, without knowing it.

This all takes place in the present tense, in a temporal Zone in which the moment, oblique as it may be, can be imagined as continually happening.

Gravity's Rainbow is a story about missing the promised end. Something pro-found is being argued about the Aristotelian investment in climax, recognition, peripety, conflict. Why must stories end with character isolated by a deed? Pyn-chon's enterprise comes to rest on a deeply skeptical insight into the pleasures and structures of fiction, which can provide a diversion from—indeed a calculated camouflaging of, Pynchon might argue—the "real Text" and the "power sources" that give rise to it. We pick up the novel for the love scene, the shoot-out, the orgasm, the explosion of the rocket—for the *war*. (In its parabolic arc, the V-2 marks out the very pattern of plot itself.) And we pick up a novel to choose sides, to measure ourselves against the scope of the characters and to determine which are worthy of our feeling with, or for, or against. But our investments in these "blèssed structures," as Robert Lowell calls them, can permit a vast misdirection of attention away from the larger plot and its assisting agents, from the process of globalization that seems to run of itself, a "war in progress" that goes on under the radar screen of our art and in which "business would be the true, the rightful authority."

Pynchon so constructs his novel as to make it a secret history hidden in plain sight. It is there for us to notice, if we can see through and past our desires for the usual pleasures of the text. *Text* is the key word in Enzian's vision at the ruins of the Jamf refinery:

> There doesn't exactly dawn, no but there *breaks*, as that light you're afraid will break some night at too deep an hour to explain away—there floods on Enzian what seems to him an extraordinary understanding. This serpentine slag heap he is just about to ride into now, this ex-refinery Jamf Ölfabriken Werke AG, *is not a ruin at all. It is in perfect working order.* Only waiting for the right connections to be set up, to be switched on . . . modified, precisely, *deliberately* by bombing that was never hostile, but part of a plan both sides—"*sides?*"—had always agreed on . . . yes and now what if we—all right, say we *are* supposed to be the Kabbalists out here, say that's our real Destiny, to be the scholar magicians of the Zone, with somewhere in it a Text, to be picked to pieces, annotated, explicated, and masturbated till it's all squeezed limp of its last drop . . . well we assumed—natürlich!—that this holy Text had to be the Rocket, oruru rumno orunene the high, rising, dead, the blazing, the great one ("orunene" is already being modified by the Zone-Herero children to "omunene," the eldest brother) . . . our Torah. What else? Its symmetries, its latencies, the *cuteness* of it enchanted and seduced us while the real Text persisted, somewhere else, in its darkness, our darkness . . .

Pynchon begins this paragraph by using the contraction "You're." Such a use of the second person here includes the reader—it's a form of direct address. By way of Enzian, Pynchon asks us to decode the text of the war. Enzian reads the whole thing as a sideshow staged to divert us from the "interlocks," the cartel of forces and interests that profit from war and therefore send it up. The Rocket is "only an arrangement of fetishes." It is built by IG Farben as a come-on to "call down" Allied bombers, planes that "all could have been, ultimately, IG built." "Bombing was the exact industrial process of conversion" of energy throughout the interlocking corporate global grid. "This war was never political at all, the politics was all theatre, all just to keep the people distracted . . . secretly, it was being dictated instead by the needs of technology . . . by a conspiracy between human beings and techniques, by something that needed the energy-burst of war, crying, 'Money be damned, the very life of (insert name of Nation) is at stake.'"

The key interlock Pynchon cites to make his case is quite real. As John Blum writes, in *V Was for Victory* (1976), in the 1930s the Standard Oil Company of New Jersey "agreed not to develop processes for the manufacture of artificial rubber, in exchange for a promise from IG Farbenindustrie, the large German petrochemical firm, not to compete within the United States for petroleum products." The intended result was more money for each firm. The unintended consequence was that when war did break out and especially after the Japanese captured 90 percent of the world's rubber supplies, the United States suffered a "crisis in rubber," one that hindered the war effort and deprived consumers of tires for their cars.

Against the horror of this overwhelming network of interests, Pynchon summons the power of skeptical reading itself. Skeptical reading questions, it keeps moving, it refuses to rest easy in its own conclusions. Here is Enzian again: "And if it should prove not to be the Rocket, not the IG? Why then he'll have to go on won't he, on to something else—the Volkswagen factory, the pharmaceutical companies . . . and if it isn't even in Germany then he'll have to start in America, or in Russia, and if he dies before they find the True Text to study, then there'll have to be machinery for others to carry it on . . ." *Study*, Pynchon writes. That's the saving verb. No American novel of the second half of the century comes off as more seriously studied. The difficulty we have in deciphering it is modeled for us in Enzian's journey, one that culminates not in a face-off with an antagonist but in an act of suspicious reading, an activity that must necessarily continue. "We have to look for power sources here," Enzian thinks to himself, "and distribution networks we were never taught, routes of power our teachers never imagined." *We* have to look; the argument redounds on us. There is no school that teaches this; there is only *Gravity's Rainbow*.

Near the end of his wanderings through the Zone, Slothrop finds himself on the steamer *Annubis*. There he meets Ensign Morituri. "I want to see the war over in the Pacific," Morituri tells Slothrop, "so that I can go home . . . I want only to be with Michiko and our girls, and once I'm there, never to leave Hiroshima again. I think you'd like it there. It's a city on Honshu, on the Inland Sea, very pretty, a perfect size, big enough for city excitement, small enough for the serenity a man needs." Morituri expresses the uncomplicated human wish to return to a place where ordinary human life simply goes on.

Later, well into part 4 of the novel, "The Counterforce," Slothrop finds "a scrap of newspaper headline." It contains a "wirephoto of a giant white cock, dangling in the sky straight downward out of a white pubic bush." The photo comes to us as a challenge in pattern recognition, a pattern Slothrop reads as pornographic. And it will prove, once we have deciphered its caption, to be another image in support of the case that the culture of the West has subsumed the energies of the pleasure principle into the service of the death instinct.

The headline under the caption reads:

MB DRO

ROSHI

With a little imagination, we can fill in the missing letters:

BOMB DROPPED

ON HIROSHIMA

So the dropping of the atom bomb comes to Slothrop as a fragment of yesterday's news. He has lived unaware through the transforming moment; Slothrop finds the scrap of newspaper some ninety pages after the action of the text passes though August 6, 1945, a date that also corresponds, in the complex calendar of the novel, to the Feast of the Transfiguration. For most readers the correspondence passes unattended, since it is unannounced, as so often happens, in fiction as in life, we have had the experience but missed the meaning. This is how history comes to us, as we live through it, belatedly, in fragments difficult to read. The built-in lag between the having of experience and the grasping of its meaning is like the delay between the impact of the V-2 and the hearing of its sound. Survival is a matter of keeping one's ears open, of listening—even when it seems to make no practical difference.

Pynchon so structures our awareness of the event of the bomb as to make it part of the already happened:

After such knowledge, what forgiveness? Think now
History has many cunning passages, contrived corridors

And issues, deceives with whispering ambitions,
Guides us by vanities. Think now
She gives when our attention is distracted
And what she gives, gives with such supple confusions

That the giving famishes the craving. Gives too late
What's not believed in, or if still believed,
In memory only, reconsidered passion. Gives too soon

Into weak hands, what's thought can be dispensed with

Till the refusal propagates a fear. Think
Neither fear nor courage saves us. Unnatural vices
Are fathered by our heroism. Virtues
Are forced upon us by our impudent crimes.
These tears are shaken from the wrath-bearing tree.

For Pynchon's characters, as for Eliot's Gerontion, knowledge typically arrives too late to protect them from a looming fate. There are no fully realized recognition scenes in *Gravity's Rainbow* (Enzian's vision on the Lunenberg heath comes closest to this), no pedagogical moments when knowledge is effectively passed from one generation to another. But Pynchon does offer a sense of leveling, a sort of forced human communion by way of the gathering awareness that beyond the specific fear of going about one's business under the threat of the V-2, everyone now lives under the imminence of the bomb. By virtue of their invention of the ultimate engine of death, the Elect have been absorbed into the "everybody," which is also the novel's last word.

◆   ◆

The Herero of South Africa, so efficiently colonized by the Germans at the turn of the century, are central to Pynchon's design. It was their singular fate as a people to have been the first on their continent ever gathered into a concentration camp. The belated conquest of Africa, like the earlier conquest of the New World, was set in motion by a story, a European myth of *Lebensraum* and of racial and cultural superiority that fueled the expansionist project and that rationalized the extermination of the people living in the way of empire. It is a story Leslie Silko dubs "witchery." At the heart of her novel *Ceremony* (1977), Silko interpolates a poem that lays out how witchery came to run the world. "Long time ago," the poem begins,

in the beginning
there were no white people in this world
there was nothing European.
And this world might have gone on like that
except for one thing:
witchery.

The poem tells the story of how all the witch people in the world get together and stage a contest in dark things. They show off their stuff. Then an unknown witch steps forward and says "listen: 'What I have is a story.'" Everybody laughs at her for making such a paltry offering. "*Laugh if you want to*," the witch answers, "*but as I tell the story / it will begin to happen.*"

She tells the story of the sudden appearance of "*white skin people.*" They grow away from the earth. When they look, they see only objects. They fear the world, and they destroy what they fear. They are blown across the ocean, in giant boats. They kill all the animals; they bring terrible diseases. Up in the nearby hill—the witch's conference takes place "north of Cañoncito"—they will find the "*rocks with veins of green and yellow and black.*" They "*will lay out the final pattern with these rocks . . . and explode everything.*"

"Take it back," the other witches cry. But the witch shakes her head and says, "*It's already coming. / It can't be called back.*"

The story the witch tells is nothing less than the conquest of America—from a Laguna Pueblo point of view. But it's less a history of the conquest than of the attitudes that made it possible. At the heart of the story stands racial difference itself, the conjuration of people with white skin. The original sin is not the fact of variations among kinds of human bodies, a biological given pre-dating all human stories, but the belief that racial difference *counts.* Sin—witchery—originates in the origination of the other, in the will to notice and specify someone as different. As the most pervasive form of American "othering," racism becomes in *Ceremony* a metaphor for the evilness of mind that would cut through the rich tangle of blood and history in order to harden the borders between us.

Silko herself is a product of a complex ancestry, a descendant of Laguna and Plains Indians, as well as European and Mexican forbears. Her hybrid status left her on the edge of Laguna Pueblo culture, but, through her great-grandmother and her aunts, she came to feel that "I am of mixed-breed ancestry, but what I know is Laguna." Using the pueblos and landscapes of north-central New Mexico as her sustaining locale, she was also well positioned to feel with all those in her home place who found themselves up against the color line. She understands that the damage done by witchery cuts both ways, against self and other. Witchery wants "us to believe all evil resides with white people," Betonie tells Tayo. "They want us to separate ourselves from white people, to be ignorant and helpless as we watch our own destruction. But white people are only tools that the witchery manipulates."

Silko's novel broods on the power of ideology to reproduce itself and to operate in seeming independence of human control. She offers witchery as her metaphor for the master narrative, the received version of the past that renders some people as conquerors and others as the colonized. Her poem stages a fiction in which the Native Americans of North America—the "Navajo," the "Hopi," the "Zuni," the "Sioux," the "Eskimos"—also become complicit in their own demise. They make the story up, or participate in its construction, and then it befalls them. "It was Indian witchery," Betonie asserts, "that made white people in the first place." Only by

submitting to a myth of complicity can Indians gain an enabling sense of responsibility for and therefore possible agency against the outcomes that oppress them.
The notion that race matters, one embraced by both sides of the conquest, is the
fatal move. By imagining the moment in which race is acceded to as so matter-
ing—by imagining a scene in which whiteness not only is assigned certain behavior patterns but is actually made up—Silko implies that it can be unmade.

Silko's poem provides a history of its novel's present, since the witchery it would
reveal and undo is still playing itself out, on the Indian reservations of the United
States and in the jungles of Southeast Asia. *Ceremony* begins in the troubled dreams
of a veteran returning from the war in the Pacific. (Some twenty-five thousand
Native Americans fought in the Second World War.) His name is Tayo, and he is a
Laguna Indian trying to recover from the death of his cousin Rocky and from having been ordered to shoot captured Japanese soldiers in cold blood. At the instant
in which the order is given, Tayo sees his enemy as his Uncle Josiah; he makes the
conflation between his own people and the descendents of their Asian ancestors he
has been sent to fight, and so refuses to shoot. Now he is back in New Mexico,
haunted by all that he did and did not do in "the white people's war."

The Laguna Pueblo is located in northwestern New Mexico, forty miles west of
Albuquerque. The returning soldier therefore finds himself in a Zone or at a "point
of convergence" where divergent American cultural traditions have again become
entangled, one hundred miles southwest of Los Alamos, where the bomb has just
been developed, and three hundred miles northwest of the "Trinity site," where the
bomb has recently been exploded. So while Tayo has been away fighting "the yellow man," as Bruce Springsteen calls him in "Born in the U.S.A.," his home place
has been recolonized by the ultimate expression of the westering scientific spirit. It
turns out that the government needs the Pueblo Indians one more time, not only
for their remote and sparsely populated land but for what lies under it. This is why
men in official cars, years before, paid the people "living on the Cebolleta land
grant" for rights to dig holes in their gray clay. In the closing pages of the novel,
Tayo wanders up to an abandoned mine shaft. He finds the stone "streaked with
powdery yellow uranium," the residue from the beautiful rocks the government
has taken from deep within the earth. "The pattern of the ceremony," he realizes,
"was completed there."

The pattern completes itself here, but not because Silko thinks the bomb marks
a necessary end. The decisions Tayo makes and the recognitions he experiences, in
the pages that follow this scene, contribute to Silko's larger and more subversive
project, "the struggle for the ending to the story." The bomb allows for one kind of
ceremony, one kind of ending. In the curious logic of its creation, the cultural anxieties that would deny or transcend death coalesce in an object that promises com-

plete annihilation. The very physics of the exploding bomb—its power to cover and to alter so much distance so quickly—transforms space into time, converts square miles into an instant. If, as Charles Olson (1910–70) maintains, "we must go over space, or we wither," then the bomb expresses the fulfillment of this imperative, a speeded-up manifest destiny in which space is gone over by being destroyed. Silko reads the bomb as the ultimate American ceremony, since the desire endlessly to "go over" space, or to live inside a "Platonic conception" of the self, or to remain inside Sutpen's "innocence"—all this signifies a refusal to accept the offered terms of mortal life, a refusal the exploded bomb unambiguously expresses.

Against the bomb, Silko puts forward another model of ceremony. She does this through the formal structure and the rhetorical figures of her novel. As the book opens, a reader finds herself unstuck in time and space. Adrift in Tayo's haunted consciousness and in the unmarked transitions between memories of the war, prison camp, a hospital in Los Angeles, and life in the recovered pueblo, we are also caught in an interplay of Spanish, English, Laguna, and Japanese voices. Tayo himself is a mixture of white, Spanish, and Laguna genes, part of the hybridity celebrated by Williams in *In the American Grain*. This is the Silko "tangle."

The tangle is a metaphor central to Silko's healing ceremony as well as the emerging shape of her novel. Not until the closing scene will we find relief from the boundarylessness of the opening. The lack of marked chapter divisions and the intermingling of poetry and prose create, as in Toomer's *Cane*, a structural tangle, a rich generic conflation. The call is to surrender to this fictional world and to accept its absence of walls.

At first, Tayo attempts to manage the "tangled things" by reverting to a time-honored image of self sufficiency. He thinks of a single deer, "something that existed by itself, standing alone." In this he resembles Auntie, who fights to get back to an original purity, a place and time where and when "the entanglement" of her native tongue with English "had been unwound to the source." Tayo's strategy quickly collapses, and his story advances into the hybridity of identities and the temporal fluidity native to any human life. Like Billy Pilgrim, he learns to "wander back and forth in time." But whereas for Billy being so unstuck leads to a numbing of awareness, for Tayo it becomes an invitation to experience a Pynchonesque sense of the connectedness of all moments and all things.

In an early recognition scene, the medicine man makes a case for the language appropriate to Tayo's quest. He reminds Tayo that "no word exists alone." A semiotics deriving from Native American ground delivers us to a terrain already scouted by Gertrude Stein, a world where meaning results from the entanglement of word with word and from their endless differential interplay. Just as words and languages announce a fundamental imbrication, so the ceremony, the ritual that would heal us, must acknowledge its interdependence with ceremonies that have already happened, or are to come. Tayo will one day cry with relief "at finally seeing the pattern, the way all the stories fit together—the old stories, the war stories, their stories—to become the story that was still being told. He was not crazy; he had never been crazy. He had only seen and heard the world as it always was: no boundaries, only transitions through all distances and time."

Ceremony acts to bridge division within and between cultures and individuals. For a time, a particular ceremony may come to seem like truth. But the nature of ceremony is that there is no end to it, or of the need to reinvent it. Truth, in Silko's view, is something that changes. As Betonie tells Tayo,

> The people nowadays have an idea about the ceremonies. They think the ceremonies must be performed exactly as they have always been done, maybe because one slip-up or mistake and the whole ceremony must be stopped and the sand painting destroyed . . . But long ago when the people were given these ceremonies, the changing began, if only in the aging of the yellow gourd rattle or the shrinking of the skin around the eagle's claw, if only in the different voices from generation to generation, singing the chants. You see, in many ways, the ceremonies have always been changing.

Ceremony as Silko conceives it is not so much a unique act or ritual as an attitude taken toward cultural change. "Things which don't shift and grow," Betonie says, "are dead things." Witchery counts on people clinging to the "ceremonies the way they were." Witchery is thus a kind of fundamentalism, a refusal to acknowledge that ceremonies originate in a unique historical moment in response to a specific need. Made by human beings, they can and will be and should be changed by them.

At the end, Tayo comes up with something very simple. Like Bayard Sartoris in Faulkner's "An Odor of Verbena," he refuses to repeat. He will not recapitulate the unendable ceremony of revenge. Tayo watches his friends torture another friend, grabs a screwdriver, and imagines himself breaking into the scene. But he finally does not intervene. It is a difficult decision to accept, or to interpret.

Tayo renounces the heroic and, in doing so, may remind us that the hero often brings about, in his insistence on acting, the destruction of the very thing he purports to defend:

> It had been a close call. The witchery had almost ended the story according to its plan; Tayo had almost jammed the screwdriver into Emo's skull the way the witchery had wanted, savoring the yielding bone and membrane as the steel ruptured the brain. Their deadly ritual for the autumn solstice would have been

completed by him. He would have been another victim, a drunk Indian war veteran settling an old feud; and the Army doctors would say that the indications of
this end had been there all along, since his release from the mental ward at the
Veterans' Hospital in Los Angeles. The white people would shake their heads,
more proud than sad that it took a white man to survive in their world and that
these Indians couldn't seem to make it.

Tayo refuses, once more, to be drawn into the cycle of violence and into the old,
familiar, self-destructive Indian script. Like Ellison's Invisible Man, he goes back
into his hole, biding his time, not acting. Inside the kiva, the old men invite Tayo
to tell his story and to accept once more the sustaining ceremonies of his locality,
the comforting and temporary boundaries of handmade walls.

✦   ✦

The Japanese and American national stories were finally to intersect in what
"might be taken as the greatest war story of them all," the making and dropping of
the atomic bomb. In Richard Rhodes's brilliant account, *The Making of the Atomic
Bomb*, the story becomes a romance of international collaboration and of the triumph of Western science. It turns out that physicists from Germany, Hungary,
Italy, Denmark, the United Kingdom, and the United States were the most important warriors of all. Already there, in matter, the bomb is not an invention but a
discovery, a latent power "that science found hidden in the world and made manifest." To blame science for uncovering this potential, Rhodes concludes, "confuses
the messenger with the message."

If it was science that found the bomb, it was geopolitics that determined whether
and how it was to be used. The bomb may have blown "a kind of hole in human
history," as Mary McCarthy was to write, but it was still within history that the
bomb was dropped. While there may be no rationalizing the use of the bomb,
Rhodes, the most serious student of the problem, inclines toward the view that the
dropped bombs ushered in—virtually demanded—the possibility of change, espe
cially in the monolithic and paranoid structure of the national security state. Writing in the mid-1980s, before the collapse of the Soviet Union, Rhodes holds that
"change is possible because the choice is bare: change is the only alternative to total
death."

In *Hiroshima*, John Hersey focuses on the Japanese experience of the bomb, not
on American strategy or intentions. What does it feel like, he asks, to go through
something like this? Since an answer can only come on an individual level, Hersey
chooses to tell the story of six survivors: the Red Cross surgeon who works three
days with one hour's sleep; the tailor's widow who hides her sewing machine in a
cistern; the German priest with chronic diarrhea; the pastor who ferries the

wounded across the Ota River; the hospital-owning doctor who stands in water up to his neck in order to avoid the fire; and the personnel clerk with the broken leg, "crushed by books." These people—this enemy—Hersey quietly insists, are now part of American history too.

In his last and great poem, "Epilogue" (1977), Robert Lowell ends with these lines:

> We are poor passing facts,
> warned by that to give
> each figure in the photograph
> his living name.

So here are the names:

> Dr. Terufumi Sasaki
> Ms. Hatsuyo Nakamura
> Father Wilhelm Kleinsorge
> Reverend Mr. Kiyoshi Tanimoto
> Dr. Masakaza Fujii
> Miss Toshiko Sasaki

Hersey begins with a cast call, working each of these names into his opening paragraph. He also begins with a precise time of day and with the exact date: "At exactly fifteen minutes past eight in the morning, on August 6, 1945, Japanese time, at the moment when the atomic bomb flashed above Hiroshima . . ." The world will be different after this moment, such specificity argues; the lives of the people touched by it—and who was not?—will never be the same.

Hersey went to Hiroshima in September of 1945. An entire issue of the *New Yorker* was devoted to the book that resulted. Hersey produced a short book (118 pages in its original printing in 1946) about a huge thing. He seemed to grasp from the beginning that the problem was one of scale. "There were so many." Dr. Sasaki, the sole uninjured doctor on the Red Cross hospital staff, soon comes to realize this. "In a city of two hundred and forty-five thousand, nearly a hundred thousand people had been killed or doomed at one blow; a hundred thousand more were hurt . . . Tugged here and there in his stockinged feet, bewildered by the numbers, staggered by so much raw flesh, Dr. Sasaki lost all sense of profession and stopped working as a skillful surgeon and a sympathetic man." Faced with such bewildering numbers, Hersey attempts to maintain his sense of proportion and professional decorum by merging the role of a journalist with that of a novelist.

Human scale: this is what literature returns us to. It gives us, however mythic or ironic its dimensions, man as measure of the world. This is why Hersey feels obliged to craft his report out of the conventions and strategies of a novel. In doing so, he stakes a claim to having invented a new form, the first piece of the New Journalism that was to become a dominant prose mode in the postwar years.

The big issue here is feeling, how to remain a "sympathetic" writer and therefore to create an empathetic reader. Yet one striking quality about *Hiroshima* is its tonelessness. Hersey's voice sounds "matter-of-fact." This is a phrase Hersey applies to the essay by Toshio Nakamura with which he ends the book. Hersey is looking for a tone that won't "lie." In "The Aftermath," a coda Hersey added to *Hiroshima* forty years after the explosion, he writes that Father Kleinsorge now only reads the Bible and railroad tables, "the only two sorts of texts . . . that never told lies." Given the text that Hersey initially produced, it is clear that railroad tables served him as a more powerful model than did the Bible.

Hersey attempts no overview. He strays often into the present tense. His objective is to be with the victims, to imagine Japan. Yet he must fall back on fictional devices, after all, if he is to find any way to move his reader. Fiction is a special kind of lying, a nicer knowledge of belief, as Stevens says, that knows what it believes in is not true. As Sidney maintained in his *An Apology for Poetry*, the poet "nothing affirms, and therefore never lieth." What Hersey proves alive to in his material are all the little patterns that allow an audience to this catastrophe to make sense. His is an act of noticing, the product of an attention so discreet and yet so acute that it can seem as if Hersey has made up what he has only and simply found.

For example, Hersey binds his six characters together by way of the word "flash." Each one of them sees this, except for Miss Toshiko Sasaki. At the moment of the explosion, she is in a dark office, turned away from the windows. For her, the flash becomes instead a "room . . . filled with a blinding light." The noun *flash* cannot be applied to her story; even under the most leveling set of conditions ever experienced by a community of human beings, individual cases vary. She is the exception that proves the rule, the experience that exceeds any meaning-making pattern.

Hersey is alert to small ironies. He ends "A Noiseless Flash" with the following sentence: "There, in the tin factory, in the first moment of the atomic age, a human being was crushed by books." The human being is Miss Sasaki, "her leg horribly twisted and breaking underneath her." All Hersey will allow himself here by way of commentary is the mildly portentous phrase, "in the first moment of the atomic age." The ironic questions remain unspoken, yet all-but-virtually asked. Of what good, in this new age, will all that accumulated book learning prove? And have we, in the ultimate Faustian bargain, at last turned the best of our knowing against ourselves?

Hersey locates radiant images. When Father Kleinsorge rushes back into his house, after the blast, he finds his "desk in splinters all over the room, but a mere papier-mâché suitcase, which he had hidden under the desk, stood handle-side up." He will come to regard the suitcase, which contains his breviary and the diocese account books, "as a bit of Providential interference." It will acquire "a talismanic quality." This is one way to read the meaning of the suitcase. A less credulous reader can take another kind of comfort in the image, by focusing on the container rather than the contents. The very fragility of papier-mâché, so brittle and so manmade, adds a poignancy to the awareness of just what—and who—had the fortune to survive.

Hersey begins with numbers and remains alert to the pathos in them. For one thing, the numbers keep changing:

> Statistical workers gathered what figures they could on the effects of the bomb. They reported that 78,150 people had been killed, 13,983 were missing, and 37,425 had been injured. No one in the city government pretended that these figures were accurate—though the Americans accepted them as official—and as the months went by and more hundreds of corpses were dug up from the ruins, and as the number of unclaimed urns of ashes at the Zempoji Temple in Koi rose into the thousands, the statisticians began to say that a least a hundred thousand people had lost their lives in the bombing.

If the numbers are not accurate, and, if they keep changing, of what good are they? By sticking close to the story of his six, Hersey betrays an awareness that neither literature nor statistics has ever found an effective way to quantify loss.

Hersey dramatizes his aesthetic and moral challenge, which is to see it feelingly. Everywhere there is deformation or suppression of expressive capacity. The danger for Hersey is in overcorrection, a failure of imagination in the very tone of bare attention he has summoned in order to manage the horror. By attending closely to the tones of voice adopted by others, Hersey concedes along the way the possible lapses in his own. Thus, the Japanese radio broadcast of August 7 is characterized as a "succinct announcement." Hersey doubts "it probable that any of the survivors happened to be tuned in." Those able to worry at all about what has happened discuss it in "primitive, childlike terms." An Army doctor speaks as if "he were reading from a manual." Early on, Hersey notes Mr. Tanimoto's loss of affect. Separated from his wife at the time of the bombing, he meets her, "by incredible luck," near a large Shinto shrine. "She was carrying their infant son. Mr. Tanimoto was now so emotionally worn out that nothing could surprise him. He did not embrace his wife; he simply said, 'Oh, you are safe.'"

Hersey configures his story as one about silence and speaking out. The bomb arrives with a *noiseless* flash, with a delayed noise that therefore makes it, like Pynchon's V-2, a force we are powerless to anticipate. "Almost no one in Hiroshima,"

Hersey writes, "recalls hearing the noise of the bomb." It is both the producer and the production of silence. "To Father Kleinsorge, an Occidental, the silence in the grove by the river, where hundreds of gruesomely wounded suffered together, was one of the most dreadful and awesome of his whole experience. The hurt ones were quiet; no one wept, much less screamed in pain; no one complained; none of the many who died did so noisily; not even the children cried; very few people even spoke." And this silence has been made possible by a prior and collective self-silencing, the ongoing suppression of speech and sharing of information that made it possible for Japan and the United States to prosecute the war. This silence is broken by the sound of the Emperor's voice.

In Japan the war is ended by way of an act of listening. "At the time of the Post-War, the marvelous thing in our history happened," Mr. Tanimoto later wrote. "Our Emperor broadcasted his own voice through radio directly to us." As Richard Rhodes reminds us, "his 100 million subjects had never heard the high, antique Voice of the Crane before." The "marvelous thing" here is not what is said—We surrender—but that the Emperor is *heard*. "They listened to the broadcast and when they came to realize the fact that it was the Emperor, they cried with full tears in their eyes." The listening Japanese do not cry because of the news the broadcast brings, or over the Emperor's mention of a "new and most cruel bomb." In *A Personal Matter* (1964), Oe Kenzaburo writes of his wonder at hearing the Emperor at all. He "had spoken in a *human* voice, no different from any adult's." The Japanese cry with gratitude at being able to hear the unmediated voice. "What a wonderful blessing it is that Tenno himself call on us and we can hear his own voice in person."

Hersey dramatizes, above all, the struggle between straight and secret history. The methods and motives of straight history are embodied in the Japanese radio broadcast of August 7. "Hiroshima suffered considerable damage as the result of an attack by a few B-29s. It is believed that a new type of bomb was used. The details are being investigated." Straight history relies on euphemism ("considerable damage"), on the objective case ("It is believed"), and on the passive voice ("details are being investigated"). It converts the story of human action into mere mechanical process. *Hiroshima* offers itself as an answerable example of secret history, one that gives us the human story by way of the "lies"—the techniques—of art. The secret history of war offers an interval in which we can abandon our chosen sides and empathize with the enemy. It is given to Ms. Nakamura to enact this, albeit on a homely and modest scale.

A few minutes before the bomb falls, Ms. Nakamura begins watching her neighbor tear down his house. He has been ordered to do so by the prefectural government in order to create a wider fire lane.

At first, she was annoyed with him for making so much noise, but then she was moved almost to tears by pity. Her emotion was specifically directed toward her neighbor, tearing down his home, board by board, at a time when there was so much unavoidable destruction, but undoubtedly she also felt a generalized, community pity, to say nothing of self-pity. She had not had an easy time.

In the sentences that follow, Hersey describes the death of Ms. Nakamura's husband in the war and her ongoing attempts to support her family with piecework.

We feel what we feel about this, upon hearing it. But the sentences quoted have already performed the essential task. They trace a motion much more important than the pity we might feel for any one character in a book. They enact the human capacity for moving from annoyance to pity, the power to bring the other close. And then the pity begins to ramify, into a generalized pity for the community, and then back into a pity for the self. The pity naturally and rightly circles round to the self; as Elizabeth Bishop was later to write, "Pity should begin at home." The structure of Hersey's sentence acknowledges this; there is no shame in it. Only by learning to extend to others some part of the immense reserves of hope and love and pity we each feel for ourselves, *Hiroshima* reminds us, can we begin the work of lessening the uncountable number of neighbors we have too long mistaken for enemies.

CHAPTER NINE

Civil Rights

WRIGHT ❧ GAINES ❧ BALDWIN ❧ WALKER ❧ KING ❧ CLARK

*A*nd Till was hung yesterday," Ezra Pound (1885–1972) writes in *The Pisan Cantos* (1948). Pound wrote the line from a prison camp near Pisa where he had been incarcerated after being arrested for his wartime broadcasts in support of Mussolini. The name "Till" may ring a faint bell. A footnote to canto 74 identifies him as "Louis Till, an African-American trainee at the DTC executed on July 2, 1945 . . . Till was the father of Emmet Till, whose cold-blooded murder at age fourteen by two white men in Mississippi sparked the Civil Rights Movement in the South." What a collision of worlds is here, one implausible enough to inspire wonder at the strange fetchings of Pound's poetic method, as well as to remind us that as one war ended, another kind of struggle was about to start. Richard Sieburth's footnote claims perhaps too much, since the murder of Emmet Till is only one of the many possible sparks of the movement we call civil rights. When *does* something as awesome as the civil rights movement begin? After three centuries of provocations and sparks, how was it that the mid-1950s saw the emergence of the single most dramatic and effective grassroots insurgency in American history?

If Taylor Branch is telling the story, the high points include the 1955 Montgomery Bus Boycott; the 1957 Little Rock crisis over school integration; the 1960 Greensboro, North Carolina, sit-ins; the 1961 Freedom Rides; James Meredith's attempt in 1962 to enroll at Ole Miss; the Birmingham marches—against police dogs and fire hoses—in 1963; the March on Washington later that year; the 1964 Freedom Summer and the passage of the Civil Rights Act; and the 1965 march from Selma to Montgomery with its Bloody Sunday on the Pettus Bridge.

If Charles Payne is telling the story, the high points begin, as well, with Rosa Parks refusing to give up her seat on the bus, and then move on to Septima Clark becoming director of the citizenship workshops at Tennessee's Highlander Folk School in 1956; Ella Baker's assuming direction of the Southern Christian Leadership Conference in 1957; Diane Nash's spearheading the Nashville sit-in movement, in 1960; the arrival later that year of Robert Moses and his voter registration project in Cleveland, Mississippi; Baker's arranging the founding conference of the Student Nonviolent Coordinating Committee in 1960; the refusal of the Democratic Party to seat Fannie Lou Hamer and her Freedom Party at the 1964 Atlantic City convention; and the passage of the Voting Rights Act in 1965.

The first version of the civil rights struggle is largely about mobilizing; the second, about organizing. Branch's account in *Parting the Waters (1988)* focuses on Martin Luther King Jr. and the fight for integration; Payne's *I've Got the Light of Freedom* (1995) looks to figures such as Septima Clark and Robert Moses and the winning of the right to vote. The one struggle unfolded through nonviolent direct action, amplified by dramatic and soul-wrenching photographs; the other depended on the largely invisible labor of reading and teaching and learning to sign one's name. While standing up to the man worked its revolutionary changes, so did sitting down with a book. And figures from both movements often worked together, their collective efforts resulting in the passage of the most significant change in law since the glory days of the New Deal. The two strands of the movement tested the imaginations of those who made art out of these years, since the challenge was to locate in the tradition of heroic mobilization its concealed doubts and despairs, and to recognize in quiet organizing the necessary and immeasurable presence of vision and courage. Charles Payne probably gets it right when he writes that beyond all the surviving responses to the terrible beauty of that time, "the movement was its own work of art."

* * *

Published in 1945, Richard Wright's (1908–60) *Black Boy* tells one story of how a black boy becomes a man. In doing so, it acts as an allegory of the future. The next twenty years were those in which African-American men and women—and children—found, in Wright's words, the power "to stand up and fight." This was freedom not given but taken, which is the only way freedom can ever come.

Before the taking came the waiting. My two chronologies of the civil rights movement both begin in 1955, with the period of "The Taking." They begin there because the Supreme Court decision of *Brown v. Board of Education* in 1954 made it possible to dream that change was imminent. But the groundwork for change had been laid well before that, in a history that requires me to divide my account into two successive periods in which pressure builds and is then released. The period I call "The Waiting" begins in the early 1940s as the felt realities of eight decades of unfulfilled promises reach a tipping point brought on by the war. This was a period "infected by waiting," as James Baldwin writes in "Notes of a Native Son." During these years, the executive and judicial branches were the primary agents of governmental change. The period of The Taking begins on the day Rosa Parks refuses to give up her seat on the bus. During these years, the legislative branch of the federal government engaged in the more significant initiatives.

Wright chooses to begin *Black Boy* with a scene in which Richard sets fire to his own house. "One winter morning," the book begins,

> in the long-ago, four-year-old days of my life I found myself standing before a fireplace, warming my hands over a mound of glowing coals, listening to the wind whistle past the house outside. All morning my mother had been scolding me, telling me to keep still, warning me that I must make no noise.

In the quiet house Richard's Granny lies ill. Angry, fretful, and impatient, he cries out with a glad shout when a bird wheels past a window.

> "You better hush," my brother said.
> "You shut up," I said.

His mother steps into the room and tells Richard to "keep quiet." Interested only by the fire, he begins feeding it a few straws from a broom. Soon a sheet of yellow lights the room, and Richard finds himself "hiding under a burning house."

This is the fire next time, a premonitory outbreak of tension and rage. Richard sets the fire in response to being silenced: the first thing said to him is "hush," and the first thing he says is "shut up." Silenced both at home and in the white world—later, in front of Mr. Cole, Richard will find that "I could not speak"—the narrator of *Black Boy* traces a controlled eruption as he locates the sources of his anger and the power of his voice.

Wright's family home is so inwardly divided that it is perhaps worth burning down; the family has turned against itself the anger and disgust generated by living in the Jim Crow South. Its primary mode of connecting with Richard is to beat him, or to shush him. Richard's task will be to reverse this process of internalization by finding a way to expose the sources of behavior and therefore to make the dark things plain.

Richard comes to associate the self-silencing of his people with the presence of his father. "I learned that I could not make noise when he was asleep in the day time. He was the lawgiver in our family and I never laughed in his presence." Lacking a sanctioning voice, Richard finds himself adrift in a world of "cryptic tongue" and "coded meanings." He learns about sex in the school yard, quickly memorizing "all the four letter words," and yet he finds himself unable to recite the simplest lessons in the school room. Meanwhile, after a gang of boys knocks him down and steals the family food money, his mother compels him "to stand up and fight." She sends him back on the street where, in a frenzy of fear, he scatters the gang and wins the right to the streets of Memphis. And he must learn to stand up and fight so early—he is barely six—because his father has disappeared.

Black Boy unfolds as a story of how two kinds of education compete and eventually fuse in the narrator's soul. There is the premature "racy and daring" education of the streets, as well as the painfully acquired and grudgingly offered ideas Richard takes "from books." There is a direct connection between the loss of the father and the varieties of Richard's educational experience.

Once the father disappears, Richard feels hunger. "Whenever I felt hunger I thought of him with a deep biological bitterness." The family is often without food, and Richard will grow up on a diet of mush, lard, and greens. The literal hunger for food and for the lost father becomes a pang so deep that Richard can only assuage it by converting the meaning of this lack into an appetite he himself can satisfy. We see him doing this in the sentences where he describes watching his schoolmates eat sandwiches of bread and juicy sardines. Inwardly he vows that "someday I would end this hunger of mine, this apartness, this eternal difference." Here Wright converts stomach hunger into the longing to stand with rather than apart. As the passage continues, Wright admits to a curiosity about the world so great that by the fifth grade he will be skipping meals in order to roam about. "To starve in order to learn about my environment was irrational, but so were my hungers." In such a sentence, the word "hunger" has been fully redefined—into a craving for knowledge rather than for food.

Hunger of Memory is the title Richard Rodriguez gives the story of his education. He borrows the title from the scene in *A Moveable Feast* where, on the day that she and Ernest wander through Paris and play "Do you remember" about their past good times, Hadley Hemingway remarks that "memory is hunger." She says this before they eat a big dinner at Michaud's and before Ernest discovers that even after the meal "the feeling that had been like hunger . . . was still there." Hemingway here comes upon the awareness of a hunger that cannot be filled by food, by memory, or even by love, a kind of fundamental restlessness that fuels in him, and in any writer like him, the endless work of making and knowing. Rodriguez, admiring the passage, lifted the phrase for his title. But what he took from Hemingway he could also have found in Wright.

Chapter 1 of *Black Boy* ends with the scene in which Richard is taken to ask for money from his father. Richard and his mother find themselves standing in a room with the father and a strange woman. The father remains seated during the entire scene. When the mother asks for money for his children, the father laughs. He laughs his way through the encounter, a man who has long since stopped taking himself seriously. "Give the boy a nickel," the woman says. The father reaches into his pocket and pulls one out. "Don't take it," the mother says. Richard wants to take the nickel, but he does not want to take it from his father. The mother tells her husband that he should be ashamed, and she and Richard leave. As the image of the scene surges into his mind in "the years after," Richard feels it to possess "some vital meaning which always eluded me."

The meaning, of course, has to do with why, in the America that all the living and the dead have made, black men have so often left and why they have so often not stood up for their wives and children. It is a pattern Richard will not repeat. "Leaving home" will prove to be one of the requirements of growth, but it need not entail an abandonment. When Richard eventually does leave, he will send for his family in order to care for them. The man who leaves is a pattern that culminates in Morrison's Paul D, a key black male figure in the African-American literature of the century, and a man who, although tempted to leave, finally stays and stands up to the ghosts that haunt not only Sethe's house but the African-American heart and soul.

"A quarter of a century was to elapse," Wright continues in the following paragraph, "between the time when I saw my father sitting with the strange woman and the time when I was to see him again, standing alone upon the red clay of a Mississippi plantation, a sharecropper, clad in ragged overalls, holding a muddy hoe in his gnarled, veined hands." Although Richard can still see a shadow of his face in the father's face and hear an echo of his voice in the father's voice, he realizes that "we were forever strangers, speaking a different language, living on vastly distant planes of reality." The toothless, smiling, white-haired man he sees standing against the sky "could never understand me or the scalding experiences that had swept me beyond his life." His soul is still "imprisoned" in the slow flow of the seasons. The white landowners have not handed him a chance to learn the meaning of loyalty, of sentiment, of tradition. He is a man with no regrets and no hope. And he still laughs, amused, when Richard tells him of the destinies of his wife and children. He is a man who "had gone to the city seeking life, but who failed in the city." Whereas I, his son, Wright continues, had been borne in the burning arms of that city toward the "alien and undreamed-of shores of knowing."

Wright mentions, as the passage unfolds, that "I forgave him," but the admission is gratuitous. The fact of the forgiveness has already been embodied in the form and force of the juxtaposed scenes. As we jump from the scene with the father and the strange woman to the scene with Richard and his father in the field, we are asked to feel all that the heart cannot ferry on. Richard can see and "understand" and even forgive his father, but he cannot help or change him. And the father can manage even less, since he remains still "imprisoned" and "fastened" and "chained" in a creaturely state of unknowing, a state we have seen before in Huck Finn's Pap and in Gatsby's hapless father, who turns up for his son's funeral only to spill a glass of milk. Richard has come to his awareness through "living the knowledge" that his father can never possess. The supreme tragedy of the father's experience is that because he has not sought or been granted the means to know himself, he cannot acknowledge the reality and experience of his son.

"I will acknowledge you as my son": this statement serves as the climax not only of Faulkner's *A Fable* (1954) but of his novelistic career. What else do any of us and especially Faulkner's sons crave but acknowledgment, an owning up to what is already known? *Black Boy* chronicles an unending crisis of acknowledgment. Just as Richard is not heard in the opening scene, so his father fails to recognize him as his son and the white world refuses to treat him as human. Richard must therefore discover a way to acknowledge himself, to become his own father by giving birth to a new self through the complementary experiences available to all unfathered selves, the activities of reading and writing.

In Wright's story, the search for knowledge will replace the hunger for the father. Richard learns to read early, by the age of six, but it will take him as many more years to learn what reading means. His big discovery is that reading can transform the creature into the human being. He tells us this in the pages that follow the two scenes with his father, in two paragraphs that flash forward to the time of his mature awareness. In these paragraphs he speculates on "the strange absence of real kindness in Negroes, how unstable was our tenderness, how lacking in genuine passion we were." Brooding on what he perceives to be the cultural barrenness of black life, Wright wonders if the emotions we deem human are "native with man," or if they do not have to be "fostered." *Fostered*, as in "foster" parent. The "qualities" we value in ourselves must be taught, learned, exchanged, in the way a good foster parent might raise a fatherless child. The parent Wright chooses to be fostered by does not belong to "the external world of whites and blacks." No, "it had been my accidental reading of fiction and literary criticism that had evoked in me vague glimpses of life's possibilities."

Tellingly, Richard's first scene of reading is interrupted. The young school teacher who boards with his grandmother is often seen reading, and one day Richard asks her what her book is about. She puts him off, saying he is too young. "But I want to know now," he answers. So she whispers the story of *Bluebeard and His Seven Wives*. "As she spoke, reality changed." Richard's imagination blazes into another kind of fire; "the sensations the story aroused in me were never to leave me." Just as she is about to finish, Granny steps onto the porch and shouts, "you stop that, you evil gal!" Richard is left not knowing "the end of the tale."

It may not therefore come as an entire shock when, in the following scene, as Granny scrubs his "anus," Richard says to her, "When you get through, kiss back there." While he here speaks "words whose meaning I did not fully know," he also means what he says. The "uttered words" that he cannot "recall" mark his fall into transgressive speech, a medium that drives him from his family even as it connects him with an entire history of the lost emotions of his race. For what Granny has interrupted and devalued is "the first experience in my life that had elicited from me a total emotional response." It is stories about life, Richard is coming to learn, that create the capacity to feel it and to live it.

By the age of twelve, then, Richard discovers himself possessed of a "conception of life that no experience would ever erase." It is a "conviction that the meaning of living came only when one was struggling to wring a meaning out of meaningless suffering." Implied in this construction is that meaning has to be *wrung*. The meaningless becomes the meaningful by way of a concerted act of pressure, an attempt to squeeze out. It is an artist's conception of experience—the more is made out of the "less"—and, given its emphasis on suffering, it is also a tragic sense of life.

Richard's search for knowledge is continually thwarted by a conspiracy of silence in which the things most worth knowing about—sex, emotion, family history, and race—are the most forbidden. The greatest curiosity circles around the subject of "white folks." Noticing for the first time that the railroad has a white and a black ticket line, as well as separate compartments for each race, Richard asks if he can "go and peep at the white folks." Told again by his mother to "keep quiet," he proceeds to engage her in two pages of questions about whether his light-skinned Granny, who "looks white," is white, and about the origin of the family names. At every turn the mother answers a question with a question or an irritable non sequitur. Richard insists that Granny herself must want to "find out" answers to such questions. "For what, silly?" his mother replies.

"So she could know."
"Know for what?"
"Just to know."
"But for *what*."
I could not say. I could not get anywhere.

Here Richard's mother evades the issues of knowing and being known as successfully as his father does. Richard thereby begins to realize that his parents' apparent condition of unknowing has everything to do with a tacit and deeply complex knowledge of the windings and workings of life along the color line.

For Richard, the white world presents itself as a text dying to be read. "The words and actions of white people were baffling signs to me . . . Misreading the reactions of whites around me made me say and do the wrong things." In chapter 1, Wright has already written about thumbing through books before he has learned to read and wondering about "the baffling black print." The repetition of the word "baffling" in connection with the dominant race reinforces the sense that Richard's ultimate reading project is to decipher the white world, a lifework that becomes, by way of the energy and empathy required, an experience of soul-making. The effort to render these baffling signs legible generates in Richard an invaluable endowment, something close to the capacity for emotion itself. His "fantasies" about white people become "a part of my living, of my emotional life; they were a culture, a creed, a religion." Mere mention of whites arouses in him "a vast complex of emotions." Of what else can he be speaking here than the endless work of imagining the oppressor that constitutes not only the guarantee of survival for the oppressed but that leads, in a kind of redeeming irony, toward an enlargement of soul where the black boy comes to contain an understanding of the white world in a way that it never can or will understand him?

For Wright, the end of reading is writing. *Black Boy* details Richard's first entry into print and the incomprehension of the classmates who cannot grasp why he would write fiction at all. Admitting that "nobody" told him to do it, they can only ask, "Then why did you do it?" The answer can only be, "Because I wanted to." But Richard writes as well to overcome the imposed silence and to fight back. "Why had we not fought back," he questions, after his uncle is shot. Perhaps the experience of the staged and fake fight of the battle royal, imposed on him and a fellow black worker at the optical factory, near the end of his story, enables Richard to redefine what fighting back might mean. His sudden discovery of H. L. Mencken provides him the model of another way: "this man was fighting, fighting with words." Outright black rebellion (Wright is writing in the early 1940s), he concludes, "could never win." What can and eventually will prevail is fighting through writing, a merging of the destructive and creative impulses that *Black Boy* has already demonstrated on every page.

But writing was not going to be easy; when Wright's editor submitted the manuscript of *Black Boy*, originally titled "American Hunger," to the Book-of-the-Month Club, it insisted that he revise one scene and drop part 2, "The Horror and the Glory," which dealt with the Communist Party in Chicago. Wright agreed to the changes, producing the text most readers came to know as *Black Boy*. He also added a new, brief conclusion to part 1. In the penultimate paragraph of the four pages that had been essentially forced upon him, Wright still found a way to deliver a surprising prophecy of deliverance—"that the South too could overcome."

Fighting as reading and writing—Wright's *Black Boy* anticipates the vast scene of instruction the civil rights movement was to become. Those who opposed change could only be converted, Martin Luther King Jr. continuously emphasized, if African-Americans had themselves already submitted to a profound and inner conversion. King quickly saw that the movement required black "bodies" as a means of "laying one's case before the conscience of the local and national community." But bodies could only prove effective in the street if they had already passed through "a process of self-purification." Social change could be effected when the oppressed had undergone an education of the heart. Before instructing one's enemy, one had to reschool oneself. Like the "writers" Richard Wright came to admire, the citizens who committed themselves to this process of reeducation "seemed to feel America could be shaped nearer to the hearts of those who lived in it."

Not long out of the university, Grant Wiggins has returned to Bayonne, Louisiana, to teach school. The war is over; it is the late 1940s. A young black man, Jefferson, is arrested as an accomplice in the robbery and murder of a white store owner, and Grant is drawn into the story of Jefferson's response to his death sentence. During the closing arguments at his trial, the defense argues that Jefferson is no better than a "hog" and therefore cannot be held responsible for his actions. Jefferson is unmanned by the charge. The question becomes, in the face of this indictment and of his existential fear, "Will Jefferson stand up?"

As with *Huckleberry Finn*, a novel also written four decades after the action it depicts, *A Lesson Before Dying* (1993) affords its author a crucial perspective on its subject. The knowledge of all that is to come for his people during the elapsed interval encourages Ernest Gaines (b. 1933) to structure his novel as a story about waiting. It is not always the "watchful waiting" Ralph Ellison wrote about in 1963. It is just as often a swallowing of rage.

Jefferson waits to be executed. The whites control the official calendar; it is they who decide when the condemned man will be killed, "the convenient date and time." Whites humiliate blacks by making them wait in department stores, court rooms, kitchens, cell blocks. "I decided to wait," Grant says to himself, while talking to Sheriff Sam Guidry, in Henri Pichot's kitchen. He has come to solicit permission to visit Jefferson in the penitentiary. Grant decides to wait just before Guidry walks into the kitchen and asks, "Been waiting long?" "About two and a half hours, sir," Grant answers. Less than twenty years after these fictional events, Martin Luther King Jr. could give a far different answer, in his speech in the capitol at Montgomery after the successful march from Selma, to the question about how much longer African-Americans were going to have to wait: "How long? Not long."

Gaines prefigures this spoken promise when he has the Pichot's maid reassure Grant, at the beginning of his wait, "I'm sure it won't be too long now." But of course Gaines is not prefiguring but refiguring, since he puts these words into the mouth of a character conceived over twenty years after King actually spoke them. *A Lesson Before Dying* is filled with simple statements like this that resonate forward in the life of the novel's characters with a prophetic power, even as for the author, and the reader, looking back, they herald changes long since accomplished.

Change is at the heart of Gaines's novel, especially the change of a black boy into a man. "I want a man," Miss Emma says about her godson Jefferson. By "man" she means someone who will "stand for her." Grant and Emma fight to make Jefferson stand up and acknowledge in himself a manhood systematically denied the African-American male. As Grant explains to his girlfriend Vivien, "we black men have failed to protect our women since the time of slavery. We stay here in the South and are broken, or we run away and leave them alone to look after their children and themselves. So each time a male child is born, they hope he will be the one to change this vicious circle—which he never does . . . What she wants to hear first is that he did not crawl to that white man, that he stood at that last moment and walked." The irony in the wish is that in their efforts to make it come true, Emma and her accomplice, Tante Lou, display more gumption and uprightness than any of the men in the novel, including Grant and Jefferson, and therefore prefigure the savvy self-reliance of the women who would follow them and who would prove so central to the success of the civil rights movement.

Jefferson finally will stand up: "Tell Nannan I walked." He goes to his death on his own two feet, uncomplaining and unassisted. Gaines can imagine such a wish-fulfilling ending because he knows the future. Plenty of black men and women, after waiting for so long, will go on to stand up to power. Gaines elects the metaphor of standing because so much of the courage required of those who would bring about the great change demanded the walking of a gauntlet, against billy clubs and rifles and police dogs and fire hoses in the street. So much of the fight was taken to places where it became a mortal decision whether to sit or to stand. The irony, as Martin Luther King Jr. was to point out, is that during the coming years of "creative tension" the forces arrayed against change could convert sitting and standing into a distinction without a difference. "One day the South will know that when these disinherited children of God sat down at lunch counters they were in reality standing up for the best in the American dream."

How does Jefferson locate in himself the will to stand? Gaines does not quite answer this question. It just so happens that one day, after months of visits in which Grant has solicited nothing but "It don't matter," he sees a new look—of pain—on Jefferson's face. He can see that Jefferson wants to say something. "I stood over him, waiting." Then Jefferson says, "Tell—tell the chirren thank you for the pe-pecans." Grant catches himself grinning like a fool. "I felt like crying with joy. I really did."

The joy comes from the fact of response. It is good and human to respond to care, as Jefferson finally does. But the engine of response—whatever it is that moves Jefferson from his habitual diffidence (a habit he shares with Grant, who begins his narration with the statement "I was not there," and who comes off as a man determined by negatives like "couldn't" and "wasn't") to this act of thanks—remains unexplained. It has something to do with Jefferson's decision to "rite something," even though he "don't kno what to put on paper." Jefferson's diary signals his willingness to lay claim to the self-definition and self-respect resulting from any honest attempt to put feelings on paper. And this breakthrough also has something to do with what Grant does for a living, with teaching.

Gaines chooses to narrate the execution by way of a white voice. Paul, the young deputy, tells Grant about it. After finishing, he moves in front of Grant to look him in the face.

> "You're one great teacher, Grant Wiggins," he said.
> "I'm not great. I'm not even a teacher."
> "Why do you say that?"
> "You have to believe to be a teacher."

As he waits for news of the execution, Grant reminds himself that "I will not believe." He stubbornly resists belief in "the same God or laws that men believe in who commit these murders." He means the murder of men like Jefferson who are not judged by their peers. There is something attractive in Grant's stubborn unbelief, an honest cleaving to his skepticism and his rage. But he acknowledges that in order to be free, people "must believe."

Believe in what? Not in the existing "laws" but in the power of men to change their standing by changing the law. He must believe the opposite of what President Eisenhower believed when he asserted, about the civil rights measures that came his way, that "you cannot change people's hearts merely by law." The consequence of such belief is to conclude that change comes not through courts and legislatures but through a shift in custom. But the history of the United States proves the opposite. Hearts dead set against legal changes adapt eventually to the new behaviors enjoined by the law, as they did in the interval between the fictional year in which Jefferson walks and the actual year in which Gaines imagined him. Jim Crow laws were in fact "difference made legal," as Martin Luther King Jr. wrote in 1963, a government-sanctioned hardening of the heart. American history is in fact a romance of the deep reciprocity between hearts and laws. All significant legal changes—such as the eventual realization that separate cannot be equal—are prompted by extralegal imperatives, such as compassion or shame. Justice is simply the conversion of love into statutes. As these newly enacted laws become the norm, they in turn instruct and enlarge reluctant hearts.

A good part of the romance of America is the story of the endless struggle between law and love and hate. What we call "history" is a record of the changes that occur. Frequently "history" can no more explain *how* these changes occur than Gaines can explain what makes Jefferson respond and stand up. And if history often seems to move less by knowable causes than by unfathomable ones (secretly), it is because large changes are often rooted in private, individual ones—the kind produced in acts of reading and writing, like Jefferson's, the kind recorded in literature.

"You are a great teacher," Paul says to Grant, as if to say that Grant has taught Jefferson to stand up. It is more accurate to say that he has attended at a process of education, of leading out. As an honest teacher, Grant acknowledges that while he cannot define what teaching is, he can testify that learning occurs, and that it occurs, excruciatingly enough, by way of waiting, through a patience allowing what is in some way already known to come forth. Grant thus retreats into an explanation that explains nothing, as he and Paul conclude their exchange:

> "I saw the transformation, Grant Wiggins," Paul said.
> "I didn't do it."
> "Who, then?"
> "Maybe he did it himself."
> "He never could have done that. I saw the transformation. I'm a witness to that."
> "Then maybe it was God."

Can you know who you are, if you don't know who your father is? James Baldwin's (1924–87) fictional families reverse the Faulknerian dynamic: instead of having too much father, Baldwin's sons have too little. Characters such as Gabriel Grimes in *Go Tell It on the Mountain* (1953) do fulfill a father function, but their true relation to their various sons remains undisclosed or obscure. Set all-too-terribly free in a world of unknown or shifting paternity, Baldwin's sons discover themselves to be heirs to the Lucas Beauchamp of *Go Down, Moses*, a black man who out of will and necessity has "*fathered himself*."

All-too-terribly free, I have written, because this is a freedom, and a terrifying one: the American Negro, Baldwin writes in *Notes of a Native Son* (1955), "is unique among the black men of the world in that his past was taken from him, almost literally, at one blow." When Faulkner calls Lucas "ancestryless," he does not mean that Lucas is without precursors but rather that they cannot be altogether claimed or even ascertained. The missing or unacknowledging father in Baldwin's works acts as a figure for the theft of both history and memory, and Baldwin's attempts to situate his characters with respect to their fictional fathers and himself with respect to his literary fathers can be understood as a vast recovery project, one to which he gave essential impetus but which it was left to others to forward, if not to complete.

As in *Absalom, Absalom!*, *Go Tell It on the Mountain* acquires its force through a strategic withholding of genealogical knowledge. Unlike Faulkner, Baldwin does not involve the son in the belated work of coming to know. John Grimes will remain in ignorance about his actual birth status, and the structure of the novel is meant to highlight this unchanging condition. John is an active, searching figure only in parts 1 and 3. These two sections, writes Michel Fabre, act "like the side panels of a triptych whose central panel ('The Prayers of the Saints') relates the converging stories of Johnny's aunt, stepfather, and mother." In this long central section the key recognitions occur, recognitions in which John plays no part.

The two big revelations have to do with paternity. The first, which occurs in "Florence's Prayer," is that John's father Gabriel has a "bastard" son named Royal. Gabriel's sister Florence knows this by way of a letter from Gabriel's first wife, Deborah, and the knowledge is shared with the reader in a scene where Florence discusses the letter with her husband. The second revelation comes later, in "Elizabeth's Prayer," where the narrator reveals that Johnny is himself illegitimate and is not Gabriel's son. None of this knowledge is ever conveyed to John. He never knows about Royal, and he begins and ends the novel facing Gabriel, the man he calls "father." Even though Gabriel came into John's life some years after his birth, when he marries his second wife and John's mother, Elizabeth, Baldwin makes it clear on his opening page that John's "earliest memories—which were in a way, his only memories" are of a world in which Gabriel is always already there.

In the language of the novel, Royal and John are both "bastards." A key early scene attempts a transvaluation of the meaning of this word. There is a third son in the story, Roy, Johnny's younger brother and the "legitimate" child of Gabriel and Elizabeth. Roy is as hostile toward Gabriel as Johnny is unsuccessfully solicitous. One day Roy comes home with a knife wound on his face. Mutual accusation breaks out, and Gabriel slaps Elizabeth. "You slap her again, you black bastard," Roy yells, "and I swear to God I'll kill you." Roy uses the word "bastard." The irony of the usage is that of Gabriel's three sons, Roy is the only one who is not a bastard. But of course the epithet is directed against the father, and the word sticks.

It sticks because Baldwin means to redefine the meaning of the word "bastard" in the same way that in *The Color Purple* Alice Walker means to redefine the meaning of the word "virgin." When Shug says to Celie, "You still a virgin," she does so after learning that Celie has never had an orgasm. Virginity is here redefined not as contingent upon penetration by the male but rather by the capacity for female sexual response. It has nothing to do, in this redefinition, with the gender of the partner or the purity of the responding body. Walker thus performs a tonic riff on Faulkner's claim that "it was men invented virginity not women," reminding us that virgins are of value insofar as they remain the intact possession of the male parent, an object of exchange that he can, in the marriage ceremony, "give" to another man.

A "bastard" for Baldwin is not a son born out of wedlock but a father who strikes his wife and, more crucially, a man who refuses to acknowledge his sons. No more than Walker does Baldwin cede the meanings of words to the conventions of patriarchy or the pieties of the law. Such redefinitions are also caught up in the romance of Baldwin's life story. David Baldwin, the rejecting preacher by whom James was raised, married his mother Emma three years after James was born and preferred the younger brother Sam, his son by a previous marriage.

Baldwin chooses to make his women the bearer of their culture's secret history. In the novel's two most moving scenes, Gabriel's long-suffering first wife, Deborah, and his angry sister, Florence, confront Gabriel, in quite different ways, with their long-held knowledge of the same secret, the story of Esther and Royal, "her bastard boy." Having fathered a bastard, they both urge upon him, is not a sin, but refusing to acknowledge him is.

In the first scene, Deborah treats Gabriel with great tenderness. As a girl, she was raped by white men, and as a consequence, she and Gabriel have been unable to bear children. One day Gabriel comes home and Deborah tells him that a local boy named Royal "done got hisself killed in Chicago." She responds by speaking of Royal as just another lost black child; she gives no indication that she knows of the true relation. Gabriel begins to weep, and Deborah watches him for a long time. Then she asks her loving question: "Gabriel . . . that Royal . . . he were your flesh and blood, weren't he?" Gabriel answers "Yes." In the scene that unfolds, Deborah asks Gabriel why he let Royal go off and die by himself, why he never "said nothing." He defends himself, even accusing Deborah of being "happy" that Royal is dead. But then he asks her, "How long you been knowing about this?" Ever since Esther came to church, she answers, long before, that is, Esther and Gabriel ever slept together. She has known about Royal all along. She has even hoped that Gabriel might want "to own that poor boy," so that she could "have raised him like my own." And she has said nothing, biding the time, and letting Gabriel cling to his secret. *Own*, Deborah says: not "own" as in "to possess," but as in "to acknowledge."

It is hard to imagine a scene more expressive of a crushing love. For what is the kind of love Deborah displays here but the keeping of one's counsel even unto the heart's utter hurt, a refraining from the unburdening of a knowledge the partner is not yet ready to assume? Gabriel's secret is here revealed to be an open one; Deborah even tells him that she knows he stole from their money box to pay for Esther's journey north. Deborah stages a recognition scene at great cost to herself while allowing her husband to maintain his dignity and to release his grief. By way of this display of tact and courage, Baldwin makes a profound point about the emotional division of labor that obtains in so many American homes, the strange and wonderful willingness of women to initiate the work of making feelings plain.

Yet her love is also crushing because it makes no room for Gabriel's growth, which might have occurred had he been confronted earlier with the matter of his son. In the second scene, Florence comes at Gabriel with the same story, but she does so in anger. "I been carrying this letter now . . . for more than thirty years," she tells Gabriel, in a confrontation occurring not long before the novel ends. It is the letter Deborah wrote to her about Royal's story. Gabriel denies that his life is "in that letter." He wants to exist instead inside God's forgiveness. But Florence stands for history rather than for the consolations of religion. "It's time you started paying," she says. Florence believes that all past actions count. "You think whatever you done already, whatever you doing right at that *minute*, don't count." Gabriel's is the old, familiar American belief that the past can be wished or forgotten away.

Florence threatens to out Gabriel, to show the letter to Elizabeth. But we never see her deliver on the threat. We never even get to read the letter. As in the scene with Deborah, a character decides on a course of *not telling*. Florence's point is not about the content of the past, but the attitude taken toward it. What was done matters, certainly, but what matters even more is the will to own up to it. It matters much more to Florence that Gabriel be made to confront the fact of the thing done than that he make a public confession about it. In a 1970 conversation with Margaret Mead, Baldwin disavowed any interest in white "atonement" for the sins of the fathers, calling instead for the "recognition of where one finds oneself in time or history or now."

The failure to acknowledge the son operates in Baldwin's work as a figure for a collective refusal to own up to the force and shape of the American past. It is not a problem confined to the lives of black people. It is, in fact, a bigger problem for white people, Baldwin argues, since the systematic exclusion of and discrimination against blacks is the largest possible instance of a willed amnesia and self-alienation that can only cripple the nation. "Depthless alienation from oneself and one's people is, in sum," Baldwin writes, "the American experience."

Baldwin explores this alienation in *Notes of a Native Son*. That work can perhaps best be approached, however, by comparing it to one that treats another crisis of acknowledgment, a crisis occurring between brothers. In his 1957 story "Sonny's Blues," Baldwin makes it plain that division *between* the races is no more a problem than division *within* the race and *within* the black self.

"He's my father, ain't he?" Roy asks in *Go Tell It on the Mountain*. "But he don't never listen to me—no, I all the time got to listen to him." The words could come right out of "Sonny's Blues." "I hear you," Sonny says to his brother. "But you never hear anything *I* say." Sonny says this to a man who is by profession a school teacher, a paid listener. Long before we meet Sonny we are made aware that the brother, who is also the narrator, struggles with his elected task. "I listened to the boys outside," he says. They are playing and laughing in the schoolyard. "Their laughter struck me perhaps for the first time." *For the first time*, that is, he hears the lack of joy in the laughter. He has not been paying attention. "I hadn't wanted to know," he has already admitted, two paragraphs earlier. Know what? Know things he cannot find "any room for . . . anywhere inside me," things like Sonny's pain, as expressed in his music.

Music is not simply a matter of generating sound. It is an act of expression arising out of an act of listening. Everybody carries around, Sonny argues, a "storm inside." But you can't talk it and you can't make love with it and so you have to play it, and then, when you try, "you realize *nobody's* listening. So *you've* got to listen." Listen, Baldwin means, to the music of suffering. Sonny and his brother do agree on one thing: everybody suffers. Sonny is angry that people have to suffer "that much." Rather glibly, the brother replies: "But there's no way not to suffer—is there, Sonny?"

This is the rhetorical question that sets Sonny off. The point, he answers, is not that everybody suffers—the point is that "*everybody* tries not to." So they take heroin, or try not "to know," or play the blues. What distinguishes people—what gives them their character and their personal style—is the form the resistance to suffering takes. The heroes, often artists, are those in whom intense listening and response are inseparably tied. The artists not only have suffered but also have listened to the "terrible" pain of others and have acknowledged it in a response both personal and communal.

The whole effort of the story is to have the brother acknowledge Sonny's music, to get him to the nightclub, to have him listen. He hasn't been listening, not to Sonny or to the world. He doesn't even know who Charlie Parker is. The process whereby this acknowledgment occurs is twofold. Before the brother can hear Sonny's blues, he has to learn how to listen to the others in the street for whom he has made no room inside himself, and in this lesson Sonny is his teacher. The brother, looking down through his apartment window, sees Sonny listening intently to the music of a small street revival. Instructed by this example, he is then able to listen to Sonny when he comes upstairs. It is the first genuine conversation they have had, and it further enables the narrator to hear his brother's music.

At the club, before Sonny begins to play, the brother says to himself, "All I know about music is that not many people ever really hear it." The music begins, creating a "dialogue," first among the players on the stage. Sonny can only play his difficult blues in response to the attentive urging of the other players. When the group finally begins playing the blues, the "tale" told by the music is not new—it's about suffering and delight and even triumph—but "it always must be heard."

"And this tale," the narrator continues, "has another aspect in every country." We are not in another country; we are here, in the United States of 1957, and the music that is beginning to come forth is the kind that "could help us to be free if we would listen." It's not so much the still, sad music of humanity as it is the long, black song, the one that on this night opens the listener to the memory of the stones on the road his mother walked, of the moonlit road on which his father was killed, and of his own little girl, dead from polio. In granting access to all this, Sonny's blues serve here as a figure for the power of art to connect the listener to the "long line" of the neglected past.

The movement of the verbs in Baldwin's closing paragraphs makes the point: "I heard . . . I saw . . . I felt." The narrator moves from hearing the music to seeing people and scenes from his past to having feelings about all of that. Then the "tears begin to rise." He reverses the motion of the opening paragraph of the story, the one in which he hasn't "wanted to know" or to feel, the one in which he can't find "any room . . . inside me." Sonny is by comparison a hero of openness—as a boy he is "bright and open"—an almost masochistically permeable figure who makes room inside himself for "torment" and who then sends that suffering and that knowledge back out, transformed, as music.

It is a music that goes "all the way back." Music is cultural memory translated into moving sound. The brother finally hears, in Sonny's music, that "freedom lurked around us." And the reason jazz is the music Sonny prefers to play, and plays at the story's end, is because jazz, like good conversation, is about listening and responding. "The dry, low, black man said something awful on the drums, Creole answered, and the drums talked back." An eloquent expression of contained black pain, jazz also celebrates an ongoing American dialogue between traditions that continually invents "new ways to make us listen."

To listen is to respond. When the narrator truly hears his brother's music, he sends him up a drink, a Scotch and milk the waitress sets on the piano near Sonny's head. "He didn't seem to notice it, but just before they started playing again, he sipped from it and looked toward me, and nodded." It is the long-sought acknowledgment. This connection frees a terrible and beautiful power. Sonny puts the drink back on the piano. The musicians begin again, and the narrator regards the glass: "For me, then, as they began to play again, it glowed and shook above my brother's head like the very cup of trembling."

The reference is to the Old Testament Book of Zechariah, which encourages Jews recently returned from exile with the prospect of a revivified Jerusalem:

"Behold, I will make Jerusalem a cup of trembling unto all the people round about" (12:2). At the end of Baldwin's story the exiles are American blacks in 1957, and the narrator hears in his brother's jazz the promise of another rising. The story, written at the hinge point between the Waiting and the Taking, ends in prophecy.

The essays in *Notes of a Native Son* act as a call to remember. "Alienation" is the word Baldwin uses to describe the resistance to memory; it works in the essays as a synonym for "repression" or "forgetting." The American confusion is not grandiose but personal, based as it is on the Gatsby-like and "very nearly unconscious assumption that it is possible to consider the person apart from all the forces which have produced him. This assumption, however, is itself based on nothing less than our history, which is the history of the total, and willing, alienation of entire peoples from their forebears." Such willed alienation binds the alienated even more surely to that from which they believe themselves to have been set free, since the iron law in all such transactions is that the repressed will return. At the heart of this alienation lies the failure to integrate the fact and experience of black Americans into the nation's family romance.

This failure operates as a signal instance of what I have been calling throughout this study the American "innocence." The innocence inheres in Florence's belief that history "don't count." The failure very much remains a family affair; after writing of "white Americans," Baldwin says of the Negro that "he is bone of their bone, flesh of their flesh; they have loved and hated and obsessed and feared each other and his blood is in their soil. Therefore he cannot deny them, nor can they ever be divorced." Baldwin's prophetic call is for an integration already long since accomplished. His task is to remind the American reader of an intimacy between the races running so deep and going so far as to render absurd the mere fact of social segregation. The call to the white reader is not "Set me free" but "Acknowledge me." I—the black American—am the most secret part of you. The work Americans are being called on to complete, in the mid-1950s, is not simply the legislation, important as it is, of new civil rights. It is a work of spiritual exploration and reintegration, a psychoanalysis of the American soul.

In the closing pages of *Notes of a Native Son*, Baldwin makes this case by way of a revived dead metaphor, a punctuation mark, and another redefinition of a word. "Stranger in the Village" concludes by invoking "the darker forces in human life." The American vision of the world allows "little reality" for these forces. Baldwin goes on to write about our propensity to "paint moral issues in glaring black and white," as in the positing of "an evil empire." The words "darker" and "black and white" are clearly metaphors, tropes that we have long since agreed on as adequate to invoking a very complex case—the case, that is, of the felt dimensions of our inner, largely unconscious lives, and of the forces ruling them. They are also dead metaphors, words we use without acknowledging the figurative weight they carry. And it is our tendency to reduce experience to such terms, and with such carelessness, that perhaps best reveals us and the damage we are so unknowingly prepared to do.

The damage flows from the ways in which a structure of imagery so casually deployed also conditions the perception and treatment of the not-white. For the notion that bad things are "dark" or "black" has nothing to do with bad things themselves—they have no color—and everything to do with the aspect of those Americans designated as "Negro." It is as if everything "dark" and "black" about themselves that white people attempt to cut away becomes inevitably confused with Americans designated as "black." This is why Baldwin goes on to complete the sentence from which I have already quoted by concluding that this "American vision of the world . . . owes a great deal to the battle waged by Americans to maintain between themselves and black men a human separation which could not be bridged." One of our most characteristic modes of thinking—our black-and-white moralizing—is a direct product and symptom of "the interracial drama." The structure of imagery in "Sonny's Blues" invites us to push beyond such thinking. The tension between "lights" and "darkness" set up in the opening paragraph is resolved in the closing one, where, having had their say, the musicians "talk up there in the indigo light."

Americans like binaries: good and evil, past and present, black and white. Baldwin's contribution is to remind us that our most cherished binary has long since broken down. "One of the things that distinguishes Americans from other people is that no other people has ever been so deeply involved in the lives of black men, and vice versa." He goes on to claim, in the essay's closing sentences, that "it is precisely this black-white experience which may prove of indispensable value to us in the world we face today. This world is white no longer, and it will never be white again." Baldwin makes two deft moves here. First, he replaces his earlier formulation, "black and white," with the hyphenated "black-white." Second, he inverts, by dint of positioning and repetition, the implicit hierarchy of meanings built into the accepted usage of the word "white."

The hyphen matters because it achieves through a modest stylistic shift a visual and rhythmic reminder that black and white are already intimately joined, separated by much less than the word "and." The repetition of the word "white" matters because, by the time it takes its place in the final sentence of the essay, it has come to mean something like "simple." Baldwin is saying two things at the very end: that the world can never again think of itself as unmixed in color, and that, more importantly, it can never again think that color mixing much matters, can never again in good faith indulge in the overly simple "black and white" thinking that has always been so inadequate in covering the human case.

❦   ❦

Alice Walker (b. 1944) lived out the mixing of the races in a very public way. In 1966 she met Mel Leventhal, the fellow civil rights worker with whom she traveled to Greenwood, Mississippi, and who became her husband the following year. One of her most powerful early stories anticipated this experience. In an interview in *Black Women Writers at Work*, Walker says, "I wrote 'The Child Who Favored Daughter' . . . out of trying to understand how a black father would feel about a daughter who fell in love with a white man. Now, this was very apropos because I had just come out of a long engagement with a young man who was white, and my father never accepted him. I did not take his nonacceptance lightly. I knew I needed to understand the depth of his antagonism . . . Ironically, it was over that story, in a sense, that I met the man I did, in fact, marry. We met in the movement in Mississippi." Walker began the story and met Mel Leventhal when she was twenty-two years old.

Throughout her early twenties Walker found herself in the position she writes about in "Child," where the disapproval of the father is embodied in the law. The crime is to have "given herself." *Give* is the operative word in Walker's story. The daughter's crime is to claim the right "to give her love" to whomever she pleases. She thereby not only breaks the father's heart but usurps his generative power as the "*giver of life.*" She challenges the assumption that a creator has the right to control his creatures, as her giving becomes the equivalent of an aggressive form of taking. She takes control over her own body and therefore of the system that has marked it out as the supreme possession of the man who made her. The story thus announces what had already become the case: the willingness of black women to resist all forms of social control in their quest to achieve for their people a full set of "civil" rights.

"The Child Who Favored Daughter" consists of a core story and its repetition. The father in the story once had a sister named "Daughter" whom he loved "with his whole heart." She was a giver. "She would give him anything she had." But she would also "give anybody anything she had," including the very white man in whose cruel, hot, and lonely fields the brother works. Broken by the collapse of this affair, Daughter returns home to madness and suicide. The women in the brother's life subsequently face a "sullen barrier of distrust and hateful mockery." He cannot forgive his sister for "the love she gave that knew nothing of master and slave." Then, years later, when he learns of his daughter's affair with a white man, he beats her and begs her to "deny the letter" he has found. She refuses, and in an emotion "burning with unnamable desire," he kills her by cutting off her breasts.

In Walker's story, the father wants his daughter to deny her letter. The scene between Florence and Gabriel in *Go Tell It on the Mountain* also turns on the power of a document, a letter that threatens Gabriel and binds him to his suppressed history. It is in such fugitive sources that American literature often locates the answerable record of the nation's past. One thinks of Celie's discovery of Nettie's letters, midway through *The Color Purple*, or the letter Charles Bon plants on his body for a grieving Judith to find, or the newspaper clipping about Sethe that Stamp Paid shows to Paul D. Walker's story begins with such a document: "She knows he has read the letter."

If the daughter's body is the object of the father's unnameable desire, the "words of the letter" are the focus of his rage. "It is rainsoaked, but he can make out 'I love you' written in a firm hand across the blue face of the letter. He hates the very paper of the letter and crumples it in his fist." The father has somehow found his daughter's letter to her lover. How it has come to him matters less than that he believes it to be his; fathers are men made out of words, and the language belongs to them, as the third sentence of Walker's story reminds us: "*Father, judge, giver of life.*" The daughter approaches the father—she is walking toward him—through names, names that she rehearses in her head and that convey his power to originate and punish. Her fate will resemble Louvinie's, the slave woman in *Meridian* (1976) who has her tongue cut out after telling too powerful a story, one "bursting . . . with delight." The daughter's transgression has been *to write* about her desire, and the father's deepest wish is that she will eat her words: "She is his daughter, and not Daughter, his first love, if she will deny the letter. Deny the letter; the paper eaten and the ink drunk, the words never wrung from the air." By refusing to eat her words and therefore to swallow her voice, this unnamed woman renounces the role of daughter and dies asserting not only the claims of desire but her right to articulate it.

Slave narratives often turn on the moment when the slave becomes lettered. "The Child Who Favored Daughter" reveals that the literacy plot is alive and well. From colonial times, slaves had been governed by antiliteracy laws, statutes generated "in an attempt to prevent the forging of passes but also to head off insurrection." Slave owners understood early on the connection between the power to read and write and the will to organize and to rebel. Eugene Genovese makes the point by way of ex-slave Josiah Henson, who recognized that learning how to read had made him "more anxious than before to do something for the rescue" of his people.

Walker updates the literacy plot by relocating it within the black family and by deploying it as a figure for the struggle between repression and desire. The father's attempts to deny his daughter access to language evoke the slaveholder's attempt to deny it to the slave. The reproduction of slavery within the black family flows not only from the father's ironic internalization of the oppressor and his violence toward black bodies, but from his fear of the destabilizing power of words themselves, their tendency to expose secrets and to articulate feelings threatening to all hierarchies, including the family of which any father is the traditional head. By intercepting his daughter's letter, the father not only anticipates the blocking husband in *The Color Purple*, who will hoard Nettie's letters to Celie, but also attempts to staunch an unstoppable verbal outpouring. "Write" is the last thing Nettie says to Celie, before she disappears out of her life for thirty years, and acceding to the imperative marks the crucial step from slavery to freedom. Celie does *write*. Walker's work dramatizes the power of letters to change a woman's—and therefore a people's—place.

❦   ❦

There was one American letter that almost didn't make it into the canon. It was scribbled in the margins of the *Birmingham News*, in response to a story with the headline "White Clergy Urge Local Negroes to Withdraw from Demonstration." The response filled every available margin of the paper, wrapping around "pest control ads and garden club news." It overflowed onto pages borrowed from a California entertainment lawyer. Friends at a nearby motel deciphered the prisoner's "chicken scratch handwriting" and typed up the results. With the help of an old Negro trusty at the jail, a smuggling relay was set up, with the lawyer bringing typed draft back and carrying new copy out. The letter quoted from Saint Augustine and T. S. Eliot. It was published without fanfare in the June 1963 issue of the Quaker journal *Friends*. A month later reprint rights to the letter were being sold to the *Atlantic Monthly*.

Martin Luther King Jr.'s (1929–68) "Letter from Birmingham Jail" announces that the Waiting has long since been superseded by the Taking. "Freedom is never voluntarily given by the oppressor," he reminds us, "it must be demanded by the oppressed." The letter's basic rhetorical move is to consign the word "wait" to quotation marks. It is no longer a word King himself can use without irony. "For years now I have heard the words 'Wait!'" Those who would counsel him to "wait" live inside "a tragic misconception of time," King argues. There is nothing in the flow of time that will inevitably cure all ills, and belief that necessary changes will come in God's good time is in fact a self-serving "myth of time" promoted by "people of good will." Direct action is always "untimely." The very course of American history testifies to the efficacy of the untimely act.

"And the war came," Lincoln writes in his Second Inaugural Address, about the how and the why and above all the when of the coming of the Civil War. The "And," that is, can be read as a simple conjunction, where history is merely about one thing following another, a weak parataxis. Or the "And" can be read as meaning something like "therefore," where the war comes as the terrible and earned and ut-terly predictable consequence of the four-score and five years of American history preceding it. Like all huge and altering events, it has a timely untimeliness. The only appropriate time for social change is *now*. "Now is the time," King writes, and then he repeats himself: "Now is the time."

King addresses his letter above all to himself. The story told by Taylor Branch in his great narrative history is of a man of immense patience, one inclined less to de-cision than to vacillation. The big question about King's career has to do with the eight-year gap between the success of the 1955 boycott and his jailing in Birming-ham in 1963. During these years King often participated in acts of "determined legal and nonviolent pressure." But, in the years following the boycott, King did also appear to be waiting for a "Now" in which he could engage as fully with history as he had in the great months of 1955. The Birmingham marches in 1963 provided him with the moment of maximum untimeliness, an interval of "creative tension" in which his own tendency to "wait" on events finally found release in an "unavoid-able impatience." In the letter, the huge periodic sentence beginning with the words "But when you have seen vicious mobs lynch your mothers and fathers . . ." consti-tutes for King the necessary refresher course in American history that explains and sanctions his present will to act. It is as if in those eight years King himself had been asked to compress and reenact the experience of the "more than 340 years" during which his people had "waited . . . for our constitutional and God-given Rights." He did so, and the letter came.

One reason Rosa Parks found the strength not to stand and surrender her seat on the bus in December of 1955 was because in July of that year she had attended a two-week interracial conference held at the Tennessee Highlander Folk School. Workshops at the school were run by Septima Clark (1898–1987). King makes reference to Clark's efforts in "Letter from Birmingham Jail": "in preparation for direct action," he writes, "we decided to go through a process of self-purification. So we started having workshops on non-violence." And Alice Walker was to make indirect reference to these workshops in *Meridian* when she has Meridian say to Truman that "revolution would not begin . . . with an act of murder—wars might begin that way—but with teaching." More than any other figure, it was Septima Clark who defined the workshop as the central scene of instruction for the civil rights movement and who reconceived teaching as an effective form of fighting.

Born in Charleston, South Carolina, Clark devoted her life to learning how to teach. She prizes her role as teacher so highly that in her memoir, *Ready from Within* (1986), Clark decides to skip over the first forty-nine years of her life and shifts in her third paragraph to the year 1947, when her teaching really caught fire. "I want to start my story with the end of World War II because that is when the civil rights movement really got going."

In 1947, Clark returns to Charleston to teach in the public schools. She is a widow with a grown son. At a childhood education meeting in Washington, D.C., in 1952, she first hears about a place "where blacks and whites could meet together and talk." She visits Highlander Folk School, near Chattanooga, in the summer of 1954. Returning the next summer as a teacher there, she meets Rosa Parks. Rosa is shy, almost diffident. "She wouldn't talk at all at first." But she has already shown her initiative in her work with the integrated Freedom Train and, finally, with Septima's encouragement, consents to tell the workshop about it. "Three months after Rosa got back to Montgomery, on December 1, 1955, she refused to get up from her seat on the bus."

Back in Charleston, Clark is getting into trouble of her own. As a member of the NAACP she runs afoul of a newly enacted law prohibiting any city or state employee from such membership. Dismissed from her job, she sends out 726 letters to black teachers asking them to tell the state that the law is unjust. She receives twenty-six replies. Only five teachers go with her to confront the superintendent. "I don't know why I felt that the black teachers would stand up for their rights. But they wouldn't."

Septima learns a "good lesson" from this experience. "I considered that one of the failures of my life because I think I tried to push them into something that they weren't ready for. From that day on I say, 'I'm going to have to get the people trained. We're going to have to show them the dangers or the pitfalls that they are in, before they will accept.' And it took many years."

When Clark arrives at Highlander, she enters a world of teacher-training. As Director of Workshops, her job is to train people to go out and found Citizenship Schools. The schools then turn nonvoters into voters. Clark quickly realizes that "you couldn't get people to register and vote until you teach them to read and write."

In 1940, 2 percent of the African-Americans living in the twelve states of the South were "actually qualified to vote." In the heart of the old Confederacy, C. Vann Woodward writes, blacks were "effectively prevented from registering even when they had the courage to try." In 1954, only fourteen votes were cast by black voters in the thirteen Mississippi counties with mainly black populations. Those who did manage to vote were required to answer a twenty-one-question form and to interpret one of the 285 sections of the state constitution.

Clark helped to change all this. Between 1957 and 1970 she was instrumental in starting 897 Citizenship Schools. In 1962 the five major civil rights groups came together to form the Voter Education Project. Ten years later, the first two blacks were elected to Congress since Reconstruction.

"I changed too," Septima claims as she traveled through the Deep South, visiting already-trained teachers and recruiting new ones.

> Working through those states, I found I could say nothing to those people, and no teacher as a rule could speak with them. We had to let them talk to us and say to us whatever they wanted to say. When we got through listening to them, we would let them know that we felt that they were right according to the kind of thing that they had in their mind, but according to living in this world there were other things they needed to know. We wanted to know if they were willing then to listen to us, and they decided that they wanted to listen to us.

Clark comes to change through listening. She promptly incorporates this lesson into her teaching style. Rather than imposing a strict curriculum, Clark learns to start with what her students already know. "Students would talk about whatever they had done that day—started a vegetable plot, dug potatoes." They tell her "what they would like to learn." It might be how to make out a bank check, or about why the pavement stops where the black section of town begins. "The first night they gave us their input, and the next morning we started teaching them what they wanted to do." "We were never telling anybody," Clark says, "we used a very nondirective approach."

Clark's methods convert the classroom into what it always is, at its best, a site of "sudden recognition." She recognizes that useful knowledge is not so much imposed as brought forth. A teacher works with "the kind of thing" students already have "in their mind," the kind of thing Grant Wiggins is able to help Jefferson locate in himself. Good teachers are recognized for what they have always been, those who "can teach their own capacity to learn." Clark's work becomes, like the work of Robert Moses in Greenwood, and in McComb, and in Clarksdale, a triumph of listening: "his ability to listen and to think and more than anybody else to consolidate," writes Charles Payne, "let you talk about what you wanted to talk about." The result was a lasting empowerment. "In the very act of working for the impersonal cause of racial freedom, a man experiences, almost like grace, a large measure of personal freedom."

Clark's big word is "change," and teachers tend to develop, she comes to see, in response to their students. This is the basic dynamic of the act of learning we call teaching: one is instructed by those one is trying to help. "We had to change," Clark admits, about the pressure put on teachers by students at the training center. This change led to a collapse of the distinction between leaders and followers. In response to those who want Dr. King to lead all the marches, she says, "You're there . . . Can't you do the leading in these places?" Believing that every marcher is a potential leader, Clark also believes "that you develop leaders as you go along, and as you develop these people let them show forth their development by leading." The goal is a continual elevation of the base into the superstructure, the conversion of students into teachers, followers into leaders.

Clark first spoke up in print in *Echo in My Soul*. Published in 1962, the book was written out of the middle of the struggle, when everything still hung in the balance. Her collaboration with Cynthia Stokes Brown, *Ready from Within: A First Person Narrative*, appeared in 1986, a year before her death. Brown writes that Clark "told me this story when she was eighty-one years old, from how she remembered and interpreted her life in 1979."

Ready from Within is the superior book. It gains from what Brown calls "a feminist perspective" acquired by Clark in the years after writing *Echo in My Soul*. Its form also acts as a knowing extension of its content. *Ready from Within* divides itself into two parts, "The Movement" and "The Beginning and the End." By choosing to "start my story . . . when the civil rights movement really got going," Clark argues that a life story really gets going when it engages history. "I spent forty years growing up," Clark says. But the core of her story is what happens after that, the years from 1954 to the early 1960s. It was then, by opening herself to her students, that Clark experienced "growth like most people don't think is possible." She brought about change in others by opening up to change in herself, and so she came to embody the truth that "the measure of a person is how much they develop in their life." In believing this, Clark joins the visionary company of romantic developers who, beginning with Wordsworth, invented something new in human experience by learning to revalue change by calling it growth, and then by reminding us, as Sam Shepard does at the end of *Buried Child*, that "you can't force a thing to grow."

Nor can you force a nation to give what cannot be "given." Faulkner's last strong novel understands this, marking his major contribution to the literature of civil rights. In the 1948 *Intruder in the Dust*, Lucas Beauchamp is the man accused and imprisoned, stuck, like Mark Twain's Jim, in his own kind of smokehouse. Like Jim, he sits still, but unlike Jim, he controls outcomes. It is by dint of his wit and will that he enlists the aid of his white allies, gains his freedom, and also succeeds in paying for it. The novel thus explores, once again, the paradox in Huck Finn's awful phrase, "to set a free nigger free." Like Twain, Faulkner realizes that you cannot set a man free if you have the power to do so, since having the power—along with the history of having had it—stands altogether in the way of the project. You can't *give* anyone his freedom. And if he hasn't somehow got it—if he has to be given it—how then can he ever get it?

Faulkner approaches these questions through the metaphor of payment. "Gave," "pay," "cost," "receipt"—on these words the action turns. They are meant to invoke the history of a country in which people have once been sold. Lawyer Gavin Stevens believes that the South owes Lucas and his people, and he doubts whether the police can help. "I can only say that the injustice is ours, the South's. We must expiate and abolish it ourselves, alone and without help nor even (with thanks) advice. We owe that to Lucas whether he wants it or not." Gavin here appears to endorse a continued period of watchful waiting, one in which the South would somehow reform itself without any outside pressure. But Lucas has other plans, just as Martin Luther King Jr. and Septima Clark had other plans.

Because he knows that no amount of material reparation can repay his people for its bitter past, Lucas insists on paying for what is done on his behalf at every step of the way. He will accept no "gifts." One acceptable form of repayment is the acknowledgment of what was done. Thus, in the last sentence of the novel, Lucas speaks the two words that can stand in for and act as the formal recognition of the price he and his people have paid and continue to pay for their American arrival: "My receipt."

During the years of the Waiting and the Taking, nobody "gave" anybody any thing. "*Giver*" is the word that sticks in Alice Walker's throat; she knows, with Emerson, that "we do not quite forgive a giver." King's lieutenant Bayard Rustin refused the metaphor of the gift as early as 1957, after King showed him a draft of a speech he was preparing for the Prayer Pilgrimage in Washington, D.C. "Give us the ballot!" King had written. "Martin," Rustin replied, "colored people don't want to have somebody 'give' them anything anymore."

Black Americans did the only thing that could be done—they took their freedom. They took it by schooling themselves in what would work, and then by putting their bodies where their beliefs were. The Civil Rights Act was signed, after the longest filibuster in the history of the Senate, on July 2, 1964. The Voting Rights Act was passed a year later. On that day, C. Vann Woodward writes, "Jim Crow as a legal entity was dead." But something James Baldwin had written, a decade earlier and in another country, hung uneasily in the air. "Nothing is more unbearable, once one has it, than freedom." On August 11, 1965, five days after President Johnson signed the second of the two greatest pieces of social legislation passed in the second half of the twentieth century, Watts went up in flames.

CHAPTER TEN

Love and Separateness

WELTY ❦ PETRY ❦ DOUGLAS ❦ MARY MCCARTHY
❦ FRIEDAN ❦ STEINBECK

*I*n the year Rosa Parks refused to give up her seat on the bus, Eudora Welty (1909–2001) published *The Bride of the Innisfallen,* a gathering of short stories containing "The Burning," in which two half-mad sisters hang themselves after their house has been burned by Union soldiers. Left behind is their slave, Delilah. She stirs the feathery ashes and finds in them "Phinney's bones." These are the remains of her child, conceived on her by the brother of the sisters and kept upstairs by them as a sort of mad offspring in the attic. Then Delilah starts walking—north, perhaps—"her treasure stacked on the roof of her head."

Before Delilah finds the bones, she has a vision. From the burned house she retrieves a Venetian mirror and stares into it. Delilah sees in the mirror the shape and consequence of Southern history itself, a world held up by "black men," "men now half-split away, flattened with fire." She sees Jackson before Sherman came. She sees "what men had done to Miss Theo and Miss Myra and the peacocks and to the slaves, and sometimes what a slave had done and what anybody could now do to anybody." One of Welty's foreseeing, turbaned women, Delilah has, as Peter Schmidt puts it, her "sibylline epiphany." She sees what Dilsey sees: "I seed de beginnin, en now I sees de endin." It is a vision of peace and pain and decline and fall, of the price that has been paid and is being paid—now, in 1955—and that will go on being paid for the actions of the past.

I do not propose to read Welty as a sibyl of race, although she has much to say about it. It is what she reveals about the lives of women that makes her, even more, such a pivotal and prophetic figure. On a first approach to her work, it does not perhaps seem so. Her decorated prose can act, like Stevens's self-confessed "gaudiness," as a feinting maneuver, as if she were chary of seriousness. As R. P. Blackmur once said about Stevens, she wants to make supreme statements discreetly, so that their beauty will show before their force. "That horror may evolve out of gentility"—this, according to Joyce Carol Oates (b. 1938), is the Welty effect. Yet the horrors in Welty—especially the experience of rape—are treated with a lightness that disarms them of their stigmatizing power. The freedom lies in choosing how to *take* things.

Welty did her strongest work in the short story, where by dint of sheer length we are not invited to linger on the losses. Those written between 1940 and 1955 take as their project a search for new outcomes for the inherited plot of a woman's story. "The Wide Net" (1942), "At the Landing" (1943), and the sequence of *The Golden Apples* (1949) form the heart of this achievement.

Few American writers more resist plot summary. A prose that so fends off reduction to the "what happened" has something profound to tell us about the search for meaning itself. However, insofar as Welty works by contraries and the resolution of them, her work also invites the very sort of attention it appears to discourage. I will in any case proceed by treating the stories as an imitation of an action, in the hope that the very awkwardness of the approach might turn something up.

As "The Wide Net" opens, Hazel Jamieson has "vanished." After staying out all night, her husband William returns home to find a note saying that she will no longer put up with him and that she is "going to the river to drown herself." William and his friends get out the wide net and drag the river. William dives deep and into "the true trouble that Hazel had fallen into," a sense of "elation that comes of great hopes and changes." Hazel, it turns out, is pregnant, she can do nothing about it, "and so it had turned into this." The men make a party; they catch and cook a passel of fish. But they fail to "catch Hazel." "Who says Hazel was to be caught?" Doc asks.

When William returns home, he hears his voice called. Hazel is standing in the bedroom doorway; she has been hiding about the house all the time. "It was the same as any other chase," Welty writes, "in the end." And Hazel promises to "do it again if I get ready." In the meantime, the couple has moved to the front porch. The story ends with Hazel taking him by the hand and leading him back inside.

John Updike's (1932–2009) *Rabbit Run* (1960) ends with a one-word sentence: "Runs." Welty uses the same word in the first story in *The Golden Apples*: "That's just what I *know* King MacLain'd do—run." Running away is what men like Harry Angstrom and King MacLain do; to run is the province of the male. The single biggest thing Welty's story imagines is that women, too, can run.

But of course the woman comes back, or never leaves at all; as Elizabeth Bishop was to write, in "Questions of Travel," "*the choice is never wide and never free.*" This is especially true for women like Hazel Jamieson. The kind of running they accomplish has more to do with an internal mobility, an exploration of the eddies and rapids of the spirit.

"Make or break," we say. We perhaps ought better to say, "break *to* make." "The Wide Net" ends as it proceeds, as a comedy of remarriage. As so often in American fiction, families act as allegories of the nation, a structure that needs to be broken apart, in a kind of civil war, in order to be made.

"The Wide Net" is dedicated to John Fraizer Robinson, the man Welty accompanied to San Francisco in 1946 and whom she did not marry. Such a fact has at best an ambiguous status in Welty's self-described "sheltered life." The shape of that life is of two singular dedications: to her work, and to her mother. The four great books of stories came out in 1941, 1943, 1949, and, finally, 1955, the year in which Welty's mother suffered a difficult recovery from an eye operation. Welty published only three stories in the next fifteen years. Her mother died in 1966. In 1970, she brought out *Losing Battles*, her longest novel. Then came *The Optimist's Daughter* in 1972 and *One Writer's Beginnings*, her autobiography, in 1984. There had been three more novels along the way, *The Robber Bridegroom* (1942), *Delta Wedding* (1946), and *The Ponder Heart* (1954). Welty was to travel widely well into her forties, but she always returned to and called home the town of Jackson, Mississippi, where her parents, natives of Ohio and West Virginia, had settled in 1904.

Published a year after "The Wide Net," "At the Landing" is perhaps Welty's most radical and disturbing story. Jenny lives with her grandfather up the hill from the river landing. She is "shy." She also lives with the awareness that "one day she would be free to come and go." Meanwhile, Jenny never performs "any act, even a small act, for herself . . . It might seem that nothing began in her own heart." One day, in watching fisherman Billy Floyd, her innocence leaves her. Her every sight of him betrays desire for which she has no words. "But if innocence had left, she still did not know what was to come."

What comes is the rape that in Welty so often comes. But it is not quite taken as a rape, and that is the difficult and elusive point. For the experience Welty visits upon her heroines we need an undiscovered word. Whatever happens to these women, they somehow remain, like Jenny, "inviolate." Looking at Billy mastering the horse, Jenny has an insight "about love." "She had the knowledge come to her that a fragile mystery was in everyone and in herself." Welty calls this a "moral knowledge," and by this she alludes to "the uncanny sensation," as Mary McCarthy puts it, "of the *otherness* of a separate being," an otherness beyond the reach of any touch. So, when the touching comes, it perhaps changes little. Welty places emphasis instead on having felt "what was in another heart besides her own," as Jenny does when she watches Billy play with the albino Mag. Not for nothing is Jenny's maiden name Lockhart.

Something in us cannot be touched, like the "lump of amber" Jenny will later hold in her hands. "There was no way at all to put a finger on the center of light." What we love and acknowledge in another is a separateness:

Suddenly it seemed to him that God Himself, just now, thought of the Idea of
Separateness. For surely He had never thought of it before, when the little white

heron was flying down to feed. He could understand God's giving Separateness first and then giving Love to follow and heal in its wonder; but God had reversed this, and given Love first and then Separateness, as though it did not matter to Him which came first.

Love and Separateness are not the opposed terms that an easy reading of this famous passage from "A Still Moment" (1942) might suggest. It is out of her perception of Billy's separateness that Jenny in fact discovers her love. By way of having her character watch Billy, Welty redefines love as a continual interplay of greeting and letting go.

Jenny's grandfather dies. She walks by the river with Billy and feels clumsy. She hears the little pulse of blowing bubbles from a mussel hidden in the river and realizes that "a clear love is *in the world.*" Then the rain begins to fall, and Billy saves her in his boat from the rising water. He lifts her onto a dry place, where she sleeps. When she wakes, "he violated her and still he was without care or demand and as gay as if he were still clanging the bucket at the well." He cooks fish and wild meat and Jenny eats in "obedience" to him. "For him it was all a taking freely of what was free."

But what is it to her? While she eats in obedience, she also eats "greedily" and "eagerly." She feels "not as sorrowful as she might have been." As a marriage needs to be broken and opened in order to be made, so does the inviolate self. In either case, if there is a touching involved, it is of two separatenesses.

Jenny returns to the flooded house and spends days in an "ecstasy" of cleaning. Time heals her of "the shock of love." The experience Welty calls "love" comes, as it must come, as a shock. Jenny feels herself closing down again, like a house with all its rooms dark, where "someone would have to go slowly from room to room," lighting each one.

Jenny leaves the landing that July. At the river, she sits with the fishermen. Again there is the smell of fish being cooked and wild meat. Men are throwing knives at a tree. The men put her in a houseboat and one by one come "in to her." Out of that space, which we cannot see, come cries and male laughter, "and somehow both the harsh human sounds could easily have been heard as rejoicing."

"Could easily have been heard," Welty writes. The emphasis falls on the nature of the response. How we hear these sounds depends on how we take things, in this world. The freedom we have, when all the other freedoms have fallen away, Welty everywhere intimates, is to structure the nature of our own response. As she was to write in *One Writer's Beginnings*, her stories are made out of "my responses to the real experiences of my own life." And her response, Welty everywhere suggests, is her responsibility.

"Nothing is done to oneself that one does not accept." This is what Pilar says to Maria about her rape by the Facists, in *For Whom the Bell Tolls*. "By some contemporary standards of sexual politics," Michael Kreyling writes, "the ending of 'At the Landing' condones rape." Kreyling reads Jenny's initiation as a necessary one, a tonic ushering from innocence to experience. But surely Welty positions rape on a continuum of things done to the self that the self finds the resources to respond to in an unscripted way. Welty's most daring argument is that a response can determine the meaning of an action. She never locates the event of a rape in the consciousness of the intruder. And in taking rape the way they take it, Welty's women deprive rape of its shame and so invite a transvaluation of the reader's response to the imagined experience as well.

It is perhaps less a question then of getting over a developmental hurdle than of the ever-present power, exerted above all by the least powerful among us, to assign meaning to experience. Welty's women dare *not* to be traumatized. And they locate the power to do so in the place where their author locates it, in the last sentence of her autobiography: "For all serious daring starts from within." Despite what happens to them, Welty's women keep coming back at men, as does Rosamond, another abducted woman who at the end of *The Robber Bridegroom* tracks down her husband and who declares in triumph, "I came and found you!" These are not women, to use Joan Didion's mordant formulation about the "wounded birds" of "The Women's Movement" (1972), "too delicate to deal at any level with an overtly heterosexual man."

Jenny uses the word "mystery" when she first comes upon love. The words "mystery" and "secret" have a distracting history in Welty's work, one that culminates in *One Writer's Beginnings*, where she allows that "one secret is liable to be revealed in the place of another that is harder to tell, and the substitute secret when nakedly exposed is often the more appalling." Welty implies here that the keeping and exposing of secrets is a kind of game. An obsession with "concealment," as she calls it in "A Memory," is just what she writes her way beyond, because the pursuit of mystery can be a fatal thing, as it proves to be in "A Still Moment." In laying hold of a man, the outlaw Murrell "meant to solve his mystery of being," but the only result of this assault on another man's "secret" is that it kills him. It turns out that there is no mystery to uncover; there is simply a condition to be shared. In "Circe," Welty invokes this "mortal mystery," which is the awareness that we are going to die and the fact that most of us bear up under this fact. When Bowman comes upon "a fruitful marriage" in "Death of a Traveling Salesman," he comes upon this sort of mortal mystery. "There was nothing remote or mysterious here—only something private. The only secret was the ancient communication between two people." The purpose of the stories is not to expose mysteries, but to count the many ways in which we consent to go through time together.

At the heart of Welty's vision is the woman who goes into water. Sometimes she goes in like Ophelia, borne down by the weight of male projection and the beauty myth; sometimes, like Adrienne Rich (b. 1929), as a willful and courageous diver into the wreck of conventional hope. The central story in *The Golden Apples* turns on the moment when Easter, an orphan, an unmothered girl, drops into Moon Lake.

Loch Morrison, the only boy at the camp, dives in after her. Back on shore, he administers first aid. Loch "fell upon her and drove up and down upon her, into her, gouging the heels of his hands into her ribs again and again." The girls watch Loch work, "astride Easter."

Later, in "The Wanderers," Virgie Rainey will choose, on the day of her mother's funeral, to go into water. "She took off her clothes and let herself into the river." In this elected moment of immersion, she experiences a joining with the "All" and a happy sense of "the vanishing opacity of her will." She trembles "at the smoothness of a fish or a snake that crossed her knees." She acts out a mature acceptance of both solitude and the desire for pleasure in the body, one well beyond the reach of the girls at Moon Lake.

The girls are asked to watch a rescue that looks like a rape. Water for Welty is the transformative element; when you come out of it you may be changed. "Transformation" is what her characters simultaneously spurn and crave. The change is often violent. The girls at Moon Lake spend their week trying to promote emotions in themselves, but in the end they cannot do so on their own. A sexual other is also needed. Welty sees that her culture has turned girls into Andromedas, virgins chained to the rock of convention. So a "Perseus" has to be found, and what he carries with him is Medusa's head.

The girls watching Loch "hated him" and "almost, they hated Easter." They hate that they have been awakened to Easter's "secret voice" and to "her terrible mouth," from which "a snake would come out."

There are many ways to read the Medusa myth. In *The Glory of Hera* (1968), Philip Slater moves beyond a phallic reading of the writhing snakes. As a boundary symbol—Slater focuses on the snake's mouth and capacity to shed its skin—a head of snakes can evoke the fear of being swallowed up, as well as of being penetrated. Moon Lake is itself such a place, with "bottomless parts" where "snakes harmless and harmful, were freely playing now." It is the uncanniness of her own body that the girl confronts when she looks at the Medusa. One "secret" Perseus wields when he flaunts the severed head is the engulfing and terribly open secret of female sexuality itself, before which women as well as men can be turned to stone.

In *One Writer's Beginnings*, Welty reads her stories as held together by a "sort of tie—a shadowing of Greek mythological figures, gods and heroes that wander in various guises, at various times, in and out, emblems of the characters' heady dreams." Beyond its dominating Perseus and Medusa myth, *The Golden Apples* offers a carnival of such ties: Danae and her shower of gold, Atalanta and her golden apples, Circe and the men as swine. But the book is mythopoeic rather than mythographic; Welty's interest is not in cataloguing the contemporary parallels but rather in the process of mythmaking itself. The word "myth" comes from mythos, the Greek word for "story," and Welty means to direct attention toward the root meaning of the word. Myths are not fixed and dead patterns, like the constellations into which so many mythical figures have been gathered. They can operate instead in our lives as the overdetermined and therefore ambiguous and therefore freeing stories they always already are. Myths are stories we inherit in order to revise, to read more meaning *into*. They are not templates for behavior, but suggestive precedents by way of which we discover the power of our own "visioning."

This is precisely what Virgie Rainey does. In *The Golden Apples*, we first see her in a bedroom with a sailor, having sex. She claims that pleasure. Then "June Recital" backtracks to fill in her girlhood. It is the story of a student and a teacher. Miss Eckhart creates "a dedicated place" where Virgie can master the piano. A woman passes along the tradition of making art to another woman, and the debt, as with any successful pedagogy, is owed by the teacher to the student. Virgie "was the one who made things evident about Miss Eckhart." And when Miss Eckhart plays the sonata, the effect, like the rescue at Moon Lake, is "violent." Art, like sex, opens us to "more than the ear could bear to hear or the eye to see." Later, Miss Eckhart will slap her own mother when she mocks her daughter's standard line of thanks to Virgie, "*danke schoen*." The slap is at once a reproach for all that her mother has not taught her and an affirmation of the compensating reciprocities of the teacher-student bond.

There is no Greek myth that figures such a scene; there is no Greek myth in which an older woman unlocks or acknowledges the power in a younger one. Welty has to make up her own myth. Or, more accurately, Welty ends her book by giving us a woman immersed in the process of making one. It is as if in imaging her characters, Welty splits herself in two. "Inasmuch as Miss Eckhart might have been said to have come from me, the author, Virgie, at her moments, might have always been my subject." Welty concludes her autobiography with this recognition. Refiguring this split, imagining new demarcations that can accommodate a woman's full wants and needs, is precisely that act of the mind we see Virgie engaged in when she ponders the Perseus-Medusa myth at the end of *The Golden Apples*.

In "The Wanderers," the story with which *The Golden Apples* closes, Virgie's mother has died and the town of Morgana gathers for the funeral. Virgie moves about the house and encounters her neighbors, but she makes no real contact. Irrelevant things get said to her, like "You should marry now." In response to another careless comment, Virgie hears herself making a life decision: "Going away."

Before Katie Rainey dies, in a scene that comes early in "The Wanderers," she has a sensation and a vision:

> There was a simple line down through her body now, dividing it in half; there should be one in every woman's body—it would need to be the long way, not the cross way—that was too easy—making each of them a side to feel and know, and a side to stop it, to be waited on, finally.

Welty sets the mother's vision alongside the daughter's, the one Virgie has in the closing pages, on the courthouse steps. Virgie remembers that among her pictures from Europe, Miss Eckhart had one that "showed Perseus with the head of Medusa." She remembers the male vaunting, the pride in the lifted arm and the triumph over the uncanny monster. Then she thinks about the line made by the hero's sword:

> Cutting off the Medusa's head was the heroic act, perhaps, that made visible a horror in life, that was at once the horror in love, Virgie thought—the separateness. She might have seen heroism prophetically when she was young and afraid of Miss Eckhart. She might be able to see it now prophetically, but she was never a prophet. Because Virgie saw things in their time, like hearing them—and perhaps because she must believe in the Medusa equally with Perseus—she saw the stroke of the sword in three moments, not one. In the three was the damnation—no, only the secret, unhurting because not caring in itself—beyond the beauty and the sword's stroke and the terror lay their existence in time.

Perseus makes a horizontal cut, the cross way. He severs the head from the body. This is the age-old myth of the West, the separation of higher from lower, head from body, God from creature, soul from self, man from woman. The myth posits an above and a below and disguises hierarchies as binaries. What would it mean, Welty asks, if we were split vertically, from head to toe, the long way?

A lengthwise split still leaves *two whole halves*. It is an image, perhaps, of a self divided in such a way that it can keep company with itself. Thoreau and Hurston imagine such a self, in writing about solitude and ecstasy. Welty's stories are full of doublings, or moments when people see themselves in mirrors. In such moments, "opposites," as Virgie perceives, "were close together." Even "Love" and "Separateness," the opposites that first surface in "A Still Moment," may not be very far apart. Welty offers up at the end of "The Wanderers" a way of reading experience in which "the hero and the victim," "hate" and "love," the "hideous and the delectable" all emerge as ineluctable partners in a dance of difference.

In the final paragraph of "The Wanderers," as Virgie sits in the rain on the courthouse steps, she is joined by an old "wrapped-up Negro woman with a red hen under her arm."

> Then she and the old beggar woman, the old black thief, were there alone and together in the shelter of the big public tree, listening to the magical percussion, the world beating in their ears. They heard through falling rain the running of the horse and bear, the stroke of the leopard, the dragon's crusty slither, and the glimmer and the trumpet of the swan.

Welty ends her book with an act of listening. Two women here heed the percussion of the world, the endless "beat of time." They form another set of joined opposites, being "alone and together," as well as black and white. They hear the sounds that five mythological creatures make. These are the echoes given off in the mind as it listens to the ongoing recycling of the stories humans make, a process as unending as the Morgana gossip that builds out the life of the town. Here, as the myths and gossip around Virgie reach almost a breaking point, she and an old black woman hover on the threshold of a looming destiny, as they pay heed to the voices great within them, and to the traditions becoming theirs to shape.

＊　＊

Academic historians have long argued that the women's movement was given an essential push by African-American freedom-taking. Of course, the fight for suffrage preceded even the Civil War, and its accomplishment in 1920 did not signal the end of anything for activist women. But the phase that gives rise to modern feminism—marked by the passage of Title VII in 1964, the founding of NOW in 1966, and the passage of *Roe v. Wade* in 1973—does appear to take energy and heart from the struggle called "civil rights."

The perception contains a surprising irony, one articulated by Septima Clark. Of the many reasons why the civil rights movement could not sustain itself, Clark mentions only one: "The way men looked at women." The devaluation of women's work and power is reflected in the many standard histories of the movement, which focus on the actions of men. Ella Baker claims that getting things moving in the key black institution, the church, depended "on women, not men. Men didn't do the things that had to be done"—things like staying up all night on the Thursday after Rosa Parks was arrested in order to type and mimeograph flyers calling for a one-day bus boycott, as did Jo Ann Robinson and her colleagues on the Women's Political Council. Baker believed that the movement had come to depend too much on incidents "involving violence," since violence "was more likely to be considered a story." The undramatic work of organizing and teaching simply didn't make the news. "Success is registered," Baker argued, "in terms of . . . how much prestige and recognition you have," and she also saw that progressive movements can falter once they gain a certain level of media attention, as if that attention marked the realization of the goal.

"In those days," Clark writes, "I adored Dr. King." Over the years, she undergoes a shift in "perspective." "The way I think now about him comes from my experience in the women's movement." Twenty years later, Clark sees that "this country was built up from women keeping their mouth's shut." It was built from the proposition—one Hurston's Joe Starks embodies—that men talk and women listen. Clark herself "used to feel that women couldn't speak up." The silencing of both women and black people was broken in the 1950s. Clark recenters the history of that time in the breaking of the first silence when she claims that "the civil-rights movement would never have taken off if some women hadn't started to speak up."

In the same year that Welty began writing the stories that would be gathered into *The Golden Apples*, Ann Petry (1908–97) delivered an early and prophetic act of speaking up. Graduating from the Connecticut College of Pharmacy in 1931, Petry worked in the family business until her marriage and move to New York in 1938, where she began to publish articles in the *Amsterdam News* and short stories in *The Crisis*. Her work in P.S. 10 in Harlem brought her close, for the first time, to the lives lived by America's urban blacks. The result was *The Street* (1946), the first novel by an African-American to sell more than a million copies. Set in wartime New York, *The Street* explores how it feels to be an African-American woman in this time and place, especially one possessed of a body that attracts the attention of men.

The novel opens with Lutie Johnson's search for a place to live. She settles on three "dark, dirty" rooms in a Harlem walk-up. She will live there with Bub, her eight-year-old son. Lutie is trying to make it on her own after the breakup of her marriage to Jim, one that foundered when she was forced to work away from home as a maid in a Connecticut suburb. As Lutie attempts to make a home and a living on her own, Bub is drawn into a mail-stealing scheme that lands him in the Children's Shelter. Lutie goes to nightclub entrepreneur and would-be boyfriend Boots Smith, to get money for a lawyer. When Boots proposes to trade money for sex, she flies into a rage and kills him with an iron candlestick. Believing that a child whose mother is a murderer doesn't stand a chance in the world at all, Lutie buys a one-way train ticket to Chicago.

The Street departs from the fiction of its day in its mature and matter-of-fact sexual awareness. The third-person voice tells us that Lutie has a "tall long-legged body." Of course, Lutie can't hear this voice, but what she can detect is the continual flow of feeling directed at her in the gazes of black and white men. She feels the su-per's "eyes traveling over her—estimating her, summing her up, wondering about her." She reads the "fat curve" of Lil's breasts and doesn't hesitate to imagine "a lot of other things that Lil could teach" her son. She quickly sees that her Connecticut employer pays more attention to men other than her husband. And she abides the slander put out by white women at luncheon parties about colored wenches "al-ways making passes at men."

The very frankness of her gaze protects Lutie against puritanical reaction. She wishes her husband there at the train and knows that then "he would have put his arms around her and really kissed her." When she receives Pop's letter about "*Jim's carrying on with another woman*," she heads right home. "Month after month and that black bitch had been eating the food she bought, sleeping in her bed, making love to Jim." Lutie's refusal of euphemism keeps her acutely aware of the force of "desire" in human life.

Blake and Freud put so much emphasis on "an improvement of sensual enjoy-ment" because they saw that if people had a decent access to the body and its sexual desires, then they had already done a lot of courageous work in clearing away the mystifications and prohibitions with which culture binds them. Clarity about sex makes it possible to be clear about other things.

Her blackness, Lutie comes to see, reduces the range of her job choices. In order to save her family, Lutie has to leave it. In her absence, Jim betrays her. He betrays her not only because she is absent but because he has even fewer economic options than she does. "The women work," Lutie thinks to herself, "because the white folks give them jobs—washing dishes and clothes and floors and windows. The women work because for years now the white folks haven't liked to give black men jobs that paid enough for them to support their families. And finally it gets to be too late for some of them. Even wars don't change it. The men get out of the habit of working and the houses are old and gloomy and the walls press in. And the men go off, move on, slip away, find new women. Find younger women."

Lutie's perceptions are diagnostic. She sees that in the urban black world of the 1940s, there is no division of labor. "Here on this street women trudged along overburdened, overworked, their own homes neglected while they looked after someone else's while the men on the street swung along empty-handed, well dressed, and carefree." In such passages Lutie becomes a heroine of analysis, a fig-ure who not only suffers her world but who insists on making its workings plain. She sees how history works, where the experience of individual lives accumulates into a systematic bias perceptible only, perhaps, to a novelist's eye.

Lutie's killing of Boots Smith is an act of murder that is also an act of analysis. Petry surrounds the scene with a sense that the act is understood. Lutie has come to Boots for money he will not lend her but with which he proposes to buy her sexual services. Petry writes that "she was angry with him . . . for being a procurer for Junto," the white man Boots works for. Lutie yells at Boots, and he begins slapping her. Her vision blurs, but it clears as she picks up the candlestick. Boots "was the person who had struck her," but as her "angry resentment" builds he becomes "a handy, anonymous figure" of everything she has fought against. "A lifetime of pent-up resentment went into the blows." As she continues striking Boots, Lutie strikes at all the things Boots "represented."

Lutie's act is representative. She commits the act on behalf of herself and people like her, striking out against a history of loss and abuse. This is Petry's answer to Bigger Thomas's killing in *Native Son* (1940), an act in which another black character strikes out against a figure Eldridge Cleaver was later to call the Ogre. For Bigger and for Cleaver, the Ogre is the culturally implanted fantasy image of the white woman. For Lutie, the Ogre is not so much the black man as it is all the "things" this encounter with him calls up and represents. Knowing this, Petry does not allow her character to mystify the deed, as Dreiser's Clyde Griffiths is temporarily allowed to do after killing Roberta. On the subway, looking back at the killing, Lutie wonders, "Had she killed Boots by accident?" She concludes that "the first blow was deliberate and provoked." "The impulse to violence had been in her for a long time." It is a recognition worthy of Sethe, in *Beloved*, who never apologizes for or rationalizes her act and who ascribes it to the simple motive of taking her babies and putting them where they will be safe. Lutie and Sethe are connected not only by their capacity to act but by their insistence on "clear understanding."

No more than Dreiser or Farrell does Petry represent her main character's working life. She focuses instead on Lutie's failed search for something satisfying to do. After Lutie gives up her job as a maid, she works on a hand presser in a laundry while studying shorthand and typing at night. She passes the civil service exam and becomes a file clerk. What she really wants to do is sing, and the pursuit of this desire brings her into a murderous association with Boots Smith.

Lutie's subsistence-level income leaves her unavailable to anything as highfalutin as the free play of "the market." She has neither the money nor the time to become a consumer. Her world is cut off from the myths and realities of economic mobility; its black citizens live in a caste system in which virtually any white is above any black, and where the races live in distinct enclaves. Even the wealthy Mrs. Hedges remains marooned in her second-floor apartment on the street. Petry details a world in which the barriers to progress are more social than economic, and where the social includes her status as both an African-American and a female. For such a citizen, Petry predicts, the fight for women's rights will be difficult to distinguish from the fight for civil rights.

Petry images Lutie's predicament as an "ever-narrowing space." Because he is white, male, and unencumbered—and living in Paris—Henry Miller (1891–1980) can write in *Tropic of Cancer* (1934) about life in a city as a continual experience of "sufficient space." Because she is black, female, and encumbered, Lutie experiences New York as a space of "closing in." The architecture of the novel returns to rooms, walls, streets. The rooms are small and ugly. "The walls seemed to come in toward her, to push against her." And the street is, like Joe Christmas's, not a dead end but a "circle, and she could keep going around it forever and keep on ending up in the same place, because if you were black and you lived in New York and you could only pay so much rent, why, you had to live in a house like this one."

As Lutie's horizon contracts, her sense of space becomes personified, animated. "Streets like the one she lived on were no accident. They were the North's lynch mobs," she thinks. When Boots tries to pimp her to Junto, she imagines him with a brick in his hand, the "final one needed to complete the wall that had been building up around her for years." While she is out working, Lutie thinks, the street even usurps the most cherished of human roles, becoming "both mother and father" to "your kid."

Lutie remains confined to the horizontal, to the street. One way out—or up—would be to pass as white. Near the beginning of Nella Larsen's (1891–1964) *Passing* (1929), an African-American woman finds herself stuck on a hellish Chicago street. Irene Redfield chooses to step onto an elevator and is thereby "wafted upward on a magic carpet to another world, pleasant, quiet, and strangely remote from the sizzling one that she had left below." Like Gatsby's ladder to the stars, Irene's elevator tempts the taker with a breezy lightness of being. And, like Gatsby's ladder, it can only be traveled "alone," affording a transcendence upward for which the riser pays a severe price.

Lutie chooses to remain below, in part because she has a child. None of Petry's characters escape being "walled in," and African-American fiction will have to wait until Gloria Naylor's (b. 1950) *The Women of Brewster Place* (1982) before a group of black characters, all women, tears down the encroaching wall. But the reader of Petry's novel is granted a mobility denied its inhabitants, one gained through Petry's generosity with point of view. As the third-person narration shifts among standpoints, we are allowed to move among isolated subjectivities and to discover the connections between them.

Chapter 4 gives us the world according to Jones, the super; chapter 5, his girlfriend Min; chapter 9, Bub, the son; chapter 10, Mrs. Hedges, the madam; chapter 11, Boots Smith; and, in the culminating act of imagination, chapter 14 gives us ten pages narrated on behalf of the white schoolteacher Mrs. Rinner. These shifts in point of view are as complicated as anything in Faulkner or Pynchon and anticipate, in their range and daring, the chiming monologues of Anna Deavere Smith's (b. 1950) *Twilight* (1993). What counts is the fact rather than the content of such diversifications. The case being made is simple and profound: "it all depended on where you sat how these things looked." Because the people of New York sit in such different places, places largely determined, they see things differently, and their perspectives do not coincide, or even intersect. But the abundance of ways of looking imagined and embodied in Petry's novel can remind her reader that the multiplication of standpoints is one way in which fiction approximates the condition we call "democracy," a condition that in 1940s New York remained more available in a book than on a street.

✦   ✦

Lutie's awareness of sex as a fact in human life provides her with a tool for analysis that allows her access to the linked issues of race and class. Lutie may be the most politically aware female character in the novels of her day. But she is so far ahead of her time that she has no movement with which she can join and no formal language with which to make a move from her immediate experience of "sex" to an understanding of the ways in which the meanings attached to bodily differences gather into the problem of "gender."

Lutie's capacity for analysis stands in stark contrast to the abilities imagined by Mary McCarthy, whose female characters suffer from "the problem that has no name." "The chains that bind" her characters, as Betty Friedan (1921–2006) was to write in *The Feminine Mystique* (1963), are in the "mind and spirit," "made up of mistaken ideas and misinterpreted facts, of incomplete truths and unreal choices." In *The Group*, also published in 1963, McCarthy says about Priss that "she seemed to have no mind of her own." This is the worst thing McCarthy can say about a character, and she sees it as being the case for most of her women. Nine years later, Adrienne Rich reissues the call. As she writes in "When We Dead Awaken: Writing as Re-Vision" (1971), "Until we can understand the assumptions in which we are drenched we cannot know ourselves." By whatever power—preferably their own—women need to be raised up out of institutionalized forms of oppression. Consciousness also needs to be raised; Friedan and Petry and McCarthy link up with Welty's search for a new female mythos or story, a new way of knowing the self.

One of the surprises of American literature is that it contains so few satisfying scenes in which a mother instructs a daughter, especially in the facts of life. In "Indian Camp," Hemingway gives us a boy who learns too much, too soon. It turns out that girls are lucky to learn much at all, early or late. "At the heart of her vision is the failed or simply missed mother-daughter exchange." Michael Kreyling writes this about Eudora Welty, but the claim applies to most of the writing women who come before or after her.

Early on in *One Writer's Beginnings*, Welty asks her mother a question: "Where do babies come from?" She hopes that her mother will tell her "what she'd promised for so long." The mother tells Eudora that "the mother and the father had to both *want* the baby." The daughter senses that "she was not really *telling* me." It turns out that "something" saves the mother from telling, every time. Usually it's the interrupting voice of the male neighbor, who routinely breaks into song. Then, "on the night we came the closest to having it over with," the daughter herself short-circuits the exchange. "She started to tell me without being asked, and I ruined it by yelling, 'Mother, look at the lightning bugs!'" Eudora chooses to be distracted. "I had missed my chance. The fact is she never did tell me."

Of course, as so often in Welty, a character's action expresses more than a single-minded wish; the scene can be read as about more than a failure to listen. The young Welty may in fact hear her mother's reluctance and so interrupt in order to protect her from having to tell. Or she may sense that she herself is not quite ready to handle an answer to the question. As so often is the case in such scenes, the party being instructed already contains a grasp of the desired knowledge. The daughter's interruption *is* an answer to her question, since lightning bugs, in blinking forth, are looking to attract a mate. Moreover, because the scene is not closed down by an answer, it can spiral beyond itself toward a secret even "harder to tell," the story, which then follows, of the early death of Welty's brother. Like Nick Adams, Welty learns that life ends before she learns anything useful about how it begins, as well as learning that these two secrets—we call them "death" and "sex"—are "connected."

Most mother-daughter exchanges are not so subtly structured. And so the question arises, as it does for Cassie Morrison in Welty's "June Recital," "Should daughters *forgive* mothers?" Forgive them for what? For being caught up, perhaps, in an inherited chain of unlived lives and untold secrets in which the daughter continues to pay for all that the mother never got or never knew. In *Of Woman Born* (1976), Adrienne Rich contends that since the mother is "the one through whom the restrictions and depredations of a female existence were perforce transmitted," she can stand in "for the victims in ourselves, the unfree woman, the martyr." How might a daughter receive instruction from a mother, so imagined? Welty in any case concludes, "I doubt that any child I knew was told by her mother any more than I was about babies. In fact, I doubt that her own mother ever told her any more than she told me."

The daughter's dilemma culminates in Dorothy Allison's (b. 1949) *Bastard Out of Carolina* (1992), where, instead of soliciting knowledge from the mother, an abused daughter almost destroys herself by trying to protect her mother from it. "My tongue swelled in my mouth. I didn't want anyone to know anything. Mama,

I almost whispered, but clamped my teeth together." The stifled whisper follows a rape scene into which the mother has just stumbled and which she will find the power to overlook when she decides, finally, to leave her daughter and go off with the rapist, who is also her husband and therefore the daughter's stepfather.

◆   ◆

Untransmitted knowledge is a core subject in the fiction of Ellen Douglas (b. 1921). Like Welty, Douglas was born in Mississippi and settled eventually in Jackson. Like Faulkner, she was to situate much of her work in a fictional Mississippi place, Homochito County. Marriage and motherhood occupied Douglas during the 1950s, and her first story was not published until 1961. A first novel followed a year later. Early on she adopted the pseudonym "Ellen Douglas," choosing not to publish under her married name, Josephine Ayres Haxton.

Writing during the years in which Welty composed *One Writer's Beginnings*, Douglas uses the diary form as a figure for a female rage driven inward. In *A Lifetime Burning* (1982), a woman anguished by her husband's affair with a younger man consigns her thoughts to a diary, one addressed to her children. Then Corinne finds another diary, hidden long ago by her husband's grandmother, a suicide. It details the female bind. "When I married, no one had told me how children are made or how they come into the world. My education was entrusted to him. I will not consign a daughter of mine to such a fate." The notebook ends with the husband's death and the grandmother's temporary delivery into a "sane world."

But there is a second notebook. With her brutal, loveless husband—the instructing "him"—ten years dead, the grandmother finds herself forced back again into the diary form. She has much to tell, about the young girls set running like foxes by a neighbor who likes to watch his daughters chased by slaves, and about her own father, who now threatens to take away her children out of the conviction that she has formed an "unnatural" sleeping arrangement with her cousin Maria. Hers is a story of the "perfidy, the heartlessness, the hypocrisy, the self-righteousness of real men." She counsels her "Sisters in pain" to "hate them." But she does not, despite her earlier resolve, speak out; she consigns her story to the future "finder" of her writing. "I know why I will leave this notebook hidden here. I have no one to give it to, no one to whom I may allow myself to speak out. Not my daughters. I cannot bear to speak to my daughters. God keep them from the need to understand my life. But I will leave these pages, will put down the record, as Crusoe, alone on his island, put down his record, not knowing who might find it after his solitary life was spent." In this way, female self-silencing at once transcends and reproduces itself.

However, as Corinne admits in the following entry, "there was no diary. Or rather, the diary is mine, my invention." The invented diary provides a "plausible" explanation for the mystery of the grandmother's death. And so it forms a surmise within the larger diary Corinne directs at her children, itself an "imaginary conversation" that may never be delivered. At the end of that process lies an even more imaginary hope, a hope shared no doubt by male as well as female parents for a scene of instruction that so rarely arrives, when "someone will ask questions and we'll get to the bottom of it all." Corinne goes on to stage just such a scene, with her three children challenging their mother on her versions of the past. But that scene too is imaginary, in her head, as she admits to her diary: "The questions, the comments, after all are mine, not yours."

Will the children ever someday read all this? By way of these "imaginary" scenarios, Douglas draws a profound distinction between the experience of the uninstructed child in the narrative and the experience of the reader of it. The unsaid only has force in a novel like *A Lifetime Burning* if it is *written down*; for the author to make her point about the failure of a character-to-character exchange, the unsayable has, in some measure, to be spelled out on the page. The dallying with "false surmise," as Milton puts it in "Lycidas," is at the heart of the enterprise we call literature. The strategy interposes a little ease, allows for wishes and hopes and curiosities to roam. Thus, even after Corinne takes back a "*true lie*," as she calls it, the burden and pleasure of the fantasy have nevertheless made themselves felt. The character's loss is the reader's gain, since she or he is encouraged to imagine and confront all that remains incommunicable within Douglas's fictional world.

❦   ❦

Mary McCarthy (1912–89) takes as her subject the uninstructed daughter. She also scrutinizes the ways in which women collaborate in their state of unknowing. "The subordination of women is brought about by countless small acts," Dr. Spock was to argue in the year McCarthy divorced Edmund Wilson, and McCarthy proves deeply attentive to such acts. But her original contribution is a bracing willingness to blame the victim.

Like Welty, McCarthy also deploys a myth. Instead of Medusa, she chooses Persephone. At its core, the myth reveals the mother as complicit in or somewhat helpless before the daughter's fate. Demeter's brother Zeus is also Persephone's father, and he connives with his brother, Hades, in the abduction of his daughter. Demeter is only partially successful in rescuing Persephone from the hell of initiation, and all because the daughter has eaten a few pomegranate seeds, has shown appetite. Mother and daughter get their love back part-time, for the warmer seasons of the year. The daughter is abducted by patriarchy before self-protective instruction by the mother can begin.

"She would leave him, she thought, as soon as the petunias had bloomed." McCarthy's "The Weeds" (1944) opens with this sentence. The unnamed wife of the story has been reaching out "unthinkingly" for such a plan, "as doubtless Perse-phone's hand had strayed toward a pomegranate seed." She does run off, only to find that she has "exchanged the prison of the oppressor for the prison of the self." So she returns to her husband. Her garden is gone. "In ten days the weeds had swallowed it." The weeds are, in fact, her garden. They are what she proves compe-tent to make; the garden as she originally planted it looks "like a letter written by a child who has lost his ruler."

A woman leaves a husband and then comes back. Alice Munro was to begin *Runaway* (2004) with such a story, and of course Welty had already written it, in "The Wide Net." McCarthy makes the story new by focusing on the wife's inepti-tude in choosing to go, or grow.

Incompetence is the open secret of *The Group*. McCarthy's eight Vassar gradu-ates don't know how to do much of anything. The whole experience of being a woman in the world—how to dress, think, make love, nurse a baby, or toilet train a toddler—appears to be located outside of them. After Kay dies, the Group even debates whether her corpse should be fitted out with a brassiere.

"Knowledge" in this world might make for "composure," Dottie thinks to her-self, and for her sexual knowledge comes through a man. Dick tells her to relax in an "instructive voice." The initiation goes well, and Dottie experiences "uncontrol-lable contractions that embarrassed her, like the hiccups." Dick has to tell her what's happened; "You *came, Boston,*" he says.

McCarthy's rage that such things still need to be spelled out to women—set in the 1930s, the story reads like a chronicle of the 1950s—will tilt her prose toward the clinical awkwardness of an instruction manual.

Like Professor Mulcahy before his student in *The Groves of Academe* (1952), Mc-Carthy herself feels "a harsh desire to initiate that innocence." "Get yourself a pes-sary," Dick mutters to Dottie, as he propels her out the apartment door. She hears the word as "peccary." So much for her higher education, the one that has in-structed her in "ancient fertility rites." At the doctor's office, where Dottie has gone to be fitted, McCarthy loses patience with her character and subjects her to the in-dignity of a show-and-tell: "The woman doctor would insert it, and having made sure of the proper size, she would teach Dottie how to put it in, how to smear it with contraceptive jelly and put a dab in the middle, how to crouch in a squatting position, fold the pessary between thumb and forefinger of the right hand, while parting the *labia majora* with the left hand, and edge the pessary in." The insistence on procedure here may mask the fact that this all takes place in an imaginary fu-ture, by way of a "would." The scene imagines an initiation by a woman doctor that never actually happens.

In the event, the doctor is male and the pessary jumps out of Dottie's hand and shoots across the room. She cannot bring herself to ask her most burning question, about what it means if a man makes love to you and does not kiss you once. Dottie buys her contraceptives, calls Dick a few times, and, receiving no answer, leaves the equipment under a park bench.

McCarthy's fiction proceeds from an assumption that nothing is, or can be, learned. Even were her characters provided timely instruction, they would not significantly change. By her own admission, the adoption of a "comic" mode mandates such a view. In her essay "Characters in Fiction" (1961), McCarthy claims that "the capacity to learn, from experience or instruction, is what is forbidden to all comic creations." The irony is that McCarthy did not see herself as comic, and that her performance as a public intellectual completely belied this view of human character. The blindness of her insight was in not taking herself as the best available instance of a self that did and could learn, as a woman with a knife in her brain.

McCarthy presents the midcentury's most striking case of the critic as artist. At Vassar College, she was informed that her mind was "critical" rather than "creative." She shares with Oscar Wilde a sneaking and half-serious suspicion, one expressed in "The Critic as Artist," that "it is very much more difficult to talk about a thing than to do it." To do would be to write novels, or stories, or plays; to talk would be to write criticism about them. McCarthy began reviewing books for *The Nation* and *The New Republic* soon after her graduation from Vassar in 1933 and went on to become the drama critic for *Partisan Review*. The meaning of the career inheres in the contrast between the ferocious intelligence displayed in the critical work and the cluelessness deplored in the fiction. What the performance lacks in empathy—unlike Welty, McCarthy does not love her characters—it makes up for in knowingness. The tension between doing a thing and talking about it is built into the structure of McCarthy's most engaging book, *Memories of a Catholic Girlhood* (1957).

A gathering of eight autobiographical sketches, *Memories* tells the story of Mary's upbringing at the hands of good and bad grandparents after the death of her mother and father in the influenza epidemic of 1918. Each sketch except the last is followed by an italicized critique. The first critique begins, "*There are several dubious points in this memoir.*" The alternating pattern of remembrance and critique allows for an ongoing deconstruction of what Mary has just constructed. The net effect is of a scrupulosity that cares more about "*untruthfulness*" than about the "*temptation to invent.*" The critic here triumphs over the artist, except at the very end of the book, where the last chapter is allowed to stand without an appended interrogation.

In "To the Reader," Mary also affirms the complete adequacy of her early education. Apparently an American girl *can* learn. The most arresting evidence of this possibility comes in the passage where Mary celebrates the advantages of being schooled in "Catholic history" in a Protestant nation. It's a far cry from the curriculum dished out to Studs Lonigan at St. Patrick's:

> Nor is it only a matter of knowing more, at an earlier age, so that it becomes a part of oneself; it is also a matter of feeling. To care for the quarrels of the past, to identify oneself passionately with a cause that became, politically speaking, a losing cause with the birth of the modern world, is to experience a kind of straining against reality, a rebellious nonconformity that, again, is rare in America, where children are instructed in the virtues of the system they live under, as though history had achieved a happy ending in American civics.

McCarthy delivers here a concise defense of the importance to the growing soul of a "secret history" called up by and concealed within the happy endings of our self-congratulatory narratives, as well as a lucid display of the adversarial imagination to which she made such a pungent contribution.

❦　❦

In *Grand Expectations* (1996), James T. Patterson argues that "the hastening of the sexual revolution was perhaps the most important cultural change to emerge from the 1960s." The word "revolution" bespeaks a change dramatically accomplished. Yet during the ensuing decades American culture proved remarkably willing to reimpose innocence on its daughters. Even as I write these sentences, in 2005, the "abstinence-only" sex education movement and the proponents of "intelligent design" continue to shape the curriculum of the public schools. The writers of the 1950s remain acutely aware that "important cultural change" must continually be fought for. And now that a war on terror has marshaled political discourse into our "good" and their "evil," a rhetoric of binary assumptions once again tempts us with its promise of separate and therefore inherently unequal sex roles and functions.

In *Homeward Bound* (1988), Elaine Tyler May has written convincingly of the connection between cold war fears and the retreat to a conservative model of the nuclear family. Containment of communism abroad appeared to require containment of female energies at home. One of the novels that most successfully explored the ironies and costs of these intertwined ventures was Steinbeck's *East of Eden* (1952).

Steinbeck finished *East of Eden* in the year before the republic summoned Ike. The "police action" in Korea was underway and the Army-McCarthy hearings were not far off. The United States was a scared country, one busily projecting monsters. You could see it in every horror film that came down the pike. Although the novel runs its course in the decades before World War I, *East of Eden* finds ways to express a healthy sense of cold war paranoia. It pits Steinbeck's emerging myth of the "lonely mind" against his earlier interest in group action and social solidarity. In this he enacts the shift toward the right—the reluctant or gleeful rejection of the New Deal consensus and values—that was to prove the most profound political development of the postwar years. Of the pioneers in the Salinas Valley he can write:

> I think that because they trusted themselves and respected themselves as individuals, because they knew beyond doubt that they were valuable and potentially moral units—because of this they could give God their own courage and dignity and then receive it back. Such things have disappeared perhaps because men do not trust themselves anymore, and when that happens there is nothing left except perhaps to find some strong sure man, even though he may be wrong, and to dangle from his coattails.

At the other extreme lay the dangers of the "mass method": "In our time mass or collective production has entered our economics, our politics, and even our religion, so that some nations have substituted the idea collective for the idea God. This in my time is the danger." Between fascism and communism lay the ground cultivated by the old familiar American Adam, the "exploring mind of the individual human."

Despite such pronouncements, the imagination of the novel pays less heed to international relations than to life on the home front. While busy fighting wars, both cold and hot, 1950s America invested its conscious energy in the domestic pursuit of happiness, and the structure of *East of Eden* reflects this. When its war comes, it comes merely as a backdrop, a place for one inconvenient hero to die offstage while another stays home and pairs off with the girl.

The book to read alongside *East of Eden* is *The Feminine Mystique*. Steinbeck and Friedan were both autodidacts, inspired amateur sociologists who disdained the consensus models of the academy and pushed on instead into a radical critique of love at home. Steinbeck deploys Cathy Trask as an exemplar, in Friedan's words, of "a yearning that women suffer in the middle of the twentieth century in the United States."

The end of World War II marked a sudden decline in the power of women in the public world, and Friedan's book rehearses the statistics. The marriage rate in the United States was the highest in the Western world in the years 1944 to 1948; the average marriage age of women dropped to twenty by the end of the 1950s. Meanwhile, the "proportion of women attending college in comparison with men dropped from 47 percent in 1920 to 35 percent in 1958." The birth rate would soar in the 1950s; by decade's end it was approaching India's. The baby boom peaked in 1957. In the wake of the Kinsey Report and the new self-consciousness about female response, so ably detailed by Mary McCarthy, sex became a project. Yet the blue laws stayed on the books, and the birth control pill was not approved for marketing by the FDA until 1960. It was not until 1965 that the state could no longer restrict the access of married persons to contraceptives.

The best-selling novels of the period—books such as Herman Wouk's (b. 1915) *Marjorie Morningstar* (1955) and Rona Jaffe's (1931–2005) *The Best of Everything* (1958)—teased female readers with the prospect of a career while finally delivering their heroines to the higher calling of homemaking. These are the years in which home economics became entrenched as a high school subject. *Homemaking in the High School* (1961), first published in the 1930s, went through numerous postwar editions and promised "to develop persons capable of maintaining a satisfying home and family life in a free society." *Betty Crocker's Picture Cook Book* appeared in 1950, complete with images that made food preparation routine and even glamorous. By 1950 an ideology of femininity had firm control of the American imagination. Here is Friedan:

> The feminine mystique says that the highest value and the only commitment for women to make is the fulfillment of their own femininity. It says that the great mistake of Western culture, through most of its history, has been the undervaluation of this femininity. It says that femininity is so mysterious and intuitive and close to the creation and origin of life that man-made science may never be able to understand it. But however special and different, it is in no way inferior to the nature of man; it may even in certain respects be superior. The mistake, says the mystique, the root of women's troubles in the past is that women envied men, women tried to be like men, instead of accepting their own nature, which can find fulfillment only in sexual passivity, male domination, and nurturing maternal love.

Systematically, and with a cold fury, Steinbeck's Cathy Trask sets out to defy the temptations of the feminine mystique. From the start of her life, she disdains to define herself *in relation*. She refuses to cede what Friedan calls her "private image" to a public role. Her self-containment, imaged by Steinbeck as a bodily inversion, seems almost willful: "Before her puberty her nipples turned inward." As an adolescent, she will not fit in. "She never conformed in dress or conduct." If caught in the biological trap, she will refuse to mother. While pregnant, there is "no quickening of milk glands," and, on her birth bed, she bites the hand that helps her. Having insisted without shame on abortion, she walks away from the task of child-raising. She has no interest in keeping house and lets Lee nurse and cook. She uses Faye's crochet hook not to make booties but to probe her "clitoris"; Steinbeck measures the shock of the gesture with the frankness of his term.

Cathy will not enjoy sex—she will profit from it. She becomes a whoremistress. Like the women in prewar magazine fiction, as described by Friedan, she defines herself through her career. In running her own business and controlling her money, she refigures the male realm of fulfillment and reminds us that the "oldest profession" is, after all, female. In her ghastly and tormented independence, and in her indifference toward any balance between the claims of love and separateness, Cathy becomes the shadow, the prophetic image of an as yet unacknowledged and gathering female rage.

In writing about Richard Yates's (1926–92) *Revolutionary Road* (1961), another fiction about female confinement, James Wood has argued that the novel turns on "the single question of whether a wife should be allowed to work." A decade earlier, Steinbeck had foreseen this as a question that would loom over the 1950s. The Cathy he imagines is a heroine of work. She achieves business success, but success purchased, once again, as it was for Mary Austin's Seyavi, by having to choose between love and work. Of the three things with which, if you have had them, as Austin argues in "The Walking Woman," you could live without all the rest, Cathy gets only one. Steinbeck and Yates continue to imagine American women as forced to choose *between*.

Of course, Steinbeck presents Cathy as a "monster" in her not seeming to care about Austin's other two "things." She simply walks away from love and children. Here is a woman who rapes herself, incinerates her parents, beds down with her brother-in-law, shoots her husband, and abandons her twin boys: Eve and Tamar and Delilah and Jezebel are rolled into one. Steinbeck's opening sentence about her gets it right: "I believe there are monsters born in the world to human parents." This is right because it presents and does not explain, since, through Cathy, Steinbeck attempts to create an affront to the interpretative schemes that police the category we call "human."

"Most children abhor difference," Steinbeck maintains. But Cathy is difference, stands for it, and spends her life "using her difference." In his most sophisticated paragraph on Cathy, Steinbeck advances the theory that she inhabits a unique and separate language:

> When I said Cathy was a monster it seemed to me that it was so. Now I have bent close with a glass over the small print of her and reread the footnotes, and I wonder if it was true. The trouble is that since we cannot know what she wanted, we will never know whether or not she got it. If rather than running toward something, she ran away from something, we can't know whether she escaped. Who knows but that she tried to tell someone or everyone what she was like and could not, for lack of a common language. Her life may have been her language,

formal, developed, indecipherable. It is easy to say she was bad, but there is little meaning unless we know why.

If Cathy can be read as a feminist heroine, the passage argues that she can also be read as a postmodern one.

Vladimir Nabokov's (1899–1977) *Lolita*, published in 1955, arrives at a similar destination by way of a far different route. As Frederick Whiting has convincingly shown, *Lolita* reveals "how the innocence of children had been elevated to the premier trope of national vulnerability," and the novel does so by inventing its own version of the "monstrous," a pedophile who gets outmaneuvered by a nymphet. What Humbert Humbert cannot abide is that the object of his desire would show the agency of a subject; in doing so, Lolita, like Cathy Trask, becomes one more of the unlikely but instructive heroines of the 1950s.

Cathy, then, is not a failure of characterization but a critique of standard notions of it. Through her, Steinbeck dissolves confidence in a stable, knowable self. For character, he substitutes the notion of discourse. As a formal feature *of* the novel, Cathy gets constructed out of "small print" and "footnotes." She is researched, closely read. As a character *in* the story, Cathy and her otherness become functions of something "formal, developed, indecipherable," something defiant and demanding of interpretation. In a novel so committed to speech and the act of translation, Cathy remains untranslatable, beyond the assurances of a common language. The banality of her evil only reinforces its uncanny power. And if individuals are distinguished by relative "difference" rather than by intrinsic essence, why not locate the prime exemplar of this difference in the very site of the homelike, in the body and person of the mother?

The opening page of *East of Eden* defines the mother as the word whose presence is everywhere and identity nowhere:

> I remember that the Galiban Mountains to the east of the valley were light gay mountains full of sun and loveliness and a kind of invitation, so that you wanted to climb into their warm foothills almost as you want to climb into the lap of a beloved mother.

The beloved mother projected here proves entirely fugitive, since no human figure in the novel will embody her. Sam Hamilton calls Liza "mother," but she is his wife. On meeting Cal and Aron, Abra volunteers to "be your mother." Kate calls Faye "poor little mother." Lee's birth story can deliver only "the tattered meat of my mother." *Mother*: something about private and public history corrupts and consumes the meaning of the word. The ultimate slippage applies to Cathy. We see her give birth. Yet nothing highlights the inadequacy of the term more than those moments in which Adam and Aron throw it at her. "You are the mother of my sons." "My mother is dead." The more Cathy gets reduced to this role, the more she defies it. "Mother" is a word for which no referent here can be found; it constitutes a meaning only through the history of its contradictory and ironic usages.

In the decade in which the "Reproduction of Mothering" was to regain so much steam, stories such as "The Wanderers" and novels such as *The Street* began to expose the cultural arrangements and historical forces that made it difficult for mothers to "mother" their children, or for women to achieve a balance between love and separateness. What comes between the woman and her elected task is often an abusive or neglecting or simply absent male—what comes between, we perhaps too glibly say, is "patriarchy." And the coming between, as the decades ahead would discover, is not culturally specific but uncannily widespread, a narrative the United States shares with the China of Kingston's *The Woman Warrior* and the Japan of Hisaye Yamamoto's (b. 1921) *Seventeen Syllables* (1988). This narrative culminates in *Beloved*, in a story about a woman described by her author as having "an excess of maternal feeling, a total surrender to that commitment." One of the consistent features of American fictions about motherhood was that it remained for women themselves to free themselves from such excesses and such surrender.

CHAPTER ELEVEN

Revolt and Reaction

MAILER ✦ DIDION

*F*rom a postmillennial perspective, the big thing about the sixties is not the
good accomplished in that decade but the reaction it appears to have induced. No other decade in the twentieth century carries such symbolic weight.
One's politics can be measured by one's take on that time. The divide between the
red and the blue states has largely to do with this: the sixties gave Americans an
unprecedented access of power in relation to the world; or, the sixties opened the
gates of excess and misrule. A positive take on the decade might invoke the rise
of the women's movement, environmentalism, gay liberation, and the rights of
people with disabilities. A negative view recalls the rise of drug abuse, the breakdown of the public schools, the spread of pornography, and the culture of divorce.
Vietnam and one's response to it remain the touchstone, the iceberg that still
cruises through our dreams. There is no question that because of that time Americans became more free. There is little question as well that many of them also became more lost.

The decade of the sixties was singularly rich in visionary sociology, books such
as Herbert Marcuse's *One-Dimensional Man*, Paul Goodman's *Growing Up Absurd*,
R. D. Laing's *The Politics of Experience*, and Norman O. Brown's *Love's Body*. The
literature of race and civil rights continued to make its story heard, and I have already cited the contributions made during this decade by James Baldwin, Eldridge
Cleaver, Martin Luther King Jr., Alice Walker, and Septima Clark. Vonnegut pub-
lishes *Slaughterhouse-Five* in 1969, while, four years later, Pynchon gives us what
may be the great novel of the sixties sensibility in *Gravity's Rainbow*. *Ariel* is published in 1965, as radical a book of poetry as the period was to afford. Bishop's poetic career runs athwart the decade, while giving little direct attention to it. Michael
Herr begins sending his "dispatches" to *Esquire* in 1968, but he waits to gather them
into the supreme book on the Vietnam experience until 1977. All this and more
belong in any full account of the sixties, as does the subsequent work done by the
young who were shaped by living through that time, a generational legacy about
which I have written in my book on storytelling and the Vietnam generation.

In this chapter I confine my attention to two American writers. While these two
represent only a part of the whole, the intensity of imaginative performance risked

by each makes them more than qualified to stand in for those who sought during this time to convert experience into art. Norman Mailer (1923–2007) celebrates what is gained during these years; Joan Didion (b. 1934) measures what the changes cost. But he is not blue while she is red; American literature does not square off over the decade in any either-or way. Didion and Mailer publish their works of scaled invention in 1968, and each balances in a distinctive way a sense of ground gained with a presentiment of loss. They represent a necessary dialectic, between the wisdom born of excess and the damage done by it. Their common enemy is received thought and language, empty convention, cliché. Even in their most conforming moments, they insist on entering into convention with a unique and personal style.

◆   ◆

Since the subject is Norman Mailer, it will only do to plunge in. We are in *The Armies of the Night*, chapter 5, "Toward a Theater of Ideas," when the book (the career, really) finally takes off, our hero being obliged "to notice on entering the Ambassador Theater that he had an overwhelming urge to micturate." The Master of Ceremonies—one of the many roles he will play in the book, along with Novelist, Journalist, Historian, Participant, and Left Conservative—decides he will have to find the Room before he goes on stage. On the way upstairs he tells a young man from *Time* that he has come to Washington "to protest the war in Vietnam,"

> and taking a sip of bourbon from the mug he kept to keep all fires idling right, stepped off into the darkness of the top balcony floor, went through a door into a pitch-black men's room, and was alone with his need. No chance to find the light switch for he had no matches, he did not smoke. It was therefore a matter of locating what's what with the probing of his toes. He found something finally which seemed appropriate, and pleased with the precision of these generally unused senses in his feet, took aim between them at a point twelve inches ahead, and heard in the darkness the sound of his water striking the floor. Some damn mistake had been made, an assault from the side doubtless instead of the front, the bowl was relocated now, and Master of Ceremonies breathed deep of the great reveries of this utterly non-Sisyphian release—at last!!—and thoroughly enjoyed the next forty-five seconds, being left on the aftermath not a note depressed by the condition of the premises. No, he was off on the Romantic's great military dream, which is: seize defeat, convert it to triumph. Of course, pissing on the floor was bad, very bad . . .

How odd and wonderful that in a scene of such awkwardness Mailer is able to discover the fearful symmetry between the sole self and the body politic. A man trying to relieve himself in the dark misses his aim and instead hits the floor. In one unlooked-for moment he thereby blunders upon a conceit that answers the question of not why, but how, we are in Vietnam.

"At his best," Richard Poirier writes about Mailer in *The Performing Self*, "he risks contamination. He does so by adopting the roles, the styles, the sounds that will give him the measure of what it's like to be alive in this country." Even to his own harm and embarrassment, Mailer offers himself up as a sacrificial figure, one whose comically bad behavior can embody a truth about his country's tragically misguided behavior in war.

Why Are We in Vietnam? (1967) is the title of the book Mailer holds in one hand throughout the pissing scene; he carries a coffee mug full of bourbon in the other. "Look Ma, no hands!" he seems to be saying, as he brings this story back to us. The story is an allegory, of course. Let us count the ways in which Mailer's performance here parallels his country's performance in Vietnam: he is operating in ignorance, in the dark; he cannot locate his objective; he resorts to the Romantic's conversion of "defeat" into "triumph"; he relies on fancy words—euphemisms, really, like "micturate," when the honest verb "piss" more accurately covers the case; once he starts, he cannot stop.

The pissing scene at once models a liability toward error and a corrective response to it. If Mailer here makes a mistake, he also admits it to be one. The passive construction "Some damn mistake had been made" mimics, instead, the decision of those who conducted the war to mystify the issue of responsibility. In so openly mobilizing his abjection, Mailer shows that embarrassment can lead to education. The very bravado that propels the imperial self into the "pitch-black" can be matched by having the courage of one's mistakes. Of course, there has to be a willingness to "confess straight out to all aloud"; strength only arises from the acknowledgement of vulnerability. "From gap to gain is very American," Mailer will go on to write, and yet the lesson seems lost on those who dictate his country's foreign policy.

In *Cannibals and Christians* (1966), Mailer asserts that "form is the record of a war," and that "it is the character of the war which creates the particular style of the form." Given the character of the war Mailer here attempts to comprehend, the Vietnam War, the only style he can reasonably adopt is the mock-heroic. For a man so obsessed by courage—the word appears thirteen times in "The White Negro" (1955)—such a stance entails a massive curtailment. Mailer admits early on his marginal status here: "To write an intimate history of an event which places its focus on a central figure who is not central to the event, is to inspire immediate questions about the competence of the historian." He then proceeds to provide the terms of analysis required for an understanding of the pissing scene. We've had the experience, but perhaps missed the meaning, so Mailer puts a name to his predicament and argues that only the "not central" self can resolve the ambiguities of the event:

> An eyewitness who is a participant but not a vested participant is required, further he must be not only involved, but ambiguous in his own proportions, a comic hero, which is to say, one cannot happily resolve the emphasis of the category—is he finally comic, a ludicrous figure with mock-heroic associations; or is he not unheroic, and therefore embedded somewhat tragically in the comic?

If Mailer cannot be the hero of history, he can act as a "bridge," perhaps even a *pons asinorum*. Mailer nominates himself for this compound role and then asks the reader to come along: "Let us then make our comic hero the narrative vehicle for the March on the Pentagon." The gesture is so disarming we can scarcely resist it.

In accepting that he has "no position" here, Mailer stands in for the war-resisting reader. The satisfying thing for a hero to do is to go to war. To refuse to go, and to burn your draft card instead, as the young men Mailer so much admires will later do, young men he sees as "committing their future either to prison, emigration, frustration, or at best, years where everything must be unknown," is to elect a far more ambiguous stance as a man and as a citizen. It is to fight for one's country by refusing to fight in its wars. For the literal act of picking up a gun, resistance to the war substitutes civil disobedience in the street. And yet as Mailer's list of the possible futures facing draft-card burners makes clear, such protest does entail considerable physical and emotional risk.

How in the United States do you fight the fighting of a war? The answer, when it comes, arises from Mailer's scrupulous attention to the convergence between real and symbolic action. The action Mailer has come to perform, to be arrested in a March on the Pentagon, occurs as a sort of afterthought. After crossing Memorial Bridge and reaching the North Parking Area, he turns and runs from the threat of Mace in the eyes. Then he gathers himself and makes "a point of stepping neatly and decisively over" a low rope. Confronted by an MP, he begins sprinting, like a back cutting around a secondary. After being brought to a halt, he is grabbed by two U.S. Marshals, "and they set off walking across the field at a rabid intent quick rate, walking parallel to the wall of the Pentagon, fully visible on his right at last, and he was arrested, he had succeeded in that." By slipping in the arrest by way of a paratactic phrase, Mailer modestly offers it up as just one more in a series of events. He again proves himself a master of missing the moment, as when, as he admits earlier, he had wandered off during the day of the 1963 Civil Rights March just before Martin Luther King Jr. began, "I have a dream." The "real" action of the book occurs elsewhere, in Mailer's bridging—yes, even his pontificating—of two modes of action.

In his speech at the Ambassador Theater, Mailer maintains that the upcoming march "will be at once a symbolic and a real act." As we read on into *Armies*, the distinction between the symbolic and the real shimmers and begins to disappear. In "technology land," as Mailer calls the United States, an act has become impossible to distinguish from a gesture. The war in Vietnam is itself a performance, a show of strength meant to intimidate assumed enemies with the nation's resolve. The problem with the performance is that it is not recognized as being one, and so it confuses, as Mailer himself had been accused of doing in *Advertisements for Myself* (1960), "the life of action with the life of acting out." The only cure for such geopolitical acting out is an enforced self-consciousness about the nation's reasons for and ways of acting.

In *Armies*, Mailer betrays little interest in policy and its rationales; he reads the war instead as an expression of a rising resentment that will generate, in time, the foot soldiers of the Reaction. "They had won the country, and now they were losing it to the immigrants who had come after and the descendants of slaves." Vietnam, in short, is "where the small town had gone to get its kicks." And so the nation's true enemy is an enemy within, not communism but "certainty," the gathering force of a politics of fundamentalism and resentment. The best weapons against such a soul-killing certainty are speculation, metaphor, surmise, and play, the carnival unleashed by Mailer's mock-heroic and self-interrogating art.

Theater, then, is Mailer's antidote to war. "Mailer walked to the stage." No other sentence in the book better captures his joy in performance and his acceptance of it as what there is to do. "The only path of escape known in all the worlds of God is performance," Emerson wrote, in "Worship." "Escape from what?" we might ask. From the illusion, perhaps, that life permits unmediated action. Mailer imagines American culture as wholly mediated and ritualized and as one in which Vietnam is really a sideshow, a performance staged by "corporation land" to distract from the ongoing wars at home. *Armies* celebrates the inescapability of performance, while deploring the style and substance of the production that is Vietnam.

Mailer is not called on to risk the kind of courage displayed by the young men who burn their draft cards. But he can offer up his artistic performance as a model of how to live through this difficult time. Politics, sex, art—by the late sixties all have become existential, dependent on a performance whose end is unknown. "We are up, face this all of you," Mailer tells his audience, "against an existential situation—we do not know how it is going to turn out." Mailer's searching and improvisational style proves the appropriate vehicle for a national crisis that is also an existential one. As he says, "The clue to discovery was not in the substance of one's idea, but in what was learned from the style of one's attack." Neither the war-resister nor the writer knows "what was going to happen next," and yet each must act anyway. "Just as the truth of his material was revealed to a good writer by the cutting edge of his style . . . so a revolutionary began to uncover the nature of his true situation by trying to ride the beast of his revolution."

"Revolution" is a melodramatic term for what was being attempted in those heady days. It turns out that you will be hard-pressed, in the United States, to match the risks taken and the ground gained by the founding Revolution itself, an existential act that created a nation that would prove remarkably adept at permitting and thereby containing dissent. In such a political-cultural situation, Mailer understands that social change is often the product of symbolic acts. The American paradox is that after the founding Revolution the only successful revolutions are those that remain within the law. The civil rights movement had already proven this. It chose to reject the "reality" of revolutionary violence for the "symbolic" force of nonviolence and for the willingness to be arrested, and so changed the world.

The antiwar movement was not to be as successful, in part because of the violence called forth in the fighting of it. "When you look back upon those years," Mailer was to say, some thirty-five years later, in conversation with Howard Norman, "all roads lead to Kent State." By this he means that Vietnam would become, as Michael Herr argues in *Dispatches*, "the turnaround point" in which American history had "come back to form a containing perimeter." Violence directed outward was turned around, by the National Guard, on young Americans seeking to protest the war. Four of these young were killed at Kent State, in Ohio, on the first weekend in May of 1970. These actions were taken as the direct result of decisions made along a chain of command, a chain beginning and ending at the White House. After the spring of 1970, the antiwar movement could no longer take for granted those "liberties to dissent" that Mailer counts on and acts upon during his days in the streets. But neither could its most extreme advocates point to anything accomplished by the some 250 bombings carried out nationwide in the eight months leading up to the shootings at Kent State.

Mailer's chance to perform becomes the measure of a working democracy, one that honors the ritual of civil disobedience by arresting protestors rather than shooting them. This is a book about the privilege to make art, one deeply grateful for the still-intact traditions that allow a man like Mailer to march in the streets without being shot. It thus fulfills Robert Lowell's (1917–77) prediction, made in 1966, that "we will soon look back upon this troubled moment as a golden time of freedom and license to act and speculate." *The Armies of the Night* becomes Mailer's angry and affectionate love letter to a fleetingly permissive cultural moment and to a country that offers him "the opportunity to grow up a second time."

This is precisely what he accomplishes in one great sentence in "A Half-Mile to Virginia," the longest in Mailer's work and one that deserves its place alongside the most ambitious and moving sentence Faulkner ever wrote, a sentence in which Mailer not only crosses a bridge but builds one, as in the central metaphor of standing under a "mythical arch":

In any event, up at the front of this March, in the first line, back of that hollow square of monitors, Mailer and Lowell walked in this barrage of cameras, helicopters, TV cars, monitors, loudspeakers, and wavering buckling twisting line of notables, arms linked (line twisting so much that at times the movement was in file, one arm locked ahead, one behind, then the line would undulate about and the other arm would be ahead) speeding up a few steps, slowing down while a great happiness came back into the day as if finally one stood under some mythical arch in the great vault of history, helicopters buzzing about, chop-chop, and the sense of America divided on this day now liberated some undiscovered patriotism in Mailer so that he felt a sharp searing love for his country in this moment and on this day, crossing some divide in his own mind wider than the Potomac, a love so lacerated he felt as if a marriage were being torn and children lost—never does one love so much as then, obviously, then— and an odor of wood smoke, from where you knew not, was also in the air, a smoke of dignity and some calm heroism, not unlike the sense of freedom which also comes when a marriage is burst—Mailer knew for the first time why men in the front line of a battle are almost always ready to die: there is a promise of some swift transit—one's soul feels clean; as we have gathered, he was not used much more than any other American politician, litterateur, or racketeer to the sentiment that his soul was not unclean, but here, walking with Lowell and Macdonald, he felt as if he stepped through some crossing in the reaches of space between this moment, the French Revolution, and the Civil War, as if the ghosts of the Union Dead accompanied them now to the Bastille, he was not drunk at all, merely illumined by hunger, the sense of danger to the front, sense of danger to the rear—he was in fact in love with himself for having less fear than he had thought he might have—he knew suddenly then he had less fear now than when he was a young man; in some part of himself at least, he had grown; if less innocent, less timid—the cold flame of a perfectly contained exaltation warmed old asthmas of gravel in the heart, and the sense that they were going to face the symbol, the embodiment, no, call it the true and high church of the military-industrial complex, the Pentagon, blind five-sided eye of a subtle oppression which had come to America out of the very air of the century (this evil twentieth century with its curse on the species, its oppressive Faustian lusts, its technological excrement all over the conduits of nature, its entrapment of the innocence of the best—for which young American soldiers hot out of high school and in love with a hot rod and his Marine buddies in his platoon in Vietnam could begin to know the devil of the oppression which would steal his soul before he knew he had one) yes, Mailer felt a confirmation of the contests of his own life on this March to the eye of the oppressor, greedy stingy dumb valve of the worst of the Wasp heart, chalice and anus of corporation land, smug, enclosed, morally blind Pentagon, destroying the future of its own nation with each day it augmented in strength, and the Novelist induced on the consequence some dim unawakened knowledge of the mysteries of America buried in these liberties to dissent—What a mysterious country it was. The older he became, the more interesting he found her.

If the truth of a good writer's material is revealed by the cutting edge of his style, then Mailer surely achieves that revelation here. The core sentence is, simply, "Mailer and Lowell walked." The power of the sentence arises from the grammatical devices used to keep it going for a page and a half (parentheses, semicolons, dashes, participles, along with a somewhat creaky comma splice); from the range and audacity of its allusions (this struggle evokes the French Revolution, the Civil War, and the Union Dead, the latter a direct reference to the 1960 poem by his march mate Lowell); from its command of sensory metaphor ("an odor of wood smoke" as synecdoche for a lost, pioneering America); from its deceptive but welcome pause after the word "grown" (the semicolon that follows the word reformulates the claim "he had grown" into a more qualified act of self-celebration, into "he had grown; if less innocent, less timid"); from its righteous anger issuing in obscenity (the Pentagon may be an "anus," but it is also a seeing asshole, an "eye" that echoes Norris's "octopus," with its single, "cyclopean" eye); from the deployment of the trope of divorce (he feels on this day a "freedom which also comes when a marriage is burst" and then discovers that the political recapitulates the personal, that many are feeling divorced from their country); and from its being followed by a short sentence that recasts it in ten words: "The older he became, the more interesting he found her."

Mailer ends, then, by admitting that he is growing in his love. Growth is the central activity enacted here, where growth permits union, of citizen with nation, of husband and wife, and, especially, of self with ego-ideal: it is "some divide in his own mind" that Mailer is crossing on this day. Mailer succeeds in making the rhythm and argument of his sentence a figure for a balance, carefully achieved, between the forces that would join us together and those that can and perhaps should hold us separate and apart. There is no rule for such accommodation; politics, like marriage and like the writing of books, requires a spirit of adventure, a willingness to experiment, and an openness to the field.

The sentence acts as testimony to Mailer's achieved growth, as a man and as an artist, just as the shape changing of the Pentagon, which every day augments in strength, testifies to a runaway corporate power. The sentence creates a bridge; form here *is* action. By keeping all these thoughts and associations and sensations aloft in one syntactic unit, Mailer achieves his historical sublime, an ingathering and an interfusing. America is in divorce; Civil War has come again. "The two halves of America were not coming together, and when they failed to touch, all of history might be lost in the divide." But the integrating power of the sentence argues otherwise and so enacts a comedy of remarriage in which Mailer once again plights his troth to a wayward but deeply loved "her."

For Mailer, sex had been the realm where union is achieved. In *Armies*, sex operates as a metaphor for various kinds of failed union; it has little to do with bodies actually copulating. Mailer is at his best when sex acts as tenor rather than vehicle; little can be sillier than his ruminations on the good orgasm. Some lessons of the flesh do, however, still obtain; Mailer delays the "real climax" of his story until quite late in the book. By then, a reader has de-invested in such an outcome anyway, since Mailer's thoughts about his wife are more compelling than any description of lovemaking might be. He loves her but he does not "know her." Whitman captures this paradox in "Crossing Brooklyn Ferry," where the buildings of New York compel a similar admission: "We fathom you not—we love you." So with the country: "Mailer finally came to decide that his love for his wife while not at all equal or congruent to his love for America was damnably parallel." Like many American men, Mailer feels bound to conclude that no country can be "altogether awful" when it has produced women so subtle, supple, mysterious, fine-skinned, tender, and wise, and that such women, like the country itself, may and indeed perhaps must be loved precisely insofar as they cannot be known. And the immediate point being made about such loves is that they are never felt more strongly than when they are being torn and lost. Divorce can be a kind of fortunate fall.

The Armies of the Night begins with a phone call to Mailer from author-novelist Mitchell Goodman, who is calling to ask for something that will be easy to refuse and expensive to perform. A few months later, in October of 1967, Mailer finds himself arm in arm with Robert Lowell and Dwight Macdonald, walking across the Potomac. This "History as a Novel" actually begins before the phone rings, with a long quotation from *Time* magazine, a journalistic account of the event in which Mailer is described as its "anti-star." Mailer quotes the article and then writes: "Now we may leave *Time* in order to find out what happened."

Mailer begins with what Michael Herr calls "straight history." Book One of *Armies* counters this reductive and dismissive account with a secret history in which a man "not central" to the event claims to be the measure of the event. Then,

in Book Two, Mailer returns to the methods of straight history and attempts a ret-
rospective, inclusive overview. Event is reduced to diagram; the narrative contracts
around the bureaucracies of resistance. This attempt breaks down in chapter 6 of
Book Two, where Mailer abandons it and concludes that

> an explanation of the mystery of the events at the Pentagon cannot be developed
> by the methods of history—only by the instincts of the novelist. The reasons are
> several, but reduce to one. Forget that the journalistic information available from
> both sides is so incoherent, inaccurate, contradictory, malicious, even based on
> error that no accurate history is conceivable. More than one historian has found
> a way through chains of false fact. No, the difficulty is that the history is inte-
> rior—no documents can give sufficient intimation: the novel must replace his-
> tory at precisely the point where experience is sufficiently emotional, spiritual,
> psychical, moral, existential, or supernatural to expose the fact that the historian
> in pursuing the experience would be obliged to quit the clearly demarcated lim-
> its of historic inquiry.

The long list of adjectives defining the experience at the Pentagon reminds us that
history, to mean anything, must be a matter of feeling, and that feelings are precisely what Mailer's stance and style have been designed to call up. For a writer who
had spent twenty years presenting himself as the central man, the one novelist of
his generation willing to act on his emotions in public, the opportunity afforded by
the March on the Pentagon might have seemed less than promising, since it afforded him only a "not central" role. But in this massive correction of his drive toward the heroic, an emotional stepping-down he has the imagination to accept and
exploit, Mailer is liberated to produce the one book that best captures the feeling
of living through that time. And the feeling it calls up is a searing love of country
coupled with a desire to be divorced from it.

  And so the chance came. The sixties gave Mailer what he wanted, a breakout
from the "years of conformity and depression" and into a time he prophecies in
"The White Negro," "a time of violence, new hysteria, confusion and rebellion."
That the sixties failed to change the world in all the ways that might have been
imagined does not negate the value of what was achieved. "Rites of passage" do accomplish their secret work, as Mailer argues near the end of *Armies*, and these
particular rites were to leave him and many Americans with a sense of being "forever different." Those of us who organized, marched, applied for conscientious
objector status, and then went on to lead comfortable, middle-class lives were
changed, and forever. We live differently, especially in our domestic arrangements,
because of those days. Their full fruit has not yet been harvested, but it will eventually be brought in. Like Mailer, most of us continued to believe in marriage, how-

ever many marriages some of us have attempted. Like Didion, as we shall see, many of us also put our minds and hearts into the task of raising children. These were conventional moves to make, and they might appear to bespeak the failure of some promised revolution in politics, or at least in consciousness. But what we discovered during the closing decades of the century is that it is possible to live convention with a difference. What we lost, during the sixties, was an innocent faith in our nation's straight history and its purity of intent; what we gained was a sense that a restructuring, in our local lives and communities, might begin to show the way toward social change.

Yes, the decade was followed by the Reaction. But to blame the sixties for the response it "provoked" is to misunderstand action and its responsibilities. What Mailer and those allied with him chose to do was their responsibility; what the forces arrayed against them chose to do and continue to do, "in response," is theirs.

✦   ✦

"A scale model of Vietnam": this is what Mailer provides in the pissing scene. America's longest war—George Herring gives its dates as 1950–75—was not to be won. Its prosecution involved, to use Mailer's word, too many "mistakes." The first mistake was conceptual. The containment theory assumed that Vietnam was one of a series of dominos, which, if it fell, would lead to the spread of communism throughout Southeast Asia. The theory overlooked the fact that Vietnam and China were longtime enemies and that a victory by the North would not necessarily have led to the extension of China's hegemony. Other mistakes were tactical, or organizational. South Vietnam was a weak and corrupt ally, not an integrated polity. It provided, finally, little to fight for. American firepower set itself the task of defeating a guerilla army, but the nature of the power brought to bear was often ill-suited to the task involved. Troop morale was undermined by the rotation of "short timers" in and out of units; instead of being given a chance to cohere into a fighting force, most soldiers entered and exited Vietnam on a unique, year-long stint. The list could go on. But it can be wrapped up by saying that the biggest mistake was a failure of historical imagination, an insistence on denying that a communist insurgency was also, given the long history of Vietnam's struggle to define itself as a political entity, a war of national liberation. It was a failure, once again, to empathize with the enemy; we were aiming, finally, in the wrong direction.

The phrase "a scale model of Vietnam" comes from Joan Didion's *Slouching towards Bethlehem* (1968), although the phrase is not hers. It surfaces in a leaflet circulating on the streets of Haight-Ashbury, one from which she quotes in her title essay. Only by way of a quotation does Didion allow "Vietnam" to first enter her text, but the war shadows everything. It is with her when she visits the National Memorial Cemetery of the Pacific, in 1966, when she watches them "bringing in bodies now from Vietnam." She has just come from Pearl Harbor, where she begins "to cry" in an uncharacteristic outflow of feeling. To someone who questions why "a sunken ship should affect me so," rather than, say, John Kennedy's assassination, she can only say that she belongs to a different and an older generation. When she watches the new graves being dug up in the crater of the extinct volcano, she watches more as a parent than a child of that moment.

The Southeast Asian War is not quite Didion's war—she was a little too young for World War II, a little too old for Vietnam. Contra Mailer, she is not much interested in the seriousness of war resistance. As devoted as she may be to cultural critique, Didion is equally compelled by the traditional demands of motherhood, despite the difficulties she admits to in trying to provide her daughter with a "family life." She homes in on her responsibility for the more self-destructive forms of acting out in her time, and especially in her home place, and on what she judges to be the failure of one generation to raise another one capable of doing much more than fleeing the burdens of its unique history.

Abandoning her characteristic reserve, Didion breaks out, in the title essay "Slouching towards Bethlehem," into an indictment that is also a statement of faith:

> We were seeing the desperate attempt of a handful of pathetically unequipped children to create a community in a social vacuum. Once we had seen these children, we could no longer overlook the vacuum, no longer pretend that the society's atomization could be reversed. This was not a traditional generational rebellion. At some point between 1945 and 1967 we had somehow neglected to tell these children the rules of the game we happened to be playing. Maybe we had stopped believing in the rules ourselves, maybe we were having a failure of nerve about the game. Maybe there were just too few people around to do the telling. These were children who grew up cut loose from the web of cousins and great-aunts and family doctors and lifelong neighbors who had traditionally suggested and enforced the society's values. They are children who have moved around a lot, *San Jose, Chula Vista, here.* They are less in rebellion against the society than ignorant of it, able only to feed back certain of its most publicized self-doubts, *Vietnam, Saran-Wrap, diet pills, the Bomb.*
>
> They feed back exactly what is given them. Because they do not believe in words—words are for "typeheads," Chester Anderson tells them, and a thought which needs words is just one more of those ego trips—their only proficient vocabulary is in the society's platitudes. As it happens I am still committed to the

idea that the ability to think for one's self depends upon one's mastery of the language, and I am not optimistic about children who will settle for saying, to indicate that their mother and father do not live together, that they come from "a broken home." They are sixteen, fifteen, fourteen years old, younger all the time, an army of children waiting to be given the words.

The sixties are for Didion a "social crisis" inseparable from a massive rejection of articulation. "Wow" has become a descriptive term. This "revolution" is followed by the Reaction, one perhaps secretly hoped for by some of those who resisted. Didion's sense of the sixties as a misguided children's crusade veers toward Pynchon's in *Vineland* (1990), where campus radical Frenesi Gates carries on an affair with Federal Prosecutor Brock Vond, who swoops down in his helicopter to carry her off for hot weekends. It's a "Leda and the Swan" myth, where Leda actively consents to her rape by the powers that be. Pynchon's sad and arresting argument has it that many of the rebels of the sixties were actually in love with the very authority they set out to resist. "Brock Vond's genius was to have seen in the activities of the sixties left not threats to order but unacknowledged desires for it." Why else, Pynchon asks, are the energies of revolt followed by the "Nixonian Repression," and then by an even greater one? "The personnel changed, the Repression went on, growing wider, deeper, and less visible, regardless of the names in power." The best response, his story seems to conclude, is to retreat to a safe place, as does Zoyd Wheeler, and try to do a decent job raising a child.

The unassailable fact, one more evident in 1990 than available to the farsighted Didion in 1968, is that the energies of the sixties—energies summoned by the deep seriousness of the civil rights and antiwar movements—were not able to organize themselves into a long-term and effective political force. Of course, a more generous historical perspective would discover that the reaction began in the 1930s, against the New Deal, burst forth as McCarthyism in the late 1940s, went into abeyance in the Eisenhower years, and then surfaced again with Goldwater in 1964, only to lose that battle and then to go on and win the larger political war. The so-called excesses of the sixties were then invoked by the winners to provide the cultural rationale for a politics of resentment masquerading as a compassionate conservatism.

Didion sounds the word "children" seven times in her seminal passage; her stance toward the atomization of America is downright parental. And she includes herself in the failure, as part of the "we" who, once they have seen all this, cannot pretend that things are otherwise. In "On Going Home," the short essay soon to follow, Didion as much as admits that she can no longer promise her daughter a world of cousins and rivers and great-grandmother's teacups, a passage that echoes the "web of cousins and great-aunts and family doctors and lifelong neighbors" she notates the loss of here.

The children of the sixties are a product, then, of how they have been raised; they are the children of Cork and Lucile Miller, the couple in "Some Dreamers of the Golden Dream" who have misplaced the future and started looking for it in bed. The malady from which the Millers suffer afflicts most of Didion's subjects in *Slouching*, and it can be summed up as living in a naïve relation to one's own story. Like the children in Haight-Ashbury, "their only proficient vocabulary is in the society's platitudes." So the lovers in this suburban sublime say things like "Don't kiss me, it will trigger things." They do it all "in the name of 'love'; everyone involved placed a magical faith in the efficacy of the very word." However, since their language and their sense of narrative are received rather than constructed—since they take no responsibility for making their own story or even noticing that they are in one—the Millers and their intimates are condemned to repeat and therefore to pass on to their children only disabling illusions.

"This is a story about love and death in the golden land." So Didion begins. She will repeat the gesture, as in "Here is a story that is going around the desert tonight," or "I want to tell you a Sacramento story." Didion signals the importance of the gesture on the second page of the book, where the sentence openings "This is" and "Here is" are each repeated three times. By so openly offering her reader a story *as a story*, Didion prevents any naïve absorption into the text and encourages us to accept it all as something made. She has found a story in these materials, one that exists only by way of the strength of her stance and style. The Didion effect, then, is of a direct and somewhat offhand offering. How could we not accept? The price of acceptance is to discover that "we," too, are implicated in a scene from which the narrative voice had seemed willing to place us at a safe and ironic distance.

Didion believes that words make you free. Atomization can be met with articulation. Without words and the mastery of them, the self remains trapped in cliché. This is the burden of any decent English class, and it is a conservative one. This is why Didion falls back on words like "rules" and "game," choices that cast the problem as one of knowing certain conventions and therefore how to play within bounds.

Didion signals her obsession with articulation in "A Preface," where she labels herself "neurotically inarticulate." The precision of her writing continually demonstrates the irony of this claim. But her writing also seeks out occasions to demonstrate the truth of the claim, to reveal the power of the "disorder" of which she writes to challenge even her mastery of the language. The most moving of these moments involve the abstract noun "something," as in the self-consuming conclusion to "On Morality": "Of course we would all like to 'believe' in something." This word haunts the end of the essay and specifies Didion's refusal to give such longings a name. Then there is the crescendo of "something's" in her astonishing paragraph on the uncanny appeal of Howard Hughes:

> Why do we like these stories so? Why do we tell them over and over? Why have we made a folk hero of a man who is the antithesis of all our official heroes, a haunted millionaire out of the West, trailing a legend of desperation and power and white sneakers? But then we have always done that. Our favorite people and our favorite stories become so not by any inherent virtue, but because they illustrate something deep in the grain, something unadmitted. Shoeless Joe Jackson, Warren Gamaliel Harding, the *Titanic: how the mighty are fallen.* Charles Lindbergh, Scott and Zelda Fitzgerald, Marilyn Monroe: *the beautiful and damned.* And Howard Hughes. That we have made a hero of Howard Hughes tells us something interesting about ourselves, something only dimly remembered, tells us that the secret point of money and power in America is neither the things that money can buy nor power for power's sake (Americans are uneasy with their possessions, guilty about power, all of which is difficult for Europeans to perceive because they are themselves so truly materialistic, so versed in the uses of power), but absolute personal freedom, mobility, privacy. It is the instinct which drove America to the Pacific, all through the nineteenth century, the desire to be able to find a restaurant open in case you want a sandwich, to be a free agent, live by one's own rules.

The "something" here is deep, unadmitted, interesting, and only dimly remembered. By keeping the speculation aloft for so long, by refusing to deliver on the concrete referent behind the thing, Didion encourages us to provide the answer for ourselves, an answer all the more damning when it comes, after the parenthesis, in a sentence and a half that redefines the central promise of America as, also, its deepest sickness.

The God term "freedom" is shadowed, it turns out, by its satanic twin, "mobility." The promised pursuit of happiness—Didion later will label it "a consumption ethic"—leads, too often, to this, to a state of paranoid isolation and narcissistic craving in which, as another prophet from the sixties went on to tell us, freedom is just another word for nothing left to lose.

Mobility as illness: this is the theme of the opening paragraph of "Slouching towards Bethlehem," one that invokes a world of bankruptcies and public auctions and abandoned homes and adolescents drifting from "city to torn city, sloughing off both the past and the future as snakes shed their skins." The dozen or so references to snakes in the volume have less to do with venom than with skin shedding.

To "simply *move on*," as James Pike does in *The White Album* (1979), is for Didion the worst thing you can do, not because it is immoral, but because it is careless. Fitzgerald's utmost pejorative is also Didion's; theirs is a world in which the best people play by the rules and wipe away the obscene word scrawled on the steps of a deceased friend's home by the . . . children.

And yet Didion shares with Fitzgerald the capacity to take great risks for her characters, to extend her sympathy in unexpected directions, and to implicate herself in an appreciation of the vast, meretricious beauty she also condemns. At the end of her stay in Haight-Ashbury, Didion is taken by Otto into a living room where a child is reading a comic book. "Five years old," Otto says. "On acid." Didion tells us the child's name and a little about her situation. Her mother has been giving her acid and peyote for a year. People with self-respect know the price of things, Didion will argue, and the price the journalist must pay here, in order to bring the story back for us, is to fail to reach out or even to articulate. "I start to ask if any of the other children in High Kindergarten get stoned, but I falter at the key words." This courageous exposure of the limits of her professional stance and her personal nerve overwhelms all irony and generates a sense of pity for all involved, even perhaps for the paralyzed narrator herself.

Didion's self-consciousness about the stories she tells and her elected stance toward them culminate in "John Wayne, A Love Story." Of course, she has seen the movies before she meets the man, and she has been especially moved by hearing him tell the girl in a picture called *War of the Wildcats* that he will build her a house " 'at the bend in the river where the cottonwoods grow.' As it happened I did not grow up to be the kind of woman who is a heroine in a Western, and although the men I have known have had many virtues and have taken me to live in many places I have come to love, they have never been John Wayne, and they have never taken me to that bend in the river where the cottonwoods grow. Deep in that part of my heart where the artificial rain forever falls, that is still the line I wait to hear."

In this stunning confession, the irony is inseparable from the awe. We each very possibly carry within us, Didion's admission suggests, nostalgia for such an illusion. In Didion's case, she waits for a settled domestic happiness in a Western space with a man of unquestioned "sexual authority," which is, of course, pretty much what Lucile Maxwell thought she was getting when she settled down with Gordon Miller in the San Bernardino Valley. Unlike Lucille, Didion knows that such outcomes exist only in stories, as an image of the desired rather than the possible.

In the same year that Frank Kermode gave the lectures that would become *The Sense of an Ending* (1967), Didion thus provides a heart-stretching example of the key distinction made in his book, the one about the difference between believing in a myth and believing in a fiction. Both are constructs—stories—but a myth is a story that one believes in some sense to be true, while a fiction is a story that one knows to be constructed. The only kind of belief still available to a mind like Didion's, a mind so skeptical and yet so drawn to the power of the reigning illusions, is the "nicer knowledge of / Belief," as Wallace Stevens calls it, "that what it believes in is not true."

Given Didion's awkward and self-consuming confession, it is all the more moving that she chooses to end her book by marrying and settling down, with a man and in the West. She decides, at the end, to play by the rules. "Here is a story," finally, about herself.

"What I want to tell you is what it is like to be young in New York," Didion writes in "Good-Bye to All That." Then, in the following sentence, she explains "why I no longer live there." Her account of these years allows the reader no suspension of disbelief; the "love" for New York is shadowed from the start by her knowing "that it would cost something sooner or later." Loss is preemptive and ever present in Didion; the question is not whether but when it will come. This is an effect she learned from Hemingway; given their continual insinuation of future pain into the experience of present pleasure, in reading them we enjoy, at best, a sense of suspicious calm.

By twenty-eight New York has come to seem old to her. She begins to hurt the people she cares about and to insult those she does not. A friend writes down

a psychiatrist's name and address for me, but I did not go.
   Instead I got married, which as it turned out was a very good thing to do but badly timed . . .

The husband, never named, comforts her in her despair and suggests that they get out of the city for a little while. "It was three years ago that he told me that"—she is writing in 1967—"and we have lived in Los Angeles since." At the height of the adventure of the sixties, our heroine decides to marry, to go home to her native California, to settle down.

Didion will one day tell us that she went on to "find meaning in the intensely personal nature of my life as wife and mother." She tells us this in *The Year of Magical Thinking* (2005), the book she will write in the wake of her husband's death and her daughter's descent into an eventually fatal illness. Only in this book does she describe the day of her wedding on "a January afternoon when the blossoms were showing in the orchards off 101," or will she write about the deeply loved routines of married life, the setting of the table, the lighting of the fire, the dinner with John. They will be married thirty-one days short of forty years. "People with self-respect," she has long since told us, "have the courage of their mistakes. They know the price of things." What she could not have foreseen, and could only come to know through hard and bitter experience, is that one of the prices to be paid, when you love a man who dies at the dinner table of a sudden massive coronary event, is having to survive the loss of him.

The climax of the story Didion chooses to tell about her marriage, in *Slouching towards Bethlehem*, comes as an afterthought, as in Mailer's "and he was arrested." The paragraph break before "Instead I got married" makes the act feel even more arbitrary, and more sudden. As in Bishop's "Crusoe in England," most of the courtship and sexual love are consigned to the white space between one line, or paragraph, and another. But it is not reticence that Didion celebrates here. She falls back on the conventions and "rules" of story itself. "Badly timed," she writes. But the out-of-the-blue marriage is perfectly timed, if you are a reader looking for a satisfying ending to Didion's book. *Slouching towards Bethlehem* finishes as comedy, with a happy ending in which a new society is born out of the old.

"Was anyone ever so young," Didion writes, and she seems eager to mature. Yet she everywhere mourns the loss of an earlier self and the fact of "the promises we break as we grow older." When the big change comes, it is not the earned product of growth; the sudden marriage provides nothing as vulgar as "closure." By opting for the most conventional story ending of all, Didion also forecasts the choice that so many survivors of the sixties, however radical in their politics, would go on to make. By making so little of it and yet by locating the event at just the right narrative moment, Didion once again acknowledges how our lives are so often driven by the wish that they might conform to the shapes of stories, especially "happy" ones. Now, at the end of her book, however she has arrived at this point, Didion may be ready to begin, to raise and teach the rules to a child of her own.

The difference between Mailer and Didion comes down to many things, but one of the things that matters is whether you prefer paying or growing. "Pay or grow," Mailer writes in *Advertisements for Myself*, and by the "or" he seems to mean that we must each choose to do the one thing or the other. In his sentence about crossing the Potomac, Mailer is moved by his own sense of having grown, as if this were work for a man. In so many of her sentences about how life goes, Didion is struck by the necessity to pay, especially if one is to maintain one's self-respect. "Price" is the key word in her essay on that subject, as in the phrase "anything worth having has its price." For Didion, change is almost always loss; for Mailer, change brings with it the promise of growth. This is one reason that while he finds mostly hope in the sixties, she finds mostly loss.

Both writers do share something important, besides their commitment to the disciplines imposed by the possession of a personal style. They share a "growing sense," in Mailer's words, "of apocalypse in American life." Didion's title, borrowed from Yeats's "The Second Coming," signals as much. In "On Morality," she even quotes with relish the apocalyptic longings Mailer expresses on behalf of his hero at the end of *The Deer Park* (1955). "*Where are we headed?*" she is asked on a book tour, and although she scorns the question, she answers it, in her way. For what comes, for Didion, as for Mailer, is the Reaction, and about this, too, they are prescient. While he divines the big-time resentments of the folks from the small towns, she finds herself "listening to a true underground, to the voice of all those who have felt themselves not merely shocked but personally betrayed by recent history. It was supposed to have been their time. It was not." These "secret frontiersmen" and their eschatological visions will evolve into the shock troops of what Pynchon will call the Nixon and the Reagan and the Bush Repressions, roused to passionate intensity by "an obscure grudge against a world they think they never made."

When commentators adduce the sixties as the subtext of our contemporary politics, it is to Mailer and Didion that we can turn for a full understanding of the claim. By capturing accurately how it felt then, these two writers purchase the authority to tell us what that time means now. And the choice we face, in looking back on and integrating the sixties, is not a choice between, but of. Mailer embodies the one choice, and Didion embodies the other. It is the best kind of tragic choice, between two conflicting goods.

CHAPTER TWELVE

The Postmodern

SHEPARD ✤ BEATTIE ✤ CARVER ✤ DELILLO ✤ GADDIS

*T*he postmodern structure of feeling can be characterized by a series of refusals:

—the refusal of the old master narratives;
—the refusal of the distinction between high and popular culture;
—the refusal of the pure or the generic for the hybrid;
—the refusal of the normative for the differentiated;
—the refusal of the universal for the particular and the local;
—the refusal of the unified individual for the non-self-identified subject;
—the refusal of weighty allusion for light-hearted pastiche;
—the refusal of the natural or the essential for the constructed.

These refusals can feel, to some, like losses, especially a loss of the self's felt sense of power in relation to the world. And the sense of coming after, of having survived the passing of a more passionate historical interval, can induce nostalgia, as when Frederic Jameson reads postmodernism "as the substitute for the sixties and the compensation for their political failure." Koba Mercer questions the felt extent of this so-called cultural shift, where "predominant voices in postmodern criticism have emphasized an accent of narcissistic pathos by which the loss of authority and identity on the part of a tiny minority of intellectuals is generalized and universalized as something that everybody is supposedly worried about."

The five authors assembled in this chapter do share a concern, if not a worry, about one of the most "normative" and "natural" and "essential" of cultural institutions—the American family. Sam Shepard's (b. 1943) work traces the difficulty, in a culture of performing selves, of compelling "recognition" from a parent. Ann Beattie's (b. 1947) work also unfolds as a drama of attachment, one in which friendship replaces kinship, and children are stood in for by "things." Raymond Carver (1938–88) and Don DeLillo (b. 1936) discover a surprising empathy for the figure of the "wife" as they explore the challenge of imagining—or being imagined by— the assigned partner of the "husband." William Gaddis (1922–98) attempts to reconcile his readers to the anxieties swirling around the prefix "post-," urging upon them an acceptance of being belated and indebted to circumstances of personal origin in the same way that postmodern writers stand in a belated and indebted relation to the work that comes before them.

❖   ❖

Shepard's plays explore the troubled relation between our fear of performance and our lust for attention. They do so by taking the careful measure of the spaces between us; there is nothing casual about the physical positions of the bodies on his stage. The blocking explicit in his stage directions and implicit in his scene dynamics advances a complex argument about the possibilities for character and action in his world. Exits and entrances reveal themselves as perilous moments of definition or self-loss. Characters seek without knowing it an instant of distinction or notice. Shepard's management of the exclamation "Where do I stand!" reveals a conception of life as an unending and usually unwitting competition for space and for love.

Shepard's most celebrated play won the Pulitzer Prize in 1979 and takes as much of its power from how the actors move as from what they say. The subject of *Buried Child* could be called "the stark dignity of / entrance." The phrase is from the William Carlos Williams poem in which he imagines the way a new shoot shoulders the earth crumbs and pushes up into the light. *Buried Child* ends with Halie's lovely speech about how shoots and people come into the world:

> Good hard rain. Takes everything straight down deep to the roots. The rest takes care of itself. You can't force a thing to grow. You can't interfere with it. It's all hidden. It's all unseen. You just gotta wait til it pops up out of the ground. Tiny little shoot. Tiny little white shoot. All hairy and fragile. Strong though. Strong enough to break the earth even. It's a miracle, Dodge. I've never seen a crop like this in my whole life. Maybe it's the sun. Maybe that's it. Maybe it's the sun.

If Shepard ends his play with an appeal to a sustaining natural order, it is because the cultural space of the family has so utterly botched the task of nurturance. What makes us grow, draws us out? The play foregrounds such questions by focusing on the birth of each character into the space of the stage. The moment of truth is the one of coming on to the set.

A summary of actor entrances in *Buried Child* might read like this:

> Lights come up on a living room, with stairs upward to the left and a screen porch to the right. Wife Halie begins speaking upstairs, unseen, and husband Dodge talks back from his seat on the couch at center stage. Dodge yells for son Tilden, and Tilden "*enters from stage left, his arms loaded with fresh corn.*" Halie finally enters slowly, down the stairs, and "*continues talking.*" She does so after introducing by report another character we will never see, dead son Ansel. Near the end of act 1, son Bradley drags himself in on his wooden leg. He slips, enters

from the screen porch "*laboriously*," shaves and bloodies his father's scalp. Act 2 begins with Shelly's offstage laughter. She and her boyfriend, long-lost grandson Vince, enter the house unnoticed. The final entrance is effected by Tilden as he again carries something onto the stage, the last character to be granted entrance, the bundle of the buried child.

If kinds of entrance bespeak types of character, we might advance the following reading of the play: Halie is the perpetually absent mother, a voice that speaks without noticing or listening. Dodge is the present but absent father, the paternal force who never leaves the stage and whose death will occasion no notice. Ansel exists only as rumor, the fantasy child who replaces the one his mother actually conceived and buried. Bradley's noise and violence measure his actual impotence. Stranger Shelly sneaks on and off and so will fend off this uncanny family by finding it temporarily "familiar." Vince must revise his unremarked first entrance with a second, forcing the recognition—only Halie briefly grants it—his initial homecoming fails to evoke. The buried child appears in the play's last scene—its father, Tilden, presents it to its mother, Halie—so as to bring an end to the repressions set in motion in the first scene.

The major interruption in the play is Vince's second entrance; as act 3 winds down, he cuts his own door through the screen porch and climbs, knife in mouth, into the central space. By doing so, he also cuts short a recognition scene, Dodge's articulation of the story behind the buried child. But "interruption" may be too strong a word for what happens here. No one recurs to and picks up the dropped stitch of Dodge's story; attention simply shifts to Vince. An interruption can best occur during a continued and focused act of attention, and this is what Shepard's plays do not provide. Instead, the inattentiveness of character quickly schools the audience to expect a series of arresting distractions.

"Me—to play": Hamm's first line in Beckett's *Endgame* (1957) might well be the motto for Shepard's people. They insist on playing, on keeping the performance alive, without any solid faith or even interest in being comprehended or known. Attention without recognition—this is what they desperately, unhappily want. In *Buried Child*, *recognize* proves the operative verb. The verb gets attached to Vince, the unremembered son and grandson, but its reach extends to everyone, from the Halie who "doesn't really notice the two men" in her living room to the death of Dodge, "*completely unnoticed*," against the TV. "I recognize the yard," Vince says. "Yeah but do you recognize the people?" Shelly replies. Tilden's answer to the question "Do you recognize him?" refuses Vince any fatherly recognition: "I had a son once but we buried him." Shelly persists in forcing the issue with Dodge, but he turns it into a comic interrogation:

DODGE, *watching T.V.* Recognize who?
SHELLY. Vince.
DODGE. What's to recognize?

To learn, see, know again—this is the burden of the verb. Shelly insists on keeping the fiction of recognition alive in a world where no original cognition occurred that might be had again. Recognition is a promise of drama, the experience Aristotle thought distinguished it from other literary genres. Shepard's conception of drama is so pure that his characters have been reduced to the desire to perform in spite of the absence of an action to be imitated. The outcome is no outcome, no *anagnorisis* of *cognitio*. The recognition that would lead to catharsis and hence to the end of drama and the need for drama—this is what Shepard's plays do not give, and in this may reside their postmodernism.

While watching a Shepard play, we are not witness, then, to a world of character isolated by a deed. Things happen; there is plenty of noise and motion on the set. The scenery is relentlessly domestic or mundane; we are not allowed the escape hatch of thinking the action merely an allegory or a dream. Props play an abundant part. The major elements on stage at the end of *Buried Child* are less the actors than a wooden leg, a blanket, a bouquet of roses. It is as if in the moment of discovering the expressive possibilities of the physical space of the stage this playwright had lost faith in the conventions of drama. The surviving given is the impulse to perform, and Shepard's theater thus becomes not a space for the imitation of an action but one for acting out.

It is precisely the "give-and-take" of which the boy speaks in *The Rock Garden* (1964) that is absent from these performances, especially the mutuality of verbal exchange. Dialogue becomes the desired and feared thing in Shepard, a state the achievement of which could signal a scary breakthrough to a new way of being. "You gotta talk or you'll die," Tilden maintains. No one fails to talk in these plays, or at least to make noise: they are "Dyin' for attention," in the words of *The Tooth of Crime* (1972). These characters speak like actors, bypassing the intimacy of conversation for the insistence of monologue. Speech is directed outward, not to be heard but overheard. Talking forces with little to say press for a piece of turf onstage. The most poignant of questions may be Salem's "Are you listening" in *La Turista* (1967). And yet Shepard does not supply her utterance with a question mark; Salem produces it within an uninterruptible monologue. The typography of the play's final pages gives a sort of answer, nevertheless: two columns of print each assigned to one speaker. The lines are meant to be spoken simultaneously; here the "back" does not wait for the "forth."

These are style matches, and victory depends less on physical strength than on the invention and deployment of a unique language. In *The Tooth of Crime*, the duel unfolds between two visions of the power and status of words. For Hoss, language expresses; for Crow, it constitutes. Hoss displays a psyche; Crow inhabits a discourse. The values of sincerity and authenticity vie with those of arbitrariness and recombination. Or, we might say, the values of modernity compete with and are defeated by, in the action of the play, the forces of postmodernity. The price of Crow's victory is utter loneliness; he wins and becomes stellified, a star revolving in unpeopled space.

But these contesting plays—and *True West* (1980) is the other strong example—actually eschew victory for standoff. At the end one man appears to have beaten or talked down the other, but the real situation is an uneasy parity, a kind of endless struggle of the brothers. *True West* gets divided into nine scenes, with each scene in turn divided into mood units by the word "*pause.*" The lack of strong act or scene divisions or even of a simple rising action testifies to repetitive rather than climactic outcomes. And if shame is the ultimate weapon in *The Tooth of Crime* and in *True West*, it may be because the vision of conflict proves so relentlessly male, so located in the performance anxieties of a gendered ego. When Crow says of Hoss that "he was backed up by his own suction," he simply points to the same vacuum of doubt behind any or every man, as Shepard sees it.

The appearance of the mother at the end of *True West* confirms this. Hers may be the most astonishing entrance in Shepard's work. It is as if Lee and Austin have been fighting in order to grab a little of her notice, and this is what she cannot give. Her focus relentlessly elsewhere, she is the ever-present absent Shepard mother, the woman for whom there is no here here. Shepard's plays repeat the uncanny continual return of the prodigal parent:

> AUSTIN *makes more notes,* LEE *walks around, pours beer on his arms and rubs it*
>   *over his chest feeling good about the new progress, as he does this*
> MOM *enters unobtrusively down left with her luggage, she stops and stares at the*
>   *scene . . .*

It will take five utterances from the sons before Mom finally speaks: "I'm back." If the moment of coming on stage is epiphanic for a Shepard character, none enter with a greater sense of diffidence than these perpetually missing persons, the women whose bland, insistent unnoticing voices seem beyond the register of dramatic change or affect. "I don't recognize any of you": the voice is Shelly's, in *Buried Child*, but she speaks for most of Shepard's characters and virtually all of his parents, especially the female ones. These anti-Oedipal dramas deny that the self can be found—recognized—at home. If so many of the plays dramatize the avoidance of love, it is because at the beginnings of things stands a parent who refuses to be an audience for her child.

To gain notice, to assert manhood, to be loved—the drive toward performance is perhaps Shepard's most overdetermined, one pressed on him by all the complexities of his being. And although the wish to be loved seems, to me, the most comprehensive, performance is finally for Shepard an excess, a gratuitous human impulse beyond explanation or the need for it. That we perform is the redundant truth; why we do so, he, this least analytical of dramatists, usually wonders not. As Shepard says of his friend Bob Dylan, "The point isn't to figure him out but to take him in." Of course, this very act of taking in turns out to be the act of recognition so many of Shepard's characters cannot themselves perform.

◆   ◆

Ann Beattie likes lists. As she says of one of her characters, "she often counted things." Things, Beattie thinks we believe, have the power to relieve our anonymity by making our differences plain. Hers is a sustained meditation on the status of things in our culture, on the status we have because of the things we own. Beattie devotes herself to imagining characters for whom the possession of things serves as distraction from possession in and by love.

A story in *Distortions* (1976), her first collection of short stories, shows a character distracted from people by things. "A lot of things haven't been going the way I figured," a man named David says. Then he corrects himself. "Not really things. People." Beattie's work can be read as an act of growing resistance to this confusion. Finding a workable balance between people and possessed objects proves a balance difficult to achieve, given that hers is a world in which value typically floats, like the space borne astronauts mentioned so frequently in *Secrets and Surprises* (1978). In launching her career at a time when the value of objects had become fully unmoored by advertising into the weightlessness of the market, Beattie seemed destined to write about a scene in which, as in "Taking Hold," Reeboks have replaced Rilke. (The same story mentions the Nylons, the Walkman, the Honda Accord.) Beattie's things do not do anything. Their power is registered by their aura, and the status we gain by knowing their names—gilt by association. This immersion in a "chaos of first names" and brand names supports Blanche Gelfant's claim that "of all Beattie's qualities the most distinctive is contemporaneousness." In this continual state of up-to-dateness, people have become generic, interchangeable, while objects have become capitalized.

Beattie's is as sophisticated an account of class and commodification as her generation is likely to give or to get. When critics lament the loss of a political vision in post-sixties America, hers is some of the first work that should be summoned to counter the claim. Beattie has given us a critical and sympathetic look at the new class flung up by postindustrial capitalism. Fred Pfeil argues that "the overwhelming majority of those United States citizens who in 1980 were between 25 and 35 years of age were members of that class." Barbara and John Ehrenreich have dubbed it the "professional-managerial class," or PMC. According to Pfeil, this class experiences the decline of the Oedipal ego (see Shepard's absent fathers and ubiquitous but unnoticing mothers); adopts television as its lingua franca; perceives no strong line between high and popular culture; does work that is bureaucratized, contingent (a series of "projects"), and largely mental; and suffers from "deindividuation," a sense that the self has been displaced into and can best be represented by received codes and clichés. Beattie's work records the strain it takes to live such a life, as her prose "mimes the ceaseless process of the consumerized self's construction, fragmentation, and dissolution at the hands of a relentless invasive world of products."

Beattie's most hopeful work tries to oppose the woes of consumption with the risks of production. True production is making, the addition to the world of a thing not there before. American culture has consistently made this task difficult for women, who must chart their way between two equally demanding kinds of making: creation and procreation. Each entails a unique product, a work of art (or some equally valuable made thing) or a child.

Beattie wants to clear a space in which a woman can satisfyingly make. Yet her characters seem permanently shadowed by the sense of what Ezra Pound calls "the not done," by a sense, however much they have made, of "the diffidence that faltered." They are threatened not only by the looming consequences of what they have made but also by the fear, often supported by an authorial judgment, that they have chosen to make the less than fulfilling thing.

Beattie is wary of vertical human ties, of identity as something forged across a generation gap. The positive word for horizontal attachment is *friendship*, and in "Friends," Beattie exposes her generation's tropism toward affiliation within an age cohort. "Friends" proves, however, a story nearly impossible to follow. Here the collapse of the gap produces a maze of relationships so horizontal that they become interchangeable. People function in such stories as replacement parts. One solution is to become lovers, as Perry and Francine temporarily do—to impose some erotic tension on the mess. Another way out of the chaos of first names is one that Beattie's work will go on to prize more openly: taking care.

For all her attention to fraternity, Beattie has from the beginning exercised a deeply *parental* imagination. But caring for children entails enormous risks. In her books a child is often abused or lost. *Distortions* ends with two children burning in a boat. In *Chilly Scenes of Winter* (1976), her first novel, Charles must mother his mother. A couple in the title story in *Secrets and Surprises* has lost a child to leukemia. In *Falling in Place* (1980), a brother shoots a sister. The first story in *The Burning House* (1982) deals with a brain-damaged child. Jane refuses to play "the perfect little mother" in *Love Always* (1985) and is killed. The first couple we meet in *Where You'll Find Me* (1986) mourns a dead daughter. In *Picturing Will* (1989), the father goes to jail, the mother retreats into fame, and the boy becomes the project of the stepfather. Children are lost even before they are born: Beattie fills her stories with abortion, infertility, miscarriage.

Since parents in her fictional worlds often find themselves sharing the responsibility for a damaged child, Beattie's theme might seem to be the lost innocence of children. Yet she rarely writes convincingly from the perspective of a child. Her interest, rather, is in the effect of the idea or the event of a child on an adult mind and heart. Her adults are asked to imagine—to picture—children, and they usually fail. The work is less about a child's liability to fall than an adult's refusal to rise to the occasion, as she puts it in *Picturing Will*, of being a parent.

"Forgetting a child": the phrase comes from "Janus," Beattie's most concentrated short story. The story first appeared in *The New Yorker* in 1985 and was republished in the 1987 collection *Where You'll Find Me*. In the story, the phrase about forgetting a child forms part of a simile, one in which the central character searches for a comparison worthy of her attachment to a beloved thing. In these seven pages, Beattie engages in a complex study of the limits and powers of a caring human attention.

Andrea, a real estate agent, owns a remarkable bowl. The story begins with a sentence about it: "The bowl was perfect." Her husband is asked not to put his keys in it. Andrea places the bowl in houses she is trying to sell, and it seems to bring her luck. One day she leaves it behind; this is like "forgetting a child." She gets it back and begins to fear for "the possibility of the disappearance." At the story's end, we learn that the bowl was a gift from a lover, and that when Andrea would not decide in his favor, he left her and called her "two-faced," a Janus.

The story encourages at least two possible readings:

In a world based on "the pleasure of new possessions," the bowl is the ultimate thing. It is clearly compensatory; both Andrea and her husband have "acquired many things to make up for all the lean years." Yet it is not a thing like the other things named here—the Bonnard, the Biedermeier, the Leica. It is a thing that is not a status object. Andrea feels grateful toward it, judges it "responsible for her success." She fantasizes a "relationship" with the bowl and becomes obsessed by its possible loss. The very structure of the story, beginning and ending with a paragraph focused on the bowl, suggests Andrea's secondariness. Beattie has fashioned a story to record once again the ways in which people in a world of "prospective buyers" become functions of their things.

Or: The bowl is a shape to fill a lack. In it Andrea finds compensation for not having a child. Clearly aligned with a woman's inner space—"There was something within her now, something real, that she never talked about"—the bowl figures forth Andrea's unspoken decision about motherhood. "It was meant to be empty." Andrea's responses to the bowl reverse those called forth by a standard developmental sequence. She begins by granting the bowl independence, falls into an anxiety of attachment, recalls the moment of its conception—her lover's "I bought it for you." In this reading, Beattie has then once again fashioned a story to record the ways in which a woman's imagination recurs to a displaced drama of generation.

Yet these are inadequate readings of the story and of Beattie's career. The bowl is compensatory in yet another way. In the absence of the departed lover, his gift becomes the object of Andrea's displaced feelings. And yet this is precisely what she, in a classic case of self-protective repression, cannot allow herself to know. The key element in the story's structure, then, is Beattie's placement of the information about the lover as giver of the bowl. By withholding this crucial knowledge until the final paragraphs of the story, Beattie choreographs a recognition, but one that revises the traditional recognition scene in that only the reader—and not Andrea—has the experience of revelation.

Beattie's deliberately withheld disclosure accomplishes two things: it opens an ironic gap between the reader's and the character's understanding, a gap that makes Andrea's passionate and mysterious attachment to the bowl an object of pathos; and it allows the reader to share for the bulk of the story Andrea's bemused and shifting fascination with the loved thing. The latter consequence implicates us at least temporarily in the impossibility of exposition and in the necessity of *reading*. Reading involves a take on something, a submission to the wonder of unexpected supply. The bowl suggests "motion," and Andrea keeps circling it. Reader and character are caught up in an activity in which viewpoints shift. In the first sentence of the story, the bowl is seen as "perfect." At the end, it is seen somewhat differently: "In its way, it was perfect: the world cut in half, deep and smoothly empty." The repetition of the adjective calls to mind the story's beginning, measures the distance we have traveled, admits the modification achieved, and asserts the integrity of a mind that continues to revise its perceptions without repudiating any one of them.

"Janus" marks Beattie's movement from irony to ambiguity. In thinking about her husband and herself, Andrea notes that "while ironies attracted her, he was more impatient and dismissive when matters became many-sided or unclear." Two stances emerge here: irony, or single-mindedness. Both are reductive, modes of simplification. Neither proves adequate in a story with language so flagrantly interpretative:

> It was both subtle and noticeable—a paradox of a bowl. Its glaze was the color of cream and seemed to glow no matter what light it was placed in. There were a

few bits of color in it—tiny geometric flashes—and some of these were tinged with flecks of silver. They were as mysterious as cells seen under a microscope; it was difficult not to study them, because they shimmered, flashing for a split second, and then resumed their shape.

It would be a mistake to focus too much on the image here. Beattie's stories are rhetorical, not iconic. She wants to throw us back on the status of our response, rather than to make us "notice," as she writes at the end of this paragraph, "some object." Like our most famous verbal icons—Keats's urn or Stevens's jar—these things are summoned in order to tease us *out* of thought, or into thought about how we think. The men in Andrea's life want to reduce the "many-sided" to the "two-faced," but Andrea reveals that through the act of attending to a thing we assume whatever irreducibility we have, give possibility its being. In its continual unstillness—its surges of warmth and chill, ascriptions of likeness and difference, findings of satisfaction and lack—Beattie's story becomes the story of the act of the generous and open mind.

This is the story's meaning until its final paragraph adds a further one. Once we have learned of the lover, his gift of the bowl, and his abrupt departure, we are prepared to gain a fuller understanding of Andrea—and a deeper empathy for her:

> Time passed. Alone in the living room at night, she often looked at the bowl sitting on the table, still and safe, unilluminated. In its way, it was perfect: the world cut in half, deep and smoothly empty. Near the rim, even in dim light, the eye moved toward one small flash of blue, a vanishing point on the horizon.

Now the asserted perfection of the bowl is slightly modified: "In its way, it was perfect."

And Andrea, like the bowl, is also cut in half, deep and smoothly empty as a consequence of having both betrayed her husband and lost her lover. In this state of aftermath she is "still and safe," but "unilluminated." She has displaced her love for persons onto an object, gaining stability, but ceasing to glow. The only remaining light in the dark room is valedictory and comes from the bowl. The small blue flash at the rim resembles both the departing lover and a diminishing self.

In a story of remarkable concentration, its final paragraph achieves the figural concision of a poem. And in the almost interior perspective achieved by Beattie's third-person narrative here, the reader trembles on the other side of the thin membrane separating Andrea from self-knowledge. Our recognition of her lack of recognition accounts for the ending's poignance. And yet it does not invite us to judge or dismiss, but to feel with this woman who has, at least for now, fallen into a confusion characteristic of her moment:

Could it be that she had some deeper connection with the bowl—a relationship of some kind? She corrected her thinking: how could she imagine such a thing, when she was a human being and it was a bowl? It was ridiculous. Just think of how people lived together and loved each other . . . But was that always so clear, always a relationship?

How could she imagine such a thing? Beattie shows us precisely how, and in doing so the work of the career goes beyond the representation of the postmodern condition and into the realm of diagnosis and cure.

Reading "Janus" returns us once again, then, to Beattie's true and indisputably claimed ground, to the story of how we keep a thing in mind. "What she believed was that it was something she loved." "Janus" and the career of which it is a part can be read as an inquiry into the sustained act of attention we call love. Her characters and narrators usually let their attention lapse, and irony rushes in. But in "Janus," a character's flawed but passionate devotion to her study becomes a figure for Beattie's devotion to her craft, and for her best reader's commitment to reading the products of it. This is love, after all—to keep looking and studying and caring and going back to retrieve something forgotten even while the possibility of damage and disappearance persists. Love is risk, the chancing that what we give over to the love "object" may not be acknowledged, valued, or reciprocated. And whether it is the child we conceive and rear or the moving rather than the static story we write for a reader yet unknown, each must be sent out into the world protected only by the power of our care.

✦   ✦

A big question in Raymond Carver studies is whether to prefer the expansive, openly emotional stories of *Will You Please Be Quiet Please?* (1976), *Furious Seasons* (1977), and *Cathedral* (1983) or the lean, elliptical work in *What We Talk About When We Talk About Love* (1981). Compositional history often betrays no single intention: an inveterate reviser, Carver was in the habit of revisiting his stories to shorten or enlarge them. "I like to mess around with my stories," he maintained in *Fires* (1983). Discernible over the span of the career, as William Stull argues, is "a dialectic of expansion, contraction, and restoration." Further complicating any narrative of Carver's development is the matter of Gordon Lish, the editor at *Esquire* who published "Neighbors" in 1970 and who later, at McGraw-Hill, pushed for the "minimalist" style of Carver's third and, to my mind, best book.

The pattern of fat-lean-fat suggests that Carver's minimalist work may form an exception to his general rule. Yet this is also the work for which he was first singled out and by which he is most vividly remembered. The debate over whether and how the stories might be minimalist belongs to the dusty past; the term is in any case a somewhat dunderheaded simplification of the rich effects these stories produce. Carver's leaving out of things in no way equates to a waning of affect. A close comparison of the fat and lean versions of one story reveals that omission in Carver can work, as in Hemingway, to make the reader "feel more."

"There are about four versions of 'So Much Water So Close to Home,'" Carver has said. "The version that appeared in *Spectrum* and then in the *Pushcart Prize* anthology is different from the version in both *What We Talk About* and *Fires*. They're all different stories, and they have to be judged differently." As Gunter Leypoldt points out, there are at least "five published versions" of this story. He also convincingly demonstrates that for the purposes of comparison there are "only two versions," since Carver's "longer versions" of the story, as he shows, "are virtually identical." The unique and much-reduced version published in the 1981 *What We Talk About When We Talk About Love* is a stronger work, I believe, than the longer and original text.

The shorter version is stronger because it asks more of the reader. In version 1, emotions and feelings are directly named; in version 2, they must be inferred. This is a necessary rather than an arbitrary effect, since the story is about a woman attempting to imagine a man's experience. As Claire reaches out to Stuart in trying to grasp what happened on the fishing trip, so the reader must reach out to Claire, supplying her with motive and affect in the face of slim evidence. In each version Claire is the narrator, but only in the shorter version does this act of the mind—precisely because of all that the mind does not know—work as a medium of dramatic recognition.

Carver begins the story with the effect of an action: "My husband eats with a good appetite." In version 1, Carver omits the indefinite article and extends the sentence with a conjunction: "but he seems tired, edgy." In here attempting to divine what Stuart feels from what he does, Claire preempts the work of interpretation for us. The "but" also moves the story out of the simple present and into the passive tense. But the power of the opening depends on our felt sense of Claire's abbreviated temporal horizon, a reach of knowledge so limited as to be confined to verbs like "eats," "chews," "looks," "wipes," and "shrugs." Tenses here create tension, a condition from which Claire, as well as the reader, desires relief.

The action producing this effect is the story of the fishing trip, from which Stuart has returned the night before. "I WAS asleep when he got home." We aren't told about the moment of return until the third section of version 2. (The ten pages of version 2—as compared to the eighteen pages of version 1—are spaced into nine discrete sections, each marked by a capitalized word.) Sex is exchanged—"I turned and opened my legs"—but information isn't. In version 1, Claire does wake up once

Stuart returns, and she follows him into the kitchen, where he is drinking a beer. Not until the next morning does the story of the trip get told.

In neither version are we permitted access to the scene of instruction. This is Carver's key use of the "ellipse," as he called it, an effect that "goes back to Hemingway of course." Carver offers up the fact but not the content of Stuart's telling *after* Claire has already told us: in the second section of version 2, which we will have just read, she attempts her narration of the fishing trip. On this formal matter the two versions openly diverge, and they do so in their treatment of the reader. In version 1, Stuart asks Claire to sit down, "and then he told me." Version 2 contains no such solicitous moment. Claire gets up to the sound of the slammed telephone receiver and asks, "What is going on?" Then Carver delivers his key sentence, which is also a paragraph: "It was then that he told me what I just told you." In neither version do we get an account of the fishing trip in Stuart's words.

There is no "you" in version 1, no reader directly addressed. There, we remain unacknowledged spectators of the long-underway dissolution of a marriage. Carver can summon the "you" in version 2 because, by virtue of the way Claire delivers her narration there, we have been allowed to become cocreators of it. *What I just told you*, she says. The "what" points back to the great second section of the story, in which the fishing trip has just been imagined, and designates it as the key act of intimate telling, an intimacy shared by reader and narrator rather than by husband and wife:

> He and Gordon Johnson and Mel Dorn and Vern Williams, they play poker and bowl and fish. They fish every spring and early summer before visiting relatives can get in the way. They are decent men, family men, men who take care of their jobs. They have sons and daughters who go to school with our son, Dean.
>
> Last Friday these family men left for the Naches River. They parked the car in the mountains and hiked to where they wanted to fish. They carried their bedrolls, their food, their playing cards, their whiskey.
>
> They saw the girl before they set up camp. Mel Dorn found her. No clothes on her at all. She was wedged into some branches that stuck out over the water.
>
> He called the others and they came to look. They talked about what to do. One of the men—my Stuart didn't say which—said they should start back at once. The others stirred the sand with their shoes, said they didn't feel inclined that way. They pleaded fatigue, the late hour, the fact that the girl wasn't going anywhere.
>
> In the end they went ahead and set up the camp. They built a fire and drank their whiskey. When the moon came up, they talked about the girl. Someone said they should keep the body from drifting away. They took their flash-lights and went back to the river. One of the men—it might have been Stuart—waded in

and got her. He took her by the fingers and pulled her into shore. He got some
nylon cord and tied it to her wrist and then looped the rest around a tree.

The next morning they cooked breakfast, drank coffee, and drank whiskey,
and then split up to fish. That night they cooked fish, cooked potatoes, drank
coffee, drank whiskey, and took their cooking and eating things back down to
the river and washed them where the girl was.

It may prove difficult for me adequately to express my admiration for the work accomplished in this passage, one of the supreme examples of the isolating pathos of
gender. Claire here attempts to answer an age-old question: Why do men go fishing? The answer might seem obvious: to get away from women. And yet what they
catch, of course, is a woman. In this harrowing fable about the return of the repressed, Carver reveals the vast American enterprise of lighting out for the territory as the illusion it has always been, since it is shadowed by and in this case directly confronted with that from which it would escape. The identity of our heroes
of "beset manhood," as Nina Baym puts it—our Nattys and our Nicks and our Stu-
arts—proves not imperial but relational, dependent for its very sense of "freedom"
on the Coras and the Helens and the Claires left behind.

Those who are left behind are also left to imagine the lives of those who leave.
In "When We Dead Awaken," Adrienne Rich envisions just the sort of awakening
Claire experiences here, one in which she begins to resee her place in a world of
men. The reader comes upon these paragraphs after the opening scene in the
kitchen and so understands them as narrated by Claire on the morning after Stuart's return. This means that Claire has had only a few hours in which to process
what "he told" her. Out of this very lack of information and this brief amount of
time, we watch her construct a deeply moral and comprehending narrative.

So Carver also "goes back to Hemingway" by refiguring the central trope of
"Indian Camp." Once again, a story turns on an unspeaking and unspeakable female body. In Hemingway, the Indian woman's screams are deemed "not important," and Nick looks away. It is as if Nick is simultaneously asked to acknowledge
and to repress some primal crime. The result, nevertheless, is that the woman is the
thing left out. Carver marks an advance on Hemingway in that in "So Much Water
So Close to Home" the female body at the center of things is spoken for, finally, and
by an empathetic female voice.

Claire's narrative purchases authority by being honest about what it doesn't
know. Phrases like "my Stuart didn't say which" and "it might have been Stuart"
punctuate her retelling with an open admission of surmise. The surmises remind
us that Claire is working with self-interested hearsay even as they implicate *and*
exonerate Stuart. The adjective "my" also echoes the opening word of the story and

then drops out of the second mention of Stuart, as if to indicate that Claire is moving away from a clinging possessiveness. Against her "my," and in the first four sentences of the section, Claire juxtaposes four repeated "they's." As the pronoun continues to be repeated throughout the passage, it takes on the ominous, chiming tone of an obscene epithet.

Claire uses repetition, then, to create irony. The first time she calls the "they" "family men," the phrase functions as a simple cliché. But by the time she repeats the cliché in the second paragraph—"Last Friday these family men"—the phrase has begun to deserve scare quotes. Family men are precisely what they will turn out not to be, either in their loyalty to the home place or in their willingness to "take care," not of their jobs, but of another "family man's" daughter.

My students are invariably appalled by this scene, and their discomfort comes to rest on the sentence in which the men "took their cooking things and eating things back down to the river and washed them where the girl was." "Why is this so shocking?" I ask. "Because it's an act of pollution," one of my students once answered. What the men do here is just plain dirty.

The moment's force comes from the juxtaposition of the naked pathos of the girl's body with the banal act of washing dishes; it's an unholy mixture of sacred and profane. This grotesque act of housekeeping reminds us of the division of labor on which traditional marriage depends, and of the price female bodies too often pay in the maintaining of it. In an earlier story in *What We Talk About When We Talk About Love*, "Tell the Women We're Going," Carver uncovers the murderous dynamic between staying "married" and the male wish to be "going." It is men who want to go; as Claire points out, the girl in the river, clearly the victim of rape and murder, isn't "going anywhere."

But Claire is going somewhere. The shock of the experience has converted her into a mental traveler, one capable of new empathies and judgments. So she will imagine herself in the creek like the girl, "right in it, eyes open, face down." The discovery of her potential victimhood is superseded by the felt sense of solidarity. "My head swims," she tells us, about the sensation she feels after attending the girl's funeral. Here the literal picturing of herself in water has been refigured into a metaphor that once again places her there even as it names the hard-won sense of vertigo that is the price she must henceforth pay for having allowed herself to develop an imagination. And the key act of imagination, again, is when she places the men and their dishes by the girl in the river. This is surely not a piece of information conveyed to her by Stuart; such women's work would be beneath his notice. It is something Claire makes up, her strikingly adequate image for the spreading stain of violation. It is as if in one courageous sentence Claire imagines the existence and the transgression of a new taboo.

In version 1, there is no repetition of the phrase "family men." There is no "my" modifying the word "Stuart." The two surmises are there, but the second surmise is blunted by the interpolation of a too-obvious "I don't know who" before the phrase "it might have been Stuart." The washing of the dishes where the girl was is an image common to both versions, but in version 1, Carver italicizes his point in the sentences that follow, where he has the men tell *coarse* stories and speak of *vulgar* or *dishonest* escapades out of the past. The adjectives here label the behavior. While the narrator of version 1 is a more reflective and editorializing presence, the gain in her self-awareness is a loss for the reader, who feels less for being told how to feel.

Carver scholars agree that Gordon Lish "cut, rearranged, and rewrote freely" in order to produce the style of version 2. What they don't agree on is what this means. Richard Ford (b. 1944) makes the unassailable point that once Carver accepted such revisions, he made them his own. "They're all different stories," Carver said about the versions of "So Much Water So Close to Home," "and they have to be judged differently." The quote acknowledges difference and invites judgment. I judge the version in *What We Talk About When We Talk About Love* as more affecting than the others and have given my reasons for doing so. But a case against the mode of the story can certainly be made, as does Adam Meyer when he argues that "deletion here leaves the reader less sure about the direction in which the story is headed." Carver himself came to judge version 1 as "fuller somehow and more generous and maybe more affirmative." This evaluation of his own career resembles my evaluation of Hemingway's, where I am relieved by the fuller and more generous and more openly awkward style of *For Whom the Bell Tolls*, despite its renunciation of the theory of omission that distinguished the early work. It all depends on where you think a writer should *go*. In Carver's case, however, it is difficult to argue for a clear line of development when the volumes of stories that mark the major swerves follow so closely upon each other: 1976, 1977, 1981, 1983. Carver himself appears to look on the stories in *What We Talk About* as his least characteristic, and he was happy to move away from them. Lish had perhaps pushed him in a "minimalist" direction he chose, finally, not to take. Whichever "Carver" one prefers, his "low postmodernism," as Philip Simmons calls it, turns out to be a very contingent affair.

*   *

Jack Gladney lives with his wife Babette and their children from various marriages. He teaches Hitler Studies at the College-on-the-Hill. The family flees an "airborne toxic event" during which Jack is exposed to its poisons. He begins to worry, more than ever, about dying, just as he discovers that Babette has been taking a drug called Dylar. She pays for the Dylar by granting sexual favors to supplier

Willie Mink. Jack shoots Mink in a motel room and also wounds himself. Nobody dies, and at the end he finds himself back in the supermarket, shopping, absorbed by the white noise of everyday consumer life.

So much for the novel's "plot": the characters in Don DeLillo's *White Noise* (1985) are drawn to the word, as when Jack asserts to his assembled department heads that "all plots tend to move deathward," or when Murray Siskind later contradicts him and says, "To plot is to live." Either way, the issue of the novel's having a plot is out of the bag. This tone of deadpan cultural knowingness gives the novel its "postmodern" (DeLillo uses the word in chapter 30) quality by converting its big emotions and occurrences into instances of themselves. At any moment the book can digress into "talking theory," as Jack and Murray do on their campus walks. By building in the commentary traditional novels leave it to the critic to supply, *White Noise* may leave us with the question, what is left to be said?

Perhaps that the commentary makes little difference. Within the first twenty pages, we visit, for instance, "THE MOST PHOTOGRAPHED BARN IN AMERICA." "No one sees the barn," Murray tells Jack; "we're not here to capture an image, we're here to maintain one." It's a rueful gloss on Walter Benjamin's "The Work of Art in the Age of Mechanical Reproduction," with the barn standing in for the artistic masterpiece toward which, before the invention of photography, a pilgrimage had to be made. In a world of endless reproduction, the work of art begins to erode, to become a mere item for casual consumption, to lose what Benjamin calls its "aura." Murray, well schooled in theory, goes on to make the point. "Because we've read the signs" about the barn, the ones advertising its most photographed status, "we can't get outside the aura. We're part of the aura. We're here, we're now."

And yet, DeLillo's plot obviously moves toward something real, something beyond the casual reproduction of images. That something "is part of the nature of physical love," the question, in a companionable marriage, of "who will die first." We are still left, for all the mediations and the cracking wise, with the burden of all plots, the fact and timing of our deaths and of the deaths of the people we love. There at least is reality that will not dodge us.

The question comes up because Jack has been exposed to the toxic event and because Babette senses that life is always nothing more than one. Something toxic will, eventually, get each of us. Her fears are what we once called "existential." In the great and moving chapter 26, husband and wife confront each other about the Dylar. Jack wants to know why she is sneaking the drug, and Babette tells him that about a year and a half earlier she had begun to experience a "condition" that would not go away. So she sought out a "Mr. Gray" and offered herself as test subject for a drug that would cure her of the condition. The exchange involved one "grubby" indiscretion, Babette's offering of her body for the Dylar.

On hearing this, Jack feels "a sensation of warmth creeping up my back and radiating outward across my shoulders." He tries to fend it off by deploying mock-sex talk: "Then he entered you." But Babette won't let him retreat to irony and dismisses his "stupid usage." The jealousy is bad enough, but on top of it Jack begins to feel a hollow coldness, "an inkling of what she'd been talking about all along"— not the sexual betrayal, but the "human condition" for which she was willing to go to such extremes.

And then she tells him: "I'm afraid to die," she said, "I think about it all the time." Jack argues that "this is not a reasonable fear" and maintains that "everyone fears death." But Babette is not comforted: "I fear it right up front," she answers. Jack proves more injured than worried, resentful that the woman he thinks of as lacking in "guile" has been "able to conceal such a thing." He also feels competitive with her. "Baba, I am the one in this family who is obsessed by death." They continue talking, comparing their respective fear-of-death symptoms. They clench "in an embrace that included elements of love, grief, tenderness, sex and struggle." Then Jack plays his trump card. He tells Babette about his exposure to Nyolene D; he tells her that it is he, not she, who is "tentatively scheduled to die." Babette climbs on top of him, sobbing. "The warm tears fell on my lips. She beat me on the chest . . . She took my head in her hands, gently and yet fiercely, and rocked it to and fro on the pillow, an act I could not connect to anything she'd ever done, anything she seemed to be."

Hence, Babette does something, from Jack's perspective at least, unprecedented. It is not a mere reproduction of "anything." Of course, there are commonly lived experiences and frequently read plots that can provide a context for understanding how she does respond here, and that require no cultural knowingness for doing so. Babette is experiencing an emotion, and her ability to have one may rest, in part, on what she has learned by encountering characters in literary plots. This in no way invalidates the genuineness of her response; it is only in this way, to reverse the formula DeLillo deploys on his last page, that the living speak to the dead. If emotions, as Eliot says, are always in danger of being lost, then the work of the living is to refind and to refeel them, as Babette does here. That such an emotion may be a reproduction of an earlier one only marks it as a token of the respect the living are able to pay to those no longer capable of having emotions at all.

To plot is to agree that life can be shaped so as to convincingly mean something. We pay for this gain in meaning with a death, since for plots to be fulfilled they must, like lives, also end. Jack argues that "all plots move in one direction," toward death, but Murray counters by saying that "to plot is to affirm life, to seek shape and control." Fictional endings may herald mortal endings but are finally quite distinct from them. They are provided for us precisely so that we might rehearse,

by way of them, for the big ending. As Wallace Stevens writes, "One likes to practice the thing."

In ending, fictional stories actually extend and give life by calling forth all of
those feelings—including the fear of losing life—that make life livable and worth
living. And the story that DeLillo ends up producing is of one of the most believable and flawed and good marriages in American fiction. Marriage as enacted by
Babette and Jack is about accepting the fate of going through time together, toward
death. Adultery, perhaps the key plot element of the traditional novel, functions
here as mere counterplot, a digression from the momentum of mortality and one
that gives the Gladneys' story a chance for unlooked-for emotional discoveries and
a greater sense of extension in time.

The point of the thing resides in words like "going through" and "together." Jack
inaugurates the sorrowing and passionate exchange with his wife by announcing
that "it's time for a major dialogue." And then they have one; nobody runs out of
the room. People still talk to each other in DeLillo's novel as if talking still desperately mattered, and they do so in alarmingly frank ways, often articulating awarenesses lying behind speech. This is where the perpetual resorting to metacommen-
tary reveals itself as more than a coy device. DeLillo gives voice to his startlingly
prescient observations as the ever-present but unheard melodies of our diurnal
round, a body of knowledge we may carry with us by virtue of being situated within
contemporary culture, but one that rarely can rise to or even need rise to the level
of speech. This may be the postmodern "language of waves and radiation," as De-
Lillo calls it in the novel's closing paragraph, or it may be the still, sad music of humanity as it lives out its mortal days. We all live within the range of both kinds of
vibration, but only an ear like DeLillo's can enable us to hear it.

◆   ◆

Although published in 1955, William Gaddis's *The Recognitions* had to wait until
the 1970s to be . . . recognized. Frederick Karl designates Gaddis one of the Tri-
bunes, a lonely forerunner of a movement to come. "It is only from within the current postmodern context that we can really begin to read *The Recognitions*," John
Johnston wrote in 1990. Reviews of the novel were so uncomprehending and dismissive that Gaddis was to include in *JR* (1975) coded swipes at Glandvil Hix (Gran-
ville Hicks) and M Axswill Gummer (Maxwell Geismar). Delayed recognition ac-
counted, in part, for the gap in Gaddis's career, as he was forced into public relations
and corporate speech writing in order to support himself and did not publish a second novel until twenty years after his first. The National Book Award given to *JR*
also served as a belated nod to the earlier and more extraordinary performance.

Cynthia Ozick argues that the substance of Gaddis's work is "nearly always rage,
mostly rage about false belief," and Wyatt Guyon's career as a painter in *The Recog-*

nitions can be read as the product of an almost religious fury. Wyatt reacts against Aunt May's belief that "to sin is to falsify something in the Divine Order." Her real hostility is to making of any kind as a sort of competition with God. Wyatt becomes a great forger in order to confound the distinction between making and falsification. He affirms the value of "mortal creative work" even as he acknowledges the probable impossibility of making anything "original."

Alone in her room, Esme the poet imagines a beyond "where nothing was created, where originality did not exist: because it was origin." Her nostalgia, like that of Milton's Satan, is to get back to a primal before, to production without reproduction. Satan rejects absolutely the notion of having an origin: "We know no time," he asserts, "when we were not as now." His behavior in *Paradise Lost* can be read as a reaction-formation against the very idea that he was *made*.

Gaddis views the copying inherent in any act of artistic making not as sin but as an unavoidable necessity. The great musicians may touch "the origins of design with recognition," but for everybody else it is no more possible to return to an origin than it is to be wholly original. Since we are all influenced—profoundly "origined"—no real anxiety can flow from the fact. One is reminded of the parable about the woman and the notion of the world resting on the back of a giant turtle. "And what does the turtle rest on?" she asks. "It's turtles"—copies—"all the way down."

So copying is what there is to do. But copy in what spirit? Do we copy in a sense of despair at the funhouse mirrors of postmodernism, or with a sense of tragic joy in the work of making the world human while also acknowledging that every act of making is obligated, belated, derivative? In his principled forgery, Wyatt resembles the protagonist of Borges's "Pierre Menard, Author of the *Quixote*" (1939). Borges quotes as evidence of Menard's completed labors one sentence of the *Quixote*, which Menard has been able to compose not by copying the original but by producing "a few pages which would coincide—word for word and line for line—with those of Miguel de Cervantes." As a parable about literary history, "Pierre Menard" has fathered many refigurings, from Harold Bloom's (b. 1930) *The Anxiety of Influence* to John Barth's (b. 1930) "The Literature of Exhaustion." Yet the author of this "Fiction" chooses rather to place the emphasis elsewhere, in a playful celebration of all that it took to create, "in the twentieth century," the later text. "Cervantes' text and Menard's are verbally identical," Borges writes, "but the second is almost infinitely richer."

Borges concerns himself less with the anxiety or exhaustion inherent in being a belated author than with the endowments and capacities inherent in being a belated reader. As André Maurois argues in his Preface to *Labyrinths* (1964), the coincidence between Menard and Cervantes "becomes so total that the twentieth-century author rewrites Cervantes' novel literally, *word for word*, and without referring to the original. And here Borges has this astonishing sentence: 'The text of Cervantes and that of Menard are verbally identical, but the second is almost infinitely richer.' This he triumphantly demonstrates, for this subject, apparently absurd, in fact expresses a real idea: the *Quixote* that we read is not that of Cervantes, any more than our *Madame Bovary* is that of Flaubert. Each twentieth-century reader involuntarily rewrites in his own way the masterpieces of past centuries. It was enough to make an extrapolation in order to draw Borges's story out of it." While Maurois makes a profound point about the power of readers to adapt to their belatedness, he does so while making a curious and perhaps even a disastrous error, since he *misquotes* the "astonishing" sentence from Borges (Maurois substitutes "The text of Cervantes" for Borges's "Cervantes' text") that makes the case for the richness of word-for-word rewriting.

The *Quixote*, at least, actually exists as a thing that might be copied, however much Borges resists using the verb. But Gaddis ups the ante on Borges by having Wyatt Guyon paint copies of Flemish originals that never ever were. As Wyatt says to art critic Basil Valentine, the painting he has "been forging all this time never existed." What he has been creating, with great care, are *simulacra*. Verbs like "copy" and "forge," as Borges foresaw, fall short of expressing this complex relation of maker and work. Yet both Borges and Gaddis cling to the notion that such efforts deserve "to be taken seriously" before the world, that there remains, despite our station in time, "something worth doing."

For the reader of *The Recognitions*, the something worth doing is to keep going. Having just spent two weeks at the beach with the novel, I must confess that they were the most difficult of my reading life. This is a book of 956 pages, almost half a million words. The most I could manage was 150 pages a day. The novel lacks the elements that might keep a reader going: annotated scene shifts, identification of the speaking voice, likeable characters, a manageable quantity of allusion, a followable plot. At some point, the resolve to finish it becomes a moral decision. And then the reader is rewarded, in the big recognition scene, by a confluence between the experience being had *in* the novel and the experience being had *of* it. On page 896, Wyatt, now renamed Stephen Asche, tells the "distinguished novelist" Ludy that we can only atone for our own sins by "living it through." He is talking about an old man who raped an eleven-year-old girl and who has now returned to be near her remains, at the monastery of San Zwingli. It is important to go where one has sinned, but not in the hope that one can directly repay the loss. As Agnes Deigh says earlier, "we do not, ever, pay for our own mistakes. We pay for the mistakes of others." The dynamic of sin and atonement depends on an acceptance of displacement and the impossibility of reciprocal payback.

This is a serious rather than a trivial instance of postmodern alterity: the working out of the harm we have caused does not return to its origin but is displaced outward among unimaginable strangers. "I have to go on," Stephen tells Ludy. The old man has told him to do this. Why go? Ludy asks. To go out and be where one has sinned, like the old man who has returned to the scene of his crime. He returns not to directly repay, but to begin the process of paying forward. "He learned only through her suffering," Stephen tells Ludy. "If that was the only way he could learn? So now do you see why he sends me on? . . . once you're started in living, you're born into sin, then? And how do you atone? By locking yourself up in remorse for what you might have done? Or by living it through." *By living it through*, Stephen repeats, four more times. "To have lived it through," he ends, "and live it through, and deliberately go on living it through."

Gaddis's reader is like a traveler across Spain ("Spain is a land to flee across"), or a pilgrim through a John Ashbery (b. 1927) poem, a pursuer of "destinations one after another whose reason for being so cease upon arrival, and he must move on, to provide that interim of purpose with which each new destination endows the journey." Destination here merges into an ongoing destiny, like those "moments of insight" in Ashbery's "The Task," moments that "melt / In becoming, like miles under the pilgrim's feet." In the final words of his novel, Gaddis admits that because of the difficulty of the score he has produced, it is one likely to be "seldom played." Gaddis here anticipates that his excesses or "sins" as a novelist can only be expiated by future generations of patient and enduring readers. The call made by the old man upon Stephen is paralleled by the call made by Gaddis upon his audience: reading it through.

If *The Recognitions* "can legitimately lay claim to being the first American 'postmodern' novel," as John Johnston argues, then Gaddis's contribution to this shift in structures of feeling can be said to be a moral one. Nothing about the condition he evokes relieves us from the burden of having to "pay for our mistakes," or for what Stephen calls our "sins." Gaddis retains the vocabulary if not the experience of belief. His richest frame of reference is church history. He writes like an Eliot who never makes the return to faith, relying on the lives of the saints and their passionate commitment as a standard against which the unseriousness of his historical moment can be measured. His then is a grieving, reluctant postmodernism. The later novels abandon this mood, recognizing the nostalgia for a lost wholeness as a nostalgia. Formally, this shift is registered as a turn into dialogue.

Gaddis may well prove, as Steven Moore maintains, "the greatest writer of dialogue in the history of the novel," but his dialogue novels enact the death of dialogue itself, as talk reduces in them to a sort of monologic white noise. *JR* ends with the desperate cry, "Hey? You listening . . . ?" The endless production of self-regarding voice acts as a formal extension of the novel's content, its vision of 1970s

American culture as a merry-go-round of credit where what matters is the circula-
tion of money rather than the worth of anything it might stop to buy. As Johnston
has it, "both speech and capital thus become part of the same runaway system."
More despairing in its vision of making than *The Recognitions*, the novel is filled
with outright plagiarists and failed artists, such as Thomas Eigen, who steals his
idea for a play from a screenwriter. In a terrifying reprise of Frost's "Home Burial,"
the 1985 *Carpenters Gothic* deploys the breakdown of give-and-take between husband and wife as a means of exploring "fictions" and their "serviceable" or "desperate" uses. In his fourth and last novel, *A Frolic of His Own* (1994), Gaddis returns
to an artist figure and allows him a minor triumph.

Oscar Crease has written a play about the Civil War. While our initial impression of the play may be a dubious one, Jonathan Raban argues that "it is, we are
made to feel, the best play, the best reckoning with the paradox of his own history,
that its author (call him Gaddis, or Eigen, or Oscar Crease) could make under the
circumstances." Reading *A Frolic of His Own* thus involves changing one's mind,
since the play-within-the-novel that at first seems a parody of *Gone with the Wind*
(1936) gradually enforces a revaluation of its worth, into something more like an
awkward but heartfelt homage to *Absalom, Absalom!*

A Hollywood studio has made a movie with suspicious borrowings from the
play, and Oscar is suing them for the alleged theft. Meanwhile, Oscar is both the
logical defendant and the actual plaintiff in a personal injury case in which he
claims to have been run over by his own automobile while trying to hotwire it.
Meanwhile, his father, a judge, is being harassed out of election to the next highest
level of the bench by a public outcry over his decision in a case involving a dog that
became trapped in a steel sculpture named Cyclone Seven. Meanwhile, Oscar's
brother-in-law Harry, an attorney, is working himself to death in pursuit of promo-
tion to senior partner at the firm of . . .

Law is what we have instead of war: Oscar's *Once at Antietam*—in the play, long
passages of which interrupt the present action of the novel, ancestor Thomas
Crease sends up a substitute to fight in his place in both the Northern and Southern armies, and both men are killed at Antietam—acts as an exemplum of the
continuous uncivil war of litigation life in the end-of-the-century United States has
become. Gaddis's characters speak in a tone of continuous complaint, a hectoring
of self and other that reduces experience to injury. And Oscar's play provides more
than an inflated parallel to his embittered present: what gets glorified in it as a civil
war, one fought in order to fulfill the true spirit of the law as the founder's understood it (despite their original compromising inclusion of the three-fifth's clause
and their general willingness to shore up sectionalism by way of the Great Compromise in which all states, even the smallest ones, were allotted two representa-

tives in the Senate), turns out to be one more family fight, a struggle over legacy arising from a perceived slight that itself turns out to be a simple misunderstanding—or willful misreading—of Oscar's own family history, a history on which the play is more than loosely based. To use attorney Harry Lutz's word, the ongoing civil war in which Americans permit themselves to indulge in various legal frolics of their own originates from little more than a child's "resentment."

The casualty of all this argufying is listening itself. What is going on here does not stop; Gaddis offers over 500 pages without chapter divisions, and the characters, unmarked by any "she said's," cease speaking only when they are cut off. The breathlessness of the style marks the sense of the other not as conversational partner but as "mere interruption." Oscar continually repeats the word "listen," but he interjects it as an imperative meaning "Shut up." "Don't interrupt me Christina listen," he says. Gaddis's signal contribution to our moral understanding is to get us to recognize that the form of our speech matters more than its content, and that the way in which we hold or share the floor is a profound measure of our spiritual development.

The law itself is frequently reduced to mere verbiage: "Words, words, words, that's what it's all about." The quote recycles a famous line from *Hamlet*, another work sensitive to the cruelty in "the law's delay." It is the endlessness of litigation Gaddis seems to despair of, the momentum of a game in which the players have long since lost control of the rules or of their motives for consenting to play in the first place. They fight back with a stubborn querulousness, and their words have less to do with the creation of portable meaning than with the assertion of presence or the execution of force. Law becomes the pitiful or pitiable resort of an aggression denied the release of violence and of a narcissism unable to tolerate the smallest slight.

Yet, while the speakers here resist accommodating another voice, Gaddis structures his novel as a self-interrupting form. The reader moves among unmarked dialogue, passages from Oscar's play, legal opinions, the text of a deposition. Each interval marks a rhetorical occasion in which "words, words, words" are stylized in an effective way. This "pattern of repeated interruptions" asks the reader to remain as open and flexible as most of the characters stay predictable and closed. When Oscar finds himself haunted "by the sense that 'reality may not exist at all except in the words in which it presents itself,'" he may be experiencing language as the postmodern prison-house at its most extreme. When we read about him feeling this, we are reminded that Gaddis has offered us, instead, a playing field.

The so-called difficulty of American postmodern poetry, drama, and fiction generates an empowering paradox: you cannot ask this much of a reader and also convincingly argue that "discourse" or "system" deprives the self of all agency. As I

have attempted to demonstrate, a Shepard play or a Gaddis novel achieves comple-
tion only in the mind of an audience that is also a cocreator, one that feels, as
Longinus has it in "On Sublimity," as if "we have created what we have only heard."
The Recognitions provides a careful formulation of this postmodern sublime: in
moving through the novel, readers can experience "that sudden familiarity, a sort
of . . . recognition, as though they were creating it themselves, as though it were
being created through them while they look at it or listen to it." Readers can only
feel as though they are creating it for themselves if they in some way already possess the knowledge and power to do so. And this enforced awareness is precisely
the kind of recognition these works so generously offer us. As Otto the playwright
notes to himself, "Orignlty not inventn bt snse of recall, recgntion pttrns alrdy
thr." Gaddis's postmodernism thus also reveals itself as the newest Neoplatonism,
an embracing of knowledge as the unacknowledged but, in some way, already
known.

Longinus and Plato: how odd and wonderful that a discussion of the postmodern would lead us back to the great promoter and the great mistruster of the pleasure of the text. And yet that is where these writers take us. Knowledge here belongs to the province of the "re-," an act of the mind that can only happen because
it is happening again. In the terms I have laid out in the present book, "recognition"
then would be the name these authors give to the movement beyond innocence,
beyond our wanting not to know what we know. No unbound knowing is possible,
and any anxiety of influence may be superfluous, since we stand in such an un-
original relationship to our very selves. And yet this recognition of the workings of
recognition carries with it its sublime compensations, since it can only come to us
by way of our absorption into and identification with the work of creation, as we
live it through. The writers summoned in this chapter thus convert the postmodern sense of belatedness into a continual *re*-cognition of the capacities and powers
of the reading self, as it comes to know what it knows.

CHAPTER THIRTEEN

Studying War

CORMAC MCCARTHY ✦ HERR

*N*ear the end of *The Face of Battle* (1976), John Keegan speculates on what it takes for a battle to be won. It must involve the "moral collapse" of the enemy, a collapse that becomes final only if the battle has been hard-fought. "Easy victories, between equals, almost never stick." The battles of Agincourt, Waterloo, and the Somme were hard-fought, and so could end. The German victory over the French in 1870 came too easily, and so provoked its catastrophic second act, the entrenched resistance of the one army against the other in World War I. Battle requires, Keegan writes, "a mutual and sustained act of will by two contending parties . . . if it is to result in a decision."

Americans are good at fighting hard and are used to winning. According to some, in fact, "winning is the only thing." Of course, the really difficult battles in life—against the fear of death, or one's own selfishness and pride—are not struggles that can be "won." Nevertheless, Americans are given to reducing the terms of existence to those of a zero-sum model. Our obsession with winning and losing can even diminish war itself to the status of a game. "War is the ultimate game," Cormac McCarthy's (b. 1933) judge maintains, in a speech the author invites us to take seriously. But to think so, McCarthy repeatedly shows, is to avoid having to take in the ultimate product of war, human death. Hemingway anticipates McCarthy in this. In *Death in the Afternoon*, he distinguishes between the Spanish and the American taste in games: "We, in games, are not fascinated by death, its nearness and its avoidance. We are fascinated by victory and we replace the avoidance of death by the avoidance of defeat. It is a very nice symbolism but it takes more cojones to be a sportsman when death is a closer party to the game."

In his book *Perpetual War for Perpetual Peace* (2002), Gore Vidal lists the annual interventions in which, in every year since the surrender of the Japanese in Tokyo Bay, the United States has sent combat troops into another country. The list is long: Korea, Lebanon, Guatemala, Taiwan, Nicaragua, Panama, El Salvador, Vietnam, Cambodia, Laos, Somalia, the Philippines, Thailand, Cuba, Grenada, Haiti, the Dominican Republic, Columbia, Bosnia, Pakistan, Afghanistan, Iran, Iraq. The list provides evidence enough that despite the daily capitalist struggle in which we set out to "beat" the competition, Americans still long for and so manage to seek out, if only vicariously through the soldiers they send abroad, the emotions that become available through being at war.

Perhaps this is because war redeems life from "flat degeneration." The claim may seem strange coming from as pacific a soul as William James. But James saw earlier than most that our being at war has everything to do with how war makes us feel. A succinct and positive expression of the case is actor George C. Scott as General George S. Patton: "How I love it so." Those who deplore war "ought to enter more deeply into the ethical view of their opponent," James argues, and are also called on to imagine, in James's eloquent and yet now infamous phrase—infamous after being quoted by Jimmy Carter as a cure for the national malaise of the late 1970s—a "*moral equivalent to war.*"

We will not be competent to imagine such an equivalent until we acknowledge the emotions to which war appeals. The great writers about war do this; they have "no secrets," as Michael Herr (b. 1940) writes, "about it or the ways it could make you feel." One thing commonly felt is a passionate and sometimes rivalrous affiliation between men, a connection that runs so deep that it can deny many reentry into the "complicated world of defined alliances," as Hemingway writes in "Soldier's Home," of domestic life. Two books that openly and honestly confront the feelings called up by war, Cormac McCarthy's *Blood Meridian* (1985) and Herr's *Dispatches* (1977), are the subject of this chapter.

* *

"Poor Mexico," Porfirio Diaz once said, "so far from God, so close to the United States." Cormac McCarthy claims as his terrain the "boundary lines between our country and Mexico" and takes as his subject the way American men are compelled south across these lines, in a kind of unending replay of the nation's first war of empire. The two great countries that now meet at the Rio Grande may have been sundered by initial patterns of settlement, but McCarthy's riders continually trespass on that divide, as they become heroic and doomed geographers of spatial and emotional affinities lying deeper than the lines on any map.

The central action of *Blood Meridian* is set in 1849, at the beginning of the end of America's genocide against the "indian" and at the end of the beginning of the imperial thrust against Mexico, the Caribbean, and Central America. "The war's over," someone says about the recently concluded hostilities between Mexico and the United States, but that two-year-long conflict proves no more than a formal chapter in an ongoing American tropism toward violence directed south. The shocking atrocities committed in the novel both by and against Comanche and Apache and Mexican and American bodies are to be understood, then, not as gratuitous but as a terrible and unending result, the fully earned consequence of the 350 years of post-Columbian North American history that precedes them. No other continent was so successfully wrested by violence from one people by another, an enterprise transforming every locale on it into a "blood" meridian. And by virtue of that history, so McCarthy's vision would seem to argue, citizens of the United States are condemned to live in the chaotic and perpetual state of the "postwar."

At sixteen, the kid falls in with a band of scalphunters led by Glanton and "the judge." They kill most everything they meet—with guns, knives, rocks, hands, feet. By the end, the kid and the judge are trying to kill each other. During the kid's recovery from an arrow wound in San Diego, the judge disappears. Narrative time now speeds up ("in June of that year he was in Los Angeles") and then begins to leap, in the space of a few pages, over entire decades: "In the late winter of eighteen-seventy eight he was on the plains of North Texas." McCarthy ends his Border Trilogy with a similar elision and compression. At the conclusion to *Cities of the Plain* (1998), Billy Parham ages fifty years in one paragraph, as an action taking place in the early 1950s suddenly vaults into "the spring of the second year of the new millennium." In either case, the very casualness of the tone, in which a character's middle age is so swiftly subsumed, cauterizes the wound in time it creates, marking what follows as epilogue and sealing off the now amputated past in Mexico as the inimitable and passionately lived interval.

The kid's stunned fascination with the judge creates the potential for an Ishmael-Ahab–like bond, except that the kid does not and has no desire to command the narrative voice. He possesses no language with which he might speak back to the judge. "Was it always your idea," the judge says to him, before their final confrontation, where the kid will kill him in an outhouse, "Was it always your idea, he said, that if you did not speak you would not be recognized?" The task of speaking back falls to the third-person narrative voice, a highly rhetorical instrument at once accommodating of and resistant to the judge's seductive fatalism.

That voice could be described as Hemingway doing a parody of Faulkner. McCarthy's Faulknerian elements of style are his most obvious and egregious: a hushed and breathless syntax that can issue in sentences of a page in length; portentous, idea-ridden dialogue; a fondness for the big and arcane word; a gift for frequent and far-fetched comparisons. McCarthy embraces some of these habits more closely than others. Or, to put it more accurately, by dint of repeating them, he alerts us to their limitations and salvages what part of them he can in order to reveal the paratactic and world-accepting and therefore Hemingwayesque heart of his vision, a vision most eloquently expressed by the oft-repeated sentence "They rode on." In such formulations, the narrative voice brackets its and the judge's excesses *as* excesses and sides with the ineloquence and nonviolent "clemency" of the kid.

McCarthy's gift for comparison is perhaps the most salient of these elements of style. By the novel's fifth paragraph, the narrator is seeing steamboats "like cities adrift." Later, the sun will rise "like the head of a great red phallus." One paragraph gets six similes: "hard as iron," "like a ghost army," "like shades of figures erased upon a board," "like pilgrims exhausted," "bright as chrome," and "like reflections in a lake." McCarthy likes to end a sentence with "like," as in "They halted and made a dry camp without wood or water and the wretched ponies huddled and whispered like dogs."

McCarthy deploys simile, it could be argued, as an antidote to the profound divisiveness of war, the perpetual collision of monad against monad. His similes bind the hard particulars of the world into "unguessed kinships." Since the human bodies he conjures up resist such projection, he lavishes his figures largely on the landscape, animating his chosen space in an unparalleled embrace of the pathetic fallacy. Rock and star and wind become suffused with a consciousness so intense as to reverse the normal relation of figure and ground. Faulkner uses simile to explore the inner lives of even his most obsessive characters, but McCarthy deploys it in order to contrast a deadness of human soul with the uncanny aliveness of "the bones of things" in a burned-out place.

Or, conversely, the animation of nature through simile projects a world of "malign" intent. The judge continually makes notes and sketches in a leather notebook. Asked what he aims to do with them, he replies "that it was his intention to expunge them"—by "them" he means the things the images represent—"from the memory of man." A conversation about representation ensues. Webster praises the judge's pictures as "like enough the things themselves." But he adds the proviso that "no man can put all the world in a book." The judge takes his point and then recalls an old Huero who, sketched by the judge, felt "unwittingly chained . . . to his own likeness" and who then compelled the judge to bury the portrait in the floor of a cave.

McCarthy uses "likeness" here to mean *representation* rather than *comparison*. The point would appear to be that representation involves a pathetic and self-doomed act of imitation. The judge, although he indulges in creating representations, has a horror of them, since they reveal the gap between word or image and the represented thing. Nothing that man can make can alter the book of things in which his fate is already written. "I dont want in your book," Webster says to the judge. "My book or some other book said the judge. What is to be deviates no jot from the book wherein it's writ." By "book" the judge seems to mean body, the material self in which a mortal fate is indelibly inscribed. "Whether in my book or not, every man is tabernacled in every other and he in exchange and so on in an endless complexity of being." In certain moods, even a writer as cheerful as Emerson might agree. If "Nature" refers to essences unchanged by man and "Art" refers to "the mixture of his will with the same things," then man's "operations taken together are so insignificant, a little chipping, baking, patching, and washing, that in an impression so grand as that of the world on the human mind, they do not vary the result." The result for all of us, of course, is death. And this realization, then, is one origin of violence: a rage at the powerlessness of representation to free man from his fundamental "likeness" to every other human under the sign of death.

The striking out against the mortal body serves, in *Blood Meridian*, as a ritual confrontation with this felt fact. Violence *is* the human ritual: as the judge will later claim, "A ritual includes the letting of blood. Rituals which fail in this requirement are but mock rituals." That the ritual repetition-compulsion of violence avails nothing—confers no more life—only further incites it. War appeals because it channels the individual "taste for mindless violence" by way of a crusading or patriotic script, thus the rationalizing claim made by the captain who first recruits the kid for Mexico: "We are to be the instruments of liberation in a dark and troubled land."

The judge's casual will to kill also expresses his desperate wish to know. "Whatever in creation exists without my knowledge," he tells Toadvine, "exists without my consent." Not having been present at the creation, or his own, the judge can only take revenge on his place in time by gaining the "knowledge enormous," as Keats writes, that will make a god of him. He collects "specimens" so as to bring them into the reach of "men's knowing." The goal is to rout out "the existence of each last entity" and to make it stand naked before man's knowledge, thereby positioning man in the place of the original creator. Knowing is "taking charge."

The project inevitably fails and so collapses into a demonic parody of itself, with the judge not only wasting his erudition on the desert air but opting, finally, for the paranoid opposite of true knowing, the Ahabian belief that a design of darkness is better than no design at all. The world, because it will not submit to the judge's will to know it by subsuming its infinite variety, becomes "a malign thing set against him." McCarthy's will to divine similitude in dissimilitude, such a life-giving and interconnecting enterprise in the hands of a true poet, is carried by the judge to its self-consuming extreme, and so reveals a potential darkness at the heart of the will toward figuration itself, since to compare one thing to another can be to do a kind of violence to it.

How does the judge come to have such cold blood? Perhaps because he suffers from "the primary illness of separation of thinking from feeling," as Truman Capote (1924–84) writes about one of the motiveless murderers in his "True Account." Sam Kashner, brooding on the casual neglect of his teacher, William Burroughs (1914–97), makes a similar assessment: "Burroughs's voice was the voice of

American violence, I thought. It seemed to separate knowledge from feeling, which always brought cruelty." This separation or dissociation of sensibility is an illness from which the writing of a Capote or a McCarthy or a Herr seeks, also, to deliver us.

What angers the judge about the kid is his "indifference" to questions of knowing and design and his refusal to adopt a theory about the world. No less violent than the judge, the kid indulges in no rationale for his behavior. He simply participates in the fight for survival McCarthy represents as the condition of living, in his time, in the American Southwest. His great gift is to "go on."

"See the child," *Blood Meridian* begins. The novel's protagonist is introduced as the "kid." "So you're the man," the captain will say to him, as he signs up for the filibustering expedition. Child/kid/man: the child may be "father of the man," as the narrative maintains in the second paragraph, but the novel leaves somewhat open the question as to whether the kid's experience south of the border allows him to evolve from the one into the other.

The primary evidence for growth resides in the kid's continual resistance to the judge's vision and style. He may not have much of a voice—the judge does all the impressive talking—but he does know how to watch and, finally, to listen. The kid begins as a wary watcher of his father: "The boy crouches by the fire and watches him." When the judge turns up, the kid is part of the "All" who "watched the man." At chapter's end, the judge returns his gaze: "As the kid rode past the judge turned and watched him." Perpetually on the watch, Glanton's band seeks always to know whether its enemies are ahead or behind. "They did not know how far the Mexicans were behind them and they did not know how far the Apaches were ahead." The extreme watchfulness of the characters not only ensures their survival but mimics the narrative voice and its mordant and unblinking gaze.

During their violent standoff in Southern Arizona, as the judge calls out to him from his hiding place, the kid adds listening to watching. "Hello called the judge . . . The kid lay listening." As the judge fires his rifle, he calls out points of jurisprudence. He expounds on laws pertaining to property rights.

> Then he spoke of other things. The expriest leaned to the kid. Dont listen he said.
>
> I aint listenin.

The kid has by now learned that the danger lies less in the judge's bullets than in his words. So he does and does not listen, saving his life by attending to the judge's movements and, by refusing to assent to his words, saving his soul.

As he listens to the judge's speech on war, in chapter 17, the reader is tested in a similar way. These three pages are the most likely to be excerpted and lifted up as the argument of the whole. But the novel possesses, in fact, another model for "Argument," the model followed by Milton in *Paradise Lost*, where each book—or, in this case, chapter—is headed by a series of phrases that herald and condense the upcoming action. These brief formulas—as in "The judge on war"—tend to give more shape and point to an episode than it may internally possess. But without them, we would be truly lost. McCarthy provides us with an "Argument" precisely in order to acknowledge, through a counterpointing outline, the unstoppable parataxis of the whole.

The judge and John Keegan have surprisingly convergent views on what it is that makes men fight. Keegan comes round to quoting the famous adage, originally applied to Waterloo, that the battle of the Somme was won on the playing fields of Eton. The English officer corps that in 1916 so effectively motivated its soldiers to run forward toward almost certain death was an extension of the English public school tradition where every man learned what was expected of him, and he learned it by playing games. "They organized games for the men, and took part themselves, because that was the public school recipe for usefully occupying young males in their spare time." Man "loves games," the judge says. "Let him play for stakes." The stakes, of course, are highest in the game of war, where the merit lies not in the game itself but in "the value of that which is put at hazard." All games aspire to the condition of war "for here that which is wagered swallows up game, player, all":

> This is the nature of war, whose stake is at once the game and the authority and the justification. Seen so, war is the truest form of divination. It is the testing of one's will and the will of another within that larger will which because it binds them is therefore forced to select. War is the ultimate game because war is at last a forcing of the unity of existence. War is god.

It is tempting to take this speech seriously and to explicate it. But it would be a mistake. The judge is not so much wrong as he is beside the point, since McCarthy's novel has already revealed that war is above all about business: what motivates Glanton's men to fight is a bounty of $100 a scalp. That men can also cite and even believe in other reasons for going to war besides making money—a rage against the created order, as in the judge's case, or the glamour of risk, or a fear of dishonor, or patriotism, or simply loyalty to their fellows—does not obviate the fact that war is kept going by the profits to be made from it. This is why Tobin, the expriest to whom the judge directs his speech, answers the judge with a nonanswer: "The priest does not say."

Arrow-shot and anguishing in the sands by the river, the kid is asked a question and gives a reply:

What do you want to do?
Go on.

Go on. "On" is the kid's word, just as "They rode on" is McCarthy's truest and least affected sentence. Above all, the kid is committed to on-ness. He is in the world and imagines no other one. "I wonder if there's other worlds like this," the old buffalo hunter muses to the kid, near the end of the story. "Or if this is the only one." The first words the kid speaks in the novel express his deep and unself-conscious refusal to protest against his lot and therefore answer, in advance, the old hunter's question. "I just got here," the kid says, in response to a question about the quantity of the rain in Nacogdoches. He will express no premature opinions; he will be in the here and endure it. The kid's not-talking and his watching and listening and fighting to stay alive embody, even if he does not so put the case to himself, his acceptance of life in existential time.

Billy Parham also meets a judge figure in the epilogue to his story, and he is asked to listen to another advocacy of fate. His response is like the kid's: "I better get on." Like the judge, the man Billy meets by the underpass hates the fact that "one thing leads to another." He erects an argument against this fact by citing the ability to map out a life as proof that "its shape was forced in the void at the onset." But Billy knows, even if he cannot say so, that the human ability to make a "narrative" out of a life after it is lived in no way alters the fact that as it is lived every moment is experienced as a step to the block, a going on into unmapped futurity. "Living it through" remains, in William Gaddis's phrase, the human work. McCarthy's lexicon in *Blood Meridian*, so graced with arresting ornament—who else summons the vocabulary of "arcature" or "whang" or "ciborium"—serves as a massive distraction from a much more deeply felt sense that going on is what there is to do, as he once again admits in the final sentence: "*Then they all move on again.*"

And so the kid comes to understand something beyond the judge's knowing: that killing is serious and therefore finally to be avoided precisely because we live in a world in which we are going to die. And because he, unlike the judge, does not reject the materiality of an open-ended and time-bound creation, the kid knows clemency. The judge accuses the kid of having a flaw in the fabric of his heart in that he has reserved "some corner of clemency for the heathen." In a book where the blow has largely replaced the touch, we are continually surprised by upspringings of clemency, the little nameless unremembered acts of kindness and love Wordsworth called the best part of a good man's life. The hermit shares his "mess" with the kid and, unasked, ties a bag of food to his mule. The kid helps Brown with his arrow wound and lets Shelby live. He shares his horse with Tate.

Sarah unhesitatingly washes the idiot in the river. In his last act of clemency, the kid offers to convey a survivor out of a company of slaughtered penitents. She is an old woman in a faded rebozo, kneeling in a nearby niche in the rocks. He tells her he will take her to a safe place. Then he reaches out and touches her arm. She moves slightly. "She was just a dried shell and she had been dead in that place for years."

So ends chapter 22. It is the chapter in which the kid loses track of the judge, time speeds up, and he ages twelve years. The following and final chapter begins: "In the late winter of eighteen seventy-eight he was on the plains of north Texas." The kid is suddenly forty-five. He has grown older, but has he grown? Has his way advanced upon the judge's way? *Way* is perhaps the word to end with. The kid accepts the world as a way. Like Casy in *The Grapes of Wrath*, he sees being human as being "always on the way." The judge, on the other hand, rages against life as a mere way and seeks a way out. Even though the kid kills the judge in the closing pages of the novel, McCarthy gives the judge the last word. Or rather, the narrator tells us what the dancing judge is saying. "He says that he will never die." This sentence is followed by the words "THE END."

Although "He says that he will never die" can be said to be the book's last sentence, it is not the last word. An "Epilogue" follows, in which the kid consents once again to move on. In the final paragraph of the novel proper, McCarthy summons the judge for one last performance. "He is naked dancing." McCarthy indicates the surreality of this closing scene by shifting out of the past and into the present tense. "He never sleeps, he says. He says he'll never die." This is a fantasy, not an event. It is a vision of the judge's vision of life and of the terrifying persistence of his idea. The judge can be killed, but his idea cannot. And that idea, from which so much slaughter flows, is that there is or should be another and a better world, one in which we do not die. If any "idea" lies at the root of war, it is this one, since it is an idea that justifies making war against the mortal terms of life itself.

✦   ✦

"Poor Vietnam," we might also say, "so close to China, so far from the United States." Our not knowing that the border between China and Vietnam is the key fact in that country's geography led us into a war there founded on a "bloody innocence," as Michael Herr has it, an innocence as complete as the one that would, fifty years later, take so little account of the divisions between Sunni and Shiite in Iraq. Again and again, to quote McCarthy's sentence, "we are to be instruments of liberation in a dark and troubled land." The same fight in a different theater—was not Vietnam, a war in which we continued to export our racism westward, not also a war fought in "Indian country," the site where the Trail of Tears, as *Dispatches* suggests, "was headed all along"?

This may be why Herr begins his book with a map made by another empire:

There was a map of Vietnam on the wall of my apartment in Saigon and some nights, coming back late to the city, I'd lie out on my bed and look at it, too tired to do anything more than just get my boots off. That map was a marvel, especially now that it wasn't real anymore. For one thing, it was very old. It had been left there years before by another tenant, probably a Frenchman, since the map had been made in Paris. The paper had buckled in its frame after years in the wet Saigon heat, laying a kind of veil over the countries it depicted. Vietnam was divided into its older territories of Tonkin, Annam and Cochin China, and to the west past Laos and Cambodge sat Siam, a kingdom. That's old, I'd tell visitors, that's a really old map.

If dead ground could come back and haunt you the way dead people do, they'd have been able to mark my map current *and burn the ones they'd been using since '64, but count on it, nothing like that was going to happen. It was late '67 now, even the detailed maps didn't reveal much anymore; reading them was like trying to read the faces of the Vietnamese, and that was like trying to read the wind. We knew that the uses of most information were flexible, different pieces of ground told different stories to different people. We also knew that for years now there had been no country here but the war.*

We were fighting then, as we are fighting now, in the first decade of the twenty-first century, over lines drawn on a map by European or North American powers. But to look at such a map is to see it dissolve into a palimpsest, as Herr's overlaying of old lines upon "current" ones makes clear. These layered visual histories of struggle carry their coded messages, as when Herr remembers to designate Siam as a kingdom, the only country on the map not to have been colonized. And there's that word "China," one that divides and swallows up the "territories" of Vietnam. The French may have invaded the region in the late nineteenth century, but the Vietnamese had been fighting off the invading Chinese for almost two thousand years. The words as well as the lines on a map, however old, compel interpretation, and they reveal a map to be what it always is: an aerial view of blame. Looking, then, must eventually give way to reading—to a committed and self-aware willingness to interpret—as it does in Herr's second paragraph.

⁕   ⁕

The informing text behind so many Vietnam stories is Joseph Conrad's, the voice that can say "And this also has been one of the dark places on the earth." So reads the first sentence uttered by Marlowe in *Heart of Darkness* (1902). If it sounds as if Marlowe is talking about the Congo, he is in fact speaking of London. The point being made is that the "darkness" of Africa is a projection, a metaphor allowing the colonizer to dump his shadow on the colonized. Marlowe goes in search of Kurtz, but the darkness he finds in Africa is one he always already carries with him.

The form of Conrad's novel proves a resilient one: the troubled memoir of the survivor who has outlived his attraction toward the charismatic hero. This structure allows for displacement and distance, an elegy for somebody else. And yet the splitting or doubling of the central character—the profound identification between the teller and his fascinating subject—allows as well for a self-elegy, a mourning for the possibilities in the speaker that have not survived the "horror" of his war.

Marlowe/Kurtz, Fowler/Pyle, Herr/Flynn—the line of descent is a compelling one. Graham Greene rewrites *Heart of Darkness* down to the point of leaving the surviving man facing the alarming charms of the hero's Intended. In the early 1950s, English journalist Fowler lives happily in Saigon with his Vietnamese lover, Phuong. Into their peace comes Pyle, a young American bent on developing a third force that can tip the balance between the Communists and the French. Pyle steals Phuong away from Fowler, and Fowler arranges to have him killed. After its flurries of engagement, the book begins and ends with Fowler and Phuong upstairs alone, in personal space, as she fixes him an opium pipe.

The Quiet American (1955) may be the greatest novel written about America in Vietnam, despite the fact that it antedates the arrival of U.S. ground troops there by almost ten years. Its greatness lies, in part, in Greene's confounding the stories of "War and Love." A few pages from the end, Fowler says, "I can't worry much about people in history." But he has himself already entered history, and for personal reasons. He arranges Pyle's death in order to recover Phuong and then discovers that history and the personal cannot again be separated. He learns that one has to take sides, "if one is to remain human."

Pyle takes sides from the start and yet remains so "armored by his good intentions and his ignorance" as to be destroyed by what he tries to save. He is fully engaged, albeit by an imaginary Vietnam. What he knows he has gotten from the wrong books, and Fowler endeavors to strip him of his innocence: "That was my first instinct—to protect him. It never occurred to me that there was greater need to protect myself. Innocence always calls mutely for protection when we would be so much wiser to protect ourselves against it." Pyle has the kind of innocence that thinks that a man is required to jeep through enemy territory in order to inform another man that he plans to steal his girl. He treats Fowler as if he were merely an opponent in a "game." Confidently astride history, with big plans for redirecting the war, Pyle gets derailed by his inexperience of the personal and dies because he does not know, with Fowler, that "we are incapable of honour" in love.

In renewing Marlowe's Congo vision, Greene thus prophesies the future as well. He creates the best case yet made against an American innocence that would have appalled Conrad and that proved to be the downfall of our intervention in Vietnam. This innocence can be defined as an absence of awareness about one's position in a narrative, Pyle's uncritical belief in the power and originality of his Vietnam war story.

In 1979, Michael Herr adapted the plot and tone of *Heart of Darkness* for the screenplay of *Apocalypse Now*. But he had already paid Conrad homage in the war-torn form of *Dispatches*, the one book by an American that most successfully takes on not only Vietnam but also the traditions that had already fully imagined it. Herr's book works not simply because it is outraged but because it remembers. If the theme of salvaged love drops out, the narrator-hero structure remains. Herr centers his book squarely in the problem of survival; Herr's Vietnam, like the kid's Mexico, is about the gain in loss of living on.

Herr admits that he is telling an "old story." His is the story of a "survivor" who spent his war watching it. Herr went to Vietnam in 1967 and spent a little more than a year there, most of it with the Marines, witnessing the siege of Khe Sanh and the destruction of Hue, the old imperial capital. *Esquire* had hired his services with no particular deadline or assignment—just "cover" the war. "Talk about impersonating an identity, about locking into a role, about irony: I went to cover the war and the war covered me; an old story, unless of course you've never heard it."

The most dramatic moment in the first chapter comes when Herr amplifies the meaning of the verb *to cover*—when he slides over to the wrong end of the story. "We covered each other," he says about life with the grunts, "an exchange of services that worked all right until one night when I slid over to the wrong end of the story, propped up behind some sandbags at an airstrip in Can Tho with a .30-caliber automatic in my hands, firing cover for a four-man reaction team trying to get back in." So "Breathing In" ends with Herr picking up a gun, as his drama of detachment temporarily ends: "I wasn't a reporter, I was shooter." In the morning after the fire-fight, Herr sees the empty clips lying around his feet and cannot "remember ever feeling so tired, so changed, so happy."

The clarity of these emotions proves unique in *Dispatches*, a transport unavailable when looking at pain. Herr never suffers a serious wound, although he will panic badly on one occasion. A mortar round comes in, and "when we fell down on the ground the kid in front of me put his boot into my face." The kid's profuse apology sends Herr into a terror spiral: "somewhere in there I got the feeling that it was him, somehow he'd just killed me. I don't think I said anything, but I made a sound that I can remember now, a shrill blubbering pitched to carry more terror than I'd ever known existed, like the sounds they've recorded off of plants being burned, like an old woman going under for the last time." Herr has in fact suffered a bloody nose. His big moment of physical pain and fear proves bathetic, the wrong end of the story.

Herr's job and his story are not to shoot and be shot, and his book works because he cannot do his job with a single mind. It is precisely this failure—and his awareness of it—that saves him from innocence. Yet it does not lead to ironic detachment. Doubleness comes in many forms, and one of them is empathy.

"Put yourself in my place": Herr quotes this request before telling the head-wound story on himself, and it is the implicit request made to him by every GI he meets, "the story . . . always there . . . and always the same." Being a good reporter, a journalist, it turns out, means staying *un*detached, feeling with. " 'Must be pretty hard to stay detached,' a man on the plane to San Francisco said, and I said, 'Impossible.' " Herr's "Impossible" advances a claim about the status and purpose of witness, one made on behalf of all those who, at whatever distance, watched and survived the war. The claim comes straight out of Wilfred Owen and his muddy trenches: that when it comes to war, "the Poetry is in the pity."

Vietnam writing by combatants makes, typically, the opposite move and invests energy in the act of not feeling and in detailing the defenses that hold pain at bay. Drugs supply one way out. In *Meditations in Green* (1983), Stephen Wright's (b. 1946) narrator not only smokes pot but identifies with the uncontested being of a plant: "Vegetable bliss." Pitch-black humor offers another way, as in Gustav Hasford's (1947–93) conversion of the war in *The Short-Timers* (1979) into a sick joke, a world made "safe for hypocrisy." Silence provides a third, as in Larry Heinemann's (b. 1944) *Paco's Story* (1986), where a body reduced to "bloody confetti" finds its story not only stolen by others but, anyway, "more than the tongue can tell." Herr gets liberated to tell precisely by what limits him, the precariously safe haven of the journalist's stance. He can put himself in a soldier's place because he is not already in it and so converts his book into a meditation on its persistent activity—looking—and on looking's biggest subject—pain.

Herr's earliest act of witness, one he buries midway through the book, in the first section of "Illumination Rounds," deals with his not being able to see. He is "new, brand new, three days in-country" and taking his first ride in a Chinook helicopter:

> And across from me, ten feet away, a boy tried to jump out of the straps and then jerked forward and hung there, his rifle barrel caught in the red plastic webbing of the seat back. As the chopper rose again and turned, his weight went back hard against the webbing and a dark spot the size of a baby's hand showed in the center of his fatigue jacket. And it grew—I knew what it was, but not really—it got

up to his armpits and then started down his sleeves and up over his shoulders at the same time. It went all across his waist and down his legs, covering the canvas on his boots until they were dark like everything else he wore, and it was running in slow, heavy drops off of his fingertips.

This scene replays one on Conrad's Congo steamer, in which Marlowe sees "something big" appear in the air, the helmsman step "back swiftly," and then him fall at Marlowe's feet. The helmsman has been hit and killed not by a bullet but a spear. The narrator's literal description of the motions of the wounded body captures the terrifying sense that in such dark places, until we lose our innocence, we will have the experience but miss the meaning.

Given the casual notation through which the sentences about the boy in the helicopter unfold, Herr gets the reader to take the same, unknowing trip. Knowledge by definition is belated and comes too late to rescue or to save. Words like *bullet* or *blood* are facts language here cannot quite summon, although it can manage the uncanny and domesticating metaphor of the baby's hand. The growing darkness of the blood captures the way knowledge will come to Herr in Vietnam, its irrevocable stain, its inevitable spread. All that is left, as Conrad writes in the preface to *The Nigger of the 'Narcissus,'* and as Herr repeats, is an act of witness: "I didn't go through all of that not to see."

Shame and the look: if Herr connects the two, he does so by way of exposing his profession's lust for guilty pleasure. Looking, like desire, is an act that is never ended. Of dead bodies, Herr begins by imagining a moment "when you finally started seeing them." But "even when the picture was sharp and cleanly defined, something wasn't clear at all, something repressed that monitored the images and withheld their essential information. It may have legitimized my fascination, letting me look for as long as I wanted; I didn't have a language for it then, but I remember now the shame I felt, like looking at first porn, all the porn in the world. I could have looked until my lamps went out and I still wouldn't have accepted the connection between a detached leg and the rest of a body, or the poses and positions that always happened, (one day I'd hear it called 'response-to-impact'), bodies wrenched too fast and violently into unbelievable contortion." In Vietnam, Herr discovers the endlessness of looking, its uncanny resemblance to the rhythms of desire.

"I went there behind the crude but serious belief that you had to be able to look at anything, serious because I acted on it and went, crude because I didn't know, it took the war to teach it, that you were as responsible for everything you saw as you were for everything you did." When the distinction between seeing and doing collapses, journalistic "objectivity" is revealed as the weak fiction it has always been.

Herr's text finds no stance free from responsibility and so delivers a timeless trea-
tise on the ethics of journalism as well as a historically specific analysis of the implication of any onlooking American in the war in Vietnam.

We come to *Dispatches* the way Herr went to Vietnam, to see, to know, to be
turned on—and we leave it responsible for everything we have read. The book gets
us to perform a witness act. But it does not indulge in the "mistake of thinking that
all you needed to perform a witness act were your eyes." Feeling is the thing, and if
we do not move from looking to feeling, and bring feeling to the aid of knowing,
then we have refused to take the trip; we have stayed home.

Of course, "home" is the ultimately false position, the place that, after Vietnam,
ceases to exist. The States are, as Herr calls San Francisco, "the other extreme of the
same theater." The Vietnam books that play up the distinction between the war and
home are the least convincing, like James Webb's (b. 1946) *Fields of Fire* (1978).
After the crafted pathos of Webb's battle scenes, the final tableau at a stateside peace
rally tries and fails to make a point about dissent at home undermining the fighting
abroad. But the burden of fighting as Webb has revealed it, and as nearly every
book about combat reveals it, is not in its purpose but its passion, a self-justifying
activity that knows less about politics than the brotherhood of pain. Men in Vietnam fought out of the solidarity with other men that war will always create, a solidarity experienced in a different way by those in the peace movement, a struggle
reflecting a legitimate domestic disquiet and entailing its own substantial although
not mortal risks. Robert Stone's (b. 1937) *Dog Soldiers* (1973) made, early on, the essential case for Vietnam as a war also fought at home. The aptly named Converse
simply switches from one theater to another, an America as spaced out and drugged
out as its Southeast Asian double. As Herr says in the last line of his book, "Vietnam Vietnam Vietnam, we've all been there."

The continual and unresolved issue for Herr is that he has chosen harm's way:
"'You fucking guys,' he said, 'you guys are *crazy!*'" This is said by an exhausted
Marine who judges Herr crazy for electing to share his pain. And this is the man
who gives Herr "the look that made you look away." "I realized that after all this
time, the war still offered at least one thing that I had to turn my eyes from." Herr
suffers his failure of vision precisely when made to remember that the pain he
looks at belongs to somebody else. The wounded Marine who "forgives" him for
being a reporter may inflict even more damage:

> We were on the ground when those rounds came, and a Marine nearer the trench
> had been splattered badly across the legs and groin. I sort of took him into the
> trench with me. It was so crowded I couldn't help leaning on him a little, and he
> kept saying, "You motherfucker, you cocksucker," until someone told him that I

wasn't a grunt but a reporter. Then he started to say, very quietly, "Be careful, Mister. Please be careful."

As readers, we are placed at a double remove: our task is to watch a man watch another's pain. Herr provides an exemplum of this task in a moment at Khe Sanh when a Marine walks out of a shelled triage tent:

> A Marine came out and stood by the flap for a moment, an unlighted cigarette hanging from his mouth. He had neither a flak jacket nor a helmet. He let the cigarette drop from his lips, walked a few steps to the sandbags and sat down with his legs drawn up and his head hanging down between his knees. He threw one limp arm over his head and began stroking the back of his neck, shaking his head from side to side violently, as though in agony. He wasn't wounded.

As we read into these sentences, we prepare ourselves for the uncovering of a wound. But the kind of pain we see the Marine suffer is not a physical pain. He is feeling for another, back inside the tent. In this chain of imaginings, the reader watches Herr watch a Marine who in turn shares the "agony" of a man we cannot see. In moments like this, Herr connects with the possibilities of witness and reveals that the respective distance from the point of impact does not prevent hurts from being felt.

"I couldn't look at the girl": this sentence, perhaps Herr's most terrifying and most honest, echoes backward toward Hemingway's "Indian Camp," where Nick "didn't look at it," and forward into all the inevitable future moments of looking away. It comes near the end of "Illumination Rounds," as Herr visits the province hospital at Can Tho:

> One of the Vietnamese nurses handed me a cold can of beer and asked me to take it down the hall where one of the Army surgeons was operating. The door of the room was ajar, and I walked right in. I probably should have looked first. A little girl was lying on the table, looking with wide dry eyes at the wall. Her left leg was gone, and a sharp piece of bone about six inches long extended from the exposed stump. The leg itself was on the floor, half wrapped in a piece of paper. The doctor was a major, and he'd been working alone. He could not have looked worse if he'd lain all night in a trough of blood. His hands were so slippery that I had to hold the can to his mouth for him and tip it up as his head went back. I couldn't look at the girl.
>
> "Is it all right?" he said quietly.
>
> "It's okay now. I expect I'll be sick as hell later on."
>
> He placed his hands on the girl's forehead and said, "Hello, little darling." He thanked me for bringing the beer. He probably thought that he was smiling, but

nothing changed anywhere in his face. He'd been working this way for nearly twenty hours.

"Is it all right?" the doctor asks. He speaks out of the middle of this scene to an un-wounded journalist, asks him about his pain. He takes time to imagine what Michael Herr may be feeling. As if it mattered. As if, compared with what the girl below him must be feeling, it mattered. He turns aside from one act of pity into another, and then he turns back to the girl.

The brilliance of this scene is that Herr is able to recognize this story *as* a story and thus to raise a casual aside into one of the most moving examples of the capacity for pity in the literature of war, a pity so far beyond the call of duty that it feels terrifyingly, limitlessly sublime. Meanwhile, the girl's eyes are wide and dry. They have been permanently opened. Meanwhile, Herr looks away. But not before he has looked and made us look as well. Two kinds of vision collide here—one beyond and the other still burdened by feeling, and they are mediated by the doctor's two sayings, his seemingly endless love.

Herr gives this little story a structure because the pain requires it if it is to be felt. As in Tim O'Brien's (b. 1946) Vietnam books, *story* is for Herr a privileged word. "They all had a story," the grunts did, "and in the war they were driven to tell it." This is what Herr can do. The Marines know he will survive. So he must absent himself from felicity awhile, and draw his breath in pain, *To tell my story.* "Okay, man, you go on, you go on out of here you cocksucker, but I mean it, you tell it! You tell it, man. If you don't tell it . . ." The first story Herr tells is one he repeats—it is told to him by a Marine—and it proves exemplary: "Patrol went up the mountain. One man came back. He died before he could tell us what happened." Herr will incorporate into his later stories a number of moves found in this one. Vietnam stories are short, dispatches. They are fragmentary, broken off. They refuse to moralize the tale. And they foreground their own untellability, presume that either the speaker or the listener will fail to survive or connect. Herr finds this story as "resonant as any war story I ever heard" and will build his style out of it.

Herr's Vietnam proves less a shape than an echo in time. Its romance comes from its evocation of earlier moments, the way it intersects with the rhythms and shapes of American history and popular culture. A story of fatal repetitions and continuities, Vietnam replays the national experience as William Carlos Williams might have dreamt it if he had waited fifty more years to write *In the American Grain*:

> You couldn't find two people who agreed on when it began, how could you say when it began going off? Mission intellectuals like 1954 as the reference date; if you saw as far back as War II and the Japanese occupation you were practically a historical visionary. "Realists" said that it began for us in 1961, and the common

run of Mission flak insisted on 1965, post-Tonkin resolution, as if all the killing that had gone on before wasn't really war.

Anyway, you couldn't use standard methods to date the doom; might as well say that Vietnam was where the Trail of Tears was headed all along, the turn-around point where it would touch and come back to form a containing perimeter; might just as well lay it on the proto-Gringos who found the New England woods too raw and empty for their peace and filled them up with their own imported devils. Maybe it was already over for us in Indochina when Alden Pyle's body washed up under the bridge at Dakao, his lungs all full of mud; maybe it caved in with Dien Bien Phu. But the first happened in a novel, and while the second happened on the ground it happened to the French, and Washington gave it no more substance than if Graham Greene had made it up too. Straight history, auto-revised history, history without handles, for all the books and arti- cles and white papers, all the talk and the miles of film, something wasn't an-swered, it wasn't even asked. We were backgrounded, deep, but when the back-ground started sliding forward not a single life was saved by the information. The thing had transmitted too much energy, it heated up too hot, hiding low under the fact-figure crossfire there was a secret history, and not a lot of people felt like running in there to bring it out.

"It began . . . it began . . . maybe it . . . bring it out." There are too many "it's" here, twelve all told, compared to the one usage of the concrete term "Vietnam." As the sentences unfold, the little two-letter abstract noun begins to toll like a bell, sound-ing out a warning against the very desire for certainty the passage acknowledges and also refuses to satisfy. Through his repetition of this one word, Herr dramatizes the insistent presence of the elusive, essential, undesired *it*, the missing of which sustains a willful and fatal innocence.

"It," of course, is the war—or, rather, an adequate narrative of it. The passage broods on when the war could be said to have begun. Stories need origins; without a beginning, a point from which to "date the doom," an experience cannot be lifted out of the overcoming flow of incoming information. But beginnings, like endings (did the war end in 1973, when the United States signed a peace treaty and with-drew its troops, or in 1975, when the last helicopter left the embassy roof?), are al-ways fictions imposed on the data stream by the historian's or the storyteller's art, and the kinds of beginnings and endings chosen reflect the author's moral, emo-tional, and political stance, as well as something perhaps deepest of all—his intel-lectual courage. Only visionaries, Herr admits, reach far forward, or far back: "straight history" artificially brackets off an "it" like Vietnam from the long per-spectives. "Secret history" listens instead for the rhymes and the fatal continuities, attending always to Henry James's reminder that when it comes to answerable art or responsible life, "relations stop nowhere."

Herr's great passage about the war between straight and secret history provides a demonstration and justification of his method. If he confounds history and fiction, Dien Bien Phu with Alden Pyle, if he looks at Vietnam with CinemaScope eyes, if Vietnam makes Wingy Manone snap into his head one minute and *Fort Apache* the next, it is because the war is being fought by a culture in which experience has become *mediated*, an interpenetration of movies and music and high school versions of history and raw experience so thorough that the point, as Stein argues in *Lord Jim* (1900), is no longer to sort out the data but "in the destructive element immerse." If Herr begins by trying to preserve distinctions between the mediated and the actual, as when he looks at that very old map, he will end by collapsing them: "Out on the street I couldn't tell the Vietnam veterans from the rock and roll veterans. The Sixties had made so many casualties, its war and music had run power off the same circuit for so long they didn't even have to fuse." Vietnam was a war fought out of a massive and collective illusion, one constructed out of and fed by the romantic confusion of a culture unable to draw the line between the world and its projections onto it.

So what survives? Brotherhood, perhaps, the sheer generational experience of affiliation, of going through time together. "There was a brotherhood working there," Herr writes in "Colleagues," and he reserves his least complicated emotions for the beloved comrade, Sean Flynn. Out of Flynn's story, he constructs a discreet elegy for a lost friend and a gone vocation, the practice and project of journalism.

We meet Flynn early on, near the beginning of "Breathing In." "Sean Flynn could look more incredibly beautiful than even his father, Errol, has thirty years before as Captain Blood, but sometimes he looked more like Artaud coming out of some heavy heart-of-darkness trip, overloaded on the information, the input! The input! He'd give off a bad sweat and sit for hours, combing his mustache through with the saw of his Swiss Army knife." Flynn's "Credentials" get established less through the assertion of his personal beauty than the fact of his origin in a prince of popular culture. He is a reminder, a rhyme, not of an event or person that happened in time but of one forever stellified on screen. He is the embodiment of glamour. And the war needs it, cannot, in fact, escape it, as the wounded Tim Page argues at the end of "Colleagues":

> Take the glamour out of war! I mean, how the bloody hell can you do *that*? Go and take the glamour out of a Huey, go take the glamour out of a Sheridan ... Can *you* take the glamour out of a Cobra or getting stoned at China Beach? It's like taking the glamour out of an M-79, taking the glamour out of Flynn.

Herr sustains Flynn's glamour by withholding him from the reader. He emerges slowly, as Kurtz and Sutpen do, although without the menace. The glamour of these figures resides in their mystery, a sense that they are silent centers that cannot be known. Such figures embody the mystery of character itself, its opacity and otherness in contrast to all we so awkwardly know about their narrators. Flynn's celebrity forces him to seek his friends "among those who never asked him to explain himself": if he had a past "he didn't like to talk about it. Sometime during his years in Vietnam, he realized that there really were people whom he cared for and could trust, it must have been a gift he never expected to have, and it made him someone who his father, on the best day he ever had, could have envied."

Herr obviously loves Flynn, but he does not claim to know him. There is something unrepresentable about Flynn, and that is just as well, since Herr discovers through Flynn that love may only be possible in the presence of partial knowledge. On trying to get at Flynn, he will simply call him "special." For a man so gifted with words, this is high praise indeed, since it suggests that Flynn has silenced Herr's word-arsenal.

If Flynn is not known or conveyed, his loss is survived. One day he just disappears, a fact Herr withholds from the "Colleagues" chapter and reveals only once he is back home:

> I have pictures of Flynn but none by him, he was in so deep he hardly bothered to take them after a while. Definitely off of media, Flynn; a war behind him already where he'd confronted and cleaned the wasting movie-star karma that had burned down his father. In so far as Sean had been acting out, he was a great actor. He said that the movies just swallowed you up, so he did it on the ground, and the ground swallowed him up (no one I ever knew could have dug it like you, Sean), he and Dana had gone off somewhere together since April 1970, biking into Cambodia, "presumed captured," rumors and long silence, MIA to say the least.

April 1970 was of course the month in which President Nixon announced on national television that "this is not an invasion of Cambodia" even as he also announced that we would be invading Cambodia. Flynn rode straight into the mess stirred up there, one that culminated in the killing fields.

Herr follows the sentences about Flynn's disappearance with a paragraph that begins "*There it is.*" He goes on to give the etymology of the phrase. No extended elegy for Flynn; Herr just turns away. The elegy has been the entire book, its looming recognition that Vietnam means the discovery and the loss of glamour. And what is lost with Flynn and his lost war is the glamour of journalism itself.

Dispatches traces Herr's transformation from journalist to survivor, and his survival as a witness leads him to question the value and purpose of straight journalism as a form. If he went to Vietnam as a war correspondent, he found that "conventional journalism could no more reveal this war than conventional firepower could win it, all it could do was take the most profound event of the American decade and turn it into a communications pudding." Some sort of excess was required, a disruption of form. The result was New Journalism: the time had come to adapt the resources of fiction in order to get at the news. "The news media," Herr maintains, "were ultimately reverential toward the institutions involved," especially when it came to covering war. So it is perhaps not a surprise that Hersey's *Hiroshima* can be considered the first piece of New Journalism, a mode that erupted into life in the 1960s in the careers of Truman Capote, Norman Mailer, Joan Didion, Hunter Thompson (1937–2005), and Tom Wolfe (b. 1931). Each of these writers renounces the myth of "objectivity" and each claims as a right and a privilege the job of conveying, in Didion's words, "*how it felt to me.*"

Because conventional journalism had failed "to cover" the story, even so distinguished a reporter as Neil Sheehan (b. 1936) of the *New York Times* felt impelled to slide over "to the wrong end of the story," in Herr's phrase, and to become, while remaining a working journalist, an activist-citizen. In 1971 he risked wiretapping and jail by helping to release the Pentagon Papers, the "top-secret history of the United States role in Indochina," a history commissioned in 1967 by Secretary of Defense Robert McNamara. Even then, for all their value in exposing the actual story of American behavior in Southeast Asia, the documents Sheehan brought to light could not, as Mailer writes, "give sufficient intimation," and so Sheehan found himself impelled even further, going on to write one of the most comprehensive books about the lived experience of Vietnam, *A Bright Shining Lie: John Paul Vann and America in Vietnam* (1988).

Vann "died believing he had won his war," while Sheehan tried to expose its secrets and to stop it by doing so. Sheehan thus shows empathy for a character whom he could well have deemed to be a kind of enemy. The resulting book proves impossible to classify—is this journalism, or biography, or cultural criticism, or spilt memoir? The kind of book it of course most resembles is one of the great American novels. In choosing to tell the story of the war by way of the story of a single man, a man Sheehan deems to be the war's "one compelling figure," Sheehan falls back on one of the time-honored structuring devices in that novelistic tradition, the Interpreted Design. Out of his deep study of the Vietnam war, Sheehan finds himself entering the realm of imagining into which the experience of war so often delivers our strongest writers, a realm of unlooked-for affiliations discernible only through the unconventional conventions of art.

CHAPTER FOURTEEN

Slavery and Memory

MORRISON

Beloved (1987), the anchoring text in the "Lincoln to Morrison" course I teach every year, comes late, and when I get to it I ask my students, "Why do this work, when it is so painful?" In focusing so relentlessly on the lived experience of slavery, the novel may seem to promise little but pain. But the novel actually tells a love story, a comedy with a tragedy at its heart. That an experience so traumatic becomes, in the end, so affirmative reveals something profound about why we read literature. If death is the mother of beauty, pain is the mother of understanding and acknowledgment. Reading any difficult text involves us in a continual act of reality-testing in which the mind learns to take pleasure in its own disillusionment. Literature dispels illusion, and it is illusion—false belief—that too often makes us unhappy and sick. "We must disenthrall ourselves," Lincoln wrote in the second year of the Civil War, "and then we shall save our country." The disenthrallment offered by literature also helps us to save ourselves, to free the heart and mind from the seductive and debilitating American "innocence" and into the more abundant life we seek.

As a love story, *Beloved* offers up an image of what most of us want for our lives. Yet the only way to find and keep love, the novel reminds us, is to acknowledge all that stands in the way of doing so. "To get to a place where you could love anything you chose—not to need permission for desire—well now, *that* was freedom." Paul D thinks this to himself as he watches Sethe circle him, in the climactic scene in the novel. He thinks this because he has long since learned, as Du Bois wrote at the beginning of the century, that slavery was above all about "the freedom to love."

Beloved begins with the homecoming of the lover. Sethe and Paul D have not seen each other in eighteen years; Ulysses returns to Penelope—except that Sethe hasn't been waiting for him. In the old days in Kentucky, at Sweet Home, Paul and Sethe were friends, not lovers. Paul has spent the long years since the end of the war as a "walking man," staying one step ahead of the violence at his back. "The best thing," he has come to believe, "was to love a little bit," and he has hidden his heart away in a tin tobacco box. And yet somehow, "not even trying, he had become the kind of man who could walk into a house and make the women cry." Sethe quickly opens up to him and tells him the terrible story of the Sweet Home boys stealing her milk. Paul takes her in his arms and presses his cheek against the branches of her chokecherry tree, the pattern of scars left on her back by her Sweet Home whipping. "And he would tolerate no peace until he had touched every ridge and leaf of it with his mouth, none of which Sethe could feel because her back skin had been dead for years. What she knew was that the responsibility for her breasts, at last, was in somebody else's hands."

Sethe and Paul D get together quickly, with little hesitation or ceremony. By the end of the first chapter, they are upstairs in bed. It will take the entire length of the novel, however, for them really to get together. By so swiftly delivering on the possibility of love, and then by taking it away, as she does once Beloved arrives, Morrison (b. 1933) invokes one of fiction's promised ends and incites in the reader a desire for it. Expecting a happy ending becomes a central pleasure of the text. The finding, losing, and refinding of the connection between Sethe and Paul bracket the mother-daughter story. The structure of Morrison's novel thus reinforces the Walking Woman's claim that there are "three things which if you had known you could cut out all the rest," and that of the three, adult sexual love is "the best."

Standing in the way of Paul putting "his story next to hers," as he finally consents to do in the closing chapter, is one of Austin's other "three things." "This story is about, among other things," Morrison has written, "the tension of being yourself, one's own Beloved, and being a mother." More pointedly, Morrison sees Sethe as having "an excess of maternal feeling, a total surrender to that commitment." Sethe has to work through her ambivalences about self-love and especially mother-love before she can put her story next to Paul's. And Morrison makes this the work of the novel because slavery played itself out as a developmental catastrophe, one that denied female slaves the freedom to love male slaves, certainly, but above all the freedom to love their children.

Under slavery, motherhood is the unsafe place, and the women who survive it seek out spaces they can control, like Denver's boxwood bower or Baby Suggs's "clearing." In the climactic moment, Sethe will take her babies and put them where they will be "safe." In stealing her milk, the Sweet Home boys attack Sethe in her most vulnerable place, in her motherhood. The "green breast of the new world," as Fitzgerald calls it at the end of *Gatsby*, comes down to this, Morrison argues, to the rape of a dark body by a white one.

Sethe sees her own mother only "a few times out in the fields and once when she was working indigo." The mother, however, does manage one brief scene of instruction. She carries Sethe behind the smokehouse, opens her dress, lifts her breast, and points under it. "Right on her rib was a circle and a cross burnt right in the skin. She said 'This is your ma'am. This,' and she pointed. 'I am the only one got this mark now. The rest dead.'" Sethe's mother may seem here to reduce herself to a scar. But a brand so precariously close to her unavailable breast, and however acquired, actually signifies her solidarity with other slaves so marked and her resistance to being marked *as a slave*. For her stubbornness she will eventually be hung, and as the young Sethe searches through the pile of mangled bodies she will be yanked away by Nan, who survived the middle passage with Sethe's mother. Nan then tells Sethe a story she will, like a Faulkner character, one day repeat, the story of being taken up many times by the crew and of becoming pregnant, the story of another mother compelled by the conditions of slavery to kill her children.

Beloved reverses the Sutpen repudiation plot. The novel becomes an orgy of reconnection, of acknowledgment. "A fully dressed woman" with "new skin" walks out of the water, and Sethe is a goner. When Beloved returns, she becomes the objective correlative of all that slave mothers have been denied, the chance to care in safety. But, finally, getting Beloved back is a fantasy, an illusion that must be put by. In this world, we are not permitted the literal recovery of our losses. What we are given is memory, "historical imagination" if you will, the human faculty whereby loss can be acknowledged and worked through, hence the importance of storytelling in the novel's structure, a structure built out of scenes where one character actively solicits an account of the past.

"Tell me," Beloved whispers to her sister Denver, "Tell me how Sethe made you in the boat." "To tell, to refine and tell again," Morrison writes, in words she could have found in Faulkner. Morrison's debts to Faulkner have been openly acknowledged. "As for Faulkner," she said in 1994, "I read him with enormous pleasure. He seemed to me the only writer who took black people seriously." In 1955 she earned a master's degree at Cornell with a thesis on suicide in Faulkner and Virginia Woolf. In *Beloved*, Morrison appropriates and adapts Faulkner's methods in order to bring to fulfillment a project he so powerfully began. That project is to reveal the experience of slavery as the living and changing and too often dangerously unacknowledged content of the American mind.

Beloved exposes the power of unacknowledged presences. Faulkner is a precursor acknowledged on virtually every page, and this openness to influence by a writer whose presence in Morrison's work some might find unsettling provides just one instance of the ways in which the novel converts its method into a balm for its anguished subject. Slavery, *Beloved* argues, is the shadow inhabiting our every act. Yet, except for Amy, the novel's main characters are black. The inquiry centers on the effect of slavery on the African-American heart and soul. Yet *Beloved*, like *Absalom, Absalom!*, is a reader's book, one in which, regardless of her race, she is drawn into an act of cocreation in which the hurts of the characters are not only imagined but felt.

Cocreation is required because Morrison deliberately withholds the shape and meaning of the Sweet Home experience. We begin in the middle of a haunting and do not learn its proximate cause until the end of part 1. Only a few pages in, Morrison does mention "a baby's fury at having its throat cut." But this is no more helpful than Faulkner also mentioning on his page 8 a nephew who shot his sister's fiancé "to death before the gates to the house." Paul D turns up very early on, but his escape from the chain gang is not narrated until 120 pages in. Morrison and Faulkner share a conviction that transformative novelistic narration requires deferral. In 1992, Morrison recalled working up a lecture on *Absalom* "that took me forever, which was tracking all the moments of withheld, partial, or disinformation, when a racial fact or clue *sort* of comes but does not quite arrive . . . Do you know how hard it is to withhold that kind of information but hinting, pointing all of the time?"

Along with a strategy of withholding, Faulkner and Morrison also share a will toward summary that their best work fights against. Faulkner writes in *Absalom* about being torn between taking his time and getting things over with:

> It (the talking, the telling) seemed (to him, to Quentin) to partake of that logic-
> and reason-flouting quality of a dream which the sleeper knows must have oc-
> curred, stillborn and complete, in a second, yet the very quality upon which it
> must depend to move the dreamer (verisimilitude) to credulity—horror or plea-
> sure or amazement—depends as completely upon a formal recognition of and
> acceptance of elapsed and yet-elapsing time as music or a printed tale.

By submitting to this same sense of formal recognition, Morrison draws her reader into a conjecture-ridden read. Out of the scraps of information she intermittently doles out, her reader can slowly construct a quilt of memories. The method induces a hunger for narrative coinciding with a growing capacity to remain in a state of suspense. As Morrison writes in the 1993 afterword to *The Bluest Eye* (1970), "the reader is thereby protected from a confrontation too soon with the painful details, while simultaneously provoked into a desire to know them."

The supreme moment in *Absalom* occurs when Quentin and Shreve and Henry and Charles become compounded. This is achieved through the imaginative struggle of the two young men in the present to understand the actions of two young men in the past. If the novel works—if we accept the offered gambit—the reader becomes the fifth party to this union.

Morrison's novel offers us just such an intimacy with the text. But the force of her retelling must necessarily differ from Faulkner's, since his characters, like Quentin, "have had to listen to too much," while Morrison's have been told far too little. Storytelling tends to create or release anxiety in Faulkner. Because her characters have been denied access to their history, Morrison can instead convert storytelling into a kind of erotics, the satisfying of an appetite. Hearing and telling arise out of conditions of craving, of hunger and thirst. "'Tell me,' Beloved said. 'Tell me how Sethe made you in the boat.'" The structure of this small exchange anticipates the crucial acts of storytelling on which the fate of the characters will hinge.

Denver tells Beloved about the white woman Amy, with her little arms and her good hands. In the telling, Denver begins herself to see what she is saying: the image of her mother, the nineteen-year-old slave girl, walking through the dark woods to find her children with another baby inside her and the dogs and guns behind. "Denver was seeing it now and feeling it—through Beloved. Feeling how it must have felt to her mother. Seeing how it must have looked." The power to feel a story here depends on the felt presence of the *auditor's* response. "The monologue became, in fact, a duet as they lay down together, Denver nursing Beloved's interest like a lover whose pleasure was to overfeed the loved." Denver speaks, Beloved listens, and the two do the best they can "to create what really happened, how it really was." Later, in the early chapters of part 2, the duet becomes a trio as Morrison moves to what she calls an "unuttered . . . three-way conversation" in which interlocking monologues by Sethe, Denver, and Beloved converge around the repetition of the limit words "mine" and "join."

Absalom and *Beloved* turn upon two great and fatal questions: Why did Henry kill Charles Bon? Why does Sethe kill Beloved? Of course, *why* is too small a word to contain the anxiety of unknowing these novels provoke, where answers arrive in the form of further questions. Because history compels acts of violence that have everything or nothing to do with a character's free will? Because race is the shadow under our every act? These questioning answers may ease certain anxieties, but they pale in importance to all that is felt and learned in the activity of arriving at them.

Morrison's fame will come to rest, I believe, on the end of part 1 of *Beloved*, the sequence of chapters offering three differing perspectives on Sethe's act. The first of these chapters opens as follows:

> When the four horsemen came—schoolteacher, one nephew, one slavecatcher and a sheriff—the house on Bluestone Road was so quiet they thought they were too late. Three of them dismounted, one stayed in the saddle, his rifle ready, his eyes trained away from the house to the left and to the right, because likely as not the fugitive would make a dash for it. Although sometimes, you could never tell, you'd find them folded up tight somewhere . . .

Morrison brings us close by holding us at a distance; a phrase like "the fugitive" signifies that this third-person voice speaks on behalf of a white slave catcher's point of view. "You could never tell," Morrison writes; we are talked to as if we were one of the horsemen. They—Sethe and her children and Baby Suggs and Stamp Paid, all of whom go unnamed here—are part of "them." By using the word "nigger" twice in the unfolding paragraph, Morrison firmly positions the reader with schoolteacher and his men.

Why first approach Sethe's act in this way? An answer begins to take shape only after we have read to the end of part 1, up to and through Paul's parting "So long." Once we have done so, we can recalibrate our shock at the callousness of the four horsemen chapter, because we can see that Morrison, like Sethe, chooses to begin by "circling" her subject, and that she begins at the furthest circumference. She begins, that is, by speaking in the voice of the law, and on behalf of the practical application of it by those whose interests it is intended to serve.

But the law is "late," late for the apocalypse it unwittingly brings down, late because it sees only with its own "eyes." Because it sees this Ohio family as made up of mere "creatures," worth less than a "snake or a bear," it cannot anticipate the human response to its arrival. Finally delivered into the presence of Sethe's act, we therefore get mostly aftermath:

> Inside, two boys bled in the sawdust and dirt at the feet of a nigger woman holding a blood-soaked child to her chest with one hand and an infant by the heels in the other. She did not look at them; she simply swung the baby toward the wall planks, missed and tried to connect a second time, when out of nowhere—in the ticking time the men spent staring at what there was to stare at—the old nigger boy, still mewing, ran through the door behind them and snatched the baby from the arch of its mother's swing.

The unfeeling in the onlooking eyes here grants Morrison a terrible freedom; total lack of empathy allows for a clinical disposition of the unspeakable. As the narration coldly blocks out the scene, all is reduced to a sense of missed opportunity. At the same time, the inquisitive reader—if by this time such a stance is still imaginable—is provided with a silent movie of "what happened" in the shed.

Then the questions begin. The focal figure for the white point of view here is schoolteacher's nephew, the one who stole Sethe's milk. He will perform the role of Blake's Idiot Questioner, asking things that if you "had to ask," as Sethe later thinks to herself, if you "didn't get it right off," then they can never be explained. "What she go and do that for?" the narrator asks, on the nephew's behalf. The question is asked again. Then, in its third iteration, Morrison finally puts it in quotation marks—into the nephew's mouth—and adds two words: "What she want to go and do that for?" As the question finally becomes the nephew's own, it also supplies itself with a kind of answer. In adding the words "she want," the nephew acknowledges Sethe's act as more than a reflex and frames it as a question of wanting, of expressed desire.

Schoolteacher sees immediately "that there was nothing there to claim." Sethe is doing all the claiming, as the prose reiterates some twenty pages later, by way of Paul's sense that "more important than what Sethe had done was what she claimed." When her eyes roll back into her head, after schoolteacher turns away, Sethe temporarily experiences the loss of her point of view, a power and a privilege she will, in the pages that follow, authoritatively reclaim.

Morrison shifts the point of view in the four horsemen chapter soon thereafter, with the sentence beginning "Baby Suggs noticed who breathed." Our characters have their names again. Baby Suggs and Stamp Paid enter the shed and begin tending to the children. She takes Denver, the "crying baby," to Sethe and tells her, "It's time to nurse your youngest." Sethe aims "a bloody nipple into the baby's mouth." Denver here begins her soul-wrenching education; transmission is always a mixture: there is always blood in the milk. "Aiming," Morrison writes, as if Sethe now considers her breast a weapon. If the site of nurturance has also been the occasion of her most painful dirtying, Sethe is also learning to mobilize her mother-love as a force of supreme resistance.

"That ain't her mouth," the following chapter begins. Paul D says this to Stamp Paid, the man who ferried Sethe across the Ohio during her escape from Sweet Home and who snatches Denver from the arch of her mother's swing. Stamp has just brought Paul a newspaper clipping "with a picture drawing of a woman who favored Sethe except that was not her mouth." We are back in the present action of the novel, in 1873 rather than in 1855, the year in which Beloved is killed. And yet despite the leap in time and the abruptness of its opening, the chapter seems to follow the four horseman chapter in inevitable sequence, in part because the narrative has at this point left us stranded in Paul's position, filled with questions that we perhaps may be sober enough, unlike the nephew, not to ask.

The newspaper clipping chapter brings the reader closer to Sethe's act. Yet the chapter turns on all that is not said, on Stamp's strategic response to Paul's "ain't," his resistance to knowing. Stamp is the teacher and Paul the student, and there is a document at the heart of this scene of instruction. Paul cannot read, but he knows enough about newspapers to know that when a black face appears in one the story is not about something anybody wanted to hear.

Meeting Paul's resistance, and respecting it, Stamp does not tell. As with the nephew's questions, the chapter turns upon three repetitions, with the fourth one being the charm. "He was going to tell him about," Morrison writes, "He was going to tell him that," "He was going to tell him that." Morrison follows her "about's" and "that's" with sentences telling the reader what is not being told to Paul. Deploying the rhetorical device called "occupatio"—talking about something while saying you're not going to talk about it—Morrison asks much more from her reader here than Stamp asks from his listener.

"So Stamp Paid did not tell him how she flew," Morrison writes in the fourth pass at the telling, "snatching up her children like a hawk on the wing; how her face beaked, how her hands worked like claws, how she collected them every which way: one on her shoulder, one under her arm, one by the hand, the other shouted forward into the woodshed filled with just sunlight and shavings now because there wasn't any wood." Once again, the scene in the shed comes to us in an oblique and less than satisfying manner. We never in fact get to the shed; the prose focuses on Sethe's collecting of her children, breaking off once she disappears into the shed in part because Stamp will also arrive there too late. While the metaphor of the mother as a clawed and beaked hawk may sound reductive, it actually prepares the way for the "She just flew" action in the subsequent chapter, one providing the most sympathetic description of Sethe's aggressive motherly vigilance.

Morrison acknowledges the asymmetrical demands the chapter has made of her character and her reader by ending it with a reversal. "So Stamp Paid didn't say it all. Instead he took a breath and leaned toward the mouth that was not hers and slowly read out the words that Paul couldn't." Here, at the end, the reader is locked out. We watch Stamp read words we are not given. Paul is asked to listen and to take the knowledge in. He continues his resistance: "that ain't her mouth." As if in frustrated response to the limits of Paul's imagination, Morrison closes out the chapter with a violently reductive paragraph:

> Stamp looked into Paul's eyes and the sweet conviction in them almost made him wonder if it had happened at all, eighteen years ago, that while he and Baby Suggs were looking the wrong way, a pretty little slavegirl had recognized a hat, and split to the woodshed to kill her children.

While the paragraph begins with that look into Paul's eyes, with Stamp's attempt to fathom their capacities, it ends by evoking the newspaper's wholly unsympathetic account. Sethe kills, in part, to free her children from the anonymity of white violence but becomes, in the process, mere news for an uncomprehending white audience. Yet her act cries out to be understood in a context of defiance. She takes away life before its dignity can be cancelled. The coolly dismissive phrasing here manages to capture some of this. "Split to the woodshed" may sound offhand, but the verb rides on the force of a terrifying pun; the comprehending, empathetic reader is witnessing a mother's heart being split in half. And "to kill" is exactly right. This is what Sethe does: she kills. She does not "murder." I caution my students that in putting words on Sethe's act they must be careful only to apply those that strictly fit the case. "Murder" judges as it classifies, and shifts the register into the domain of law. "Kill" describes what Sethe does, no more, no less.

The climactic chapter in *Beloved* takes us into Sethe's kitchen. Paul D brings her the clipping, and she responds by delivering up the most complex account of why she took and put her babies where they'd be safe.

As so often in Morrison, we find ourselves arriving in the middle of a conversation. "She was crawling already when I got here," the chapter begins. Morrison cleaves to this strategy in fidelity to her sense that we are all always late, that things start before they seem to, that history is more infinite than the future. Being thrown into the middle of things not only captures our felt experience; it also encourages readiness, openness, and a willingness to move forward with only partial knowledge.

The third and final version of Sethe's act belongs to her, as Morrison has written earlier, because "she alone had the mind for it and the time afterward to shape it." Sethe has been preparing for this encounter, then, for eighteen years. As much as the story may be Sethe's, Morrison does not surrender it up entirely to a first-person voice. While the chapter begins with Sethe speaking, and while she tells a good part of it, Morrison understands that Sethe cannot and should not narrate the killing scene itself.

Instead, Sethe approaches the truth by circling it. "She was spinning. Round and round the room." Paul sits at the table while Sethe spins around him, "circling him the way she was circling the subject." Morrison does not mean to suggest that Sethe is incapable of giving us the story in every detail. Sethe's circling honors instead the responsibility of reading. By the time we arrive at Sethe's chapter, we know much more about Sethe's act than Paul has been willing to take in. We have even been asked to see it, from the perspective of cruel indifference, as "a nigger woman holding a blood-soaked child to her chest." We have been offered, above all, the experience of the entire foregoing novel. If we have read well, in a Faulknerian spirit, we do not need to ask Paul's question, "Did it work?" By now we know that Sethe's act cannot be understood from any single moment or perspective, but only from within the entire circle of the American experience. And we have already collected, as Sethe does when she gathers her children, enough bits and parts of knowledge of slavery to understand not only why Sethe kills or attempts to kill, but enough to judge that act an unassailable choice.

Such recognitions await us, as we read on into the encounter between Sethe and Paul. The floor belongs to Sethe; Paul says nothing until near the end, when he manages to squeeze out his pathetic "Your love is too thick." But he nevertheless plays a crucial role, the same role Beloved plays in the storytelling scene with Denver. He listens, and he looks. His seemingly friendly attention brings out the story:

"Perhaps it was the smile, or maybe the ever-ready love she saw in his eyes—easy and upfront, the way colts, evangelists and children look at you—that made her go ahead and tell him what she had not told Baby Suggs, the only person she felt obliged to explain anything to." She goes on to lay claim to her experience. "I did it. I got us all out." Then, in his moment of deepest understanding, Paul takes what she had said and refers it back to his own experience; as we say, he *identifies*. "Paul D did not answer because she didn't expect or want him to, but he did know what she meant." As he remembers Alfred, Georgia, and the men who could stop you from hearing doves or loving moonlight, he however reaches in his inner theater a conclusion far different from what similar experience has taught Sethe. She becomes "big," but Paul concludes that the apt response is to protect yourself and love "small." What begins in identification ends in divergence. Morrison reveals the power of story to bring people together even as, given their inevitably differing ways of taking things, it can drive them apart.

Paul nevertheless assists Sethe in where she means to go, all the way back into the shed. When she gets there, her voice breaks off and the third-person voice takes over. We read this consummate paragraph as if the narrator had herself bumped into Sethe's "rememory":

> Sethe knew that the circle she was making around the room, him, the subject, would remain one. That she could never close in, pin it down for anybody who had to ask. If they didn't get it right off—she could never explain. Because the truth was simple, not a long-drawn-out record of flowered shifts, tree cages, selfishness, ankle ropes and wells. Simple: she was squatting in the garden and when she saw them coming and recognized schoolteacher's hat, she heard wings. Little hummingbirds stuck their needle beaks right through her head-cloth into her hair and beat their wings. And if she thought anything it was No. No. Nono. Nonono. Simple. She just flew. Collected every part of life she had made, all the parts of her that were precious and fine and beautiful, and carried, pushed, dragged them through the veil, out, away, over there where no one could hurt them.

"Simple:" Morrison writes, with the colon promising an answer. Yet what follows has nothing to do with motive. It is a conditioned response, an unfree choosing of freedom. Experience, after all, must be listened to: the hummingbird wings Sethe feels sending needles into her head are a reexperiencing of the "needles" in her scalp that one day overtook Sethe at Sweet Home, when she overheard school-teacher enumerating her animal characteristics. Having felt that anger and that shame, she has learned from it, internalized it as bodily knowledge, and now refuses such a dirtying for her children. Morrison also permits herself an allusion

Sethe could not have intended, a reference forward to Du Bois and his "veil." Sethe's daughter, like Burghardt Du Bois, is carried by death back through "the veil," as Du Bois wrote and as Morrison echoes, away from a "sea of sorrow." A novel that *follows* Faulkner so faithfully throughout chooses, in the crucial instance, to *anticipate* Du Bois. When Sethe carries her daughter through the veil, she could not have known—the mind of a novel that cannot see beyond 1873 cannot have known—that some thirty years later Du Bois would establish the veil as a central figure in the African-American experience. We witness here one of those sleights of hand that only literary genius can accomplish; as Borges argues, "every writer *creates* his own precursors." Morrison has listened so well to Faulkner's narrative strategies and to Du Bois's arguments as to make it difficult, after *Beloved*, to read either *Absalom, Absalom!* or *The Souls of Black Folk* except through her powerful refigurations.

"The existing monuments form an ideal order among themselves," Eliot writes in "Tradition and the Individual Talent," an order "which is modified by the introduction of the new (the really new) work among them." In 1987, much of the American tradition was modified, and had to be read anew, in the light of Morrison's astonishing intervention. Refigurations such as hers are at the center of the present book, insofar as I read the American procession as a continuing act of troping upon tropes, of thinking in fictions that extend prior fictions, acts of imagination that disenthrall by providing more enabling enthrallments. In *Beloved*, Morrison openly and triumphantly acknowledges her indebtedness to the existing monuments, while giving the most complete and compelling answers to the questions posed by them, answers to questions Paul D cannot even bring himself to ask.

The quality of Morrison's answers foregrounds the difference between the white and the black experience of slavery. Faulkner's ultimate social usefulness is in showing how slavery destroyed white families; Morrison's, in showing how it destroyed black ones. But *destroys* is really the proper tense. *Absalom* and *Beloved* continue to operate as forces for change in the American present because they implicate us all in the ongoing cultural and social disaster. The point driven home by Morrison's answer is a brutal one: *It is better to die than to live like that.* As Harriet Jacobs wrote, in the years when the war clouds gathered, "Death is better than slavery." And Morrison's novel takes the proposition from generality back to its source in excruciating experience. The intensity and extremity of the emotional recognitions choreographed in *Beloved* ought to instruct us toward a way of feeling and acting about the questions of the day, from inner-city violence to affirmative action. Every American lives with Sethe's answer. And the force of that answer has everything to do with how Morrison's novel makes a reader think and feel while moving through it.

Eliot uses the word "monument" for the intervening and enduring work of art. Morrison felt herself compelled to write her novel because the existing order of American literature, despite the interventions of Jacobs, Twain, Du Bois, and Faulkner, did not, when she began *Beloved* in 1983, contain an adequate memorial to slavery. So she claimed, in an interview given in 1988:

> There is no place you or I can go, to think about or not think about, to summon the presences of, or recollect the absences of slaves; nothing that reminds us of the ones who made the journey and of those who did not make it. There is no suitable memorial or plaque or wreath or wall or park or skyscraper lobby. There's no three hundred foot tower. There's no small bench by the road . . . And because such a place doesn't exist (that I know of), the book had to.

Early on in *Beloved*, Morrison writes of a "picture" that "if you go there and stand in the place where it was, it will happen again; it will be there, waiting for you." Morrison calls such experience "rememory." Sethe tells Denver, "If a house burns down, it's gone, but the place—the picture of it—stays, and not just in my rememory, but out there, in the world." Denver then asks, "Can other people see it?" "Oh yes," Sethe answers. "Someday you be walking down the road and you hear something or see something going on. So clear. And you think it's you thinking it up. A thought picture. But no. It's when you bump into a rememory that belongs to somebody else." Combining the verb "remember" and the noun "memory," rememory is both an act and a thing. Like a ghost, it is a presence that haunts places. Yet it has an uncanny physicality; we can "bump" into it. In contrast to private memory, rememory is communal and intersubjective, something anybody can experience and perhaps no one can avoid.

In its inherent redundancy, the word "rememory" evokes maddening recurrences. And as long as ghostlike open secrets remain unacknowledged, they retain the power to disrupt and obstruct. We will continue to bump into them, be haunted by them. Functioning as the opposite of a "monument," rememory remains fugitive yet present, invisible yet palpable to the touch. If it is possible for a nation to have a rememory, then for the United States it would be slavery, and if an adequate memorial to that experience finally exists, one that when we go there it will happen again, demanding a full response, it is *Beloved*.

Pa Not Pa

KINGSTON ✦ WALKER ✦ ELLISON ✦ LEE ✦ RODRIGUEZ

*Y*ou must not tell anyone," *The Woman Warrior* (1976) begins. A mother then proceeds to give a daughter a story she is not to pass on. "In China your father had a sister who killed herself. She jumped into the family well. We say that your father has all brothers because it is as if she had never been born."

This is the mother's first pass at the story, and it takes a brief paragraph. She then explains why the aunt took her own life. Years after the aunt's husband had sailed for America, the Gold Mountain, the aunt became pregnant. On the night "the baby was to be born," the villagers raid the house. They break and scatter everything. "The next morning, when I went for the water," the mother continues, "I found her and the baby plugging up the family well."

Maxine Hong Kingston (b. 1940) tells her twice-told tale in fewer than three pages. The remaining sixteen pages of the chapter circle back on the aunt, filling in the daughter's—Kingston's—response to what she has been told. She approaches the aunt through "imagining." As the "Perhaps" sentences unfold, she thinks of her aunt dreaming of a lover. In judging her final act, she gives the aunt the benefit of the doubt: "Carrying the baby to the well shows loving. Otherwise abandon it. Turn its face into the mud." Faced with an act almost as difficult to interpret as Sethe's act, Kingston finds the generous word. And she sees as well that "the real punishment was not the raid swiftly inflicted by the villagers, but the family's deliberately forgetting her." Kingston's work becomes, as a consequence, "to name the unspeakable," to free the forever-hungry aunt from neglect by devoting "pages of paper to her."

Nothing in Kingston's subsequent body of work matches the power of "No Name Woman," the title she gives to the opening section of *The Woman Warrior*. While she spends an immense amount of narrative capital very swiftly here, she can do so because the aunt's response will remain her core story—a woman assuming or being denied voice. Hence the terrifying scene in the final section of the book, where a young Maxine assaults a girl who would not talk "in school," cornering her in the lavatory, squeezing her cheeks, and pulling her ears so as to force her out of silence. "I have a terrible time talking," Kingston has already informed us. When she was small her mother cut her tongue; she sliced the frenum. Maxine develops a "pressed-duck voice." The "quiet girl" scene affords her the chance to take revenge against a tradition that so successfully silences women while burdening them with a knowledge they "must not tell." The challenge becomes to work the narrative around to a place where, as Kingston does on the last page of her memoir, we can hear "a woman's voice singing."

"No Name Woman" creates a paradigm for a recurring and failed recognition scene, one in which a parent hides a secret behind another secret easier to tell. The deeper secret always involves paternity, the "true" identity of the father. The mother collaborates in the maintenance of the secret; "she never listens," Kingston writes about her mother in *The Fifth Book of Peace* (2004); "she's the one does the talking." The bearer of the secret is an unlistened-to or "unwanted" daughter. Because she is unlistened to and unwanted, and because of the sexual double messages of which her experience is constituted, this daughter-narrator is uniquely positioned to hear and to name the unspeakable and so to uncover the family as, in Robert Stone's phrase, "an instrument of grief." In a postfeminist age, where the usefulness and authority of the male have been seriously eroded, the daughter-narrator tells us how the family does—or does not—continue to work. As she does so, she becomes a *self-listener*, a woman who uncovers, as Kingston does, "no higher listener . . . but myself."

The deeper secret can be summed up in one sentence from *The Color Purple*: "Pa not pa." These are stories in which the father has gone missing, or has been mistaken, or proves in some way false. "The truth always kills the father," Robert Penn Warren writes in *All the King's Men* (1948), and these narratives routinely uncover a truth about the difficulty of performing "Pa," the ineluctability of fatherhood. They remind us that patriarchy has always persisted as a brittle but stubborn concept, an assignment of power to a figure who exists largely in imagination and who is often simply not at home.

The secret behind the story of "No Name Woman" is that Kingston's father had once been traded for a girl. While Kingston makes only brief reference to this incident in "No Name Woman," she gives it a detailed retelling at the beginning of *China Men* (1980). Ah Goong, Maxine's paternal grandfather, "wished for a happy daughter he could anticipate seeing in the evenings after work." Ba Ba, his youngest son and Kingston's father-to-be, has just been born. When the neighbors give birth to "the loveliest dainty of a baby girl," he says, "Let's trade." His wife discovers the switch and undoes the exchange. "Dead man," she rages, "trading a son for a slave." So the secret behind the secret—what Amy Tan might call the "long-cherished wish"—is that hidden within the Chinese preference for sons over daughters lies a secret so subversive as to undermine even the status and standing of the father. The daughter is not "good leftover stuff," as Amy Tan (b. 1952) calls her own daughter-narrator in *The Joy Luck Club* (1989), but turns out to be, in a vast reaction formation against a cultural practice so tied to the arbitrariness of gender, the child most deeply wanted.

✦   ✦

The Color Purple (1982) begins with the rape of a daughter by a father. By Celie's second letter, mama is dead. Sister Nettie is soon driven away, and Pa marries off Celie with as much ceremony as one might use in selling a cow. Before Nettie leaves, she issues one injunction: "Write." Celie faithfully does so, continuing to send letters into a void of unresponse, since her husband Mr. _____ routinely intercepts all correspondence from Nettie, now living in Africa. Once Shug discovers the purloined letters, Celie shifts from the status of writer to reader and does not contribute another letter to the narrative until Nettie drops the bombshell that "Pa is not our pa!"

Celie's story begins with a sudden blow. She comes to consciousness through the body and discovers, as Alice Walker did in her own life, "how alone woman is, because of her body." Rape is the originating act, the beginning of Walker's book and of Celie's story. It hurts her into language. "I am fourteen years old. ~~I am~~ I have always been a good girl." In the wake of the rape, Celie has become not only self-expressing but self-revising. But the fall into sex carries no consoling knowledge: "First he put his thing up gainst my hip and sort of wiggle it around. Then he grab hold my titties. Then he push his thing inside my pussy. When that hurt, I cry." Pa's "thing" is mystified by the lack of a name, as are the bouts of pregnancy that somehow befall Celie. "When I start to hurt and then my stomach start moving and then that little baby come out my pussy chewing on it fist you could have knock me over with a feather." Lacking a mother's instruction, Celie experiences her body as an alien space, the site of her father's desire and her mother's anger. Abrupt and concrete, her sentences yearn toward a verbal and emotional vocabulary that can convert sensation into emotion and that can deliver Celie into the possibility of feeling rather than watching her life.

✦   ✦

The opening two letters of *The Color Purple* can be read as restaging Trueblood's dream from chapter 2 of Ralph Ellison's *Invisible Man* (1952). Trueblood, a black sharecropper, recounts the story in his own words to the narrator and the white man for whom he acts as a chauffeur, Mr. Norton. Ellison positions the dream much in the way Walker does the rape of Celie, as an ur-story, an originating fantasy out of which the novel that follows seems to spring.

It is so cold in Trueblood's cabin that the family of three sleeps together: "Me on one side and the ole lady on the other and the gal in the middle." Trueblood thinks about the daughter's new boyfriend and then hears her say, "'Daddy,' soft and low in her sleep." He gets to thinking about living with an old girlfriend along the river, and the sound of riverboats, and the way the sound came close up like seeing a wagon full of watermelons "split wide open-alayin' all spread out and cool and sweet." His daughter squirms and throws her arm across his neck. He turns his back to move away and slips into a dream. It is a dream of "fat meat," and a "white lady," and running "through a dark tunnel." Trueblood wakes to find his daughter "scratchin' and tremblin' and shakin' and cryin'" beneath him. He now tries to "move without movin'." He pulls away, but "she didn't want me to go then." Wife Kate wakes up and brains him with an ax. Trueblood runs away and returns to find both women pregnant. Now white folks "gimme more help than they ever give any other colored man." "What I don't understand is how I done the worse thing a man can do in his own family and 'stead of things gittin' bad, they got better."

Ellison structures his story for a white listener: Mr. Norton is its audience, and Trueblood's melodrama gets put forward, in part, as a burlesque of the listener's stereotyping expectations. Celie writes to no audience but God and so tends to diminish rather than heighten the violence of her story. Still, the two stories can be compared. In both, there is the same triad of father, mother, and girl child. There is the same seduction of proximity, the fatal home space. In both, initiation equals betrayal. Both are masterpieces of dialect, spoken by eloquent but seemingly uncomprehending voices. And Trueblood and Celie each present themselves as victims of incestuous desire. It befalls them, like a force from without.

Ellison's point may be that men are also alone because of their bodies, that they are no more the subjects of their desire than are women, and that fathers and daughters are functions of reciprocal yearnings they neither understand nor control. And yet, as W. T. Lhamon has shown, there is more to Trueblood than abject performance. "Trueblood is mature," Lhamon argues, "his desires neither simple nor pure, and love is just one among many contending forces playing on him. Ellison's tone catches his wrong and does not forgive him . . . When the two women shun him in his own yard, we see they are right. Nevertheless, Trueblood's suffering and increasing self-understanding fascinate us." Trueblood is helped through his dark night of the soul by looking up at the stars and beginning to sing the blues, a falling back on a cultural resource allowing "him to survive all the surrounding scorn and his own self-hatred." He falls back on the consoling words, melodies, and rhythms of the long black song.

Walker borrows the Ellison story but drops the reciprocity. Celie never answers "Pa" in any way. She is innocent, deprived of all desire. Her education will thus necessarily consist largely of sex education, a process of sisterly intimacy in which Shug helps Celie discover how the parts of her body work and teaches her the names they are known by. As she gains this crucial self-knowledge, the romance of incest will diminish into the ugliness of rape; Celie discovers that "Pa is not our pa," and the story she is caught in loses the dimensions of family romance.

But, of course, this *is* the family romance. Every family romance imagines that Pa is not pa, replacing in the child's fantasy the blood parents with those of "better birth." Walker has once again invented a story in which the father is not the father, in which the daughter gets her fairy-tale wish, of another, better man being her true begetter. Yet Celie reacts to the crucial letter from Nettie as if it were a negation, a loss:

> Dear God,
>   That's it, say Shug. Pack your stuff. You coming back to Tennessee with me. But I feels daze.
>   My daddy lynch. My mama crazy. All my little half-brothers and sisters no kin to me. My children not my sister and brother. Pa not pa.
>   You must be sleep.

This is Celie's shortest and most "spontaneous" letter. As in *Clarissa*, the climax of the story is marked by the breakdown of epistolary style. Letters become "Papers," fragments, outcries. A writer so careful about tenses loses all track of them; the lack of verbs here bespeaks a spiritual vertigo. Unlike Clarissa's story, however, Celie's moves toward unmasking rather than defeat.

Celie quickly composes herself and goes to see her father. "For the first time in my life," the following letter begins, "I wanted to see Pa." Celie and Shug drive to Pa's house and confront him on his front porch. Celie comes right out with it:

> Nettie in Africa, I say. A missionary. She wrote to me that you ain't our real Pa.
>   Well, he say. So now you know.

Swift and light as that the ties give, and Celie learns of finalities beyond the grave. The power of the moment lies in its bathos, Pa's cruelly casual offhand response. The whole issue of fatherhood is consumed and discarded by his deadpan "So now you know." As if he could care less. As if—as is of course the case—he never cared. Everything looks permanent until its secret is known.

Clarissa's story culminates in rape and its fatal consequences; Celie's begins in rape and culminates in empowering knowledge. What she comes to know is that there is no secret, no gnosis, no hidden knowledge or power on which a father is founded. The power is secrecy itself, and Pa's stands as a metaphor for the power lodged in any parent, which is simply to remain mysterious, hidden, unknown. Were we ever to "know" a parent, he or she would retain no more power than does Pa, the man who merely pretends to the role and in a moment of surprising insight simply shucks it off. Families are founded on secrets, and the power they have over us, Walker argues, is less in some irresistible blood tie than the leveraged ignorance of all we do not know.

If in her novel Walker imagines the social world as a conflict between men and women, her receptiveness to work by male writers ought to qualify Michael Awkward's claim that, in reading *The Color Purple*, "it is most fruitful to concentrate primarily on *maternal* influences." Beyond Walker's obvious debt to Samuel Richardson, why does she begin by dedicating her book to Stevie Wonder, calling upon him to "*show me how to do like you*"? And why does she open her novel by restaging a dream from a novel by Ralph Ellison? Walker has Celie say "I make myself wood," a clear reference back to Po Sandy in Charles Chesnutt's *The Conjure Woman*, a character who also, in an attempt to deaden pain, says "I wisht I wuz a tree." She borrows from Eldridge Cleaver an emphasis on sexual "access" as a defining variable in human power relations. Hortense Spillers was nearly alone, in 1985, when she questioned the model of the black female literary tradition as an unanxious sisterhood. According to Spillers, Hurston and Walker and Morrison "engage no allegiance to a hierarchy of dynastic meanings that unfolds in linear succession and according to our customary sense of 'influence.'" If Walker's fiction explores the relationship, as she wrote in 1973, "between parents and children, specifically between fathers and daughters," her use of sources reveals her as a writer willing and able to locate enabling literary fathers as well as mothers.

Nowhere is this clearer than in Walker's choice of a title. The color "purple" derives, of course, from "Bona and Paul," the culminating story in Jean Toomer's *Cane*. Throughout *Cane*, color functions as Toomer's major figure for "difference," the sense of difference Paul falls into when he suddenly feels "apart from the people around him." In his closing monologue, Paul attempts to counter this felt experience of difference with the imagined notion of a supremely blended color, of which purple becomes the ultimate example. As Paul leaves the Gardens, they have become "purple like a bed of roses would be at dusk."

Walker treats purple, on the other hand, not as a figure for difference or for the collapse of it. Shug presents it rather as a figure for passion, for unbidden response. Responding is what we are obliged to do, Shug argues: "I think it pisses God off if you walk by the color purple in a field somewhere and don't notice it." Purple here gets assigned outward, onto creation, and away from the body and any concern with its possible hues. By refiguring purple as the color of fulfilled pleasure rather than of resolved or unresolvable difference, Walker argues that for the characters in her tradition the matter of color need not preempt the pursuit of one's happiness.

Still, for all her openness to influence across the gender line, sisterhood remains for Walker the most compelling venue. By the end, *The Color Purple* has come to substitute affiliation for filiation, a sibling community based on the exchange of words rather than blood ties reinforced by secrets. Human bonds become a matter of reciprocal belief, not a function of natural inheritance. As Celie says to Nettie in her longest and most eloquent letter, "How can you be dead if I still feel you?" The very structure of the book, divided as it is between the styles of two quite different correspondents, suggests the possibility of exchange despite the obstacles thrown up against it.

As in Eaton's "Mrs. Spring Fragrance," we are invited once again to listen to "the secret talk of women." And, once again, this vast creative work is rendered secret through no wish of its own but by the resistances of an unappreciating man. In this experience, Celie and Nettie stand in for an entire tradition. "*The Color Purple* makes clear," Deborah McDowell argues, "that the black woman writer has written primarily without an audience capable of accepting and appreciating that the full, raw, unmediated range of the black woman's experience could be appropriate subject matter for art." Instead, the daughter in "The Child Who Favored Daughter" is commanded by her father to swallow her offending words; instead, one sister's correspondence is secreted from another by an intercepting male. While Walker's growth as an artist has clearly been forwarded by men, the women in her fiction must look largely for assistance from other women.

Walker therefore ends her novel with a recognition scene not between parent and child but between two sisters. The challenge is to reunite a family without relying on the traditional glue of hierarchy or guilt. In Walker's sense of an ending, no one hurries home. Those who approach "walk real slow up the walk to the house." Those who wait, wait just as patiently. Celie tells it this way:

> I try to speak, nothing come. Try to git up, almost fall. Shug reach down and give me a helping hand. Albert press me on the arm.
>
> When Nettie's foot come down on the porch I almost die. I stand swaying, tween Albert and Shug. Nettie stand swaying tween Samuel and I reckon it must be Adam. Then us both start to moan and cry. Us totter toward one nother like us use to do when us was babies. Then us feel so weak when us touch, us knock each other down. But what us care. Us sit and lay there on the porch inside each other's arms.
>
> After while, she say *Celie.*
>
> I say *Nettie.*
>
> Little bit more time pass.

The moment of return occurs among equals, and the core of it is an act of basic acknowledgment, the saying of the living names. No one need make the first move, like the erring son who bethinks himself to "arise and go to my father." The reunion is halting, tentative. Walker carefully notates the blocking because this reunion is above all a redemption of touch. If being manhandled starts the book, being woman-embraced ends it. Letters are no longer needed, because desire is being brought home, and the salutation to this last letter ends with an end, not a comma but a period. What follows is not a letter but Celie's answered prayer, a fulfilled wish sent not out but up, one ending in "Amen."

The ending is earned on the level of the sentence, especially the fourth from the last. Celie is wondering about how the various sets of grandchildren now see the story's aging adults: "And I see they think me and Nettie and Shug and Albert and Samuel and Harpo and Sofia and Jack and Odessa real old and don't know much what going on." What the grandchildren think doesn't matter; it's how Celie says this that matters. All sorts of lines could be drawn between the proper nouns in this sentence, and the lines would make an impressive and confused family tree. But Walker commits the names to Celie's unpunctuated parataxis: they float together in a mere series, all on one syntactic line. In this horizontal vision of relation, Walker sees only *next to*, not above or below. Everybody seems a sibling. If this sentence and the story of which it is a part argue that the generations ought to collapse into a generation—the family into a brotherhood and a sisterhood—Walker has earned the right to the fantasy by converting her literary fathers and mothers into brothers and sisters who contribute without rancor to the resonance of her work of art.

❦   ❦

In *The Daughter's Seduction* (1982), Jane Gallop argues that one of the binding forces of the nuclear family is an unconscious and mutual "seduction" of the daughter by the father and the father by the daughter, a seduction in which the only way to "avoid scaring" the father away "is to please him, and to please him one must submit to his law which proscribes any sexual relation." Hence the double bind so characteristic of female sexuality in our culture, a sexuality the culture continually arouses and punishes. And hence the novel's fascination with the fate of the daughter, a figure who suffers the contradictions that maintain the American Innocence, a vast enterprise of complicity passing itself off as an engine of disinterested concern.

Chang-rae Lee's (b. 1965) *A Gesture Life* (1999) can be read as a prolonged and unwilled recognition scene during which a male narrator fails to maintain his deeply cherished innocence, a heavily policed ego ideal threatened by two "unwanted daughters," his adopted daughter Sunny and the Korean comfort woman he meets and betrays during the Second World War. Doc Hata's narration is shaped by his attempt to repress what he did, and did not do, with and for these two daughters. The effort results in a gesture life, a series of anxious performances in which a man tries to pass for what he is not.

Passing could be said to be *the* American story, since the myth of self-making assumes the possibility of "passing" out of one's born form. Living out his days as the retired owner of a medical and surgery supply store in northern New Jersey, not far perhaps from where Philip Roth's Swede Levov will pursue his suburban dream, Doc Hata is an ethnic Korean attempting to pass as Japanese and, in the process, to become an American. But Doc Hata has a daughter and a past that refuse to play along with his act. As the repressed returns, we are drawn into a series of disclosures whereby the hero, who is also the narrator, is stripped of so many illusions about the self as to vanish from the page, as he does in the novel's final sentence, where he ceases to be a subject at all: "Come almost home."

Doc Hata is twice accused of leading a gesture life. "You, Lieutenant, too much depend upon generous fate and gesture," Captain Ono tells him, during the Pacific War. "There is no internal possession, no embodiment. Thus you fail in some measure always." If this is so, why, one might ask, is Franklin Hata telling this story? What is the motive or impulse behind the gesture of narrative, and what is accomplished by way of it? Can it become, in Sam Shepard's phrase from *The Tooth of Crime*, a "true gesture"?

The narration certainly does convey the price of leading a gesture life: alienation from memory and feeling, the failure of erotic relationships, separation from a child and her children, the eventual loss of a hard-earned American place. As in *Gatsby*, women suffer the most collateral damage from a hero's investment in some idea of himself that goes into loving them: by the end Anne Hickey, Mary Burns, K, and Sunny's almost-born daughter all will be dead. All of this happens as the narrative unfolds. But the real drama here is in how the act of telling his story disturbs the narrator's cherished innocence, a condition he finally defines as a stunningly willful hiding from knowledge already possessed: "innocence, wanting not to know what I know."

The personal story is tangled up with national histories: the Japanese annexation of Korea in 1905, and the oppression of and condescension to the one nation by the other; the Second World War, and the Korean "comfort women" forced to provide sex to Japanese soldiers; Korean postwar immigration to the United States, which began in earnest in the 1970s, although Doc Hata emigrates at least a decade before that. In this romance of immigration and attempted assimilation, Doc Hata's key gesture is to suppress his Korean origins and to pass as a Japanese man now wishing to become an American.

"Most of us were ethnic Koreans," Doc Hata tells us in an aside, in chapter 4, but the emphasis throughout falls on his upbringing in Japan and the treatment he receives from his adoptive parents, the Kurohatas. His habit is simply to omit from any account of himself his country of origin; when the comfort woman K says,

"You are a Korean," he answers, "I am not." "I am a Japanese," he will readily assert, as he does when Sunny accuses him of making a "whole life out of gestures and politeness." "She came from Japan," Doc Hata maintains, early on, about his adopted daughter. "I wish I hadn't spoken inaccurately about Sunny to Mrs. Hickey," he thinks to himself as he walks away from the encounter. *Lied* might be the more accurate word here, since we will eventually learn that Sunny, like her father, also comes from Korea.

When Doc Hata, in his turn, decides to adopt a child, he insists that it be a daughter, finding himself "strangely unmovable on the issue." He claims that "my desire for a girl was unknown to me" until at the adoption agency "the words suddenly" stream from his mouth. The stronger desire might seem to be that the adoptive child be Japanese, so as to sustain his fantasy of being not Korean. But he feels a strange relief after being told "there were no Japanese children available" and agrees to settle for a girl from the city of Pusan, in Korea. So he acts out, in spite of and even against all self-knowledge—in all *innocence*—his deepest wish, to acquire a daughter to replace another Korean "daughter" lost in the war.

When do things go irretrievably wrong? Continually, Lee's novel answers—as long as one persists in leading a gesture life. A good example is the moment when Doc Hata first sees Sunny. "I was disappointed, initially," he tells us. She is Korean, all right, he has acceded to that. But he also sees that she is the product of "a night's wanton encounter between a GI and a local bar girl." "It was obvious," he continues, "how some other color (or colors) ran deep within her." Even more than her father, Sunny is a hybrid, and given her "wavy black hair and dark-hued skin," she is probably the child of a Korean mother and an African-American father. He also tells us that Sunny senses, on their first encounter, "the blighted hope in my eyes." He sees, right away, that Sunny *sees*—sees, above all perhaps, that she is not K. Those un-innocent about love may have learned to acknowledge every finding as a refinding, but Doc Hata cannot accept that love is always directed at a substitute, even as he so willfully sets out to acquire one. There is no going back from such a reaction and its subsequent denial; the life Doc Hata and Sunny construct together will be false, and she will abandon it as soon as she is able.

Near the end of Roth's *The Human Stain*, Nathan Zuckerman concludes that "writing personally is exposing and concealing at the same time." In attempting to conceal, Doc Hata's narration also continually exposes, as when it uncovers his inhibitions about racial and cultural fusion in the adoption scene. Behind all the surface composure lies the great Pacific war, in which he served willingly in the Japanese army, a memory horde that, once it begins to revisit the narrator, insists on being fully remembered.

Doc Hata's first detailed memory of the war comes unbidden, as he stands outside the house where he has just seen his daughter having sex. "My heart flooded black, and at that moment I wished she were nothing to me." Then the woman turns on a light, and Doc Hata realizes "it wasn't Sunny at all." "It was a great relief," Doc Hata says, a relief, he means, to have discovered that the woman he has been watching is not Sunny. The memory that then rises up in his mind can be seen as a kind of punishment for having indulged in a sexual fantasy about his female child. "It was a great relief. And there, as I stood on the ruined cobble of the patio under a wide starless sky, the reports of music and voices playing off the hidden trees, an image of another time suddenly appeared to me, when I began my first weeks of service in the great Pacific war."

Somehow his anxiety and relief over Sunny provoke this image, and Doc Hata proves respectful of its power. He allows the image to enter his narration and to play itself out. At the center of this remembering of the war is a dead girl, a Korean comfort woman who jumps from the second floor of a "welcoming house." This memory will be followed by the scene in which Sunny returns to her father's house and they talk, for the first time, about his experience of the war. She tells him she intends to leave his house and to take nothing from him. He warns her about "what can become of young women." It is then we begin to get full chapters about the war, chapters in which the narrator moves reluctantly and inexorably closer to the memory of what became of K.

Present calls up past here in a clear logic of association, although that logic appears to be lost on the man who generates it. Nevertheless, he consents to follow where it leads. Doc Hata's resistance to having certain memories does structure the sequence of disclosures, and it delays the disclosure of the most painful memory until the last. His present struggles with the daughter he still spurns and craves open up cracks in his defenses and lead him back into a recovery of what can happen not only to young women but to young men. Sunny is the repetition that makes clear a secret at the heart of culture and the heart of war, its dependence for its operations on a pool of "unwanted daughters," in the phrase K applies to herself and those like her.

In remembering, Doc Hata approaches the subject of the comfort women through a series of euphemisms, as is his habit. He has been posted as paramedical officer to a camp in the foothills outside Rangoon. There he talks with Corporal Endo, who is addicted to pornography, about the expected "new arrivals." They are next referred to as "female volunteers." In a similar attempt to avoid seeing and naming a thing for what it is, Doc Hata will deny the obvious evidence that K is, as Sunny will become at seventeen, pregnant. "You think you love me but what you really want . . . is my sex," K tells him, after he has "descended upon her" with a lust he chooses to give another name. Called on by K to commit an act rather than to persist in a life of gesture—to kill her—he refrains for "sentimental" reasons, where the sentimental is understood as a failure of feeling, a refusal to understand that killing K will spare her from a dirtying fate. When the moment arrives in which he must render K's death, the narrator will avoid directly reporting it, falling back instead on the event of coming upon her remains. This very scene, so poignantly rendered at the end of chapter 14, may in fact be offered up by Lee as the experience by way of which the man called Franklin Hata is forever bound to a euphemistic gesture life:

> I walked the rest of the way to the clearing. The air was cooler there, the treetops shading the falling sun. Mostly it was like any other place I had ever been. Yet I could not smell or hear or see as I did my medic's work. I could not feel my hands as they gathered, nor could I feel the weight of such remains. And I could not sense that other, tiny, elfin form I eventually discovered, miraculously whole, I could not see the figured legs and feet, the utter, blessed digitation of the hands. Nor could I see the face, the perfected cheek and brow. Its pristine sleep still unbroken, undisturbed. And I could not know what I was doing, or remember any part.

Unwittingly, perhaps even mechanically, the narrator falls back on the expressive eloquence of the negative: "I could not . . . I could not . . . I could not . . . I could not." Yet under the cover of these negatives the reader is invited to do the very thing the narrator tells us he could not do. Sublime precisely because of all they will not image or say, these sentences nevertheless ask us to engage in an act of gathering. So much comes to rest on the final syllable here, on the word "part." The narrator may well imagine that he will not remember any part—any aspect— of this experience, but we have already experienced a more harrowing sense of the word "part," as we at once discover the miraculous wholeness of the baby's body and find ourselves protected by the decorum of Lee's prose from having to account for the scattered remains of the mother's. We may notice, as well, the inspired use of the word "digitation" here. A digit can be number or a division of a limb, but "digitation" evokes the articulations of the hands, the part of the body distinguishing us from the other animals and that is such an essential tool in the healer's art.

By this point in our reading experience of Lee's novel, we may have learned to translate the indirection of the narrator's voice into an expression of all it seeks to omit. Perhaps Lee here even attempts to enact, by way of Doc Hata's urgent but withholding prose, a model for historical recovery in which horror can be summoned and felt without a descent into the sensational or the pornographic. The knowledge thereby conveyed exists not so much on the page as in the persisting reader.

One dead baby calls up another: Doc Hata's story, like so many great stories, is structured around unacknowledged repetitions, as the secret of K's story is revealed in the place of another even harder to tell. Just as a sexual fantasy about Sunny calls up the first memory of K, so the full recovery of the K story will in turn call up the most deeply buried memory of Sunny. Only after narrating the final scenes with K does Doc Hata recall his arranging for Sunny "to take care of her difficulty." Despite the doctor's insistence that she is "past an acceptable point," the father pressures his seventeen-year-old daughter into an abortion during which he stands in as a nurse. "I forced her to do it," he says. This scene comes to us as the last significant action in the book; what follows is epilogue.

Lee understands that his narrative should not and cannot narrate the procedure itself. "What was done" is wisely left out. Some recognition scenes derive their power from respecting taboos against certain kinds of representation. But of course they only escape being evasions if, as Hemingway argues, one knows that one is omitting. Only then can the reader sense the omission and therefore feel more than she understands. There is no need to recount every part of Sunny's abortion; what we are asked to feel instead is the cost to Sunny of her father's soul-killing obsession with how things might look.

Lee's handling of the scene reverses the strategy applied to K's death. We may not be asked to look, but Doc Hata is not spared: "What I saw that evening at the clinic endures, remaining unaltered, preserved." As he assists with the operation, Doc Hata at once fulfills and kills off the hope of realizing his double ambition, to be both a doctor and a father. He has seen and insisted on being present to "what no decent being should ever look upon and have to hold in close remembrance." He therefore fully earns his adopted Japanese name, Kurohata. Once in New Jersey, Franklin Hata had shortened his name to "Hata," which means "flag." But he never really loses the "Kuro," which means "black." When, as he says in the novel's closing paragraph, "I will fly a flag," he really means a black flag, of himself as contagion, in a visible last judgment on his life. It has been a life, it is his achievement to acknowledge, in which his will to pass as something other than he is has blocked every access to love.

Hunger of Memory: The Education of Richard Rodriguez (1982) ends with a recognition that the narrator's parents are no longer really parents, or at least that Pa is no longer Pa. It is Christmas night. Richard, now living on his own, has returned to his parents' house for the day. As the grown children begin to leave, his mother seems sad to him.

> How sad? Why? (Sad that we are all going home? Sad that it was not quite, can never be, the Christmas one remembers having had once?) I am tempted to ask her quietly if there is anything wrong. (But these are questions of paradise, Mama.)

My brother drives away.

"Daddy shouldn't be outside," my mother says. "Here, take his jacket out to him."

She steps into the warmth of the entrance and hands me the coat she has been wearing over her shoulders.

I take it to my father and place it on him. In that instant I feel the thinness of his arms. He turns. He asks if I am going home now. It is, I realize, the only thing he has said to me all evening.

With these words, the book ends.

In restaging the conclusion of *Paradise Lost*, Richard Rodriguez (b. 1944) imagines family life as a continual expulsion from paradise. The parents stay, while the children, like Adam and Eve, must, simply, "go." The father's job has been simplified down to one thing: to remind the son that it is time to be "going home," where home is necessarily somewhere else, a place removed from the father's warm, still innocent, and—Richard feels the thinness of the arms—inadvertently diminished space. Still, nostalgia persists, as in a longing for a better Christmas than one remembers ever having had.

The parental loss of place and authority in Richard's life has been gathering itself from the memoir's opening pages, a loss accompanied by a sorrowful sense of recompense. Few writers of the century as powerfully link this gain through loss to the fall into the symbolic order. One of the achievements in *Hunger of Memory* is to convert the unique story of one Mexican-American boy's leaving home and assimilation into the dominant order into a recognition scene for any American child who has ever gone to school. It is in school, he reminds us, that the self undergoes "Americanization," a transit from the intimacies of family and into the rituals of public life. His story thereby "discloses an essential myth of childhood—inevitable pain." But "the loss" also implies the gain. "There are *two* ways a person is individualized," Rodriguez's story demonstrates. "While one suffers a diminished sense of *private* individuality by becoming assimilated into public society, such assimilation makes possible the achievement of *public* individuality."

The fall comes after the nuns visit. Not believing that English is his to use, Richard mumbles through his lessons in the classroom. One Saturday the nuns turn up and ask his parents to encourage the use of English at home. The parents instantly agree and say to their children, "*Ahora*, speak to us *en ingles*." After the game of practicing English begins, Richard happens to enter the kitchen and does not realize his parents are speaking in Spanish until, upon seeing him, "their voices change to speak English." He feels startled, pushed away. "In that moment of trivial misunderstanding and profound insight, I felt my throat twisted by un-sounded grief." The spell is broken, and he resolves to learn classroom English.

Richard's moment of alienation and decision marks the end of a process, his lovingly detailed evocation of being born into "the family voice," as Elizabeth Bishop calls it, and of then falling out of it. What happens to the six-year-old Eliza-beth in "In the Waiting Room" (1977) happens to the six-year-old Richard in the kitchen. In a moment of overhearing he detects a linguistic incongruity that plunges him into a sudden sense of individuation ("you are an *I*," Bishop writes) and strange belonging ("you are one of *them*"). No other American writer has more carefully notated the process of individuation and assimilation as one of heard and lost *sound*.

"I was a listening child," Rodriguez writes in "Aria," "careful to hear the very different sounds of Spanish and English. Wide-eyed with hearing, I'd listen to sounds more than words." Remaining a child longer than most, he lives "in a world magically compounded of sounds," frightened by the voices of *los gringos*, delighted by the sounds of Spanish at home. Turning this tension into play, the family pieces new words together by taking an English verb and giving it Spanish endings. "The voices of my parents and sisters and brother. Their voices insisting: *You belong here. We are family members. Related. Special to one another. Listen*!" Spanish remains for Richard "the language of joyful return."

Richard's education begins with a moment of hearing. On the day he first enters a classroom, a nun says in a friendly but oddly impersonal voice, "'Boys and girls, this is Richard Rodriguez.' (I heard her sound out: *Rich-heard Road-ree-guess*.) It was the first time I had heard anyone name me in English." Now surrounded by the "high sound of American voices," he is unable to form the English words he tries to voice into "distinct sounds." And he is unsettled by his parents' attempts to speak English, especially in the moment of hearing his father talking to a teenaged atten-dant. "I do not recall what they were saying, but I cannot forget the sounds my fa-ther made as he spoke." His words slide together, his voice rushes, it reaches falsetto notes. Richard looks away, tries "not to hear anymore." The first chance he gets, he runs ahead in the dark.

This is his initial aural fall. Rodriguez understands the deep truth that embar-rassment leads to education, and surely no embarrassment cuts deeper than the chagrin a child can feel over the fact and behavior of the parent. The moment with the father and the attendant captures a specific Mexican-American dilemma, but it also touches on the experience of anyone who begins to hear the sound of a par-ent's voice and to feel the need to break with it.

Once Richard resolves to learn English, he stops hearing words as mere sound. "A more and more confident speaker of English, I didn't trouble to listen to *how* strangers sounded, speaking to me." He trades the *how* for the *what*, sublimity for signification. It is the Wordsworthian transaction. In *The Prelude*, another story of the growth of the writer's mind, Wordsworth links a sense of visionary power, of felt oneness with one's origins, to a language of pure sound. The child stays unfallen as long as it remains capable of a kind of unanxious hearing, open to the ghostly language of the ancient earth. And Wordsworth makes the crucial distinction between the liberating power of "how" and the profaning reductions of "what"; only in "remembering how she felt, but what she felt / Remembering not," does the soul retain a sense of "possible sublimity."

Richard will make the inevitable move to meaning. "Listening to persons who sounded eccentrically pitched voices, I usually noted their sounds for an initial few seconds before I concentrated on *what* they were saying." If there is a loss of possible sublimity in the move to content, there is perhaps also a sense of relief: one feels, at last, at home in the symbolic order. And so the shades of the prison-house begin to close upon the growing boy. "At about the same time I no longer bothered to listen with care to the sounds of English in public, I grew careless to the sounds family members made when they spoke." It will never again "be easy" for him "to hear intimate family voices."

The one cultural figure who refuses to make the transit Richard describes is the writer, who clings to the power of sound as at least half, and perhaps the more affecting half, of language. The very fact that Rodriguez can write so movingly about his history testifies to his also having resisted the fall from sound into content. If language and intimacy are "the great themes" of his past, Richard knows that "the message of intimacy could never be translated because it was not *in* the words . . . used but passed *through* them." He insists, like any serious writer, on maintaining an intimacy with his reader—a power to move him or her—based on his ability to manipulate what Frost called "sentence sound." This is what literary art does, how it works upon us. Sound often operates, of course, as "unheard" melody, to use Keats's word, one all the more powerful because it fills the being before the mind can think. The task of criticism is to return upon this transaction and to recover the ways in which we had the experience but missed the meaning.

Just to make sure we get the point, Rodriguez repeats it, and he makes an even more powerful one about intimacy, by way of the pun lodged in the verb "pass." Just as intimacy passes through words, so it itself "must finally pass." Rodriguez would dishonor those he has loved and now loves were he to claim anything else. "Intimacy is not trapped within words. It passes through words. It passes. The truth is that intimates leave the room. Doors close. Faces move away from the window. Time passes. Voices recede into the dark. Death finally quiets the voice." The very brevity of these sentences expresses an experience cut short, just as the sibilant "s's" and "c's" send up a quiet, funereal whisper. The sense rather than the sound of these sentences also does important work, rehearsing for the final scene in the book, where Richard will pass out of his parent's house. In this brilliant fusion of aural and scenic effects, Rodriguez discovers that the most intimate message passing through words is of our longing to name and hold on to what is also always passing away.

Rodriguez's key stylistic move is to break off from a plangent meditation with a self-reflexive interjection. These often come in the form of sentence fragments, his preferred syntactic shape: "Dark-skinned. To be seen at a Belgravia dinner party. Or in New York. Exotic in a tuxedo." Having just broached the issue of being "socially disadvantaged," of feeling "happy," of alienation and assimilation, Rodriguez slides away from thematic heaviness with these glib and funny sentence bits. His elegiac tone requires the continual leaven of humor. This self-interrupting voice betrays a man thinking and reveals what we might call the deep rhythm of his thought. It is as if his writing *listens to itself* and therefore feels compelled to comment on, to qualify—even to resist—the unfolding momentum.

Rodriguez even parodies this parodic strategy. In *Brown*, his third volume of memoir, he finds himself staging an imaginary production of *The Tempest*, and he breaks off from the reverie in order to ask:

> Does anybody know what I'm talking about. Ah, me. I am alone in my brown
>   study. I can say anything I like. Nobody listens.
> *Will there be anything else, sir?*
> No, nothing else, thank you.

This exchange gets at the essential quality of Rodriguez's early work, its loneliness. He writes as if there were no one else for him in this world. By virtue of his mixed heritage and his contrarian response to it, he finds himself as isolated as Caliban, another brown and eloquent presence recruited into a white world. Anticipating this, he opens *The Education* by preempting the parallel: "I have taken Caliban's advice. I have stolen their books. I will have some run of this isle." Alone in his brown study, Rodriguez projects himself as his own best audience. The making of this lonely character is his major imaginative achievement, and the burden of the career is to write past the obvious impasse.

Richard first confronts his loneliness when his scholarly project breaks down. A graduate student in English, he has gone to the British Museum to pursue his study of the pastoral, but he finds he can no longer do the work. "*Then* nostalgia began." He yearns for a time when he "had not been so alone." He goes home, to his parents' house in Sacramento, and is relieved at how easy it is to be there. But after this "early relief, this return, came suspicion." He is unable to stop thinking abstractly about his experience; he has been schooled into self-consciousness. And so he finally loses home and realizes the end of education, which is to shape "indefinite, meaningless longing" into desire. And that desire, he will one day realize, is for "the past."

The deep and perhaps unheard argument of the career is a brown history of America rooted not in "hate" but in attraction. Richard comes upon his core metaphor belatedly, in the third volume of his trilogy. The metaphor remains inextricable from the play of desire. "The reason I am interested in brown history today is because, as a boy, I was embarrassed by my sexual imagination." Rodriguez confesses to being embarrassed not by his brown skin, we may note, but by yearnings and feelings a child of any color might have.

Rodriguez deploys his "particular" story about overcoming sexual embarrassment as the dynamic on which to map a national process of acceptance, a coming to terms not so much with what America might be as with what it has always already been. It is history—not prophecy—that his country needs, a sense of the past leading back to the fact that it has always been brown, just as Mr. Secrets will make the discovery and disclose, through his writing, that he has always been gay. Unacknowledged intimacies become, then, the theme of the national story, as they are of the author's life. America begins in the kind of moment where Rodriguez's trilogy will end.

Rodriguez embraces his abiding literariness at the beginning of *Brown* by opening with a primal scene from de Tocqueville, of "two women and a child in a glade beside a spring." The child is white; "her dusky attendants," an Indian and a slave. Each woman endeavors to attract the child's attention. De Tocqueville approaches, and the "colloquy is broken." The Negress awaits, while the Indian plunges into the forest.

De Tocqueville speculates on the degradation of the African and the diffidence of the Indian. Rodriguez responds with a remonstrance: "*These women are but parables of your interest in yourself. Rather than consider the nature of their intimacy, you are preoccupied alone with the meaning of your intrusion.*" Rodriguez continually returns instead to an alternative scene, one in which an Indian woman and a white intruder withdraw, together. "White America's"—like Old Mexico's— "wettest perdition fantasy has always been consanguinity with some plum-colored thigh."

In *Days of Obligation* (1992), Rodriguez argues that in our national story the Indian is "relegated to the obligatory first chapter," after which she disappears, to return only as a "stunned remnant." But he sees an Indian every time he stares in the mirror, although he is challenged in the perception by a student at Berkeley who tells him, "You're not Indian, you're Mexican." He is, at best, cut, diluted, mixed, the product of a "stag version" of the conquest in which "the Indian must play a passive role," as the awaiting woman. Cortés will rape Malinche. But why not imagine Mexico from "an Indian" as well as a female point of view: "*I opened my little eye and the Spaniard disappeared.*" An epistemological as well as a sexual opening, the taking in and knowing of the Spaniard by a Malinche here given transgressive voice also disappears that Spaniard into a mestizo future. "Willing to marry, to breed, to disappear in order to ensure her inclusion in time," Indian Mexico, it turns out, long ago "initiated the task of the twenty-first century—the renewal of the old, the known world, through miscegenation." "It is *this* to be *moral*," Williams had argued, seventy-seven years earlier, "TO MARRY, to *touch*—to *give* because one HAS . . . to hybridize, to crosspollenize,—not to sterilize, to draw back, to fear, to dry up, to rot. It is the sun."

Rodriguez once described *Hunger of Memory* as another *Labyrinth of Solitude*, but *Brown* is also deserving of the comparison, since both books turn out to be about "the profoundest experience life can offer us, that of discovering reality as a oneness in which opposites agree." This is Octavio Paz's ambitious definition of love. And love is what Rodriguez reads into the ubiquitous American brown, "a color produced by careless desire." Brown is, above all, "making," by which Rodriguez means it is both the result of a centuries-long process of commingling and a color crying out to be made into a deeply complex rather than a muddy metaphor. Rodriguez summons and rejects the metaphor of the "mosaic" as "unerotic," for instance, because it overstresses the separateness of each part. The color of romance, brown bespeaks, in contrast, a bleeding through of bloods, tongues, customs, kinds. Brown bows to the inevitable knowledge that "there is no border." Brown is, first and last, the visible token of the coming together of old and new world bodies. "This undermining brown motif, this erotic tunnel, was the private history and making of America."

Such recognitions about the public realm call on, or perhaps result from, corresponding adjustments in the private life. Rodriguez's trilogy turns out to have a kind of plot: the loss of the family paradise and the gaining of education; the recovery of the Mexican father; the disclosure of the gay lover. *Brown* ends with Richard in bed with his male partner. "I listen to the breathing of the man lying beside me," he writes. "I know where I am."

It has been a long time coming, and some readers fault Rodriguez for having been so discreet about his erotic life. *Brown* does mark his completed coming-out, although the overt declarations, like "I was born gay," are reserved for the closing pages of the book. On the other hand, if "it takes a good reader," as Rodriguez has said, "to make a good book," then it may not challenge the limits of reciprocity to maintain that the private life Rodriguez finally shares with us has been hidden all along where all secret histories are hidden, in plain sight. You can, if you are so inclined, find evidences of it scattered everywhere, from his naming of the first chapter of *The Education* "Aria" to ending "Credo" with the word "brunch" (opera and brunch being two secular sacraments favored by gay San Franciscans); to the casual aside that "at Stanford, it's true, I began to have something like a conventional sexual life"; to his watchfulness toward the brown male laboring bodies in "Complexion." In the end, Rodriguez's choice of discreet disclosure over outright self-announcement reaches far beyond questions of sexual preference to become, as we read these deeply literary and passionately political books, a figure for the ambiguity and ubiquity of brownness itself, always with us if perhaps unnoticed, bespeaking the will of desire to blend, sublimely impure, unstaunchable.

CHAPTER SIXTEEN

After Innocence

ROTH

*I*n 1993, Philip Roth's (b. 1933) novels began winning prizes and continued winning them: the PEN/Faulkner Award for *Operation Shylock*, the 1995 National
Book Award for *Sabbath's Theater*, the Pulitzer Prize for *American Pastoral* (1997),
the Ambassador Book Award for *I Married a Communist* (1998), the PEN/Faulkner
Award, again, for *The Human Stain* (2000), and, in 2004, the Society of American
Historians' Prize for *The Plot Against America*. The end of a century seemed to
summon all Roth's powers: this was surely the Major Phase. While the work marked
a return to the more grounded realism of the early career and away from the
metafictional playfulness of the Zuckerman trilogy and *The Counterlife* (1987), it
also marked an advance, a passionate re-embrace of his country's politics and history and an attempt to recover a usable past by writing, in the American trilogy,
definitive fictional accounts of how it felt to be alive in the fifties, the sixties, and
the nineties.

How was it that Roth found in himself such autumnal strength? One answer has
to do with the two autobiographies produced by him as he began to deal with losing
his parents, his health, and his marriage to Claire Bloom. The first of these, *The Facts*
(1988), does moderately interesting work, but the second, *Patrimony* (1991), so triumphantly succeeds, I will argue, as to open up the richest decade of the career.

The impulse to write the story of the life was anything but new, for Roth; many
of his books, as Debra Shostak says of *The Counterlife*, can also be called "an imitation of autobiography." Confusing the boundaries between his imagined fiction
and his actual life could be said to be what Roth's project is all about. And yet the
two autobiographies do mark a turn, one in which an act of *uncovering* propels the
novelist into prophetic strength.

What is uncovered comes down to two words: mother and father. *The Facts* begins with a letter from Roth's alter ego, Nathan Zuckerman, a letter that wonders
"if this book was written . . . as a palliative for the love of a mother who still, in my
mind, seems to have died inexplicably—at seventy-seven in 1981." (Bess Roth did
in fact die of a heart attack in 1981.) *The Facts* begins with this surmise only to turn
away from it. The mother proves as absent as are most of the women in Roth's fiction, absent in the sense that they are not given the status of subjects interesting for

their own sake but who function rather as objects or as screens for projection by a self-absorbed and inescapably male narrative voice. Bess Roth—or whatever the author of *The Facts* might have chosen to call her—is given no more freestanding identity in this "palliative" than is Josie Jensen, the wife Roth exorcises by writing this minimally displaced version of his actual marriage to Margaret Roth, a marriage that ended in life, as it does in *The Facts*, with the wife's death in an automobile accident.

With the father, however, it is different. Roth focuses in *Patrimony* on father loss, and he tries to stay there. The second memoir records the years of Herman Roth's decline and death, from a brain tumor, at the age of eighty-five. In the course of the story, Roth is saved from a huge heart attack by an emergency quintuple by-pass operation, at the age of fifty-six.

The father's bequest is a stance and a style. He is "the vernacular," a sense of things Roth has long since incorporated. He is also something a little new, the "un-blinking." Roth chooses the word carefully, as a way of forecasting that the upcoming novels will often turn, as does *Patrimony*, on a transgressive act of looking. Philip is helping his father bathe himself:

> I looked at his penis. I don't believe I'd seen it since I was a small boy, and back then I used to think it was quite big. It turned out that I had been right. It was thick and substantial and the one bodily part that didn't look at all old. It looked pretty serviceable. Stouter around, I noticed, than my own. "Good for him," I thought. "If it gave some pleasure to him and my mother, all the better." I looked at it intently, as though for the very first time, and waited on the thoughts. But there weren't any more, except my reminding myself to fix it in my memory for when he was dead. It might prevent him from becoming ethereally attenuated as the years went by. "I must remember accurately," I told myself, "remember every-thing accurately so that when he is gone I can re-create the father who created me." *You must not forget anything.*

Given how much is going on here, this is a remarkably calm recognition scene. Philip faces up to the facts of life: one's parents have sex. He takes his own measure, and relaxes about it. And he comes upon "the no big deal"; he realizes that this for-bidden sight doesn't really reveal or amount to very much.

This scene can work because it follows directly on the memoir's set piece, the five pages in which the son finds the father in the bathroom—"I beshat myself"—and then cleans up the mess:

> Where his shit lay in front of the toilet bowl in what was more or less a contigu-ous mass, it was easiest to get rid of. Just scoop it up and flush it away. And the

shower door and the windowsill and the sink and the soap dish and the light fix-
tures and the towel bars were no problem. Lots of paper towels and lots of soap.
But where it had lodged in the narrow, uneven crevices of the floor, between the
wide old chestnut planks, I had my work cut out for me. The scrub brush seemed
only to make things worse, and eventually I took down my toothbrush and, dip-
ping it in and out of the bucket of hot sudsy water, proceeded inch by inch, from
wall to wall, one crevice at a time, until the floor was as clean as I could get it.

Philip finishes the job, concluding that "I couldn't have asked anything more for
myself before he died" and that once you sidestep disgust and plunge past your
phobias, "there's an awful lot of life to cherish."

Patrimony signals early on that cleaning will be the work ahead. "Ever since my
father had been alone," Roth writes, "I'd sometimes wind up," when visiting his
apartment, "after having used the toilet, scouring the sink, cleaning the soap dish,
and rinsing out the toothbrush glass." A little later he parenthetically remarks:
"(Don't talk to anyone in my family about *cleaning*—we saw cleaning in its heyday.)"
And, just before the shit scene, Philip remembers a moment when, two days earlier,
his father had yanked his new, ill-fitting dentures out of his mouth and handed them
to his son while crossing North Bond Street. Philip is astonished to find that having
the teeth in his hand is "utterly satisfying." By taking his father's dentures, slimy sa-
liva and all, he has "stepped across the divide of physical estrangement that, not so
unnaturally, had opened up between us once I'd stopped being a boy."

The kind of cleaning Roth ultimately has in mind in *Patrimony* has less to do
with an actual physical mess than with a chastening of his own style. "How clean
the sun when seen in its idea / Washed in the remotest cleanliness of a heaven /
that has expelled us and our images," Stevens writes, in "Notes toward a Supreme
Fiction" (1942), and Roth's writing here shares a similar longing for such a cleanliness. He makes this plain in the conclusion drawn at the end of the shit scene. "So
that was the patrimony. And not because cleaning it up was symbolic of something else but because it wasn't, because it was nothing less or more than the lived
reality that it was."

The shit is not "symbolic." It is not a figure for anything. No more does his father's penis, which Philip sees on the following page, conjure up any thoughts. He
simply fixes it in memory. The disavowal of figurative language in these two linked
scenes forecasts a turn in Roth's style away from a sort of showy ingenuity and toward a more unadorned and grounded voice. His big fear is of sentimental figura-
tions, of comparisons and images that invite us to look away from rather than at
the terrible beauty of the moment. Roth even decides to end his book with just
such a "figure," with the dream of himself as a child standing on a pier in Port

Newark watching a "battle-gray boat," cleared by some catastrophe of all living things, drift toward shore. In interpreting this dream, he proceeds to make an overt comparison: "my father *was* the ship."

Philip dreams this dream on the day in July when his father is to have his second MRI. But Roth withholds the dream until the final pages of his narrative, where it becomes the closing scene. It is a strategic ending, a deferral in violation of chronology made in order to make a point. And the point, I think, is that this is not the way such a book should end, that for the sake of a slippage of one letter (shi*p*/shi*t*), Roth allows his imagination to advert to what he labels "plaintive metaphor and poeticized analogy," a move his wide-awake self was "not ever likely to have licensed." Loss here may get worked up into a pretty package, but this ending provides only the sentimental parody of a eulogy, which work the body of the book has long since accomplished. To do this to his father's memory—to fancy it up with such game-playing over latent and manifest content—is to renounce the patrimony, to do something . . . unclean.

If, at his most enabling and unsentimental, Herman Roth is the "unblinking," then much rides on the moment when he himself looks away. It occurs on the evening of his wife's death, when he flees from her corpse. At the hospital he follows her stretcher into a cubicle and "could not stand to see what he saw and so he ran." This moment acts as a precedent for the more stubborn evasions of the son. The evasion begins in *The Facts*. As Zuckerman complains to Roth at the end, "just look at how you begin this thing. The little marsupial in his mother's sealskin pouch. No wonder you suddenly display a secret passion to be universally loved. But where, by the way, is the mother after that?" As in *Patrimony*, the father usurps the mother's place. On page 8 of *The Facts* we see Roth wondering whether "this book was written as a palliative for the loss of a mother," but on page 10, where the narrative proper begins, he digresses into a story about his father's appendix, and, as Zuckerman will later point out, "there is no mother" after that.

"One secret is liable to be revealed in the place of another that is harder to tell," Eudora Welty writes, in *One Writer's Beginnings*. In the structure of *Patrimony*, the mortality of the father stands in as the substitute secret for one much harder to tell, the secret of Philip's unfinished work of mourning for his mother. And the true patrimony, the largest gift conferred on the son as he grapples with the substitute secret, is to be allowed, through the process of writing his book about his father, to complete this work.

Perhaps Roth's most distinctive skill as a novelist is his ability to manage narrative time. *Patrimony* does this through a series of striking digressions. At key moments the storyteller turns aside from chronological momentum, which moves only toward death, in order to grant the reader a passage of interposed ease. The longest digression occurs in chapter 2 in response to Philip's glimpse of the shaving mug that had once been his grandfather's. Philip has just driven to his father's apartment to bring him the news about his brain tumor, but, in order to buy some time, he ducks into the bathroom and spots the shaving mug instead. Then he is off, into a nearly forty-page digression that fills us in on everything from his boyhood stamp collection to his widowed father's exploits among the retirees of Bel Harbour, Florida. The digression finally ends in the first sentence of chapter 3, where Roth signals a return to the present with a melodramatic "So."

Form here is a register of feeling—in this case, of an anxiety over having to convey a hard fact. And yet the digression actually opens itself to a secret even harder to tell, since the core memory disclosed in it involves the details of "burying my mother in May of 1981" and the actual moment of her death at a seafood restaurant. Yes, the mother does die in a digression, in a sort of side thought, but the fact that Philip recurs to such a memory, even while trying to delay facing his father, argues for how hard he is working *not* to have his mother on his mind.

While digression may look like a deferral of a difficult task, it can actually entail the assumption of one. In the first digression in the book, Philip, in driving toward his father's New Jersey apartment, has missed the fork in an exit road and found himself passing "right alongside the cemetery where my mother had been buried seven years before." While he doesn't want to leave his father waiting, he feels "unable to continue on by as though nothing unusual had happened." So he gets out of his car and goes to stand in front of his mother's grave.

Remarkable here is Roth's reluctance to narrate the moment, to turn it into a meaning-filled incident. He is there by virtue of an "accident"; he hasn't been "searching for that cemetery whether consciously or unconsciously." He ends the scene with a general rumination rather than in a personal reminiscence, shifting out of first- and into a more inclusive second-person form of address. About the best he can manage, as he almost too obviously stages a scene of a son desperately trying to avoid feeling anything, is to acknowledge that "at a cemetery you are generally reminded of just how banal your thinking is." Later on, Roth will judge the moment at the cemetery to be "*narratively* right." While this may console the writer in Roth, it does little for the ungrieving son, who persists in reading only a minimal importance into "an event *not* entirely random and unpredictable."

The scene is much more than narratively right; it is emotionally necessary. While Philip may say that at the cemetery "I didn't expect to learn anything new," a process has begun. It is a process his father must announce when, on the evening after an abortive visit to a retirement home, the son overhears him crying out, "Mommy, Mommy, where are you, Mommy?" Through an empathetic ventriloquism, Herman Roth calls out to his dead wife on behalf of his living son.

Patrimony is a lonely text, a story of two men marooned in their losses, but the son is far lonelier than the father, since he is a man who will live and die without children. He is therefore a man not much used to having to administer care, and so, when the work of cleaning up begins, the revelations come fast upon him. On the day following the shit scene, Philip draws a bath for his father. "I sat on the edge of the tub while the water ran, testing the temperature with my fingers—my mother, I remembered, used to test it with her elbow." So, very delicately—the process is summoned with an offhand dash—Philip begins to mother his father. He begins to find in himself that tenderness and that care. The next day, he overhears his father on the phone, saying "Philip is like a mother to me." Surprised at first by the "description," Philip quickly accepts it as "discriminating." This is one comparison he does not question; it proves, in fact, the crucial instance of his father's "unblinking" style.

Such acceptances allow Philip to experience the care of the self. After his heart attack, as he imagines himself "giving suck to my own newborn heart," Philip finally and fully identifies with his mother. In these scenes of "delirious maternal joy . . . I was as near to being the double of my nurturing mother as . . . I had come to feeling myself . . . interchangeable with . . . my failing father."

It is a striking feature of the English language that no synonym for "patrimony" exists when the gifts come from the mother's side. Roth's changing understanding of how fiction might work, in the years subsequent to the writing of the two memoirs, can nevertheless be seen as an inheritance from his mother. A signal feature of his early and mid-career had been the Rothian rant, those magnificent, uninterruptible monologues. Herman Roth embodies this "ruthlessness," this "I've Gotta Be Me" sensibility. In a conversation with Joanna Clark, on the day his father finally gives him the shaving mug, Philip acknowledges that he took something far different from his mother. "He got a lot of mileage out of never recognizing the differences among people. All my life I have been trying to tell him that people are different one from the other. My mother understood this in a way that he didn't. Couldn't. This is what I used to long for in him, some of her forbearance and tolerance, this simple recognition that people are different and that the difference is legitimate." In the fictional work to come, this integration of the mother's perspective results in the transformation of Zuckerman, Roth's main self-character, from a talker into a listener. Talking about himself, as he does so brilliantly in the Zuckerman trilogy, will give way, in the American trilogy, to the patient pursuit of and careful audition to stories about somebody else, stories that reveal "difference," the need to acknowledge it, and the effort to bridge it, as the work we are in.

Roth's is a monologic sensibility continually striving to be dialogic. His fictional forms seek to grant admission to a voice and a vision other than his own. They strain to admit that "difference." But, up until the early 1990s, Roth's furious integrity is largely able to make room only for characters who are objects of ridicule or mirrors of Roth. Perhaps the completed mourning for his mother, fully enacted in *Patrimony*, encouraged him to make this turn. Perhaps the most we can say is that the death of his parents, the end of his second marriage, the first heart attack, and the recovery from a Halcion addiction, so movingly chronicled in the opening pages of *Operation Shylock*, correlate with a growing openness to difference. It is pleasant to believe that beyond the prayer shawls, and the shaving mug, and the vernacular, and the shit, the real patrimony (is it a "matrimony"?) is the ease and the power and the openness to difference expressed in the late career.

The shit scene in *Patrimony* has such force, in part, because it is a repetition. "That happened to me one other time in my life," Herman Roth informs his son, as he is being bathed by him. It happened in 1956, after the father had been entrusted by Metropolitan Life with an office of forty employees. A middle-of-the-night phone call brought news that somebody had broken into the office, and before "I could make it to the toilet," Herman continues, "the same thing happened." Roth then goes on to document his father's vexed history at the insurance company.

It is a history of anti-Semitism. Roth recounts an exchange of letters on the subject in which the company rejects any claim of "religious bias." He cites a federal campaign in the 1960s "against alleged religious discrimination in insurance companies." When the Met Life CEO claims "innocence" of any such practices, Herman Roth responds by saying that "there are just a couple of little holes in his sense of history." But Herman also says that "they've been awfully good to me" and that his rise in the company was a kind of wonder.

"The hell it is," Philip replies. "You worked. You sweated blood for them." You even "beshat" yourself for them, he might have added. "You have a history and so do they. The difference is that you own up to yours, you say that you were 'nothing,' but they don't like to admit to theirs, if those letters are any indication."

Owning up to history is the work of Roth's novels of the 1990s. The American trilogy takes on, in sequence, the 1960s, the 1950s, and the 1990s. Roth's ability to conduct such a persuasive survey can be traced directly back, as I have argued, to the breakthrough accomplished in *Patrimony*, and to its carefully structured sequence of revelations. First, Philip inherits the shit and all that comes with it. What the son takes on in the one scene allows him to give point and force to the father's story in the pages immediately following. The CEO's straight history may be full of little holes, but by dint of diligent research—afternoons are spent in the archives of the American Jewish Committee digging into discrimination in the insurance industry—Roth brings forward a secret history that divests the reader of his "innocence." And this is what he will continue to do in the novels that follow.

In *The Plot Against America*, Herman Roth defines history as "everything that happens everywhere." Like the son at the beginning of *Patrimony*, the father makes a "wrong turn," on entering Washington, D.C., and the family suddenly finds itself at the Capitol. "We had driven right to the very heart of American history; and whether we knew it in so many words, it was American history, delineated in its most inspirational form, that we were counting on to protect us." Of course, inspirational history does no such thing; the Roths are expelled from their hotel and harassed at the restaurant. Mere proximity to the monuments and seats of government has about as much power to "protect"—the word appears frequently in the novel—as does life insurance. The only way history can protect us, Roth's novel argues, is by our knowing it.

The vast counter-history offered up in *The Plot Against America* takes on meaning and force only if we continually correct it and therefore perceive the ironies in it by reminding ourselves of what really did happen in 1940. And the allegory becomes richer if we perceive Roth's treatment of the past as also comprising a history of the present, a displaced fable of the threats to mobility and privacy and civil liberty conjured up in the early years of the twenty-first century by so-called threats to what Philip calls "the homeland." Apart from the aid to memory provided by the postscript, the novel can only work if read from "the historical perspective of the knowing reader." Such a reader's fate, as Roth writes in *The Counterlife*, is "to be innocent of innocence at all costs."

Roth's counterfactual history of the 1940s also reminds us that the alternative to innocence is not certainty. By making up a past in which Lindberg wins over Roosevelt, Roth reminds us that the past could well have happened otherwise, that our sense of what "happened" remains a matter of interpretation and debate, and that all histories—including my own—are very contingent affairs.

❖   ❖

A high school sports star, Seymour Irving Levov marries the local beauty queen, inherits and runs with pleasure his father's glove-making business in Newark, and fathers a daughter named Merry. For his blue-eyed, blond good looks, people call this fair-complexioned Jewish boy "the Swede." The Swede's *"simple and most ordinary"* life, as Zuckerman calls it, falls apart in 1968, after the Newark riots have burned down the inner city and his daughter, as a protest against the Vietnam War, attempts to bomb the Rimrock post office and thereby kills a local doctor. Zuckerman, aging and impotent and from the same lost Newark neighborhood, runs into the Swede in his second life, in 1985, after he has regrouped from the collapse of his marriage to Dawn and gone on to father three sons. At the Swede's request, the two men meet and Swede narrates the loss of Newark Maid and its devastating effect on his father. Ten years later, at his forty-fifth high school reunion, Zuckerman runs into Swede's brother Jerry and learns that Swede has just died of prostate cancer. Jerry also fills him in on the heartbreaking backstory, and Zuckerman comes to believe that "the father was the cover. The burning subject was the daughter." "*This* was what he had summoned me to talk about," Zuckerman concludes, "had wanted me to help him *write* about." And so he sets out to reconstruct the story of Swede's great fall, the story that forms the heart of *American Pastoral*.

Swede Levov is Roth's most compelling unknowing reader. He embodies a truth he cannot know: that the American Dream contains within it the seeds of the American Tragedy. Swede, we might simply say, is destroyed by his "Swedian innocence." His unquestioning faith in the good fortune it is his privilege to live out, so the argument might go, provokes in his daughter an all-consuming reaction. The novel invites such a reading, in which Swede's loss of his daughter is seen to result from "some failure of his own responsibility." And yet the knowing reader of *American Pastoral* may also resist such a reading, since in the attempt to explain Swede's fall, we reduce "the inexplicable" to something manageable and comforting and thereby reproduce a version of the very innocence that destroys the Swede.

Swede did—or didn't do—something to or for Merry: his story is a tragedy of parenting. This, at least, is where Zuckerman begins. "I am thinking of the Swede's great fall and of how he must have imagined that it was founded on some failure of his own responsibility. This is where it must begin." Zuckerman finds himself thinking of the "mysterious, troubling, extraordinary historical transition" between the triumphant days of wartime and the explosion of the daughter's bomb in 1968. Such disasters must be caused, Zuckerman reasons, must be the product of "a single transgression." "And, inexplicably, which is to say lo and behold, I found him in Deal, New Jersey," driving back from the beach with his daughter. Zuckerman then produces—imagines—the kiss scene.

A lot is going on here. First, Zuckerman's explanatory scheme is assigned to Swede; he portrays himself as simply imagining from his hero's perspective. Second, the key incident that will be summoned as the moment of tragic fall is wholly constructed by Zuckerman. As he has already told us, "anything more I wanted to know, I'd have to make up." Readers may remember the kiss scene as just one more reported incident; my students, in trying to understand Swede, usually overlook the scene's status as a dream. But Zuckerman uses an ellipsis to clearly mark the scene as occurring in a kind of dissolve, a fade-out into surmise. "To the honeysweet strains of 'Dream,' I pulled away from myself, pulled away from the reunion, and I dreamed . . . I dreamed a realistic chronicle." The scene Zuckerman then proceeds to imagine has no more verifiability than does the scene between Gatsby and Daisy at the end of chapter 6 of *The Great Gatsby*, where Nick, an equally speculative narrator who also introduces his reverie by way of an ellipsis, imagines the moment of Gatsby kissing Daisy as its own kind of fall.

In Zuckerman's dream, Swede leans over and kisses Merry on her "stammering mouth." He does so in answer to her request. She is eleven. After the disaster, when Swede goes "obsessively searching for the origins of their suffering," it is this "anomalous moment," Zuckerman conjectures, that Swede "remembered."

Zuckerman stages this scene, I believe, as a precise example of how not to imagine the past. This is a novel profoundly hostile to reductive explanations, of the history of a person or of a country. Reductive explanations send Merry out on her quest, and she will be the one finally to challenge her father in his search after them. "You can't explain away what I've done by motives, Daddy. I certainly wouldn't explain away what *you've* done by motives." This response drives Swede a little crazy. "Then *you* explain it," he cries out. "Explain it to me, *please.*"

This may be the cry of even the knowing reader as well. Explanations are, after all, what he comes for. Isn't it Roth's job to connect act and consequence? And isn't one of the largest questions in American historiography a desperate question about the 1960s: How did we get there, and how did we get from there to here?

The most reductive and capricious and therefore politically effective answer to the question has come from the political right, which managed to write the history of the sixties as a disaster of misrule and then to mobilize this so-called wrong turning as the subtext of national politics from Reagan to the second Bush. Toni Morrison is eloquent on this point, arguing, in the 1996 Jefferson Lecture, that "killing the sixties, turning that decade into an aberration, an exotic malady ripe with excess, drugs and disobedience, is designed to bury its central features—emancipation, generosity, acute political awareness and a sense of shared and mutually responsible society." Roth may even seem to court such a reduction by making Merry so unattractive and by surrounding her story with questions about parenting. Maybe the sixties really did involve a failure of authority and maybe the needed thing is a return to those core "values" that the period is seen, in the "loss-of-authority" narrative, as abandoning. Such a view would align Roth with Joan Didion at her most stringent, with her belief that at some point between 1945 and 1967 we somehow neglected to tell our children the rules of the game we happened to be playing.

Merry herself rejects such an explanation. Whatever she did and whatever she became, she will not blame it on a cliché about generational rebellion.

The central metaphor of the novel grows out of the brilliant descriptions of Swede's glove-making business in Newark. The details of glove manufacture, attended to so lovingly by Swede and Zuckerman, are meant to express the lost golden age of downtown Newark, a time of fine craftsmanship, relative economic stability, and even cordial working relations among races and classes. All this is then swept away by the social dislocations of the 1960s. Roth dramatizes this loss without trying to explain it. Newark stands in for any American's Gone Good Place, the sustaining home so often swept away by the engines of change.

A good explanation is like a glove that fits. A glove is a thing placed over another thing in order to give it a more pleasing shape, to "protect" it. And straight history, with its glib and reassuring explanations, is what we pull over the pain and chaos of the past in order to make sense of "the inexplicable," Swede's eventual phrase for what his daughter has become.

Historical interpretations and novelistic structures grow out of similar attempts to explain. But how we go about the business of explaining the past to ourselves makes all the difference. The major innovation of Roth's American trilogy is to have narrator Zuckerman direct his attention away from himself and onto a hero: Swede Levov, Ira Ringold, Coleman Silk. A relentless interrogation of an inexplicable self gives way to an interest in a potentially explicable other. That Swede cannot finally be explained isn't really the point; Zuckerman's empathetic will to overcome Swede's "opacity" is what arrests and moves us. Wanting to know another and coming to accept that you cannot is a much more soul-making discovery than the preemptive postmodern assumption that all is always indeterminate. It connects the most generous impulses behind reading with Frank Kermode's eloquent definition of love: "the power by which we apprehend the opacity of persons to the degree that we will not limit them by forcing them into selfish patterns." The Interpreted Design, as David Minter calls it, continually enjoins just such a motion of heart and mind, as the reader discovers that a narrator's quest to know a hero is gradually supplanted by a narrator's willingness, in spite of and even because of all that cannot be known, to love.

Still, there is much to be said for knowing. Roth's novel chooses not so much to reject explanations as to multiply them. The resulting flurry of explanatory schemes celebrates the richness of the interpreting mind, rather than the limits of its reach.

The recurring speech act in *American Pastoral* is the interrogative. The novel ends with Zuckerman's heart-felt cry: "And what is wrong with their life? What on earth is less reprehensible than the life of the Levovs?" Questions reach out toward answers, and Roth provides his share of them—not to the question "What's made Merry Merry?" but rather to the question "How might I go about framing an answer to this question?" We will more than likely do so according to an idea about how to read experience. We frame such an answer not by reaching for what Roth calls "the handiest empty-headed idea," but by engaging one of the great explanatory schemes. A psychoanalytic reading might begin to construct an answer to the question in Dawn's overshadowing beauty and in the father's uncomprehended Oedipal feelings for his daughter. A Marxist reading could focus on the tension between the material comforts of Old Rimrock and the eventual poverty to which Merry consigns herself. A performative theory of identity might see Merry, like Sheila Salzman, as simply "acting the role of herself." A reader-response approach could process the narration as a self-consuming artifact, where the man who is making it up admits to nothing so readily as that "I was wrong."

What about a historical explanation? That Merry is a product of the past and present history of her American place? "Out of what context did these transformations arise?" Zuckerman asks, early on. To this question no American novelist of the closing decade of the twentieth century has made a more comprehensive response. A response, however, is not necessarily an answer. Does the emergent "American berserk" result from the trauma of the Vietnam War, an event that can be read as producing not only Merry's bombs but also, in *The Human Stain*, Les Farley's will to murder? Is it the lingering effect of anticommunism and the Cold War, a native-born paranoia that not only destroys Ira Ringold in *I Married a Communist* but leads in *The Plot Against America* to the election of Lindberg? The deeper explanation may be something corrupting in the very prosperity of the 1990s, a decade that saw, by the year 2000:

—a reduction of acid rain by one-half from 1970;
—a decline in smog by a factor of one-third;
—retroviral drugs that transformed AIDS into a survivable illness;
—a record 68 percent of American homes as owner-occupied;
—a reduction of the poverty rate to 11.3 percent of the population;
—85 million households with one or more cars or trucks;
—and charitable giving at an all-time high.

Is Merry's distress a reaction to this—to the unassailably "good life" that most Americans lived toward and finally fulfilled during the Clinton years? (The assumption behind such an apparently anachronistic question is that "historical" novels do not simply chronicle a past but also encode a history of the moment of their production.) Where do stories start, where do explanations begin? Driving home from the clinic and his wife's suicidal depression, Swede "wondered if it wasn't better for her to identify what had happened to her in 1949, not what has happened to her in 1968, as the problem at hand." Michael Herr might answer that "you couldn't use standard methods to date the doom." Nineteen forty-nine is the year in which Dawn won the state beauty pageant and so found herself derailed from the "normal." It is perhaps as good a place as any to begin the story of her fall. All that is involved is a narrative choice, of one beginning over another.

By virtue of this passage, Roth once again affirms that the most capacious explanations are narrative ones, those "blèssed structures," as Robert Lowell calls them, generated in and by fiction. Roth's fictions protect us from "drowning . . . in inadequate explanations" by allowing those explanations to have their say and thereby to expose the limitations of any one "idea" about life to explain life. "Searching for an explanation," as Swede does for five years after the bombing, is a measure of his care. But settling on one explanation not only is a kind of death but can lead to murder, as it does for Merry. The Interpreted Design appeals to Roth because it resists both an easy postmodern indeterminacy and the innocence of ideological forms of reductive thinking. The narrative explanations provided by novels with such a design have force and value because they immerse the reader in the very fascination and bewilderment being explored. The opening paragraphs of *The Great Gatsby* provide perhaps the most familiar example of such a stance, where Nick continually shuttles between wonder and judgment. No explanation of a character and his fate is of much worth if it is one from which a reader is invited to stand aside. Or, as Zuckerman argues: "To let your hero's life occur within you when everything is trying to diminish him . . . to implicate yourself . . . in the bewilderment of his tragic fall—well, that's worth thinking about."

✦   ✦

The final novel of the American trilogy ends with the image of the self alone with America—and with Les Farley. *The Human Stain* juxtaposes two varieties of loneliness: Zuckerman's choice of the "creative remove," and Coleman Silk's choice of the Imperial Self. Coleman may dance Zuckerman back into life, and each man may briefly assuage the loneliness of the other, but Coleman's is finally the deeper loneliness, since it is based on a lie. To lie is to be lonely, since nobody then can "know" you.

In an attempt to relieve *his* sense of the burden of Coleman's loneliness, Zuckerman stages a scene in which Coleman unburdens himself of his secret. Silk shares it with his lover, Faunia Farley, but, as with the kiss scene in *American Pastoral*, the episode is clearly made up. Coleman never does share his secret with Zuckerman, who imagines the disclosure to Faunia directly after he has belatedly come to know it, at Coleman's funeral. Zuckerman then assumes that Coleman "*had* to have" told Faunia "the truth about the beginning," and so proceeds to invent a scene in which he finally says to her, "What would you think . . . if I told you I wasn't a white man?" Zuckerman therefore gives us the recognition scene long after he has shared with the reader its resultant knowledge; early in the second chapter, we learn that Coleman comes from "a model Negro family." So *The Human Stain* offers up two plots: Coleman's story of passing and the process of Zuckerman's coming to know it. "He has a secret," Zuckerman finds himself thinking about Coleman, when he runs into him at Tanglewood. But he does not begin work—he is not prompted to write Coleman's story—until "some three months later, when I learned the secret and began this book." Our narrator consents to tell the story only once he has learned its secret, and the narrative thereby produced is less about uncovering a secret than it is about watching how brilliantly one can be kept.

Roth thereby reverses Faulkner's strategy in *Absalom, Absalom!*, where the secret of a man who is passing as white is withheld from the reader until the closing pages of the book. Faulkner's purpose in withholding this conjecture—Charles Bon's "blood" remains, of course, of uncertain origin—is to implicate the reader in the emotional field of a Sutpen-like "innocence" that perpetuates race as the constructed and destructive and thereby tragic open secret of American life. Roth's purpose in revealing Coleman's secret so early on is to implicate readers in a different way, to enlist us as an audience for Coleman's successful performance of whiteness.

Because he does get away with it. Coleman pays a huge price for his choice, of course, the loss of any contact with his biological family. He marries Iris Gittelman and tells her that "he was Jewish." And his wife will die, although not as a result of secret-keeping, but rather from her anguish over the treatment of Coleman subsequent to an incident when his secret accidentally surfaces through a sort of slip of the tongue, when he asks, about two of his nonattending students, "Do they exist or are they spooks?" Still, even up to the day of Coleman's funeral, a discerning Zuckerman remains taken in by a performance that only the sight of Coleman's sister Ernestine allows him to see through. "I could tell she wasn't white," he says to himself. It is then she tells Zuckerman much of the family history he has already relayed to us.

The great shift between 1936 and 2000 is that race has become a condition one can comically perform rather than tragically suffer. Joe Christmas and Charles Bon, like Rena Walden before them, may pass, for a time, but they will eventually pay a fatal price for doing so. By the time Roth comes to write his novel, passing has become less a matter of an intractable color line and more a figure for performative notions of identity. *The Human Stain* has little to say about the actual experience of being black in the United States; its focus is on the sheer willfulness and bravado of Coleman's act. And this performativity, we are in turn reminded, lies at the heart of the American Dream. It is also Gatsby's story, where the successful act of passing as a "son of God" or anything but the child of one's parents reveals itself as the fantasy at the heart of our national family romance.

Coleman's resistance to playing an assigned role and a predetermined identity strongly resembles Roth's own early rebellion against the assigned label of Jewish (rather than American) author, hence the effrontery of *Portnoy's Complaint* (1967), with its annihilating portraits of father and mother. If the gesture of rebellion against the family generates the trajectory of the early career, the integration of the parental legacy underwrites, as I have argued, the beauty and force of Roth's major phase. But Roth does not insist that his characters fall into line with his late wisdom. Each continues, instead, to pursue his or her uniquely adaptive and destructive version of the American Dream. If "all" one wants, like Coleman, is "to be free," for instance, then the living out of this dream will entail a lot of collateral damage, since the fantasy simply represses rather than undoes all those "arbitrary" (it is Coleman's word) designations, like race, that remain so "rigidly unalterable." The very respectability being sought by dreamers of the American Dream arises, then, out of something sleazy, if not soul-killing, since the status one gains in realizing it comes at the price of leaving so much behind that it can involve, as it does in Coleman's case, the breaking of a mother's heart.

✦ ✦

"Everything looks permanent," Emerson writes, "until its secret is known." Gatsby's and Sutpen's and Coleman's keeping of a personal secret reenacts their country's habit of hiding its history from itself. Roth's American trilogy reveals the impermanence and volatility of a national identity founded on such secrets. In *The Human Stain*, he exposes the prurience at the heart of our righteousness and tracks the eruptions of our suppressed longings in the "ecstasy of sanctimony" that occurs over something as small as . . . "a president's penis." This sanctimony leaves our daughters (Merry and Faunia), above all, exposed to the most violent degradations, since as the bearers of our innocence they pay the heaviest price when, as is inevitable within the sexual order Roth imagines, they are subjected to the loss of it.

Roth sets the context for Coleman's story early on, establishing a field of allusion as rich as anything in Eliot or Pynchon. "If you haven't lived through 1998, *you* don't know what sanctity is," he maintains, and then he goes on to provide the field of knowledge out of which such knowing might arise, alluding in fewer than three pages to "Bill Clinton's secret"; a nude Miss America in *Penthouse* (Vanessa Williams); two home run gods, one white and one brown (Mark McGuire and Sammy Sosa); Hawthorne's "persecuting spirit"; Senator Lieberman's concern for the TV-watching habits of his ten-year-old daughter; William Buckley on Eloise and Abelard; Ayatollah Khomeni's fatwa against Salman Rushdie; and Christo's mammoth building wraps, not to speak of the head quote already provided, from *Oedipus the King*. Each of these allusions touches on matters of repression or scandal, or, in the case of McGuire and Sosa, on a seemingly innocent competition that is also a register of the deepest tensions in American life. This is stuff, Roth's chapter title suggests, "Everybody Knows." They know about it from reading the headlines or the sports pages. But they can only know what it all means—how it hangs together in a significant pattern—if they read a novel with the connection-making powers of *The Human Stain*.

In the novel's closing scene, Zuckerman, on his way to visit Coleman's sister, spots a gray pickup and parks next to it. He walks into the winter woods until he comes to a frozen lake. There he sees a solitary figure bending over a hole in the ice with an abbreviated fishing rod in his gloved hands. It is Les Farley, and the pickup is the "murder weapon" with which, three months earlier, he ran Coleman and Faunia off the road. Zuckerman will never get to Ernestine's house; the book ends with this digression, perhaps one of the last and most purposeful turnings aside in this happily deviant career.

As the two men converse, Zuckerman sees that Les has used a four-foot-long length of corkscrew blade, "an auger," to drill through the ice. "It's a clean place," Les remarks. "As long as I can keep it a secret." Les goes on to talk about his service in Vietnam, thereby sharing "a secret of his that is even bigger than the secret of this pond." He talks about the 250 B-52s lost over North Vietnam. "But the government'll never tell you that." The government doesn't even inform him that he suffers from PTSD; it is "a colored girl at the VA" who tells him "how it was going through my subconscious." "The subconscious mind," he continues. "You can't control it. It's like the government. It *is* the government. It's the government all over again. It gets you to do what you don't want to do."

This menacing encounter culminates in the moment when Les raises the auger's long bright bit right up to Zuckerman's face. Zuckerman begins to shuffle backward as Les reminds him that now he knows about the "secret spot." "It's safe with me," Zuckerman promises. Once safely back on shore, he turns to look back and then delivers the final sentences:

> Just facing him, I could feel the terror of the auger—even with him already seated
> back on his bucket: the icy white of the lake encircling a tiny spot that was a man,
> the only human marker in all of nature, like the X of an illiterate's signature on a
> sheet of paper. There it was, if not the whole story, the whole picture. Only rarely,
> at the end of our century, does life offer up a vision as pure and peaceful as this
> one: a solitary man on a bucket, fishing through eighteen inches of ice in a lake
> that's constantly turning over its water atop an arcadian mountain in America.

The sense of an ending is very strong here. Roth correlates the end of his trilogy with the end of the twentieth century and with the end of Zuckerman's comfortable creative remove, since as he backs away from Les he knows that "I was going to have to go elsewhere to live."

Roth refigures here the endings of *In Our Time* and *The Great Gatsby*, which also offer up a vision of a solitary figure in a landscape. Nick Adams's "good place" and Nick Carraway's "new world" here become Les Farley's "secret place." Whether Hemingway's Nick will fish the swamp, or Fitzgerald's Nick will again find something commensurate to his capacity for wonder—these are questions left open. As they exit their narratives, both characters turn, like Zuckerman, and look back. By way of these acts of turning, each author acknowledges that what is really being sought is not the "plenty of days coming," as Nick Adams imagines, but rather something, as Fitzgerald writes of Gatsby, already "behind him."

What is really being sought, of course, as the last two words of *The Great Gatsby* tell us, is "the past." This is the true American secret place; this is the legacy that bears us "ceaselessly back," as Les finds himself "waking up in the middle of the night back in Vietnam." In Les's terms, it is a subconscious mind that insists on haunting us with a secret history until we turn and acknowledge it.

Zuckerman's sense of terror at the end of *The Human Stain* arises here from being threatened by an instrument that aggressively penetrates. Feeling "completely bested" by Les's huge screw, Roth, by way of Zuckerman, retreats. With such a tool, "the sharpness is everything." After forty years of championing the appetites of the phallic auger, Roth appears to have temporarily exhausted an interest in knowing as penetration. Zuckerman has long since admitted to being impotent, and the loss of the ability to penetrate in one way is offset by an almost motherly solicitude for his wayward subject. The turn that begins in *Patrimony* has been fully accomplished; with Coleman, as with Swede, Roth deploys a mode of imagining that foregrounds the pleasures and the limits and the dangers of trying to know, one substituting empathy for edge.

Roth offsets the terror of the auger with the "pure and perfect" beauty of the scene. What the auger discloses is a water that "cleans itself." Nature's self-sustaining processes here work independently of any human control—as did "the green breast of the new world," before the Dutch sailors stepped onto it. This is why Fitzgerald has them hold their breath, hesitate, before they take possession. A fall occurs once they do so, as the green breast begins its transformation into the dark fields of the republic. The water of the lake may be the kind that can clean itself, but that the natural world can continue to do so in a place so stained by human touch is one of the more persistent American illusions. Man leaves his mark, his "X." And the messes left behind by history, like those created by the "careless" Tom and Daisy, require a caring human presence to clean them up.

For all the sense of a paradise lost, or about to be lost, Roth suffuses his ending with a kind of hope. The hope is contained not only in words like "arcadian," but in a pun hidden within the repeated sounding of the word "auger." Augury is the art of prophecy; the augurs of ancient Rome were the official interpreters of signs and portents, as, for the modern nation, its novelists have become. Les's sharp drill not only excavates a past; it prophecies a future. Roth means for the vision here to reach both ways, back into the determining and forward into the evermore about to be. He is the rememberer, but he is also the augur. And the augury Roth provides at the end of *The Human Stain* and throughout the books of the 1990s grows out of his deep study of the culture of the American past and his awareness that this past is always present. As Northrop Frye reminds us, in *Anatomy of Criticism*, upon such study the renewal of a nation depends: "The culture of the past is not only the memory of mankind, but our own buried life, and study of it leads to a recognition scene, a discovery in which we see, not our past lives, but the total cultural form of our present life. It is not only the poet but his reader who is subject to the obligation to 'make it new.'"

Like the "X" on a sheet of paper, writing can be seen as marring an original and virginal whiteness; no exemption can be issued for the writer from our collective responsibility for the conquest of America. But the specific kinds of marks a writer leaves behind make, in the struggle for and against national self-recognition, all the difference. By refusing to see the "whole picture," "illiterate" writing pollutes and degrades our personal and our public spaces. Illiterate writing cannot see the whole picture because it is incapable of reading the "whole story," the history of the nation as told in its literature. The literacy Roth here invokes is not simply a matter of being able to read and write. It is a matter of having the energy and courage to read and write the necessary words, those that can reach forward with hope because they have looked unblinkingly back.

Roth here imagines at the end a lake of cold, clear water. This water "is like what we imagine knowledge to be," Elizabeth Bishop writes, in "At the Fishhouses" (1947):

If you tasted it, it would first taste bitter,
then briny, then surely burn your tongue.
It is like what we imagine knowledge to be:
dark, salt, clear, moving, utterly free,
drawn from the cold hard mouth
of the world, derived from the rocky breasts
forever, flowing and drawn, and since
our knowledge is historical, flowing, and flown.

Under Roth's hand, Bishop's salt becomes "extracold" fresh water. Whether the prophetic figure stands at seaside or lakeshore, the medium of the vision is much the same. The taste of such water is bitter, and it burns. It is so cold that it is hot, and it is cold because the lessons it imparts are unsentimental. The knowledge figured here is only to be gained from immersion in the kinds of writing that Bishop and Roth offer us. Like Roth's lake of dark, clear water, or like Bishop's indifferent sea, this writing engages in an ongoing and purifying ritual, as it reminds us that the only way toward a more "peaceful" American future is by listening to and recirculating the sharp-edged auguries of the past.

A Personal Note

We take what we need from the books we read, and what we need changes. Our culture continually changes its mind about what counts in—and as—literature as well. This book records the reading experience of a man of sixty who began the formal study of American literature over forty years ago, in the mid-1960s. I am amazed to see where a career as a student and teacher has brought me, from the all-male lecture halls at Yale where I never heard a word about African-American literature to the more modestly appointed spaces at the University of Maryland, where, in my classes, women and people of color sit next to white men, and where writers like Toni Morrison and Chang-rae Lee anchor the syllabi in my lectures and graduate seminars. The exclusive lists of the Great Tradition have given way to the universe of the Expanding Canon.

All this has been for the good, and I am glad to have been a part of it. Of course, over the years I have had to continually reeducate myself. When I first offered a course in "Twentieth-Century American Literature," in 1975, my ignorance of the advertised subject distracted me from the presumption of its scope. I typed up a reading list of five poets: Frost, Stevens, Eliot, Pound, and Williams. Twenty of the enrolled students, after inspecting the syllabus, stood up and walked out of the room. Not in protest against the story having been reduced to five dead, white males. No, what they wanted was fiction. I continued teaching the course, eventually dropping Pound and adding Hemingway, Fitzgerald, Faulkner, and Warren. It was all I knew, and good things came out of it, like Jahan Ramazani, a would-be government major who switched to English after taking my course in 1977 and who, twenty years later, would replace Richard Ellmann as the editor of the *Norton Anthology of Modern and Contemporary Poetry*.

My pedagogical moment came when, in 1979, my friend Angela Davis turned around in a faculty meeting and complained to my face that my syllabus contained no African-American writers. The comment rankled; I was embarrassed at being called out, and not quite sure how to respond, since I had read very few of the authors she thought I should teach. This was still standard at the time at Virginia, although things had begun to change rapidly in other departments. But the English Department then had no full-time black faculty, and none of its senior members ever put any pressure on me, or even handed me a book, that might have suggested a change of course.

Not getting tenure—in 1980—knocked me off of the academic ladder and into working for the state humanities council in Charlottesville. Our job was to hand out small grants to libraries, schools, museums, and community groups in all the far corners of Virginia. We had black officers on the board, like Jessie Brown from Hampton Institute, and black people walking in the door, like Stanley Johnson, an ex-con looking to start a reading program in the Lynchburg jail. Suddenly I had a new constituency—not just the mostly white faces staring back at me in a UVA classroom. Here we were, in the heart of the old Confederacy, trying to get people to read and think about their collective past, and there was no way to avoid seeing that slavery was the heart of it. I read John Hope Franklin's *From Slavery to Freedom*, and I began to realize that I knew next to nothing about Virginia, or America. I sent out a call for proposals on "Black History in Virginia," teamed up with historian Armstead Robinson and a local high school teacher, and sat in that summer while ten teachers from around the state began to learn about the story behind the official story.

Trying as well to keep my writing self alive, I began thinking about my home state of California. At first I thought I wanted to write a novel about growing up in San Bernardino. Being a researcher by nature, I began some background reading and discovered the work of John Muir. Muir had a great story—he discovered the first living glacier in the high country above Yosemite and founded the Sierra Club in 1892—and also turned out to have written a number of books. They were pretty good books, but they did not meet the definition of "literature" I had been trained to enforce. The same held true for other California writers I stumbled across, like explorer John C. Frémont and mountain man Zenas Leonard. They seemed to occupy some nether space between literature, history, and memoir; they were hybrid and sometimes awkward and only intermittently gifted with style. But they were indubitably part of the story. So I began to expand my sense of what counted as imaginative work and came to believe that any study of a literary region had to be catholic in its taste and willing to solicit testimony from all kinds of unlooked-for places. The California book eventually came out, and even won a prize, but it dealt with no writers of color, and there was only one woman in it.

It is strange to realize how late it was in the century before I really began to open myself to the work of the century. By the time I arrived at Maryland, in 1987, I had become conscious of the need to broaden my course offerings. I think Jean Toomer was the first writer of color to appear on one of my syllabi, for a course on the 1920s, largely because he shared with Hemingway and Fitzgerald both the style and the concerns of high modernism. It was not until after starting my next book, on artists from the Vietnam generation, that I made my first full study of an African-American author. I had always believed in Elizabeth Bishop's call to "read ALL of somebody." Surveying the literary landscape in 1987, I fixed upon Alice Walker as the salient African-American author of her generation, and I plunged in. Her work led me back to Cleaver, Ellison, Larsen, Chesnutt, Du Bois, and Jacobs. But my big discovery was that she was in conversation with Faulkner and O'Connor. *The Color Purple* also presented itself as deeply responsive to the ways in which people talk and listen to each other, to how knowledge is exchanged or withheld. I began to see that the American tradition was vaster than I had imagined, that its "minority" and "canonical" strains could not be separated, that relations stop nowhere.

When I came to write *Five Fires*, in the mid-1990s, it all blew wide open. A short and sweet book about race and catastrophe in California of course required that I immerse myself in Asian-American and Mexican-American literature. The batting order in *The Fall into Eden*, my first book on California, now looked woefully inadequate, as did its exceedingly hothouse quality, its subtle readings largely closed off from any history except literary history. By now I had learned that any "text" has its rhetoric and its style, and that memoirist Juana Machado and merchant Lai Chun-chuen can sometimes tell us as much about the past, and how it is coded in language, as a Gertrude Atherton or a Bret Harte.

Anyone who has managed to make it through this book will recognize that Faulkner and Morrison are its anchoring authors, and not simply because they are each prolific and profound. They are central to my project for two reasons: because they each grasp, as fully as any of the assembled writers, the pedagogical romance at the heart of reading; and because their interrelationship has come to model, for me, the ways in which a tradition is sustained and renewed.

I wish I could remember when I first read *Beloved*; it was some time in the early 1990s. I had long been a student of Faulkner and had come to believe that the central scenes in his work are those shared by Quentin and Shreve in *Absalom, Absalom!* While reading *Beloved*, I realized that I had not yet fully understood the power and value of these scenes, and that only after experiencing the three chapters at the end of part 1, especially the scene with Sethe and Paul D in the kitchen, had I come to understand Faulkner's call for a "happy marriage of speaking and hearing," those empathetic and pedagogical moments in which two young men accomplish a generous retelling of the past and invite the reader to become a cocreator in the process.

This was the essence of reading, and the value of reading American literature, as I had come, slowly and sometimes grudgingly, to understand it. There was no longer any way to read the greatest white American novelist of the twentieth century except through the greatest black American novelist of the twentieth century.

At Yale, around the time Chloe Wofford was becoming Toni Morrison, I had been a student of Harold Bloom. As so often throughout my career, he now came to aid me. I remembered one of his favorite quotations from Borges: "every writer *creates* his own precursors." Influence does not simply flow one way, from the past toward the present. It also flows backward; the truly great and new work of art, as Eliot maintains, not only enters tradition but alters it.

In my reading of the American procession, the Faulkner-Morrison relation provides the most dramatic example of this process of entering and altering. Faulkner had tried valiantly to imagine slavery and its cost to the white soul. But he could only imagine so far; as he writes in "Pantaloon in Black," there are things that "no white man could ever read." Not until Morrison came along, and created Sethe and Stamp Paid and Paul D, did an American novelist do what Faulkner anticipated but could not achieve—to imagine the terrible cost of slavery to the black soul. Morrison learned from Faulkner not only the importance of centering the inquiry around a violent and mystifying act but the even greater importance of converting the reader's method of approach to this act into the novel's most anguished subject. But Faulkner needed Morrison as much as she needed him. He could allow us to approach the question of why Henry shoots Charles, or why Quentin kills himself. But only Morrison could circle the question of why Sethe kills Beloved, and thereby enable a reader like myself to approach the deepest and yet most open secret in American life.

So it was I came to see that beyond Bishop's call to read "ALL of somebody" there lay a further call: "Read ALL of everybody." For all I thought I knew about Faulkner, I was never able to really read him, to see the ways in which he bravely succeeded and honestly fell short, until I read Morrison. It was all one tradition—one house—and my understanding of any part of it depended on a knowledge, always partial and ever expanding, of the whole.

Each member of the visionary company of readers keeps the imagination alive and builds his or her own sense of things. In this big and sometimes awkward book of mine, I offer my reader a version of my tradition. The point is not to believe me, but to continue the work. Still, I am glad to have written these pages, happy that they now form a small part of the world we share. See, I hold them toward you.

To the Reader

ix "a special kind of": Morrison, *Toni Morrison: Conversations*, 25.

x "I associate": Eliot, *The Waste Land and Other Poems*, 52.

xi "corporation land": Mailer, *The Armies of the Night*, 114.

xi "innocence": Faulkner, *Absalom, Absalom!*, 182.

xii "compounded": Ibid., 289.

xii "'And now,' Shreve said": Ibid., 261.

xii *"So it's the miscegenation"*: Ibid., 293.

xii "spot of Negro blood": Ibid., 254.

xiii "the two of them": Ibid., 250.

xiii "the work we are": Lincoln, *Lincoln: Speeches and Writings, 1859–1865*, 687.

xiii "string of historical facts": Lincoln, *Lincoln: Speeches and Writings, 1832–1858*, 430.

xiii xiv "evidences of design": Ibid., 426.

xiv *"sacred right of self"*: Ibid., 427.

xiv "slavery": Ibid., 427.

xiv "the join": Morrison, *Beloved*, 213.

xiv "combination": Roosevelt, 79.

xiv "While one can do": Ellison, *Shadow and Act*, 140.

xiv "as for the Negro": Ibid., 43.

xiv "the greatest artist": Ibid., 42.

xv "Eliot, Pound, Gertrude Stein": Ibid., 140.

xv "Faulkner has given us": Ibid., 273.

xv "into the depth of": Ibid., 273.

xv "to set a free": Clemens, 292.

xv "affiliation": Said, 16.

xvi "'Tell me'": Morrison, *Beloved*, 76.

xvi "Denver was seeing it": Ibid., 78.

Chapter 1 • *The Body and the Corporation*

1 "You couldn't find two": Herr, 49–50.

2 "yellow man": Springsteen.

2 "None of the books": Bishop, *Bishop: Poems, Prose, and Letters*, 151.
2 "'The problem with 'straight history'": Ted Kaouk, final exam for ENGL 631, May 2009.
3 "By the time Krebs": Hemingway, *In Our Time*, 69.
3 "You'll lose it": Hemingway, *The Sun Also Rises*, 245.
3 "It was a history": Hemingway, *In Our Time*, 72.
3 "*separate peace*": Ibid., 63.
3 "a depreciation of all": Henry James, "Henry James's First Interview."
4 "a chance to pay": Norris, *Norris: Novels and Essays*, 660.
4 "All—the—traffic—will": Ibid., 854.
4 "*offered at various figures*": Ibid., 670.
4 "came in on it": Ibid., 732.
4 "Instantly the revolvers and": Ibid., 993.
5 "stand in . . . in *one*": Ibid., 728.
6 "I would like to": Chambers, 15.
7 "Up went our land": Ibid., 17.
8 "that combination between business": Roosevelt, 79.
8 "combination, concentration intensive and": Brandeis, 3.
8 "history is more infinite": Rody, 4.
8 "*How it felt to me*": Didion, *Slouching towards Bethlehem*, 134.
9 "great fiction shows us": Welty, *Welty: Stories, Essays, & Memoir*, 810.
9 "Another summer I determined": Rodriguez, *Hunger of Memory*, 63.
9 "It is forms that": Godard.
9 "pivotal event": Norris, *Norris: Novels and Essays*, 1163.
9 "all of a sudden": Franklin Walker, 266.
9–10 "that abrupt swoop of terror": Norris, *Norris: Novels and Essays*, 786.
10 "expectation in preference to": Coleridge, 77.
10 "preparation of effect": Norris, *Norris: Novels and Essays*, 1163.
10 "At first, it was": Ibid., 989.
10 "Presley withdrew to watch": Ibid., 986.

Chapter 2 • Double Consciousness

12 "white scholars . . . colored": Johnson, *Johnson: Writings*, 13.
12 "the best ragtime player": Ibid., 71.
12 "the old slave songs": Ibid., 86.
12 "into the interior": Ibid., 101.
12 "some terrible crime": Ibid., 112.
12 "unbearable shame": Ibid., 115.
12 "Then I met her": Ibid., 119.
12 "I love you": Ibid., 123.
12 "We were married the": Ibid., 126.
12 "I am an ordinary": Ibid., 127.
13 "ivory whiteness": Ibid., 13.
13 "sword thrust": Ibid., 14.

13 "it fooled many readers": Johnson, *The Autobiography* (Dover Thrift Edition), iii.

14 "beings 'of an inferior order'": Chesnutt, *Chesnutt: Stories, Novels, & Essays*, 379.

14 "a negro": Ibid., 362.

14 "give up the world": Ibid., 460.

14 "*deliberately withheld meaning*": Aiken, 48.

15 "tall, dark, with straight": Chesnutt, *Chesnutt: Stories, Novels, & Essays*, 269.

15 "had clamorously warned all": Ibid., 270.

15 "a few years after": Ibid., 269.

15 "strikingly handsome": Ibid., 272.

15 "ivory": Ibid., 273.

15 "negro child": Ibid., 274.

15 "the subject of the": Chesnutt, *The House Behind the Cedars*, ed. William C. Andrews, vii.

15 "something familiar": Chesnutt, *Chesnutt: Stories, Novels, & Essays*, 274.

15 "It must be Rena": Ibid., 275.

15 "scarcely": Ibid., 276.

15 "a distinction which is": Ibid., 901.

16 "son": Ibid., 278.

16 "electric spark": Ibid., 279.

16 "that stain": Ibid., 284.

16 "by others of better": Freud, "Family Romances," *The Standard Edition*, vol. 9, 239.

16 "a new man": Chesnutt, *Chesnutt: Stories, Novels, & Essays*, 287.

16 "took": F. Scott Fitzgerald, 156.

16 "about the past life": Chesnutt, *Chesnutt: Stories, Novels, & Essays*, 369.

16 "a bright mulatto": Ibid., 370.

16 "impostor . . . self-made man": Sollers, 250.

17 "the old story": Chesnutt, *Chesnutt: Stories, Novels, & Essays*, 279.

17 "the family secret": Ibid., 311.

17 "along the border-line": Ibid., 342.

17 "a young cullud 'oman": Ibid., 339.

17 "a negro girl had": Ibid., 362.

17 "like a lily on": Ibid., 360.

18 "*hearsay descents*": Toomer, *The Wayward and the Seeking*, 121.

18 "identity": Chesnutt, *Chesnutt: Stories, Novels, & Essays*, 360.

18 "If there be a": Ibid., 352.

19 "to himself he never": Ibid., 373.

19 "You are aware, of": Ibid., 378.

19 "'I am white' replied": Ibid., 379.

19 "no external sign": Ibid., 373.

19 "privilege": Ibid., 381.

19 "the populous loneliness of": Ibid., 312.

19 "A young culled 'oman": Ibid., 461.

20 "To get to a place": Morrison, *Beloved*, 162.

20 "the freedom to love": Du Bois, 370.

20 "When I began this": Rodriguez, *Brown*, xv.

21 "The one, a gray-haired": Du Bois, 383.

21 "intimacy": Ibid., 489.

21 "detached scientist": Lewis, 226.

21 "dangerous": Du Bois, 532.

21 "dark sister struggling in": Ibid., 534.

21 "coiling twisted rope": Ibid., 535.

22 "The red stain of": Ibid., 368.

22 "to be both a": Ibid., 365.

22 "The negro is a": Ibid., 364.

22 "meeting and mingling": Lawrence, *Women in Love*, 139.

22 "a star balanced with": Ibid., 144.

22 "MERGING": Lawrence, *Studies in Classic American Literature*, 187.

22 "recognition of souls": Ibid., 186.

23 "Union": Vidal, *Lincoln*, 22.

23 "merge . . . double self into": Du Bois, 365.

23 "logic of metaphor": Crane, 163.

24 "herein lie buried many": Du Bois, 359.

24 "divine event": Ibid., 366.

24 "to set a free": Clemens, 292.

24 "not yet darkened": Du Bois, 509.

24 "I took and put": Morrison, *Beloved*, 164.

24 "Well sped, my boy": Du Bois, 510.

25 "He knew no color-line": Ibid., 509.

25 "collected every bit of": Morrison, *Beloved*, 163.

25 "bitter meanness": Du Bois, 510.

25 "*my book not fall*": Ibid., 547.

25 "Within the Veil": Ibid., 507.

25 "Criticism of writers by": Ibid., 395.

25 "weary of the race": Ibid., 398.

25 "So thoroughly did he": Ibid., 393.

25 "the deformation of mastery": Baker, 50.

25 "mastery of form": Ibid., 33.

26 "critical . . . thawing out": Washington, 143.

26 "I delivered my message": Ibid., 187.

26 "effective medicine": Ibid., 143.

26 "the revelation": Du Bois, 363.

26 "The exchange was merry": Ibid., 363.

26 "I was born a": Washington, 1.

26 "calmly told him 'Booker Washington'": Ibid., 20.

27 "In order to lift": Ibid., 69.

27 "use their hands": Ibid., 84.

27 "a few quilts and": Ibid., 130.

27 "we must do something": Ibid., 73.

27 "My whole former life": Ibid., 174.

28 "great leap": Ibid., 128.

28 "In all things that": Ibid., 129.

28 "agitation of questions of": Ibid., 131.

28 "a white man": Ibid., 2.

28 "the productions of our": Ibid., 128.

28 "beauty and dignity": Ibid., 86.

28 "to love work for": Ibid., 87.

28 "They had not fully": Ibid., 84.

28 "in tilling a field": Ibid., 129.

Chapter 3 • Pioneering Women

31 "a woman in it": Austin, *Stories from the Country of Lost Borders*, 205.

31 "the earth is no": Ibid., 3.

31 "of fullest understanding": Ibid., 261.

31 "All this time the": Ibid., 204–5.

31 "If it were not": Ibid., 210.

32 "to write a story": Ibid., 203.

32 "There was a mine": Ibid., 204–5.

32 "one of the very": Ibid., 205.

32 "For her the heart": Ibid., 206.

32 "I sat within the": Ibid., 207.

32 "the one thing the": Ibid., 207.

32 "honored . . . his destiny": Ibid., 208.

32 "not use it": Ibid., 209.

32 "The crux of the": Ibid., 206.

32 "He had never known": Ibid., 207.

33 "name": Ibid., 207.

33 "wife and his children": Ibid., 209.

33 "I have *missed* you": Ibid., 209.

33 "wish for a personal": Ibid., 256.

34 "She came and went": Ibid., 255.

34 "the contradiction of reports": Ibid., 256.

34 "three things which if": Ibid., 258.

34 "The flock traveled down": Ibid., 259.

34 "I stayed with Filon": Ibid., 261.

35 "she danced and dressed": Ibid., 96.

35 "Love and work": Erickson and Smelser, 4.

35 "three things . . . were good": Austin, *Stories from the Country of Lost Borders*, 258.

35 "I do not know": Ibid., 261.

35 "To work and to": Ibid., 262.

36 "Much of our trouble": May, 168.

36 "the secret talk of": Eaton, 18.

36 "the first Asian American": Amy Ling quoted in Eaton, 11.

36 "could not help receiving": Ibid., 18.

37 "For a long time": Ibid., 20.

37 "Friday was nice": Bishop, *Bishop: Poems, Prose, and Letters*, 155.

37 "ears": Eaton, 18.

37 "This is America, where": Ibid., 22.

37 "incommunicable": Cather, *Cather: Early Novels and Stories*, 937.

37 "a man's story like": Austin, *Stories from the Country of Lost Borders*, 202.

38 "something . . . from replying": Eaton, 27.

38 "a wooden building": Lai, 34.

38 "I offer the real": Eaton, 23.

38 "listening to repeating": Stein, *The Making of Americans*, 291.

38 "genius": Stein, *Stein: Writings 1903–1932*, 661.

39 "wandering": Ibid., 173.

39 "Sometimes you seem like": Ibid., 164.

39 "internal difference, / Where the": Dickinson, vol. 2, 235.

39 "Slowly every one in": Stein, *The Making of Americans*, 284.

39 "history of learning to": Ibid., 294.

39 "Sometimes it takes many": Ibid., 291.

39 "finding that no one": Ibid., 483.

39 "always looking": Ibid., 484.

39 "bottom": Ibid., 290.

39 "deeply moved": Stein, *Stein: Writings 1903–1932*, 712.

40 "Vocabulary in respect to": Stein, *Stein: Writings 1932–1946*, 326.

40 "completely not interesting": Ibid., 314.

40 "servile": Ibid., 319.

40 "there is nothing more": Borges, *Selected Non-Fictions*, 32.

40 "poignant incidents": Stein, *Stein: Writings 1903–1932*, 710.

40 "Nor should emotion itself": Ibid., 866.

40 "we are driving to": Bishop, *Bishop: Poems, Prose, and Letters*, 66.

40 "the sequence of motion": Hemingway, *Death in the Afternoon*, 22.

40 "Hitherto she had been": Stein, *Stein: Writings 1903–1932*, 781.

41 "wild quality": Ibid., 682.

41 "Melanctha Herbert was a": Ibid., 125.

41 "Rose," "black," "yellow," "white": Ibid., 124.

41 "Sometimes the thought of": Ibid., 125.

42 "regular": Ibid., 70.

42 "She did not belong": Ibid., 71.

42 "There was a time": Stein, *The Making of Americans*, 302.

42 "the cause of women": Stein, *Stein: Writings 1903–1932*, 743.

43 "*the linguistic sign is*": de Saussure, 67.

43 "construct something / Upon which": Eliot, *The Waste Land and Other Poems*, 67.

43 "execution is always individual": de Saussure, 13.

43 "build therefore your own": Emerson, 48.

44 "the classic is the": Williams, *Imaginations*, 356.

44 "I was something that": Cather, *Cather: Early Novels and Stories*, 724.

44 "rudeness . . . rests all upon": Williams, *In the American Grain*, 109.

45 "The historical sense compels": Eliot, *Selected Prose of T. S. Eliot*, 38.

45 "We have no books": Williams, *In the American Grain*, 109.

46 "one is forced on": Ibid., 220.

46 "walls . . . touch": Ibid., 157.

46 "parsimoniously . . . gave magnificently": Ibid., 108.

46 "sperm": Ibid., 58.

47 "It is *this* to": Ibid., 121.

47 "thick Indian blankets": Cather, *Cather: Later Novels*, 296.

47 "fragments of their desire": Cather, *Cather: Early Novels and Stories*, 567.

47 "holidays": Cather, *Cather: Later Novels*, 158.

48 "The difficulty was that": Ibid., 285.

48 "constantly refined tradition": Ibid., 299.

48 "could not present more": Ibid., 286.

48 "figura": Auerbach, 49.

48 "Live in the layers": Kunitz, 218.

48 "liminal landscape of changing": Kolodny, "Letting Go of Our Grand Obsessions," 9.

49 "And the silver of": Cather, *Cather: Later Novels*, 303.

49 "old warlike church": Ibid., 337.

49 "contagious diseases": Ibid., 352.

49 "a long tradition": Ibid., 332.

50 "repugnance . . . hospitable shelter": Ibid., 358.

50 "I have seen the": Ibid., 434.

50 "admitted its mistake": Ibid., 458.

50 "She exists wherever a": Glasgow, vi.

50 "without joy": Cather, *Cather: Later Novels*, 271.

50 "Something he knew he": Wharton, 1291.

50 "extra tasks": Freud, *The Standard Edition*, vol. 22, 117.

50 "a man's love and": Ibid., 134.

50 "A boy's mother . . . is": Ibid., 118.

51 "The petitioners are entitled": *Lawrence v. Texas*.

51 "We were reluctant to": Cather, *Cather: Later Novels*, 222.

51 "my friendship with Outland": Ibid., 133.

51 "He was standing in": Ibid., 459.

51 "It was the discipline": Ibid., 427.

51 "They have a great": Ibid., 431.

51 "celibacy": Ibid., 365.

52 "A life need not": Ibid., 432.

52 "What is lonely is": Bradley, 142.

52 "Just when I thought": Bishop, *Bishop: Poems, Prose, and Letters*, 155.

Chapter 4 • Performing Maleness

53 "*No end and no*": Hemingway, *In Our Time*, 21.

54 "hell": Ibid., 111.

54 "good place": Ibid., 139.

54 "not important": Ibid., 16.

54 "Already there was something": Ibid., 139.

55 "*Be a man my*": Ibid., 143.

55 "The Thing Left Out": Julian Smith, 135.

55 "about coming back from": Hemingway, *A Moveable Feast*, 76.

55 "In the morning the": Hemingway, *In Our Time*, 145.

55 "Max *please believe me*": Reynolds, *Hemingway: The American Homecoming*, 49.

56 "things": Hemingway, *In Our Time*, 17.

56 "At the lake shore": Ibid., 15.

56 "Nick did not watch": Ibid., 17.

56 "The German word 'unheimlich'": Freud, *On Creativity and the Unconscious*, 124.

56 "among its different shades": Ibid., 129.

57 "is a word the": Ibid., 131.

57 "the 'uncanny' is that": Ibid., 123–24.

57 "He did not feel": Hemingway, *In Our Time*, 155.

57 "This *unheimlich* place . . . however": Freud, *On Creativity and the Unconscious*, 152–53.

57 "interne": Hemingway, *In Our Time*, 17.

58 "the man who lived": Wolff, 97.

58 "In the early morning": Hemingway, *In Our Time*, 19.

59 "The real end . . . was": Hemingway, *A Moveable Feast*, 75.

59 "*goes without saying*": Barthes, 143.

59 "Do you believe in": Hemingway, *For Whom the Bell Tolls*, 250.

59 "divine events from the": Ibid., 252.

59 " 'Then,' Pilar went on": Ibid., 256.

60 "the dignity of movement": Hemingway, *Death in the Afternoon*, 192.

60 "earliest thing": Hemingway, *The Short Stories of Ernest Hemingway*, 365.

61 "I've been cleaning out": Ibid., 366.

61 "Do you remember . . . the": Hemingway, *For Whom the Bell Tolls*, 336.

62 "I do not care": Ibid., 337.

62 "retreats . . . holding attacks": Hemingway, *Selected Letters, 1917–1961*, 608.

62 "one that misused the": Hemingway, *For Whom the Bell Tolls*, 338.

63 "more a consequence of": Michaels, 96.

63 "the crime of death and birth": Yeats, 235.

64 "threshing around": Hemingway, *The Short Stories of Ernest Hemingway*, 335.

64 "My heart's broken": Ibid., 336.

64 "unsound on sex": Ibid., 490.

64 "whole matter": Ibid., 491.

64 "own education in those": Ibid., 491–92.

64 "direct sexual knowledge": Ibid., 490–91.

64 "What was it like": Ibid., 497.

65 "You'll lose it": Hemingway, *The Sun Also Rises*, 245.

65 "to do that business": Hemingway, *For Whom the Bell Tolls*, 469.

66 "the rest of the": Hemingway, *A Farewell to Arms*, 117.

66 "I am an old": Hemingway, *For Whom the Bell Tolls*, 16.

66 "nothing is done to": Ibid., 73.

66 "high plateau": Ibid., 467.

67 "I go with thee": Ibid., 463.

67 "Go, go . . . stand up": Ibid., 464.

67 "he could never be": Hurston, *Hurston: Novels & Stories*, 333.

Chapter 5 • *Colored Me*

68 "Hair—braided chestnut": Toomer, *Cane*, 27.

69 "*to-be-looked-at-ness*": Mulvey, 2186.

69 "No one ever saw": Toomer, *Cane*, 5.

69 "she feels my gaze": Ibid., 10.

69 "thereafter wavered in the": Ibid., 14.

69 "Wherever they looked, you'd": Ibid., 15.

70 "staring": Leroy Jones, 6.

70 "run your mind over": Ibid., 7.

70 "Through the bloody September": Faulkner, *Collected Stories of William Faulkner*, 169.

70 "Happen? What the hell": Ibid., 171–72.

70 "In a world ordered": Mulvey, 2186.

71 "Primeval Mitosis": Cleaver, 163.

71 "dynamic of history": Ibid., 164.

71 "Race fears are weapons": Ibid., 174–75.

71 "I will have sexual": Ibid., 153.

71 "sisters": Ibid., 189.

71 "the Ogre": Ibid., 19.

72 "She whispered in my": Jacobs, 31.

72 "patriarchal institution": Ibid., 62.

72 "reconciler": Toomer, *The Wayward and the Seeking*, 54.

72 "a spiritual fusion analogous": Ibid., 18.

72 "Suddenly he knew that": Toomer, *Cane*, 75.

72 "between those who elect": Emerson, 896.

73 "the most heterogeneous ideas": Eliot, *Selected Prose of T. S. Eliot*, 60.

73 "similitude in dissimilitude": Wordsworth, 460.

73 "forming new wholes": Eliot, *Selected Prose of T. S. Eliot*, 64.

73 "John's body is separate": Toomer, *Cane*, 50.

73 "The poet must become": Eliot, *Selected Prose of T. S. Eliot*, 65.

73 "an unmixed human race": Toomer, *The Wayward and the Seeking*, 121.

73 "I talk": Toomer, *Cane*, 114.
73 "sweetheart": Ibid., 81.
73 "I traced my development": Ibid., 46.
73 "I'd like to know": Ibid., 76.
74 "He is a candle": Ibid., 70.
74 "Art and Helen clot": Ibid., 77.
74 "I came back to": Ibid., 78.
75 "whitewashed": Ibid., 81.
76 "gaze": Ibid., 116.
76 "double consciousness": Emerson, 205.
76 "characteristics . . . emotional endowment": Locke, 19.
77 "there is little evidence": Ibid., 259.
77 "misunderstanding an attitude": Ibid., 255.
77 "history must restore what": Ibid., 231.
77 "fusion": Ibid., 206.
78 "humiliating": Hemenway, 183.
78 "racial health": Ibid., xii.
78 "tragedy of color": Ibid., 336.
78 "stand off": Hurston, *Hurston: Folklore, Memoirs, and Other Writings*, 9.
78 "a lot of hope": Hemenway, 3.
78 "the art people create": Ibid., 159.
79 "It did not do": Ibid., 215.
79 "I tried to embalm": Ibid., 231.
79 "the most convincing . . . novel": Jordan, 5.
79 "best thing": Morrison, *Beloved*, 273.
79 "makes": Hurston, *Hurston: Novels and Stories*, 311.
79 "Janie talked": Ibid., 180.
79 "love game": Ibid., 267.
79 "mine too": Ibid., 258.
79 "long side": Ibid., 283.
79 "They all leaned over": Ibid., 328.
79 "Phoeby's hungry listening helped": Ibid., 23.
79 "leaned above the page": Stevens, *Stevens: Collected Poetry & Prose*, 279.
79–80 "She had to go": Hurston, *Hurston: Novels and Stories*, 328.
80 "misunderstanding": Ibid., 329.
80 "A mood come alive": Ibid., 175.
80 "the family voice": Bishop, *Bishop: Poems, Prose, and Letters*, 113.
80 "mouf on things": Hurston, *Hurston: Novels and Stories*, 179.
80 "stop and say a": Ibid., 177.
80 "eager to feel and": Ibid., 180.
80 "envy": Ibid., 175.
80 "understandin'": Ibid., 180.
81 "that was the end": Ibid., 184.
81 "didn't know Ah wuzn't": Ibid., 181.
81 "Dat's you": Ibid., 182.

81 "chasm of misgiving and": Johnson, *Johnson: Writings*, 14.
81 "shadow": Du Bois, 363.
81 "big voice": Hurston, *Hurston: Novels and Stories*, 244.
81 "big arguments": Ibid., 284.
81 "It must have been": Ibid., 209.
81 "You need tellin' ": Ibid., 232.
82 "Too busy listening tuh": Ibid., 244.
82 "When you pull down": Ibid., 238.
82 "put jus' de right": Ibid., 221.
82 "nature . . . caution": Ibid., 227.
82 "to live by comparisons": Ibid., 332.
82 "She was stretched on": Ibid., 183.
83 "make myself wood": Alice Walker, *The Color Purple*, 23
83 "ebony chain of discourse": Gates, 256.
83 "I wishst I wuz": Chesnutt, *Chesnutt: Stories, Novels, & Essays*, 22.
83 "God happened to Mary": Austin, *Earth Horizon*, 51–52.
83 "in a tree forever": Glück, 13.
83 "tree": Morrison, *Beloved*, 15.
83 "With thinking we may": Thoreau, 429.
84 "absolute awareness of self": Cavell, 101.
84 "What *we* know as": Ibid., 105–56.
84 "a friend of my": Morrison, *Beloved*, 272.
84 "Ah reckon you wish": Hurston, *Hurston: Novels and Stories*, 304.
85 "flaws": Awkward, 38.
85 "They seemed to be": Hurston, *Hurston: Novels and Stories*, 305.
85 "beauty . . . has gradually grown": Thoreau, 360.

Chapter 6 • *The Rumor of Race*

86 "I just mean that": Warren, *Talking with Robert Penn Warren*, 138.
87 "a novelist, perhaps unconsciously": Steinbeck, *Steinbeck: A Life in Letters*, 553.
87 "best of all talking": Faulkner, *Faulkner: Novels 1942–1954*, 140.
87 "then he was twenty-one": Ibid., 187.
88 "rhetoric of retellings": Faulkner, *Sartoris*, "Afterword" by Lawrance Thompson, 310.
88 "As usual": Ibid., 19.
88 "Do I have to": Faulkner, *Faulkner: Novels 1926–1929*, 557.
88 "those who can, do": Faulkner, *Faulkner: Novels 1936–1940*, 474.
88 "*I have heard too*": Ibid., 171–72.
89 "Again. Sadder than was": Faulkner, *Faulkner: Novels 1926–1929*, 950.
89 "*Maybe nothing ever happens*": Faulkner, *Faulkner: Novels 1936–1940*, 216.
89 "brother seducer . . . brother avenger": Irwin, 37.
89 "born too late": Faulkner, *Faulkner: Novels 1936–1940*, 17.
89 "*deliberately withheld meaning*": Aiken, 48.
89 "impotent yet indomitable frustration": Faulkner, *Faulkner: Novels 1936–1940*, 5.

89 "But why?": Ibid., 9.
90 *"why God let us"*: Ibid., 8.
90 "If we shall suppose": Lincoln, *Lincoln: Speeches and Writings, 1859–1865*, 687.
90 "peculiar and powerful interest": Ibid., 686.
91 "overpassing": Faulkner, *Faulkner: Novels 1936–1940*, 261.
91 "deliberately withheld": Ibid., 218.
91 "none to ask her": Ibid., 104.
92 "the best way out": Frost, *The Poetry of Robert Frost*, 64.
92 "From a little after": Faulkner, *Faulkner: Novels 1936–1940*, 5.
92 "one true sentence": Hemingway, *A Moveable Feast*, 12.
92 "time is your misfortune": Faulkner, *Faulkner: Novels 1926–1929*, 956.
92 "will not go behind": Frost, *The Poetry of Robert Frost*, 34.
92 *"coffee-colored face"*: Faulkner, *Faulkner: Novels 1936–1940*, 113.
93 *"furious immobility"*: Ibid., 116.
93 *"eggshell shibboleth of caste"*: Ibid., 115.
93 "white, brittle and eggshell-thin": Ellison, *Shadow and Act*, 273.
93 *"There is something in"*: Faulkner, *Faulkner: Novels 1936–1940*, 11–12.
93 *"instrument"*: Ibid., 111.
94 "Out of quiet thunderclap": Ibid., 6.
94 "shot the fiance to": Ibid., 8.
94 "her husband and the": Ibid., 23.
95 *"I'm going to tech"*: Ibid., 154.
95 *"But let flesh touch with"*: Ibid., 115.
95 "adjunctive or incremental": Ibid., 199.
95 "His trouble was innocence": Ibid., 182.
95 "wanting not to know": Lee, 290.
96 "Rabble Crew": Takaki, 64.
96 "abominable mixture and spurious": Ibid., 67.
96 "sound Negro": Ibid., 68.
96 "nigger": Faulkner, *Faulkner: Novels 1936–1940*, 186.
96 "He had learned the": Ibid., 187.
97 "How it was the": Ibid., 192.
97 "to combat them you": Ibid., 197.
97 "repeat the past": F. Scott Fitzgerald, 116.
97 "to a certain starting": Ibid., 117.
98 "you re-read, tedious and intent": Faulkner, *Faulkner: Novels 1936–1940*, 83–84.
98 "It (the talking, the": Ibid., 17–18.
98 "Henry loved Bon": Ibid., 74.
98 "probation": Ibid., 80.
98 "they cannot marry because": Ibid., 242.
99 "I don't believe it": Ibid., 280.
99 "seen and touched parts": Ibid., 270.
99 "the pure and perfect incest": Ibid., 80.
99 "maybe the war would": Ibid., 282.
99 "Don't you know yet": Ibid., 283.

99 *"mother was part negro"*: Ibid., 292.

100 *"nigger . . . to sleep with"*: Ibid., 294.

101 "the great imaginative leap": Kartiganer, 98.

101 "It might have been": Faulkner, *Faulkner: Novels 1936–1940*, 250.

101 "Shreve ceased. That is": Ibid., 275.

101 "He ceased again. It": Ibid., 289.

102 *"So it's the miscegenation"*: Ibid., 293.

102 "Think of his heart": Ibid., 272.

103 *"a might-have-been"*: Ibid., 118.

103 "stick to the nicer": Stevens, *Stevens: Collected Poetry & Prose*, 291.

103 "truth . . . simple": Morrison, *Beloved*, 163.

Chapter 7 • *The Depression*

105 "No I don't like": Conrad, *Heart of Darkness*, 29.

105 "The American public does": Howells in Thomas, v.

105 "his unhappy life": Dreiser, *Dreiser: An American Tragedy*, 923.

105 "the beauty of the": Ibid., 924.

105 "Dreiser is widely regarded": Denby, 178.

106 "work itself resists representation": Denning, 244.

106 "there were three things": Austin, *Stories from the Country of Lost Borders*, 258.

106 "To work and to": Ibid., 262.

106 "himself above the type": Dreiser, *Dreiser: An American Tragedy*, 16.

106 "the manufacturing end of": Ibid., 210.

107 "the one really important": Ibid., 200.

107 "various processes": Ibid., 212.

107 "Oh I got up": Dugan, 82.

108 "And over all the": Dreiser, *Dreiser: An American Tragedy*, 271.

108 "the call . . . of sex": Ibid., 273.

108 "she might even be": Ibid., 120.

109 "It excited him too": F. Scott Fitzgerald, 156.

109 "Her voice is full": Ibid., 127.

109 "stinging sense of what": Dreiser, *Dreiser: An American Tragedy*, 251.

109 "'Happiness' is, after all": Didion, *Slouching towards Bethlehem*, 210.

109 "In your rocking chair": Dreiser, *Dreiser: Sister Carrie, Jennie Gerhardt, Twelve Men*, 173.

109 "his count of enchanted": F. Scott Fitzgerald, 98.

110 "He knew that when": Ibid., 117.

110 "Platonic conception": Ibid., 104.

110 "eventually he took Daisy": Ibid., 156.

110 "repeat the past": Ibid., 116.

110 "some idea of himself": Ibid., 117.

110 "So we beat on": Ibid., 189.

111 "Clyde had a soul": Dreiser, *Dreiser: An American Tragedy*, 193.

111 "You can get someone": Ibid., 482.

111 "cowering sense of what": Ibid., 506.

112 "I had just begun": Yezierska, *Bread Givers*, 1.

112 "fat from the soup": Ibid., 10.

112 "so busy working for": Ibid., 12.

112 "the problem of Father": Ibid., 296.

112 "The prayers of his daughters": Ibid., 9.

112 "silent aloofness": Ibid., 242.

112 "I stepped into the": Ibid., 151.

112 "This door was life": Ibid., 159.

112 "was the only immigrant": Drucker, vol. 2, 1689.

112–113 "to learn, to know": Yezierska, *Bread Givers*, 201.

113 "I want the knowledge": Ibid., 181.

113 "I had lived the": Ibid., 202.

113 "I had to give": Ibid., 208.

113 "It's from him": Ibid., 279.

113 "Mental Fight": Blake, 95.

113 "tyranny": Yezierska, *Bread Givers*, 295.

114 "If only such an": Dreiser, *Dreiser: An American Tragedy*, 507.

114 "It would have to": Ibid., 531.

114 "The blackness of this": Ibid., 546.

114 "the darkest and weakest": Ibid., 533.

114 "But you must choose": Ibid., 536.

114 "nor had he intentionally": Ibid., 683.

114 "an anguished state in": Denby, 184.

115 "false belief": Ozick, 395.

115 "Because their moods were": Dreiser, *Dreiser: An American Tragedy*, 271.

115 "Of the opinion of": Ibid., 426.

115 "What we did had": Hawthorne, 170.

116 "People with self-respect": Didion, *Slouching towards Bethlehem*, 145.

116 "It was a lie": Dreiser, *Dreiser: An American Tragedy*, 910.

116 "Clyde . . . was called upon": Ibid., 492.

117 "dejected": Ibid., 493.

117 "the most troubled and": Ibid., 492.

117 "How far he had": Ibid., 493.

117 "Oh, why had he": Ibid., 493–94.

117 "the world from which": Ibid., 494.

117 "I am part of": F. Scott Fitzgerald, 184.

117 "loss of some 104": Kennedy, 167.

118 "the most radical piece": Lichtenstein, *Walter Reuther*, 50.

118 "sole voice": Lichtenstein, *State of the Union*, 51.

118 "perhaps the New Deal's": Kennedy, 378.

119 "March whistled stinging snow": Di Donato, 11.

119 "fifteen chisel point intoned": Ibid., 17.

119 "pushing the job": Ibid., 25.

119 "sealing up the mute": Ibid., 26.

119 "The stone has fixed": Ibid., 68.

119 "father's trowel": Ibid., 95.

119 "He reached the trowel": Ibid., 96.

119 "in futile search of": Ibid., 273.

119 "all shall be shut": Ibid., 279.

120 *"lend a myth to"*: Crane, 34.

120 "sentence to stone": Di Donato, 189.

120 "The work his parents": Dreiser, *Dreiser: An American Tragedy*, 12.

120 "A mood of opposition": Farrell, 124.

120 "a mood of opposition": Dreiser, *Dreiser: An American Tragedy*, 113.

120 "For years he had": Mailer, *The Armies of the Night*, 117.

121 "'I was affected by": Ibid., 83.

121 "Has given my heart": Frost, *The Poetry of Robert Frost*, 221.

121 "our moods do not": Emerson, 406.

121 "vacillating, indefinite, uncertain mood": Dreiser, *Dreiser: An American Tragedy*, 551.

121 "I felt . . . I felt": Himes, *If He Hollers Let Him Go*, 102, 103, 110.

121 "I started drawing in": Ibid., 101.

121 "fragile": Ibid., 102.

121 "a dead absolute quiet": Ibid., 103.

121 "better": Ibid., 110.

121 "pressure": Ibid., 167.

121 "Race was a handicap": Ibid., 3.

122 "I noticed a closed": Ibid., 177.

122 "The irritation ironed quickly": Ibid., 48.

122 "room of being": William James: *William James: Writings 1902–1910*, 532.

122 "white folks sitting on": Himes, *If He Hollers Let Him Go*, 150.

122 "All of a sudden": Ibid., 9.

122 "Los Angeles hurt me": Himes, *The Quality of Hurt*, 73.

123 "would not employ Negroes": Blum, 183.

123 "discrimination in the employment": Ibid., 188.

123 "The air was so": Himes, *If He Hollers Let Him Go*, 20–21.

123 "advantage": Ibid., 25.

123 "I ain't gonna work": Ibid., 27.

123 "the size of it": Ibid., 38.

123 "Looks like this man": Ibid., 203.

124 "with a girl beside": Farrell, 311.

124 "elation": Ibid., 313.

124 "sorrow": Ibid., 314.

124 "low": Ibid., 320.

124 "too many feelings": Ibid., 380.

124 "Perhaps he had scorned": Ibid., 318.

124 "break in the stock": Ibid., 824.

124 "Both of these days": Ibid., 825.

124 "with a sweet caporal": Ibid., 5.

124 "St. Patrick's meant a": Ibid., 7.

125 "It meant Bertha trying": Ibid., 6.

125–126 "allowed me to shape": Rodriguez, *Hunger of Memory*, 72.

126 "he couldn't even say": Farrell, 90.

126 "heart's speech": Ibid., xxi.

126 "An American writer of": Ibid., x.

126 "the story of Studs": Ibid., xx.

126 "welcome as useful hands": Gleason, 28.

127 "Their lives were dedicated": Farrell, xx.

127 "America was a fine": Ibid., 734.

127 "negroes, Indians, Mexicans, Irish": Takaki, 149.

127 "I never thought": Farrell, 454.

128 "He felt a little": Ibid., 244.

128 "He wondered if the": Ibid., 499.

128 "passing the time": Ibid., 639.

128 "asking himself how many": Ibid., 743.

129 "ward of the state": Kennedy, 202.

129 "I have used a": Steinbeck, *Steinbeck: A Life in Letters*, 98.

129 "great shadows": Steinbeck, *Steinbeck: Novels and Stories 1932–1937*, 569.

129 "unshaded light": Ibid., 547.

129 "Something . . . grows out of": Ibid., 743.

129 "slow sullen movement": Steinbeck, *Steinbeck: A Life in Letters*, 98–99.

129 "great big soul": Steinbeck, *Steinbeck: The Grapes of Wrath and Other Writings 1936–1941*, 654.

129 "Been tryin' to start": Ibid., 619.

129 "I'll be all aroun'": Ibid., 656.

130 "The most precious thing": Steinbeck, *Steinbeck: A Life in Letters*, 410.

130 "from 'I' to 'we'": Steinbeck, *Steinbeck: The Grapes of Wrath and Other Writings 1936–1941*, 371.

130 "Ma looked to Tom": Ibid., 309.

130 "She let him have": Ibid., 324.

131 "the family unbroke": Ibid., 390.

131 "revolt": Ibid., 389.

131 "We'll go in the": Ibid., 584.

131 "Spen' all my time": Ibid., 659–60.

131 "Seems like our life's": Ibid., 660.

132 "Why have you got": Ibid., 553–54.

133 "Pa's voice took on": Ibid., 554.

134 "we was holy when": Ibid., 296.

Chapter 8 • *The Second World War*

135 "Thirty Years War": Churchill, iii.

135 "astray . . . in the never-endingness": Styron, 17–18.

135 "I would hate to": Vonnegut, 2.

136 "the psychological and emotional": Fussell, *Wartime*, ix.

136 "the real war is": Ibid., 290.

136 "Because the soldier's history": Fussell, *The Norton Book of Modern War*, 313.

136 "It was a savage": Fussell, *Wartime*, 132.

137 "the war of machines": Kennedy, 615.

138 "In our isolated world": Jeanne Wakatsuki Houston and James D. Houston, 194.

139 "For forty years, California": Starr, 36.

139 "alternate present": Dick, 97.

140 "there had not been": Sone, 157–58.

141 "succeeded in provoking a": Starr, 49.

141 "taste the silence": Mori, 25.

142 "it is her day": Ibid., 166.

142 "She is still alive": Ibid., 25.

142 "Long ago children, I": Ibid., 15.

142 "Turn back?": Ibid., 16.

142 "If there were no": Ibid., 21.

143 "Come back": Ibid., 20.

143 "It was all impersonal": Rhodes, 711.

144 "happiest moment": Vonnegut, 168.

144 "moonlike ruins": Ibid., 167.

144 "horse pitiers": Ibid., 169.

144 "When Billy saw the": Ibid., 170.

144 "look at any moment": Ibid., 23.

144 "in the present . . . above": Emerson, 270.

144 "know how the Universe": Vonnegut, 101.

144 "one moment follows another": Ibid., 23.

144 "natality": Arendt, 8.

144–145 "Billy, with his memories": Vonnegut, 131.

145 "Billy cried very little": Ibid., 170.

145 "The Poetry is in": Owen, 3.

145 "Pity the men who": Vonnegut, 171.

145 "*Listen*": Ibid., 19.

145 "listening": Ibid., 146.

145 "God is listening": Ibid., 147.

145 "powerful psychosomatic responses": Ibid., 152.

146 "skyline . . . intricate and voluptuous": Ibid., 129.

146 "dirty picture of the": Ibid., 35.

146 "to imagine what was": Ibid., 144.

146 "Billy thought hard about": Ibid., 152.

147 "assertion-through-structure": Pynchon, *Gravity's Rainbow*, 10.

147 "Keep cool, but care": Pynchon, *V*, 393.

147 "Slothrop sits on a": Pynchon, *Gravity's Rainbow*, 694.

147 "There is also the": Ibid., 738.

147 "the connectedness of the": Mendelson, 144.

147–148 "maybe for a little": Pynchon, *Gravity's Rainbow*, 648.

148 "they will meet face": Ibid., 564.

148 "Enzian on his motorcycle": Ibid., 734.

149 "the real Text": Ibid., 520.

149 "power sources": Ibid., 521.

149 "blèssed structures": Lowell, *Collected Poems*, 838.

149 "a war in progress": Pynchon, *Gravity's Rainbow*, 165.

149 "There doesn't exactly dawn": Ibid., 520.

150 "agreed not to develop": Blum, 132.

150 "crisis in rubber": Ibid., 226.

150 "And if it should prove": Pynchon, *Gravity's Rainbow*, 524–25.

150 "We have to look": Ibid., 521.

150 "I want to see": Ibid., 480.

151 "a scrap of newspaper": Ibid., 693.

151 "After such knowledge, what": Eliot, *The Waste Land and Other Poems*, 21–22.

152 "everybody": Pynchon, *Gravity's Rainbow*, 760.

152 "Long time ago": Silko, 133.

152 "listen: 'What I have": Ibid., 135.

153 "north of Cañoncito": Ibid., 133.

153 *"rocks with veins of"*: Ibid., 137.

153 "Take it back": Ibid., 138.

153 "I am of mixed-breed ancestry": Velie, 106.

153 "us to believe all": Ibid., 132.

154 "the white people's war": Ibid., 36.

154 "point of convergence": Ibid., 246.

154 "Trinity site": Ibid., 245.

154 "the yellow man": Springsteen.

154 "living on the Cebolleta": Silko, 243.

154 "streaked with powdery yellow": Ibid., 246.

154 "the struggle for the": Ibid., 232.

155 "we must go over": Olson, 114.

155 "tangled things": Silko, 7.

155 "the entanglement": Ibid., 69.

155 "wander back and forth": Ibid., 18.

155 "no word exists alone": Ibid., 35.

156 "at finally seeing the": Ibid., 246.

156 "The people nowadays have": Ibid., 126.

156 "It had been a": Ibid., 253.

157 "might be taken as": Kennedy, 656.

157 "that science found hidden": Rhodes, 783.

157 "confuses the messenger with": Ibid., 784.

157 "a kind of hole": Mary McCarthy, "Letter to the Editor," *Politics*, 367.

157 "change is possible because": Rhodes, 785.

158 "crushed by books": Hersey, 16.

158 "We are poor passing": Lowell, *Collected Poems*, 838.

158 "At exactly fifteen minutes": Hersey, 1.
158 "There were so many": Ibid., 25.
159 "matter-of-fact": Ibid., 225.
159 "the only two sorts": Ibid., 117.
159 "room . . . filled with": Ibid., 16.
159–160 "desk in splinters all": Ibid., 22.
160 "a talismanic quality": Ibid., 66.
160 "Statistical workers gathered what": Ibid., 80–81.
160 "succinct announcement": Ibid., 49.
160 "he were reading from": Ibid., 50.
160 "by incredible luck": Ibid., 30.
160 "Almost no one in": Ibid., 5–6.
161 "To Father Kleinsorge, an": Ibid., 36.
161 "At the time of": Ibid., 64–65.
161 "his 100 million subjects": Rhodes, 745.
161 "They listened to the": Hersey, 65.
161 "new and most": LaFeber, 255.
161 "had spoken in a": Oe Kenzaburo, viii.
161 "What a wonderful blessing": Hersey, 65.
161 "Hiroshima suffered considerable damage": Ibid., 49.
162 "At first, she was": Ibid., 8.
162 "Pity should begin at": Bishop, *Bishop: Poems, Prose, and Letters*, 153.

Chapter 9 • Civil Rights

163 "And Till was hung": Pound, 8.
163 "Louis Till, an African American": Ibid., 122.
164 "the movement was its": Payne, 256.
164 "to stand up and": Richard Wright, *Wright: Later Works*, 17.
164 "infected by waiting": Baldwin, *Baldwin: Collected Essays*, 69.
165 "One winter morning, in": *Wright: Later Works*, 3.
165 "hiding under a burning": Ibid., 5.
165 "I could not speak": Ibid., 192.
165 "I learned that I": Ibid., 10.
165 "cryptic tongue": Ibid., 7.
165 "coded meanings": Ibid., 24.
166 "racy and daring": Ibid., 25.
166 "Whenever I felt hunger": Ibid., 16.
166 "someday I would end": Ibid., 126.
166 "To starve in order": Ibid., 127.
166 "Do you remember": Hemingway, *A Moveable Feast*, 53.
166 "memory is hunger": Ibid., 57.
166 "Give the boy a": *Wright: Later Works*, 33.
167 "the years after": Ibid., 33–34.
167 "Leaving home": Ibid., 173.

167 "A quarter of a": Ibid., 34.
167 "had gone to the": Ibid., 35.
168 "I will acknowledge you": Faulkner, *Faulkner: Novels 1942–1954*, 988.
168 "the strange absence of": *Wright: Later Works*, 37.
168 "native with man": Ibid., 45.
168 "the external world of": Ibid., 413.
168 "But I want to": Ibid., 38.
168 "As she spoke, reality": Ibid., 39.
168 "the end of the tale": Ibid., 40.
168 "anus . . . When you get": Ibid., 41.
168 "uttered words": Ibid., 42.
169 "the first experience in": Ibid., 40.
169 "conception of life that": Ibid., 100.
169 "white folks": Ibid., 46.
169 "looks white": Ibid., 47.
169 "find out . . . For what": Ibid., 48.
169 "The words and actions": Ibid., 196.
169 "the baffling black print": Ibid., 22.
170 "fantasies . . . a part of": Ibid., 74.
170 "nobody . . . Then why did": Ibid., 167.
170 "Why had we not": Ibid., 55.
170 "this man was fighting": Ibid., 248.
170 "could never win": Ibid., 252.
170 "that the South too": Ibid., 415.
171 "a process of self-purification": King, 291.
171 "seemed to feel America": *Wright: Later Works*, 414.
171 "hog": Gaines, 8.
171 "watchful waiting": Ellison, *Shadow and Act*, 124.
171 "the convenient date and": Gaines, 158.
171 "I decided to wait": Ibid., 47.
171 "How long? Not long": King, 230.
171 "I'm sure it won't": Gaines, 44.
172 "I want a man": Ibid., 13.
172 "stand for her": Ibid., 167.
172 "we black men have": Ibid., 166–67.
172 "Tell Nannan I walked": Ibid., 254.
172 "creative tension": King, 291.
172 "One day the South": Ibid., 302.
172 "It don't matter": Gaines, 186.
172 "I was not there": Ibid., 3.
172 "couldn't . . . wasn't": Ibid., 5.
173 "rite something": Ibid., 226.
173 "You're one great teacher": Ibid., 254.
173 "I will not believe": Ibid., 251.
173 "you cannot change people's": Woodward, 163.

173 "difference made legal": King, 294.

174 " 'I saw the transformation": Gaines, 254.

174 *"fathered himself "*: Faulkner, *Faulkner: Novels 1942–1954*, 91.

174 "is unique among the": Baldwin, *Baldwin: Collected Essays*, 124.

174 "ancestryless": Faulkner, *Faulkner: Novels 1942–1954*, 81.

175 "like the side panels": Fabre, 120.

175 "earliest memories—which were": Baldwin, *Baldwin: Early Novels & Stories*, 9.

175 "You slap her again": Ibid., 46.

175 "You still a virgin": Alice Walker, *The Color Purple*, 81.

175 "it was men invented": Faulkner, *Faulkner: Novels 1926–1929*, 936.

176 "her bastard boy": Baldwin, *Baldwin: Early Novels & Stories*, 208.

176 "done got hisself killed": Ibid., 141.

176 "Gabriel . . . that Royal": Ibid., 142.

176 "happy": Ibid., 143.

176 "to own that poor": Ibid., 144.

177 "I been carrying this": Ibid., 206.

177 "in that letter": Ibid., 207.

177 "It's time you started": Ibid., 208.

177 "atonement . . . recognition of where": Bigsby, *Critical Essays on James Baldwin*, 128.

177 "Depthless alienation from oneself": Baldwin, *Baldwin: Collected Essays*, 89.

177 "He's my father, ain't": Baldwin, *Baldwin: Early Novels & Stories*, 23.

178 "I hear you": Ibid., 852.

178 "I listened to the": Ibid., 832.

178 "I hadn't wanted to": Ibid., 831.

178 "you realize *nobody's* listening": Ibid., 857.

178 "But there's no way": Ibid., 856.

178 *"everybody* tries not to": Ibid., 857.

178 "All I know about": Ibid., 861.

179 "tale . . . it always must": Ibid., 862.

179 "could help us to": Ibid., 863.

179 "bright and open": Ibid., 831.

179 "torment": Ibid., 861.

179 "all the way back": Ibid., 863.

179 "The dry, low, black": Ibid., 862.

179 "He didn't seem to": Ibid., 863–64.

179 "For me, then, as": Ibid., 864.

180 "Alienation": Baldwin, *Baldwin: Collected Essays*, 100.

180 "white Americans . . . he is": Ibid., 89.

180 "the darker forces in": Ibid., 128.

181 "the interracial drama": Ibid., 129.

181 "talk up there in the": Baldwin, *Baldwin: Early Novels & Stories*, 863.

181 "One of the things": Baldwin, *Baldwin: Collected Essays*, 129.

182 "I wrote 'The Child": Tate, 186–87.

182 "given herself": Alice Walker, *In Love and Trouble*, 39.
182 *"giver of life"*: Ibid., 35.
182 "with his whole heart": Ibid., 38.
182 "sullen barrier of distrust": Ibid., 40.
182 "deny the letter": Ibid., 44.
182 "burning with unnamable desire": Ibid., 45.
183 "She knows he has": Ibid., 35.
183 "words of the letter": Ibid., 42.
183 *"Father, judge, giver of"*: Ibid., 35.
183 "bursting . . . with delight": Alice Walker, *Meridian*, 43.
183 "She is his daughter": Alice Walker, *In Love and Trouble*, 44.
183 "in an attempt to": Genovese, 562.
183 "more anxious than before": Ibid., 563.
184 "Write": Alice Walker, *The Color Purple*, 19.
184 "pest control ads and": Branch, 738.
184 "chicken scratch handwriting": Ibid., 740.
184 "Freedom is never voluntarily": King, 292.
184 "wait . . . a tragic misconception of": Ibid., 296.
184 "myth of time": Ibid., 295.
184 "untimely": Ibid., 289.
184 "And the war came": Lincoln, *Lincoln: Speeches and Writings, 1859–1865*, 686.
185 "Now is the time": King, 296.
185 "determined legal and nonviolent": Ibid., 292.
185 "unavoidable impatience": Ibid., 293.
185 "more than 340 years": Ibid., 292.
185 "revolution would not begin": Alice Walker, *Meridian*, 188.
186 "I want to start": Clark, *Ready from Within*, 23.
186 "where blacks and whites": Ibid., 30.
186 "She wouldn't talk at": Ibid., 32.
186 "Three months after Rosa": Ibid., 34.
186 "I don't know why": Ibid., 37.
186 "good lesson": Ibid., 38.
186 "you couldn't get people": Ibid., 53.
186 "actually qualified to vote": Woodward, 141.
187 "I changed too": Clark, *Ready from Within*, 53.
187 "Students would talk about": Payne, 74.
187 "what they would like": Clark, *Ready from Within*, 63.
187 "sudden recognition": Clark, *Echo in My Soul*, 19–20.
187 "can teach their own": Payne, 167.
187 "his ability to listen": Ibid., 334.
187 "In the very act": Ibid., 331.
187 "We had to change": Clark, *Ready from Within*, 64.
187–188 "You're there . . . Can't you": Ibid., 77.
188 "that you develop leaders": Ibid., 78.
188 "told me this story": Ibid., 19.

188 "start my story": Ibid., 103.
188 "you can't force a": Shepard, *Seven Plays*, 132.
189 "I can only say": Faulkner, *Faulkner: Novels 1942–1954*, 438.
189 "My receipt": Ibid., 470.
189 "we do not quite": Emerson, 536.
189 "Give us the ballot!": Branch, 217.
189 "Jim Crow as a": Woodward, 186.
189 "Nothing is more unbearable": Baldwin, *Baldwin: Early Novels & Stories*, 222.

Chapter 10 • Love and Separateness

190 "Phinney's bones": *Welty: Stories, Essays, & Memoir*, 595.
190 "black man . . . men now": Ibid., 593.
190 "what men had done": Ibid., 594.
190 "sibylline epiphany": Schmidt, 223.
190 "I seed de beginnin": Faulkner, *Faulkner: Novels 1926–1929*, 1106.
190 "gaudiness": Stevens, *Letters of Wallace Stevens*, 263.
190 "That horror may evolve": Joyce Carol Oates, 71.
191 "vanished": Welty, *Welty: Stories, Essays, & Memoir*, 204.
191 "the true trouble that": Ibid., 217.
191 "and so it had": Ibid., 223.
191 "catch Hazel": Ibid., 224.
191 "It was the same": Ibid., 226.
191 "Runs": Updike, 309.
191 "That's just what I": Welty, *Welty: Stories, Essays, & Memoir*, 332.
191 "*the choice is never*": Bishop, *Bishop: Poems, Prose, and Letters*, 75.
192 "sheltered life": Welty, *Welty: Stories, Essays, & Memoir*, 948.
192 "shy": Ibid., 292.
192 "one day she would": Ibid., 293.
192 "any act, even a": Ibid., 294.
192 "But if innocence had": Ibid., 296.
192 "inviolate": Ibid., 297.
192 "the uncanny sensation of": Mary McCarthy, *The Groves of Academe*, 134.
192 "what was in another": Welty, *Welty: Stories, Essays, & Memoir*, 298.
192 "lump of amber": Ibid., 309.
192 "Suddenly it seemed to": Ibid., 239.
193 "a clear love is": Ibid., 303.
193 "he violated her and": Ibid., 304.
193 "For him it was": Ibid., 305.
193 "ecstasy": Ibid., 306.
193 "someone would have to": Ibid., 307.
193 "in to her": Ibid., 312.
193 "my responses to the": Ibid., 944.
194 "By some contemporary standards": Kreyling, 79.
194 "For all serious daring": Welty, *Welty: Stories, Essays, & Memoir*, 948.

194   "I came and found": Welty, *Welty: Complete Novels*, 87.
194   "wounded birds . . . too delicate": Didion, *The White Album*, 116.
194   "one secret is liable": Welty, *Welty: Stories, Essays, & Memoir*, 857.
194   "concealment": Ibid., 93.
194   "meant to solve his": Ibid., 232.
194   "mortal mystery": Ibid., 642.
194   "a fruitful marriage": Ibid., 155.
194   "There was nothing remote": Ibid., 156.
195   "fell upon her and": Ibid., 441.
195   "astride Easter": Ibid., 440.
195   "She took off her": Ibid., 530.
195   "the vanishing opacity of": Ibid., 531.
195   "Transformation": Ibid., 480.
195   "hated him": Ibid., 445.
195   "bottomless parts": Ibid., 435.
196   "sort of tie": Ibid., 943.
196   "visioning": Ibid., 326.
196   "a dedicated place": Ibid., 348.
196   "was the one who": Ibid., 354.
196   "violent": Ibid., 365.
196   "more than the ear": Ibid., 364.
196   *"danke schoen"*: Ibid., 368.
196   "Inasmuch as Miss Eckhart": Ibid., 946.
197   "You should marry now": Ibid., 536.
197   "Going away": Ibid., 542.
197   "There was a simple": Ibid., 519.
197   "Cutting off the Medusa's": Ibid., 554–55.
197   "opposites were close together": Ibid., 546.
198   "the hero and the": Ibid., 555.
198   "hate . . . love": Ibid., 556.
198   "hideous and the delectable": Ibid., 555.
198   "Then she and the": Ibid., 555–56.
198   "The way men looked": Clark, *Ready from Within*, 79.
198   "on women, not men": Payne, 92.
198   "involving violence": Ibid., 394.
199   "Success is registered": Ibid., 379.
199   "In those days": Clark, *Ready from Within*, 78.
199   "this country was built": Ibid., 82.
199   "the civil rights movement": Ibid., 83.
199   "dark, dirty": Petry, 10.
199   "tall long-legged body": Ibid., 27.
200   "eyes traveling over her": Ibid., 13.
200   "fat curve": Ibid., 10.
200   "a lot of other": Ibid., 19.
200   "always making passes at": Ibid., 40–41.

200 "he would have put": Ibid., 34.
200 "*Jim's carrying on with*": Ibid., 52.
200 "Month after month and": Ibid., 54.
200 "an improvement of sensual": Blake, 38.
200 "The women work": Petry, 388–89.
200 "Here on this street": Ibid., 65.
201 "she was angry with": Ibid., 428.
201 "was the person who": Ibid., 429.
201 "A lifetime of pent-up": Ibid., 430.
201 "Had she killed Boots": Ibid., 434.
201 "clear understanding": Ibid., 183.
202 "ever-narrowing space": Ibid., 323.
202 "sufficient space": Miller, 321.
202 "closing in": Petry, 160.
202 "The walls seemed to": Ibid., 79.
202 "circle, and she could": Ibid., 407.
202 "Streets like the one": Ibid., 323.
202 "final one needed to": Ibid., 423.
202 "both mother and father": Ibid., 407.
202 "wafted upward on a magic carpet": Larsen, 8.
203 "it all depended on where": Petry, 199.
203 "the problem that has": Friedan, 30.
203 "The chains that bind": Ibid., 31.
203 "she seemed to have": Mary McCarthy, *The Group*, 256.
203 "Until we can understand": Rich, *Arts of the Possible*, 11.
203 "At the heart of": Kreyling, 231.
204 "Where do babies come": Welty, *Welty: Stories, Essays, & Memoir*, 855.
204 "what she'd promised for": Ibid., 854.
204 "the mother and the": Ibid., 855.
204 "connected": Ibid., 857.
204 "Should daughters *forgive* mothers?": Ibid., 368–69.
204 "the one through whom": Rich, *Of Woman Born*, 235.
204 "I doubt that any": Welty, *Welty: Stories, Essays, & Memoir*, 856.
204 "My tongue swelled in": Allison, 297.
205 "When I married, no": Douglas, 142.
205 "sane world": Ibid., 143.
205 "unnatural": Ibid., 149.
205 "perfidy, the heartlessness, the": Ibid., 150.
205 "finder . . . I know why": Ibid., 144.
205 "there was no diary": Ibid., 151.
206 "imaginary conversation": Ibid., 160.
206 "The questions, the comments": Ibid., 163.
206 "*true lie*": Ibid., 46.
206 "The subordination of women": Spock and Rothenberg, 30.
206 "She would leave him": Mary McCarthy, *The Hounds of Summer*, 10.

207 "exchanged the prison of": Ibid., 22.

207 "In ten days the": Ibid., 28.

207 "like a letter written": Ibid., 10.

207 "Knowledge . . . composure": Mary McCarthy, *The Group*, 56.

207 "instructive voice": Ibid., 38.

207 "uncontrollable contractions": Ibid., 39.

207 "You *came*, Boston": Ibid., 42.

207 "a harsh desire to": Mary McCarthy, *The Groves of Academe*, 15.

207 "Get yourself a pessary": Mary McCarthy, *The Group*, 52.

207 "ancient fertility rites": Ibid., 35.

207 "The woman doctor would": Ibid., 57.

208 "the capacity to learn": Mary McCarthy, *On the Contrary*, 289.

208 "critical . . . creative": McKenzie, 76.

208 "it is very much": Wilde, 359.

208 *"There are several dubious"*: Mary McCarthy, *Memories of a Catholic Girlhood*, 47.

208 *"untruthfulness"*: Ibid., 11.

208 *"temptation to invent"*: Ibid., 3.

209 *"Nor is it only"*: Ibid., 25.

209 "the hastening of": Patterson, *Grand Expectations*, 712.

210 "lonely mind": Steinbeck, *Steinbeck: Novels 1942–1952*, 446.

210 "I think that because": Ibid., 320.

210 "mass method": Ibid., 445.

210 "exploring mind of the": Ibid., 446.

210 "a yearning that women": Friedan, 15.

210 "proportion of women attending": Ibid., 16.

211 "The feminine mystique says": Ibid., 43.

211 "Before her puberty her": Steinbeck, *Steinbeck: Novels 1942–1952*, 386.

211 "She never conformed in": Ibid., 387.

211 "no quickening of milk": Ibid., 503.

211 "clitoris": Ibid., 561.

212 "the single question of": Wood, 92.

212 "I believe there are": Steinbeck, *Steinbeck: Novels 1942–1952*, 385.

212 "Most children abhor difference": Ibid., 387.

212 "using her difference": Ibid., 386.

212 "When I said Cathy": Ibid., 503.

213 "how the innocence of": Whiting, 834.

213 "monstrous": Nabokov, 131.

213 "I remember that the": Steinbeck, *Steinbeck: Novels 1942–1952*, 309.

213 "mother": Ibid., 180.

213 "be your mother": Ibid., 677.

213 "poor little mother": Ibid., 562.

213 "the tattered meat of": Ibid., 692.

214 "You are the mother": Ibid., 652.

214 "My mother is dead": Ibid., 763.

214 "an excess of maternal": Morrison, *Conversations with Toni Morrison*, 252.

Chapter 11 • Revolt and Reaction

216 "to notice on entering": Mailer, *The Armies of the Night*, 29.
216 "to protest the war": Ibid., 31.
217 "At his best, he": Poirier, *The Performing Self*, 14.
217 "confess straight out to": Mailer, *The Armies of the Night*, 31.
217 "form is the record": Mailer, *Cannibals and Christians*, 371.
217 "To write an intimate": Mailer, *The Armies of the Night*, 53.
218 "bridge": Ibid., 54.
218 "no position": Ibid., 118.
218 "committing their future either": Ibid., 74.
218 "a point of stepping": Ibid., 129.
218 "and they set off": Ibid., 131.
219 "will be at once": Ibid., 47.
219 "technology land": Ibid., 15.
219 "the life of action": Mailer, *Advertisements for Myself*, 367.
219 "They had won the": Mailer, *Cannibals and Christians*, 17.
219 "where the small town": Mailer, *The Armies of the Night*, 153.
219 "Mailer walked to the": Ibid., 36.
219 "The only path of": Emerson, 1075.
219 "corporation land": Mailer, *The Armies of the Night*, 115.
219 "We are up, face": Ibid., 38.
219 "The clue to discovery": Ibid., 25.
219 "what was going to happen next": Ibid., 87–88.
220 "When you look back": conversation with Howard Norman, 2003.
220 "we will soon look": Lowell, *The Letters of Robert Lowell*, 479.
220 "the opportunity to grow": Mailer, *Advertisements for Myself*, 346.
221 "In any event, up": Mailer, *The Armies of the Night*, 113–14.
222 "cyclopean": Norris, *Norris: Novels and Essays*, 617.
223 "The two halves of": Mailer, *The Armies of the Night*, 157–58.
223 "real climax": Ibid., 268.
223 "We fathom you not": *American Poetry: The Nineteenth Century*, vol. 2, 870.
223 "Mailer finally came to": Mailer, *The Armies of the Night*, 171.
223 "anti-star": Ibid., 3.
223 "Now we may leave": Ibid., 4.
224 "an explanation of the": Ibid., 255.
224 "years of conformity and depression": Mailer, *Advertisements for Myself*, 338.
224 "a time of violence": Ibid., 356.
224 "Rites of passage": Mailer, *The Armies of the Night*, 280.
225 "A scale model of": Didion, *Slouching towards Bethlehem*, 101.
226 "bringing in bodies now": Ibid., 194.
226 "to cry": Ibid., 192.
226 "a sunken ship should": Ibid., 192–93.
226 "We were seeing the": Ibid., 122–23.
227 "Brock Vond's genius was": Pynchon, *Vineland*, 269.

227 "Nixonian Repression": Ibid., 71.

227 "The personnel changed, the": Ibid., 72.

228 "Don't kiss me, it": Didion, *Slouching towards Bethlehem*, 16.

228 "in the name of": Ibid., 18–19.

228 "This is a story": Ibid., 3.

228 "Here is a story": Ibid., 159.

228 "I want to tell": Ibid., 185.

228 "neurotically inarticulate": Ibid., xvi.

229 "Of course we would": Ibid., 162.

229 "Why do we like": Ibid., 71.

229 "a consumption ethic": Ibid., 210.

229 "city to torn city": Ibid., 84.

230 "simply *move on*": Didion, *The White Album*, 57.

230 "Five years old": Didion, *Slouching towards Bethlehem*, 127.

230 "at the bend in": Ibid., 30.

231 "nicer knowledge of": Stevens, *Stevens: Collected Poetry & Prose*, 291.

231 "What I want to tell": Didion, *Slouching towards Bethlehem*, 227.

231 "that it would cost": Ibid., 228.

231 "a psychiatrist's name and": Ibid., 237.

231 "It was three years": Ibid., 238.

231 "find meaning in the": Didion, *The Year of Magical Thinking*, 191.

231 "a January afternoon when": Ibid., 53.

231 "People with self-respect have": Didion, *Slouching towards Bethehem*, 145.

232 "Was anyone ever so": Ibid., 227.

232 "the promises we break": Ibid., 186.

232 "Pay or grow": Mailer, *Advertisements for Myself*, 350.

232 "anything worth having has": Didion, *Slouching towards Bethlehem*, 146.

232 "growing sense of apocalypse": Mailer, *The Armies of the Night*, 224.

233 "*Where are we headed?*": Didion, *The White Album*, 179.

233 "listening to a true": Ibid., 95.

233 "secret frontiersmen": Ibid., 98.

233 "an obscure grudge against": Ibid., 101.

Chapter 12 • *The Postmodern*

234 "as the substitute for": Jameson, xvi.

234 "predominant voices in postmodern": Mercer, 424.

235 "Where do I stand!": Shepard, *Seven Plays*, 245.

235 "the stark dignity of": Williams, *The William Carlos Williams Reader*, 16.

235 "Good hard rain": Shepard, *Seven Plays*, 132.

235 "*enters from stage left*": Ibid., 68–69.

235 "*continues talking*": Ibid., 73.

236 "*laboriously*": Ibid., 82.

236 "familiar": Ibid., 110.

236 "Me—to play": Beckett, 2.

236 "doesn't really notice the": Shepard, *Seven Plays*, 131.

236 "*completely unnoticed*": Ibid., 90.

236 "Do you recognize him?": Ibid., 92.

237 "DODGE, *watching T.V.*": Ibid., 100.

237 "give-and-take": Shepard, *The Unseen Hand and Other Plays*, 44.

237 "You gotta talk or": Shepard, *Seven Plays*, 78.

237 "Dyin' for attention": Ibid., 238.

237 "Are you listening": Ibid., 264.

238 "he was backed up": Ibid., 252.

238 "AUSTIN *makes more notes*": Ibid., 52.

238 "I'm back": Ibid., 53.

238 "I don't recognize any": Ibid., 122.

239 "The point isn't to": Shepard, *Rolling Thunder Logbook*, 100.

239 "she often counted things": Beattie, *Secrets and Surprises*, 36.

239 "A lot of things": Beattie, *Distortions*, 214.

239 "chaos of first names": Gelfant, 40.

239–240 "the overwhelming majority of": Pfeil, 98.

240 "professional-managerial class": Ehrenreich and Ehrenreich, 9.

240 "mimes the ceaseless process": Pfeil, 110.

240 "the not done": Pound, 100.

240–241 "the perfect little mother": Beattie, *Love Always*, 100.

241 "Forgetting a child": Beattie, *Where You'll Find Me*, 108.

241 "The bowl was perfect": Ibid., 105.

241 "the possibility of the": Ibid., 110.

241 "two-faced": Ibid., 112.

241 "the pleasure of new": Ibid., 107.

241 "responsible for her success": Ibid., 109.

241 "prospective buyers": Ibid., 105.

241–242 "There was something": Ibid., 109.

242 "It was meant to": Ibid., 107.

242 "I bought it for": Ibid., 111.

242 "motion": Ibid., 106.

242 "In its way, it": Ibid., 112.

242 "while ironies attracted her": Ibid., 109.

242 "It was both subtle": Ibid., 106.

243 "Time passed. Alone in": Ibid., 112.

244 "Could it be that": Ibid., 109.

244 "What she believed was": Ibid., 110.

244 "I like to mess": Carver, *Fires*, 188.

244 "a dialectic of expansion": Stull in Meyer, 123.

245 "There are about four": Carver, *Conversations with Raymond Carver*, 187.

245 "five published versions": Leypoldt, 323.

245 "My husband eats with": Carver, *What We Talk About When We Talk About Love*, 78.

245 "but he seems tired": Carver, *Where I'm Calling From*, 160.

245 "I WAS asleep when": Carver, *What We Talk About When We Talk About Love*, 82.

246 "ellipse": Carver, *Conversations with Raymond Carver*, 126.

246 "and then he told": Carver, *Where I'm Calling From*, 163.

246 "What is going on?": Carver, *What We Talk About When We Talk About Love*, 82.

246 "He and Gordon Johnson": Ibid., 80–81.

247 "beset manhood": Baym, 3.

248 "right in it, eyes": Carver, *What We Talk About When We Talk About Love*, 83.

248 "My head swims": Ibid., 87.

249 "I don't know who": Carver, *Where I'm Calling From*, 162.

249 "cut, rearranged, and rewrote": Leypoldt, 318.

249 "They're all different stories": Carver, *Conversations with Raymond Carver*, 125.

249 "deletion here leaves the": Meyer, 103.

249 "low postmodernism": Leypoldt, 323.

249 "airborne toxic event": DeLillo, 117.

250 "all plots tend to": Ibid., 26.

250 "To plot is to": Ibid., 291.

250 "postmodern": Ibid., 227.

250 "talking theory": Ibid., 290.

250 "THE MOST PHOTOGRAPHED BARN": Ibid., 12.

250 "Because we've read the": Ibid., 13.

250 "is part of the": Ibid., 15.

250 "condition": Ibid., 191.

250 "grubby": Ibid., 194.

251 "human condition": Ibid., 195.

251 "I'm afraid to die": Ibid., 196.

251 "this is not a": Ibid., 196.

251 "everyone fears death": Ibid., 197.

251 "guile": Ibid., 5.

251 "able to conceal such": Ibid., 197.

251 "in an embrace that": Ibid., 199.

251 "tentatively scheduled to die": Ibid., 202.

251 "The warm tears fell": Ibid., 203.

251 "all plots move in": Ibid., 199.

251 "to plot is to": Ibid., 292.

252 "One likes to practice": Stevens, *Stevens: Collected Poetry & Prose*, 104.

252 "language of waves and": DeLillo, 326.

252 "It is only from": Johnston, 134.

252 "nearly always rage, mostly": Ozick, 395.

253 "mortal creative work": Gaddis, *The Recognitions*, 33.

253 "where nothing was created": Ibid., 299.

253 "the origins of design": Ibid., 322.

253 "a few pages which": Borges, *Labyrinths*, 39.

253   "Cervantes' text and Menard's": Ibid., 42.
253–254   "becomes so total that": Ibid., xi–xii.
254   "been forging all this": Gaddis, *The Recognitions*, 385.
254   "to be taken seriously": Gaddis, *A Frolic of His Own*, 13.
254   "something worth doing": Ibid., 461.
254   "we do not, ever": Gaddis, *The Recognitions*, 556.
255   "I have to go": Ibid., 892.
255   "He learned only through": Ibid., 896.
255   "Spain is a land": Ibid., 769.
255   "moments of insight": Ashbery, 13.
255   "can legitimately lay claim": Johnston, 136.
255   "the greatest writer of": Moore, 6.
255   "Hey? You listening . . . ?": Gaddis, *JR*, 726.
256   "both speech and capital": Johnston, 148.
256   "fictions": Gaddis, *Carpenter's Gothic*, 157.
256   "serviceable": Ibid., 121.
256   "desperate": Ibid., 157.
256   "it is, we are": Raban, 168.
257   "resentment": Gaddis, *A Frolic of His Own*, 348.
257   "mere interruption": Ibid., 346.
257   "Don't interrupt me Christina": Ibid., 408.
257   "Words, words, words, that's": Ibid., 161.
257   "pattern of repeated interruptions": Ibid., 197.
257   "by the sense that": Ibid., 29.
258   "we have created what": Longinus, 139.
258   "that sudden familiarity, a": Gaddis, *The Recognitions*, 535.
258   "Orignlty not inventn bt": Gaddis, *A Frolic of His Own*, 123.

Chapter 13 • *Studying War*

259   "moral collapse": Keegan, 302.
259   "Easy victories, between equals": Ibid., 301.
259   "a mutual and sustained": Ibid., 302.
259   "We, in games, are": Hemingway, *Death in the Afternoon*, 22.
260   "flat degeneration": William James, *William James: Writings 1902–1910*, 1284.
260   "How I love it": *Patton* (1970), Twentieth-Century Fox.
260   "ought to enter more": William James, *William James: Writings 1902–1910*, 1288.
260   "no secrets about it": Herr, 228.
260   "complicated world": Hemingway, *In Our Time*, 71.
260   "boundary lines between our": Cormac McCarthy, *Blood Meridian*, 34.
260   "The war's over": Ibid., 29.
261   "in June of that": Ibid., 316.
261   "the spring of the": Cormac McCarthy, *Cities of the Plain*, 265.
261   "Was it always your": Cormac McCarthy, *Blood Meridian*, 328.

261 "They rode on": Ibid., 90.
262 "like cities adrift": Ibid., 4.
262 "like the head of": Ibid., 44.
262 "hard as iron": Ibid., 46.
262 "unguessed kinships": Ibid., 247.
262 "the bones of things": Ibid., 116.
262 "malign": Ibid., 330.
262 "that it was his": Ibid., 140.
262 "like enough the things": Ibid., 141.
263 "the mixture of his": Emerson, 8.
263 "A ritual includes the": Cormac McCarthy, *Blood Meridian*, 329.
263 "taste for mindless violence": Ibid., 3.
263 "We are to be": Ibid., 34.
263 "Whatever in creation exists": Ibid., 198.
263 "knowledge enormous": Keats, 355.
263 "specimens": Cormac McCarthy, *Blood Meridian*, 198.
263 "taking charge": Ibid., 199.
263 "a malign thing set": Ibid., 330.
263 "the primary illness of": Capote, 354.
263–264 "Burroughs's voice was the": Kashner, 176.
264 "indifference": Cormac McCarthy, *Blood Meridian*, 328.
264 "See the child": Ibid., 3.
264 "So you're the man": Ibid., 32.
264 "father of the man": Ibid., 3.
264 "All . . . watched the man": Ibid., 6.
264 "As the kid rode": Ibid., 14.
264 "They did not know": Ibid., 218.
264 "Hello called the judge": Ibid., 289.
264 "Then he spoke of": Ibid., 293.
265 "The judge on war": Ibid., 241.
265 "They organized games for": Keegan, 279.
265 "loves games": Cormac McCarthy, *Blood Meridian*, 147.
265 "the value of that": Ibid., 249.
265 "The priest does not": Ibid., 250.
266 "What do you want": Ibid., 278.
266 "I wonder if there's": Ibid., 317.
266 "I just got here": Ibid., 6.
266 "I better get on": Cormac McCarthy, *Cities of the Plain*, 285.
266 "one thing leads to": Ibid., 269.
266 "its shape was forced": Ibid., 285.
266 "narrative": Ibid., 283.
266 "arcature": Cormac McCarthy, *Blood Meridian*, 153.
266 "whang": Ibid., 159.
266 "ciborium": Ibid., 192.
266 "*Then they all move*": Ibid., 337.

266 "some corner of clemency": Ibid., 299.

266 "mess": Ibid., 19.

267 "She was just a": Ibid., 315.

267 "In the late winter": Ibid., 316.

267 "always on the way": Steinbeck, *Steinbeck: The Grapes of Wrath and Other Writings 1936–1941*, 344.

267 "He says that he": Cormac McCarthy, *Blood Meridian*, 335.

267 "bloody innocence": Herr, 20.

267 "Indian country": Ibid., 255.

268 "*There was a map*": Ibid., 3.

268 "And this also has": Conrad, *Heart of Darkness*, 5.

269 "I can't worry much": Greene, 187.

269 "if one is to": Ibid., 174.

269 "armored by his good": Ibid., 163.

269 "That was my first": Ibid., 37.

269 "game": Ibid., 112.

270 "Talk about impersonating an": Herr, 20.

270 "We covered each other": Ibid., 67.

270 "I wasn't a reporter": Ibid., 68.

270 "when we fell down": Ibid., 31.

270 "somewhere in there I": Ibid., 31–32.

271 "Put yourself in my": Ibid., 31.

271 "the Poetry is in": Owen, 31.

271 "Vegetable bliss": Stephen Wright, 3.

271 "safe for hypocrisy": Hasford, 59.

271 "bloody confetti": Heinemann, 26.

271 "more than the tongue": Ibid., 163.

271 "new, brand new, three": Herr, 167–68.

272 "something big": Conrad, *Heart of Darkness*, 46.

272 "I didn't go through": Herr, 256.

272 "when you finally started": Ibid., 19.

272 "even when the picture": Ibid., 18.

272 "I went there behind": Ibid., 20.

273 "mistake of thinking that": Ibid., 66.

273 "the other extreme of": Ibid., 6.

273 "Vietnam Vietnam Vietnam, we've": Ibid., 260.

273 "You fucking guys": Ibid., 205.

273 "the look that made": Ibid., 208.

273 "I realized that after": Ibid., 206.

273 "We were on the": Ibid., 110.

274 "A Marine came out": Ibid., 123.

274 "One of the Vietnamese": Ibid., 184–85.

275 "They all had a": Ibid., 29.

275 "Okay, man, you go": Ibid., 207.

275 "Patrol went up the": Ibid., 6.

275 "You couldn't find two": Ibid., 49–50.

277 "relations stop nowhere": Henry James, *The Novels and Tales of Henry James*, vol. 1, 213.

277 "in the destructive element": Conrad, *Lord Jim*, 208.

277 "Out on the street": Herr, 258.

277 "There was a brotherhood": Ibid., 223.

277 "Sean Flynn could look": Ibid., 8.

277 "Take the glamour out": Ibid., 248.

278 "among those who never": Ibid., 195.

278 "he didn't like to": Ibid., 196.

278 "special": Ibid., 194.

278 "I have pictures of": Ibid., 253–54.

278 "*There it is*": Ibid., 254.

279 "conventional journalism could no more": Ibid., 218.

279 "The news media were": Ibid., 214.

279 "top-secret history of": Sheehan, *The Pentagon Papers*, ix.

279 "died believing he had": Sheehan, *A Bright Shining Lie*, 790.

279 "one compelling figure": Ibid., 13.

Chapter 14 • *Slavery and Memory*

280 "We must disenthrall ourselves": Lincoln, *Lincoln: Speeches and Writings 1859–1865*, 415.

280 "To get to a": Morrison, *Beloved*, 162.

280 "walking man": Ibid., 46.

280 "The best thing": Ibid., 45.

280 "not even trying, he": Ibid., 17.

281 "And he would tolerate no": Ibid., 17–18.

281 "his story next to": Ibid., 273.

281 "This story is about": Morrison, *Conversations with Toni Morrison*, 254.

281 "an excess of maternal": Ibid., 252.

281 "clearing": Morrison, *Beloved*, 87.

281 "green breast of the": F. Scott Fitzgerald, 189.

281 "a few times out": Morrison, *Beloved*, 60.

281 "Right on her rib": Ibid., 61.

282 "A fully dressed woman": Ibid., 50.

282 "Tell me": Ibid., 76.

282 "To tell, to refine": Ibid., 99.

282 "As for Faulkner, I": Morrison, *Toni Morrison: Conversations*, 101.

283 "a baby's fury at": Morrison, *Beloved*, 5.

283 "that took me forever": Morrison, *Toni Morrison: Conversations*, 74.

283 "It (the talking, the": Faulkner, *Faulkner: Novels 1936–1940*, 17–18.

283 "the reader is thereby": Morrison, *The Bluest Eye*, 213.

284 "Denver was seeing it": Morrison, *Beloved*, 78.

284 "unuttered . . . three-way conversation": Morrison, *Conversations with Toni Morrison*, 249.

284 "When the four horsemen": Morrison, *Beloved*, 148.

285 "So long": Ibid., 165.

285 "Inside, two boys bled": Ibid., 149.

285 "had to ask": Ibid., 163.

285 "What she go and": Ibid., 150.

286 "that there was nothing": Ibid., 149.

286 "more important than what": Ibid., 164.

286 "Baby Suggs noticed who": Ibid., 151.

286 "crying baby": Ibid., 152.

286 "That ain't her mouth": Ibid., 154.

286 "with a picture drawing": Ibid., 155.

286 "He was going to": Ibid., 157.

287 "So Stamp Paid did": Ibid., 158.

288 "She was crawling already": Ibid., 159.

288 "she alone had the": Ibid., 78.

288 "She was spinning. Round": Ibid., 159.

288 "circling him the way": Ibid., 161.

288 "Did it work?": Ibid., 164.

289 "Perhaps it was the": Ibid., 161.

289 "Paul D did not": Ibid., 162.

289 "Sethe knew that the": Ibid., 163.

289 "needles": Ibid., 193.

290 "every writer *creates* his": Borges, *Labyrinths*, 201.

290 "The existing monuments form": Eliot, *Selected Prose of T. S. Eliot*, 38.

290 "Death is better than": Jacobs, 62.

291 "There is no place": Morrison, *Toni Morrison: Conversations*, 44.

291 "picture . . . rememory": Morrison, *Beloved*, 36.

Chapter 15 • Pa Not Pa

292 "You must not tell": Kingston, *The Woman Warrior*, 3.

292 "The next morning, when": Ibid., 5.

292 "imagining": Ibid., 8.

292 "Perhaps": Ibid., 6.

292 "Carrying the baby to": Ibid., 15.

292 "the real punishment was": Ibid., 16.

292 "to name the unspeakable": Ibid., 5.

292 "pages of paper to": Ibid., 16.

292 "in school": Ibid., 173.

292 "I have a terrible": Ibid., 165.

292 "pressed-duck voice": Ibid., 192.

293 "a woman's voice singing": Ibid., 209.

293 "she never listens": Kingston, *The Fifth Book of Peace*, 249.

293   "an instrument of grief": Stone, *A Flag for Sunrise*, 107.

293   "no higher listener . . . but": Kingston, *The Woman Warrior*, 204.

293   "The truth always kills": Warren, *All the King's Men*, 354.

293   "wished for a happy": Kingston, *China Men*, 17–18.

293   "the loveliest dainty of": Ibid., 18.

293   "Let's trade": Ibid., 19.

293   "Dead man": Ibid., 21.

293   "good leftover stuff": Tan, 323.

294   "Write": Alice Walker, *The Color Purple*, 19.

294   "Pa is not our": Ibid., 182.

294   "how alone woman is": Alice Walker, *In Search of Our Mother's Gardens*, 248.

294   "I am fourteen years": Alice Walker, *The Color Purple*, 1.

294   "First he put his": Ibid., 1–2.

294   "When I start to": Ibid., 3.

294   "Me on one side": Ellison, *Invisible Man*, 42.

295   "split wide open-alayin'": Ibid., 43.

295   "fat meat": Ibid., 45.

295   "scratchin' and tremblin' and": Ibid., 46.

295   "move without movin'": Ibid., 47.

295   "What I don't understand": Ibid., 51.

295   "Trueblood is mature": Lhamon, xxx.

296   "Dear God": Alice Walker, *The Color Purple*, 183.

296   "For the first time": Ibid., 184.

296   "Nettie in Africa, I": Ibid., 187.

297   "it is most fruitful": Awkward, 137.

297   "*show me how to*": Alice Walker, *The Color Purple*, v.

297   "I make myself wood": Ibid., 23.

297   "I wisht I wuz": Chesnutt, *Chesnutt: Stories, Novels, & Essays*, 22.

297   "access": Cleaver, 153.

297   "engage no allegiance to": Spillers in Pryse and Spillers, 198.

297   "between parents and children": Alice Walker, *In Search of Our Mother's Gardens*, 256.

297   "difference": Toomer, *Cane*, 75.

297   "purple like a bed": Ibid., 78.

297   "I think it pisses": Alice Walker, *The Color Purple*, 203.

298   "How can you be": Ibid., 267.

298   "*The Color Purple* makes clear": McDowell, 43.

298   "walk real slow up": Alice Walker, *The Color Purple*, 293.

299   "And I see they": Ibid., 295.

299   "avoid scaring . . . is to": Gallop, 71.

299   "unwanted daughters": Lee, 245.

300   "Come almost home": Ibid., 356.

300   "You, lieutenant, too much": Ibid., 266.

300   "true gesture": Shepard, *Seven Plays*, 251.

300   "innocence, wanting not to": Lee, 290.

300 "Most of us were": Ibid., 72.
301 "You are a Korean": Ibid., 234.
301 "I am a Japanese": Ibid., 95.
301 "strangely unmovable on the": Ibid., 74.
301 "I was disappointed, initially": Ibid., 204.
301 "writing personally is exposing": Roth, *The Human Stain*, 345.
302 "My heart flooded black": Lee, 104.
302 "it wasn't Sunny at": Ibid., 105.
302 "welcoming house": Ibid., 111.
302 "what can become of": Ibid., 145.
302 "new arrivals": Ibid., 159.
302 "female volunteers": Ibid., 161.
302 "You think you love": Ibid., 300.
302 "descended upon her": Ibid., 295.
303 "sentimental": Ibid., 266.
303 "I walked the rest": Ibid., 305.
304 "to take care of": Ibid., 338.
304 "past an acceptable point": Ibid., 342.
304 "I forced her to": Ibid., 283.
304 "What was done": Ibid., 344.
304 "What I saw that": Ibid., 345.
304 "I will fly a": Ibid., 356.
304 "How sad? Why? (Sad": Rodriguez, *Hunger of Memory*, 194.
305 "Americanization": Ibid., 27.
305 "While one suffers a": Ibid., 26.
305 "*Ahora*, speak to us": Ibid., 21.
306 "the family voice": Bishop, *Bishop: Poems, Prose, and Letters*, 150.
306 "I was a listening": Rodriguez, *Hunger of Memory*, 13.
306 "in a world magically": Ibid., 16.
306 "The voices of my": Ibid., 18.
306 "the language of joyful": Ibid., 16.
306 "Boys and girls, this": Ibid., 11.
306 "high sound of American": Ibid., 14.
306 "I do not recall": Ibid., 15.
306–307 "A more and more": Ibid., 22.
307 "remembering how she felt": Wordsworth, 214.
307 "At about the same": Rodriguez, *Hunger of Memory*, 25.
307 "be easy . . . to hear": Ibid., 28.
307 "the great themes": Ibid., 32.
307 "the message of intimacy": Ibid., 31.
307 "sentence-sound": Frost, *The Selected Letters of Robert Frost*, 111.
307 "unheard": Keats, 372.
307 "must finally pass": Rodriguez, *Hunger of Memory*, 39.
308 "Dark-skinned. To be": Ibid., 3.
308 "Does anybody know what": Rodriguez, *Brown*, 38.

308 "I have taken Caliban's": Rodriguez, *Hunger of Memory*, 3.
308 "*Then* nostalgia began": Ibid., 71.
308 "early relief, this return": Ibid., 72.
309 "hate": Rodriguez, *Brown*, 195.
309 "The reason I am": Ibid., 203.
309 "particular": Ibid., 12.
309 "two women and a": Ibid., 1.
309 "colloquy is broken": Ibid., 2.
309 "*These women are but*": Ibid., 3.
309 "White America's wettest perdition": Ibid., 107.
309 "relegated to the obligatory": Rodriguez, *Days of Obligation*, 3.
309 "stunned remnant": Ibid., 4.
309 "You're not Indian, you're": Ibid., 5.
310 "stag version": Ibid., 8.
310 "an Indian": Ibid., 22.
310 "Willing to marry, to": Ibid., 24.
310 "initiated the task of": Ibid., 25.
310 "It is *this* to": Williams, *In the American Grain*, 121.
310 "the profoundest experience life": Paz, 202.
310 "a color produced by": Rodriguez, *Brown*, xi.
310 "making": Ibid., 38.
310 "mosaic . . . unerotic": Ibid., 63.
310 "there is no border": Ibid., 122.
310 "This undermining brown motif": Ibid., 133.
310 "I listen to the": Ibid., 229.
310 "I was born gay": Ibid., 224.
310 "it takes a good": Rodriguez, "Violating the Boundaries," 446.
311 "brunch": Rodriguez, *Hunger of Memory*, 110.
311 "at Stanford, it's true": Ibid., 130.

Chapter 16 • *After Innocence*

312 "an imitation of autobiography": Shostak, 210.
312 "if this book was": Roth, *The Facts*, 8.
313 "the vernacular": Roth, *Patrimony*, 181.
313 "I looked at his": Ibid., 177.
313 "I beshat myself": Ibid., 173.
313 "Where his shit lay": Ibid., 174.
314 "I couldn't have asked": Ibid., 175.
314 "Ever since my father": Ibid., 25–26.
314 "(Don't talk to anyone": Ibid., 37.
314 "utterly satisfying": Ibid., 152.
314 "How clean the sun": Stevens, *Stevens: Collected Poetry & Prose*, 329.
314 "So *that* was the": Roth, *Patrimony*, 176.
314 "figure": Ibid., 237.

315 "battle-gray boat": Ibid., 235.

315 "my father *was* the": Ibid., 236.

315 "plaintive metaphor and poeticized": Ibid., 237.

315 "could not stand to": Ibid., 33.

315 "just look at how": Roth, *The Facts*, 167–68.

315 "there is no mother": Ibid., 168.

315 "One secret is liable": Welty, *Welty: Stories, Essays, & Memoir*, 857.

316 "So": Roth, *Patrimony*, 65.

316 "burying my mother in": Ibid., 30.

316 "right alongside the cemetery": Ibid., 19.

316 "unable to continue on": Ibid., 20.

316 "at a cemetery you": Ibid., 21.

316 "*narratively* right": Ibid., 74.

316 "I didn't expect to": Ibid., 20.

316 "Mommy, Mommy, where are": Ibid., 50.

317 "I sat on the": Ibid., 176.

317 "Philip is like a": Ibid., 181.

317 "giving suck to my": Ibid., 226.

317 "He got a lot": Ibid., 126.

318 "That happened to me": Ibid., 178.

318 "religious bias": Ibid., 183.

318 "against alleged religious discrimination": Ibid., 185.

318 "innocence": Ibid., 184.

318 "there are just a": Ibid., 187.

319 "everything that happens everywhere": Roth, *The Plot Against America*, 180.

319 "wrong turn": Ibid., 57.

319 "We had driven right": Ibid., 58.

319 "the historical perspective of": Roth, *Operation Shylock*, 84.

319 "to be innocent of": Roth, *The Counterlife*, 318.

319 "*simple and most ordinary*": Roth, *American Pastoral*, 31.

320 "the father was the": Ibid., 80.

320 "Swedian innocence": Ibid., 4.

320 "some failure of his": Ibid., 88.

320 "the inexplicable": Ibid., 266.

320 "I am thinking of": Ibid., 88.

320 "a single transgression": Ibid., 89.

320 "anything more I wanted": Ibid., 74.

320 "To the honeysweet strains": Ibid., 89.

321 "stammering mouth": Ibid., 91.

321 "obsessively searching for the": Ibid., 92.

321 "You can't explain away": Ibid., 251.

321 "killing the sixties, turning": Morrison, *What Moves at the Margin*, 175–76.

322 "opacity": Roth, *American Pastoral*, 77.

322 "the power by which": Kermode, 144.

322 "And what is wrong": Roth, *American Pastoral*, 423.

322 "What's made Merry Merry?": Ibid., 137.
322 "the handiest empty-headed idea": Ibid., 241.
323 "acting the role of": Ibid., 379.
323 "I was wrong": Ibid., 21.
323 "Out of what context": Ibid., 44.
323 "American berserk": Ibid., 86.
323 "wondered if it wasn't": Ibid., 179.
323 "you couldn't use standard": Herr, 49.
323 "normal": Roth, *American Pastoral*, 180.
324 "drowning . . . in inadequate explanations": Ibid., 151.
324 "Searching for an explanation": Ibid., 152.
324 "To let your hero's": Ibid., 88.
324 "creative remove": Roth, *The Human Stain*, 19.
324 "*had* to have": Ibid., 337.
324 "What would you think": Ibid., 341.
324 "a model Negro family": Ibid., 86.
324–325 "He has a secret": Ibid., 212.
325 "some three months later": Ibid., 213.
325 "innocence": Ibid., 136.
325 "he was Jewish": Ibid., 130.
325 "Do they exist or": Ibid., 6.
325 "I could tell she": Ibid., 316.
325 "son of God": F. Scott Fitzgerald, 104.
326 "all . . . to be free": Roth, *The Human Stain*, 126.
326 "arbitrary": Ibid., 120.
326 "rigidly unalterable": Ibid., 121.
326 "Everything looks permanent until": Emerson, 404.
326 "ecstasy of sanctimony": Roth, *The Human Stain*, 2.
326 "a president's penis": Ibid., 3.
326 "If you haven't lived": Ibid., 2.
326 "Bill Clinton's secret": Ibid., 3.
327 "murder weapon": Ibid., 344.
327 "an auger": Ibid., 346.
327 "It's a clean place": Ibid., 347.
327 "As long as I": Ibid., 348.
327 "a secret of his": Ibid., 352.
327 "But the government'll never": Ibid., 353.
327 "a colored girl at": Ibid., 354.
327 "how it was going": Ibid., 355.
327 "secret spot": Ibid., 359.
327 "It's safe with me": Ibid., 360.
327 "Just facing him, I": Ibid., 361.
327 "I was going to": Ibid., 360.
328 "good place": Hemingway, *In Our Time*, 139.
328 "new world": F. Scott Fitzgerald, 189.

328 "secret place": Roth, *The Human Stain*, 360.

328 "plenty of days coming": Hemingway, *In Our Time*, 156.

328 "behind him": F. Scott Fitzgerald, 189.

328 "waking up in the": Roth, *The Human Stain*, 355.

328 "completely bested": Ibid., 359.

329 "The culture of the": Frye, 346.

329 "If you tasted it": Bishop, *Bishop: Poems, Prose, and Letters*, 52.

A Personal Note

332–333 "read ALL of somebody": Bishop, *One Art*, 596.

334 "no white man could": Faulkner, *Faulkner: Novels 1942–1954*, 102.

Library of America editions have been used, in most cases, as the authoritative text.

Aaron, Daniel. *The Unwritten War: American Writers and the Civil War.* Madison: Univ. of Wisconsin Press, 1987.

Aiken, Conrad. "William Faulkner: The Novel as Form." In *Faulkner: A Collection of Critical Essays (Twentieth-Century Views).* Englewood Cliffs, NJ: Prentice Hall, 1966.

Allison, Dorothy. *Bastard Out of Carolina.* New York: Plume, 1996.

Apocalypse Now (film). United Artists. 1979.

Arendt, Hannah. *The Human Condition.* Chicago: Univ. of Chicago Press, 1958.

Ashbery, John. *The Double Dream of Spring.* New York: Dutton, 1970.

Auerbach, Eric. *Mimesis: The Representation of Reality in Western Literature.* Princeton: Princeton Univ. Press, 1953.

Austin, Mary. *Earth Horizon.* Boston: Houghton Mifflin, 1932.

———. *Experiences Facing Death.* Indianapolis: Bobbs-Merrill, 1931.

———. *The Land of Little Rain* (1903). In *Stories from the Country of Lost Borders,* ed. Marjorie Pryse. New Brunswick: Rutgers Univ. Press, 1987.

———. *Lost Borders* (1909). In *Stories.*

Awkward, Michael. *Inspiriting Influences: Tradition, Revision, and Afro-American Women's Novels.* New York: Columbia Univ. Press, 1989.

Baker, Houston. *Modernism and the Harlem Renaissance.* Chicago: Univ. of Chicago Press, 1987.

Baldwin, James. *Giovanni's Room* (1956). In *Baldwin: Early Novels & Stories.* New York: Library of America, 1998.

———. *Go Tell It on the Mountain* (1953). In *Baldwin: Early Novels & Stories.*

———. *Notes of a Native Son* (1955). In *Baldwin: Collected Essays.* New York: Library of America, 1998.

———. "Sonny's Blues" (1957). In *Baldwin: Early Novels & Stories.*

Band of Brothers (television series). HBO. 2001.

Baraka, Amiri. *Dutchman and the Slave: Two Plays.* New York: Harper Perennial, 1971.

Barth, John. "The Literature of Exhaustion." In *The Atlantic,* 220.2, August 1967.

Barthes, Roland. *Mythologies.* New York: Farrar, Straus & Giroux, 1972.

Baym, Nina. *Feminism and American Literary History*. New Brunswick: Rutgers Univ. Press, 1992.

Beattie, Ann. *The Burning House*. New York: Random House, 1982.

———. *Chilly Scenes of Winter*. New York: Doubleday, 1976.

———. *Distortions*. New York: Doubleday, 1976.

———. *Falling in Place*. New York: Random House, 1980.

———. *Love Always*. New York: Random House, 1985.

———. *Picturing Will*. New York: Random House, 1989.

———. *Secrets and Surprises*. New York: Random House, 1978.

———. *Where You'll Find Me*. New York: Simon & Schuster, 1986.

Beckett, Samuel. *Endgame* (1957). New York: Grove Press, 1958.

Benjamin, Walter. "The Work of Art in the Age of Mechanical Reproduction" (1936). In *Illuminations: Essays and Reflections*. New York: Schocken, 1969.

The Best Years of Our Lives (film). Samuel Goldwyn. 1946.

Bigsby, C. W. E. "The Divided Mind of James Baldwin." In *Critical Essays on James Baldwin*, ed. Fred. L. Standley and Nancy V. Burt. Boston: G. K. Hall, 1988.

———. *Modern American Drama, 1945–2000*. New York: Cambridge Univ. Press, 2001.

The Birth of a Nation (film). David W. Griffith Corp. 1915.

Bishop, Elizabeth. *Bishop: Poems, Prose, and Letters*. New York: Library of America, 2008.

———. *One Art: The Letters of Elizabeth Bishop*, ed. Robert Giroux. New York: Farrar, Straus & Giroux, 1995.

Biskind, Peter. *Seeing Is Believing: How Hollywood Taught Us to Stop Worrying and Love the Fifties*. New York: Pantheon, 1983.

Blake, William. *The Poetry and Prose of William Blake*, ed. David V. Erdman. Garden City, NY: Doubleday, 1970.

Bloom, Harold. *The Anxiety of Influence*. New York: Oxford Univ. Press, 1973.

Blum, John Morton. *V Was for Victory: Politics and American Culture during World War II*. New York: Harcourt Brace Jovanovich, 1976.

Borges, Jorge Luis. *Labyrinths*. New York: New Directions, 1964.

———. *Selected Non-Fictions*, ed. Eliot Weinberger. New York: Penguin, 1999.

Bradley, A. C. "Wordsworth." In *Oxford Lectures on Poetry*. Bloomington: Indiana Univ. Press, 1961.

Branch, Taylor. *Parting the Waters: America in the King Years, 1954–63*. New York: Simon and Schuster, 1988.

Brandeis, Louis D. *Other People's Money and How the Bankers Use It* (1914). New York: Harper & Row, 1967.

Brown, Norman O. *Love's Body* (1966). Berkeley: Univ. of California Press, 1990.

Brown, William Wells. *Clotel; or, The President's Daughter* (1853). New York: Penguin, 2003.

Brown v. Board of Education of Topeka (Supreme Court Case). 1954.

Capote, Truman. *In Cold Blood*. New York: Random House, 1965.

Carver, Raymond. *Cathedral*. New York: Knopf, 1983.

———. *Conversations with Raymond Carver*, ed. William L. Stull and Marshall Bruce Gentry. Oxford: Univ. Press of Mississippi, 1990.

———. *Fires: Essays, Poems, Stories.* New York: Vintage, 1983.

———. *Furious Seasons.* Santa Barbara: Capra Press, 1977.

———. *What We Talk About When We Talk About Love.* New York: Knopf, 1981.

———. *Where I'm Calling From: Selected Stories.* New York: Vintage, 1988.

———. *Will You Please Be Quiet, Please?* New York: McGraw-Hill, 1976.

Cather, Willa. *Death Comes for the Archbishop* (1927). In *Cather: Later Novels.* New York: Library of America, 1990.

———. *My Ántonia* (1918). In *Cather: Early Novels and Stories.* New York: Library of America, 1986.

———. *The Professor's House* (1925). In *Cather: Later Novels.*

———. *The Song of the Lark* (1915). In *Cather: Early Novels and Stories.*

Cavell, Stanley. *The Senses of Walden.* New York: Viking, 1974.

Chambers, Mary E. Letter to the Visalia *Delta* in "The Struggle of the Mussel Slough Settlers for Their Homes!" Visalia, CA: Delta Printing Establishment, 1880.

Chesnutt, Charles. *The Colonel's Dream* (1905). In *Chesnutt: Stories, Novels, & Essays.* New York: Library of America, 2002.

———. *The Conjure Woman* (1899). In *Chesnutt: Stories, Novels, & Essays.*

———. *The House Behind the Cedars* (1900). In *Chesnutt: Stories, Novels, & Essays.*

———. *The House Behind the Cedars*, ed. William C. Andrews. Athens: Univ. of Georgia Press, 2000.

———. *The Marrow of Tradition* (1901). In *Chesnutt: Stories, Novels, & Essays.*

Chopin, Kate. *The Awakening* (1899). Boston: St. Martin's, 1993.

Churchill, Winston. *The Gathering Storm.* Boston: Houghton Mifflin, 1948.

Clark, Septima. *Echo in My Soul.* New York. E. P. Dutton, 1962.

———. *Ready from Within.* Trenton, NJ: Africa World Press, 1986.

Cleaver, Eldridge. *Soul on Ice.* New York: McGraw Hill, 1968.

Clemens, Samuel. *Adventures of Huckleberry Finn* (1884). Norton Critical Edition. New York: W. W. Norton, 1999.

Coleridge, S. T. C. *The Literary Remains of Samuel Taylor Coleridge.* Vol. 2, ed. Henry Nelson Coleridge. London: Pickering, 1836–39.

Conrad, Joseph. *Heart of Darkness* (1902). New York: W. W. Norton, 1973.

———. *Lord Jim* (1900), ed. Cedric Watts. Peterborough, ON: Broadview Press, 2001.

———. *The Nigger of the 'Narcissus.'* (1897). In *The Nigger of the 'Narcissus' and Other Stories.* New York: Penguin, 2007.

Cott, Nancy F. *No Small Courage: A History of Women in the United States.* New York: Oxford Univ. Press, 2000.

Crane, Hart. *Complete Poems & Selected Letters.* New York: Library of America, 2006.

Dear, I. C. D., and M. R. D. Foot, eds. *The Oxford Companion to World War II.* New York: Oxford Univ. Press, 1995.

DeLillo, Don. *White Noise.* New York: Penguin, 1985.

Denby, David. "The Cost of Desire: Theodore Dreiser's 'An American Tragedy.'" In *The New Yorker,* April 21 and 28, 2003.

Denning, Michael. *The Cultural Front: The Laboring of American Culture in the Twentieth Century.* New York: Verso, 1997.

de Saussure, Ferdinand. *Course in General Linguistics*, ed. Charles Bally and Albert

Sechehaye, in collaboration with Albert Riedlinger; trans. Wade Baskin. New York: McGraw-Hill, 1966.

Dick, Philip K. *The Man in the High Castle* (1962). In *Dick: Four Novels of the 1960s*. New York: Library of America, 2007.

Dickinson, Emily. *American Poetry: The Nineteenth Century*. Vol. 2. New York: Library of America, 1993.

Didion, Joan. *Slouching towards Bethlehem*. New York: Farrar, Straus & Giroux, 1968.

———. *The White Album*. New York: Simon and Schuster, 1979.

———. *The Year of Magical Thinking*. New York: Random House, 2005.

Di Donato, Pietro. *Christ in Concrete*. New York: Bobbs-Merrill, 1937.

Dos Passos, John. *Manhattan Transfer* (1925). Boston: Houghton Mifflin, 2003.

———. *U. S. A.* (1936). In *Dos Passos: U. S. A., The 42nd Parallel, 1919, The Big Money*. New York: Library of America, 1996.

Douglas, Ellen. *A Lifetime Burning* (1982). Baton Rouge: LSU Press, 1995.

Douglass, Frederick. *Douglass: Autobiographies*. New York: Library of America, 1994.

Dreiser, Theodore. *An American Tragedy* (1925). In *Dreiser: An American Tragedy*. New York: Library of America, 2003.

———. *Sister Carrie* (1900). In *Dreiser: Sister Carrie, Jennie Gerhardt, Twelve Men*. New York: Library of America, 1987.

Drucker, Sally Ann. Introduction to "Anzia Yesierska." In *The Heath Anthology of American Literature*. Vol. 2. Lexington, MA: D. C. Heath & Co., 1990.

Du Bois. W. E. B. *The Souls of Black Folk* (1903). In *Du Bois: Writings*. New York: Library of America, 1985.

Dugan, Alan. *Poems Seven: New and Complete Poetry*. New York: Seven Stories Press, 2003.

DuPlessis, Rachel Blau. *Writing beyond the Ending: Narrative Strategies of Twentieth-Century Women Writers*. Bloomington: Indiana Univ. Press, 1985.

Eaton, Edith Maud. *Mrs. Spring Fragrance and Other Writings*, ed. Amy Ling and Annette White-Parks. Urbana: Univ. of Illinois Press, 1995.

Ehrenreich, Barbara and John. "The Professional-Managerial Class." In *Between Labor and Capital*, ed. Pat Walker. Boston: South End Press, 1979.

Eliot, T. S. *Selected Prose of T. S. Eliot*, ed. Frank Kermode. New York: Harvest Books, 1975.

———. *The Waste Land and Other Poems*, ed. Helen Vendler. New York: Penguin, 1998.

Ellison, Ralph. *Invisible Man*. New York: Random House, 1952.

———. *Shadow and Act*. New York: Random House, 1964.

Emerson, Ralph Waldo. *Emerson: Essays and Lectures*. New York: Library of America, 1983.

Equiano, Oluadah. *The Interesting Narrative and Other Writings*. New York: Penguin, 2003.

Erickson, Erik, and Neil J. Smelser. *Themes of Work and Love in Adulthood*. Cambridge, MA: Harvard Univ. Press, 1980.

Fabre, Michel. "Fathers and Sons in James Baldwin's *Go Tell It on the Mountain*." In

James Baldwin: A Collection of Critical Essays. Englewood Cliffs, NJ: Prentice Hall, 1974.

Farrell, James T. *Studs Lonigan.* Urbana: Univ. of Illinois Press, 1993.

Faulkner, William. *Absalom, Absalom!* (1936). In *Faulkner: Novels 1936–1940.* New York: Library of America, 1990.

———. *Collected Stories of William Faulkner.* New York: Random House, 1950.

———. *A Fable* (1954). In *Faulkner: Novels 1942–1954.* New York: Library of America, 1994.

———. *Flags in the Dust* (1973). In *Faulkner: Novels 1926–1929.* New York: Library of America, 2006.

———. *Go Down, Moses* (1942). In *Faulkner: Novels 1942–1954.*

———. *Intruder in the Dust* (1948). In *Faulkner: Novels 1942–1954.*

———. *Light in August* (1932). In *Faulkner: Novels 1930–1935.* New York: Library of America, 1985.

———. *Sartoris* (1929). New York: Signet-Harcourt Brace, 1964.

———. *The Sound and the Fury* (1929). In *Faulkner: Novels: 1926–1929.*

———. *The Unvanquished* (1938). In *Faulkner: Novels 1936–1940.*

Fiedler, Leslie. *Love and Death in the American Novel* (1960). Urbana: Dalkey Archive Press, 1998.

Fitzgerald, Frances. *America Revised.* New York: Vintage, 1980.

———. *Fire in the Lake: The Vietnamese and the Americans in Vietnam.* Boston: Little, Brown, 1972.

Fitzgerald, F. Scott. *The Great Gatsby* (1925). In *The Great Gatsby: The Authorized Text,* ed. Matthew J. Bruccoli. New York: Simon & Schuster, 1995.

The Fog of War (film). Sony Pictures Classics. 2003.

Fort Apache (film). Argosy Pictures. 1948.

Franklin, John Hope, and Alfred A. Moss. *From Slavery to Freedom: A History of African Americans* (1947). New York: Knopf, 2000.

Freud, Sigmund. "Family Romances" (1908). In *The Standard Edition.* Vol. 9, ed. James Strachey. London: Hogarth Press, 1964.

———. "Femininity" (1933). In *The Standard Edition.* Vol. 22.

———. "The 'Uncanny'" (1919). In *On Creativity and the Unconscious.* New York: Harper & Row, 1958.

Friedan, Betty. *The Feminine Mystique.* New York: W. W. Norton, 1963.

Frost, Robert. *The Poetry of Robert Frost.* New York: Holt, Rinehart and Winston, 1969.

———. *The Selected Letters of Robert Frost,* ed. Lawrance Thompson. New York: Holt, Rinehart, Winston, 1964.

Frye, Northrop. *Anatomy of Criticism.* Princeton: Princeton Univ. Press, 1957.

Fussell, Paul. *The Great War and Modern Memory.* New York: Oxford Univ. Press, 1975.

———, ed. *The Norton Book of Modern War.* New York: W. W. Norton, 1990.

———. *Wartime: Understanding and Behavior in the Second World War.* New York: Oxford Univ. Press, 1989.

Gaddis, William. *Carpenter's Gothic.* New York: Penguin, 1985.

———. *A Frolic of His Own.* New York: Simon & Schuster, 1994.

———. *JR* (1975). New York: Penguin, 1993.

———. *The Recognitions* (1955). New York: Penguin, 1993.

Gaines, Ernest. *A Lesson Before Dying.* New York: Random House, 1993.

Gallop, Jane. *Feminism and Psychoanalysis: The Daughter's Seduction.* Ithaca: Cornell Univ. Press, 1982.

Gates, Henry Louis, Jr. *The Signifying Monkey: A Theory of Afro-American Literary Criticism.* New York: Oxford Univ. Press, 1988.

Gelfant, Blanche. *Women Writing in America: Voices in Collage.* Hanover, NH: Univ. Press of New England, 1984.

Genovese, Eugene D. *Roll, Jordan Roll: The World the Slaves Made.* New York: Vintage, 1976.

Glasgow, Ellen. *Barren Ground* (1925). New York: Farrar, Straus & Giroux, 1957.

Gleason, William A. *The Leisure Ethic: Work and Play in American Literature, 1840–1940.* Palo Alto: Stanford Univ. Press, 1999.

Glück, Louise. *The Triumph of Achilles.* New York: Ecco Press, 1985.

Godard, Jean-Luc. *Histoire(s) du Cinéma.* Gaumont. 1988–98.

Goodman, Paul. *Growing Up Absurd.* New York: Random House, 1960.

Greene, Graham. *The Quiet American* (1955). New York: Viking, 1956.

Griswold v. Connecticut (Supreme Court Case). 1966.

Harvey, Brett. *The Fifties: A Woman's Oral History.* New York: HarperCollins, 1993.

Hasford, Gustav. *The Short-Timers.* New York: Harper & Row, 1979.

Hawthorne, Nathaniel. *The Scarlet Letter* (1850). New York: Penguin, 2003.

Heinemann, Larry. *Paco's Story.* New York: Farrar, Straus & Giroux, 1986.

Heller, Joseph. *Catch-22.* New York: Simon & Schuster, 1961.

Hemenway, Robert E. *Zora Neale Hurston: A Literary Biography.* Urbana: Univ. of Illinois Press, 1977.

Hemingway, Ernest. *Death in the Afternoon.* New York: Scribners, 1932.

———. *A Farewell to Arms.* New York: Scribners, 1929.

———. *For Whom the Bell Tolls.* New York: Scribners, 1940.

———. *in our time.* Paris: Three Mountains Press, 1924.

———. *In Our Time.* New York: Scribners, 1925 and 1930.

———. *A Moveable Feast.* New York: Scribners, 1964.

———. *Selected Letters, 1917–1961,* ed. Carlos Baker. New York: Scribners, 1981.

———. *The Short Stories of Ernest Hemingway.* New York: Scribners, 1954.

———. *The Sun Also Rises.* New York: Scribners, 1926.

Herr, Michael. *Dispatches.* New York: Knopf, 1977.

Herring, George C. *America's Longest War: The United States in Vietnam, 1950–1975.* New York: Knopf, 1979.

Hersey, John. *Hiroshima* (1946). New York: Vintage, 1989.

Himes, Chester. *If He Hollers Let Him Go* (1945). New York: Thunder's Mouth Press, 1986.

——. *The Quality of Hurt: The Autobiography of Chester Himes*. Vol. 1. New York: Doubleday, 1972.

Hollinger, David A. *Postethnic America: Beyond Multiculturalism* (1995). New York: Basic Books, 2006.

Houston, Jeanne Wakatsuki, and James D. Houston. *Farewell to Manzanar*. Boston: Houghton Mifflin, 1973.

Hunter, J. Paul. "Steinbeck's Wine of Affirmation in *The Grapes of Wrath*." In *The Grapes of Wrath (The Viking Critical Library)*. New York: Penguin, 1972.

Hurston, Zora Neale. *Mules and Men* (1935). In *Hurston: Folklore, Memoirs, and Other Writings*. New York: Library of America, 1995.

——. *Their Eyes Were Watching God* (1937). In *Hurston: Novels and Stories*. New York: Library of America, 1995.

Irwin, John T. *Doubling and Incest / Repetition and Revenge: A Speculative Reading of Faulkner's Novels*. Baltimore: Johns Hopkins Univ. Press, 1975.

Jacobs, Harriet. *Incidents in the Life of a Slave Girl* (1861). Norton Critical Edition, ed. Nellie Y. McKay and Frances Smith Foster. New York: W. W. Norton, 2001.

Jaffe, Rona. *The Best of Everything* (1958). New York: Penguin, 2005.

James, Henry. *Henry James Letters*, ed. Leon Edel. Vol. 4. Cambridge, MA: Harvard Univ. Press, 1984.

——. "Henry James's First Interview." In *The New York Times*, March 21, 1915.

——. "The Preface to Roderick Hudson." In *The Novels and Tales of Henry James*. Vol. 1. New York: Scribners, 1907.

James, William. "The Moral Equivalent of War" (1910). In *William James: Writings 1902–1910*. New York: Library of America, 1987.

——. *Pragmatism* (1907). In *William James: Writings 1902–1910*.

Jameson, Frederic M. *Postmodernism, or, the Cultural Logic of Late Capitalism*. Durham: Duke Univ. Press, 1991.

Johnson, James Weldon. *The Autobiography* (Dover Thrift Edition). New York: Dover, 1995.

——. *The Autobiography of an Ex-Colored Man* (1912). In *Johnson: Writings*. New York: Library of America, 2004.

Johnston, John. "Toward Postmodern Fiction." In *William Gaddis: A Collection of Critical Essays*, ed. Harold Bloom. Philadelphia: Chelsea House, 2004.

Jones, James. *From Here to Eternity*. New York: Scribners, 1951.

Jordan, June. "On Richard Wright and Zora Neale Hurston." In *Black World* 23, August 1974.

Karl, Fredrick R. *American Fictions: 1940–1980*. New York: Harper & Row, 1983.

Kartiganer, Donald. *Fragile Thread: The Meaning of Form in Faulkner's Novels*. Amherst: Univ. of Massachusetts Press, 1979.

Kashner, Sam. *When I Was Cool: My Life at the Jack Kerouac School*. New York: HarperCollins, 2004.

Keats, John. *The Poems of John Keats*, ed. Jack Stillinger. Cambridge: Belknap Press, 1978.

Keegan, John. *The Face of Battle: A Study of Agincourt, Waterloo, and the Somme*. New York: Penguin, 1983.

Kennedy, David M. *Freedom from Fear: The American People in Depression and War, 1929–1945*. New York: Oxford Univ. Press, 1999.

Kermode, Frank. *The Sense of an Ending: Studies in the Theory of Fiction*. New York: Oxford Univ. Press, 1968.

King, Martin Luther, Jr. "Letter from Birmingham Jail." In *A Testament of Hope: The Essential Writings and Speeches of Martin Luther King, Jr.*, ed. James. M. Washington. San Francisco: HarperCollins, 1991.

Kingston, Maxine Hong. *China Men*. New York: Knopf, 1980.

———. *The Fifth Book of Peace*. New York: Vintage, 2004.

———. *The Woman Warrior*. New York: Knopf, 1976.

Kolodny, Annette. *The Land before Her: Fantasy and Experience of the American Frontiers, 1630–1860*. Chapel Hill: Univ. of North Carolina Press, 1984.

———. *The Lay of the Land: Metaphor as Experience and History in American Life and Letters*. Chapel Hill: Univ. of North Carolina Press, 1975.

———. "Letting Go of Our Grand Obsessions: Notes toward a New Literary History of the American Frontiers." *American Literature*, vol. 64, no. 1, March 1992.

Kreyling, Michael. *Understanding Eudora Welty*. Columbia: Univ. of South Carolina Press, 1999.

Kunitz, Stanley. *The Collected Poems*. New York: W. W. Norton, 2000.

Lacan, Jacques. *Feminine Sexuality: Jacques Lacan and the Ecole Freudienne*, ed. Juliet Mitchell and Jacqueline Rose. New York: W. W. Norton, 1985.

LaFeber, Walter. *The Clash: U.S.-Japanese Relations throughout History*. New York: W. W. Norton, 1997.

Lai, Mark H., Genny Lim, and Judy Yung. *Island: Poetry and History of Chinese Immigrants on Angel Island, 1910–1940*. San Francisco: San Francisco Study Center, 1980.

Laing, R. D. *The Politics of Experience*. New York: Pantheon, 1967.

Larsen, Nella. *Passing* (1929). New York: W. W. Norton, 2007.

Lawrence, D. H. *Studies in Classic American Literature* (1923). Cambridge: Cambridge Univ. Press, 2003.

———. *Women in Love* (1920). New York: Viking, 1975.

Lawrence v. Texas (Supreme Court Case). 2003.

Lee, Chang-rae. *A Gesture Life*. New York: Penguin, 1999.

Lewis, David Levering. *W. E. B. Du Bois: Biography of a Race, 1868–1919*. New York: Henry Holt, 1993.

Leypoldt, Günter. "Reconsidering Raymond Carver's 'Development': The Revisions of 'So Much Water So Close to Home.'" *Contemporary Literature*, vol. 43, no. 2, Summer 2002.

Lhamon, W. T., Jr. *Deliberate Speed: The Origins of a Cultural Style in the American 1950s*. Cambridge, MA: Harvard Univ. Press, 1990 and 2002.

Lichtenstein, Nelson. *State of the Union: A Century of American Labor*. Princeton: Princeton Univ. Press, 2003.

———. *Walter Reuther: The Most Dangerous Man in Detroit*. Urbana: Univ. of Illinois Press, 1997.

Lincoln, Abraham. "A House Divided: Speech Delivered at Springfield, Illinois, at the Close of the Republican State Convention, June 16, 1858." In *Lincoln: Speeches and Writings, 1832–1858*. New York: Library of America, 1989.

———. "Second Inaugural Address." In *Lincoln: Speeches and Writings, 1859–1865*. New York: Library of America, 1989.

Locke, Alain. *The New Negro* (1925). New York: Atheneum, 1980.

Longinus. "On Sublimity." In *The Norton Anthology of Theory and Criticism*. New York: W. W. Norton, 2001.

Loving v. Virginia (Supreme Court case), 1967.

Lowell, Robert. *Collected Poems*. New York: Farrar, Straus & Giroux, 2003.

———. *The Letters of Robert Lowell*, ed. Saskia Hamilton. New York: Farrar, Straus & Giroux, 2005.

Lyotard, Jean-Francois. "Defining the Postmodern" (1986). In *The Norton Anthology of Theory and Criticism*. New York: W. W. Norton, 2001.

Mailer, Norman. *Advertisements for Myself*. New York: G. P. Putnam's Sons, 1959.

———. *The Armies of the Night*. New York: Penguin, 1968.

———. *Cannibals and Christians*. New York: Dial Press, 1966.

———. *The Deer Park*. New York: G. P. Putnam's Sons, 1955.

———. *The Executioner's Song*. Boston: Little, Brown, 1979.

———. *The Naked and the Dead*. New York: Rinehart and Company, 1948.

———. *Why Are We in Vietnam?* New York: G. P. Putnam's Sons, 1967.

Marcuse, Herbert. *One-Dimensional Man*. Boston: Beacon Press, 1964.

May, Elaine Tyler. *Homeward Bound: American Families in the Cold War Era*. New York: Basic Books, 1988 and 1999.

McCarthy, Cormac. *All the Pretty Horses*. New York: Vintage, 1992.

———. *Blood Meridian*. New York: Random House, 1985.

———. *Cities of the Plain*. New York: Vintage, 1998.

———. *The Crossing*. New York: Knopf, 1994.

McCarthy, Mary. "Characters in Fiction." In *On the Contrary*. New York: Farrar, Straus & Cudahy, 1961.

———. *The Group*. New York: Harcourt Brace, 1963.

———. *The Groves of Academe*. New York: Harcourt Brace, 1952.

———. *The Hounds of Summer and Other Stories*. New York: Avon, 1981.

———. "Letter to the Editor." *Politics*, 3:10 (November 1946).

———. *Memories of a Catholic Girlhood* (1957). New York: Harvest Books, 1972.

McDowell, Deborah E. *"The Changing Same": Black Women's Literature, Criticism, and Theory*. Bloomington: Univ. of Indiana Press, 1996.

McKenzie, Barbara. *Mary McCarthy*. New Haven: Twayne, 1967.

McPherson, James M. *Battle Cry of Freedom: The Civil War Era*. New York: Oxford Univ. Press, 1988.

Mendelson, Edward. "The Sacred, the Profane, and the *Crying of Lot 49*." In *Pynchon: A Collection of Critical Essays*. Englewood Cliffs, NJ: Prentice Hall, 1978.

Mercer, Kobena. "'1968': Periodizing Postmodern Politics and Identity." In *Cultural Studies*, ed. Lawrence Grossberg, Cary Nelson, and Paula Treichler. New York: Routledge, 1992.

Meyer, Adam. *Raymond Carver*. New York: Twayne, 1995.

Michaels, Walter Benn. *Our America: Nativism, Modernism, and Pluralism*. Durham: Duke Univ. Press, 1997.

Miller, Henry. *Tropic of Cancer* (1934). New York: Random House, 1983.

Minter, David. L. *The Interpreted Design as a Structural Principle in American Prose*. New Haven: Yale Univ. Press, 1969.

Moore, Steven. *A Reader's Guide to William Gaddis's 'The Recognitions.'* Lincoln: Univ. of Nebraska Press, 1982.

Mori, Toshiro. *Yokohama, California* (1949). Seattle: Univ. of Washington Press, 1985.

Morris, Edmund. *The Rise of Theodore Roosevelt* (1979). New York: Random House, 2001.

Morrison, Toni. *Beloved* (1987). New York: Plume-Penguin, 1988.

——. *The Bluest Eye* (1970). New York: Plume-Penguin, 1994.

——. *Conversations with Toni Morrison*, ed. Danille K. Taylor-Guthrie. Jackson: Univ. Press of Mississippi, 1994.

——. *Playing in the Dark: Whiteness and the Literary Imagination*. Cambridge, MA: Harvard Univ. Press, 1992.

——. *Sula*. New York: Knopf, 1973.

——. "This Amazing, Troubling Book." In *Adventures of Huckleberry Finn*. Norton Critical Edition. New York: W. W. Norton, 1999.

——. *Toni Morrison: Conversations*, ed. Carolyn C. Denard. Jackson: Univ. of Mississippi Press, 2008.

——. *What Moves at the Margin: Selected Nonfiction*, ed. Carolyn C. Denard. Jackson: Univ. of Mississippi Press, 2008.

Mulvey, Laura. "Visual Pleasure and Narrative Cinema" (1975). In *The Norton Anthology of Theory and Criticism*, ed. Vincent B. Leitch. New York: W. W. Norton, 2001.

Munro, Alice. *Runaway*. New York: Knopf, 2004.

Nabokov, Vladimir. *Lolita* (1955). In *Nabokov: Novels 1955–1962*. New York: Library of America, 1996.

Naylor, Gloria. *The Women of Brewster Place*. New York: Penguin, 1982.

Norris, Frank. *McTeague* (1899). In *Norris: Novels and Essays*. New York: Library of America, 1986.

——. "The Mechanics of Fiction" (1901). In *Norris: Novels and Essays*.

——. *The Octopus* (1901). In *Norris: Novels and Essays*.

Oates, Joyce Carol. "The Art of Eudora Welty." In *Eudora Welty: A Collection of Critical Essays*, ed. Harold Bloom. Philadelphia: Chelsea House, 1986.

Oates, Stephen B. *Let the Trumpet Sound: A Life of Martin Luther King*. New York: Harper & Row, 1982.

O'Brien, Tim. *If I Die in a Combat Zone* (1973). Rev. ed. New York: Dell, 1979.

——. *The Things They Carried*. New York: Houghton Mifflin/Seymour Lawrence, 1990.

Oe Kenzaburo. *A Personal Matter* (1964). New York: Grove Press, 1994.

Olsen, Tillie. "I Stand Here Ironing" (1956). In *Tell Me a Riddle*. New Brunswick: Rutgers Univ. Press, 1995.

Olson, Charles. *Call Me Ishmael*. New York: Reynal and Hitchcock, 1947.

Owen, Wilfred. *The Collected Poems of Wilfred Owen*. New York: New Directions, 1963.

Ozick, Cynthia. "On William Gaddis." In *Conjunctions: Two Kingdoms*, vol. 41, 2003.

Patterson, James T. *Grand Expectations: The United States, 1945–1974*. New York: Oxford Univ. Press, 1996.

———. *Restless Giant: The United States from Watergate to Bush v. Gore*. New York: Oxford Univ. Press, 2005.

Patton (film). Twentieth-Century Fox. 1970.

Payne, Charles. *I've Got the Light of Freedom: The Organizing Tradition and the Mississippi Freedom Struggle* (1995). Berkeley: Univ. of California Press, 2007.

Paz, Octavio. *The Labyrinth of Solitude* (1961). New York: Penguin, 1999.

Petry, Ann. *The Street*. Boston: Houghton Mifflin, 1946.

Pfeil, Fred. *Another Tale to Tell: Politics and Narrative in Postmodern Culture*. New York: Verso, 1990.

Plath, Sylvia. *Ariel*. New York: Harper & Row, 1965.

Plessy v. Ferguson (Supreme Court Case). 1896.

Poirier, Richard. *The Performing Self: Compositions and Decompositions in the Languages of Contemporary Life*. New York: Oxford Univ. Press, 1971.

———. *A World Elsewhere: The Place of Style in American Literature*. New York: Oxford Univ. Press, 1966.

Pound, Ezra. *The Pisan Cantos* (1948), ed. Richard Sieburth. New York: New Directions, 2003.

Pryse, Marjorie, and Hortense Spillers. *Conjuring: Black Women, Fictions, and Literary Tradition*. Bloomington: Indiana Univ. Press, 1985.

Pynchon, Thomas. *Gravity's Rainbow*. New York: Viking, 1973.

———. *V*. New York: Lippincott, 1963.

———. *Vineland*. Boston: Little, Brown, 1990.

Raban, Jonathan. "At Home in Babel." In *William Gaddis: A Collection of Critical Essays*, ed. Harold Bloom. Philadelphia: Chelsea House, 2004.

Ramazani, Jahan. *The Norton Anthology of Modern and Contemporary Poetry*. Third Edition. New York: W. W. Norton, 2003.

Reynolds, Michael. *Hemingway: The American Homecoming*. New York: Blackwell, 1992.

———. *Hemingway's First War: The Making of a Farewell to Arms*. Princeton: Princeton Univ. Press, 1976.

Rhodes, Richard. *The Making of the Atomic Bomb*. New York: Simon & Schuster, 1986.

Rich, Adrienne. *Collected Early Poems*. New York: W. W. Norton, 1993.

———. *Of Woman Born: Motherhood as Experience and Institution* (1976). New York: W. W. Norton, 1986.

———. "When We Dead Awaken: Writing as Re-Vision" (1971). In *Arts of the Possible: Essays and Conversations*. New York: W. W. Norton, 2001.

Robinson, Marilynne. *Housekeeping*. New York: Farrar, Straus & Giroux, 1981.

Rodriguez, Richard. *Brown: The Last Discovery of America*. New York: Penguin, 2002.

———. *Days of Obligation: An Argument with My Mexican Father*. New York: Knopf, 1992.

———. *Hunger of Memory: The Education of Richard Rodriguez*. New York: Knopf, 1982.

———. "Violating the Boundaries: An Interview with Richard Rodriguez" by Timothy S. Sedore. *Michigan Quarterly Review*, vol. 38, no. 3, Summer 1999.

———. "What a Wall Can't Stop." *The Washington Post*, Sunday, May 28, 2006.

Rody, Caroline. *The Daughter's Return: African-American and Caribbean Women's Fictions of History*. New York: Oxford Univ. Press, 2001.

Roe v. Wade (Supreme Court Case). 1973.

Roosevelt, Theodore. *An Autobiography* (1913). New York: Macmillan, 1914.

Roth, Philip. *American Pastoral*. New York: Random House, 1997.

———. *The Counterlife*. New York: Farrar, Straus & Giroux, 1987.

———. *The Facts: A Novelist's Autobiography*. New York: Penguin, 1988.

———. *The Human Stain*. Boston: Houghton Mifflin, 2000.

———. *I Married a Communist*. Boston: Houghton Mifflin, 1998.

———. *Operation Shylock*. New York: Simon & Schuster, 1993.

———. *Patrimony*. New York: Simon & Schuster, 1991.

———. *The Plot Against America*. Boston: Houghton Mifflin, 2004.

———. *Portnoy's Complaint* (1969). In *Roth: Novels 1967–1972*. New York: Library of America, 2005.

———. *Sabbath's Theater*. Boston: Houghton Mifflin, 1995.

Royce, Josiah. *The Feud of Oakfield Creek*. Boston: Houghton Mifflin, 1887.

Sacks, Sheldon. *Fiction and the Shape of Belief*. Berkeley: Univ. of California Press, 1967.

Said, Edward. *The World, the Text, and the Critic*. Cambridge, MA: Harvard Univ. Press, 1983.

Saving Private Ryan (film). Dreamworks and Paramount. 1998.

Schmidt, Peter. *The Heart of the Story: Eudora Welty's Short Fiction*. Oxford: Univ. Press of Mississippi, 1991.

Scott v. Sanford (Supreme Court Case). 1857.

The Searchers (film). C. V. Whitney Pictures. 1956.

Sheehan, Neil. *A Bright Shining Lie: John Paul Vann and America in Vietnam*. New York: Random House, 1988.

———. *The Pentagon Papers*. Neil Sheehan, Hedrick Smith, E. W. Kenworthy, and Fox Butterfield. New York: Bantam, 1971.

Shepard, Sam. *Rolling Thunder Logbook*. New York: Viking, 1977.

———. *Seven Plays*. New York: Bantam, 1981.

———. *The Unseen Hand and Other Plays*. New York: Bantam, 1986.

Shostak, Debra. *Philip Roth: Countertexts, Counterlives*. Columbia: Univ. of South Carolina Press, 2004.

Silko, Leslie Marmon. *Ceremony*. New York: Penguin, 1977.

Sinclair, Upton. *The Jungle* (1905). Tucson: See Sharp Press, 2003.

Slater, Philip E. *The Glory of Hera: Greek Mythology and the Greek Family*. Princeton: Princeton Univ. Press, 1968.

Smith, Anna Deavere. *Twilight: Los Angeles, 1992*. New York: Doubleday, 1994.

Smith, Julian. "Hemingway and the Thing Left Out." In *The Short Stories of Ernest Hemingway: Critical Essays*, ed. Jackson R. Benson. Durham: Duke Univ. Press, 1975.

Sollers, Werner. *Neither Black nor White but Both: Thematic Explorations of Interracial Literature*. New York: Oxford Univ. Press, 1997.

Sone, Monica. *Nisei Daughter*. Boston: Little, Brown, 1953.

South Pacific (film). Twentieth-Century Fox. 1958.

Spock, Benjamin, and Michael B. Rothenberg. *Dr. Spock's Baby and Child Care*. Sixth Edition. New York: Penguin, 1992.

Springsteen, Bruce. *Born in the U.S.A.* Columbia Records. 1984.

Starr, Kevin. *Embattled Dreams: California in War and Peace, 1940–1950*. New York: Oxford Univ. Press, 2002.

Stein, Gertrude. *The Autobiography of Alice B. Toklas* (1933). In *Stein: Writings 1903–1932*. New York: Library of America, 1998.

———. *The Making of Americans* (1925). Norman: Illinois State Univ. Press, 1995.

———. *Stein: Writings 1932–1946*. New York: Library of America, 1998.

———. *Three Lives* (1909). In *Stein: Writings 1903–1932*.

Steinbeck, John. *East of Eden* (1952). In *Steinbeck: Novels 1942–1952*. New York: Library of America, 2002.

———. *The Grapes of Wrath* (1939). In *Steinbeck: The Grapes of Wrath and Other Writings 1936–1941*. New York: Library of America, 1996.

———. *In Dubious Battle* (1936). In *Steinbeck: Novels and Stories 1932–1937*. New York: Library of America, 1994.

———. *Steinbeck: A Life in Letters*, ed. Elaine Steinbeck and Robert Wallsten. New York: Penguin, 1975.

Stevens, Wallace. *Letters of Wallace Stevens*. New York: Knopf, 1966.

———. *Stevens: Collected Poetry & Prose*. New York: Library of America, 1997.

Stone, Robert. *Dog Soldiers*. Boston: Houghton Mifflin, 1973.

———. *A Flag for Sunrise*. New York: Knopf, 1981.

Styron, William. *The Long March*. New York: Vintage, 1955.

Sundquist, Eric J. *To Wake the Nations: Race in the Making of American Literature*. Cambridge, MA: Harvard Univ. Press, 1993.

Takaki, Ronald. *A Different Mirror: A History of Multicultural America*. Boston: Little, Brown, 1993.

Tan, Amy. *The Joy Luck Club*. New York: Putnam, 1989.

Tate, Claudia, ed. *Black Women Writers at Work*. New York: Continuum Intl. Pub. Group, 1984.

Thomas, Keith. *The Oxford Book of Work*. New York: Oxford Univ. Press, 1999.

Thoreau, Henry David. *Thoreau: A Week, Walden, Maine Woods, Cape Cod*. New York: Library of America, 1985.

Toomer, Jean. *Cane* (1923). New York: Liveright, 1975.

———. *The Wayward and the Seeking: A Collection of Writings by Jean Toomer*, ed. Darwin Turner. Washington, DC: Howard Univ. Press, 1980.

Updike, John. *Rabbit Run*. New York: Knopf, 1960.

Velie, Alan R. *Four American Indian Literary Masters: N. Scott Momaday, James Welch, Leslie Marmon Silko, and Gerald Visenor*. Norman: Univ. of Oklahoma Press, 1982.

Vidal, Gore. *Lincoln*. New York: Random House, 1984.

———. *Perpetual War for Perpetual Peace*. New York: Thunder's Mouth Press, 2002.

Vonnegut, Kurt. *Slaughterhouse-Five*. New York: Delacorte Press, 1969.

Walker, Alice. *The Color Purple*. New York: Harcourt Brace Jovanovich, 1982.

———. *In Love and Trouble: Stories of Black Women*. New York: Harcourt Brace Jovanovich, 1973.

———. *In Search of Our Mother's Gardens: Womanist Prose*. New York: Harcourt Brace Jovanovich, 1983.

———. *Meridian*. New York: Harcourt Brace Jovanovich, 1976.

Walker, Franklin. *Frank Norris: A Biography*. Garden City, NY: Doubleday, 1932.

Warren, Robert Penn. *All the King's Men*. New York: Harcourt Brace Jovanovich, 1946.

———. *Talking with Robert Penn Warren*, ed. Floyd C. Watkins, John T. Hiers, and Mary Louise Weeks. Athens: Univ. of Georgia Press, 1990.

Washington, Booker T. *Up from Slavery* (1901). Oxford World's Classics. Oxford: Oxford Univ. Press, 1995.

Webb, James. *Fields of Fire*. Englewood Cliffs, NJ: Prentice Hall, 1978.

Welty, Eudora. *The Bride of the Innisfallen* (1955). In *Welty: Stories, Essays, & Memoir*. New York: Library of America, 1998.

———. *A Curtain of Green* (1941). In *Welty: Stories, Essays, & Memoir*.

———. *Delta Wedding* (1946). In *Welty: Complete Novels*. New York: Library of America, 1998.

———. *The Golden Apples* (1949). In *Welty: Stories, Essays, & Memoir*.

———. *Losing Battles* (1970). In *Welty: Complete Novels*.

———. *One Writer's Beginnings* (1984). In *Welty: Stories, Essays, & Memoir*.

———. *The Optimist's Daughter* (1972). In *Welty: Complete Novels*.

———. *The Ponder Heart* (1954). In *Welty: Complete Novels*.

———. *The Robber Bridegroom* (1942). In *Welty: Complete Novels*.

———. *The Wide Net* (1943). In *Welty: Stories, Essays, & Memoir*.

Wharton, Edith. *The Age of Innocence* (1920). In *Wharton: Novels*. New York: Library of America, 1986.

———. *The House of Mirth* (1905). In *Wharton: Novels*.

Whiting, Frederick. " 'The Strange Particularity of the Lover's Preference': Pedophilia, Pornography, and the Anatomy of Monstrosity in *Lolita*." In *American Literature*, vol. 70, no. 4, December 1998.

Whitman, Walt. *American Poetry: The Nineteenth Century, Vol. 1: Philip Freneau to Walt Whitman*. New York: Library of America, 1993.

Wilde, Oscar. "The Critic as Artist" (1891). In *The Artist as Critic: Critical Writings of Oscar Wilde*, ed. Richard Ellmann. Chicago: Univ. of Chicago Press, 1982.

Williams, William Carlos. *Imaginations*. New York: New Directions, 1970.

———. *In the American Grain* (1925). New York: New Directions, 1956.

———. *The William Carlos Williams Reader*, ed. M. L. Rosenthal. New York: New Directions, 1966.

Winchell, Donna Haisty. *Alice Walker*. New York: Twayne, 1992.

Wolfe, Tom. *The Bonfire of the Vanities*. New York: Farrar, Straus & Giroux, 1987.

Wolff, Tobias. *Old School*. New York: Knopf, 2003.

Wood, James. "Like Men Betrayed: Revisiting Richard Yates's 'Revolutionary Road.'" *The New Yorker*, December 15, 2008.

Woodward, C. Vann. *The Strange Career of Jim Crow* (1955). New York: Oxford Univ. Press, 2001.

Wordsworth, William. *Selected Poems and Prefaces*. Boston: Houghton Mifflin, 1965.

Wouk, Herman. *Marjorie Morningstar*. New York: Doubleday, 1955.

Wright, Richard. *Black Boy* (1945). In *Wright: Later Works*. New York: Library of America, 1991.

———. *Native Son* (1940). In *Wright: Early Works*. New York: Library of America, 1991.

Wright, Stephen. *Meditations in Green*. New York: Scribners, 1983.

Yamamoto, Hisaye. *Seventeen Syllables and Other Stories*. Latham, NY: Kitchen Table / Women of Color Press, 1988.

Yates, Richard. *Revolutionary Road*. New York: Little, Brown, 1961.

Yeats, W. B. *The Collected Poems*. New York: Macmillan, 1983.

Yezierska, Anzia. *Bread Givers* (1925). New York: Persea Books, 1975.

———. *Red Ribbon on a White Horse*. New York: Scribners, 1950.